School Law

27th Edition

Information about the New York State Education
Law, Regulations and Decisions of the Commissioner
of Education, and Other Laws and Legal Opinions Relating
to Education for the Guidance of School Boards and
School Administrators in New York State

**New York State
School Boards Association**

**New York State
Bar Association**

This publication is intended to provide information about general questions pertaining to various statutory enactments and administrative decisions affecting public schools. It is not intended to provide the answers to specific questions. The answers to the questions are necessarily brief and are intended to call attention to the applicable law rather than provide a definitive review. Laws are changed by each session of the New York State Legislature and United States Congress, and interpretive court decisions are handed down continually. To obtain answers to specific legal questions, seek legal advice from your school board's attorney.

Printed in the United States of America

ISBN 1-56452-053-6

12M-Ham-9/98

School Law

27th Edition

Contents

Preface ix
Acknowledgment x
General Information and Abbreviations xi
Introduction xiii
    New Statutory and Regulatory Law xiii
    New Case Law xx

1. The Structure of the New York State School System 1
    Legal Framework 1
    The University of the State of New York 3
    The New York State Board of Regents 3
    The New York State Education Department 4
    The Commissioner of Education 6
    Local School Districts 8
    The Parent-Teacher Association 12

2. School Boards 13
    Powers and Duties 18
    Membership 21
    Board Vacancies 25
    Ethics and Conflicts of Interest 27
    Incompatibility of Office 32
    Board Meetings 34
    School District Records 43
    School Board Policies 50

3. School Board Organization 53
    The School District's Officers 54
    Shared Decision Making 58

4. Annual and Special School District Meetings 65
    The Annual Meeting and Election 65
    Adoption of the School District Budget 70
    Election of School Board Members 77
    Special School District Meetings 83
    Qualifications of Voters 85
    Voter Registration 87
    The Voting Process 89
    Voter Challenges 93
    Absentee Ballots 95

5. Boards of Cooperative Educational Services (BOCES) 99
    BOCES Board Membership 100
    Annual Meeting 103
    Duties and Powers of a BOCES Board 104
    BOCES Services 107
    BOCES Budget 110

6. The District Superintendent 115

7. School Administrators 123
    Superintendent of Schools 130
    Principals 135

8. Teachers 137
    Teachers' Qualifications 137
    Teachers' Rights and Responsibilities 142
    Teacher Certification 148
    Tenure and Tenure Areas 160
    Probationary Teachers and the Granting of Tenure 166
    Seniority Rights and Excessing 176
    Disciplining Tenured Teachers 184
    Teachers' Compensation and Benefits 192

9. Noninstructional Employees 201
    The Civil Service 201
    Discipline of Noninstructional Employees 212
    Security Guards 217

10. Employee Relations 219
    Contracts of Employment 219
    The Taylor Law 224
    Employee Representation Under the Taylor Law 226
    The Collective Bargaining Process 234
    Improper Practices 244
    Grievances 248
    Family and Medical Leave Act 250

11. Retirement 255
    General Provisions 256
    Teachers' Retirement System 263
    Employees' Retirement System 268
    Social Security 270

12. Students 273
    School Attendance 273
    Student Residency 283
    Homeless Children 287
    Student Health and Welfare 291

Missing and Abused Children 301
Sex Offender Registration Act ("Megan's Law") 303
Students' Constitutional Rights 305
Student Discipline 313
Student Employment 325
School Lunch and Breakfast Programs 327

13. Students with Disabilities 333
      Basic Definitions and Applicable Laws 333
      The School District's Responsibilities 338
      The Committee on Special Education 345
      Parental Challenges 350
      Disciplining Students with Disabilities 354
      Preschool Children with Disabilities 357

14. Instruction and Curricula 361
      Curriculum 365
      Instructional Resources 381
      Academic Achievement 387
      School Assistance to College-bound Students 393

15. School District Reorganization 395
      Reorganization Procedures 397
      Impact of Reorganization 401

16. School Buildings, Grounds and Equipment 405
      Acquisition and Disposal of School Property 406
      Construction and Renovation of Facilities 410
      Closing of School Buildings 416
      Use of Public School Buildings, Grounds and Equipment 417
      Conduct on School Property 425
      Commercialism in the Public Schools 428

17. School Building Safety 431
      Emergency Management 431
      Building Structure Safety 433
      Workplace Safety 436
      Hazardous Materials and Toxic Substances 439
      Indoor Air Quality 446
      Asbestos 448

18. School District Liability and School Insurance 459
      Negligence 461
      Civil Rights Liability 467
      Employment Discrimination 470
      Sexual Harassment 472
      Defense and Indemnification 475
      Insurance 478

19. Fiscal Management 485
    Cash Management 488
    Reserve Funds 491
    Investment of School District Funds 495
    The District Budget 496
    Purchasing 502
    Borrowing 507

20. Assessment and Collection of Taxes 515
    Assessment 516
    Tax Exemptions 519
    Determining the Tax Rate 524
    Tax Collection 526
    Industrial Development Agencies 529

21. State Aid 533
    Types of State Aid 535
    Calculation and Distribution of State Aid 541

22. Transportation 545
    Bus Routes 550
    School Buses 552
    School Bus Safety 555
    School Bus Drivers 560
    Purchase and Lease of School Buses and Transportation Services........... 567
    State Aid for Transportation 571
    Transportation to Nonpublic Schools 572

23. Religion in the Public Schools 577
    Prayer and Moments of Silence 579
    Religious Observances 584
    Religious Symbols 587

24. Nonpublic Schools and Home Instruction 591
    Nonpublic Schools 595
    Services for Nonpublic School Students 595
    Home Instruction 599

25. Federal Laws and Public Schools 607

Bibliography 615

Index 619

Preface

This is the 27th edition of *School Law*. Like its 26 predecessors, it provides school board members, administrators and others who use it with accurate, up-to-date, clearly written information on common legal problems most school districts face.

This edition of *School Law* has been revised to reflect the latest additions in relevant law and cases. Additionally, this edition includes 25 chapters instead of 26. Information that had appeared in a chapter on city school districts in previous editions has been incorporated into other chapters throughout the book.

This is the third time that we welcome the New York State Bar Association as co-publisher of *School Law*. We thank them for their review of this book and their helpful suggestions. The State Bar Association's sound reputation as a legal publisher continues to enhance the scope and content of this handbook.

School Law, 27th Edition, should help school board members develop a more effective understanding of their roles as board members. It should also provide the public with a greater understanding of the myriad legal details involved in operating a school district.

Sources for the information contained in this handbook include New York State law, the Rules of the Board of Regents, decisions and regulations of the commissioner of education, opinions of the state comptroller, federal laws and regulations, and court decisions from all levels of the judicial system.

The purpose of *School Law* is to provide practical help on complicated issues. *School Law* does not attempt to answer every question that may arise and, indeed, cannot, because conditions vary from one district to another.

The material in this edition of *School Law* has been thoroughly checked by staff members of the New York State School Boards Association. However, local attorneys or the Association should be consulted about complex legal issues. Remember, what is contained within the pages of this handbook is not the law, but, rather, a discussion of it.

Timothy G. Kremer
Executive Director

Acknowledgment

This handbook was originated in 1945 as an outgrowth of the doctoral thesis of the late William J. Hageny, Distinguished Service Professor Emeritus, State University of New York, College at New Paltz, New Paltz, New York. We have appreciated Dr. Hageny's work on the handbook from its inception until 1988 and his contributions to creating a ready school law reference for board members, administrators and attorneys alike. The handbook is an effort to make school law accessible and understandable to all.

Dr. Hageny's past contributions to education include Chairman of the Department of Educational Administrator and Professor of Education, State University of New York, College at New Paltz; Executive Secretary of the Mid-Hudson School Study Council; and Member of the Board of Trustees, Ulster County Community College. He served as president of the New York Collegiate Association for the Development of Educational Administration, New York State Association of Secondary School Principals and Council of Administrative Leadership. He also served for many years as Chief School Administrator of Haldane Central School Cold Spring, New York. Dr. Hageny graduated from Hobart College and Syracuse University and received his doctorate from Columbia University.

School Law

General Information

This 27th edition of *School Law* is a compendium of information about New York State school law arranged according to 25 topics, represented by the chapter headings, in a question-and-answer format. The questions are numbered according to the chapters in which they appear and their order in those chapters. When question numbers are referred to, they are set in boldface type (**14:5**).

There are two considerations to remember when using *School Law*. First, all legal references throughout the handbook are to the New York State Education Law unless noted otherwise in unnumbered footnotes at the beginning of chapters or sections. Second, when a specific number of days is referred to in a statute or elsewhere in the law, Saturdays, Sundays and holidays are included when calculating such days unless otherwise stated in specific provisions of the law or the period of time is two days or less (Gen. Constr. Law § 20), or the period of time specified ends on a Saturday, Sunday or a public holiday, in which case the specified time will occur on the next succeeding business day (Gen. Constr. Law § 25-a).

Abbreviations

The following abbreviations represent sources that are cited frequently in *School Law*.

Case Law Citations

United States Supreme Court

U.S.	United States Reports
S.Ct.	Supreme Court Reporter
U.S.L.W.	United States Law Week

Federal Courts of Appeals

F., F.2d, F.3d	Federal Reporter

Federal District Courts

F.Supp.	Federal Supplement

New York State Court of Appeals

N.Y.2d	New York Reports

New York State Supreme Court, Appellate Division

A.D.2d	Appellate Division Reports

New York State Lower Courts

Misc.2d	New York Miscellaneous Reports

Other Reports

Educ. Dep't. Rep.	(State) Education Department Reports
Fair Empl. Prac. Case	(BNA) Fair Employment Practice Cases
IDELR	Individuals with Disabilities Education Law Reporter
Opn. Att'y Gen.	Opinions of the New York State Attorney General
Opn. St. Compt.	State Comptroller's Opinions
PERB	Public Employment Relations Board's
	Official Decisions, Opinions and Related Matters
SRO	State Review Officer Decisions
St. Dep't. Rep.	State Department Reports
WL	Westlaw Online Services

Statutory Citations

Federal

USC	United States Code
Pub. Law	Public Law
CFR	United States Code of Federal Regulations

State

NYCRR	New York Code of Rules and Regulations
8 NYCRR	Regulations of the Commissioner of Education

New York State Law

Arts & Cult. Aff. Law	Arts and Cultural Affairs Law
Civ. Prac. L. & R.	Civil Practice Law and Rules
Civ. Rights Law	Civil Rights Law
Civ. Serv. Law	Civil Service Law
Educ. Law	Education Law
Elec. Law	Election Law
Exec. Law	Executive Law
Gen. Constr. Law	General Construction Law
Gen. Mun. Law	General Municipal Law
Jud. Law	Judiciary Law
Lab. Law	Labor Law
Local Fin. Law	Local Finance Law
NYS Const.	New York State Constitution
Pub. Health Law	Public Health Law
Pub. Off. Law	Public Officers Law
Real. Prop. Law	Real Property Law
Real Prop. Tax Law	Real Property Tax Law
Retire. & Soc. Sec. Law	Retirement and Social Security Law
State Fin. Law	Sate Finance Law
Tax Law	Tax Law

INTRODUCTION

Since *School Law 26th Edition* was published in 1996, there have been a number of legislative and case law changes at both the federal and state levels that directly or indirectly affect public education in New York. While most of these changes have been incorporated into the main body of this book, some have also been included in the introduction because of their significance.

This introduction is organized into two main sections: new statutory and regulatory law, and new case law. So that information could be included up to the last minute, the introduction has not been included in the index. The information in this introduction is current through August 17, 1998.

New Statutory and Regulatory Law

Not every statute and regulation that has been enacted since *School Law 26th Edition* was published can be summarized in this section. What is included here are the most significant ones, beginning with the federal level and progressing to the state level.

Federal Statutes

The Individuals with Disabilities Education Act (IDEA) was reauthorized in 1997. IDEA confers an enforceable substantive right to public education in participating states upon children with disabilities, and conditions federal financial assistance upon compliance with the substantive and procedural requirements of the act. The 1997 amendments are substantial and have caused school districts across the state to change their practices and procedures concerning the education of students with disabilities.

School districts should be aware that more changes in this area are on the horizon in light of the fact that at the time this publication went to press, the United States Department of Education was in the process of amending its regulations to conform with the amended federal law. In addition, New York State must amend its laws and regulations to be consistent with the federal requirements.

State Statutes

Board of Cooperative Educational Services (BOCES)

Chapter 436, Part A, section 13 of the Laws of 1997 requires a BOCES to prepare, and append to the proposed administrative budget made available for public inspection, a BOCES report card measuring the academic and fiscal performance of the BOCES. This report card must also be distributed to newspapers of general circulation and distributed at the annual meeting, as well as disseminated in any other manner required by the commissioner of education. It must include, at a minimum, any information of the BOCES regarding pupil performance and expenditure per pupil required to be included in the annual report by the regents to the governor and the Legislature, as specified in the law, as well as any other information required by the commissioner.

Chapter 436, Part A, section 14 of the Laws of 1997 permits any non-component school district, including the Big 5 districts, upon consent of the BOCES and with the approval of the commissioner of education, to participate as a component district of the BOCES serving its geographic area or an adjoining BOCES for the sole purpose of purchasing instructional support services.

Personnel Issues

Chapter 172 of the Laws of 1997 extends, until June 30, 1999, the applicability of injunctive relief in public employment improper practice cases.

Chapter 511 of the Laws of 1998 extends to teaching assistants and teacher aides the right to be placed on a preferred eligibility list should such an individual be laid off as a result of the transfer of a program from a board of cooperative educational services (BOCES) to a school district or vice versa.

Retirement Issues

Chapter 68 of the Laws of 1998 extends from May 15, 1998 to May 15, 1999 the prohibition against diminishing the health insurance benefits or contributions made on behalf of retirees and their dependents unless a corresponding diminution of benefits or contributions is made to active employees.

Chapter 91 of the Laws of 1998 increases the maximum retirement earnings allowed for retirees employed in public service to $15,500 for the 1999 tax year.

Chapter 266 of the Laws of 1998 reduces the amount of service necessary to receive normal retirement benefits from 25 to 20 years. The new law permits certain Tier III retirees, who retired on or before September 1, 1983 to opt for Tier IV benefits.

Chapter 330 of the Laws of 1998 extends the time within which Tier IV members of the New York State Teachers' Retirement System may apply for disability retirement.

Chapter 388 of the Laws of 1998 provides a death benefit to the beneficiaries of certain vested members of the state retirement system who die while not in public service.

Chapter 389 of the Laws of 1998 reduces the period of time a public employee must serve prior to vesting in the state retirement system. Under the new law, a public employee need only serve five years to vest in the state retirement system.

Chapter 390 of the Laws of 1998 provides a pension supplement for certain retirees from the state retirement system.

School District Budget Vote and School Board Member Elections

Chapter 436, Part A of the Laws of 1997 provides that all school districts (excluding the Big 5 districts) must hold a public hearing on the budget at least seven but not more than 14 days prior to the annual meeting and election or special district meeting at which a school budget vote will occur. The proposed budget must be presented in three components: a program component, a capital component and an administrative component. It also establishes a statewide uniform voting date for the budget vote and school board elections, the third Tuesday in May, except as otherwise specified in the law.

Chapter 436, Part A, sections 23 and 28 of the Laws of 1997 provides that no school board may submit a proposed budget or any proposition involving the expenditure of money to the voters more than twice. If the voters fail to approve the budget after the second submission, the school board must adopt a contingency budget.

Chapter 436, Part A, sections 24 and 29 of the Laws of 1997 provides that the expenses incurred for interschool athletics, field trips and other extracurricular activities, including associated transportation expenses, are ordinary contingent expenses. It also provides that the administrative component of the contingency budget, as well as the contingency budget in its entirety, may not exceed certain monetary limitations set forth in the law.

Chapter 28 of the Laws of 1998 corrects the Legislature's unintentional deletion of language in the Education Law pertaining to the time school budget and board members elections must take place. With the exception of small city school districts and school districts that are not divided into election districts and which conduct their election by a show of hands or voice vote, unless the hour and place has been previously fixed by a vote of a previous district meeting, the school district election must be held during at least six consecutive hours after 6 a.m., two hours of which must be after 6 p.m. as determined by board resolution.

School Property Taxes and Exemptions

Chapter 168 of the Laws of 1997 authorizes local governments to exclude veterans disability compensation from the calculation of income for the determination of real property tax exemptions for senior citizens.

Chapter 183 of the Laws of 1997 authorizes school districts, except small city school districts, to grant a tax exemption for certain historic real property. The exemption is phased out over a 10-year period.

Chapter 199 of the Laws of 1997 authorizes school districts to adopt a resolution to allow school property taxes to be paid in three installments. A formula for the amount of each installment is set forth in the law.

Chapter 293 of the Laws of 1997 authorizes school districts to adopt a resolution to exclude converted condominium units from receiving a beneficial real property assessment under certain provisions of the Real Property Tax Law.

Chapter 315 of the Laws of 1997 authorizes school districts to adopt a resolution permitting a real property tax exemption to persons with disabilities whose incomes are limited due to their disabilities.

Chapter 515 of the Laws of 1997 authorizes school districts to appoint a district official to correct errors on the tax roll and to determine the amount of refund due up to $2,500.

Chapter 298 of the Laws of 1998 increases by $1,000 the maximum income eligibility level for real property tax exemptions granted to senior citizens under section 467 of the Real Property Tax Law. The optional annual income eligibility cap that a school district can adopt for the full fifty percent reduction was increased from $18,500 to $19,500, and for the minimum reduction, the amount was increased from $26,900 to $27,900.

Chapter 361 of the Laws of 1998 authorizes school districts to adopt a resolution to provide an infrastructure (i.e., streets, storm and sanitary sewers, drainage facilities) exemption for certain residential building lots.

Chapter 418 of the Laws of 1998 requires a separate line on tax statements for taxes levied for free association libraries.

School Tax Relief Program (STAR)

Chapter 389, Part B of the Laws of 1997 establishes the state school tax relief program (STAR). This program is a state-funded exemption from school property taxes for owner-occupied, primary residences. The program has two components: the "enhanced" program for income-eligible senior citizens and the basic program for all other property owners. It also requires school districts to provide information about the STAR exemption to each person who owns a residence in the district.

Chapter 56, Part A, sections 1 and 2 of the Laws of 1998 increases the base figure of the enhanced STAR exemption to $50,000 for school years 1998-99, 1999-2000 and 2001-01. It also defines income for purposes of the STAR enhanced exemption.

Chapter 570 of the Laws of 1998 provides that an individual otherwise eligible for the STAR exemption because of eligibility under the senior citizens' exemption authorized by section 467 of the Real Property Tax Law, will not be denied the exemption if the individual turns 65 after the taxable status date, but on or before December 31 of the same calendar year.

Transportation

Chapters 318 of the Laws of 1997 and Chapter 94 of the Laws of 1998 require that all school buses purchased or acquired after September 1, 1997 have the telephone number, including the area code, of the owner and/or operator printed on the rear of the vehicle.

Chapter 436, Part A, sections 71-73 of the Laws of 1997 establishes a comprehensive school bus driver safety training program. It also requires all school districts to certify to the commissioner that its school bus drivers have successfully completed the school bus driver training program established under the law and the commissioner's regulations.

Chapter 464 of the Laws of 1997 permits school districts to award contracts for mobile instructional units through either competitive bidding or the request for proposals process.

Chapter 472 of the Laws of 1998 authorizes school districts to lease motor vehicles to be used to transport students to and from school and/or board of cooperative educational services for one school year, or for up to five years with voter approval. No voter approval is required in the Big 5 school districts.

Other New Laws

Chapter 436, Part A, section 58 of the Laws of 1997 establishes the universal prekindergarten program.

Chapter 536 of the Laws of 1997 prohibits a school district from charging parents for the cost of assessments or evaluations used to admit students to gifted and talented programs.

Chapter 20 of the Laws of 1998 permits certain physical therapist assistants to provide therapy to students without the direct on-site supervision of a physical therapist.

Chapter 289 of the Laws of 1998 enhances the penalties for the sale of a controlled substance on or near child day care centers, nursery schools, and prekindergarten and kindergarten facilities.

Chapter 353 of the Laws of 1998 requires school districts to have adequate asthma emergency equipment and pharmaceuticals on the premises of each school in the district, such as, but not limited to, oxygen pumps, back-up inhalers and nebulizers. It allows students afflicted with asthma to bring to school and use asthma medication during the school day.

Chapter 400 of the Laws of 1998 clarifies that the provisions of the Education Law which apply to the powers and duties of the trustees of school district public libraries, also apply to the trustees of such libraries in small cities.

Chapter 401 of the Laws of 1998 requires the State Education Department to include, as part of the health education course at the senior high school level, instruction on certain types of cancers, including breast, skin and testicular cancer.

The Board of Regents and State Regulations

Curriculum

At press time, the State Education Department was in the process of revising part 100 of the commissioner's regulations which governs curriculum in public schools in the state. The final regulations are not expected to be issued until February 1999.

Graduation Requirements

The Board of Regents has adopted 28 learning standards to guide the development of local school curricula in the following areas: English/ language arts; health, physical education, and family and consumer sciences; career development and occupational studies; mathematics, science and technology; the arts; languages other than English; and social studies. In November of 1997, the Regents approved a proposal to revise the state's graduation requirements and directed the State Education Department to promulgate regulations accordingly. The regulations are expected to be issued in February 1999.

Once the new graduation requirements are fully phased in, Regents competency tests will be eliminated and all students entering the ninth grade in 2001 will be required to pass Regents examinations in English, science, mathematics, U.S. history and government, and global history. Completion of additional Regents examinations will result in an advanced designation on a student's high school diploma.

Teacher Certification

The New York State Board of Regents has approved the final report of the Task Force on Teaching which establishes a new teacher certification system. The following is a summary of some of the changes.

Effective September 2000, until February 2, 2003, individuals who do not hold any certificate will be issued a professional certificate in place of the existing permanent certificate based on the current requirements for the permanent certificate. Teachers with a provisional certificate issued prior to the enactment of the new regulations will remain eligible for a permanent certificate.

Beginning February 2, 2003, the commissioner of education will issue an initial certificate valid for up to five years upon satisfaction of the following criteria:

1. Completion of an approved program of teacher education.
2. Completion of a bachelor's degree and a master's degree.
3. Except under certain exceptions, a recommendation for certification from an authorized institution awarding master's degrees.
4. Achievement of qualifying scores on the revalidated Liberal Arts and Sciences Test (LAST), Assessment of Teaching Skills (ATS), and Content Specialty Test (CST).

A teacher candidate completing all of the requirements for the initial certificate with the exception of a master's degree will receive a transitional certificate which will enable the candidate to teach for up to two years while completing the master's degree, provided that the first year is mentored teaching.

Beginning February 2, 2003, the commissioner will issue a professional certificate upon a candidate's completion of the following criteria:

1. The equivalent of one year of mentored teaching.
2. Three years of satisfactory teaching experience beyond the mentored experience which will include annual professional reviews.

Effective September 1, 2003, the commissioner will no longer issue temporary licenses. Prior to the 2003 termination date, there will be certain limitations imposed concerning the ability of districts to employ temporary licensed teachers. Effective September 1, 1999, no new teachers with temporary licenses may be employed in schools under registration review (SURR schools).

Effective February 2, 2003, a new teacher certification structure with new certificate titles will be put into place.

A state Professional Standards and Practices Board, which will replace the existing Teacher Education, Certification and Practices Board (TECAP) and assume its functions, will be established.

Effective September 1, 1999, all school districts will be required to develop a plan to provide their teachers with substantial professional development programs which are directly related to student learning needs as identified in the School Report Card, state initiatives and implementation of New York State standards and assessments. The plan must be approved by the commissioner.

All teachers receiving a professional certificate on or after September 1, 2000, will be required to successfully complete at least 175 hours of professional development every five years. Each district must maintain a professional development transcript for each teacher affected by the 175-hour requirement. Failure to satisfy this requirement may result in the revocation of the professional certificate and termination from employment.

A new teacher evaluation system will be established through state regulations. School districts may require additional criteria at the local level.

New Case Law

This section touches on the most significant federal and state cases that have been decided since *School Law 26th Edition* was published.

Age Discrimination in Employment Act (ADEA)

The United States Supreme Court ruled that former employees may sue under the Age Discrimination in Employment Act (ADEA), even when they have signed a release of all claims against the employer, if the release does not meet the specific requirements of the Older Workers Benefit Protection Act (OWBPA). In addition, under such circumstances, the former employee is not required to "tender back" the benefits paid in exchange for the release prior to initiating a lawsuit (*Oubre v. Entergy Operations, Inc.,* 118 S.Ct. 838 (1998)).

The U.S. Court of Appeals for the Second Circuit upheld a district's local retirement incentive plan which required participating teachers to retire at the end of the school year in which he or she is first eligible to retire under the state's retirement system. According to the court, the district's plan did not violate the ADEA because it was voluntary, it was made available for a reasonable period of time, and it did not arbitrarily discriminate on the basis of age (*Auerbach v. Board of Education of the Harborfields Central School District*, 136 F.3d 104 (2nd Cir. 1998)).

Aid to Parochial Schools

The U.S. Supreme Court ruled that sending public employees into parochial schools to provide Title I services, including remedial instruction and counseling, does not violate the Establishment Clause of the First Amendment to the United States Constitution (*Agostini v. Felton*, 117 S.Ct. 1997 (1997)). The Court reversed its prior rulings in *Aguilar v. Felton*, 473 U.S. 402 (1985) and a portion of its ruling in *School District of the City of Grand Rapids v. Ball*, 473 U.S. 373 (1985)).

Americans with Disabilities Act (ADA)

The U.S. Supreme Court ruled that the Americans with Disabilities Act (ADA) applies to individuals infected with the human immunodeficiency virus (HIV), even though the individual may have no visible symptoms of the disease (*Bragdon v. Abbott*, 118 S.Ct. 2196 (1998)).

Attendance Policies

The commissioner of education upheld a school district's attendance policy which contained an appeal process to allow a student to challenge the application of the policy by demonstrating the existence of "extenuating circumstances." The appeal process was only available to (1) allow a student to challenge the number of absences on his or record, (2) ensure that no violation of the federal Individuals with Disabilities Education Act (IDEA) or section 504 of the Rehabilitation Act has occurred, and (3) to give students a "last chance" under the policy by waiving the maximum allowable absence limit for "extenuating circumstances." According to the commissioner, since the policy and the appeal process did not differentiate between excused and unexcused absences, the district's policy was deemed valid (*Appeal of Ehnot*, 37 Educ. Dep't Rep. 648 (1998)).

Collective Bargaining

The New York State Court of Appeals handed down three relevant decisions in this area. In the first, the court ruled that a school board, which had, by resolution, reluctantly directed its superintendent to execute a contract after the Public Employment Relations Board and the courts ruled that the board's right of ratification had been lost because one of the district's negotiators failed to support ratification, did not have a separate right to legislatively approve the funding provisions of the agreement (*Board of Educ v. Buffalo Teachers Fed'n*, 89 N.Y.2d 370 (1996), *motion for reargument denied*, 89 N.Y.2d 983 (1997)).

In the second, the court ruled that although the Civil Service Law gives public employers the flexibility to appoint any one of the three highest scoring individuals on a competitive class eligible list, a school board may agree, during the negotiations process, to include a provision in the collective bargaining agreement which requires the appointment of the highest scoring individual, even though public employers are not required to negotiate with the union over the issue (*Matter of Professional, Clerical, Technical Employees Ass'n (Buffalo Board of Education)*, 90 N.Y.2d 364 (1997)).

In the third, the court ruled that section 209-a(1)(e) (the Triborough Amendment), which provides that upon the expiration of a collective bargaining agreement, a public employer shall continue all of the terms of the expired agreement until a new agreement is negotiated, does not violate the State Constitution (*Matter of the City of Utica (Zumpano)*, 91 N.Y.2d 964 (1998)).

Employment Discrimination Procedure

In *Robinson v. Shell Oil Company* (117 S.Ct. 843 (1997)), the U.S. Supreme Court expanded the protection of Title VII to protect former employees who have filed employment discrimination complaints from retaliation by their former employer.

Megan's Law

The U.S. Court of Appeals for the Second Circuit upheld the community notification provisions of the Sex Offender Registration Act (*Doe v. Pataki*, 120 F.3d 1263 (2nd Cir.), *cert. denied*, 118 S.Ct. 1066 (1998)). However, a lower federal district court has issued an injunction which prevents the implementation of the notification provisions of the law for individuals convicted before January 21, 1996.

Name-Clearing Hearings

According to the U.S. Court of Appeals for the Second Circuit, a probationary administrator who received negative evaluations and reasons for termination which the court concluded damaged the administrator's professional reputation to such a degree as to virtually preclude her from getting another job as an administrator in the future was entitled to a name-clearing hearing (*Donato v. Plainview-Old Bethpage CSD*, 96 F.3d 623 (2nd Cir. 1996), *cert. denied*, 117 S.Ct. 1083 (1997)).

Negligence Liability

The New York State Court of Appeals ruled that the rape of a 12-year-old student by a third party during a school field trip was a "foreseeable" result of the district's negligent supervision of the student and restored a $2.25 million jury verdict against the district (*Bell v. Bd. of Educ. of the City of New York*, 90 N.Y.2d 944 (1997)).

Parochial School Students

In *Russman by Russman v. Mills*, 1998 WL 417452 (2nd Cir.), the U.S. Court of Appeals for the Second Circuit ruled that the Individuals with Disabilities Education Act (IDEA) does not require public school districts to provide special education services to students who are voluntarily enrolled in private schools on the premises of their private school. However, the court remanded the case back down to the federal district court to determine whether either the Free Exercise Clause of the First Amendment or state law requires school districts to provide such services on the premises of the private school.

Preferred Eligibility Lists

A teacher recalled from the preferred eligibility list (PEL) and placed in a part-time position after being excessed from a full-time position is entitled to a new seven-year period on the PEL from the date the school district abolishes his or her part-time position, according to the Appellate Division, Second Department (*Avila v. Bd. of Educ. of the North Babylon UFSD*, 240 A.D.2d 661 (2nd Dep't 1997), *appeal denied*, 91 N.Y.2d 801 (1997)).

Religious Freedom Restoration Act

The U.S. Supreme Court declared the Religious Freedom Restoration Act unconstitutional. The law had required governmental entities, including school districts, to demonstrate a compelling governmental interest to justify imposing a burden on an individual's rights under the Free Exercise Clause of the First Amendment (*City of Boerne v. Flores*, 117 S.Ct. 2157 (1997)).

School Board Member Legislative Immunity

The U.S. Supreme Court ruled that local legislators, such as school board members, have absolute immunity from civil liability in connection with lawsuits arising out of their performance of legislative activities (*Bogan v. Scott-Harris*, 118 S.Ct. 966 (1998)).

Section 803

The New York State Court of Appeals ruled that under section 803 of the Retirement and Social Security Law, a teacher's burden of proving by "substantial evidence" that he or she did not participate in a procedure informing that individual of his or her right to join the public retirement system is satisfied merely by the individual's own statement that he or she was never informed of the right to join the retirement system. At that point, the burden shifts to the employer to challenge the credibility of the individual's assertion or by producing evidence to the contrary (*Scanlan v. Buffalo School District*, 90 N.Y.2d 662 (1997)).

Legislation which would have extended the filing deadline for retroactive membership in the state retirement systems until December 31, 1999, was vetoed by Gov. George Pataki, who cited the fiscal impact on school districts as a primary reason for his disapproval.

Sex Discrimination

The United States Supreme Court handed down a number of relevant decisions with regard to sex discrimination. In the first, the high court ruled that employees may sue their employer under Title VII for sexual harassment in cases where the alleged harasser and victim are of the same gender, and that the victim need not demonstrate that the harasser is a homosexual (*Oncale v. Sundowner Offshore Services, Incorporated*, 118 S.Ct. 998 (1998)).

The Supreme Court also ruled that an employer may be held vicariously liable for the sexual harassment of an employee by a supervisor even in cases where the employer did not know that the harassment was taking place (*Burlington Industries v. Ellerth*, 118 S.Ct. 2257 (1998); *Faragher v. City of Boca Raton*, 118 S.Ct. 2275 (1998)). However, in cases where the complaining employee suffers no economic harm as a result of the harassment, employers may be able to defend themselves by demonstrating that they exercised reasonable care to prevent and promptly correct sexually harassing behavior and that the employee unreasonably failed to take advantage of opportunities provided by the employer to report the harassment (*Faragher v. City of Boca Raton*).

Finally, the high court ruled that monetary damages are not available for teachers on student sexual harassment under Title IX unless an official of the district who has authority to institute corrective measures on the district's behalf has actual notice of, and is deliberately indifferent to, the teacher's misconduct (*Gebser v. Lago Vista Independent School District*, 118 S.Ct. 1989 (1998)).

Student Discipline

The New York State Court of Appeals upheld the one-year suspension of a student who was searched and determined to have brought a gun to school. The student argued that the suspension was improper because the district was permitted to admit the gun as evidence against him in the student disciplinary proceeding, even though in a prior Family Court proceeding, the court ruled that the seizure of the gun was unconstitutional and inadmissible in that proceeding. The Court of Appeals determined that the school officials were not precluded from reaching their own conclusion concerning the legality of the search, and were not bound by the determination of the Family Court (*Matter of Juan C. v. Cortines*, 89 N.Y.2d 659 (1997)).

The commissioner of education also ruled on several cases related to student discipline. In the first, the commissioner ruled that school districts may not condition a student's return to school on participation in counseling services and are not authorized to impose community service as a penalty in student disciplinary proceedings (*Appeal of Alexander*, 36 Educ. Dep't Rep. 160 (1996)).

Second, the commissioner ruled that school officials lacked the authority to suspend a student who permanently withdrew from school prior to his scheduled disciplinary hearing since there was no longer a "pupil-school relationship." However, he noted that if the student re-enrolled, the district could seek a suspension at that time (*Appeal of Rosenkranz*, 37 Educ. Dep't Rep. 330 (1998)).

Finally, the commissioner ruled that a school district lacked the authority to impose a lifelong ban from school grounds against a student as a penalty in a student disciplinary proceeding (*Appeal of McNamara*, 37 Educ. Dep't Rep. 326 (1998)).

Students with Disabilities

The parents of a student with a disability were not entitled to tuition reimbursement for their unilateral placement of their child in a residential placement, according to the U.S. Court of Appeals for the Second Circuit. In reversing a lower federal court decision, the Court of Appeals found that the parents failed to demonstrate the inadequacy of the district's proposed placement and stated, "The inadequacy of an IEP [individualized education program] is not established . . . simply because parents show that a child makes greater progress in a different program." In its decision the court also ruled that when a court is reviewing a determination of a hearing and/or state review officer, it must examine the administrative record and any new submissions by the parties with particular attention to whether a preponderance of the objective evidence indicates that the student has made progress or regressed in his or her program (*Walczak v. Florida UFSD*, 142 F.3d 119 (2nd Cir. 1998)).

By comparison, in *Muller v. Committee on Special Education of the East Islip UFSD*, 145 F.3d 95 (2nd Cir. 1998), the court ruled that when a case presents a mixed question of law and fact, the administrative determination is subject to a de novo review.

Meanwhile, the U.S. Supreme Court agreed to take a case that will decide whether public school districts must provide constant nursing services to students with disabilities under the Individuals with Disabilities Education Act (IDEA). The lower court ruled that continuous nursing care is a related service needed to ensure that the student receives a free, appropriate education under IDEA (*Cedar Rapids Community School District v. Garret F.*, 106 F.3d 822 (8th Cir.), *cert. granted*, 118 S.Ct. 1793 (1998)).

Tenure and Seniority

A number of relevant decisions were handed down in this area, beginning with the state's highest court. The New York State Court of Appeals ruled that a teacher who is transferred to another tenure area without his or her consent may knowingly and voluntarily waive his or her right to have service in the later tenure area credited for purposes of seniority, in the teacher's prior tenure area. Under such circumstances, a district may grant seniority credit for such service to the teacher in the second tenure area (*Kaufman v. Fallsburg CSD*, 91 N.Y.2d 57 (1997)).

The court also ruled that a teacher who served as a per-diem substitute teacher in place of another teacher on leave for an indefinite time, and who taught continuously every school day for at least one full semester before her formal appointment to a probationary term, was entitled to "Jarema credit" for that time (*Speichler v. Board of Cooperative Educational Services, Second Supervisory District*, 90 N.Y.2d 110 (1997)).

The Appellate Division, Second Department ruled that a district may not require all prospective teachers in the district to sign a waiver of their tenure rights as a condition to being hired by the district (*Costello v. Bd. of Educ. of East Islip*, 673 N.Y.S.2d 468 (2nd Dep't 1998)).

The commissioner of education ruled that a school board member may not abstain from voting on whether to grant tenure to an employee based solely on the board member's philosophical objection to the state's tenure system (*Appeal of Craft & Dworkin*, 36 Educ. Dep't Rep. 314 (1997)).

Use of School Facilities by Outside Religious Groups

The U.S. Court of Appeals for the Second Circuit ruled that a public school district which had a policy which prohibited the use of school facilities for religious worship or instruction, and did not deviate from this policy, was not required to permit access to its facilities to outside groups for religious worship or instruction (*Bronx Household of Faith v. Community School District No. 10*, 127 F.3d 207 (2nd Cir. 1997), *cert. denied*,

1998 WL 85986 (U.S.)).

At press time, there was a case pending before this same court which raises the issue as to whether a school district which had a policy which prohibited the use of school facilities for religious worship and instruction could refuse access to its facilities for such uses when school officials had erroneously allowed its facilities to be used for such purposes in the past. The lower court ruled that despite the past practice, the school district was not required to grant access to its facilities for religious worship and instruction (*Full Gospel Tabernacle v. Community School District 27*, 97 F.Supp. 214 (S.D.N.Y. 1997); but see *Liberty Christian Center, Inc. v. Watertown School District*, 1998 WL 328378 (N.D.N.Y.)).

1. The Structure of the New York State School System

Legal Framework

1:1. What is the overall legal framework for the provision of education in New York State?

The legal framework of New York State's education system consists of several levels of authority and resembles a pyramid. The base, which carries the most authority, is the federal government. Its authority resides in the United States Constitution, federal laws and regulations, and federal court decisions. The next level, the state, relies on the New York State Constitution, state laws and regulations, including the rules of the state Board of Regents, regulations and decisions of the commissioner of education, and state court decisions.

Legal authority for and jurisdiction of school boards are at the top of the pyramid. As local entities, school boards have the narrowest band of authority and may set policy only in areas in which their jurisdiction is not superseded by federal or state authority.

1:2. How do the federal and state governments affect the operation of school districts in New York State?

The Tenth Amendment to the United States Constitution leaves the function of education to the individual states by providing that "the powers not delegated to the United States by the Constitution, nor prohibited by it to the States, are reserved to the States respectively, or to the people."

Although not as common as state laws, federal statutes place certain responsibilities on local school districts. For example, under the federal Individuals with Disabilities Education Act (IDEA), districts have certain duties with regard to providing education to students with disabilities (see, e.g., 20 USC §§ 1400-1487). Federal regulations established by federal agencies also stand as the law of the land unless challenged and overturned by federal courts, or changed or overruled by the particular agency.

The basis for free public education in New York State is contained in article 11, section 1, of the state constitution, which declares that the Legislature "shall provide for the maintenance and support of a system of free common schools, wherein all the children of this state may be educated." Article 11 provides the legal authority given to the Board of

1

Regents and to the Legislature to provide for the maintenance and support of public schools.

Both the governor and the Legislature have proposed and enacted numerous statutes in the Education Law that affect education at the state level. The following statutes specify the authority of the state's school boards:

· Section 1604, for trustees of common school districts.
· Section 1709, for union free school board members.
· Section 1804, for central school district boards.
· Section 1950 for boards of cooperative educational services (BOCES).
· Articles 51, 52 and 52a for city school district boards.

In addition, the Legislature has delegated authority to the New York State Board of Regents through the Education Law. The Regents and the State Education Department (SED) also can establish policy by adopting rules and regulations within the limitations of state law. These regulations have the authority of law unless overruled by decisions of the state's courts or the Legislature, or until superseded by the promulgating agency.

The state delegates powers to school districts as it does to municipalities. School districts are considered branches, agencies or political subdivisions of the state government (*Burlaka v. Greece Central School District*, 167 Misc.2d 281 (1996); *Koch v. Webster Central School District*, 112 Misc.2d 10 (1981)). School boards must develop and implement policies in some areas and may do the same in other areas where the state and federal governments have not spoken.

1:3. What is the structure of the federal court system?

The United States district courts are the courts of original jurisdiction in the federal court system. The United States courts of appeals review cases from the district courts and original orders of various administrative agencies. The Second Circuit Court of Appeals has jurisdiction over New York.

The decisions of a United States district court and a United States court of appeals are not binding on jurisdictions outside of those in which their rulings are made, although they may provide some persuasive value when a court in another jurisdiction has a similar issue before it.

The highest court in the nation is the United States Supreme Court, which has jurisdiction over the decisions of the federal district courts, the courts of appeals and the highest state courts. The Supreme Court may, in very limited instances, such as where a state is a party, exercise original jurisdiction over certain cases.

1:4. What is the structure of the New York State court system?

The supreme court is one of New York State's courts of original jurisdiction and has authority over most civil and criminal matters. Each
county in the state has a supreme court. Other courts of original jurisdiction in the state exist, but the supreme court generally hears cases
outside the jurisdiction of these other courts.

The Appellate Division of the New York State Supreme Court is charged
primarily with hearing appeals from the state supreme courts and other
state courts of original jurisdiction. There are four appellate divisions in
New York State.

The New York State Court of Appeals is the highest court in the state.
Most of the appeals reviewed by this court come from the appellate
divisions.

The University of the State of New York

1:5. What is the University of the State of New York?

The University of the State of New York consists of all public and private
elementary and secondary schools in the state; all privately and publicly
controlled institutions of higher education, including the schools in the
State University of New York (SUNY) system; and all libraries, museums
and other educational and cultural institutions admitted to or incorporated by the University (§ 214). It is vested with broad regulatory powers
and is governed by the Board of Regents (§ 201; see also *Moore v. Board of
Regents*, 44 N.Y.2d 593 (1978)). The University of the State of New York
should not be confused with the State University of New York (SUNY).

1:6. What is the State University of New York (SUNY)?

The State University of New York (SUNY) was established in 1948
(§ 352). It consists of 34 state-operated and statutory campuses, and 30
community colleges. SUNY is governed by a 16-member board of trustees;
15 are appointed by the governor with the advice and consent of the state
Senate, and one member is president of the Student Assembly of the State
University (SASU), ex officio (§ 353(1)). The board of trustees appoints a
chancellor who heads SUNY (§ 353(3)).

The New York State Board of Regents

1:7. What is the New York State Board of Regents?

The New York State Board of Regents is the governing body of the
University of the State of New York. There are 16 Regents on the board,
which was established by the state Legislature in 1784 and is the oldest

continuous state educational agency in the United States.

The Regents exercise legislative functions over the state educational system, determine its educational policies and, except as related to the judicial functions of the commissioner of education, establish rules for carrying out the state's laws and policies relating to education and the functions, powers, duties and trusts granted to or authorized by the University of the State of New York and the State Education Department (§ 207).

The Regents also sponsor a Regents College Examinations (RCE) program. Through this nationwide, nontraditional program, adults earn credit toward college degrees in such areas as nursing, liberal arts, business and technology.

1:8. How are members of the Board of Regents chosen?

There are 16 members of the Board of Regents. Each is elected to a five-year term by a concurrent resolution of both houses of the state Legislature. One Regent is selected from each of the state's 12 judicial districts and four Regents are chosen from the state at large (§ 202).

1:9. What are the Regents' powers and duties?

The Regents have broad authority over all the state's educational institutions (*Moore v. Board of Regents*, 44 N.Y.2d 593 (1978)). The Regents appoint the commissioner of education, who also becomes the president of the University of the State of New York (§ 302; 8 NYCRR § 3.5). They establish and enforce educational and professional standards in the interests of the people of the state.

In the performance of these functions, the Regents are empowered to charter, register and inspect any school or institution under the educational supervision of the state (§§ 215, 216), to license practitioners in 38 major professions (§ 6504), and to certify teachers and librarians (§§ 3004, 3006).

The Regents meet monthly (except in August), usually in Albany. They serve without compensation, but are reimbursed for travel and other expenses. They elect their own chancellor and vice chancellor (§ 203). There are no ex officio Regents; that is, members of the Regents do not serve simply by virtue of their holding an elected or appointed position (§ 202).

The New York State Education Department

1:10. What is the New York State Education Department?

The New York State Education Department, under the direction of the commissioner of education, is the administrative arm of the University of the State of New York. It is charged with carrying out legislative mandates and the Regents' policies.

1:11. What is the function of the State Education Department?

The State Education Department (SED) is charged with the general management and supervision of all public schools and all the education work of the state (§ 101), from prekindergarten to graduate school, and is responsible for setting educational policy, standards and rules. SED also supervises the state's nonpublic schools, oversees the 38 licensed professions, provides vocational and educational services to people with disabilities, guides local government records programs, and operates the State Archives, Library and Museum.

1:12. How is the State Education Department organized?

The principal functions of the State Education Department (SED) are carried out within six major areas: Office of Management Services; Office of Cultural Education; Office of Elementary, Middle, Secondary and Continuing Education; Office of Higher and Professional Education; Office of the Professions; and the Office of Vocational and Educational Services for Individuals with Disabilities. The following two areas directly pertain to elementary and secondary education.

The **Office of Elementary, Middle, Secondary and Continuing Education (EMSC)** is responsible for strengthening local capacity to develop and implement a comprehensive and coordinated system of quality services for more than 2.8 million public school students in 4,000 schools, 714 school districts, and 38 BOCES (boards of cooperative educational services); more than 479,000 private school students in 2,145 schools; and more than 200,000 adult learners.

It works with schools to set high standards for student academic achievement, provides curriculum materials and curriculum-based state-wide tests used by virtually all schools, and helps districts identify, receive, and use state and federal grant and aid programs.

EMSC is organized into two interdisciplinary regional field teams — one in New York City and one in Albany, identified as the Regional School Services Office. Each regional field team represents the coordination and integration of all EMSC programs and services.

The **Office of Vocational and Educational Services for Individuals with Disabilities (VESID)** promotes educational and vocational achievement for students with disabilities, ages three to 21. It administers special education programs and services in New York's school system and provides support for families, educators and other staff. VESID's vocational rehabilitation program provides specialized programs and services that assist youth and adults with disabilities in preparing for, finding and adjusting to employment. VESID also supports businesses that are interested in hiring and maintaining a skilled workforce.

VESID administers 35 independent living centers across the state and 15 early childhood direction centers. VESID also oversees statewide networks responsible for providing training and information to parents, educators and others involved in educating preschool and school-aged students with disabilities. VESID's headquarters are in Albany, and it maintains 15 district offices throughout the state.

For more information about these departments, contact SED at 518-474-3852, or via its website at http://www.nysed.gov.

The Commissioner of Education

1:13. What is the role of the commissioner of education?

The commissioner of education is the president of the University of the State of New York and the chief executive officer of the State Education Department and the Board of Regents (§ 305(1); 8 NYCRR § 3.5; see **1:5, 1:7, 1:10-11.**)

1:14. What are the commissioner of education's powers and duties?

The commissioner of education's powers and duties are contained primarily in section 305 of the Education Law. They include enforcement of laws relating to the educational system, execution of all educational policies determined by the Board of Regents, issuance of regulations, supervision of all schools and institutions subject to the provisions of the Education Law, grant and annulment of teaching certificates, review of appeals and petitions pursuant to section 310, and execution of such other powers and duties as determined by the Board of Regents.

1:15. What are the commissioner's regulations?

The commissioner's regulations are rules that govern how the schools, institutions and other entities under the commissioner's jurisdiction are to be operated. They have the effect of law on the schools of the state unless they are overturned by the courts. They are officially compiled and published by the New York Department of State and are found in Title VIII of the Official Compilation of Codes, Rules and Regulations of the State of New York (8 NYCRR). They include, among other things, certification requirements for teachers, curriculum requirements, mandates on the building of schools, and standards for the various professions.

1:16. How is an appeal brought to the commissioner of education?

Any person believing himself or herself to be aggrieved by an official act of any officer or school authority, or by any action taken at a meeting concerning any matter under the Education Law or pertaining to the schools of the state, may appeal to the commissioner of education (§ 310). For example, that person must be aggrieved in the sense that he or she has suffered personal damage or injury to his or her rights *(Appeal of McCarthy,* 30 Educ. Dep't Rep. 264 (1991); *Appeal of Goldstein,* 29 Educ. Dep't Rep. 42 (1989); *Matter of Weinick,* 23 Educ. Dep't Rep. 362 (1984); *Matter of Coleman,* 23 Educ. Dep't Rep. 124 (1983)).

All appeals to the commissioner must be brought within 30 days after the decision or act complained of, or from the time knowledge of the cause of the complaint came to the person appealing the decision. However, the commissioner, in his sole discretion, may excuse a failure to commence an appeal in a timely manner for good cause (8 NYCRR § 275.16). The party against whom an appeal is filed and served must answer the appeal within 20 days of service (8 NYCRR § 275.13).

The commissioner will not determine moot or advisory questions but will determine only actual matters in controversy *(Appeal of a Student with a Disability,* 36 Educ. Dep't Rep. 248 (1996); *Appeal of Goldin,* 35 Educ. Dep't Rep. 446 (1996); *Appeal of Evans,* 33 Educ. Dep't Rep. 572 (1994); *Appeal of Sileo,* 28 Educ. Dep't Rep. 313 (1989); *Matter of Dobert,* 24 Educ. Dep't Rep. 36 (1984); *Matter of a Handicapped Child,* 24 Educ. Dep't Rep. 223 (1984)).

The commissioner will not decide the constitutionality of a statute *(Appeal of St. Cyr,* 27 Educ. Dep't Rep. 351 (1988); *Matter of Van Druff,* 21 Educ. Dep't Rep. 635 (1982)) or violations of the Open Meetings Law, Freedom of Information Law and the Family Education Rights and Privacy Act *(Appeal of Miller,* 36 Educ. Dep't Rep. 390 (1997); *Appeal of Boyle,* 35 Educ. Dep't Rep. 162 (1995); *Appeal of Nolan,* 35 Educ. Dep't Rep. 139 (1995); *Appeal of Winchell,* 35 Educ. Dep't Rep. 221 (1995)).

In addition, the commissioner will not resolve "novel questions of constitutional law" in an administrative appeal *(Appeal of Almedina,* 33 Educ. Dep't Rep. 383 (1993); *Ware v. Valley Stream High,* 75 N.Y.2d 114 (1989)).

Once it is decided, an appeal to the commissioner will not be reopened by the commissioner unless it is established that there is new and material evidence that was not available at the time of the original proceedings or that the original decision was rendered under a misunderstanding of the facts (8 NYCRR § 276.8; *Appeal of Wroblewski,* 36 Educ. Dep't Rep. 294 (1997); *Appeal of Bach,* 34 Educ. Dep't Rep. 18 (1994);

Appeal of Strada, 33 Educ. Dep't Rep. 666 (1994); *Appeal of Cook*, 27 Educ. Dep't Rep. 246 (1988)).

The procedures regarding appeals to the commissioner of education are detailed in "Handbook 1 – Regulations of the Commissioner of Education Relating to Appeals and Other Proceedings Before the Commissioner and the State Review Officer" (State Education Department, rev. Nov. 1, 1996). It is available from SED's Office of Counsel at 518-474-8927.

1:17. Are the commissioner of education's decisions reviewable by the courts?

Yes. The actions of the commissioner of education are subject to court review, the same as those of other state officials. The commissioner's decisions are subject to review in the courts by means of a proceeding under Article 78 of the Civil Practice Law and Rules. The commissioner's decisions are published in Education Department Reports (Educ. Dep't Rep.). Ordinarily they can be found in any county courthouse law library, or they can be obtained by writing directly to the State Education Department's Publications Sales, Education Building, Room 309, 89 Washington Avenue, Albany, NY 12234.

Local School Districts

Editor's Note: For additional information about school districts, see A Guide to the Reorganization of School Districts in New York State *(Albany, N.Y.: State Education Department, 1993).*

1:18. What is a common school district?

A *common school district* is a school district first created by legislative action in 1812 to operate elementary schools (kindergarten through eighth grade). Even though they lack legal authority to operate a high school, common school districts remain responsible for ensuring a secondary education for their resident children.

A common school district is administered by either a sole trustee or a school board of three trustees (§ 1602(1)). The number of members of the board of trustees of a common school district may be increased or decreased as set forth in law (§ 1602; see **2:5**).

1:19. What is a union free school district?

A *union free school district* is a school district generally formed from one or more common school districts to operate a high school program, which common school districts cannot do. First authorized by legislation in 1853, union free school districts are administered by a school board of between three and nine members. The number of members of the board of education of a union free school district may be increased or decreased as set forth in law (§§ 1702, 1703; see **2:5**).

Currently, not all union free school districts operate a secondary school program, and some have been established solely as special act school districts to serve children who reside in specified child-care institutions (see **1:23**).

1:20. What is a central school district?

A *central school district* is a school district formed by combining any number of common, union free and central school districts. First established in 1914, the central school district is the most common form of district organization in the state. Like union free districts, central school districts may operate a high school. Their school boards may consist of five, seven or nine members (§ 1804(1)). The number of board members may be increased or decreased as set forth in law (§ 1804(3); see **2:5**).

1:21. What is a central high school district?

A *central high school district* is a school district that provides only secondary education to children from two or more common or union free school districts. Only three such districts exist in the state, and the Legislature has prohibited the formation of additional such districts, except in Suffolk County.

A central high school district's governing board is composed of representatives from each of its participating districts (the number of members of such board shall be not less than five). A central high school district is part of a supervisory district (§§ 1912-1914; see **6:2**).

1:22. What is a city school district?

A *city school district* is a school district whose school boundary lines are identical with that of a city. There are two types of city school districts: those with a population under 125,000 and those with a population of 125,000 or more (§§ 2501, 2550). The enlargement of a city school district by the addition of a group of union free and common school districts results in an *enlarged city school district* (§ 1526).

Article 51 of the Education Law applies to city school districts with less than 125,000 inhabitants. Their governing boards may consist of five, seven or nine members (§ 2502(2)).

Article 52 of the Education Law applies to cities with populations of 125,000 or more. There are five in New York State, commonly referred to as the Big 5 school districts: Buffalo, New York City, Rochester, Syracuse and Yonkers. Rochester and Syracuse have seven-member boards, chosen by the voters at either a general or municipal election (§§ 2552, 2553(2)). Yonkers has a nine-member school board, each member appointed by the mayor (§§ 2552, 2553(3)). Buffalo has a nine-member school board: one member elected by the qualified voters of each member of the six city school subdistricts, and three members elected in a citywide, at-large election by the qualified voters (§ 2553(10)(c)).

The New York City Central Board of Education has seven members (§ 2590-b(1)(a)). Five of them are appointed by the city's borough presidents, and two are appointed by the city's mayor. The central board is charged with establishing and maintaining the following kinds of schools or classes to meet the needs and demands of the city: free elementary schools, high schools, training schools, technical schools, vocational and industrial schools, kindergartens, nursery schools, night schools, part-time or continuation schools, schools for adults, schools for physically or mentally disabled children, as well as schools for delinquent children or such other schools or classes as the board deems necessary to meet the needs and demands of the city (§ 2554(9)).

In addition, New York City has 32 community school boards, each composed of nine elected members. The community school boards are responsible for prekindergarten, nursery, kindergarten, elementary, intermediate and junior high schools (§ 2590-e). Special provisions relating to their governance are found in article 52-A of the Education Law.

1:23. What is a special act school district?

Special act school districts are those that are created by a special act of the Legislature rather than through a procedure provided in the Education Law. In general, these districts have been established on the grounds of charitable institutions caring for children and youth.

They are designated by the state Legislature as public school districts authorized to receive state financial aid. For example, Abbott House in Westchester County is known legally as Union Free School District No. 13, and Mother Cabrini School in Ulster County is known legally as West Park Union Free School District. Section 3602 of the Education Law outlines the details on apportionment of state aid for such districts.

1:24. What is a board of cooperative educational services (BOCES)?

A *board of cooperative educational services (BOCES)* is a voluntary, cooperative association of school districts in a geographic area that have

banded together to provide educational or business services more economically than each district could offer by itself. Each BOCES is governed
by a board of between five and 15 members elected by the component
school boards (see chapter 5 for more detailed information).

1:25. What is the relationship of a school district to local and county governments?

The relationship between a school district and local or county
government is a multifaceted one that is based on the necessity for
close communication and cooperation regarding the development and
administration of programs and services to be provided by the governmental bodies to the schools of the district.

In addition to their concern regarding the education of the students of
their districts, school boards must perform a variety of functions related
to the security, safety, health and well-being of their students. Thus,
boards must work with numerous agencies of local governments, such as
the police and fire departments as well as health, fiscal, taxation and
civil defense authorities.

Many school districts also find they work closely with county government bodies, such as planning and zoning commissions, in the selection
and acquisition of school sites, and in the construction of school buildings
and related structures or additions.

1:26. Who determines the official name of a school district?

The Education Law provides that school districts, other than city
school districts, adopt simplified legal names subject to the approval of
the commissioner of education. It requires the commissioner to issue, on
request, documents certifying the name of a school district and the names
of the towns and counties in which the territory of the district is located,
or in the case of school districts other than city school districts, which
are wholly or partly located within a city, the names of the city, as well
as the towns and counties in which the territory of the district is located
(§ 315).

The name of a centralized school district is designated by the commissioner in the centralization order (§ 1801). However, the name of a central
school district established or reorganized by such an order may be changed
by the district's school board if a written request is filed with the commissioner at least 14 days before the establishment or reorganization of the
district (§ 315; see **15:2** on centralization).

The Parent-Teacher Association

1:27. What is the parent-teacher association's relationship to the public schools?

The New York State Congress of Parents and Teachers, otherwise known as the parent-teacher association (PTA), is a voluntary group of citizens that acts in an advisory capacity to school boards, superintendents and principals. School boards are responsible for the administration of the schools and the development of the policies that govern their operation.

Section 2590-d(2)(a) of the Education Law states that a New York City community school board must provide for either a parent association or a parent-teacher association in each school under its jurisdiction and maintain regular communications with each association. In addition, community school boards must provide to all parent associations and parent-teacher associations information on student achievement, including but not limited to: annual reading scores, comparison of the achievement of students in comparable grades and schools, as well as the record of achievement of the same children as they progress through the school. This information may not be disclosed in a manner which would identify individual pupils (§ 2590-d(2)(b)).

1:28. May PTA members serve on school boards?

Yes. Service as an officer or member of a PTA does not bar individuals from membership on a school board. However, a member of the PTA who is a teacher within the same district may not serve, as teachers may not serve on the school board of the district in which they are employed (§ 2103(4); see **2:18**).

1:29. Where can information about the PTA and its publications be obtained?

Information about the PTA can be obtained from the New York State Congress of Parents and Teachers, Inc., One Wembley Square, Albany, N.Y. 12205; telephone 518-452-8808.

2. School Boards

2:1. What is a school board?

A school board is a corporate body that oversees and manages a public school district's affairs, personnel and properties. (§§ 1601, 1603, 1701, 2502(1), 2551). Its members are elected by the residents of the school district the board oversees (see **2:3**).

The term *corporate body* indicates that a school board is treated as a corporation, a legal entity that has an existence distinct and apart from its members and has the capacity for continuous existence without regard to changes in its membership. As such, the legality of a school board's contracts as well as the validity of its policies and resolutions do not depend on its individual members. Board members do not assume any personal liability for the school district even though they may be personally liable for certain conduct (see **18:1-2; 18:18**). Generally, school board members take official action only by majority vote at an official meeting (see **2:12**).

2:2. What is the composition of a school board?

A school board is composed of its elected members. One member is elected by the board at its annual reorganizational meeting to serve as president (see **3:1-3**). At its discretion, the board also may elect a vice president, who exercises the duties of the president in case of that officer's absence or disability. If the office of president becomes vacant, the vice president acts as president until a new president is elected (§ 1701).

2:3. How many school board members serve on a school board?

It depends on the type of school district. As the voters of the district determine, a common school district may have from one to three trustees (§§ 1602(1), 2101(1)). A union free school district may have from three to nine members on its board (§§ 1702(1), 2101(2)). A central school district may have a board consisting of five, seven or nine members (§ 1804(1)). The board of a central high school district is comprised of a minimum of five members, at least one from each common school district and at least two from each union free school district within the central high school district (§§ 1901, 1914).

A small city school district with a population under 125,000 may have a board consisting of five, seven or nine members (§ 2502(2)). A large city school district's board consists of between three and nine members (§ 2552). For example:

• In Yonkers, nine school board members are appointed by the mayor from the city at large (§§ 2552(d), 2553(3)).

• In both Rochester and Syracuse, seven board members are elected by the voters at large, at either a general or municipal election, or both (§§ 2552(b),(c); 2553(2)).

• In Buffalo, a total of nine school board members are elected by the qualified voters of the city from a combination of specific districts and at-large seats. Six of these board members are elected from six subdistricts of equal population created by the Buffalo Common Council, and three members are elected from the city at large (§§ 2552(a), 2553(10)).

• Two members of the seven member New York City Board of Education (i.e., the central board) are appointed by the mayor, and the remaining five members are appointed by each of the five borough presidents (§ 2590–b(1)). The two members appointed by the mayor must reside in the city, whereas each of the five borough president appointees must reside in their respective boroughs of appointment.

• School boards for the 32 community school districts within the New York City school district have nine members each who are elected at large under the provisions of section 2590–c.

A board of cooperative educational services (BOCES) has from five to 15 members elected by the members of the school boards of the BOCES' component school districts (§ 1950(1),(2)). A more detailed discussion of BOCES members' terms, as well as other issues related to BOCES, is provided in chapter 5.

2:4. What is the term of office for board members?

It depends on the type of school district. In common school districts that have just one trustee, the trustee serves only a one-year term (§§ 1602(1), 2105(1)). However, in common school districts with three trustees, the trustees are elected for three-year terms (§§ 1602(1), 2105(2)). In union free and central school districts, board members are elected for terms of three, four or five years (§§ 1702(1),1804(1), 2105(3)).

Members of a central high school board must be members of the school board of a component district while they are members of the central high school board, but the term of office on the central high school board can be shorter than the term on the school board of the component district (*Appeal of Carbonaro*, 35 Educ. Dep't Rep. 257 (1996); see also §§ 1901, 1914).

The term of office for city board members varies among the various city school districts. In most city school districts with less than 125,000 inhabitants, the term of office of a school board member is three or five years, as determined by the district (§ 2502(2)). In the Albany City School District, a board member's term is four years (§ 2502(3)). In the Rensselaer City School District, the term is five years (§ 2502(9-a)(n)).

In city school districts with 125,000 or more inhabitants (the Big 5), the term of office of school board members is as follows:

- In Buffalo, board members elected from the city school subdistricts are elected for a period of three years, while the term of office for members of the school board elected at-large is five years (§ 2553(10)(n)).
- In New York City, community school board members are elected for a term of three years, while members of the central board are appointed to four-year terms (§§ 2590–b(1)(a), 2590–c(1)).
- In both Rochester and Syracuse, board members are elected to four-year terms (§ 2553(4)).
- In Yonkers, board members are appointed to five-year terms (§ 2553(4)).

BOCES board members generally serve three-year terms (§ 1950(2)). A more detailed discussion of BOCES members' terms, as well as other issues related to BOCES, is provided in chapter 5.

2:5. May the number of members on a school board be changed?

Yes. In common school districts that have only one trustee, two-thirds of the legal voters present and voting at any annual meeting may determine to increase the size of the board to three trustees (§ 1602(3); see also *Matter of Gillison*, 70 State Dep't Rep. 60 (1949)). In common school districts that already have three trustees, a simple majority of the voters present and voting may decrease the size of the board to one trustee (§ 1602(2)). When the voters determine to decrease the number of trustees to one, the trustees in office continue in office until their terms expire, and thereafter only one trustee will be elected (§ 1602(2)).

In union free and central school districts, a proposition to increase or decrease the size of the board of education must be put before the voters upon petition of 25 voters or five percent of the number of people who voted in the previous annual election, whichever is greater (§§ 1703(2), 1804(3); see also *Matter of Swanson*, 29 Educ. Dep't Rep. 503 (1990)). In small city school districts, the board may, on its own motion, and must, on a written petition signed by 500 qualified voters of the district, submit a proposition at the annual election to increase or decrease the number of members of the board (§ 2502(4)(a)).

Such petitions must be submitted enough in advance, according to the procedures prescribed by the board, to allow a statement giving notice of the proposition to be included in the notice of the annual meeting (§§ 1703(2), 2035(2), 2502(4)(b); see also *Matter of Presutti*, 17 Educ. Dep't Rep. 445 (1978)).

When the voters determine to increase the number of board members, the additional members are elected at a special meeting called for that purpose (§§ 1703(3), 1804(3); *Matter of District No. 4, Town of Saugerties*, 70 St. Dep't Rep. 60 (1949)), except in common and small city school districts where the additional members are elected at the next annual meeting (§§ 1602(3); 2502(4)(c)). The terms of the new members must be established so as to ensure that as nearly as possible an equal number of terms expire each year (§§ 1602(3); 1804(3); 2105(9); 2502(3), (4)(c)(3)).

In union free, central and small city school districts, if the voters approve a decrease in the number of board members, no election may be held until the number of members on the board is equal to or less than the number to which the board has been decreased. At subsequent elections, board members are to be elected for terms of no more than five years, again with the aim that an equal number of terms are to expire each year (§§ 1804(3), 2105(10), 2502(4)(c)).

For information on the boards of cooperative educational services (BOCES), see **5:5-6**.

2:6. What is the difference between a trustee and a school board member?

The term *trustee* generally refers to a member of a school board of a common school district, whereas the term *school board member* generally refers to a member of the school board of any other type of school district. These terms are sometimes used interchangeably, but the more contemporary and commonly used term is board member.

Board member is also the term used throughout this book, unless a distinction is necessary for accuracy or clarity.

2:7. Are school board members local officials or state officials?

School board members are local officials.

Section 2 of the Public Officers Law defines *state officers* as those who are elected by all of the state's voters (such as the governor, lieutenant governor, comptroller, and attorney general); members of the state Legislature; justices of the state supreme court; Regents of the University of the State of New York; and every officer, appointed by one or more state officers, or by the Legislature, and authorized to exercise his or her official functions throughout the state or without limitation to any political subdivision of the state. All others are considered to be local officers, including school board members. However, their authority and duties are defined by the state and federal constitutions and laws, as well as by rules and regulations promulgated by the Board of Regents and commissioner of education.

2:8. Are members of a school board required to take a constitutional oath of office?

Yes. School board members are not able to exercise the duties of office until they take the following oath: "I do solemnly swear (or affirm) that I will support the constitution of the United States and the constitution of the State of New York, and that I will faithfully discharge the duties of the office of . . . ., according to the best of my ability" (State Constitution Art. 13 §1). This oath must be filed with the district clerk. In the case of a board of cooperative educational services (BOCES), each board member files an oath in the office of the clerk of the county in which that member resides (Pub. Off. Law § 10).

Usually the oath is administered to newly elected school board members at the board's annual reorganizational meeting by either the president of the board or the district clerk. The fact that the oath has been administered should be noted in the board's minutes.

Members who are reelected to the school board also must take the oath at the beginning of their new term of office, just as at the beginning of the first term they held. District officers of the board, such as the president, vice president, clerk and treasurer, must be administered the oath each year at the time of their appointment or reappointment. The refusal or neglect of a public officer to file an oath of office within 30 days after the commencement of the term of office to which the person is elected, or if appointed, within thirty days after notice of appointment, causes the office to become vacant (Pub. Off. Law § 30(1)(h)).

2:9. Must school board members file statements disclosing their personal financial status?

No. The Ethics in Government Act, which requires individuals holding or running for office to make financial disclosure statements, applies to municipalities with populations of 50,000 or more, but not to school districts (Gen. Mun. Law §§ 810(1); 811). Candidates for school boards, however, are required to file campaign expenditure statements under the Education Law (§§ 1528-1531; see **4:40** for more information).

Powers and Duties

2:10. What are the powers and duties of a school board?

"A board of education has no inherent powers and possesses only those powers expressly delegated by statute or necessarily and reasonably implied therefrom" *(Appeal of Bode,* 33 Educ. Dep't. Rep. 260 (1993)).

Although there are different types of school districts, all school boards are similar in that they are responsible for the education of the children residing in their respective districts. The general powers and duties of school boards are outlined in the Education Law, which assigns different powers and duties to different types of school districts, some of which are common to various types of districts, others of which are specific to a single type of district.

School boards of common school districts are governed by section 1604. School boards of union free school districts are governed by section 1709. Central school boards are governed by section 1804, small city school districts by section 2503, large city school districts by section 2554, New York City community school boards by section 2590-e, and the New York City "central" board by section 2590-g. Additional powers and duties may be found in other laws such as the General Municipal Law, the Real Property Law and the Public Officers Law, as well as in federal law and commissioner's regulations.

Consistent with law, school boards also have the authority and duty to adopt whatever policies, rules and bylaws they deem will best meet their statutory responsibilities and secure the best educational results for the students in their charge (see, e.g. §§ 1709(1), (2); 2503(2); see also **2:78-83**). Generally, a school board is responsible for the admission, instruction, discipline, grading and, as appropriate, classification of students attending the public schools in its district; for the employment and management of necessary professional and support staff; and for purchasing, leasing, maintaining and insuring school buildings, properties, equipment and supplies (see generally § 1709). With the exception of large city school districts, school boards must also present a detailed statement of estimated expenditures (i.e., the proposed budget) for the ensuing school year, which must be submitted to the district voters annually for approval (§§ 1608, 1716, 2601-a).

2:11. What is devolution, and how does it affect the powers and duties of school boards?

Devolution is the process by which the powers and duties assigned to specific school districts at the top of the list in Figure 1 below devolve and become applicable to other types of school districts through specific provisions of the Education Law (§§ 1710, 1804(1), 1805, 1903, 2503(1), 2554(1)). As shown in this figure, districts lower on the list are granted many of the powers of districts higher on the list by reference to the powers possessed by those districts. As these powers and duties devolve down to other types of districts, they are joined by additional powers and duties that then devolve to school districts located lower on the list. The additional powers, however, do not apply to school districts located higher on the table. Powers and duties devolve down but not up.

Figure 1 Devolution		
Type of District	Education Law Article	Education Law Section(s)
Common School District	33	–
Union Free School District	35	1710
Central School District	37	1804(1), 1805
Central High School District	39	1903
Small City School District	51	2503(1)
Large City School District	52	2554(1)

Unless the Education Law provides otherwise, a particular type of school district has all of the powers and duties assigned specifically to it, as well as all of the powers and duties assigned to the other types of school districts located above it on the list. Figure 1 above indicates the order of the devolution of powers and duties of school districts. The figure also refers to the article of the Education Law that governs each type of school district, as well as the section of the Education Law that provides for such devolution.

In this handbook, a general reference or citation to powers and duties of school districts refers to those of union free school districts, as set forth in section 1709, which usually apply, through devolution, to all other school districts, with the exception of common school districts.

2:12. Do individual members of a school board have the right to take official action on the board's behalf?

Generally, no. A school board acting in its corporate capacity is required to transact its business in the same manner as the governing body of any corporation; that is, its acts are required to be authorized by resolutions or motions duly adopted or passed by a majority of the whole board (Gen. Constr. Law § 41; *Matter of Ascher*, 12 Educ. Dep't Rep. 97 (1972)).

In addition, court decisions invariably agree that a transaction has no legal effect and is not considered an official action unless made at a properly constituted meeting of the board. Therefore, unless the board has taken official action to designate an individual member as the representative of the board for a particular purpose, an individual board member has no more authority than any other qualified voter of the district (see *Appeal of Silano*, 33 Educ. Dep't Rep. 20 (1993); *Matter of Bruno*, 4 Educ. Dep't Rep. 14 (1964)).

However, occasionally the board may delegate authority to a board officer, such as an auditor (§§ 1709(20-a), 2554(2-a)). It may also delegate the power to perform ministerial acts to other district officers or employees, such as authorizing the business manager to make purchases with appropriated funds of certain items that do not require competitive bidding (8 NYCRR § 170.2(b)).

2:13. May a school board appoint a superintendent of schools?

Yes. A school board has the authority to appoint a superintendent of schools for a period of years, and may enter into employment contracts of varying duration with its superintendent as permitted by law (§§ 1604(8), 1711, 2503(5), 2554(2); see **7:17-21**). Boards may also agree to extensions of the superintendent's contract, so long as the entire term of the contract plus any extensions does not exceed the maximum term authorized by statute (*Appeal of Boyle*, 35 Educ. Dep't Rep. 162 (1995); see also **7:19**).

2:14. May an outgoing school board extend a superintendent's contract and thus bind successor boards?

Yes. The commissioner of education has ruled that even last-minute extensions of a superintendent's contract by an outgoing board, while not democratic, are legal and bind a successor board, because there is specific statutory authority permitting multi-year contracts with a superintendent (*Appeal of Dillon*, 33 Educ. Dep't Rep. 544 (1994); *Appeal of Knapp*, 34 Educ. Dep't Rep. 207 (1994); see **7:20**).

By contrast, a retirement agreement between an outgoing board and its clerk was properly rescinded by a new board, according to the commissioner, who ruled that the incentives amounted to a gift of public funds because the clerk was planning to retire in any event (*Appeal of Fiore*, 34 Educ. Dep't Rep. 619 (1995)).

2:15. May a school board remove its superintendent?

Generally, yes. The board, however, must comply with any applicable provisions set forth in law or in the superintendent's contract (see also **7:24-25**).

2:16. What are the school board's responsibilities with respect to a school census?

In the cities of New York, Buffalo and Syracuse, the board of education must take a school census for the purpose of enforcing the provisions of the compulsory education law (§ 3240). In small city school districts, each board of education also serves as a permanent census board which has a duty to maintain a continuous census of all children residing in the district from birth to 18 years of age, and of children with disabilities to the age of 21. The census board is required to provide information to the commissioner of education (§ 3241(1)).

All other school districts are simply authorized, rather than required, to take a census of all children residing in the district from birth to 18 years of age (§ 3242). They still have an obligation to locate and identify students with disabilities residing in their district and establish a register of such students entitled to attend school or receive preschool services (§ 4402(1)(a); 8 NYCRR § 200.2(a); see also **13:8**).

2:17. May a school board establish a school camp?

Yes. An individual school district, or two or more school districts jointly, may establish and operate a school camp on school land or land acquired for that purpose. The camp may be used to furnish education in subjects deemed proper by the board, as well as to provide physical training, recreation and maintenance for all children of school age whether they attend public or private school. Districts may charge a reasonable fee to cover costs of food and instructional materials, although the law requires that provision be made for children who cannot afford these fees (§§ 4501-4502).

Membership

2:18. What are the qualifications for membership on a school board?

To qualify for membership on a school board in a common, union free, central, central high school or small city school district, an individual:

- Must be able to read and write (§ 2102).
- Must be a qualified voter of the district; that is, a citizen of the United States, at least 18 years of age or older, and not adjudged

to be an incompetent (§§ 2102, 2012, 2502(7); Elec. Law § 5-106(6)). (Moreover, a convicted felon is barred from running for a seat on a board of education, if his maximum prison sentence has not expired, or if he has been not been pardoned or discharged from parole (Elec. Law § 5-106(2)).

- Must be and have been a resident (but need not be a taxpayer) of the district for a continuous and uninterrupted period of at least one year (30 days in the city of Rensselaer (§ 2502(9-a)(d)) immediately before the election (§§ 2102; 2502(7),(9)(d); see also *Appeal of Baleno*, 30 Educ. Dep't Rep. 358 (1991)).
- May not have been removed from any school district office within the preceding one year (§ 2103(2)).
- May not reside with another member of the same school board as a member of the same family (§ 2103(3); *Rosenstock v. Scaringe*, 40 N.Y.2d 563 (1976)).
- May not be a current employee of the school board (§ 2103(4); see **2:20**).
- May not simultaneously hold another incompatible public office (*Matter of Schoch*, 21 Educ. Dep't Rep. 300 (1981), see also **2:41-44**).

In large city school districts and in New York City community school districts, different rules of law and/or exceptions to the above rules may govern membership on the school board (see, for example §§ 2553(1); 2590–c(3), (4); 2590–c(4)).

2:19. May a school district impose additional requirements for school board membership?

No. A school district may not require candidates for a school board position to meet eligibility requirements in addition to those imposed by statute (*Matter of Guilderland CSD*, 23 Educ. Dep't Rep. 262 (1984)).

In one case, the commissioner of education invalidated a "gentlemen's agreement" observed by a school district for more than 60 years, under which seats of elected school board members were allocated among the communities comprising the district (*Appeal of Gravink*, 37 Educ. Dep't Rep. 393 (1998)).

2:20. May a former employee of the school district serve on the school board?

Yes. Even where the school board could address a matter directly pertaining to the former employee's personal interests, such as continuing retiree health insurance benefits, because contracts with a teachers union, which is a "voluntary nonprofit association," are exempt from the provisions of the conflict of interest law (*Application of Casazza*, 32 Educ.

Dep't Rep. 462 (1993); Gen. Mun. Law § 802(1)(f); see **2:35-40** for more information on conflicts of interest).

2:21. May an individual be a school board member if that person's spouse is employed by the district?

Yes. There is no prohibition against the employment of spouses, children or other relatives of board members to positions in the district. The Education Law, however, requires a two-thirds vote by the board to hire a teacher who is related to a board member by blood or by marriage (§ 3016). The two-thirds vote requirement does not apply and has no effect on the continued employment of a tenured teacher who is initially hired before his or her relative is elected or appointed to the school board (*Appeal of Heizman*, 31 Educ. Dep't Rep. 387 (1992)).

In one case, the commissioner ruled that a person who sought employment as a social worker, in the district where her spouse was a member of the board of education, was a teacher for the purposes of this section of law and therefore needed approval from two-thirds of the board in order to be appointed (*Appeal of McNamara*, 30 Educ. Dep't Rep. 272 (1991)).

Furthermore, due to a specific statutory exception, a "contract of employment" between the district and a relative does not create a prohibited conflicting interest for the board member (Gen. Mun. Law § 800(3)(a); *Matter of Behuniak*, 30 Educ. Dep't Rep. 236 (1991); see **2:35, 2:38**).

2:22. May a member of the clergy seek office as a member of a school board?

Yes. The United States Supreme Court declared unconstitutional any ban on the eligibility of members of the clergy to run for public office, provided they meet all the statutory qualifications (*McDaniel v. Paty*, 435 U.S. 618 (1978)).

2:23. May a school board member resign from office?

Yes. Under the Education Law, a board member or other school district officer who wishes to resign may do so at a district meeting, or by filing a written resignation with the district (BOCES) superintendent of his or her district, which becomes effective only upon the approval of the district superintendent and filing with the school district clerk (§ 2111; see also Opn. Att'y Gen. 97-1).

In addition, a board member may resign under the Public Officers Law by delivering a written resignation to the district clerk (Pub. Off. Law § 31(1)(h); *Matter of Verity*, 28 Educ. Dep't Rep. 171 (1988); see also Opn. Att'y Gen. 97-1). The clerk must then notify the school board and the state board of elections (Pub. Off. Law § 31(3),(5)). Such a resignation becomes effective on the date specified, or if no effective date is specified, then immediately upon delivery of filing with the proper officer, except that in no event shall the effective date be more than 30 days after its proper filing (Pub. Off. Law § 31(2)).

A successor may not be appointed or elected until after the resignation becomes effective *(Roberts v. Allen,* 54 Misc.2d 746 (1962)).

2:24. Once a school board member has submitted his or her resignation, may it be withdrawn?

Yes, but only with the consent of the person to whom the resignation was delivered, such as the district clerk or district (BOCES) superintendent. The school board has no authority to consent to a request to withdraw a resignation (Pub. Off. Law § 31(4); *Matter of Verity,* 28 Educ. Dep't Rep. 171 (1988)).

2:25. May a school board member be removed from office?

Yes. A board member may be removed by the commissioner of education for neglect of duty or for the willful violation or disobedience of a law or a decision, order or regulation of the commissioner of education or Board of Regents (§§ 306, 1706, 2559; *Matter of Felicio,* 19 Educ. Dep't Rep. 414 (1980); see also 8 NYCRR Part 277). New York City community school board members are subject to removal by the chancellor of the New York City schools (§ 2590-l).

A school board may also remove any of its members for "official misconduct"; that is, misconduct relating to the exercise of authority as a member of the school board (§ 1709(18); *Matter of Cox,* 27 Educ. Dep't Rep. 353 (1988)). In either event, the removal may take place only after a hearing on the charges either before the commissioner of education, at which the board member has a right to be represented by counsel (§ 306(1)), or before the board of education itself (§§ 1709(18), 2559; see **2:33, 2:40**).

The commissioner's decisions have held uniformly that school officers will be removed only when they have been judged guilty of willful, unlawful conduct. Poor judgment alone does not establish that a violation of the law was willful *(Application of Marshall,* 33 Educ. Dep't Rep. 26 (1993); *Matter of Schmucker,* 32 Educ. Dep't Rep. 643 (1993)). Ordinarily, a board member who acts in good faith on the advice of counsel will not be found to have acted with the requisite willfulness to warrant removal from office *(Appeal of McCall,* 34 Educ. Dep't Rep. 29 (1994); see also *Application of Golden,* 36 Educ. Dep't Rep. 319 (1997)). However, where the advice of counsel directly contradicts established law, reliance on such advice will "not necessarily shield a board member from removal under section 306" (*Appeal of Scarrone*, 35 Educ. Dep't Rep. 443 (1996); see also *Matter of BOCES*, 32 Educ. Dep't Rep. 519 (1993)).

The commissioner has removed a board member, for instance, for behavior that interfered with the board's ability to function in a case where a board member threatened and initiated a physical altercation with another board member during a board meeting. Such conduct breached the board member's "duty to engage in constructive discussion" on matters affecting the governance of the district (*Appeal of Kozak*, 34 Educ. Dep't Rep. 501 (1995)).

The commissioner also may withhold from any district its share of state aid for willfully disobeying any provision of law or any decision, order or regulation (§ 306(2)).

2:26. May a school board member be censured or reprimanded?

No. Nothing in the Education Law authorizes either a board of education or the commissioner of education to censure or reprimand a school board member. However, a school board may criticize the actions of a board member for exhibiting poor judgment (*Appeal of Silano*, 33 Educ. Dep't Rep. 20 (1993)).

Board Vacancies

2:27. How do vacancies occur on a school board?

In addition to the timely expiration of a board member's term of office, vacancies on a school board may occur due to death, incapacity, resignation, removal from office or refusal to serve (§ 2112; *Matter of Turchiarelli*, 31 Educ. Dep't Rep. 402 (1992); see also **2:28**).

A position may also become vacant if an incumbent board member moves to a residence outside the district (Pub. Off. Law § 30(1)(d); see also *Matter of Willard*, 23 Educ. Dep't Rep. 448 (1984)). However, "an individual's residence is not lost until a new residence is established through both intent and action" (*Appeal of Lavelle*, 28 Educ. Dep't Rep 189 (1988)).

A vacancy also will occur if a board member is convicted of a felony or crime involving his or her oath of office, is declared incompetent or refuses or fails to file an oath of office (see Pub. Off. Law § 30(1); Opn. Att'y Gen. F 97-7).

2:28. May a vacancy on a school board be declared if a member is absent from three successive meetings?

Yes. A vacancy may be declared if the record clearly shows that a board member has failed to attend three successive meetings and has no sufficient excuse for the absence (§§ 2109, 2502(8), 2553(8), 2590-c(8)(a); see *Matter of Cox*, 28 Educ. Dep't Rep. 156 (1988)). If the board member has sufficient excuse to warrant absence from the meetings, a vacancy cannot be declared.

2:29. What is the procedure to fill a vacancy that may occur on a school board?

Any school board may call a special election to fill such a vacancy within 90 days after it occurs, and if it is not so filled, the district (BOCES) superintendent may fill it by appointment in school districts under his or her jurisdiction (§ 2113(1)). Common school districts must call a special district meeting immediately to fill a vacancy (§ 1607(2)). In addition, the commissioner of education may order a special election to fill a vacancy in a union free school district (§ 2113(2)). If a vacancy is filled by a special district election, the board member elected serves for the remainder of the unexpired term (§ 2113(3)).

In union free, central and small city school districts, the school board may choose instead to appoint a qualified person to fill a vacancy (§§ 1709(17), 1801(1), 2502(6)). Consistent with the limitation on the board's authority to act as a corporate body, a vote of the majority of the whole board ordinarily is required to fill a vacancy by appointment (see **2:12**). But in small city school districts, due to a unique provision of law, only a "majority of the remaining members of the board" is needed to appoint a qualified person to fill a board vacancy (§§ 2502(6), (9)(n), (9-a)(n)). If the vacancy is filled by appointment, the new board member serves only until the next regular school district election (§§ 1709(17), 2113(3), 2502(6)).

Special rules of law govern the appointment of board members in the Albany and Rensselaer city school districts (§§ 2502(9)(n), 2502(9-a)(n)), and in large city school districts (§§ 2553(6),(7), (9)(e), (10)(n); 2590-c(8)).

A person elected or appointed to fill a vacancy takes office immediately upon filing the oath of office (§§ 1709(17), 2502(6), see also **2:8**).

2:30. Are school districts obligated to fill a vacancy when one arises?

The applicable laws impose upon union free and central school districts the power and duty to fill a vacancy (§§ 1709(17), 1804(1)), and require common school districts to immediately call a special meeting to fill the vacancy when it occurs (§ 1607(2)).

The commissioner has ruled, however, that small city school boards are not obligated to fill a vacancy because, in his view, the statutory language governing vacancies in small city schools makes filling a vacancy optional (*Appeal of Keyrouze*, 34 Educ. Dep't Rep. 468 (1995)). But in the Albany and Rensselaer city school districts, which are governed by special provisions of law not examined by the commissioner in the decision above, the law provides that whenever a vacancy occurs other than because of the expiration of a board member's term of office or because of an increase in the size of the board, the board "shall" appoint a qualified person to fill the vacancy (§§ 2502(9)(n), 2502(9-a)(n)).

Ethics and Conflicts of Interest

2:31. Must a school board adopt a code of ethics and operate according to its tenets?

Yes. The General Municipal Law requires all school boards to adopt a code of ethics for the guidance of its officers and employees that sets forth the standards of conduct reasonably expected of them (Gen. Mun. Law § 806).

The law requires school district codes of ethics to "provide standards for officers and employees with respect to disclosure of interest in legislation before the local governing body, holding of investments in conflict with official duties, private employment in conflict with official duties, future employment and such other standards relating to the conduct of officers and employees as may be deemed advisable" (Gen. Mun. Law § 806(1)(a); see also Opn. St. Comp. 82-189).

The board's code should not violate other statutes. For example, the commissioner of education has held improper a board's attempt to apply a provision of its code of ethics as an additional qualification for membership on the board, eligibility for which is governed specifically by the Education Law (*Matter of Guilderland CSD*, 23 Educ. Dep't Rep. 262 (1984)). In another case, the commissioner declared null and void that portion of a board of education's code of ethics which prohibited board members from voting on the employment contracts of their relatives (*Appeal of Behuniak*, 30 Educ. Dep't Rep. 236 (1991)).

Additional information regarding the provisions of this law, including requirements for the adoption and filing of codes of ethics, may be obtained from the New York State Department of State, Division of Legal Services, 41 State Street, 8th Floor, Albany, N.Y. 12231; telephone 518-474-6740.

2:32. Must the school district's code of ethics be distributed or filed?

Both. The superintendent of schools, as chief executive officer of the district, must distribute a copy of the code of ethics to every district officer and employee, who must enforce and comply with the code, even if they do not actually receive a copy (Gen. Mun. Law § 806(2)). The district clerk must file a copy of the code, and any amendments to it, with the office of the state comptroller (Gen. Mun. Law § 806(3)(a)).

In addition, the superintendent must ensure that the district posts a copy of the provisions of the General Municipal Law regarding conflicts of interest, in each public building in a place conspicuous to its officers and employees. However, failure to post the provisions will have no effect on the duty to comply with the law, or with its enforcement (Gen. Mun. Law § 807).

2:33. Are there certain actions by school board members, district officers and employees which are specifically prohibited by law?

Yes. Public officers and employees, including school board members, district officers and employees, are specifically prohibited from:

- Soliciting or accepting any gift worth more than $75 under circumstances where it reasonably could be inferred that the gift was intended to influence or reward official action. School districts, through their own codes of ethics, can set the figure lower than $75, though not higher (Gen. Mun. Law § 805-a(1)(a); Opn. Att'y Gen. 95-10; see also Penal Law §§ 200.00, 200.10).
- Disclosing confidential information acquired during the course of their official duties or using such information to further their personal interests (Gen. Mun. Law § 805-a(1)(b)). Allegations that a board member has disclosed confidential information must be supported by competent evidence (see *Application of Bd. of Educ. of Middle Country CSD*, 33 Educ. Dep't Rep. 511 (1994)).
- Representing clients for compensation before the board or district (Gen. Mun. Law § 805-a(1)(c)).
- Entering into contingency arrangements with clients for compensation in any matter before the school board or district (Gen. Mun. Law § 805-a(1)(d)).
- With certain limited exceptions, having an interest in any contract, lease, purchase or sale over which they have any responsibility to negotiate, prepare, authorize, approve or audit (Gen. Mun. Law §§ 800-805).

In addition to any penalty contained in any other provision of law, any person who knowingly and intentionally violates these rules of law may be fined, suspended or removed from office or employment (Gen. Mun. Law § 805-a(2)).

2:34. Can school board members be paid for their service as board members?

Generally, no. Opinions of the state comptroller have consistently held that school board members may not receive compensation for their services unless expressly authorized by an act of the state Legislature, as in the case of members of the New York City school board (Opn. St. Comp. 72-342, 71-985; § 2590-b (1)(a)).

However, school board members may be reimbursed for expenses actually and necessarily incurred in the performance of their official duties (§ 2118). Board members also may receive reimbursement to cover the costs of conferences, such as those sponsored by the New York State School Boards Association, if they are believed to be of benefit to the district and if they are authorized by a resolution approved by a majority of the board, or approved by a duly authorized designee of the board, prior to attendance at such a conference (Gen. Mun. Law § 77–b; see **19:9**).

2:35. What is a conflict of interest?

The term *conflict of interest* describes a situation in which a school board member, district officer or employee is in a position to benefit personally from a decision he or she may make on behalf of the district through the exercise of official authority or disposing of public funds. The General Municipal Law expressly makes the provisions regarding conflicts of interest applicable to school districts (Gen. Mun. Law § 800(4)).

Personal interests which are prohibited by law include:

- Interest in a contract with the school district where a school board member, district officer or employee has the power or may appoint someone who has the power to negotiate, authorize, approve, prepare, make payment or audit bills or claims under the contract unless otherwise exempted under law (Gen. Mun. Law §§ 801(1), 802).
- Interest by a chief fiscal officer, treasurer, or his or her deputy or employee in a bank or other financial institution that is used by the school district he or she serves (Gen. Mun. Law § 801(2)).

Contract is defined to include any claim, account or demand against, or agreement, express or implied, as well as the designation of a depository of public funds or a newspaper for use by the school district (Gen. Mun. Law § 800(2)).

Interest is defined as a direct or indirect pecuniary benefit that runs to the officer or employee as a result of a contract with the school district (Gen. Mun. Law § 800(3)). An officer or employee is deemed to have an interest in: a firm, partnership or association of which the officer or employee is a member or employee; a corporation of which the officer or employee is an officer, director or employee; or a corporation of which the officer or employee directly or indirectly owns or controls any stock. A school district officer or employee also is deemed to have an interest in a contract between the district and his or her spouse, minor child or dependents, except that the law specifically allows a school district officer's or employee's spouse, minor child or dependent to enter into an employment contract with the district (Gen. Mun. Law § 800(3)).

2:36. What are some examples of conflicts of interest for school board members?

A school board member had a conflict of interest, for instance, when the district purchased heating oil from the company of which the board member was president and in which he owned more than 5 percent of the stock (*Appeal of Golden*, 32 Educ. Dep't Rep. 202 (1992)). In another situation where a vice president of a corporation that both installed and continued to maintain a school telephone system was elected to a board of education, there was no prohibited conflict of interest in the contracts entered into with his corporation prior to his election, although there was a potential conflict of interest after he became a board member, depending upon his responsibilities as an officer of the company, (if any) in connection with the contracts at issue (Opn. St. Comp. 86-58).

2:37. What are some examples of situations which do not involve a conflict of interest?

Section 802 of the General Municipal Law lists several specific exceptions. One such exception provides that a contract entered into by the district with a person who later is elected or appointed to the school board remains valid, except that the contract may not be renewed (Gen. Mun. Law § 802(1)(h)). A board member may enter into a contract or multiple contracts with the school district if the total consideration paid under the contract is, or contracts are, less than $750 (Gen. Mun. Law § 802(2)(e)).

In addition, the conflict of interest provisions do not apply to employment of a school board member who is a duly licensed physician as school physician upon authorization by a two-thirds vote of the board (Gen. Mun. Law § 802(1)(i)).

A school board member who is an officer of a bank and is employed at the main office of such bank has no conflict of interest either, where the school district has designated a branch of that bank as a depository for district funds and the bank employee would never have occasion to become involved in any school district transactions occurring at the branch designated for the school district's deposits (Opn. St. Comp. 77-504).

2:38. Does an interest arising from a collective bargaining agreement constitute a prohibited conflict of interest?

No. Collective bargaining agreements fall within a statutory exception to the general rule regarding contracts with membership corporations or other voluntary, nonprofit corporations or associations, and, therefore, a personal interest arising from such a contract is not a prohibited interest under the law (Gen. Mun. Law § 802(1)(f); *Stettine v. County of Suffolk*, 66 N.Y.2d 354 (1985); see also Opn. St. Comp. 89-24)).

The commissioner of education has cited the *Stettine* case to reject petitions attacking the election of board members who are retired district employees with continuing health insurance benefits under the district's collective bargaining agreement (see *Application of Casazza*, 32 Educ. Dep't Rep. 462 (1993); *Appeal of Samuels*, 25 Educ. Dep't Rep. 228 (1985); see **2:20**). This, of course, does not affect the prohibition against current employees serving as board members (see **2:18**).

Similarly, board members voting on the collective bargaining agreements of their relatives do not have a prohibited conflict of interest (Gen. Mun. Law § 800(3), Educ. Law § 3016(2); *Appeal of Behuniak*, 30 Educ. Dep't Rep. 236 (1991); see also **2:21, 2:31, 2:35**).

2:39. How can a school board determine whether one of its members has a prohibited conflict of interest?

To decide whether one of its members has a prohibited conflict of interest, a board must determine:

- Whether there is a contract with the school district.
- Whether the board member in question has an interest in that contract.
- Whether the board member is authorized to exercise any of his or her powers or duties with respect to the agreement (see Gen. Mun. Law 801(1); see **2:35**).
- Whether any exception to the conflict of interest law is applicable (Gen. Mun. Law § 802; see also Opn. St. Comp. 89-39; see **2:37-38**).

In addition, board members are required to disclose any interest they may have or acquire in any actual or proposed contract involving the district, even though it is not a prohibited interest (Gen. Mun. Law § 803; *Matter of Ackerberg*, 25 Educ. Dep't Rep. 232 (1985)). Interests which are not prohibited but which nonetheless may create an appearance of impropriety may be properly restricted by the district's code of ethics, as long as the restriction is not inconsistent with other provisions of law (Opn. St. Comp. 88-77; *Appeal of Behuniak*, 30 Educ. Dep't Rep. 236 (1991)).

2:40. What consequences may result from a violation of the conflict of interest law?

Any contract willfully entered into by or with a school district in which there is a prohibited interest is void and unenforceable (Gen. Mun. Law § 804). Furthermore, a school board member who knowingly and willfully violates the law in this regard or fails to disclose an interest in a contract may be guilty of a misdemeanor (Gen. Mun. Law § 805) and/or subject to removal from office by the commissioner of education (see *Appeal of Golden*, 32 Educ. Dep't Rep. 202 (1992); see also **2:25**).

Incompatibility of Office

2:41. May a school board member run for or hold an additional public office?

There is no general prohibition against holding two or more public offices at the same time (Opn. Att'y Gen. 82-1 (1982)). However, two issues must be addressed: first, whether there is an express prohibition against the board member holding or running for the office in question; and second, whether the duties of the two offices may be legally incompatible (see **2:42-44**).

2:42. What makes two public offices or positions of employment incompatible with one another?

One person cannot simultaneously hold two public offices or positions of employment if one office is subordinate to the other, such that the person would essentially be his or her own boss, or if the functions of the two positions are inherently inconsistent with each other, such as serving simultaneously as the district's finance officer and as the auditor responsible for the integrity of the district's finances (see *O'Malley v. Macejka*, 44 N.Y.2d 530 (1978); Opn. Att'y Gen. 92-13).

There must be a great likelihood of a division of loyalties or a conflict of duties between the offices, not merely a possibility that such complications may arise on occasion.

The doctrine of compatibility of office does not prohibit an individual from being a candidate for election to a second office where that office is incompatible with the first, if he or she intends to resign from the first office if elected to the second. However, if there is a specific provision of law that makes two offices or positions incompatible, such a provision of law may expressly disqualify a person from even being a candidate for a second incompatible office or position (Opn. Att'y Gen. 89-62; see, for example, **2:44**). Once elected and upon accepting the second office, an individual vacates the first office automatically (Opn. Att'y Gen. 89-62; *People ex rel. Ryan v. Green,* 58 N.Y. 295 (1874)).

Even where two public offices or positions of employment are compatible, a situation may arise in which holding both offices creates a conflict of interest. If this occurs, the conflict can be avoided by declining to participate in the conflicted matter (Opn. Att'y Gen. 92-13).

2:43. Are there any positions a school board member is specifically prohibited from holding?

The Education Law specifically prohibits a board member from also holding the positions of district superintendent, supervisor, clerk, tax collector, treasurer or librarian simultaneously (§ 2103(1)), or from being an employee of his or her school board (§ 2103(4)). In union free and central school districts, however, a board member may be appointed clerk of the board and of the district (§§ 2130(1), 1804(1); *Matter of Hurtgam,* 22 Educ. Dep't Rep. 219 (1982)).

In city school districts, the Education Law provides that school board members may not hold any city office other than that of police officer or firefighter (§ 2502(7); Opn. Att'y Gen. 90-80, 87-6). Decisions determining whether an employee holds an office within the meaning of this provision turn on the presence of traditional indicia of office, such as the taking of an oath of office, the filing of an undertaking or bond, designation as an office holder in a city charter, or significant policy-making authority (Opn. Att'y Gen. 90-80, 87-6).

Additionally, a town supervisor may not be a trustee of a school district (Town Law § 23(1)). But there is no prohibition against a deputy town supervisor serving as a member of a board of education (see **2:44**).

2:44. Are there any offices that have been found to be incompatible with the office of school board member?

Yes. For example, counsel to the state attorney general has expressed the opinion that public school board members may not serve simultaneously as members of the board of education of a private school within the district (Opn. Att'y Gen. 87-58), a city's common council in small city school districts (Opn. Att'y Gen. 84-61), director of weights and measures in small city school districts (Opn. Atty. Gen. 90-80), or as county elections commissioner in any city school district (Opn. Att'y Gen. 87-50; see also Elec. Law § 3-200(4)).

The state Advisory Committee on Judicial Ethics has issued an opinion indicating that a part-time judge may not seek election to a local board of education, because the Rules of the Chief Administrator of the Courts prohibit judges from campaigning for elective office (Joint Opn. of Advisory Committee on Judicial Ethics 89-157/90-7; 22 NYCRR § 100.7).

The Advisory Committee also states that a judge who already has been elected to a school board should resign because the "position on the school board [is] one that may involve dealing with quasi-political and highly controversial issues" that are incompatible with holding judicial office (*Id.*, see also 22 NYCRR § 100.5(h)). But a part-time justice may accept "appointment" to the board of trustees of a publicly funded school district for handicapped children, because by virtue of the "appointment" the justice will not be required to compete in a public, political election in order to obtain a seat on the school board, and because in that particular type of school district there is no public referendum on the school district's budget (Joint Opn. of Advisory Committee on Judicial Ethics 94-59; 22 NYCRR § 100.5(b) (h)).

On the other hand, a school board member may serve simultaneously as trustee of a public library (*Matter of Schoch*, 21 Educ. Dep't Rep. 300 (1981); see also Opn. Att'y Gen 81-110), town assessor (Opn. St. Comp. 73–1174), employee of a BOCES (*Matter of Todd*, 19 Educ. Dep't Rep. 277 (1979), village mayor (Opn. Att'y Gen. 91-59; see also Village Law §3-300), member of a town zoning board of appeals (Opn. Att'y Gen. 84-68), member of a city school board and county director of real property tax services (Opn. Att'y Gen. 93-9), volunteer in an athletic department of the school, depending upon the significance of the volunteer's responsibilities (Opn. Att'y Gen. 92-13), and deputy town supervisor (Opn. Att'y Gen. 96-29). This is only a partial list of opinions on compatibility of office. For more information, contact the state Attorney General's Office.

Board Meetings

2:45. What types of meetings are conducted by school boards?

School board meetings fall into the following categories:

- The annual *organizational* (also commonly referred to as the *reorganizational*) meeting is when the school board elects and appoints its officers and committees for the coming year, and board members take or renew their oaths of office. In most school districts, this meeting must be held each year in July. For specific dates and times (where applicable) that school districts must hold their annual organizational meeting, see **3:2**.

• *Regular* board meetings, which are the regularly scheduled business meetings held throughout the year (see **2:47**).

• *Special* board meetings, which are not regularly scheduled and may be called by any member of the board to address a particular item or items (see **2:48**).

Board meetings are distinct from school district meetings, such as the annual district meeting, at which a school board presents its annual budget to voters in the district and at which school board elections are held, or special district meetings, called for either by the voters or by the school board for district residents to vote on specific issues and propositions. See chapter 4 for more information on school district meetings.

2:46. Must school board meetings be held within the school district limits?

No. However, meeting in a location intended to avoid the public and news media may be deemed a violation of the Open Meetings Law, resulting possibly in the annulment of any action taken at the meeting (see Pub. Off. Law §§ 103, 107(1)).

2:47. Are school boards required to hold a certain number of regular meetings?

Yes. The Education Law requires school boards to meet at least once each quarter of the year (§ 1708(1)). Most boards, however, meet at least once a month. In city school districts, monthly meetings are required (§§ 2504(2), 2563(2)).

2:48. Who may call a special meeting of the school board?

Any member of a school board has the authority to call a special meeting of the board (see *Matter of Felicio*, 19 Educ. Dep't Rep. 414 (1980)), as long as notice of the meeting is given to the other board members at least 24 hours in advance (§ 1606(3)). The notice provided normally states the purpose of the meeting, although there is no specific requirement that it do so.

A majority of the board cannot decide to hold a meeting and dispense with providing notice to the remaining members. The law requires good faith efforts to give actual notice of a special or emergency meeting to each board member. Failure to do so may result in the invalidating of any action taken at the meeting (see *Matter of Colasuonno*, 22 Educ. Dep't Rep. 215 (1982)).

If it is determined that one board member did not receive notice, however, the action taken may be sustained if the member signs an affidavit waiving notice (*Matter of Bd. of Educ. of UFSD No.1 of the Town of Hume*, 29 St. Dep't Rep. 624 (1923)). It is advisable, therefore, in situations where notice cannot be given within 24 hours, that each board member sign a waiver of notice to be entered in the minutes.

Although special meetings are ordinarily held to consider a single item of business, other items of business may be included on the agenda for that meeting by consent of the board members present. There is no requirement that the notice of a special board meeting contain any notice of a proposed agenda (*Matter of Neversink*, 10 Educ. Dep't Rep. 203 (1971)).

Care should be taken, however, to see that the special board meeting does not usurp the place of regularly scheduled board meetings for the consideration of regular school district business.

2:49. What are the requirements for holding a school board meeting?

There must be a quorum of the board and public notice of the time and place of the meeting must be given (see **2:50-53**).

2:50. What constitutes a quorum of a school board?

A *quorum* is a simple majority (more than half) of the total number of board members (Gen. Constr. Law § 41). A quorum is required for the board to conduct any business. A majority of the entire board, not simply of those present, is required for the board to take any official action (Opn. of Counsel #70, 1 Educ. Dep't. Rep. 770 (1952); see also *Appeal of Greenwald*, 31 Educ. Dep't Rep. 12 (1991); Gen. Constr. Law § 41). For example, if a board has five members and three are present at a meeting, all three would have to vote in favor of a resolution for it to pass; a two-to-one vote would not be sufficient.

Generally, a school board may not adopt a policy requiring affirmative votes by more than a majority of the whole number of the board to take official action, because neither the Education Law nor the General Construction Law authorizes a board to adopt requirements in excess of those already provided by statute (*Matter of Miller*, 17 Educ. Dep't Rep. 275 (1978); but see *Appeal of Volpe*, 25 Educ. Dep't Rep. 398 (1986)).

2:51. Can school board members vote by telephone or video conference?

No. Although there are no court decisions on this issue, according to the Director of the Committee on Open Government, voting by telephone or video conferencing technology would be a violation of the Open Meetings Law. A person's physical presence is required in order to cast a vote

(NYS Department of State, Committee on Open Government, OML-AO-#2779, July 28, 1997; see also OML-AO-#2480, March 27, 1995).

2:52. What type of notice of meetings of the school board is required?

The Education Law does not require notice of board meetings to be published (*Matter of Thomas, et.al.*, 10 Educ. Dep't Rep. 108 (1971)). However, under the Open Meetings Law, which school boards must comply with, public notice stating the time and place of any board meeting must be given to the news media and conspicuously posted in one or more designated public locations at least 72 hours before the meeting, if it has been scheduled at least one week before it occurs (Pub. Off. Law § 104(1)).

If the meeting is scheduled less than a week in advance, public notice of the time and place of every other meeting must be given to the news media "to the extent practicable" and posted conspicuously a reasonable time before the meeting (Pub. Off. Law § 104(2); *Previdi v. Hirsch*, 138 Misc.2d 436 (Sup. Ct. Westchester County, 1988)).

2:53. Is an agenda necessary for a board meeting?

Although good business practice may indicate that an agenda of the regular session is in order, an agenda is not specifically required for either regular meetings or executive sessions. Moreover, the procedure to be followed at school board meetings is left to the policies adopted by the board (*Matter of Kramer*, 72 St. Dep't Rep. 114 (1951)).

2:54. Are school board meetings open to the public?

Yes. Because school boards are public bodies, the Open Meetings Law (Pub. Off. Law § 103) requires school board meetings conducted to discuss school district business to be open to the public (see also Educ. Law § 1708(3)).

Public business includes not only binding votes of the board, but also any activity which is preliminary to such a vote or involves consideration of a matter which could be the subject of board action (Pub. Off. Law § 102; *Goodson Todman Enterprises, Ltd. v. Kingston Common Council*, 153 A.D.2d 103 (3rd Dep't 1990); but see *Hill v. Planning Bd. of Amherst*, 140 A.D.2d 967 (4th Dep't 1988)).

This rule does not apply to a casual or chance encounter by board members not intended for purposes of doing business, as long as the encounter does not become an informal conference or agenda session (*Orange County Publications, Div. of Ottoway Newspapers, Inc. v. Council of Newburgh*, 60 A.D.2d 409 (1978)). Thus, the attendance of board members at a board development retreat, for example, where no school district business is discussed, would be exempt from the requirements of this rule according to an opinion by the Committee on Open Government (NYS Department of State, Committee on Open Government, OML-AO-#1973, Sept. 13, 1991).

The public may be excluded only from properly convened executive sessions of the board (Pub. Off. Law §§ 105(2), 1708(3); see **2:58-59**).

In addition, both the Public Officers Law and the federal Americans with Disabilities Act (ADA) require that public bodies make reasonable efforts to ensure that meetings are held in facilities that permit barrier-free physical access to physically disabled persons (Pub. Off. Law § 103(b); 42 USC §§ 12102 *et seq.*).

For more information on the requirements of the Open Meetings Law, see *The Sunshine Laws,* a handbook published by the New York State School Boards Association. Questions can also be directed to the Committee on Open Government at the following address: New York Department of State, Committee on Open Government, 41 State Street, Albany, N.Y. 12231; telephone 518-474-2518.

2:55. Do people attending a public school board meeting have the right to tape the meeting?

As a general rule, yes. A state appellate court has determined that there is no justifiable basis for prohibiting the use of unobtrusive, hand-held tape recording devices at public meetings of a board of education (*Mitchell v. Bd. of Educ. of Garden City UFSD*, 113 A.D.2d 924 (2nd Dep't 1985)). In another case, a judge found that a school board's bylaw prohibiting the use of recording devices at board meetings violated public policy (*People v. Ystueta*, 99 Misc.2d 1105 (District Court, Suffolk County, 1979; see also *Feldman v. Town of Bethel*, 106 A.D.2d 695 (3rd Dep't 1984)).

2:56. Are work sessions and planning meetings of the school board open to the public?

Yes. Any meeting of at least a quorum of a public body where public business is to be conducted, even if only for the purpose of informal discussions, must be open to the public, unless it is a properly convened executive session (Pub. Off. Law §§ 102(1), 103(1); *Goodson Todman Enterprises, Ltd., v. Kingston Common Council,* 153 A.D.2d 103 (3rd Dep't 1990); see also **2:57**).

2:57. Are board committee meetings open to the public?

Yes. Meetings of committees and subcommittees of the board are subject to the Open Meetings Law and must be publicized in the same manner as other public meetings (Pub. Off. Law § 102).

Meetings of board advisory committees created by the board to make recommendations to and advise the board, however, are not generally subject to the requirements of the Open Meetings Law. Nonetheless, shared-decision-making committees, both district-wide and school-based, are subject to the Open Meetings Law (NYS Department of State, Committee on Open Government, OML-AO-#2456, Jan. 31, 1995).

2:58. What is an executive session?

An *executive session* is a portion of the school board meeting which is not open to the public. It can take place only upon a majority vote of the total membership of the board taken at an open meeting (Pub. Off. Law. §105(1)). The motion should specify the subject or subjects to be discussed (*Gordon v. Village of Monticello*, 207 A.D.2d 55 (3rd Dep't 1994)), *reversed on other grounds*, 87 N.Y.2d 124 (1995)).

Executive sessions are permitted only for a limited number of specific purposes. A board may call an executive session only on the following subjects:

- Matters which will imperil the public safety if disclosed.
- Any matter which may disclose the identity of a law enforcement agent or informer.
- Information relating to current or future investigation or prosecution of a criminal offense which would imperil effective law enforcement if disclosed.
- Discussions involving proposed, pending or current litigation.
- Collective negotiations pursuant to article 14 of the Civil Service Law.
- The medical, financial, credit or employment history of a particular person or corporation, or matters leading to the appointment, employment, promotion, demotion, discipline, suspension, dismissal or removal of a particular person or corporation.
- The preparation, grading or administration of exams.
- The proposed acquisition, sale or lease of real property or the proposed acquisition, sale or exchange of securities, but only when publicity would substantially affect the value of these things (Pub. Off. Law § 105(a-h)).

Courts have the power to declare void any action taken at an executive session that is held for reasons not specified by the Open Meetings Law (Pub. Off. Law § 107(1); *Gernatt Asphalt Products v. Town of Sardinia*, 87 N.Y.2d 668 (1996)). Moreover, the court may award reasonable attorneys fees to a party who sues a school district for a violation of the Open Meetings Law and prevails (Pub. Off. Law § 107(2); see also *Matter of Gordon v. Village of Monticello*, 87 N.Y.2d 124 (1995)).

With certain limited exceptions, no official action can be taken on issues discussed in executive session without first returning to open session (see § 1708; *Matter of Crapster*, 22 Educ. Dep't Rep. 29 (1982)). Exceptions include confidential matters pertaining to children with disabilities and voting on charges against a tenured teacher pursuant to section 3020-a(2)(a) of the Education Law (for a general discussion, see Formal Opn. of Counsel No. 239, 16 Educ. Dep't Rep. 457 (1976)).

2:59. Who is entitled to attend executive sessions?

All members of the board of education and "any other persons authorized by" the board may attend executive sessions (Pub. Off. Law §105(2); see also Educ. Law § 1708(3)). Thus, only those people who are invited by the board may attend. It should be noted in this context, however, that in both large and small city school districts, the superintendent possesses the power "to have a seat on the board of education and the right to speak on all matters before the board, but not to vote" (§§ 2508(1); 2566(1)).

It is important that a school board exercise discretion in deciding whom to invite into executive session because of important confidentiality issues. In one case, the commissioner of education ruled that the attendance at executive session of a former school board member, who was awaiting the results of an appeal of the election he lost, was in conflict with statutory and regulatory provisions providing for the confidentiality of personnel and student records *(Appeal of Whalen*, 34 Educ. Dep't Rep. 282 (1994)).

2:60. Does the public have a right to speak at school board meetings?

Although school board meetings must be open to the public (Educ. Law § 1708(3), Pub. Off. Law § 103, see also **2:54**), there is no law that requires school boards to allow members of the public to speak at school board meetings. However, the commissioner of education encourages school boards whenever possible to allow citizens to speak on matters under consideration *(Appeal of Wittenben*, 31 Educ. Dep't Rep. 375 (1992)). The board can agree to limit the time for a person to speak (see *Matter of Kramer*, 72 St. Dep't Rep. 114 (1951)).

The commissioner has ruled that a school board need not permit non-residents to speak at public board meetings, even where the board has a policy of permitting residents to speak *(Matter of Martin*, 32 Educ. Dep't Rep. 381 (1992)). However, the state Committee on Open Government has indicated that such a practice would violate the Open Meetings Law. The committee concurs with the commissioner that school boards are not required to allow members of the public to speak at board meetings in the first place, but cautions that if a school board permits public participation, it may not discriminate between residents and non-residents (NYS Department of State, Committee on Open Government, OML-AO-#2696, Jan. 8, 1997 and OML-AO-#2717, Feb. 27, 1997).

2:61. Is the president or presiding officer of the school board entitled to vote at board meetings?

Yes. A school board member does not lose a vote while serving as presiding officer. His or her vote is expected on every matter and should not be reserved only for tie votes (Opn. of Counsel No. 70, 1 Educ. Dep't Rep. 770 (1952)).

2:62. May a school board rescind action previously taken at a board meeting?

Generally, the courts have held that a school board may rescind an action it has taken at any time before such action becomes final. The New York State Court of Appeals has held, for instance, that a board may not be barred from reconsidering a prior decision not to dismiss a probationary employee (*Venes v. Community School Board*, 43 N.Y.2d 520 (1978)). By contrast, it has also held that an offer of an appointment to tenure prior to the expiration of the probationary period, together with a proposed salary, becomes binding and may not be revoked by the board (see *Weinbrown v. Board of Education of Hempstead UFSD No. 15*, 28 N.Y.2d 474 (1971)).

However, according to section 34 of *Robert's Rules of Order*, a board may not rescind a previous action which, as a result of the vote on the main motion, may not be undone. For example, a board may not undo a contract it has already agreed to by motion, and the other party of that contract has been notified of the original vote.

2:63. May school board members prevent action on a matter by refusing to vote on a motion?

If a majority of the school board votes in favor of a motion, it is approved, whether the remaining members of the board vote against it, abstain or otherwise refuse to vote (see **2:50**).

When a motion is voted on, board members are expected to be counted and must be reported in the minutes either as voting for or against each motion, or as having abstained from voting (Pub. Off. Law § 87(3)(a)).

In one case, the commissioner of education ruled that school board members may not abstain from voting on whether to grant tenure to a school employee based upon philosophical objections to the state's tenure system. Board members who abstain from voting on tenure recommendations on that basis face possible removal from office for dereliction of duty (*Appeal of Craft*, 36 Educ. Dep't Rep. 314 (1997)).

2:64. Must minutes be taken at school board meetings?

Yes. Formal minutes of all actions must be taken at open meetings. Minutes must consist of a record or summary of all motions, proposals, resolutions and other matters formally voted upon, including the result of any vote (Pub. Off. Law § 106(1)). Records of votes must include the final vote of each board member on every matter voted on (Pub. Off. Law § 87(3)(a)). There is no requirement that the minutes be comprehensive in nature, although the board may impose additional requirements by adopting a policy on minutes.

Generally, school boards are not authorized to take action in executive sessions. Where boards have such authority (see **2:58**), minutes of an executive session must be taken. However, they need only contain a record of any final determinations, the date and the vote. They need not contain any matter that is not available to the public under the Freedom of Information Law (see Pub. Off. Law § 106(2); *Plattsburgh Pub. Co., Div. of Ottoway Newspapers, Inc. v. City of Plattsburgh*, 185 A.D.2d 518 (3rd Dep't 1992)).

2:65. Is the public entitled to access the minutes of school board meetings?

Yes. According to the provisions of the Open Meetings Law, minutes of school board meetings must be available to the public within two weeks from the date of the meeting. Minutes taken at executive sessions of the board must be available to the public within one week, if they record an action taken by formal vote (Pub. Off. Law § 106; see **2:64**).

Minutes must be made available to the public even if they have not been approved by the board (NYS Department of State, Committee on Open Government FOIL-AO-#8543, Nov. 17, 1994). The law also requires that the district maintain a record of the final votes of each member of the board (Pub. Off. Law §§ 87(3)(a), 106(1)). These records may not be destroyed (see **2:75**).

Minutes may be amended in order to clarify what actually occurred at a meeting, but not to reflect a change of mind which occurred after the meeting. If there is a change of mind, according to accepted rules of order, there should follow a motion to rescind or amend the motion previously adopted, and the recision or amendment should be included in the minutes of the meeting where this occurred (see *Robert's Rules of Order* §§ 34, 47).

School District Records

Editor's Note: For more information on this subject and the Freedom of Information Law, see The Sunshine Laws, *a handbook published by the New York State School Boards Association. Questions can also be addressed to the Committee on Open Government at the following address: New York State, Department of State, Committee on Open Government, 41 State Street, Albany, N.Y. 12231; telephone 518-474-2518.*

2:66. Are school district records subject to public access and inspection?

Yes. Each school board is required by the Education Law and the Public Officers Law to have school district records available for inspection and copying at all reasonable times (§ 2116; Pub. Off. Law § 87). The Freedom of Information Law, which is part of the Public Officers Law and is also commonly referred to as FOIL, requires government bodies and agencies, including school districts, to allow the public access to official documents and records (Pub. Off. Law Art. 6, §§ 84-90). Any member of the public has the right to examine and/or copy these records or documents according to procedures adopted by the district in accordance with the law (see Pub. Off. Law § 87(1)(b)). A fee may be charged for copies (see **2:73**).

FOIL also allows districts to withhold access to certain categories of documents, including those which are required by law to be kept confidential (see Pub. Off. Law §§ 87(2), 89(7); **2:69**).

2:67. Are there any restrictions on who may access school district records?

Under FOIL, there is no restriction as to who may access district records. Although section 2116 of the Education Law provides that district records are to be available for inspection to any qualified voter, FOIL has been held to broaden the category of such persons to include individuals living outside the school district as well (*Duncan v. Savino*, 90 Misc.2d 282 (1977)).

Parents and eligible students have the right to see educational records pertaining to the student under the Family Educational Rights and Privacy Act (FERPA), also known as the Buckley Amendment (20 USC § 1232g; see also **2:70**).

2:68. What types of school district records are subject to public access and inspection?

The Education Law provides that the records, books and papers of the office of any officer of a school district are the property of the district and open for inspection and copying (§ 2116; but see *Appeal of Martinez,* 37 Educ. Dep't Rep. 435 (1998); see also **2:69**).

The Freedom of Information Law defines a record as "any information kept, held, filed, produced or reproduced by, with or for" the school district, "in any form, including but not limited to, reports, statements, examinations, memoranda, opinions, folders, files, books, manuals, pamphlets, forms, papers, designs, drawings, maps, photos, letters, microfilm, computer tapes or disks, rules, regulations or codes" (Pub. Off. Law § 86).

Only existing records are subject to disclosure. An agency does not need to prepare a record that does not already exist solely for the purpose of responding to a request for information (Pub. Off. Law § 89(3); *Curro v. Capasso,* 209 A.D.2d 346 (1st Dep't 1994)).

Examples of recorded information that may be inspected by interested citizens are school contracts, statements of expenditures and minutes of board meetings.

Each district is required to maintain a reasonably current list of documents it keeps, to enable the public to determine what records are of interest (see Pub. Off. Law § 87(3)(c)). The Committee on Open Government has suggested that school districts may use the same list as is used for retaining records under the commissioner's regulations (NYS Department of State, Committee on Open Government, FOIL-AO-#28288, June 3, 1994; see also 8 NYCRR § 185.12; 8 NYCRR Appendix I).

2:69. May any district records be withheld from public access and inspection?

Yes. While the Freedom of Information Law (FOIL) generally requires access to be given to all public records, it also specifically exempts the following records from mandatory disclosure:

- Those specifically exempted by a state or federal statute.
- Certain law enforcement documents and records.
- Records which, if disclosed, would constitute an "unwarranted invasion of personal privacy" (see Pub. Off. Law § 89(2)).
- Records which, if disclosed, would impair current or imminent contract awards or collective bargaining negotiations.
- Inter-agency and intra-agency materials which are not statistical or factual tabulations or data; instructions to staff that affect the public; final agency policy or determinations, or external audits.
- Information which, if disclosed, would endanger the life or safety of any person.
- Questions or answers to an exam which has not yet been administered.

- Computer access codes (see Pub. Off. Law § 87(2)).
- The name or home address of an applicant for appointment to public employment (Pub. Off. Law § 89(7); but see *Mothers on the Move, Inc. v. Messer,* 236 A.D.2d 408 (2nd Dep't 1997)).

Exceptions are treated very narrowly. For example, a budget examiner's worksheets have been determined to be subject to inspection as "statistical or factual tabulations," not exempt as internal documents (Pub. Off. Law § 87(2)(g)(i); see *Dunlea v. Goldmark,* 54 A.D.2d 446 (1976), *aff'd,* 43 N.Y.2d 754 (1977)).

According to the commissioner of education, the same exceptions from disclosure that are available under FOIL also apply to records requested pursuant to section 2116 of the Education Law. In other words, a school district can refuse to disclose records requested under this section, to the same extent that it could deny a FOIL request pursuant to one of the exceptions from disclosure available under FOIL (*Appeal of Martinez,* 37 Educ. Dep't Rep. 435 (1998)).

2:70. Are students' records accessible under FOIL?

No. FOIL exempts from disclosure records that are specifically exempted by federal or state statute (Pub. Off. Law § 87(2)(a)). Under the federal Family Educational Rights and Privacy Act (FERPA) (also known as the "Buckley Amendment"), only parents or eligible students (meaning any student who has reached 18 years of age or is attending an institution of post-secondary education) have the right to see educational records pertaining to the student. Disclosure to anyone else without the written consent of the parent or eligible student is limited except as provided by law (see 20 USC § 1232g *et seq.*; see also 34 CFR Part 99). For example, under FERPA, students' school health records, report cards and disciplinary files are categorized as privileged documents generally not to be disclosed except as provided by law.

Districts may disclose what is known as "directory information," that is, personally identifying information about students such as their names and addresses, but only after giving public notice of the categories of information that have been designated as directory information, and giving parents or eligible students a reasonable period of time in which to inform the district that such directory information should not be released without their consent (20 USC § 1232g(a)(5)(A),(B)). Districts may also disclose student records without parental consent in certain situations, such as to other school officials who have "legitimate educational interests" and certain other state and federal officials (20 USC § 1232g(b)). Moreover, all school records are subject to inspection by court order or pursuant to any lawfully issued subpoena, provided that parents and students are notified by the school district in advance of compliance with the court order or the subpoena (20 USC § 1232g(b)(2)(B)).

Federal funds may be denied to any school district that violates the provisions of FERPA (20 USC § 1232g (a)(1)(A), (a)(2), (b)(1), (b)(2), (f)).

2:71. Are 3020-a settlement agreements available to the public under FOIL?

Yes. Generally, agreements settling disciplinary charges are subject to disclosure under FOIL. However, certain portions of such agreements should be reviewed and edited before disclosure to the public in order to protect privacy, including charges that were denied and charges mentioning the names of other employees or students (*LaRocca v. Board of Educ. of Jericho Union Free School District*, 220 A.D.2d 424 (2nd Dep't 1995); but see *Anonymous v. Board of Educ. for the Mexico CSD*, 162 Misc.2d 300 (Sup. Ct. Oswego County 1994); *Buffalo Evening News, Inc. v. Bd. of Educ. of the Hamburg CSD* (Sup. Ct. Erie County 1987)).

2:72. Do school board members have access to school employees' personnel records?

Yes, under certain circumstances. The commissioner's regulations provide that any board member may request that personnel records be examined by the board in executive session, but only for inspection and use in the deliberation of specific matters before the board and if certain procedures are followed (see 8 NYCRR Part 84).

According to these regulations, information obtained from employees' personnel records by school board members may be used only to help make decisions on personnel matters, such as appointments, assignments, promotions, demotions, pay, discipline or dismissal; to aid in the development and implementation of personnel policies; and to enable the board to carry out its legal responsibilities (8 NYCRR § 84.3; *Matter of Krasinski*, 29 Educ. Dep't Rep. 375 (1990)). A school board that permitted a nonboard member in attendance at executive session to have access to personnel records violated the regulation (*Appeal of Whalen*, 34 Educ. Dep't Rep. 282 (1994)).

Any board member may request that the superintendent bring the personnel records of a designated employee or group of employees to the public board meeting. The board must then decide to meet in executive session to examine the records. Even if a majority of the board does not wish to view the records, a single member or minority of the board may insist that a majority of the board meet in executive session so that the interested members may do so *(Gustin v. Joiner,* 95 Misc.2d 277, *aff'd,* 68 A.D.2d 880 (2nd Dep't 1979)). Records are brought by the superintendent to the executive session and returned to the superintendent at the end of the session (8 NYCRR § 84.2).

Under other circumstances, an individual board member has no greater right of access to district records than any other member of the public *(Matter of Bruno,* 4 Educ. Dep't Rep. 14 (1964)). Therefore, that board member would be able to access only that which is available under FOIL (see *Buffalo Teachers Federation, Inc. v. Buffalo Bd. of Educ.,* 156 A.D.2d 1027 (4th Dep't 1989), *appeal denied,* 75 N.Y.2d 708 (1990)).

2:73. Are there specific procedures that must be followed to gain access to school district records?

School districts are required under FOIL to adopt procedures by which interested citizens may review district records. These procedures must specify the times when and places where records are available, the names or titles of persons responsible for providing records and any fees for copying records. Copying fees may be the actual cost of reproduction, excluding fixed overhead costs, up to 25 cents per 9-inch-by-14-inch page, or any fee specified by law (Pub. Off. Law § 87(1)(b)).

Interested persons must make their request for records in writing to the school district and must identify the desired records in sufficient detail for the request to be honored. Requests should be directed to the records access officer who is the individual school districts must designate by law to be responsible for ensuring compliance with FOIL (Pub. Off. Law § 87(1)(b)).

The school district must respond within five days of the receipt of a written request by making the record available, by issuing a written denial, or by acknowledging the request and stating approximately when the request will be granted or denied (Pub. Off. Law § 89(3)).

School districts also must maintain a procedure for people to appeal the denial of records. The procedure must allow a person to appeal a denial within 30 days to the individual designated by the school board to receive and decide such appeals. Within 10 days of receipt of the appeal, that person must either provide the record requested or a written explanation of the reason for the further denial (Pub. Off. Law § 89(4)(a)).

The district must provide a "particularized and specific justification for denying access" or a "factual basis" for claiming an exemption *(Rushford v.*

Oneida-Herkimer Solid Waste Authority, 217 A.D.2d 966 (4th Dep't 1995)). The district must also file each appeal and its outcome with the Committee on Open Government (Pub. Off. Law § 89(4)(a)), at the following address: New York State, Department of State, Committee on Open Government, 41 State Street, Albany, N.Y. 12231.

Anyone who is dissatisfied with the district's final decision on a request for access to records may appeal the decision to the supreme court of the appropriate county (Pub. Off. Law § 89(4)(b)). The commissioner of education does not hear appeals regarding alleged violations of the FOIL, FERPA, or the Open Meetings Law (*Appeal of Lindauer,* 34 Educ. Dep't Rep. 596 (1995); *Application of McDougald,* 34 Educ. Dep't Rep. 424 (1995)).

2:74. What penalties may be imposed against a school district for denying access to district records?

If records of clearly significant public interest are withheld without a reasonable basis under FOIL, the school district may be assessed reasonable attorneys' fees and other costs of litigation incurred by a person who has sued for disclosure (Pub. Off. Law § 89(4)(c); see also *Gordon v. Village of Monticello,* 87 N.Y.2d 124 (1995)).

The willful concealment or destruction of public records with the intent to prevent public inspection of such records is also a violation of section 240.65 of the Penal Law and section 89(8) of the Public Officers Law, punishable by a fine of up to $250 and/or a jail term of up to 15 days (Penal Law §§ 70.15(4), 80.05(4)).

2:75. Are there any restrictions on the destruction of school district records?

Yes. Public records must be maintained and preserved in accordance with the "Local Government Records Law" which is contained in Article 57-A of the state Arts and Cultural Affairs Law. Pursuant to this law, the commissioner of education has created a document called the "Records Retention and Disposition Schedule ED-1" with which school districts must comply (Arts & Cult. Aff. Law §§ 57.17(1); 57.23; 57.25; 8 NYCRR § 185.12; 8 NYCRR Appendix I).

Records may be destroyed only after being retained for a period specified in the Schedule ED-1 (Arts & Cult. Aff. Law § 57.25(2)). Moreover, before any records listed on the Schedule ED-1 may be disposed of, the board of education must formally adopt the Schedule ED-1 by passing a resolution (8 NYCRR Appendix I, p. vii; see p. xi for a sample resolution).

Documents which are not listed in the schedule may be destroyed only with the permission of the commissioner (8 NYCRR § 185.6(a)). Records of employee disciplinary matters, investigations and evaluations may be disposed of according to the terms of a collective bargaining agreement (8 NYCRR § 185.6(d)).

Records may be preserved on microfilm and the originals disposed of, unless they date from before 1910 or have "enduring statewide significance," according to the commissioner's criteria (8 NYCRR §§ 185.6(c), 185.7), in which case they may be destroyed only with the commissioner's approval. Film reproductions are treated legally as original documents (Arts & Cult. Aff. Law § 57.29).

The destruction of canceled bonds and notes and similar obligations is governed by regulations of the state comptroller (Loc. Fin. Law § 63.10; Opn. St. Comp. 80-351).

In addition, the district clerk must deliver all records to his or her successor (§ 2121(7); Pub. Off. Law § 80).

2:76. What is a records management officer?

A *records management officer* is a person charged with the duty of initiating, coordinating and promoting the systematic management of school district records in cooperation with other school district officers. Specific duties of this officer are outlined in the commissioner's regulations (8 NYCRR § 185.2(c); see also Arts & Cult. Aff. Law § 57.19).

The records management officer is a position with responsibilities distinct from a records access officer, who is responsible for ensuring compliance with FOIL (see **2:73**).

Local governments, including school districts, must designate a records management officer and must notify the commissioner of education of his or her name, title or position, address and telephone number within one month of the designation (8 NYCRR § 185.2(a)(2)). If the position should become vacant, the school board must designate a replacement within 60 days and again must notify the commissioner of the replacement within one month of the designation (8 NYCRR § 185.2(b)).

2:77. What can school districts do to improve the management of their records?

The state Legislature has created a Local Government Records Management Improvement Fund which will remain in effect through the year 2002. This fund benefits local governments through grants for local records management and regionally-based technical assistance (Laws of 1995, Ch. 385).

School Board Policies

2:78. What is a policy?

A *policy* is a statement that establishes standards and/or objectives to be attained by the district. A school board policy should clearly state the board's view of what it considers to be the mission of the district, the objectives to be reached and the standards to be maintained; the manner in which the district is to perform these tasks, including the allocation of responsibilities and delegation of duties to specific staff members; and the methods to be used, the procedures to be followed and the reasoning to be applied in conducting the district's business, whether by the administration, instructional staff, other employees, students, parents or the public.

2:79. What is the function of school board policies?

Policies are the means by which a school board leads and governs its school district. Policies form the bylaws and rules for the governance of the district and serve as the standards to which the board, administration and students are held accountable (see § 1709). A board's policies ensure that the school district performs its established mission and operates in an effective, uniform manner. They are legally binding and serve as the local law of the school district that may be enforced by the district. Moreover, if a school district violates its own policies, the commissioner of education may enforce the policy against the district (see *Appeal of Marek*, 35 Educ. Dep't Rep. 314 (1996); *Appeal of Joannides*, 32 Educ. Dep't Rep. 278 (1992)).

2:80. What policies are essential for the governance of a school district?

It is up to each school district to determine what policies are needed for effective governance of its district. However, there are some policies required by state or federal law or regulation, including, but not limited to:

- Conduct on school property (§ 2801).
- Smoking (Pub. Health Law §1399-o(6); see also Educ. Law 409(2)).
- Code of ethics (Gen. Mun. Law §§ 806–808, namely §806(1)).
- Access to public records (Pub. Off. Law § 87(1)(b)).
- Submission of propositions by the voters (§ 2035(2)).
- Special education (8 NYCRR § 200.2(b)).
- Preschool special education (§ 4410; 8 NYCRR Parts 200.2(b)).
- Limited English proficiency (§ 3204(2-a); 8 NYCRR § 154.4).
- Child-abuse prevention and reporting procedures (§ 3209-a).
- Student records (20 USC § 1232g).
- Student conduct and discipline (8 NYCRR § 100.2(l)).

- Drug-free workplace (20 USC § 3171).
- Incidental teaching, if the district makes an incidental teaching assignment without seeking approval of the commissioner of education (8 NYCRR § 80.2(c)(7)(iii)).
- Interpreters for hearing-impaired parents (§ 3230(2); see also 8 NYCRR 200.1(mm)(2),(5)).
- Title I programs (34 CFR Part 75).
- Purchasing or procurement of goods and services that are not subject to competitive bidding (Gen. Mun. Law § 104-b).
- Nondiscrimination on the basis of sex (Title IX of the federal Education Amendments of 1972, 20 USC §1681 *et seq.*; see also 34 CFR § 106.9).
- Investments (Gen. Mun. Law § 39).
- Student suspension for possession of firearms (Educ. Law § 3214(3)(d); 20 USC § 8922-(a)).
- Alcohol and drug testing of bus drivers (49 CFR Part 382).
- Family and Medical Leave Act (FMLA) (29 USC § 2611 *et seq.*, see also 29 CFR §§ 825.300, 825.301).

2:81. Must certain policies be reviewed annually?

Yes. School boards are required to conduct an annual review of their policies on student conduct and discipline (8 NYCRR §100.2(l)(2)), purchasing (Gen. Mun. Law § 104-b(4)) and investments (Gen. Mun. Law § 39(1). The Association recommends that districts schedule these reviews on the calendar and ensure that they have the information needed to make a reasonable assessment of the current effectiveness of the policy and whether any changes may be warranted.

2:82. Must school boards maintain policy manuals?

No. Districts may be required to adopt policies on certain issues, but they are not required to maintain or organize them in any particular manner. However, it is a common practice to organize and number policies in a single manual for ease of reference and access for the board, district staff and the public.

2:83. What is the difference between a policy and a regulation?

Policies are statements by the board establishing standards and/or objectives to be attained by the district. Policies can only be adopted or amended by the vote of a majority of the board members at an open meeting. Regulations are generally more detailed directives developed by the administration to implement the board's policies. Policies give direction and goals for the district, while regulations give specific orders and procedures to be followed to move in that direction and to attain those goals. Unless otherwise specified by the bylaws of the board of education, it is the power and duty of the superintendent to enforce all provisions of law, rules and regulations relating to the management of the schools and other educational, social and recreational activities under the direction of the board of education (§§ 1711(2)(b), 2508(2)).

It is important that board policies be both broad enough to allow administrators to exercise discretion in dealing with day-to-day problems, yet specific enough to provide clear guidance. It is equally important that regulations be written to implement, but not modify, the board's policies.

2:84. What services does the New York State School Boards Association provide to assist local school boards in developing policies?

The New York State School Boards Association offers a variety of services to assist local school boards in developing and maintaining policy manuals for more effective decision making and administration. It offers an online *School Policy Encyclopedia,* which contains comprehensive discussions of legal requirements and constraints from state and federal statutes, court decisions and commissioner's regulations on nearly every area of school district governance and operations. It also contains sample school board policies and administrative regulations. *School Policy Encyclopedia* provides school boards with a foundation on which to develop school board policies.

If a district requires more in-depth assistance in developing a comprehensive policy manual, the Association's policy staff will work with its board to develop a manual specifically designed for the district.

In addition, for districts that have completed their custom policy manuals, the Association offers a policy update service to keep the manual current.

3. School Board Organization

3:1. What is the annual school board reorganizational meeting?

The annual school board reorganizational meeting is the school board's initial meeting. Here, the organization of the board is established, and school board officers and other district officers are appointed. In addition, boards often appoint other personnel, such as the internal auditor, school attorney, records access officer and records management officer, and designate depositories for district funds and newspapers for required notices (§§ 1701; 2502(9)(o)).

The annual reorganizational meeting is different from the annual district meeting, which involves the presentation of the district's annual budget to the voters and the election of school board members (see **4:1**).

3:2. Is there a specific time set by law for the annual school board reorganizational meeting?

Yes. In union free and central school districts the reorganizational meeting must be held on the first Tuesday in July. If that day is a legal holiday, then the meeting must be held on the first Wednesday in July (§ 1707(1)). Alternatively, a board of education in these districts may, by resolution, decide to hold the annual reorganizational meeting at any time during the first 15 days in July (§ 1707(2)).

The annual reorganizational meeting of central high school districts in Nassau County must be held on the second Tuesday in July (§ 1904).

In city school districts with less than 125,000 inhabitants, the reorganizational meeting is held the first week in July, unless otherwise specified by law (§§ 2504(1); 2502(9)(o); 2502(9-a)(o)).

In large city school districts the reorganizational meeting occurs on the second Tuesday in May, unless otherwise specified by law (§§ 2563(1); 2553(9)(f); 2553(10)(o)).

3:3. What school board officers are chosen at the annual reorganizational meeting?

A school board is required by law to elect a president and may, at its discretion, elect a vice president (§§ 1701; 2504(1)).

The board may exercise fairly broad discretion in determining its internal organization, officers and staff. It may appoint staff assistants and a school attorney, designate board and/or advisory committees to assist in a wide variety of functions, and employ consultants as desired for the efficient management of its work.

3:4. May a school board vest in a vice president all the powers of the president of the board in the event of the president's absence or disability?

Yes. Section 1701 of the Education Law authorizes a school board to elect one of its members as vice president with the power to exercise the duties of the president in case of his or her absence or disability.

3:5. What happens when there is a vacancy in the office of president?

When there is a vacancy in the office of president, the vice president shall act as president until a new president is elected (§ 1701).

3:6. May a school board govern through the appointment of standing committees?

No. While there is no state law that either prohibits or requires standing committees, board committees that constitute less than a quorum of the entire board cannot make legal decisions for the board as a whole (Gen. Constr. Law § 41; *Appeal of Greenwald*, 31 Educ. Dep't Rep. 12 (1991); see **2:12***).

A school board may appoint advisory committees to assist in addressing specific problems or issues. Those asked to serve on these committees should understand clearly that their role is advisory and that the final decision in all cases rests ultimately with the board.

Certain advisory committees are required by law or commissioner's regulations, and their composition and duties are prescribed therein. For example, in union free and central school districts, the Education Law requires visitation committees to visit every school under the board's jurisdiction at least once annually (§ 1708(2)). The commissioner's regulations require each school board to establish an AIDS advisory council to advise the board concerning the content, implementation, and evaluation of an AIDS instruction program (8 NYCRR §§ 135.3(b)(2), (c)(2)(i)).

The School District's Officers

3:7. Who are the school district's officers?

The school district's officers are individuals who are elected or appointed to administer the district's affairs. In addition to school board members and trustees, school district officers include district superintendents, superintendents of schools, school district clerks, treasurers and tax collectors employed by the school district (Art. 43, §§ 2(13); 2506; Town Law § 38).

3:8. Which school district officers are appointed by the school board?

School district officers appointed by the school board generally include a clerk, treasurer, tax collector and auditor (§§ 2130, 1709(20–a); 2503 (15); 2526). A critical appointment made by the board is that of a superintendent of schools who, as chief executive officer of the board, is responsible for the day-to-day administration of the school district (§§ 1604(8); 1711; 2507; 2508; 2554(2); 2590-e). The superintendent is not necessarily appointed at the board's reorganizational meeting, because he or she usually is appointed for a period of years (see **7:17**).

3:9. Is the school board's legal counsel or school attorney a school district officer?

No. The school attorney and those in similar positions are not school district officers (*Matter of McGinley*, 23 Educ. Dep't Rep. 350 (1984), citing *Matter of Harrison CSD v. Nyquist*, 59 A.D.2d 434 (3rd Dep't 1977), *appeal denied*, 44 N.Y.2d 645 (1978)).

3:10. What are the qualifications of school district officers?

The general rule is that school district officers must be able to read and write and must be a qualified voter of the district (§ 2102; for further information on the qualifications for school board members, see **2:18**).

Residency in the school district is not a statutory requirement for the district superintendent, superintendent of schools, district clerk, treasurer or tax collector (§ 2102). Therefore, these school district officers are not required to be qualified voters of the district.

3:11. May a member of a school board be appointed clerk of the district?

Yes. The school board has the power to appoint either one of its members or another individual as clerk (§ 2130(1); *Matter of Hurtgam*, 22 Educ. Dep't Rep. 219 (1982)).

3:12. May the school board appoint someone to fulfill the district clerk's duties if the current clerk is unavailable?

Although the Education Law specifically does not provide for the appointment of a deputy or acting clerk, certain duties of the district clerk must be carried out, notwithstanding the clerk's temporary incapacitation. For example, the notice of an annual meeting must be given whether or not the clerk is available to carry out this function (§ 2004(1)).

Therefore, by practical necessity, a board may designate an individual to carry out the district clerk's duties when he or she is incapacitated or otherwise unavailable.

3:13. May the offices of school tax collector and school district treasurer be held by the same person?

No. Each of the offices of school tax collector, school district treasurer, school district clerk and school district auditor, if one is appointed, must be held by separate individuals (§ 2130; 8 NYCRR § 170.2(a)).

3:14. May the school board appoint a deputy treasurer?

Yes. The board may appoint a deputy treasurer to serve at its discretion to sign checks in lieu of the treasurer or other officer required to sign such checks, in case of their absence or inability. The deputy treasurer also must execute and file an undertaking in the same manner and amount as required of the treasurer (§ 1720(2); see also **3:21**).

3:15. May the school board appoint a bank to act as the district's treasurer?

No. The school district's treasurer must be a person. However, a school board, by resolution, may enter into a contract to provide for the deposit of the school district's periodic payroll in a bank or trust company for disbursal by the district in accordance with provisions of section 96–b of the Banking Law (§§ 1719, 1720).

3:16. Must the school board designate a bank or trust company as an official school district depository?

Yes. The school board must designate one or more banks or trust companies as depository(ies) for district funds in accordance with section 10 of the General Municipal Law. The board resolution designating a depository must specify the maximum amount which may be kept on deposit at any time in each designated bank or trust company. These designations and monetary amounts may be changed at any time by further resolution (Gen. Mun. Law § 10(2)).

3:17. May the board designate a bank or trust company to fulfill its financial needs if an officer of that bank or trust company has been appointed as the school district's treasurer?

The general rule is that a school board may not designate a bank or trust company as a depository, paying agent, registration agent or its agent for investment of its funds if the school district's treasurer or his or her deputy or employee has an interest in that bank or trust company. This would constitute a prohibited conflict of interest (Gen. Mun. Law § 801(2); see § 802(1)(a) for exception; see **3:23**).

3:18. May the school board appoint one of its members to sign checks?

Yes. The school board may, by resolution, appoint a member to sign checks in lieu of the treasurer in case of his or her absence or inability, or in addition to the treasurer if the board decides to require that all checks be countersigned by another officer of the district. This board member must also execute and file a bond in the same manner and amount as is required of the treasurer (§ 1720(2); see **3:21**).

3:19. Must a school board appoint an internal auditor?

No. The position of the school district's internal auditor is a discretionary appointment of the school board. The Education Law stipulates, however, that a member of the school board, the district clerk, the district treasurer, the official responsible for the district's business management, the district's designated purchasing agent or a clerk directly involved in the accounting function, may not be appointed as the district's internal auditor (§§ 1709(20–a); 2509(4); 2526; 8 NYCRR § 170.2(a)).

3:20. Are a school district's officers required to take a constitutional oath of office?

Yes. A school district's officers, such as board members and trustees, the clerk and the treasurer, are required to take and file an oath of office with the district clerk (Pub. Off. Law § 10; see **2:8**). Usually the oath is administered at the board's annual reorganizational meeting by either the board president or the district clerk. The fact that the oath has been administered should be noted in the board's minutes.

A district superintendent also must take an oath upon the discharge of the duties of his or office but no later than five days after the date which his or her term of office begins (§ 2206; Pub. Off. Law §10).

3:21. Must certain school district officers file a bond?

Yes. The school board must establish the limits of a bond (known in the law as an "official undertaking") and require the treasurer, tax collector and auditor to file one. As an alternative, the board may include these officers in a blanket bond (§§ 2130(5); 2527; Pub. Off. Law § 11(2); 8 NYCRR § 170.2(d); see **3:14, 3:18**).

3:22. Who determines the amount of compensation received by a school district's officers appointed by the school board?

The school board determines the amount of compensation for the district treasurer, tax collector, superintendent of schools and auditor.

The board may determine the amount of compensation to be provided to the district clerk if it was not decided at the annual meeting (§§ 2123; 2130; 2506; *Appeal of Palillo*, 6 Educ. Dep't Rep. 117 (1967)).

3:23. May a school district officer do business with the school by which he or she is employed?

No, unless allowed by the conflict of interest law which is applicable to school district officers and employees as well as school board members (Gen. Mun. Law § 800 *et seq.*; see **2:35-37**).

3:24. Can the school board remove school district officers from their positions?

Both the school district's treasurer and collector serve at the pleasure of the school board, which means the board has the right to dismiss them at any time without cause (§ 2130(4); *Matter of Probeck*, 58 St. Dep't Rep. 470 (1937)). District clerks and other board officers, however, may only be removed by the commissioner of education for cause *(Matter of Motoyama,* 12 Educ. Dep't Rep. 244 (1973); see **3:25**; see also **2:25; 2:27-28** for details on the removal of board members).

3:25. What is the procedure for removing a district clerk?

The commissioner of education may remove a clerk or other school officer from office after a hearing at which the officer has a right to be represented by counsel. Removal of the clerk can be for any willful violation, neglect of duty under the Education Law or any other act pertaining to common schools or other educational institutions participating in state funds, or for willful disobedience of any decision, order, rule or regulation of the Board of Regents or the commissioner of education (§ 306).

Shared Decision Making

Editor's Note: For more detailed information on shared decision making, see A Guide to Shared Decision Making: Insights and Recommendations, *published by the New York State School Boards Association. See also "School Executive's Bulletin," Office of Elementary, Middle and Secondary Education, New York State Education Department, May 1992, pages DC 1-4.*

3:26. What is shared decision making?

The terms *shared decision making* and *school-based management* refer to a model for decision making in the schools that emphasizes both the involvement and meaningful participation of administrators, teachers and parents in the decision-making process (8 NYCRR § 100.11).

Every board of education and BOCES must have in place a district plan for the participation by teachers, parents and administrators in school-based planning and shared decision making (8 NYCRR § 100.11(b)). The adopted plan must be made available to the public and must be filed with the district superintendent and the commissioner of education (8 NYCRR § 100.11(d)(1)).

3:27. What is meant by "meaningful participation" in the decision-making process?

The commissioner's regulations provide that a school board must consult certain individuals when developing and amending the district's plan for school-based management and shared decision making. The plan the board develops with input from the district-wide committee (also referred to as the central planning committee) must outline both the creation of the school-based shared-decision-making teams and detail those educational issues on which the teams are to provide input. However, nothing in the regulations requires that a board obtain the approval of a school-based planning team before implementing a decision (*Appeal of Gillespie*, 34 Educ. Dep't Rep. 240 (1994)).

3:28. What areas must be addressed in a school district's shared-decision-making plan?

The district plan must address the following:

- The educational issues which are subject to cooperative planning and shared decision making at the building level.
- The manner and the extent of involvement of each of the parties.
- The means and standards to be used in evaluating the improvement in student achievement.
- The method of holding each party accountable for the decisions they helped make.
- The process for resolving disputes on educational issues at the local level.
- The manner in which all state and federal requirements for the involvement of parents in planning and decision making will be coordinated and met by the overall district plan (8 NYCRR § 100.11(c)).

3:29. Are there any limitations on which educational issues a shared-decision-making committee may address?

The commissioner's regulations do not define which educational issues the school-based committees must consider. A school board is expected to work together with its district-wide planning committee to define what issues the school-based shared-decision-making committee will examine.

School-based committees might consider a range of issues such as mission statements, school schedules, grouping for instruction, the allocation of discretionary resources, and links with community organizations.

In working with shared-decision-making committees, board members should be aware that while some education issues may be appropriate for input, they may not be appropriate for delegation. For example, a school board is required to formulate the school district budget, and that obligation cannot be delegated to a shared-decision-making team (§§ 1716, 1804(1); 1906(3); 2601-a; *Appeal of Kastberg*, 35 Educ. Dep't Rep. 208 (1995)). Similarly, while student performance is an appropriate issue for discussion, it is the school board that must set the course of study by which students are graded and classified (§ 1709(3); *Appeal of Orris and Kelly*, 35 Educ. Dep't Rep. 184 (1995)).

At the same time, the commissioner has found that nothing in the shared-decision-making regulation mandates that a board obtain the approval of a school-based planning team before implementing a decision. In one case, he determined a school board may establish a day care center at one of its school facilities, despite opposition from the building shared-decision-making committee (*Appeal of Gillespie*, 34 Educ. Dep't Rep. 240 (1994)).

And while there is no specific case that addresses this particular issue with regard to shared decision making, board members should also be aware that a school board cannot delegate its responsibility to grant or deny tenure to an employee *(Cohoes City School District v. Cohoes Teachers Assn.*, 40 N.Y.2d 774 (1976)). This is one example of a nondelegable duty by the board.

3:30. How often must the shared-decision-making plan be reviewed?

The plan must be reviewed biennially and amended or recertified without change, as appropriate, following the same procedures as for the original plan. The recertified or amended plan must be filed with the district superintendent and submitted to the commissioner for approval, together with a statement of the plan's success in meeting its objectives, no later than February 1 of the year in which the review occurs. The next biennial review must be completed by February 1, 2000 (8 NYCRR § 100.11(f)).

3:31. Who must be involved in the biennial review of a district's school-based planning and shared-decision-making plan?

The school board must conduct a biennial review of its school-based planning and shared-decision-making plan in consultation with its district-wide committee composed of the superintendent of schools, administrators selected by the administrative bargaining organization(s), teachers selected by the teachers bargaining organization(s) and parents selected by the school-related parent organization(s).

Parents who are employed by the district or employed by a collective bargaining organization representing teachers and/or administrators in the district may not serve on the committee. In those districts in which teachers or administrators are not represented by a collective bargaining organization, or where there are no school-related parent organizations, teachers, administrators and/or parents are to be selected by their peers in a manner prescribed by the school board or BOCES.

While the board must seek the district-wide committee's endorsement of any amendments to the plan, the board of education has the final say over the district plan (8 NYCRR §§ 100.11(b), (f)).

For further information on the biennial review process, please see "Questions and Answers Concerning the Biennial Review of District Plans for Shared Decision Making," NY State Education Department, Fall 1995.

3:32. Can a board member be a member of the district-wide committee?

No. The commissioner of education has held that the intent of the regulation is for board members to work in collaboration with the district-wide committee in developing and amending the shared-decision-making plan, and not to serve on the committee itself (*Appeal of Chester*, 35 Educ. Dep't Rep. 512 (1996)).

3:33. Who may be a member of the school-based shared-decision-making team?

According to the State Education Department, the school-based committees must be composed of administrators, teachers, parents and others who may be specified in the district-wide plan (for example students, support staff or community members).

3:34. What is the process for challenging a shared-decision-making plan?

According to the commissioner's regulations, a person who feels the school board failed to adopt, amend or recertify the plan properly may appeal to the commissioner no later than 30 days after the plan was adopted, amended or recertified. Any person who participated in the plan's development and feels that the plan fails to provide for meaningful participation in the decision-making process may also file an appeal with the commissioner (8 NYCRR § 100.11(e)(1)). The grounds for such an appeal include noncompliance with any of the six enumerated requirements of the plan (8 NYCRR § 100.11(e)(2)).

3:35. Must school districts negotiate with their unions over shared decision making?

It depends on the circumstance. The Public Employment Relations Board (PERB) has held that a school district did not violate its bargaining obligation by refusing to negotiate over teachers' participation on a shared-decision-making committee or over alleged impact of increased workload. PERB held that the teachers were not acting in their capacity as employees of the district but rather as volunteers, and that the terms for their participation on the committee was not a mandatory subject of bargaining (*Deer Park Teachers Association v. Deer Park Union Free School District,* 26 PERB ¶ 4642 (1993)).

However, where a school district has developed or implemented a plan for the participation of teachers and/or administrators in school-based shared decision making as a result of a collective bargaining agreement, any such negotiated provisions must be incorporated into the district's shared-decision-making plan required by the commissioner's regulations (8 NYCRR § 100.11(h)).

3:36. Is the shared-decision-making process subject to the Open Meetings Law?

Although there are no court decisions that address this issue, whenever a district-wide planning committee or school based shared-decision-making committee is required to have a quorum to conduct business and is actively involved in the process of formulating recommendations at any level, the meetings of that committee are subject to the Open Meetings Law, according to the state Committee on Open Government (Department of State, Committee on Open Government OML-AO-2305 (Jan. 19, 1994). Therefore, advance notice of meetings must be provided, and the meetings must be accessible to disabled persons (*MFY Legal Services Inc. v. Toia,* 93 Misc. 2d 147 (1977); Department of State, Committee on Open Government, FOIL-AO-9989 (March 26, 1997), OML-AO-2305 (Jan. 19, 1994), OML-AO-2204 (April 1, 1993).

3:37. Are the records of the shared-decision-making process subject to the Freedom of Information Law?

Although there is no case law on this particular situation, both the district-wide planning committee and school-based shared-decision-making committees are "agencies" for the purposes of the Freedom of Information Law, as indicated by the state Committee on Open Government (NYS Department of State, Committee on Open Government, FOIL-AO-9989 (Mar. 26, 1997).

4. Annual and Special School District Meetings

The Annual Meeting and Election

4:1 What is the annual meeting and election?

Historically, the annual school district meeting was an actual meeting of the residents of a school district which occurred immediately prior to or simultaneously with the vote on the proposed school district budget for the upcoming school year. However, school districts now must present the proposed budget for the ensuing school year to the voters at a public hearing held seven to 14 days prior to the date of the annual meeting and election. The public hearing replaces the annual meeting as the forum for presentation of the proposed budget to the voters (see **4:19**).

Therefore, the only remaining significance of the term "annual meeting" is that the date set by law for holding the annual meeting is the date that the budget vote and school board elections must occur.

4:2. Must a school district hold an annual meeting and election?

Yes, except large city school districts (i.e., the Big 5) and special act school districts. The purpose of the annual meeting and election is to allow qualified voters residing in the school district to vote on the school district's budget for the upcoming school year and to elect candidates to fill any vacancies on the board of education (§§ 2022(1), 2601-a(2), 2602(1)).

4:3. When is the annual meeting and election held?

With the exception of the Albany City School District, every school district in the state must hold its annual meeting and election on the third Tuesday in May. If, at the request of a local school board, the commissioner of education certifies no later than March 1 that the election would conflict with religious observances, the election may be held on the second Tuesday in May (§§ 1804(4), 1906(1), 2002(1), 2022(1), 2601-a(2)). Provisions of law which previously permitted voting on school budgets and board member elections on separate days, and/or different days of the year have been repealed.

The Albany City School District must hold its annual budget vote on the third Tuesday in May, just like other school districts to which the law applies but, by specific provision of law, members of the Albany Board of

Education are elected at a general election conducted by the Albany County Board of Elections (§§ 2502(9)(b),(p); 2602(1)). School board elections in the Big 5 take place at different dates and times as specified by law (§ 2553).

4:4. What happens if a district fails to hold its annual meeting and election on the required date?

If this happens, the school board or the district clerk must call a special school district meeting to transact the business of the annual meeting within 10 days after the time for holding the annual meeting has passed (§ 2005).

If the school board or district clerk fails to call such a special meeting, the district superintendent or the commissioner of education may order a special district meeting to conduct the business of the annual meeting. In this case, the district officers must make the reports required to be made at the annual meeting; if they do not make their reports, they may be subject to a penalty for neglect of their duties.

The officers elected at such a special meeting hold their offices only until the next annual meeting, and until their elected successors have been qualified (§ 2005; see **3:10** and **3:20** for qualification of officers).

4:5. Is there a specific time of day that the annual meeting and election must be held?

Yes. Most school districts must hold their annual meeting and election during at least six consecutive hours after 6:00 a.m., two hours of which must be after 6:00 p.m., as determined by resolution of the trustees or board of education (§ 2002(1)).

Small city school districts must hold their annual meeting and election during at least nine consecutive hours, beginning not earlier than 7:00 a.m., two hours of which must be after 6:00 p.m., as established by board resolution (§ 2602(3)).

School districts that are not divided into election districts and which conduct their election or vote by a show of hands or voice vote must hold their annual meeting and election at 7:30 p.m., unless the time is changed by a vote at a previous district meeting (§ 2002(1)). In such districts, once the proposed budget has been presented, the meeting may not be adjourned or concluded until the budget has been voted on (*Appeal of Mazzurco*, 6 Educ. Dep't Rep. 101 (1967); see also *Appeal of Kerr*, 76 St. Dep't Rep. 121 (1955)).

4:6. What happens if a school district holds its annual meeting and election on a day or time not allowed by law?

The commissioner of education may annul the results of the meeting and order a special school district meeting (see *Appeal of Glier*, 1 Educ. Dep't Rep. 695 (1961)).

4:7. May the budget vote be postponed pending settlement of collective bargaining negotiations?

No. The date for holding the annual district meeting and election is fixed by law and may not be altered to await the outcome of negotiations with a district's union (§§ 2002(1), 1804(4), 1906(1), 2022(1), 2601-a(2); see Opn. of Counsel No. 228, 8 Educ. Dep't Rep. 227 (1969)).

In cases where a budget must be presented and voted on before the settlement of contract negotiations, a school board may estimate the amount it will need to meet salary and other obligations under the contract, once the contract is settled. If insufficient funds are provided for in the budget, or if the budget is defeated, the board may appropriate an additional amount to meet these obligations. However, when the budget is defeated, the total contingency budget, including the additional amount appropriated by the board, is subject to the cap on contingency budget expenditures (§ 2023; see **19:39**; see also *Matter of New Paltz CSD*, 30 Educ. Dep't Rep. 300 (1991), citing *Matter of Fagan*, 15 Educ. Dep't Rep. 296 (1976)).

4:8. Where is the annual meeting and election held?

The annual meeting and election is held at the school(s) designated for this purpose. If the district has no school or if the school is not adequate, then it may be held in any place suitable for the occasion (§ 2002(1)).

4:9. Who calls the annual meeting and election to order?

In common school districts, the annual meeting and election is called to order by the sole trustee in districts with only one trustee, the chairperson of the board of trustees, or a person chosen by the trustee or trustees. Once the meeting is called to order, the qualified district voters present at the meeting nominate and elect one of their peers present to serve as permanent chairperson (§§ 2021(1), 2025(1)). As qualified voters, members of the school board are eligible to serve as chairperson.

In union free, central and small city school districts, a qualified voter appointed by the school board as permanent chairperson calls district meetings to order. If hours were set for voting in the notice of the meeting, the chairperson also declares the polls open and closed at the appropriate time and that no motions are in order during the hours set for voting (§§ 2025(2), 2601-a(2)).

4:10. What notice must be given to the public regarding the annual meeting and election?

The district clerk must publish notice of the date, time and place of the annual meeting and election four times during the seven weeks preceding the date of the annual meeting and election, in two newspapers having general circulation, or one newspaper of general circulation, if there is only one, with the first publication occurring at least 45 days before the date of the annual meeting and election. Therefore, in order to accomplish a timely notice, the district clerk must identify the date of the annual meeting and election, and count back 45 calendar days, then publish the first notice no later than the 45th day, and additional notices three times after that.

A newspaper of general circulation means, with narrow exceptions, a newspaper that is published at least weekly; contains news, editorials, features, advertising or other matter regarded as of current interest; that is of paid circulation; and is sent by at least second class mail (Gen. Constr. Law § 60). The fees that newspapers may charge for publishing the notice of annual meeting are set forth in section 8007 of the Civil Practice Law and Rules. A school district may not pay a claim for publication of a notice in a newspaper that does not meet the legal definition of a newspaper of general circulation (Opn. St. Comp. 93-33).

If no newspaper of general circulation is available, or if both newspapers having general circulation in the district refuse to publish the notice at the rates prescribed by law, the notice must be posted in at least 20 of the most public places 45 days before the meeting (§§ 2003(1), 2004(1), 2601-a(2)).

4:11. What must be included in the notice of the annual meeting and election?

In addition to stating the date, time and place of the annual district meeting and election (§§ 2003(1), 2004(1), 2601-a(2)), the notice also must state the following:

- The date, time and place of the public hearing on the budget now required by law (§§ 1608(2), 1716(2), 2601-a(2)).
- A statement that district residents may obtain a copy of the proposed budget at any district building, during designated hours, on each

day other than a Saturday, Sunday or holiday during the 14 days preceding the date of the annual meeting and election (§§ 1608(2), 1716(2), 2003(1), 2004(6)(d)).

- If specific propositions will be voted on, the substance of each proposition. (Note: Although a good idea, this is not a requirement under law, except where specified. For example, when a proposition to increase or decrease the number of board members will appear on the ballot at the annual meeting, the notice of annual meeting must contain a statement indicating this fact (§§ 1703(2), 2502(4)(b))).

- A statement that petitions for nominating candidates for office of school board member must be filed in the district clerk's office between 9:00 a.m. and 5:00 p.m. no later than 30 days (20 days in small city districts) before the election (§§ 2003(2), 2004(2), 2601-a(2), 2608(1))).

- Where applicable, a statement that qualified voters may apply for absentee ballots at the district clerk's office and that a list of persons to whom absentee ballots have been issued will be available for inspection in the district clerk's office during each of the five days prior to the day of the election, except Sundays, and that this same list also will be posted at the polling place(s) (§ 2004(7))).

- If the district has personal registration of voters, a statement of the time and place that the board of registration will meet to prepare the register of the school district, together with notice that any person (who is not already registered), upon proving that he or she is entitled to vote in the district, may have his or her name placed upon the register. In addition, the notice shall state that the register containing the names of qualified voters will be available for inspection in the clerk's office during each of the five days prior to the day of the election, except Sundays (§ 2004(5),(6)).

- Notice of any proposed tax to be levied in installments, prior to issuing bonds or other obligations of the district, and/or expenditure for buying, constructing or improving school buildings or grounds, and any proposed reduction or rescinding of a previously authorized tax or expenditure (§§ 416(2), 2009). Where bonds or capital notes are issued to finance a project, the notice of the meeting at which the proposed tax to finance the bonds or notes shall be voted upon must state the amount of such bonds or notes (Local Fin. Law § 41.10; *Appeal of Friedman*, 36 Educ. Dep't Rep. 431 (1997)).

4:12. What happens if the notice of the annual meeting and election does not comply with the law?

Although school districts should make every effort to comply with the legal requirements for giving notice of the annual meeting and election, if a district fails to provide adequate public notice, the results of the budget vote and/or board member elections will be upheld and will not be found illegal, unless it appears that the failure to give proper notice was wilful or fraudulent (§ 2010).

For example, in one case the commissioner refused to overturn the election results where the district had published notice in only one newspaper, not realizing until just five days before the election that the law generally requires publication in two newspapers, at which point in time it was too late to correct the error. The commissioner found that the error was not willful or fraudulent, especially since, upon discovering its error, the district mailed and hand-delivered a flyer regarding the election to district households (*Appeal of Hebel*, 34 Educ. Dep't Rep. 319 (1994)).

Adoption of the School District Budget

4:13. What kind of information must be included in the proposed school district budget?

School districts must present a detailed written statement of the amount of money which will be required for the coming school year for school purposes, specifying the several purposes and the amount of each.

Districts must present their proposed budgets in three component parts: (1) a program component; (2) a capital component; and (3) an administrative component (§§ 1608(4), 1716(4), 2601-a(3), see also 8 NYCRR §170.8). Moreover, the proposed budget must be written in plain language. This means that districts must present a complete, accurate and detailed written statement, which is easy to read and understand, informing the public regarding estimated revenues including payments in lieu of taxes and property tax refunds from certiorari proceedings, proposed expenditures, transfers to other funds, the amount of fund balance to be retained and the amount of fund balance to be used in support of budgetary appropriations as well as a comparison of the prior year's data (§§ 305(26), 1608(3), 1716(3), 2601-a(3); 8 NYCRR § 170.9).

The budget must show the total amount necessary to pay boards of cooperative educational services (BOCES). It must also include the amount of state aid to be provided and its percentage relationship to the total expenditures (§§ 1608(1), 1716(1), 2601-a(3)).

The district must attach to the proposed budget a detailed statement of the total compensation, including salary, benefits and any in-kind or other form of remuneration, to be paid to the superintendent of schools, and assistant or associate superintendents, together with a list of any administrator who will earn over $85,000 in the upcoming year. This statement must also be submitted to the commissioner within five days of its preparation on a form prescribed by the commissioner (§§ 1608(5), 1716(5), 2601-a(3)). The board is not required to itemize other employees' salaries, even if it is requested to do so at the meeting where the proposed budget is presented. However, this information is a matter of public record and, as such, is open to inspection (*Matter of Shaddock*, 73 St. Dep't Rep. 160 (1952)).

In addition, each school district must append to the proposed budget its annual Report Card, which measures the academic and fiscal performance of the school district, and which is prepared in the manner set forth by the Education Law and the commissioner's regulations. School districts must make this Report Card available to the public for inspection at school houses in the district at least 14 days before the annual meeting and election. Districts also must distribute the Report Card at the annual meeting and transmit it to local newspapers of general circulation (§§ 1608(6), 1716(6), 2554(24), 2590-e(8), 2601-a(7), see **14:71-72**).

4:14. What must be included in the program component of the proposed budget?

The program component must include, but need not be limited to, all program expenditures of the school district, including the salaries and benefits of teachers and any school administrators and supervisors who spend the majority of their time performing teaching duties, and all transportation operating expenses (§§ 1608(4), 1716(4), 2601-a(3), see also 8 NYCRR § 170.8).

4:15. What must be included in the capital component of the proposed budget?

The capital component must include, but need not be limited to, all transportation capital, debt service and lease expenditures; costs resulting from judgments in tax certiorari proceedings or the payment of awards from court judgments, administrative orders or settled or compromised claims; and all facilities costs of the school district, including facilities lease expenditures, the annual debt service and total debt service for all facilities financed by bonds and notes of the school district, and the costs of construction, acquisition, reconstruction, rehabilitation or improvement of school buildings, provided that such budget must include a rental, operations and maintenance section that includes base rental costs, total rent costs, operation and maintenance charges, costs per square foot for each facility leased by the school district, and any and all expenditures with custodial salaries and benefits, service contracts, supplies, utilities, and maintenance and repair of school facilities (§§ 1608(4), 1716(4), 2601-a(3), see also 8 NYCRR § 170.8).

4:16. What must be included in the administrative component of the proposed budget?

The administrative component must include, but need not be limited to, office and central administrative expenses, traveling expenses and salaries and benefits of all certified school administrators and supervisors who spend a majority of their time performing administrative or supervisory duties, any and all expenditures associated with the operation of the board of education, the office of the superintendent of schools, general administration, the school business office, consulting costs not directly related to direct student services and programs, planning and all other administrative activities (§§ 1608(4), 1716(4), 2601-a(3), see also 8 NYCRR §170.8).

4:17. Are school boards required to provide information about the budget for the prior school year at the time of the annual meeting and election?

Yes. A school board is required to provide a detailed, written financial statement of its expenditures and income for the preceding year, in plain language which is easy to read and understand, at the annual meeting and election (§§ 305, 1610, 1721, 2528). School boards in union free and central school districts also must publish a detailed statement of income and expenses for the preceding year during July or August, either in a newspaper of general circulation within the district or, if there is no such newspaper, then by posting the statement in five public places in the district (§ 1721). Inclusion of general items such as teacher salaries, fuel and repairs, without a detailed breakdown of each category, is sufficient. A school board's willful neglect or refusal to report its financial statement at the annual meeting will result in forfeiture of office by its members (§ 1611).

4:18. Is there a deadline by which the board of education must complete the proposed budget?

Yes. The board of education must complete the proposed budget document at least seven days before the public hearing at which the board will present the budget to the voters. Since the budget hearing must be held from seven to 14 days before the annual meeting and election, the board of education must complete the budget from 14 to 21 days prior to the date of the annual meeting and election, depending upon the hearing date selected by the board (§§ 1608(2), 1716(2), 2601-a(2)).

4:19. Are school districts required to hold a public hearing on the proposed budget?

Yes. A public hearing on the proposed budget is no longer optional. School districts must hold a public hearing on the budget at least seven days but not more than 14 days prior to the annual meeting and election (§§ 1608(1), 1716(1), 1804(4), 2022(1)).

At the public hearing, the board of education presents the proposed budget for the upcoming school year to the voters. The public hearing replaces the annual meeting as the forum for "presentation" of the proposed budget to the community (**4:1**).

Notice of the date, time and place of the public hearing must be included in the notice of annual meeting and election or special district meeting that is published or distributed (§§ 1608(2), 1716(2), see **4:10**).

4:20. Do school boards in large city school districts present a budget to the voters?

No. In large city school districts (i.e., the Big 5), school boards do not adopt a budget. Instead, they prepare an itemized estimate of the sum needed for necessary and other authorized expenses. The estimate is then filed with and acted upon by designated city officials (§§ 2576, 2590-q).

In Buffalo, it is filed with the city official authorized to receive department estimates and acted upon by such officer and the city council (§ 2576(4)).

In New York City, community school boards submit their budget estimates to the chancellor after holding public hearings on the estimates prepared by their community superintendents. The city board, upon the recommendation of the chancellor and after consultation with the community boards, files the estimates for the city school district with the mayor for action by the city council and the mayor. In addition, each community superintendent must prepare semi-annual and year-end reports which include, but are not limited to, an accounting of all funds received and expended by the subject community board from all sources. Copies of these reports are given to the city board and the community board and must be available to the public. For specific information, refer to section 2590-q(17) of the Education Law.

In Rochester, Syracuse and Yonkers, the estimate is filed with the mayor or city manager and then evaluated and dealt with in a manner similar to estimates from other city departments (§ 2576(2)).

4:21. Must the school board make a copy of the proposed school district budget available to the public before the district meeting at which it is presented?

Yes. Copies of the budget must be made available upon request to residents of the district during the 14 days immediately preceding the date of the annual meeting and election. The board of education also must include information in the notice of the annual meeting and election informing district residents that they may obtain a copy of the budget at any schoolhouse in the district, during designated hours, on each day other than a Saturday, Sunday or holiday, during the 14 days immediately preceding the date of the annual meeting and election. Furthermore, at least once during the school year, the board must include in a district-wide mailing, notice of the availability of copies of the budget (§§ 1608(2), 1716(2), 2601-a(3)). There is no legal requirement that the actual text of the budget be published in a newspaper.

4:22. Can voters change a proposed school district budget before the actual vote?

Yes, but only in school districts where the budget vote takes place by hand or voice vote. In these districts, those qualified voters present and voting may determine that a separate vote be taken for specific items on the budget. They also may vote to increase or decrease the amount of any item in the budget except for teachers' salaries or ordinary contingent expenses of the district (§ 2022(1); see also *Appeal of Rutledge*, 32 Educ. Dep't Rep. 259 (1992)).

4:23. Can a school board submit propositions to the voters that are supplemental to the budget?

Yes, subject to the two-vote limit on budget propositions (see **4:29**), school boards have the power to submit additional items of expenditure to the voters separate and apart from those specified in the proposed budget, either on the boards' own initiative or pursuant to a petition of voters (§§ 2021, 2022(2), 2035(2); see **4:24**).

4:24. Can voters submit propositions affecting the budget to be placed on the ballot?

Yes, subject to the two-vote limit on budget propositions (see **4:29**). However, the schoolboard may refuse such a proposition if its purpose is not within the power of the voters or is illegal (§§ 2008(2); 2021; *Appeal of*

Leman, 32 Educ. Dep't Rep. 579 (1993)). For example, a school board properly rejected a proposition which would require the board to submit a budget to the voters more than once before going on a contingency budget. School boards, not the voters, have the authority to determine whether to place a budget before the voters a second time, or adopt a contingency budget (*Appeal of Osten*, 35 Educ. Dep't Rep. 160 (1995)). Once an issue has been placed before the voters in a particular year, a school board may refuse to place the issue before the voters again in the same year (*Appeal of Brush*, 34 Educ. Dep't Rep. 273 (1994).

Similarly, a school board properly rejected a voter proposition which would require the school board to schedule a vote on an alternative budget proposed by a citizens' group before adopting a contingency budget. The authority to develop a budget rests with the school board, not the voters (*Appeal of Sperl*, 33 Educ. Dep't Rep. 388 (1994)).

Furthermore, where the expenditure of moneys is required by a proposition, the proposition must include specific appropriations for the items contained therein (§ 2035(2); *Matter of Sampson*, 14 Educ. Dep't Rep. 162 (1974)). Ambiguities in the proposition's language also may be grounds for the board's refusal; however, a school board may alter the language of a proposition submitted by the voters to remove any ambiguity (*Appeal of Como*, 30 Educ. Dep't Rep. 214 (1990); *Appeal of Krause*, 27 Educ. Dep't Rep. 57 (1987); *Appeal of Welch*, 16 Educ. Dep't Rep. 397 (1977)).

School boards must adopt reasonable rules and regulations concerning the submission of petitions (§ 2035(2)), including the date by which petitions must be submitted (see *Appeal of Como; Matter of Presutti*, 17 Educ. Dep't Rep. 445 (1978)), and the minimum number of signatures on a petition where the Education Law does not specify the number of signatures required for a proposition (see *Como*). This authority must be exercised with care because the commissioner of education has warned that it does not give school districts unfettered discretion to refuse such propositions (*Como*). School boards must comply with any such rules and regulations after they have been established (*Matter of Fetta*, 8 Educ. Dep't Rep. 201 (1969)).

4:25. May school boards place propositions on the ballot on matters not requiring voter approval?

If the matter is ultimately within the authority of the school board, the vote may be deemed advisory (see *Appeal of Rosenberg*, 31 Educ. Dep't Rep. 398 (1992)). However, advisory votes are discouraged because they may imply that the school board is seeking to avoid its responsibility (*Matter of Feldheim*, 8 Educ. Dep't Rep. 136 (1969)).

4:26. May a school board urge voters to vote in favor of a proposed school district budget?

No. School boards must take care to avoid spending public money to encourage voters to vote in favor of the school budget or any proposition (*Phillips v. Maurer*, 67 N.Y.2d 672 (1986)). However, boards may provide the voters with factual information about the budget and specific information about the effects of a budget's adoption or defeat in order to help them make an informed decision (*Appeal of Loriz*, 27 Educ. Dep't Rep. 376 (1988)).

The commissioner of education also has found that the use of district phones by students and administrators to call potential voters to encourage them to vote creates the appearance of improper partisan activity, where selective phone lists are used (see *Appeal of Tortorello*, 29 Educ. Dep't Rep. 306 (1990)). In the absence of partisan phone lists, the use of district phones to remind residents to vote is not improper (*Appeal of Gang*, 32 Educ. Dep't Rep. 337 (1992); see **4:74**).

However, school board members may actively support a proposed budget in their personal capacity. They have the same right as any other member of the community to express their views on public issues, as long as they do so at their own expense and on their own behalf, and do not use district funds or claim to be speaking on behalf of the board (*Appeal of Dinan*, 36 Educ. Dep't Rep 370 (1997); *Matter of Wolff*, 17 Educ. Dep't Rep. 297 (1978)).

4:27. May a school district prohibit the distribution of anonymous literature regarding the school budget?

No. The United States Supreme Court ruled that a state statute which prohibited the distribution of anonymous literature violated the First Amendment. The literature at issue expressed opposition to a proposed school tax levy and did not identify the author, but rather purported to express the views of "concerned parents and taxpayers." The individual who distributed the literature was fined $100 after a school official filed a complaint with the Elections Commission against her for violating the state law which prohibited the distribution of campaign literature which did not contain the name and address of the person or campaign official issuing the literature (*McIntyre v. Ohio Elections Comm'n.*, 514 U.S. 334 (1995)).

4:28. What happens if the voters reject the proposed school district budget?

Although it is generally considered good practice to submit a defeated budget for a second vote if the voters defeat the proposed school district budget, a school board may:

- Subject to the cap on contingency budgets (see **19:39**), prepare and adopt a contingency (or austerity) budget without going back to the voters. The board is empowered to levy a tax sufficient to pay for items that constitute ordinary contingent expenses (§§ 2022(4),(5); 2023; 2601-a(4),(5); see **19:40-42**).
- Present the original budget or a revision of the budget at a special district meeting, within the limitations set by law (see also **4:49-4:55**).
- Subject to the cap on contingency budgets (see **19:39**), adopt a contingency/austerity budget and then present one or more propositions to the voters, giving them the opportunity to vote to fund services that cannot be provided without voter approval. A separate proposition may be presented for each such service, or several services may be included in one proposition (*Appeal of Aarseth*, 32 Educ. Dep't Rep. 506 (1993)). Moreover, nothing in the law prohibits school districts from combining several unrelated objects and purposes in a single proposition (*Appeal of Friedman*, 36 Educ. Dep't Rep. 431 (1997)). Prior to submitting propositions to the voters, school districts should consult with their school attorney with respect to the contingency budget cap.

4:29. Is there any limitation on the number of times that a board of education may submit a budget or any proposition involving the expenditure of money for a vote at a district meeting?

Yes. A board of education may not submit a proposed budget, any part of such budget, or any propositions involving the expenditure of money to the voters more than twice. If the voters fail to approve a proposed budget after the second submission, or if the board elects not to put the proposed budget to a public vote a second time, the board must adopt a contingency (or austerity) budget (§§ 2022 (4),(5); 2601-a(4)).

4:30. May the commissioner of education impose a budget on school districts?

No. The commissioner of education does not have the authority to do this. However, questions as to what may be included in a contingency budget may be referred to the commissioner for a final decision (§§ 2024, 2601-a(5)(g), (6)).

Election of School Board Members

4:31. How are school board candidates nominated for election?

Nominating petitions must be signed by at least 25 qualified district voters, or 2 percent of the number of voters who voted in the previous annual election, whichever is greater (§ 2018(a)). In small city school districts, nominating petitions must be signed by at least 100 qualified voters (§ 2608(1)). The petition must include the candidate's name and residence, the residences of the people who signed the petition, the vacancy to be filled, including the name of the incumbent, and the length of the term of office to be filled (§§ 2018(a), 2608(1)).

Normally, nominating petitions are for specific seats on the school board, and candidates may be nominated for only one vacancy (§ 2018(a)). However, district voters may choose to make all seats "at large," which means that each nominee is eligible for every vacancy, rather than only for a specific seat (§ 2018(b)). In this case, nominating petitions need not state a specific vacancy (see *Appeal of Martin*, 32 Educ. Dep't Rep. 567 (1993)). A duly adopted "at large" proposition becomes effective at the next election and remains valid until repealed by the voters (§ 2018(b)).

(For information about write-in candidates, please see **4:36**.)

4:32. Do nominating petitions have to be verified?

Generally no. In school districts which conduct their school board elections pursuant to the provisions of the Education Law, it is impermissible to require that nominating petitions be verified (*Appeal of Loughlin*, 35 Educ. Dep't Rep. 432 (1996)). However, in school districts which conduct their school board elections pursuant to provisions of the Election Law, different rules may apply.

4:33. Can a person sign a nominating petition for more than one candidate for the same board seat?

Generally, yes. In most districts, there is no limit on the number of nominating petitions a district resident may sign. However, in New York City community school board elections, no person shall sign more than one nominating petition for the same board seat. In such elections, if a person does sign more than one nominating petition for the same board seat, that person's signature is invalid except upon the first petition signed (§ 2590-c(6)(a)(3); see also *Lavelle v. Gonzalez*, 93 A.D.2d 896 (2nd Dep't), *aff'd*, 59 N.Y.2d 670 (1983)).

4:34. What is the deadline for the submission of nominating petitions?

Nominating petitions must be filed in the office of the district clerk no later than 30 days (20 days in small city school districts) before the annual or special district meeting at which the school board election will occur, between 9:00 a.m. and 5:00 p.m. (§§ 2018(a), 2608(1)). Notice of the deadline for filing nominating petitions must be published in the notice of the annual or special district meeting (§§ 2003(2), 2004(2), 2007(1), 2601-a(2), 2602(2); see also **4:11**). Under certain specified circumstances, the nominating deadline may be extended (see **4:38**).

Nothing in the Education Law specifies the earliest date that candidates may begin collecting signatures on nominating petitions. In one case, the commissioner of education ruled that it was not unreasonable for a district to accept nominating petitions which contained signatures collected prior to the posting of the notice of the annual meeting, absent evidence that this practice gave some candidates an unfair advantage over others (*Appeal of Leman*, 32 Educ. Dep't Rep. 579 (1993)).

If the deadline for filing nominating petitions falls on "a Saturday, Sunday or public holiday," the filing may be performed on the "next succeeding business day" (Gen. Constr. Law § 25-a(1); see also *Appeal of Williams*, 36 Educ. Dep't Rep. 270 (1996)).

4:35. May the school board reject a nominating petition?

Yes. A nominating petition may be rejected if the nominating petition has been incorrectly filed, or if the candidate is ineligible for office or has declared an unwillingness to serve (§ 2035(2)). Although nominating petitions are presented to the district clerk, the board of education is authorized to determine whether a board candidate is eligible to serve and to reject a nominating petition from an ineligible candidate (*Appeal of Martin*, 31 Educ. Dep't Rep 441 (1992)).

4:36. Must a person have filed a nominating petition in order to be elected?

No. A person need not file a nominating petition in order to be elected to serve on a board of education. All ballots must have one blank space for each vacancy on the board of education, in which voters may write in the name of any candidate who is not listed on the ballot (§§ 2032(2)(e); 2608(2)). If the ballot does not have an open space for write-in votes, and the outcome of the election is affected as a result of the omission, the election may be nullified by the commissioner (*Appeal of Bd. of Trustees of Syosset Public Library*, 32 Educ. Dep't Rep. 460 (1993)).

There is no requirement in the Education Law that a voter place a check mark or an "x" (or any other kind of mark) next to the name of the write-in candidate (*Appeal of Titus*, 36 Educ. Dep't Rep. 407 (1997); *Appeal of Gresty*, 31 Educ. Dep't Rep. 90 (1991)). If the name of a qualified person is written on a write-in ballot, it must be counted.

Write-in ballots with minor misspellings of a candidate's name should be credited to that candidate in the absence of a showing that there is another district resident with the same or a similar name (*Appeal of Cook*, 20 Educ. Dep't Rep 1 (1980)).

Where voting machines are used, it is improper to require voters to cast write-in ballots in a separate ballot box (*Matter of Yost*, 21 Educ. Dep't. Rep. 140 (1981)).

4:37. What happens if there are no or not enough candidates properly nominated for each vacancy?

If this happens, the election must still be held, and the vacancies will be filled by the individuals with the most write-in votes (§§ 2032(2)(e); 2034(7)(a)). If there are not enough write-in candidates to fill vacancies, any remaining vacancy may be filled pursuant to the provisions of sections 1709(17), 2502(6), or 2113 of the Education Law (see **2:29-30**).

4:38. What happens if a candidate withdraws, dies or is determined for whatever reason to be ineligible for office before the election?

If a board candidate, for whom a nominating petition has been duly filed, withdraws the petition, dies or otherwise becomes ineligible to hold the office of board member at a point in time later than 15 days before the last day for the filing of nominating petitions, the district may be required to extend the nominating deadline by as much as 15 days, provided, however, that in no event may nominating petitions be filed later than 5:00 p.m. on the seventh day before the date of the election (§§ 2018(d), 2608(1)).

4:39. May a candidate who withdraws from an election resubmit his or her candidacy?

Yes, but that person must file a new petition within the same time limitations applicable to other candidates (§ 2018(a)).

4:40. Are school board candidates required to file campaign expenditure statements?

Yes. All school board candidates must file a sworn statement of all campaign expenditures on their behalf in excess of $500 with both the district clerk and the commissioner of education (§§ 1528-1531). Candidates who spend less than $500 instead may file a sworn statement indicating this to be the case with the district clerk (§ 1528). No other disclosure statement is required (see **2:9**).

The statement of expenditures in excess of $500 must list the amounts of all money or other valuable things paid, given, expended or promised by the candidate, or incurred for or on the candidate's behalf with his or her approval, and be filed with the school district clerk and the commissioner of education (§ 1528). A preliminary statement must be filed at least 10 days before the election and a final statement must be filed within 20 days after the election (§ 1529(1)). The statement must cover the period up to and including the day next preceding the day specified for the filing of the statement (§ 1529(2)).

The failure of a candidate to file a complete statement of election expenditures is an insufficient basis for setting aside the results of a school board election (*Appeal of Guttman*, 32 Educ. Dep't Rep. 228 (1992); *Matter of Pendergast*, 20 Educ. Dep't Rep. 127 (1980)). But candidates who fail to file the required statements may be ordered to do so by a justice of a state supreme court (§§ 1530-31; see also *Appeal of Donnelly*, 33 Educ. Dep't Rep. 362 (1993)).

4:41. How are school board candidates elected?

School board members are elected by a plurality of the votes cast for each vacancy (§§ 2034(7)(a)), 2502(9)(n), (9-a)(n), 2610(4)). In districts with "at-large" seats, if there are vacant positions of different lengths, positions are filled in decreasing order of the number of votes and length of office (§§ 2034(7)(c), 2502(9)(n), (9-a)(n), 2610(4)). Thus, the candidate with the highest number of votes is entitled to the position of the longest length.

In city school districts with 125,000 or more inhabitants, school board elections are conducted in accordance with section 2553 of the Education Law, except that in New York City, community school board elections are conducted pursuant to section 2590-c of the Education Law.

4:42. Must the candidates' names appear on the ballot in any particular order?

Yes. The order of the candidates' names is determined by a drawing by lot, and listed either with the specific vacancy for which they have been nominated, or all together for at-large seats. The district clerk conducts the drawing "the day after the last possible date for candidates to file a petition. In the event that any candidate is not present in person or by a person designated in a written proxy to accomplish the drawing, the district clerk shall be authorized to act as proxy" (§§ 2032(2)(b); 2608(2)).

4:43. Who gives official notice of the school board election results?

The chairperson of the meeting at which the election takes place declares the result of each ballot, as announced by the election inspectors

(§ 2034(7)(a)). If the district has been divided into election districts and voting machines are used, the election inspectors must report the results to the chief election inspector of each district, who then reports the results to the district clerk within 24 hours. The school board must then tabulate and declare the result of the ballot within 24 hours of receiving the results (§ 2034(7)(b)).

The school district clerk, in turn, notifies in writing every person elected as a school board member (§§ 2108(1), 2121(5), 2610(5)). The clerk also must report the names and post office addresses of elected board members to the town clerk of the town where the district is situated. There is a $5 penalty for failing to do so (§ 2121(5)).

4:44. What happens if an election vote is tied?

If there is a tie vote for a position on the board, the district must have a run-off election within 45 days. The only candidates in a run-off election are those who tied. No new nominating petitions are required (§§ 2034(10), 2610(6)).

4:45. Must newly-elected school board members officially accept their election to office?

No. Newly-elected school board members are considered to have accepted the office unless they file a written refusal with the school district clerk within five days after receiving notice of their election. Their presence at the meeting at which they were elected is deemed sufficient notice of their election to office (§ 2108(2)).

4:46. When does a newly-elected board member take office?

A new board member takes office when the incumbent's term of office expires, or if the seat is vacant at the time of the election, immediately after the election (§ 2105(14)).

The new board member must file an oath of office (Pub. Off. Law § 10; see **2:8**). If a new member has not filed an oath of office or is otherwise not qualified to take office when the term begins, the incumbent "holds over" in office until the new member becomes "qualified," that is, takes all the steps necessary to take office (Pub. Off. Law § 5; see *Matter of Waxman*, 19 Educ. Dep't Rep. 157 (1979)).

The failure or neglect of a board member to file an oath of office within 30 days after the commencement of the term of office to which the person is elected causes the office to become vacant (Pub. Off. Law § 30(1)(h)).

4:47. What happens if there is a dispute over the results of a school board election?

All disputes over any district meeting or election must be referred to the commissioner of education (§ 2037). The commissioner may, at his discretion, order a recount of the ballots or a new election (§§ 2034(6)(a); 2037; *Appeal of Murtagh*, 19 Educ. Dep't Rep. 179 (1979)). In fact, only the commissioner has the authority to order a recount of a vote on a school board election (*Matter of Senecal*, 22 Educ. Dep't Rep. 367 (1983); but see *Appeal of Ell*, 34 Educ. Dep't Rep. 394 (1995); see also **4:81**).

4:48. What impact does a successful challenge over the results of a school board election have on the actions taken by the board pending appeal?

In such cases, the commissioner has determined that the person initially declared the winner is a *de facto* board member during the period of time that they serve on the board while an appeal of the election results is pending. Therefore, the actions taken by the board during the pendency of the appeal are valid (*Appeal of Heller*, 34 Educ. Dep't Rep. 220 (1994); see also *Appeal of Loughlin*, 35 Educ. Dep't Rep. 432 (1996)).

Special School District Meetings

4:49. What is a special school district meeting?

A *special school district meeting* is a meeting called for a specific purpose or purposes (§§ 2006-2008). Most often, these meetings are called for holding special school board elections or resubmitting rejected budgets for voter approval.

Only matters that are included in the notice for the special school district meeting may be addressed during the meeting (§§ 2006(1), 2007(1)).

4:50. Must special school district meetings be held at a specific time?

Unlike the annual meeting and election, there generally is no designated time for holding special school district meetings. The meeting need not continue for any specific period of time, so long as enough time is allowed for all voters present at the meeting to vote on the matters before them (see *Appeal of Faulkner*, 16 Educ. Dep't Rep. 93 (1976)).

In union free and central school districts, however, a special meeting for the purpose of electing members of the board of education where there is a vacancy must be held for at least six consecutive hours between 7:00 a.m. (as opposed to 6:00 a.m. for annual elections) and 9:00 p.m., at least two hours of which must be after 6:00 p.m. A meeting may go longer than the statutory six hours so long as proper notice is given (§ 2007(4)). In *Appeal of Demos*, 34 Educ. Dep't Rep. 54 (1994), the commissioner upheld the results of a special meeting held until after 10:00 p.m.

In small city school districts, such elections must be held at least nine consecutive hours beginning not earlier than 7:00 a.m., at least two hours of which must be after 6:00 p.m. (§ 2602(3)).

4:51. How are special school district meetings called?

Generally, special district meetings are called by the school board when the board deems it necessary and proper (§§ 2006(1), 2007(1), 2602(2)), or when petitioned by 25 voters, or 5 percent of those voting in the previous annual election, whichever is greater (§ 2008(2)), for any purpose that is within the voters' power (§§ 2008(2)(a), 2021).

The commissioner of education and district superintendent also have authority to call special meetings under certain circumstances, as set forth in law (§§ 2005, 2008(1), 2113(2)). Furthermore, the commissioner of education may call a special meeting if he has annulled the results of the annual meeting or election (see *Appeal of Glier*, 1 Educ. Dep't Rep. 695 (1961)).

4:52. May a school board refuse a voters' petition to call a special school district meeting?

Yes. A school board may refuse to call a special school district meeting if its purpose is to address matters not within the power of the voters, if its purpose is illegal, or if the petition for such a meeting was not filed within 20 days after notice of a bond or note resolution was published pursuant to Local Finance Law section 81.00, or for any other reasons the commissioner of education would deem sufficient (§ 2008(2)(a-d)).

However, school boards must either accept or reject petitions for a special school district meeting within 20 days of their submission (§ 2008(2); see *Appeal of French*, 32 Educ. Dep't Rep. 100 (1992)). If a petition is accepted, notice of the meeting must be given within 20 days of the petition's receipt (§ 2008(2)).

4:53. What notice must be given to the public regarding a special school district meeting?

In common school districts, unless district residents have voted at a district meeting to prescribe another method of giving notice of special meetings, notice of a special meeting must be given to each resident by the district clerk (by hand delivery to their residence) at least six days before the meeting. Or notice can be published in two newspapers (or one if there is only one) having general circulation once in each week within the four weeks prior to the meeting, with the first publication at least 22 days before the meeting. If no newspaper is available, notice must be posted in at least 20 public places between 22 and 28 days before the meeting (§ 2006(1),(2)).

All other school districts generally must provide the same notice for a special meeting as for the annual meeting, meaning 45 days ahead of the meeting with publication once each week for four weeks in two newspapers of general circulation (§ 2007(1), see also **4:11**). However, when a special meeting is called to "re-vote" on the same budget, a modified budget or certain propositions after a defeated budget, notice is required only two weeks in advance, by publishing once each week for two weeks before the vote, with the publication being 14 days before the vote (§ 2007(3)(a)). In addition, whenever the board of education has rejected all bids for a contract or contracts for public work, transportation or purchase, the board may call a special district meeting upon two weeks notice to take further appropriate action (§ 2007(3)(a)).

4:54. What must be included in the notice of a special school district meeting?

The notice must state the date, time and place of the meeting and the matter or matters to be addressed at the meeting (§§ 2006(1), 2007(1), 2004). Special notice requirements also apply where the meeting is called to vote on the issuance of bonds or capital notes (see **4:11**).

4:55. How is a special school district meeting conducted?

Special school district meetings are conducted in the same way as the annual meeting and election. The same person who calls the annual meeting and election to order calls the special district meeting to order; written records of the proceedings must be kept; and the district clerk generally serves as the clerk of the meeting (§ 2025).

Qualifications of Voters

4:56. Who may vote at an annual meeting and election or special school district meeting?

Only qualified voters of the school district may vote on any question brought before an annual meeting and election or special school district meeting (§ 2012).

4:57. Who is a qualified voter?

A *qualified voter* is a person who is a citizen of the United States, at least 18 years old, a resident of the school district for at least 30 days prior to the meeting at which he or she offers to vote, and who is not otherwise prohibited from voting under the provisions of section 5-106 of the Election Law, for example, a person who has been adjudged to be mentally incompetent (§§ 2012, 2603). (Note: A convicted felon does have a right to vote, provided that he or she has been pardoned, his or her maximum prison sentence has expired, or he or she has been discharged from parole (Elec. Law § 5-106(2)).

In addition, in New York City, every registered voter residing in a community school district, and every registered parent of a child attending any school under the jurisdiction of the community school board of such a school district, who also meets the above requirements, may vote in a community school board election (§ 2590–c(3)).

School districts may not require voters to pay taxes or have children attending the public schools to be eligible to vote (*Kramer v. Union Free School District No. 15*, 395 U.S. 621 (1969)). Military personnel residing on a military base may also be qualified voters in the school district where that base is located (*Appeal of Kuleszo*, 30 Educ. Dep't Rep. 465 (1991)).

In districts that use personal registration, qualified voters also must either be registered with the school district's board of registration or with the county board of elections in order to vote (see also **4:61; 4:84**).

4:58. Can the chairperson of the annual meeting and election vote?

Yes, but he or she must vote before the polls are closed and cannot vote to break a tie after the polls are closed (*Matter of Dist. No. 27, Town of Canton*, 62 St. Dep't Rep. 148 (1940)).

The chairperson may also make rulings from the chair, such as declaring a motion out of order. However, a qualified voter who objects to the ruling from the chair may appeal to the entire group at the meeting for a final decision; otherwise all the voters present will be found to have agreed with the ruling of the chair (*Matter of Mazzurco*, 6 Educ. Dep't Rep. 101 (1967)).

4:59. What happens if an unqualified person votes or lies about his or her qualifications to vote?

The district may sue unqualified voters for a fine of $10 to be used for the benefit of the district (§ 2020(3)).

In addition, if it appears that the election results were affected by votes cast by unqualified persons, the commissioner of education may invalidate the vote and require a special meeting or election (*Appeal of Cobb*, 32 Educ. Dep't Rep. 139 (1992); see **4:81**).

A person who willfully makes a false statement about his or her qualifications to vote is guilty of a misdemeanor (§ 2020(1),(2)), and may be subject to a fine of up to $1,000 and/or imprisonment for up to one year (Penal Law §§ 55.10(2)(b), 70.15(1), 80.05(1)).

Voter Registration

4:60. Must school districts have a system of personal registration?

No. But school boards in union free, central and small city school districts may decide to provide for personal registration of voters in their districts (§§ 2014; 2606). Boards that adopt a resolution providing for personal registration must notify the appropriate board of elections within five days of the adoption (Elec. Law § 5-612(4)). They also must notify the board of elections of the date of school district meetings or elections at least 45 days before the meeting or election, and at least 14 days before any special meeting or election (Elec. Law § 5-612(5)).

4:61. In districts with personal registration, must voters be registered with the school district in order to vote?

Not necessarily. Although school districts may have a system of personal voter registration (§ 2014), individuals registered to vote with the county board of elections are eligible to vote at school district meetings without further registration (Elec. Law §§ 5-406; 5-612(2); *Appeal of Shortell,* 27 Educ. Dep't Rep. 190 (1987)).

The county board of elections is required to provide a list of voters to the school district at least 30 days prior to any regularly scheduled election, and a supplemental list at least 10 days before the regular election and any special election (Elec. Law § 5-612 (3)).

4:62. When and where does personal registration take place?

The time and location of voter registration is set by school board resolution. However, the last day of registration for any school district meeting or election must not be more than 14 days nor less than five days before a school district meeting. Registration must be open for at least four consecutive hours between 7:00 a.m. and 8:00 p.m., but voters may also authorize registration during the same hours children may be enrolled for a school term, or certain hours of the school day at the office of the district clerk or assistant clerk or at the district's business office (§ 2014(2); see also Educ. Law § 2606, which governs voter registration in small city school districts).

4:63. What information is included in the voter registration list?

The registration list used for each district meeting must include the names of everyone who has registered to vote at the meeting, and may include anyone who has registered and voted in prior school district meetings in the preceding four calendar years. However, the name of anyone who has died or moved out of the school district, or become otherwise ineligible to vote, must be removed (§ 2014(2)).

The registration list must include the name and street address of each voter on the list, arranged alphabetically by last name. If there is no street address, some description must be included that accurately locates the place of residence. It must also have a column or columns in which to indicate whether each person listed has voted previously in any school district election or elections or at any meetings (§ 2014(2)).

The registration list is not the same thing as a poll list (see **4:78**).

4:64. Who prepares the voter registration list?

This is prepared by the school district's board of registration (§ 2014(2)). This board consists of four qualified voters of the district appointed annually by the school board, not later than 30 days after the district's annual meeting or election, and who serve until 30 days after the annual meeting or election the following year. The board of registration is entitled to compensation at a rate fixed by the school board for each day actually and necessarily spent on the duties of the office (§ 2014(1)).

4:65. Must school districts make voter registration lists available for public inspection?

Yes. Voter registration lists must be filed in the office of the district clerk at least five days before any school district meeting or election and must be open to public inspection by any qualified voter at all reasonable times and days of the week, except Sunday, up to and including the day of the election (§ 2015(1)).

4:66. May a school district discontinue its system of personal registration?

Yes, the board may discontinue personal registration by a board resolution passed at least two months before the next school district meeting or election. However, personal registration may not then be re-instituted without voter approval (§ 2014(3)).

The Voting Process

4:67. Do the provisions of the New York State Election Law apply to school districts?

The Election Law applies to school districts only as specifically indicated in the Education Law (Elect. Law § 1-102; see Educ. Law § 2609).

4:68. Must voting booths be used at school board elections and budget votes?

Yes, in districts other than common school districts (§ 2030).

4:69. Must ballots be used in school district elections and budget votes?

Generally, yes. However, in school districts that prior to 1998 conducted their vote at the annual meeting, votes may be taken by recording the ayes and nays of the qualified voters attending and voting at the district meeting (§§ 2022(3), 2031).

4:70. May voting machines be used at the annual meeting and election or special school district meetings?

Yes. Although the use of voting machines is optional, it is considered to be in compliance with any provision of law requiring the vote to be by ballot (§§ 2035(1), 2611; *Hurd v. Nyquist*, 72 Misc.2d 213 (1972); *Matter of Nicoletti*, 21 Educ. Dep't Rep. 38 (1981)).

If voting machines are used, they must be examined by election inspectors before each election to see that all the counters are set at zero, that the ballot labels are properly placed and that each machine is in all respects in proper condition for use (§ 2035(1)).

4:71. Who provides the ballots or voting machines used at school district meetings?

Ballots are provided by the school district. When used for school board elections, ballots must contain the names of candidates who have been nominated, listed in the order determined by drawing lots (§§ 2032, 2608; see also **4:42**). A choice is indicated by an "x" or a check mark by pencil or pen in a square before the name of the candidate. One blank space must be provided under the name of the last candidate for each specific office for write-in candidates (§ 2032(d), (e); see also **4:36**)).

A voting machine or machines may be purchased by the school district or, with the consent of the county board of elections, the school district may use voting machines belonging to the county or the town in which any part of the school district is located. Rental and other terms or conditions are set by resolutions of the board of elections (§ 2035(1); Elec. Law § 3-224).

4:72. May school districts be divided into election districts?

Yes. A union free school district with personal voter registration may be divided into election districts by action of the board or by a majority vote of the qualified voters present and voting at a district meeting (§ 2017(1)). Each election district must have at least 300 qualified voters, and if possible, have a school building (§ 2017(1), (2)).

Once the decision to divide the district into election districts is made, the school board must immediately adopt a resolution dividing the district into the number of election districts as the board may determine. The resolution must be adopted at least 30 days before the annual or special meeting or election (§ 2017(2)). Voters then vote within their respective election district.

4:73. May proxy votes be cast at school district meetings?

No. There is no statutory authority permitting the use of proxy votes at school district meetings (*Matter of Kirchhof*, 70 St. Dep't Rep. 33 (1949); *Matter of District No. 1 of the Town of Pittstown*, 58 St. Dep't Rep. 423 (1937)).

4:74. Is electioneering permitted during school district elections or when voting on the school budget or propositions?

No. The Education Law prohibits electioneering on the day of the election within a 100-foot zone measured from the entrance to the polling place (§§ 2031-a; 2609(4-a)). Electioneering includes, but is not limited to such activity as distributing or displaying a candidate's campaign materials or materials on behalf of or in opposition to any propositions. It should be noted, however, that the law specifically allows a board of education to display within any polling place a copy or copies of any budget or proposition to be voted upon (§§ 2031-a(2); 2609(4-a)(b)).

District elections inspectors are required to post distance markers delineating the 100-foot zone (§§ 2031-a(1); 2609(4-a)(a); *Cullen v. Fliegner*, 18 F.3d 96 (2nd Cir. 1994). Any person who willfully violates the prohibition on electioneering may be found guilty of a misdemeanor (§§ 2031-a(3); 2609(4-a)(c)).

Calling potential voters to encourage them to exercise their right to vote, while questionable, does not necessarily constitute electioneering (*Appeal of Gang*, 32 Educ. Dep't Rep. 337 (1992)).

Holding a "[b]arbecue fund raiser at the same time as the election, even if the grill is within 100 feet of the voting booth, does not constitute electioneering in and of itself" *(Appeal of Santicola,* 36 Educ. Dep't Rep. 416 (1997)).

Similarly, holding a school concert on the night of the budget vote does not constitute electioneering, provided that the district gives notice of the concert to all district residents in the same manner and not just to those district residents whom the board believes will be supportive of the propositions on the ballot *(Appeal of Rampello,* 37 Educ. Dep't Rep. 153 (1997); *Appeal of Sowinski,* 34 Educ. Dep't Rep. 184 (1994)).

4:75. Must there be election inspectors at school district meetings?

Yes. There must be at least two election inspectors for each ballot box or voting machine in use (§ 2025(3)). However, the failure to appoint the required number of election inspectors will only be grounds for invalidating a school district election if the error affects the outcome of the election *(Appeal of Uciechowski,* 32 Educ. Dep't Rep. 511 (1993)).

In common school districts, election inspectors are elected by the voters. The election inspectors choose a chief election inspector (§ 2025(3)(a)).

In union free and central school districts, the board of education appoints the election inspectors. The board also designates a chief election inspector. Where the district is divided into election districts, the board must appoint a chief election inspector for each election district (§ 2025(3)(b)).

In small city school districts, the board of education is required to appoint three qualified voters to serve as elections inspectors for each election district, and may appoint additional elections inspectors if necessary. The inspectors themselves elect one of their number as chairman of the election, and one as poll clerk (§ 2607).

Elections inspectors appointed by the board of education may be compensated at a rate set by the board (§§ 2025(5), 2607).

Nothing in the Education Law prohibits district employees, board of education members, relatives of board members or candidates from serving as election inspectors *(Appeal of Goldman,* 35 Educ. Dep't Rep. 126 (1995); *Appeal of Bleier,* 32 Educ. Dep't. Rep. 63 (1992)).

4:76. May a school board candidate appoint poll watchers?

Yes, but only in school districts which have adopted a system of personal registration (§ 2019-a(2)(c),(d)). There is no authority for a candidate to appoint poll watchers in districts without personal registration *(Appeal of Chaplin, Jr.,* 30 Educ. Dep't Rep. 420 (1991)).

4:77. What happens if there are still people in line waiting to vote at the time for closing the polls?

All qualified voters who are present at the polling place must be allowed to vote (§§ 2033, 2609(4); see *Appeal of Fugle*, 32 Educ. Dep't Rep. 480 (1993)).

4:78. Must a poll list be made of those voting at school district meetings?

Yes. A poll list is a list maintained by the district clerk or assistant clerk(s) which contains the names and addresses of the people who have voted in a district meeting or election (§ 2029). The clerk or assistant clerk(s) must record the name and legal residences of all voters as they deposit their ballots (§§ 2029, 2609(4); see *Appeal of Gang*, 32 Educ. Dep't Rep. 337 (1992)).

Poll lists are public documents which must be made available for inspection and copying except on election day (*Appeal of Walsh*, 34 Educ. Dep't Rep. 544 (1995); *Appeal of Schneider*, 29 Educ. Dep't Rep. 151 (1989)).

4:79. Must a written record be kept of the proceedings at an annual or special school district meeting or election?

Yes. The clerk and assistant clerk(s) of district meetings must keep a true and accurate written record of all of the proceedings of the district meeting or election and file a written record with the clerk of the district within 24 hours after the meeting (§ 2025(4)).

Generally, the district clerk serves as the clerk of all district meetings and elections (§ 2025(3)). If the district clerk is not present or is unable to act, an acting clerk of the meeting must be appointed or elected in accordance with section 2025 of the Education Law.

In common school districts the voters elect assistant clerks as necessary. In union free and central school districts, the school board may appoint assistant clerks as necessary. If they are appointed by the board, the assistant clerks may be compensated at a rate set by the school board (§ 2025(5)).

4:80. How are votes counted?

The election inspectors first must count the ballots to determine if they tally with the number of names recorded on the voter list. If they exceed that number, enough ballots must be withdrawn at random by the chief election inspector to reduce the number of ballots to the number of voters. The ballots are then counted by the election inspectors who inform the chairperson of the results of the meeting (§ 2034(1), (2), (4), (5)).

4:81. What happens if a school district meeting is found to have been improperly held?

The commissioner may set aside the election results and/or may order a special school district meeting to be held (§ 2037).

There is a presumption of regularity in the conduct of school district elections. Even when someone can show that an irregularity occurred in the conduct of a school district election, the commissioner will not overturn the election results unless the complainant establishes that any alleged irregularities actually affected the outcome of the election, were so pervasive that they vitiated the electoral process, or demonstrate a clear and convincing picture of informality to the point of laxity in adherence to the education law (*Appeal of Kushner*, 36 Educ. Dep't Rep. 261 (1996)).

The burden of convincing the commissioner to set aside the results of an election rests with the person(s) challenging the election results (*Appeal of Loriz*, 35 Educ. Dep't Rep. 231 (1995); *Appeal of Horton*, 35 Educ. Dep't Rep. 168 (1995)).

Voter Challenges

4:82. In districts without personal registration, may school districts ask for proof of residency before allowing individuals to vote?

Yes. In districts without personal registration, district elections officials may, but are not required to, take an active role in ensuring voter qualifications by requiring all persons offering to vote at any school district meeting or election to provide one form of proof of residency, to be determined by the school board, such as a driver's license, non-driver I.D. card, utility bill or voter registration card. District elections officers also may require such persons offering to vote to provide their signature, printed name and address (§ 2018-c).

Challenges to the qualifications of specific individuals must be made in accordance with section 2019 of the Education Law (see **4:83**).

4:83. May a voter challenge another person's qualifications to vote in districts without personal registration?

Yes. In districts without personal registration, any qualified voter may challenge the qualifications of any other voter. If a qualified voter challenges the qualifications of another voter, then the chairman presiding at the meeting or election shall require the person offering to vote to make the following declaration: "I do declare and affirm that I am, and have been, for 30 days last past, an actual resident of this school district and that I am qualified to vote at this meeting." If the person challenged makes this declaration, then the person shall be permitted to vote, but if the person refuses, his or her vote must be rejected (§ 2019).

4:84. In those districts with personal registration, may a voter challenge another person's qualifications to vote?

Yes. In districts with personal registration, any qualified voter may challenge, *either prior to or at the district meeting,* the qualifications of any other voter. If a qualified voter challenges a person whose name is on the voter registration list, the chairperson presiding at the meeting or election shall require the person offering to vote to make the following declaration: "I do declare and affirm that I am, and have been, for 30 days last past, an actual resident of this school district and that I am qualified to vote at this meeting." If the person challenged makes this declaration, then he or she shall be permitted to vote, but if the person refuses, his or her vote must be rejected (§§ 2015(3),(4); 2019).

If, however, in a district with personal registration, a person's name cannot be found on the list of registered voters or in the registration poll ledger, then district elections officials shall not permit that person to vote, unless: (1) the person presents a court order requiring that he or she be permitted to vote in the manner otherwise prescribed for voters whose names are on the list of registered voters or in the registration poll ledger, or the person (2) submits an affidavit attesting to his or her qualifications to vote.

If the person is permitted to vote by affidavit, he or she must print on the outside of an envelope a sworn statement indicating (1) that he or she has duly registered to vote; (2) the address at which he or she is registered; (3) that he or she remains a duly qualified voter in the election district where he or she resides; (4) that his or her poll record appears to be lost or misplaced or that his/her name has been incorrectly omitted from the list of registered voters; and (5) that he or she understands that any false statement made therein is perjury punishable according to law.

A person who is permitted to vote by affidavit must vote by paper ballot, which is placed inside the envelope upon which the affidavit was written and then sealed therein until the close of the election and the canvassing of ballots (§ 2019-a(1)). "If it is determined that a voter who cast an affidavit ballot was not registered, the ballot may not be counted" (*Appeal of Vaughan,* 33 Educ. Dep't Rep 189 (1993)).

4:85. When must a challenge be made to a person's qualification's to vote?

Challenges to the qualifications of a voter, both in districts with personal registration and in districts without personal registration, must be raised no later than the time the voter presents himself or herself at the polls to vote (*Appeal of Fraser-McBride*, 36 Educ. Dep't Rep. 488 (1997)).

Absentee Ballots

4:86. May absentee ballots be used for voting at a school board election or budget vote?

Yes. School boards may, by resolution, allow the use of absentee ballots for the election of school board members, school district public library trustees, the adoption of the annual budget and school district public library budget and referenda (§§ 2018-a, 2018-b).

In general, school boards may allow the use of absentee ballots by any person who will be unable to vote in person due to illness or physical disability, hospitalization, incarceration (unless incarcerated for conviction of a felony), or travel outside the voter's county or city of residence for employment or business reasons, studies or vacation on the day of the election (§§ 2018-a(2), 2018-b(2)). Such a resolution becomes effective 60 days after its adoption and remains in effect until a subsequent resolution provides otherwise (§§ 2018-a(1), 2018-b(1)).

In districts that authorize the use of absentee ballots, the board of registration (in districts with personal registration) or district clerk or other designee of the school board (in districts without personal registration) should automatically mail an absentee ballot to each voter whose registration record on file with the county board of elections is marked "permanently disabled" (§§ 2018-a(2)(g), 2018-b(2)(g)).

No board resolution is required to authorize the issuance of absentee ballots in school districts located in Nassau and Suffolk counties, which are required by law to provide absentee ballots to individuals who otherwise are unable to vote, under circumstances as set forth in Education Law sections 2018-a and 2018-b.

The law regarding the issuance of absentee ballots in small city school districts states that school boards in small cities "may provide for absentee ballots for the election of candidates to the board of education only, in accordance with the provisions of section two thousand eighteen-a of this chapter insofar as applicable" (§ 2613). The wording of this section of law raises some doubt as to whether small city school districts have the ability to provide absentee ballots for voting on the district budget.

4:87. What is the deadline for the submission of absentee ballots?

No absentee voter's ballot will be counted unless it is received in the office of the school district clerk (clerk or designee of the school board in districts without personal registration) by 5:00 p.m. on the day of the election (§§ 2018-a(8), 2018-b(9)).

4:88. What is the procedure for voting by absentee ballot?

Except for voters whose registration is marked "permanently disabled" (see **4:86**) an individual must submit an application to receive an absentee ballot (§§ 2018-a(2)(a), 2018-b(2)(a)). The information which must be requested in the application is set by statute (§§ 2018-a(2)(a), 2018-b(2)(a)). The application must be received by the district clerk or designee at least seven days before the election if the ballot is to be mailed to the voter, or the day before the election, if the ballot is to be issued to the voter in person (§§ 2018-a(2)(a); 2018-b(2)(a)).

Upon receipt of an application for an absentee ballot, either the board of registration (in districts with personal registration) or district clerk or other designee of the board of education (in districts without personal registration) must review the application to determine if the applicant is a qualified voter and is otherwise entitled to vote by absentee ballot (§§ 2018-a(3); 2018-b(3)).

If the application is proper in all respects, the board of registration, or district clerk or other designee of the board, then mails or personally issues an absentee ballot to the voter. The board of registration or district clerk must then record the name of the voter to whom the absentee ballot was issued on the district's personal registration list or poll list (§§ 2018-a(3); 2018-b(3)).

In districts that do not use personal registration, voters may request a ballot by signed letter rather than by application so long as the district clerk or designee receives the letter not earlier than 30 days before the election nor later than seven days before the election. In this situation, the district clerk will send both an application and a ballot to the voter, and the ballot will not be counted unless the completed application is returned with it (§ 2018-b(4)).

4:89. Can a person request more than one absentee ballot application?

Yes. There is no authority under the Education Law for a school district to demand a list of the voters who will use said applications from an individual seeking multiple copies of absentee ballot applications (*Appeal of the Roxbury Taxpayers Alliance*, 34 Educ. Dep't Rep. 576 (1995)).

4:90. Does a school district have to maintain a list of those individuals who have been issued absentee ballots?

Yes. The board of registration (in districts with personal registration) must make a list of all persons to whom absentee ballots have been issued and file such list in the office of the district clerk, where it must be available for public inspection during regular office hours until the day of the election.

Similarly, the district clerk or other designee of the board of education (in districts without personal registration) must make a list of all persons to whom absentee ballots have been issued and maintain such list where it must be available for public inspection during regular office hours until the day of the election (§§ 2018-a(6)(a), 2018-b(7)(a)).

In addition, such list must be posted in a conspicuous place or places during the election (§§ 2018-a(6)(b), 2018-b(7)(b)). Placement of the list in a folder on the desk of the election inspector does not satisfy this requirement *(Appeal of Heller,* 34 Educ. Dep't Rep. 220 (1994)).

4:91. Can an absentee ballot be challenged?

Yes. Any qualified voter may, prior to the election, file a written challenge to the qualifications of any person whose name appears on the list of absentee voters prepared for transmittal to the election inspectors on the day of the election, stating the reason for such challenge (§§ 2018-a(6)(a), 2018-b(7)(a)). The written challenge must be transmitted by the clerk or designee to the election inspectors on the day of the election (§§ 2018-a(6)(a), 2018-b(7)(a)). Furthermore, on the day of the election, any qualified voter may challenge the acceptance of the absentee voter's ballot by making the challenge to the election inspectors before the close of the polls (§§ 2018-a(6)(b), 2018-b(7)(b)).

Preventing a qualified voter from exercising his or her right to object to a submitted absentee ballot may be grounds for invalidating the election results *(Appeal of Heller,* 34 Educ. Dep't Rep. 220 (1994)).

5. Boards of Cooperative Educational Services (BOCES)

5:1. What is a board of cooperative educational services?

A *board of cooperative educational services (BOCES)* is a voluntary, cooperative association of school districts in a geographic area that share planning, services and programs to provide educational and support activities more economically, efficiently and equitably than could be provided by an individual district. The geographic area covered by a BOCES is known as a supervisory district (see **6:2**).

BOCES are organized under section 1950 of the Education Law. BOCES services are focused on education for students with disabilities, career education, academic and alternative programs, summer schools, staff development, computer services (managerial and instructional), educational communication and burgeoning cooperative purchasing.

A BOCES board is considered a corporate body. All BOCES property is held by the BOCES board as a corporation (§ 1950(6)). In addition, BOCES boards are also considered municipal corporations to permit them to contract with other municipalities on a cooperative basis under sections 119-n(a) and 119-o of the General Municipal Law.

For the sake of clarity, the governing body of the BOCES will be referred to as the BOCES board throughout this chapter.

5:2. How many BOCES are there?

There are 38 BOCES in New York State.

5:3. Do all school districts belong to a BOCES?

No. Of the 705 BOCES-eligible school districts, only eight school districts did not belong to a BOCES as of March 1998. In addition, BOCES membership is not available to the Big 5 school districts (Buffalo, New York City, Rochester, Syracuse and Yonkers). However, under certain circumstances, non-component districts may participate in BOCES instructional support services (see **5:36**).

5:4. Can a school district terminate its membership in a BOCES?

There is no authority or process by which a school district can terminate its status as a BOCES component.

BOCES Board Membership

5:5. How many members are on a BOCES board?

A BOCES board may consist of between five to 15 members. The number of BOCES board members may be increased or decreased within that range by the commissioner of education (§ 1950(1),(2-b)).

5:6. How long is the term of office of a BOCES board member?

As of January 1994, BOCES board members are elected to three-year terms, except that during the transition period from the prior five-year term to the three-year term, the BOCES board may require one or more members to be elected for a term of one, two or four years, so that as nearly as possible, an equal number of board members are elected each year (§ 1950(2-b)). BOCES board members' terms commence on the first day of July following their election (§ 1950(2-b)).

BOCES board members elected prior to December 1, 1993 may complete their five-year terms of office (see "Questions and Answers on the BOCES Reform Act," State Education Department, October 1993).

5:7. Can two residents of the same component district sit on a BOCES board at the same time?

The law prohibits the election of more than one candidate residing in a particular component school district, unless the number of seats on the BOCES board exceeds the number of component school districts or an unrepresented district declines to make a nomination (§ 1950(2-a)(c)). This restriction applies, no matter which district initially nominated the person.

5:8. What are the qualifications for serving as a BOCES board member?

In order to be eligible for membership on a BOCES board, a candidate must reside within the boundaries of a component school district (§ 1950(9-a)). Any candidate nominated by a special act school district, a central high school district or any component thereof, shall be considered a resident of the district that nominated that person (§ 1950(2-a)(b)).

A candidate need not be a member of a component district school board. However, no employee of a component district is eligible for BOCES board membership (§ 1950(9)), even though a BOCES employee may serve on a component school board (*Matter of Todd*, 19 Educ. Dep't Rep. 277 (1979)).

Also, no more than one candidate per component district may be elected to serve, unless the number of BOCES seats exceeds the number of component districts or an unrepresented district declines to make a nomination (§ 1950(2-a)(c)).

5:9. How are BOCES board members nominated for office?

Members of a BOCES board are nominated by resolution of one or more of the school boards of its component districts. The resolution must be provided to the clerk of the BOCES board at least 30 days prior to the election (§ 1950(2-a)(b)).

5:10. Are there any restrictions on BOCES board nominations?

Yes. The clerk of the BOCES board must reject a nomination if the person nominated is a resident of a component school district which currently has a resident serving on the BOCES board whose term will not expire at the end of the current year, except where the number of BOCES board seats exceeds the number of component school districts or an unrepresented district declines to make a nomination (§ 1950(2-a)(b)); if the person nominated is not a resident of any component school district of the BOCES (§ 1950(9-a)); or if the person is an employee of a school district in the supervisory district (§ 1950(9)).

Any person or board member nominated by a special act school district, a central high school district or any component thereof, will be deemed a resident only of the district that nominated that person (§ 1950(2-a)(b)).

There are no limitations on the number of nominations an individual component district may make (see "Questions and Answers on the BOCES Reform Act," State Education Department, October 1993).

5:11. How are the members of a BOCES board elected?

BOCES board members are elected by their component member boards. By February 1 of each year, the BOCES board president must set the date of election in each component district. It is the same day designated for the vote on the tentative administrative budget, between April 16th and 30th. All component school boards meet on that same date, except for central high school boards which must hold their meetings the next business day (§ 1950(2-a)(b)).

The BOCES clerk then must mail an election ballot to each component district at least 14 days prior to the election. On the date designated for the election, each component board is entitled to cast one vote per vacancy, but no more than one vote per candidate. BOCES board members are elected by resolution of the component boards on the ballot prepared by the BOCES clerk (§ 1950(2-a)(c)).

Each component district must mail or deliver its completed ballot to the BOCES clerk no later than one business day after the election (§ 1950(2-a)(c)). There must be a quorum of board members voting in each component district to have a valid ballot (see "Questions and Answers on the BOCES Reform Act," State Education Department, October 1993).

The candidates receiving the plurality of votes cast are elected with the candidate receiving the highest vote total elected to the position with the longest term, and the candidate with the second highest vote total elected to the position with the next longest term, and so on. If the length of term of all positions to be filled is equal, candidates are elected in order of the greatest number of votes received until all vacancies are filled (§ 1950(2-a)(c)).

5:12. What happens in the event of a tie vote?

In the event of a tie vote, the BOCES board president must call a run-off election within 20 days of the initial vote, with only the candidates who received an equal number of votes deemed nominated. If the run-off results in a tie vote, the winning candidate is determined by drawing lots (§ 1950(2-a)(d)).

5:13. What happens if the school board of a component district is unable to obtain a quorum on the day designated for the election or fails to adopt a board resolution voting on the candidates?

If a component district fails to obtain a quorum on the date of the election, the ballot of that component school district is void, and the candidates receiving a plurality of the votes actually cast on the day of election are elected (see "Questions and Answers on the BOCES Reform Act," State Education Department, October 1993).

5:14. What happens if all of the component school districts fail to vote, so that no candidate receives a plurality?

The BOCES board position(s) will remain open until there is an election in which someone is voted in. However, each component board has a duty to elect BOCES board members, and a wilful neglect of this duty may constitute grounds for removal of the school board (see "Questions and Answers on the BOCES Reform Act," State Education Department, October 1993).

5:15. What is the procedure to fill a vacancy which might occur on the BOCES board?

If the vacancy occurs before January 1 or between five days before the date for submitting nominations to the BOCES clerk and the last day of the school year, a special election must be held on a date designated by the BOCES board president no later than 45 days after the date the vacancy occurred (§ 1950(2-a)(f)). If the vacancy occurs on or after January 1 and before the fifth day preceding the date for submitting nominations, the BOCES may appoint someone to fill the position until the next annual election (§ 1950(2-a)(f)).

When two or more BOCES have been merged or reorganized, elections may not be held to fill vacancies on the new board until a sufficient number of board member terms have expired so that the board has between five and 15 members (§ 1950(7)).

Annual Meeting

5:16. What is the purpose of the BOCES annual meeting?

The purpose of the BOCES annual meeting is to present the tentative administrative, capital and program budgets of the BOCES to school board members of component school districts prior to the vote on the tentative administrative budget, and to conduct other BOCES-wide business (§ 1950(4)(o); also see "Questions and Answers on the BOCES Reform Act," State Education Department, October 1993).

5:17. When is the BOCES annual meeting held?

The BOCES annual meeting must be held between April 1 and April 15 on a date designated by the BOCES board president. The BOCES board president must designate the date of the annual meeting by February 1 of each year.

Notice of the time, date and place of the annual meeting must be given to each of the members of the board and the clerk of each of the component districts by mail at least 14 days prior to the meeting (§ 1950(4)(o)). The BOCES must also publish such notice at least once each week within the two weeks preceding the annual meeting, the first publication to be at least 14 days before the meeting in newspapers having general circulation within the BOCES (§ 1950(4)(b)(4)).

5:18. What must the public notice of the BOCES annual meeting contain?

Notice of the BOCES annual meeting must contain the following:
- The date, time and place of the meeting (§ 1950(4)(o)).
- A statement that the tentative BOCES budgets will be presented to the component school board members at the meeting (§ 1950 (4)(b)(4)).
- A summary of the tentative BOCES capital and program budgets in a form prescribed by the commissioner (§ 1950 (4)(b)(4)).
- A summary of the tentative BOCES administrative budget in a form prescribed by the commissioner that includes the salary and benefits payable to supervisory and administrative staff of the BOCES and the total compensation payable to the district (BOCES) superintendent of schools (§ 1950(4)(b)(4)).
- When and where the tentative budgets will be available to the public for inspection (§ 1950(4)(b)(4)).

5:19. When must copies of the tentative BOCES budgets be made available?

The BOCES must provide copies of the tentative administrative, capital and program budgets and attachments to the school boards of each component school district at least 10 days prior to the annual meeting. In addition, the BOCES must comply with any reasonable requests for additional information made prior to the annual meeting.

Each component school board must make these budgets available to the residents of their respective school district, upon request (§ 1950(4)(b)(2) and (3); see also **5:29**).

Duties and Powers of a BOCES Board

5:20. What are some of a BOCES board's duties?

The following are the chief duties of a BOCES board, as listed in section 1950(4) of the Education Law:
- Appoint a district superintendent of schools and, at its discretion, provide for the payment of a supplementary salary to the district (BOCES) superintendent of schools by the BOCES (§ 1950(4)(a)(1)).
- Prepare separate tentative budgets of expenditures for program, capital and administrative costs for the BOCES in accordance with the commissioner's regulations (§ 1950(4)(b)(1)).
- Adopt the final program, capital and administrative budgets no later than May 15. After applicable state aid has been deducted,

component school districts are to be charged for their proportionate shares of the budget (§ 1950 (4)(b)(7)).

A BOCES board is also required to develop and adopt a formal policy on the acquisition, sale and disposal of personal property to be approved by the commissioner of education (§ 1950(18)).

5:21. What responsibility does a BOCES have in determining the cooperative educational needs within its supervisory district?

Each BOCES has the duty to survey the need for cooperative educational services in its supervisory district and present the findings of its surveys to local school authorities. Each BOCES must prepare long-range plans to meet the projected need for such services in the supervisory district for the next five years "as may be specified by the commissioner." The plans and annual revisions are to be submitted to the commissioner before December 1 each year. Plans for special and career education programs are to be submitted every two years, no later than the date specified by the commissioner and in a form specified by the commissioner. These plans are also to be revised annually (§ 1950(4)(c)).

5:22. What are some of a BOCES board's powers?

A BOCES board may do the following:

- Employ administrative assistants, teachers, supervisors, clerical help and other personnel recommended by the district superintendent as may be necessary to carry out its program (§ 1950(4)(e)).
- Rent, equip and furnish suitable land, classrooms, offices or buildings, with the commissioner of education's approval, in order to carry out its educational and administrative services (§ 1950(4)(p)(a)).
- Provide transportation for students to and from BOCES classes (§ 1950(4)(q)).
- Furnish any of the educational services provided for in the Education Law to school districts outside of the supervisory district, with the approval of the district superintendent of schools and the commissioner, on terms agreed to pursuant to contracts executed by the BOCES and the trustees or school boards of such districts (§ 1950(4)(r)).
- Contract with the federal government, the state government, community colleges and institutions of higher learning for the provision of career education programs (§ 1950(4)(h)(5)).
- Enter into contracts with not-for-profit corporations to participate in federal programs related to career training and experience (§ 1950(4)(h)(6)).

- Lease unneeded facilities to public or private agencies, individuals, partnerships or corporations (§ 1950(4)(p)(b)).
- Contract with the state government, community colleges, agricultural and technical colleges or other public agencies for the purpose of providing electronic data-processing services to such agencies (§ 1950(4)(h)(7)).

5:23. May a BOCES own a building?

Yes. A BOCES may own and construct buildings and obtain funds necessary for their acquisition. Purchase or acquisition of buildings, building sites or additions by a BOCES, however, depends on authorization of the "qualified voters of the board"; that is, the qualified voters of the BOCES district (§ 1950(4)(t); *Board of Educ. of East Syracuse-Minoa CSD v. Commissioner of Educ.*, 145 A.D.2d 13 (3rd Dep't 1989)). A qualified voter of the BOCES is a person who is a citizen of the United States, at least 18 years of age and a resident within the BOCES for a period of 30 days prior to the meeting at which he or she will vote (§ 1951(2)(c)). In purchasing a building site, a BOCES may not issue bonds to acquire real property.

5:24. May a BOCES contract with the New York State Dormitory Authority to construct facilities to house BOCES services?

Yes. A BOCES and its component school districts may enter into an agreement to acquire from the New York State Dormitory Authority facilities designed to house services to be provided by the BOCES, and to share the cost of the acquisition (§ 1950(13)). No such agreement may be for longer than is required to retire the obligations or to pay the Dormitory Authority in full (§ 1950(11)).

The Dormitory Authority is authorized to construct facilities where the BOCES may operate its program, to finance their cost, lease them to the BOCES, and to transfer the facilities back to the BOCES when the costs and liabilities incurred by the authority have been paid (Pub. Auth. Law §§ 1676(2)(d), 1678(15), 1689).

5:25. Do renovations of BOCES buildings require a referendum?

No. Only the acquisition or construction of additional space requires voter approval (see *Board of Educ. of East Syracuse-Minoa CSD v. Commissioner of Educ.*, 145 A.D.2d 13 (3rd Dep't 1989); § 1950(4)(t)).

5:26. May a BOCES lease its unused facilities?

Yes. A BOCES may lease its unused facilities to public or private agencies and others, with the approval of the commissioner of education, for a term of not more than five years, which is renewable with the commissioner's approval (§ 1950(4)(p)(b)).

5:27. May a BOCES rent real property?

Yes. A BOCES's authority to rent real property, however, is limited to a maximum period of 10 years, except for certain specified conditions or uses that are identified in section 1950(4)(p) of the Education Law.

Before executing a lease, the BOCES board must adopt a resolution that explains why this action is in the best interests of the supervising district, and that the rental payment is no more than fair market value as determined by the board. No such lease is enforceable against the BOCES unless and until it has been approved in writing by the commissioner of education (§ 1950(4)(p)(a)).

5:28. May a BOCES lease personal property?

Yes. A BOCES may lease personal property such as relocatable classrooms constructed on land owned by the BOCES or leased from a third party. Before executing the agreement, the BOCES board must adopt a resolution to determine that the agreement is "in the best financial interests" of the BOCES, and the resolution must state the basis for that determination. In addition, such agreements are subject to the bidding requirements of the General Municipal Law (§ 1950(4)(y)).

5:29. Are BOCES required to issue BOCES report cards?

Yes. Beginning with the 1997-98 school year, each BOCES must prepare a report card which includes measures of academic and fiscal performance of the supervisory district as prescribed by the commissioner of education. The measures for each BOCES will be compared to the statewide averages for all BOCES. The BOCES report card must be distributed publicly as required by law, including appending it to copies of the proposed administrative budget and distributing it to local newspapers (§ 1950(4)(kk)).

BOCES Services

5:30. What educational services are available through a BOCES?

Any of the following services are available through a BOCES on a cooperative basis: school nurse-teacher; attendance supervisor; supervisor of teachers; psychologist; dental hygienist; teachers of art, music and physical education; career education; guidance counselors; operation of classes for students with disabilities; student and financial accounting services;

academic and other programs and services, including summer programs and services; advanced academic courses; interactive television and other technologies; and maintenance and operation of cafeteria or restaurant service for the use of students and teachers while at school and to furnish meals to senior citizens (§ 1950(4)(d), (4)(bb), (4)(bb)(3)). These services must be requested by component districts and approved by the commissioner of education (§ 1950(4)(d)).

In addition, a BOCES may provide activities and services pertaining to the arts, training adults for employment, and activities and services regarding environmental education (§ 1950(4)(dd), (gg), (hh)). Examples of other services not specifically mentioned in the law that have been approved by the commissioner in specific situations include adult education coordinator; supervisor of education for students with disabilities; shared school business manager; coordinator of language arts; coordinator of education for gifted children; cooperative purchasing; transportation service; psychiatric consultant service; coordinator of career education; clinical programs for reading and speech correction; school health coordinator; in-service workshops; and educational communications center.

5:31. What is the procedure for securing educational services through a BOCES?

The annual procedure for securing such BOCES services is as follows:
- By February 1, component districts must file their requests for services with their BOCES (§ 1950(4)(d)(3)).
- By February 15, BOCES must submit proposed operating plans to the State Education Department (§ 1950(4)(d)(3)).
- By March 10, BOCES must notify their component school districts of the services that the commissioner of education has approved for the coming school year. This notice must include the local uniform cost for each service established in accordance with the Education Law and commissioner's regulations (§ 1950(4)(d)(3)).
- By May 1, component school districts must notify BOCES of their intent to participate in shared services and identify those services (§ 1950(4)(d)(4)).
- By June 1, BOCES must submit to the commissioner an operating plan and budget based upon component districts' requests. This must include the budgeted unit cost of programs and services calculated pursuant to the Education Law. If a BOCES receives requests for unanticipated shared services subsequent to the adoption of the budget, then it must submit an amended operating plan to the

commissioner and include a statement concerning the availability of district funds to pay for the district's share of the additional services from each superintendent who has requested the services (§ 1950(4)(d)(5)).

- By August 1, BOCES must file with the commissioner a copy of each contract for services executed with component districts (§ 1950 (4)(d)(4)).
- By September 1, BOCES must submit an annual program report and evaluation to the commissioner (§ 1950(4)(d)(5)).

5:32. May a local school board contracting with BOCES set a quota of the number of students who may enroll in particular career education courses?

No. When a school board determines to provide a program through BOCES, this has the same effect, legally, as providing that program in its own school. Of course, a board may deny admission to a student found to be unqualified for a particular course (see *Matter of Tripi*, 21 Educ. Dep't Rep. 349 (1981); see also § 4602(1)).

5:33. What is the maximum amount of time an itinerant teacher or worker may spend in a single component school district in order for the service to be approved as a shared BOCES service?

According to the State Education Department, the person whose services are to be shared may not spend any more than 60 percent or three days per week of his or her time in any one school district. A district may not expect to use most of such a person's time when engaged in a token sharing with one or two other districts.

5:34. What state aid is paid to districts to reimburse them for services purchased from BOCES?

Component districts are eligible to receive BOCES operating aid for approved services costs and administrative charges, BOCES facilities aid and BOCES rental aid. BOCES operating aid is based on prior-year approved expenditures, while aid for facilities and rental are based on current-year expenditures. Approved expenditures include salaries of BOCES employees only up to $30,000.

BOCES aid is wealth-equalized, so that districts poor in property taxes receive proportionately more than districts that are wealthy in property taxes. However, the total of the three types of aids is subject to a save-harmless provision; that is, no district will receive less BOCES aid than it received in the 1967-68 school year.

5:35. May transportation of students to BOCES be provided?

Yes. Transportation to and from classes operated by a BOCES may be provided at the request of one or more school districts. School districts and BOCES are authorized to enter into contracts with other districts, private contractors, BOCES and any municipal corporations or authorities to provide the transportation (§ 1950(4)(q)).

5:36. May a non-component district receive BOCES instructional support services?

Yes. Any non-component school district, including the Big 5, can, upon consent of the BOCES and with the approval of the commissioner of education, participate as a component district of the BOCES serving its geographic area or an adjoining BOCES for the sole purpose of purchasing instructional support services. The district must pay its share of the expenses of the program, including a charge for administration costs (§ 1950 (8-c)).

5:37. Are there any shared services the BOCES are specifically prohibited from providing?

Yes. Beginning with the 1997-98 school year, cooperative maintenance services or municipal services, including but not limited to lawn mowing services and heating, ventilation or air conditioning repair or maintenance or trash collection, or any other municipal service as defined by the commissioner of education, will not be authorized as an aidable shared service (§ 1950(4)(d)(2)).

BOCES Budget

5:38. How is the BOCES budget funded?

A BOCES budget is comprised of separate budgets for administrative, program and capital costs. After state aid and federal aid are subtracted from the cost of operating a BOCES, all component districts must share in its administrative and capital costs. Each component district's share of these costs is determined either by resident weighted average daily attendance (RWADA), real property valuation or resident public school district enrollment as defined in the Education Law. Only one method can be applied in any year, unless otherwise provided by law (§ 1950(4)(b)(7)).

In addition, component districts pay tuition or a service fee for programs in which its students participate. Generally, districts not participating in BOCES services are not required to pay for costs associated with those services, such as salaries for employees, equipment, supplies or student transportation. However, the BOCES board may allocate the cost of such services to component school districts in accordance with terms agreed upon between the BOCES board and three-quarters of the component school districts participating in the service (§§ 1950(4)(d)(4); 1951(1)).

A component district's contribution to BOCES expenditures is derived from state aid and its local tax levy.

5:39. Is there a deadline by which a BOCES board must adopt its final budget?

Yes. The final BOCES program, capital and administrative budgets must be adopted by the BOCES board no later than May 15th (§ 1950(4)(b)(7)).

5:40. What is included in the administrative budget?

By law, the administrative budget must at least include office and central administrative expenses, traveling expenses, salaries and benefits of supervisors and administrative personnel necessary to carry out the central administrative duties of the supervisory district, any and all expenditures associated with the BOCES board, the office of the district superintendent, general administration, central support services, planning and all other administrative activities.

The BOCES board also must attach to the budget a detailed statement of the total compensation to be paid to the district (BOCES) superintendent of schools, delineating the salary, annualized cost of benefits and any in-kind or other form of remuneration to be paid, plus, a list of items of expense eligible for reimbursement on expense accounts in the ensuing school year and a statement of the amount of expenses paid to the district superintendent in the prior year for purposes of carrying out his or her official duties. The commissioner's regulations further specify the content of each of the tentative budgets and the circumstances under which salaries and benefits of BOCES administrators will be budgeted under program or administration (§ 1950(4)(b)(1); 8 NYCRR § 170.3).

5:41. How is the BOCES administrative budget adopted?

A tentative administrative budget must be provided to the component districts 10 days prior to the annual meeting (§ 1950(4)(b)(2); see 5:19). Component districts must conduct a public meeting to adopt a resolution either approving or disapproving the BOCES tentative administrative budget on the same day designated by the BOCES president for the election of the BOCES board between April 16 and 30 (§ 1950(2-a)(b); see **5:11**). In the case of a central high school district, this vote will take place on the day following the designated date (§ 1950(4)(b)(5)). This resolution must be transmitted to the BOCES no later than one business day following the vote (§ 1950(4)(b)(7)).

Approval of the tentative administrative budget requires the approval of a majority of the component school boards actually voting (§1950(4)(b)(5)).

In addition to the administrative budget, component districts also review the tentative capital and program budgets.

5:42. What happens if the tentative administrative budget is not approved by the component districts?

If the majority of the total number of component school districts actually voting do not approve the tentative administrative budget, or if there is a tie vote (half the districts approve, half disapprove), the BOCES must prepare and adopt a contingency administrative budget (§ 1950(4)(b)(5)).

5:43. What are the limitations on a BOCES contingency administrative budget?

In a contingency budget for BOCES the amount of the administrative budget may not exceed the amount in the prior year's budget, except for expenditures incurred in the supplemental retirement allowances, including health insurance benefits for retirees (§ 1950(4)(b)(5)).

5:44. What is included in the BOCES program and capital budgets?

As a general rule the program budget includes costs for those BOCES shared services which have been requested by and contracted for by the component districts (§§ 1950(4)(b), 1951(1)). These costs must be based on local and statewide uniform unit costs calculated as set forth in the Education Law.

The capital budget includes, for instance, facility acquisition and construction costs; debt expenditures associated with repayment of indebtedness incurred for the acquisition of facilities and capital projects; and operation and maintenance costs such as rent, custodial salaries and benefits, and supplies and utilities. It also includes expenditures associated with the payment of court judgments and orders from administrative bodies and officers, and certain costs relating to employee retirement (§ 1950(4)(b)).

5:45. How are the BOCES program and capital budgets approved?

The BOCES tentative program and capital budgets must be provided to the component districts 10 days prior to the annual meeting (§ 1950(4)(b)(2); see **5:19**). Component districts review the tentative capital and program budgets at the annual meeting held between April 1st and April 15th, on a date, place and time designated by the BOCES president (§ 1950(4)(o)). All component school boards meet on that same date, except for central high school boards which must hold their meetings the next business day (§ 1950 (2-a(b))).

The component districts do not vote on the program and capital budgets. They only vote on the administrative budget (see **5:41-42**).

The final BOCES program and capital budgets, along with the administrative budget, must be adopted by the BOCES board no later than May 15 (§ 1950(4)(b)(7)).

5:46. Are BOCES subject to financial audits?

Yes. There are two types of audits which are to be conducted in BOCES districts:

- *State audits.* The commissioner of education shall conduct periodic fiscal audits of the BOCES and, to the extent sufficient resources are provided to SED, shall assure that each BOCES is audited at least once every three years (§ 305 (25)). In addition, the state comptroller has the authority to examine the financial affairs of a BOCES (Gen. Mun. Law §§ 30, 33-34).
- *Independent audits.* The commissioner's regulations require that BOCES obtain an annual audit, in a form prescribed by the commissioner of education, of all funds by a certified public accountant or public accountant. The auditor's final report must be adopted by resolution of the BOCES board and a copy must be filed with the commissioner of education by October 1 of each year (8 NYCRR § 170.3(a)).

6. The District Superintendent

6:1. What is a district superintendent and how does this position differ from that of superintendent of schools?

A *district superintendent* is the chief executive officer of a board of cooperative educational services (BOCES) and the general supervising officer of the supervisory district that comprises the BOCES. This person is responsible for both the BOCES and its component districts, and also performs duties assigned by the commissioner of education, serving as the State Education Department's field representative in the supervisory district. In comparison, a *superintendent of schools* is the chief executive officer of a single local school district. (See chapter 5 for more information on BOCES.)

6:2. What constitutes the supervisory district overseen by the district superintendent?

A supervisory district is made up of the total geographic area under the supervision of a district superintendent, as established under section 2201 of the Education Law.

6:3. What are the qualifications for the position of district superintendent of schools?

A district superintendent must be at least 21 years of age, a citizen of the United States and a resident of New York State (§ 2205). That person must be a graduate of a college or university from a regionally accredited institution of higher education or from an institution approved by or registered with the State Education Department and must have completed 60 semester hours in graduate courses and an approved administrative/supervisory internship under the supervision of a practicing school administrator and of a representative of the sponsoring institution of higher education (§ 3003(1)(a)(b), 8 NYCRR § 80.4)). One year of satisfactory full-time experience in a school administrative or supervisory position may be substituted for the internship (8 NYCRR § 80.4(a)(1). The individual must also have a master's degree.

At the time of his or her appointment, the district superintendent must have completed three years of teaching and/or supervision in public or nonpublic schools (§ 3003(1)(b)). Any person applying for a district superintendency on or after January 1, 1991 also must have completed two hours of course work or training on how to identify and report child abuse and maltreatment (§ 3003; 8 NYCRR § 80.4).

For exceptionally qualified persons, the commissioner may waive the stated educational requirements (§ 3003(3); 8 NYCRR § 80.4(a)(3)).

6:4. How is a district superintendent appointed?

A district superintendent is appointed by the BOCES board of a supervisory district. When a vacancy occurs and the commissioner of education has not redistricted the county to provide a smaller number of supervisory districts, the commissioner will direct the board to meet to appoint a district superintendent. This appointment is subject to the commissioner's approval (§ 2204(1), (2)). If the vacancy is not filled at this meeting, the commissioner may appoint an interim district superintendent until the BOCES fills the vacancy (§ 2204(1); see **6:9**).

6:5. Is there a maximum length for the duration of a district superintendent's employment contract?

Yes. The duration of any employment contract between a BOCES and a district superintendent may not exceed three years, unless the contract was entered into before the effective date of the Reform Act, or July 1, 1993. Copies of the agreement and any amendments thereto must be filed within five days of the contract's execution with the commissioner (§ 1950(4)(a)(1)).

Regardless of any employment contract, however, a district superintendent can be removed from office at any time by a majority vote of the BOCES board or by the commissioner of education under section 306 of the Education Law (§ 2212; see **6:7**).

6:6. Must a district superintendent take an oath of office?

Yes. The district superintendent must take a constitutional oath of office before assuming his or her duties and not later than five days after the date on which the term of office is to start. The oath may be taken before a county clerk, a justice of the peace, or a notary public, and must be filed in the office of the secretary of state (§ 2206).

6:7. May a district superintendent be removed from office?

Yes. A district superintendent may be removed from office at any time by majority vote of the BOCES board or by the commissioner of education under section 306 of the Education Law (§ 2212).

6:8. Under what circumstances does a vacancy in the office of a district superintendent occur?

Under section 2208 of the Education Law, a district superintendent's office becomes vacant when the current incumbent dies; files a written resignation with the commissioner of education and the clerk of the BOCES; accepts the office of supervisor, town clerk or trustee of a school district; or fails to take and file the oath of office. A vacancy will also occur if the district superintendent is removed from office by the BOCES board or the commissioner of education (§ 2212; see **6:7**).

6:9. How is a vacancy in the office of district superintendent filled?

When a vacancy in the office of district superintendent occurs, the commissioner of education shall, unless he or she has provided for a smaller number of supervisory districts, direct the BOCES board to meet to appoint a new district superintendent. Each board member has one vote and the person receiving the majority of all votes cast shall be appointed, subject to the approval of the commissioner. A certified copy of the proceedings and the appointment must be filed in the county clerk's office and with the commissioner of education within five days of the appointment (§ 2204(1), (2), (3); see **6:4**).

If the vacancy is not filled at this meeting, the meeting may be adjourned to a subsequent date, and the commissioner may appoint a district superintendent who serves until the board fills the vacancy. A district superintendent from one supervisory district who is appointed to be a temporary or acting superintendent in another supervisory district does not receive any compensation for duties associated with the temporary or acting position (§ 2204(1), (4)).

6:10. How is a district superintendent's salary paid?

Each district superintendent receives an annual salary of $43,499 from the state, payable by the commissioner (§ 2209(1)). In addition, the BOCES may decide to pay the district superintendent a supplementary salary (§ 1950(4)(a)). If the board decides to do so, this supplemental amount must be listed in the BOCES administrative budget that is provided to the trustees or board members of each component district (§ 1950(4)(b)(1)).

Additionally, the town supervisors in any supervisory district may vote to further increase the district superintendent's salary. This additional amount is paid by a tax levied on the towns comprising the supervisory district (§ 2209(2)).

6:11. Is there a limit or cap on a district superintendent's salary?

Yes. The total salary paid to district superintendents, including the amount paid by the state under section 2209 and the supplementary salary paid by the supervisory district, is limited to 98 percent of the total salary paid to the commissioner of education in fiscal year 1992-93 (§ 1950(4)(a)(2)). This limits the salary to approximately $128,625, or 98 percent of $131,250 (the commissioner's salary reported in fiscal year 1992-93).

The following items must also be included in the total salary cap:

• payments for life insurance having a cash value;
• payments for the employee contribution, co-pay or uncovered medical expenses under a health insurance plan;
• payments for transportation or travel expenses in excess of actual, documented expenses incurred in the performance of BOCES and state functions; and
• any other lump sum payments which are not specifically excluded from total salary by Education Law (§ 1950(4)(a)(2)).

Any variation of these limitations may subject a district superintendent to penalties, including termination (§ 2212-b).

A statement describing the district superintendent's compensation must be included in the BOCES budget prior to the BOCES annual meeting (§ 1950(4)(b)(1)).

6:12. Are there limits on other benefits provided to a district superintendent?

Yes. Under the BOCES Reform Act, a district superintendent is an employee of the state. His or her maximum vacation time and sick leave, and accrued or unused vacation or sick leave, may not exceed the maximum permitted for management/confidential employees of New York State (as of 1998, this was 200 sick days and 40 vacation days).

Further, a district superintendent may not be compensated for accrued and unused vacation credits or sick leave, or use accrued and unused sick leave for retirement service credit or to pay health insurance premiums after retirement at a rate in excess of that allowed for other management/confidential employees (§ 1950(4)(a)(2)).

However, contracts entered into prior to July 1, 1993 are not subject to this law.

6:13. May the supervisory district give pay raises to the district superintendent based upon increases in other collective bargaining agreements within the supervisory district?

No. The terms of a district superintendent's contract may not be tied to any increases paid pursuant to any collective bargaining agreements made with other employees in the supervisory district (§ 1950(4)(a)(2)).

6:14. May the commissioner of education withhold payment of the district superintendent's salary?

Yes. If the commissioner determines that a district superintendent has failed persistently to perform an official duty, he or she may withhold part or all the district superintendent's salary as it becomes due. However, the commissioner may also, in his or her discretion, pay the salary he or she has withheld to the district superintendent at a later date (§ 2211).

Pursuant to section 2112-b of the Education Law, the commissioner must withhold from a district superintendent's state salary an amount of money equal to twice the value of any violation of the salary and benefit caps, unless the commissioner determines that the violation was inadvertent in which case the commissioner shall withhold the monetary value of the violation (§§ 2212-b(2); 1950(4)(a)(2)).

6:15. May a district superintendent hold another job during his or her term of office?

No. A district superintendent may not engage in any other business or profession but must devote his or her full time to the office (§ 2213). Further, for the district superintendent to have a direct or indirect interest in any contract made with the districts that are under his or her supervision is a conflict of interest (§ 2214).

6:16. What are the district superintendent's responsibilities in the organization and operation of a board of cooperative educational services (BOCES)?

The district superintendent is the chief executive officer of the BOCES board. Where a BOCES is composed of two or more supervisory districts, the district superintendents, together with the president of the BOCES board, serve as an executive committee (§ 1950(2)).

6:17. What are the general powers and duties of the district superintendent?

Section 2215 of the Education Law states that a district superintendent's general powers and duties are to:

- Ascertain and maintain records in regard to school district boundaries. In addition, district superintendents are authorized to determine district boundary lines (*Board of Educ. of Shenendehowa CSD v. Commissioner of Educ.*, 182 A.D.2d 944 (3rd Dep't 1992)).
- Hold teacher conferences and counsel teachers in relation to discipline, school management and other school work, and matters promoting the general good of all schools of the district.

- Counsel trustees and board members and other school officers in relation to their powers and duties.
- Direct trustees and board members to "abate any nuisance" in or on the school grounds, at the direction of the commissioner of education.
- Approve the amount, or the sureties on bonds, of treasurers and tax collectors of school districts.
- Condemn a schoolhouse, at the direction of the commissioner of education (§ 412).
- Examine and license teachers pursuant to the provisions of the Education Law and conduct other examinations as directed by the commissioner of education.
- Examine any charges affecting the moral character of any teacher residing or employed within the supervisory district and to revoke that teacher's certificate pursuant to section 3018 of the Education Law.
- Take affidavits and administer oaths in all matters pertaining to the public school system, but without charge or fee.
- Take and report testimony in cases under appeal to the commissioner of education, as the commissioner directs. In such a case or in any matter to be heard or determined by the district superintendent, he or she may issue a subpoena to compel the attendance of a witness.
- Exercise at his or her discretion any of the powers and perform any of the duties of another district superintendent at the written request of that superintendent. A district superintendent also must perform such duties when directed to do so by the commissioner.
- Make an annual report to the commissioner by August 1 of each year, and submit any other reports he or she may request.
- Participate in the permanent computerized statewide school district address match and income verification system as provided by section 171 of the Tax Law and as directed by the commissioner.
- Report to the commissioner on cost-effective practices in school districts within his or her supervisory district.
- Fill, under certain circumstances, a vacancy on a school board (§ 2113).

6:18. What are the district superintendent's responsibilities in appointing teachers for probation and tenure in local districts and boards of cooperative educational services (BOCES)?

A district superintendent plays no role in appointing teachers for probation and tenure in local districts. These recommendations are made by the local superintendent of schools to the local school board.

However, the district superintendent does have the power to recommend BOCES staff members, including teachers, administrative assistants and supervisors, for a probationary period of up to three years (§ 3014(1)). The district superintendent is also charged with making tenure recommendations for those employees (§ 3014(2)).

6:19. May the district superintendent revoke a teacher's certificate?

Yes, although this authority is seldom invoked. In doing so, the district superintendent first examines the charge affecting the moral character of the teacher. The teacher is given reasonable notice of the charge, and an opportunity to defend himself or herself. If the charge is sustained, the teacher's certificate is annulled and the individual declared unfit to teach. The district superintendent must then notify the commissioner of education immediately of such annulment and declaration (§ 3018).

6:20. What are the powers and duties of the district superintendent in relation to the formation, alteration and dissolution of school districts?

A district superintendent may organize a new common or union free school district out of the territory of one or more districts that are wholly within the geographic area served by his or her BOCES "whenever the educational interests of the community require it" (§ 1504(1)). The district superintendents of two or more adjoining supervisory districts may form a joint school district out of the adjoining portions of their respective districts "when public interests require it" (§ 1504(2)).

In addition, any district superintendent may dissolve one or more school districts by order and may form a new district from this territory. He or she also may unite the territory or a portion thereof, by order, to an adjoining school district, except for a city school district (§ 1505) and/or a central school district. Annexation of a district to central school districts is completed by order of the commissioner of education (§§ 1801(2); 1802(2)).

Section 1507 of the Education Law also authorizes a district superintendent to alter district boundaries with the written consent of all the districts to be affected (*Matter of Zeltmann*, 15 Educ. Dep't Rep. 47 (1975)).

6:21. What are the district superintendent's responsibilities under school districts' emergency-management plans?

Under section 155.13(d) of the commissioner's regulations, the district superintendent is responsible for serving as the chief communications liaison among all schools within the supervisory district's territorial limits (see **17:1** for more information on emergency-management plans).

6:22. Is a district superintendent entitled to the protections of Public Officers Law section 17 which governs defense and indemnification of state employees?

Yes. A district superintendent of schools is a state employee entitled to the protections of Public Officers Law section 17 in connection with lawsuits that arise out of the performance of the district superintendent's state functions (Opn. Att'y Gen. No. F 97-10 (1997)). For further information on the issue of defense and indemnification, see chapter 18.

7. School Administrators

7:1. What are the typical school administrative positions in New York State?

Every school district in New York State may appoint a superintendent of schools (Education Law §§ 1604(8), 1711(1); 2503(5); 2554(2); see **7:17**). School districts must appoint a full-time building principal for every school, unless the commissioner of education approves an alternative mode of building administration after reviewing evidence submitted by the district (8 NYCRR §100.2(a); see **7:26**). Other common administrative positions in New York State, appointed at the option of the school board, are associate and assistant superintendents, supervisors, department chairpersons and assistant principals.

7:2. What is the required certification for school administrators in New York State?

The commissioner's regulations set out the following three classes of certificates for school administrators (8 NYCRR § 80.4):

• *School District Administrator (SDA).* The SDA class includes district superintendents, superintendents of schools, deputy, associate and assistant superintendents, and any other persons having responsibilities involving general district-wide administration (8 NYCRR § 80.4(a)).

The certificate requirements are a baccalaureate and a master's degree, including at least 60 semester hours of graduate study. Of the 60 hours, 24 must be in school administration and supervision. An approved administrative/supervisory internship also must be completed or one year of satisfactory full-time experience may be substituted for it (8 NYCRR § 80.4(a)(1)).

In addition, any person applying for a superintendent's certificate must have completed two hours of course work on or training in the identification and reporting of child abuse and maltreatment (§ 3003(4)).

Three years of teaching and/or administrative and/or supervisory and/or pupil personnel service experience in nursery school through 12th grade are also required (8 NYCRR § 80.4(a)(2)).

• *School Administrator and Supervisor (SAS).* The SAS certificate is required for principals, assistant principals, supervisors, department chairpersons and any other persons serving more than 25 percent of his or her assignment (10 periods per week) in any administrative and/or supervisory position (8 NYCRR § 80.4(b)).

The requirements for a provisional SAS certificate are a baccalaureate degree; 30 semester hours of graduate study, 18 hours of which must have been taken in school administration and supervision; and an internship of one year, or one year of satisfactory full-time experience in a school administrative or supervisory position (8 NYCRR § 80.4(b)(1)).

Three years of teaching and/or administrative and/or supervisory and/or pupil personnel service experience in nursery school through 12th grade are also required (8 NYCRR § 80.4(b)(1)(ii)).

In addition to requirements for provisional certification, permanent certification requires that an SAS candidate have completed two years of school experience in an administrative/supervisory position. Within the total program of preparation, the candidate must have been awarded a master's degree (8 NYCRR § 80.4(b)(2)).

• *School Business Administrator (SBA)*. The SBA certificate is required for deputy superintendents of schools for business, associate and assistant superintendents of schools for business and any other person having professional responsibility for the business operation of the school district, such as a school business official or administrator (8 NYCRR § 80.4(c)).

The certificate requirements are identical to those of the SDA, except that one year of satisfactory full-time experience as the chief business official, rather than one year of full-time experience in a school administrative or supervisory position of a school district, may be substituted for the internship requirement (8 NYCRR § 80.4(c)(1)).

An individual who does not hold appropriate certification may not perform administrative or supervisory duties in excess of 25 percent of his or her time (excluding preparation and lunch periods) per week (see 8 NYCRR § 80.4(b); *Matter of Connor*, 22 Educ. Dep't Rep. 313 (1982)).

7:3. May the requirements for certification as a school district administrator (SDA) be waived?

Yes. At the request of a school board or board of cooperative educational services (BOCES), the commissioner of education may waive the preparation requirements for the school district administrator certificate for a superintendent who is exceptionally qualified but does not meet all of the graduate course or teaching requirements, and whose training and experience are the substantial equivalent of such requirements (§ 3003(3); 8 NYCRR § 80.4(a)(3)).

In its formal request to the State Education Department, the board must note its approval of the request; the job description; its rationale for requesting such certification of the individual; a statement identifying the exceptional qualifications of the candidate; and the individual's completed application for certification, vitae and official transcripts of collegiate study. Such a certification, if issued, is valid only for service in the district requesting the waiver (8 NYCRR § 80.4(a)(3)).

7:4. Is there a legal procedure for decertifying a school administrator?

No, but there is a procedure, specified in Part 83 of the commissioner's regulations, to make a determination of good moral character. This could lead to the revocation, annulment or suspension of the certificate of a superintendent, teacher or other certified employee (8 NYCRR § 83.5(c)).

7:5. May districts share administrators?

Yes. Under Education Law article 40-A, school districts may arrange to share the services of a superintendent, associate superintendent, assistant superintendent or any other employee with districtwide administrative or supervisory responsibilities, with one or more other school districts (§ 1981(1)).

A shared administrator who is not in a tenure-track position is considered an employee by all districts sharing his or her services. All decisions regarding the appointment or compensation of that administrator must be made with the consent of a majority of each participating school district's board. The compensation and benefits of a shared administrator are provided by each participating school district, based on an agreed-upon formula (§ 1981(2)(a)).

For a shared administrator who may be granted tenure, the participating districts must designate one of their own as the principal employing district. That administrator is considered to be employed by the principal employing district, but decisions on the probationary appointment and compensation package must be made with the consent of a majority of each of the school boards of each participating district.

Decisions regarding the termination, discipline or tenure of that administrator are made by the principle employing district in consultation with all other participating districts. The services rendered by the shared administrator in any participating district is deemed to have been rendered in the principle employing district for all purposes, including tenure credit, seniority and discipline (§ 1981(2)(b)).

All agreements to share personnel, such as administrators, between districts must be approved by the district superintendent, or by the commissioner or his or her designee if there is no local district superintendent (§ 1981(4)).

7:6. How are school administrators appointed?

Principals, administrators and all other members of the supervisory staff of school districts must be appointed by the school board to a three-year probationary term. The appointment requires the recommendation of the superintendent of schools. This rule does not apply to superintendents of schools, associate and assistant superintendents in small city school districts, and executive directors, associate, assistant, district and community superintendents and examiners in Buffalo, New York City, Rochester, Syracuse and Yonkers (§§ 2509(1)(b), 2573(1)(b), 3012(1)(b)).

Unlike teachers, administrators who have received tenure in another school district in the state are not entitled to a shortened two-year probationary period, and must serve a three-year probationary period, according to the state education department (Opn. of Counsel, No. 235, 15 Educ. Dep't Rep. 538 (1975); see **8:74**).

7:7. Are teacher tenure areas, as defined in the Rules of the Board of Regents, applicable to school administrators?

No. Part 30 of the Rules of the Board of Regents is not applicable to administrative and supervisory personnel (8 NYCRR Part 30; *Matter of Moore*, 15 Educ. Dep't Rep. 475 (1976)). Moreover, there are no clearly defined guidelines for determining administrative and supervisory tenure areas (*Bell v. Board of Education*, 61 N.Y.2d 149 (1984)). Instead, a board of education may maintain a single district-wide "administrator" position area or establish more defined administrative tenure areas (see *Bell v. Board of Education*).

The tenure status of an administrator will be determined by the initial appointment (*Schlick v. Board of Educ. of Mamoroneck UFSD*, 227 A.D.2d 407 (2nd Dep't 1996)).

Where a school board has established more than one administrative tenure area, case law has identified factors that should be considered to determine whether certain administrative and supervisory positions must be considered to lie within the same tenure area. Among the factors to be considered are "the notice given to the individuals involved as to their tenure status, the duties of various positions, the adverse practical impact of non-recognition of a particular area and membership in collective bargaining units" (see *Matter of Plesent*, 16 Educ. Dep't Rep. 348 (1977)).

A comparison of duties and responsibilities is important in administrative tenure area cases (see, for example, *Matter of Falanga*, 17 Educ. Dep't Rep. 267 (1978)). The mere fact that two positions, such as director and chairperson, are supervisory in nature does not compel the conclusion that they are within the same tenure area (see *Matter of Plesent*).

Positions will generally be deemed to lie within the same administrative tenure area if a majority of the job duties are similar (*Coates v. Ambach*, 52 A.D.2d 261, *aff'd* 42 N.Y.2d 846 (1977)). This is commonly known as the "50 percent rule." The 50 percent rule has been applied, as well, in determining whether a particular employee serves in an administrative or teacher tenure area (*Maine-Endwell Teachers Ass'n v. Maine-Endwell CSD*, 92 A.D.2d 1052 (3rd Dep't 1983)).

Both the courts and the commissioner have held, however, that the 50 percent rule should not be rigidly applied, and that the emphasis should be on the kind, quality and breadth of responsibilities associated with the positions being compared (*Cowan v. Board of Education*, 99 A.D.2d 831 (2nd Dep't 1984); *Matter of Plesent*; *Matter of Falanga*; *Matter of Abeles*, 18 Educ. Dep't Rep. 521 (1979); *Appeal of Elmendorf*, 36 Educ. Dep't Rep. 308 (1997)).

7:8. Is an administrator entitled to credit for time spent in a substitute administrative position to shorten his or her probationary period?

No. Administrative employees do not receive so-called "Jarema credit" for time spent as a substitute administrator (*McManus v. Board of Education of the Hempstead UFSD*, 87 N.Y.2d 183 (1995); *Roberts v. Community School Board*, 66 N.Y.2d 652 (1985)). While teachers may apply Jarema credit for time spent as a substitute teacher towards the probationary period required before tenure (§§ 2509(1)(a), 2573(1)(a), 3012(1)(a); see **8:74**), administrators are not given similar rights (see §§ 2509(1)(b), 2573(1)(b), and 3012(1)(b)).

7:9. Does service as an "acting" administrator in a vacant position count toward an administrative probationary period?

Yes. A board must count as service toward a probationary period time spent by an employee assigned to a vacant position in an "acting" capacity when that employee is subsequently appointed to a probationary term in that position. The employee will be deemed to have commenced the probationary term for that particular position when appointed to fill the vacant position (*McManus v. Board of Education*, 87 N.Y.2d 183 (1995)).

7:10. Does service rendered outside an administrative tenure area pending the outcome of criminal charges count toward an administrative probationary period?

No. In *Feldman v. Community SD 32*, 231 A.D.2d 632 (2nd Dep't 1996), an assistant principal who was reassigned to the central district office during his probationary period pending the outcome of criminal charges did not receive credit for the time spent in the central district office assignment because he did not perform the duties of assistant principal during that time.

7:11. Are there specific procedures for terminating the employment of administrators or supervisors?

Yes. Education Law section 3012 governs the dismissal of administrative employees prior to the completion of the probationary term. The probationary appointment of an administrative employee may be terminated at any time on the recommendation of the superintendent and by majority vote of the school board (§ 3012(1)(b)), provided the employee is not terminated for an illegal or unconstitutional reason, and the notice requirements of section 3019-a of the Education Law are met (*Appeal of Wint*, 33 Educ. Dep't Rep. 9 (1993)).

Education Law section 3031 applies to the dismissal of probationary administrators and supervisors who are not recommended for tenure. The procedure is similar to that applicable to teachers (see **8:78-83**).

Under certain circumstances an administrator who is terminated during his or her probationary period may be entitled to a name-clearing hearing. For example, the U.S. Court of Appeals for the Second Circuit found that an administrator who received negative evaluations and reasons for termination which damaged the administrator's professional reputation to such a degree as to virtually preclude her from getting another job as an administrator in the future was entitled to a name-clearing hearing (*Donato v. Plainview-Old Bethpage CSD*, 96 F.3d 623 (2nd Cir. 1996), *cert. denied*, 117 U.S. 1083 (1997)).

Tenured administrative employees, like tenured teachers, are subject to the protections of section 3020-a of the Education Law (see **8:104-120**). Collective bargaining agreements may place further restrictions on the dismissal of administrative employees.

7:12. May a school board abolish an administrative position?

Yes, if the position is no longer necessary to the school system. School boards have broad latitude to abolish, reorganize or consolidate administrative and teaching positions (*Matter of Riendeau*, 23 Educ. Dep't Rep. 487 (1984); see *Girard v. Board of Education*, 168 A.D.2d 183 (4th Dep't 1991); *Ryan vs. Ambach*, 71 A.D.2d 719 (3rd Dep't 1979); see also **8:95**).

However, if a school board abolishes an office or position and creates another office or position with similar duties, the individual who is in the position to be abolished is entitled to be appointed to the newly-created position without reduction in salary or increment (§§ 2510(1); 2585(2);

3013(1)). This rule only applies to administrative positions to which appointments on tenure may be made (*Matter of Merz*, 21 Educ. Dep't Rep. 449 (1982)).

To determine whether two positions are similar, the degree of comparable skill, experience, training and certification required to carry out the duties and responsibilities of each position must be considered. For example, the commissioner of education has held that the positions of building principal and assistant superintendent are not similar because of the district-wide responsibilities and the additional skill, training and certification requirements of the position of assistant superintendent (*Appeal of Elmendorf*, 36 Educ. Dep't Rep. 308 (1997)).

An administrator whose position has been abolished may have the right to a pre-termination hearing before the school board where there is a possibility that the duties of the position being abolished and the duties of a position being created are similar (*Appeal of Elmendorf; Fairbairn v. Board of Education*, 876 F.Supp. 432 (E.D.N.Y. 1995); *Goldberg v. Board of Education*, 777 F.Supp. 1109 (E.D.N.Y. 1991); *DeSimone v. Board of Education*, 612 F.Supp. 1568 (E.D.N.Y. 1985)).

In addition, the administrator has the right to be placed on a preferred eligible list (PEL) of candidates for appointment to a similar position within his or her tenure area for seven years after the position is abolished (§§ 2510(3); 3013(3)).

7:13. Is a school board bound by an employment contract with a probationary administrative employee?

Yes, if one exists. The courts have ruled that a school board which has appointed a probationary administrative employee is bound by a written employment contract between that employee and the board, including those provisions concerning dismissal during the probationary period (*Averback v. Board of Educ. of New Paltz CSD*, 147 A.D.2d 152 (3rd Dep't), *appeal denied*, 74 N.Y.2d 611 (1989)).

7:14. May a school district enter into a collective bargaining agreement with its administrative employees, or a contract with its superintendent, which includes a cash payment for unused accumulated sick leave at retirement?

Yes. Sick leave is a term and condition of employment which must be negotiated with unionized employees under the Taylor Law. Because there is no express statutory prohibition against providing a cash payment for unused accumulated sick leave at retirement, the district and the union may agree to such an arrangement (*Perrenod v. Liberty Board of Educ.*, 223

A.D.2d 870 (3rd Dep't 1996); see chapter 10 for more information on the Taylor Law and collective bargaining).

Employment contracts for superintendents may also contain such a provision because the Education Law specifically authorizes contracts to contain "such terms as shall be mutually acceptable to the parties, including but not limited to, fringe benefits" (§ 1711(3); *Perrenod v. Liberty Board of Educ.*).

However, such payments may be found to violate the constitutional ban on gifts of public funds if there is no legal obligation to provide such payment under contract, collective bargaining agreement or policy prior to the accumulation of leave (*Rampello v. East Irondequoit CSD*, 236 A.D.2d 797 (4th Dep't 1997)).

Superintendent of Schools

7:15. What is a superintendent of schools?

A *superintendent of schools* is the chief executive officer of a school district (§ 1711(2)(a)). Any reference to the terms district principal, supervising principal or principal of the district generally refer to the superintendent of schools (Gen. Constr. Law § 47–a).

A *district superintendent*, on the other hand, is the chief executive officer of a board of cooperative educational services (BOCES) and is the general supervising officer of the supervisory district. The district superintendent has responsibilities for both the BOCES and the component districts that comprise the BOCES (see chapter 6 for more information on the district superintendent).

7:16. Is a superintendent a member of the school board?

No, except in city school districts. However, in all school districts, the superintendent has the right to speak on all matters before the board, but he or she does not have the right to vote on matters before the board (§§ 1711(2)(a), 2508(1), 2566(1)).

7:17. How do superintendents of schools acquire their positions in New York State?

A school board may appoint a superintendent of schools (§§ 1604(8), 1711(1), 2503(5), 2554(2)). These superintendents serve at the pleasure of the board, unless they and their boards have entered into employment contracts. Such contracts, however, may include procedures for terminating the superintendent's services prior to the end of the term (§ 1711(3); see **7:18** for more information on superintendents' contracts).

7:18. Is a contract necessary to employ a superintendent?

No. However, many school boards enter into such contracts with their superintendents. This type of contract may include terms and conditions of employment such as duties, compensation and termination of the contract (§ 1711(3); *Matter of Balen*, 20 Educ. Dep't Rep. 304 (1980)). In the absence of a contract, resolutions concerning term appointments embodied in minutes of board meetings may be used to identify the terms and conditions of employment.

A school board may not enter into a contract with a superintendent which contains any provisions relating to an increase in salary, compensation or other benefits which are based on or tied to the terms of any contract or collective bargaining agreement with the district's teachers or other district employees (§§ 1604(8), 1711(3), 2507(1), 2565(1)).

7:19. How long may a superintendent's contract last?

School districts may enter into contracts with their superintendents for terms of from three to five years (§§ 1604(8), 1711(3)).

City school districts, however, are prohibited from entering into a superintendent's contract which fixes the term or tenure of the superintendent's services. Instead, superintendents serve at the pleasure of the board unless they are appointed to a term. If appointed to a term, the term may not exceed five years in city school districts with a population of less than 250,000 and four years in Rochester and city school districts with a population of over 250,000 (§§ 2507(1), 2565(1),(3)). However, these school boards may have contracts that fix the other terms of employment, such as duties and salaries, with their superintendents (§§ 2507(1), 2565(1); *Matter of Balen*, 20 Educ. Dep't Rep. 304 (1980); *Matter of Venezia*, 19 Educ. Dep't Rep. 273 (1979)).

School boards may not circumvent the statutory limitations on the length of employment contracts for superintendents by entering into multiple contracts which, when read together, create an obligation longer than that authorized by law (*Appeal of Boyle*, 35 Educ. Dep't Rep. 162 (1995)). For example, a contract that added five more years to an existing three years remaining in a prior contract was invalid because these provisions were in effect simultaneously and extended the service of the superintendent beyond the statutory limits (*Appeal of Boyle*). However, school boards may supplant a prior contract with a new one, provided that the duration of the initial contract or the subsequent contract does not exceed the statutory limitation (*Appeal of Boyle*; *Matter of Lewiston-Porter CSD v. Sobol*, 154 A.D.2d 777 (3rd Dep't 1989), *appeal dismissed*, 75 N.Y.2d 978 (1990)).

7:20. May an outgoing board extend a superintendent's contract?

Yes. The commissioner of education has ruled that, although it may be undemocratic, it is not illegal for a "lame-duck" board to extend the superintendent's contract and even award him or her a salary increase prior to the installation of the new board (*Appeal of Dillon*, 33 Educ. Dep't Rep. 544 (1994); *Appeal of Knapp*, 34 Educ. Dep't Rep. 207 (1994)). Because such an action taken by an outgoing board is procedurally correct, a new board may not nullify it (*Appeal of Dillon*).

7:21. Must the school board of a newly-consolidated school district honor the contract of a former superintendent of one of the merged districts?

Yes. The commissioner of education has determined that a consolidated district, which is a combination of common or union free school districts merged to form a new district (see chapter 15), as the successor in interest of the districts that have merged, is obligated to honor the contract entered into by the former superintendent and the former board (§ 1804(5)(b); *Matter of Foster*, 28 Educ. Dep't Rep. 29 (1988)).

However, the consolidated district need not employ the former superintendent. Instead, it may discharge its obligation by paying the former superintendent the salary that he or she would have earned pursuant to the contract, less any income the former superintendent earns from employment elsewhere during the term of the contract (*Matter of Foster*).

7:22. What are the statutory powers and duties of a superintendent of schools?

Education Law section 1711(2) states that superintendents of schools have the following powers and duties, unless otherwise specified by the bylaws of the board of education:

- "To be the chief executive officer of the school district and the educational system, and to have the right to speak on all matters before the board, but not to vote.
- "To enforce all provisions of law and all rules and regulations relating to the management of the schools and other educational, social and recreational activities under the direction of the board of education.
- "To prepare the content of each course of study authorized by the board of education. The content of each such course shall be submitted to the board of education for its approval and, when thus approved, the superintendent shall cause such courses of study to be used in the grades, classes and schools for which they are authorized.
- "To recommend suitable lists of textbooks to be used in the schools.

- "To have supervision and direction of associate, assistant and other superintendents, directors, supervisors, principals, teachers, lecturers, medical inspectors, nurses, auditors, attendance officers, janitors and other persons employed in the management of the schools or the other educational activities of the district authorized by [the Education Law] and under the direction and management of the board of education; to transfer teachers from one school to another, or from one grade of the course of study to another grade in such course, and to report immediately such transfers to such board for its consideration and actions; to report to such board violations of regulations and cases of insubordination, and to suspend an associate, assistant or other superintendent, director, supervisor, expert, principal, teacher or other employee until the next regular meeting of such board, when all facts relating to the case shall be submitted to such board for its consideration and action.
- "To have supervision and direction over the enforcement and observance of the courses of study, the examination and promotion of pupils, and over all other matters pertaining to playgrounds, medical inspection, recreation and social center work, libraries, lectures, and all other education activities under the management, direction and control of the board of education." (For city school districts, see §§ 2508 and 2566).

With regard to the transfer of teachers, the Education Law specifically provides that a collective bargaining agreement may modify the superintendent's authority (§§ 1711(4), 2508(7), 2566(9); *Poughkeepsie City SD v. Poughkeepsie Public School Teachers' Ass'n*, 80 A.D.2d 610 (2nd Dep't 1981)).

7:23. Does the school board have the authority to change the superintendent's duties during his or her employment contract?

Generally, yes. The board retains the authority to change the superintendent's powers and duties unless the board has given up that authority in the superintendent's employment contract. Except where that authority has been removed, a board has broad latitude in establishing work requirements (*Matter of Hagen*, 17 Educ. Dep't Rep. 400 (1978)).

7:24. Under what circumstances may a school board terminate a superintendent's contract?

A superintendent's contract may be terminated through non-renewal. In this context, attention must be paid to any automatic extension, "roll-over" or "evergreen" provisions contained in the contract. Procedures for providing notice of non-renewal must be carefully observed (*Appeal of Hernandez*, 29 Educ. Dep't Rep. 508 (1990); *Matter of Northrup*, 24 Educ. Dep't Rep. 262 (1985)).

Prior to its expiration date, a superintendent's contract may be terminated for cause in accordance with the provisions of the contract and in compliance with applicable due process requirements. The services of a superintendent appointed for a specified period of time in city school districts may also be terminated for cause as long as applicable due process requirements are observed (*Matter of Brewster*, 15 Educ. Dep't Rep. 526 (1976); see **7:25**).

A superintendent's contract may also be terminated prior to its expiration date through mutual agreement between the board and the superintendent. The courts and the commissioner have held that "buy-out" agreements do not violate the constitutional prohibition against the gift of public funds (see *Ingram v. Boone*, 91 A.D.2d 1063 (2nd Dep't 1983); *Matter of Berke*, 12 Educ. Dep't Rep. 93 (1972); *Matter of Loiacono*, 11 Educ. Dep't Rep. 270 (1972)). Any documents confirming a "buy-out" or similar agreement are subject to disclosure under the Freedom of Information Law (see **2:71**).

7:25. What legal restrictions apply to dismissal proceedings against school superintendents?

Dismissal of a superintendent during the term of his or her contract or appointment requires cause and adherence to the provisions of the contract and to applicable due process procedures. Due process procedures must be followed because this kind of contract gives rise to a legally founded expectation of continued employment and is a property right within the meaning of case law (see, for example, *Appeal of Pinckney*, 35 Educ. Dep't Rep. 461 (1996); *Matter of Brewster*, 15 Educ. Dep't Rep. 526 (1976); *Matter of Driscoll*, 14 Educ. Dep't Rep. 148 (1974)).

Due process under such circumstances involves, at minimum, the right to: receive written charges and to respond in writing to such charges; be represented by counsel; a formal hearing, with the right to produce evidence and cross-examine witnesses who testify in support of the charges; obtain a transcript of such hearing; formal written findings sustaining or dismissing the charges (*Matter of De Freitas*, 14 Educ. Dep't Rep. 329 (1975)); and continued pay during suspensions pending a hearing (*Appeal of Pinckney*). The contract may modify or supplement these requirements.

It should be noted that the Education Law specifically authorizes the inclusion of procedures for termination of employment as a term of the contract between the board and the superintendent (§ 1711(3)).

One arbitrator has ruled that it is not a conflict of interest for a school board's attorney to represent the board in a disciplinary proceeding against the superintendent because the school attorney represents the board, not its employees (*Board of Educ. of the Lindenhurst UFSD v. Holzman*, Scheinman, Arbitrator, June 9, 1995).

Principals

7:26. Must there be a principal in each school?

Yes. The commissioner's regulations require that a full-time principal be employed and assigned to each school. The principal must hold appropriate certification (8 NYCRR § 100.2(a)).

If there are circumstances that do not justify the assignment of a principal to a particular school, or if another mode of building adminis-tration would be more effective, the commissioner of education may approve an alternative mode (8 NYCRR § 100.2(a)). The commissioner has determined that a district may assign one principal to a school comprised of more than one building on the same site where the buildings are in close proximity to each other (*Matter of Middle Island Principals' Ass'n*, 19 Educ. Dep't Rep. 507 (1980)).

7:27. Are school districts required to have assistant principals in school buildings?

No. There is no requirement that a school district employ assistant principals (*Matter of Ryan*, 17 Educ. Dep't Rep. 338 (1978), *aff'd*, 71 A.D.2d 719 (3rd Dep't 1979)).

7:28. Who establishes a salary schedule for the school principal?

There is no statutory or regulatory requirement that the board adopt a salary schedule for school principals. Salary specifications most frequently are embodied in a collective bargaining agreement or in the board's resolutions.

7:29. Can a school board legally reduce a principal's salary?

A school board must adhere to all the specifications, including salary, of a collectively negotiated agreement or the principal's contract.

Whether or not a contract exists, a board cannot reduce a tenured principal's salary so much that it amounts to disciplinary action, because section 3020–a of the Education Law provides the exclusive procedure for disciplinary action against tenured school district employees (*Matter of Trono*, 18 Educ. Dep't Rep. 344 (1978)).

7:30. Can a school board, acting on its own, designate its school principals as managerial employees and thereby exclude them from membership in a negotiating unit?

No. This type of designation may be obtained only upon application to the Public Employment Relations Board (PERB). Principals of schools or other administrative personnel who do not have a significant role in the formulation of district-wide policy, or who do not have a significant role in personnel administration or labor relations, may not be so designated (Civ. Serv. Law § 201(7)(a); see **10:22-24** for further information about designating managerial personnel).

8. Teachers

Teachers' Qualifications

8:1. What is the legal definition of a teacher?

No uniform definition of the term *teacher* exists. *Teacher* is most commonly understood to be any full-time member of the teaching staff of a school district. However, administrative and supervisory staff members are included within the definition in some provisions of the Education Law (see § 3101). Because the term *teacher* is defined differently within the Education Law, reference to the particular law under consideration is recommended.

8:2. What are the qualifications of a teacher?

An individual is qualified to teach in a New York State public school if he or she is a citizen of the United States, is at least 18 years of age and possesses a New York State teacher's certificate (§ 3001; see **8:26–53**). A teacher also must subscribe to an oath to support the federal and state constitutions (§ 3002).

New York State Law does not establish any qualification requirements for teachers in nonpublic schools.

8:3. May a teacher who is not legally qualified be employed by a school district?

Generally, no. A district may not employ an unqualified teacher, nor may it pay the salary of an unqualified teacher (§§ 3001(2); 3009(1); 3010); see *Winter v. Board of Educ. for Rhinebeck CSD,* 79 N.Y.2d 1 (1992); *Smith v. Board of Education,* 65 N.Y.2d 797 (1985); *Meliti v. Nyquist,* 41 N.Y.2d 183 (1976)). However, the commissioner of education may, in his discretion, "excuse the default" of a school board that employed and paid an unqualified teacher, and may legalize the past employment and authorize the payment of that teacher's salary (§ 3604(6)).

The district may employ an uncertified teacher only when a certified and qualified teacher is not available and the commissioner grants a temporary license to the teacher pursuant to and upon review of the school district's request (§ 3006; 8 NYCRR § 80.18; *Appeal of Nettles,* 31 Educ. Dep't Rep. 437 (1992); see **8:37**). However, an uncertified teacher employed by a district must be enrolled in a collegiate program toward certification by the beginning of the next semester following initial employment (see 8 NYCRR § 80.18(a)(2)(iii)(d)). No uncertified teacher may be issued more than four temporary licenses, except upon a showing of substantial progress toward certification (8 NYCRR § 80.18(h)).

A certified teacher may, however, instruct five classroom hours of teaching per week in an area for which that teacher is uncertified, pursuant to the commissioner's incidental teaching regulations, provided that, despite extensive recruitment efforts, there are no certified or qualified individuals available for the position (see 8 NYCRR § 80.2(c); **8:44**).

Any board member "who applies, or directs or consents to the application of, any district money to the payment of an unqualified teacher's salary" commits a misdemeanor (§ 3010).

8:4. Under what circumstances may a non-United States citizen teach in the public schools?

A person who is not a United States citizen is qualified to teach, provided he or she is at least 18 years of age, possesses a New York State teacher's certificate, has petitioned to become a U.S. citizen and will become a citizen of this country within the time prescribed by law (§ 3001(3)). A foreign national who cannot become a citizen solely because of an oversubscribed quota to which he or she is chargeable is likewise eligible to teach (§ 3001–a). The teacher still must meet all other qualification requirements.

In addition, a teacher from a foreign country may be qualified to teach in this state under a teacher exchange program for no more than two years (§ 3005).

The United States Supreme Court has found the citizenship requirement in the Education Law to be constitutional because of the important civic function of public school teachers in our democratic government (*Ambach v. Norwick*, 441 U.S. 68 (1979)).

8:5. May a school district refuse to employ a qualified teacher on the basis of religion, race or sex?

No. State and federal laws prohibit discrimination against applicants or current employees on the basis of race, color, national origin, sex, religion, creed or marital status. Thus, school districts may not disqualify a candidate for a teaching position based on any of these criteria (42 USC § 2000e *et seq.* (Title VII of the Civil Rights Act of 1964); 20 USC § 1681 *et seq.* (Title IX of the Education Amendments of 1972); Exec. Law § 290 *et seq.* (Human Rights Law); Civ. Rights Law § 40 *et seq.*; see **8:6-9** regarding disability and age discrimination).

Title VII prohibits unlawful employment practices such as failing or refusing to hire, discharge or otherwise discriminate against an individual with respect to employment because of his or her race, color, religion, sex or national origin (42 USC § 2000e-2). In addition, Title VII prohibits discrimination in employment on the basis of pregnancy and protects the right to reinstatement of women on leave for reasons related to pregnancy (42 USC § 2000e(k)).

Title IX bans sexual discrimination in education programs by providing for the termination of federal aid to institutions that support such discrimination (20 USC § 1681). The scope of Title IX was broadened by the Civil Rights Restoration Act of 1987 (P. L. 100–259) to permit the withholding not only of funding for specific discriminatory programs or activities within the institution, but funding from entire educational departments, organizations or institutions that support discriminatory programs or activities (20 USC § 1687).

State law also provides for equal protection of law for all persons within the state (Civ. Rights Law § 40–c(1)). School districts in particular are prohibited from making inquiries regarding the religion or religious affiliation of a candidate for employment (Civ. Rights Law § 40–a). Examples of other illegal inquiries are described in "Rulings on Inquiries," available from the New York State Division of Human Rights, 55 West 125th Street, New York, N.Y. 10027; telephone 212-961-8400.

8:6. May a school district refuse to employ an otherwise qualified teacher who has a disability?

No. State and federal laws prohibit discrimination against applicants or current employees on the basis of a disability (29 USC § 794 *et seq.* (Rehabilitation Act of 1973); 42 USC § 12101 *et seq.* (Americans with Disabilities Act); Exec. Law § 290 *et seq.* (Human Rights Law); Civ. Rights Law § 40 *et seq.*).

Section 504 of the Rehabilitation Act of 1973 prohibits discrimination based on an individual's disability by all recipients of federal financial assistance. The Americans with Disabilities Act of 1990 (ADA) is designed to eliminate both intended and unintended discrimination against individuals with disabilities in both private and governmental employment, public services, public accommodations and telecommunications. The employment provisions of the ADA cover employers with 15 or more employees. However, it is noteworthy that the ADA specifically excludes from its coverage any employee or job applicant who currently uses illegal drugs.

The United States Supreme Court has ruled that the ADA applies to people infected with the human immunodeficiency virus (HIV). This ruling signals that many people suffering from disorders from which there are not outward symptoms may be entitled to protection under the ADA (*Bragdon v. Abbott,* 118 S. Ct. 2196 (1998)).

Under New York State law, a teacher may not be disqualified for a teaching position solely because of a disability, provided the disability does not interfere with that person's ability to perform teaching duties (§ 3004; Civ. Rights Law § 40–c(2); Exec. Law § 296; see also *Antonsen v. Ward*, 77 N.Y.2d 506 (1991); *In re State Div. of Human Rights*, 70 N.Y.2d 100 (1987)).

8:7 Is a school district required to provide a reasonable accommodation to an employee with a disability?

Yes, under certain circumstances. A school district must make reasonable accommodation to the known physical or mental limitations of an otherwise qualified disabled applicant unless the school district can demonstrate that the accommodation would impose an undue hardship on the operation of its program (29 USC § 794; 42 USC § 12112; 34 CFR § 104.12(a); 45 CFR § 84.12(a); *Borkowski v. Valley Central School District*, 63 F.3d 131 (2nd Cir. 1995)).

Reasonable accommodations may include making facilities readily accessible to and usable by disabled persons, job restructuring, part-time or modified work schedules, acquisition or modification of equipment or devices, the provision of readers or interpreters, and other similar actions (42 USC § 12111(9); 34 CFR § 104.12(b); 45 CFR § 84.12(b)).

Some of the factors to be considered in determining whether a particular accommodation would cause an undue hardship are the overall size of the district's program with respect to number of employees, number and type of facilities, the size of the district's budget, and the nature and cost of the accommodation needed (42 USC § 12111(10); 34 CFR § 104.12(c); 45 CFR § 84.12(c)).

8:8. Can a teacher's age be used as a qualification for employment?

No. Age-related discrimination in hiring, promotion and other conditions of employment for employees over age 40 is prohibited by the federal Age Discrimination in Employment Act (29 USC § 623). Age-based employment qualifications for persons 18 years old or older are also barred by state law (Exec. Law §§ 291, 296); thus, districts may not specify an age requirement for any teaching position.

Additionally, mandatory retirement because of age in the public and private sectors is prohibited except in certain occupations, such as high-salaried corporate executives and tenured professors, and where age is a "bona fide occupational qualification" (Exec. Law § 296(3–a); Retire. & Soc. Sec. Law § 530).

However, an early retirement incentive plan which requires a participating teacher to retire at the end of the school year in which he or she is first eligible to retire does not violate the federal Age Discrimination and Employment Act (ADEA). The court found that in order for a retirement incentive to be lawful, it must be voluntary, it must be available for a reasonable period of time, and it may not arbitrarily discriminate on the basis of age (*Auerbach v. Board of Education of the Harborfields Central School District*, 136 F. 3d 104 (2nd Cir. 1998)).

8:9. Does a teacher have any recourse if discrimination in employment occurs?

Yes. Various provisions of state and federal law prohibit discrimination in employment, such as dismissal or refusal to hire or promote because of race, color, national origin, religion, creed, disability, sex, marital status or age (see **8:5-8**). A teacher alleging illegal employment discrimination may appeal to the state Division of Human Rights, the federal Department of Education's Office of Civil Rights, the federal Equal Employment Opportunity Commission or initiate other legal action.

8:10. May a relative of a school board member be employed as a teacher by that board?

Yes. A person related by blood or marriage to a school board member may be employed as a teacher by the district on the consent of a two-thirds majority of the board (§ 3016(2)). In common school districts, the employment of relatives of trustees as teachers must be approved by two-thirds of the voters of the district who are present and voting on the issue at an annual or special district meeting (§ 3016(1)).

There are no similar or different restrictions on the employment of relatives in nonteaching positions. For information concerning any potential conflict of interest resulting from the employment of board member relatives, see **2:21** and General Municipal Law Section 800(3)(a).

8:11. May teacher applicants be required to submit to a medical examination?

No. Such a requirement would constitute a violation of the Americans with Disabilities Act (42 USC § 12101 *et seq.*) and Section 504 of the Rehabilitation Act of 1976 (29 USC § 794 *et seq.*). However, a district may condition an offer of employment on a physical and/or psychological examination to ensure that a candidate has the physical and mental capacity to perform the duties of that position. This examination, if required, must be applied equally to all entering employees (28 CFR §§ 35.140, 41.55; 29 CFR §§ 1630.13, 1630.14; 34 CFR § 104.14).

8:12. May a district require a teacher to submit to a medical examination after the teacher has begun working for the district?

Yes, under certain circumstances. To safeguard the health of children attending the public schools, the school board or, in New York City community school districts, the superintendent can require any employee to submit to a medical examination, including a psychiatric examination, to determine that person's physical or mental capacity to perform his or her duties (§§ 913; 2568).

Refusal by a teacher to comply with an examination ordered by the school board may constitute insubordination (*McNamara v. Commissioner of Educ.*, 80 A.D.2d 660 (3rd Dep't 1981)). The board may require a teacher to submit to additional examinations if necessary to permit a doctor to render a final determination regarding that individual's fitness to teach (*Matter of Almeter*, 30 Educ. Dep't Rep. 230 (1991)).

The board may direct the examination to be conducted by its own physician or by a physician chosen by the teacher (*Matter of Hirsch*, 20 Educ. Dep't Rep. 211 (1980); *Matter of Gargiul*, 15 Educ. Dep't Rep. 360 (1976)). The teacher is entitled to be accompanied by a physician or other person of his or her choice, including a union representative. Accordingly, the teacher must be given sufficient notice to arrange for the presence of his or her physician (§§ 913, 2568; *Schiffer v. Board of Education*, 112 A.D.2d 372, *appeal dismissed*, 66 N.Y.2d 915 (1985)).

The findings of the examination must be reported to the school board (§ 913) or, in New York City, to the superintendent of schools (§ 2568) and may be used for the performance evaluation of the employee or for disability retirement.

Teachers' Rights and Responsibilities

8:13. What are teachers' customary duties?

Teachers usually perform duties that include planning educational experiences for students, providing classroom instruction, supervising students in noninstructional periods such as lunch and study hall, attending faculty and other professional meetings, participating in school conferences with parents, supervising extracurricular activities and attending school functions such as school open houses.

8:14. Is there a law that establishes a maximum length for a teacher's workday?

There are no laws that limit the hours of work a school board may establish for its teachers. However, the length of a teacher's workday is a mandatory subject of bargaining that must be negotiated with a collective bargaining unit representative, such as a teachers' union (*Troy City School Dist.*, 11 PERB ¶ 3056 (1978); see also **10:36-37**).

8:15. Do any standards exist for a teacher's daily teaching load?

Yes. The commissioner's regulations state the number of daily classroom periods of instruction for a teacher should not exceed five periods. A school district that requires teachers to instruct for more than six teaching periods a day or a daily teaching load of more than 150 pupils must justify its deviation from this policy (8 NYCRR § 100.2(i)).

The commissioner has ruled that deviation from the regulatory standards will be permitted only in unique and compelling circumstances (*Appeal of Baker*, 33 Educ. Dep't Rep. 395 (1994); *Appeal of LaForty*, 33 Educ. Dep't Rep. 161 (1993)). Districts that cannot comply with the regulation may be required to make annual reports to the commissioner on the progress made toward eventual compliance (see *Matter of Simon*, 1 Educ. Dep't Rep. 562 (1960)).

Limitations on teachers' workloads are frequently included as a provision in collective bargaining agreements.

8:16. Must teachers be given a free period for lunch?

All school districts, except New York City, must allow each teacher who is employed for more than five hours a day at least a 30-minute period free from assigned duties and scheduled, so far as practical, during the hours normally allotted for student lunch periods. Additionally, districts must schedule teaching assignments so that no full-time teacher will be assigned to continuous duty for more than five hours (§ 3029).

A collective bargaining agreement may contain a provision extending but not reducing this duty-free period (*Matter of Gordon*, 18 Educ. Dep't Rep. 518 (1979)).

8:17. May a school district unilaterally require its teachers to supervise or participate in extracurricular activities outside of regular school hours?

No. Hours of work and extra pay for extra work are mandatory subjects of collective bargaining under the Taylor Law and, thus, districts must negotiate with their teachers concerning assignment of and payment for after-school duties (*Beacon CSD*, 14 PERB ¶ 3084 (1981); see also **10:36-37**). Most school boards pay extra compensation for extracurricular supervision or participation, such as coaching athletics.

8:18. What freedom of expression rights do teachers enjoy?

School districts may discipline and dismiss employees for speech that is not on a matter of public concern or for speech which the district reasonably believes is disruptive. The district is entitled to make such a determination based on the facts surrounding the speech as the district reasonably believes them to be (*Waters v. Churchill*, 511 U.S. 661 (1994); *Connick v. Myers*, 461 U.S. 138 (1983)). The district is not required to demonstrate that the teacher's speech actually caused disruption to the district's operation; rather, the district's burden is to show that the speech threatened to interfere with the district's operations (*Jeffries v. Harleston*, 52 F.3d 9 (2nd Cir.), *cert. denied*, 116 S.Ct. 173 (1995)).

The commissioner of education has ruled that a faculty advisor to an extracurricular student newspaper could not be disciplined for allowing the publication of a cartoon depicting board members and an administrator unfavorably because the teacher was entitled to the same constitutional protection safeguarding student expression, which can only be suppressed to avoid "substantial disruption or material interference with school activities or to maintain order and discipline in the operation of its schools" (*Appeal of Board of Educ. of Wappingers CSD*, 34 Educ. Dep't Rep. 323 (1994)).

Similarly, the commissioner has also ruled that school employees may wear campaign buttons in support of school board candidates, provided there is a "minimal likelihood of disruption" because elections are a matter of public concern (*Appeal of Moessinger*, 33 Educ. Dep't Rep. 487 (1994)).

8:19. Must a teacher comply with any code of ethics or other guidelines for his or her conduct?

Yes. The General Municipal Law prohibits certain conduct by school district employees because it creates a conflict of interest (Gen. Mun. Law §§ 801, 802, 805–a). For example, an employee must not accept a gift worth more than $75 (the school board can set the limit at less than $75, though not above $75) under circumstances in which it reasonably could be inferred that the gift was intended to influence the employee, disclose confidential information or have an interest in certain types of contracts with the district.

In addition, each school district must adopt a code of ethics that provides guidance to its officers and employees regarding the standard of conduct reasonably expected of them (Gen. Mun. Law § 806). This code of ethics must provide standards as may be deemed advisable, including outside employment and holding of investments in conflict with official duties. Thus, it may proscribe certain conduct in addition to that specifically prohibited by law (Gen. Mun. Law § 806(1)(a)).

Employees of the New York City Board of Education are required by state law and board policy to submit financial disclosure statements and disclose certain other information as part of an in-depth background investigation (§ 2590–g(13), (14)). The New York State Court of Appeals has held the disclosures for background investigations are a mandatory subject of bargaining (*Board of Education of the City of New York v. New York State Public Employment Relations Bd.*, 75 N.Y.2d 660 (1990); see **10:36-37**).

8:20. What rights and obligations do teachers have over the curriculum being taught?

A school board has the power and obligation to establish curriculum within its schools (§ 1709(3)). In upholding a school district's change of its grading policy without having previously submitted the issue to a shared-decision-making committee, the commissioner explained that a school board is empowered to set the course of study by which students are graded and classified (see *Appeal of Orris v. Board of Educ. of Greenville CSD*, 35 Educ. Dep't Rep. 184 (1995)). Accordingly, teachers' claims of academic freedom to control the content of instruction must be balanced against the board's legitimate interest in establishing instructional programs.

A teacher's claim of academic freedom must be protected where the instructional material has educational value, is relevant to the curriculum and is suitable to the age and maturity of the students (*Malverne UFSD v. Sobol*, 181 A.D.2d 371 (3rd Dep't 1992); *Kingsville Independent School Dist. v. Cooper*, 611 F.2d 1109 (5th Cir. 1980)).

A district policy on academic freedom must contain specific direction regarding the use of new or different teaching methods before it becomes a basis for imposing discipline against a teacher (*Malverne UFSD*). However, the placement of a critical letter in a teacher's personnel file regarding that teacher's use of material in the classroom deemed objectionable by a school board does not rise to the level of discipline such that any right to academic freedom retained by the teacher would be chilled (*O'Connor v. Sobol*, 173 A.D.2d 74 (3rd Dep't 1991), *appeal dismissed*, 80 N.Y.2d 897 (1992)).

8:21. Are there any restrictions on a school district's imposition of a dress code on its faculty?

Yes. A school district may not unilaterally impose a dress code on its faculty. The imposition of a specific dress code for faculty is a mandatory subject of collective bargaining (Catskill CSD, 18 PERB ¶ 4612 (1985); see **10:36-37**). However, a PERB administrative law judge held a school district

may require its staff to wear photo identification cards without first negotiating the issue with the union, where the identification system relates to
the employer's mission to promote safety and accountability (*Middle
Country Secretarial Ass'n v. Middle Country CSD*, 30 PERB ¶ 4556 (1997)).

In this context, it is noteworthy that a New York appellate court ordered
reinstatement and back pay in a case where a Native American corrections
officer was dismissed for refusing to cut his hair, as required by regulation,
because of his religious beliefs. According to the court, there was no
legitimate state interest shown which outweighed the employee's right to
the free exercise of his religion (*Rourke v. NYS Dept. of Correctional Services*,
201 A.D.2d 179 (3rd Dep't 1994)).

The United States Court of Appeals for the Second Circuit, which has
jurisdiction over New York State, has held that a dress code that required a
teacher to wear a necktie does not infringe on First Amendment rights to
free expression or the right to privacy (*East Hartford Education Ass'n v. Board
of Educ.*, 562 F.2d 838 (2nd Cir. 1977)).

8:22. May a teacher in New York State administer corporal punishment to a student?

No. Corporal punishment is forbidden in public schools in New York
State, although the use of physical force is permitted where alternatives
cannot be employed reasonably (8 NYCRR §§ 19.5(a),(c); 100.2(l)(3); for
more information, see **12:117-118**).

8:23. Do teachers have the right to strike?

No. Teachers are subject to the provisions of the Taylor Law, which
prohibits strikes by police officers, fire fighters and other public employees (Civ. Serv. Law § 210). The law gives all public employees the right to
form, join and participate in labor organizations, and also grants public
employees the right to be represented by labor organizations in collective
bargaining of their terms and conditions of employment and in the
administration of grievances (see **10:12**).

The Taylor Law defines a strike or illegal job action as "any strike or
other concerted stoppage of work or slowdown by public employees" (Civ.
Serv. Law § 201(9)). A refusal by teachers to perform services in the usual
and customary manner, including voluntary activities, is an illegal job
action (*Bellmore-Merrick CSD v. Bellmore-Merrick United Secondary Teachers,
Inc.*, 85 Misc.2d 282 (1975), *aff'd*, 47 A.D.2d 815 (2nd Dep't 1975); *Haverling
CSD v. Haverling Teachers Ass'n*, 22 PERB ¶ 4554 (1989); *Pearl River UFSD*,
11 PERB ¶ 4530 (1978)). Thus, boycotts of voluntary or other assignments,
such as evening activities, extracurricular assignments, extra help, field

trips and faculty meetings, are illegal strikes (see also **10:49-50**).

In addition, the threat of refusal or the actual refusal to perform volunteer duties during collective bargaining in order to gain an advantage, known as work-to-rule, is a strike or threat of a strike that is prohibited by the Taylor Law *(Haverling CSD v. Haverling Teachers Ass'n)*.

A school district may deduct twice a teacher's daily salary for each day he or she participates in a strike (Civ. Serv. Law § 210(2)(f)). The penalty for a strike of extracurricular duties is limited to a deduction of compensation for the extracurricular work *(Baylis v. Seaford UFSD*, 22 PERB ¶ 7533 (1989); see **10:51**).

In addition, if the Public Employment Relations Board (PERB) determines that the teachers' union has violated the strike ban, it will order forfeiture of the union's membership dues deduction and agency shop fee deduction privileges (Civ. Serv. Law § 210(3)(f)).

8:24. Do teachers have the right to participate in shared decision making and school-based planning?

Yes. The commissioner has adopted regulations which require an increased level of shared decision making among teachers, administrators, parents and other members of the school community (8 NYCRR § 100.11; see **3:26–37**). The regulations require school districts to adopt a plan and to establish shared-decision-making committees at both the building and districtwide levels. They also require that teachers be members of any such committee, and that teacher members be selected by the recognized teachers union (8 NYCRR § 100.11(b); *Appeal of Wilson*, 33 Educ. Dep't Rep. 79 (1993)).

8:25. Is a school district obligated to assist a teacher facing legal action as a result of his or her conduct in the discharge of his or her official duties?

Yes (see **18:33–35**). School districts must provide an attorney and pay legal fees in a case where civil or criminal action is brought against a teacher who, in the discharge of his or her duties, takes disciplinary action against a student (§ 3028). A district's obligation extends only to charges arising out of disciplinary action by a teacher, and the applicability of the statute is determined by the actual facts underlying the incident giving rise to the allegations of misconduct and not the allegations alone *(Lamb v. Westmoreland CSD*, 143 A.D.2d 535 (4th Dep't 1988), *appeal denied*, 73 N.Y.2d 704 (1989); *Cutler v. Poughkeepsie City School Dist.*, 73 A.D.2d 967 (2nd Dep't 1980).

In addition, school districts must provide legal assistance to employees facing claims of alleged negligence or acts resulting in accidental bodily injury to any person within or outside of a school building, provided the employee at the time of the accident or injury was acting within the scope of his or her employment and/or under the direction of the school board (§ 3023). The teacher must send copies of the legal papers in the criminal or civil proceedings to the district within 10 days of being served to be eligible for district assistance (§§ 3023; 3028).

Education Law section 3811 provides that all costs and damages which are assessed against a teacher due to non-criminal conduct arising out of the good-faith exercise of his or her duties shall be a district charge, provided that the teacher gives the school district notice of the lawsuit within five days of its commencement.

However, unless the teacher gives the district written notice of the commencement of the action within five days of being served with the legal papers, the district is exempt from paying for the costs and reasonable expenses of defending the action, as well as all costs and damages adjudged against the teacher (§ 3811). These requirements do not apply to an action or proceeding brought against an employee by the school district or a criminal prosecution.

School districts also should be aware that section 18 of the Public Officers Law permits a school board to adopt a resolution to supplant or supplement the protection provided by the Education Law (see *Matter of Percy*, 31 Educ. Dep't Rep. 199 (1991)). In these instances, the notice requirements of the Public Officers Law apply.

Teacher Certification

Editor's Note: In July 1998 the Board of Regents unanimously approved the final report of the Regents Task Force on Teaching. This report will entail significant changes to the Education Law and commissioner's regulations over the next several years in the areas of teacher certification and tenure. Therefore, readers should be cautioned that some of the material in this chapter may change between now and the next edition of School Law, to be published in 2000.

The task force report includes the following recommendations:
- *A professional development plan for teachers directly related to student learning needs, developed by school districts.*
- *A new teacher certification system. Teachers receiving a professional certificate on or after September 1, 2000 will be required to complete at least 175 hours of professional development every five years.*
- *New categories of certificates for teachers. This will require the creation of new tenure areas.*

• *The establishment of a 28-member Professional Standards and Practices Board to advise the Regents and the commissioner of education on teaching-related issues. This board will replace and assume the functions of the existing Teacher Education, Certification and Practices (TECAP) Board.*

Legislation to implement the report's recommendations was to have been submitted in September of 1998, according to the report's time line. Regulations to implement new certificate titles and requirements for teacher education programs are to be enacted by September of 1999.

For more information or for a copy of the report, contact the State Education Department's website at http://www.nysed.gov.

8:26. What is a teacher's certificate?

A teacher's certificate is a license issued by the New York State Education Department that certifies that the holder meets all the necessary qualifications to teach in the public schools (§ 3004; 8 NYCRR § 80.2(d)).

8:27. Is state certification required for all public school teachers in New York State?

Yes, except in Buffalo. School districts are prohibited by law from employing a person who does not have a valid teacher's certificate (§§ 2569; 3001). Teachers employed in Buffalo must meet local requirements for licenses issued by that city in lieu of state certification, but these local requirements must meet or exceed the minimums set by the state (see § 3008; 8 NYCRR § 80.2(j)). Although teachers employed in New York City previously held local certificates, they now hold teaching certificates issued from the State Education Department (§ 2569).

8:28. In general, how much college preparation is necessary for a teaching certificate in New York State?

For provisional certification to teach in both the elementary and secondary grades, a bachelor's degree (baccalaureate) from a regionally accredited institution is necessary (8 NYCRR §§ 80.15-16). A bachelor's degree is not required of applicants for certification in the majority of career education fields (8 NYCRR § 80.5).

For a permanent certificate in elementary and secondary grades, a master's degree functionally related to the field of teaching is required. (For information on requirements for an administrator's certificate, see 7:2-3).

8:29. Must candidates pass a competency examination to become certified to teach in New York State?

Yes. However, the testing requirements for New York State teaching certificates are being amended and the changes are being phased in over several years. Under the new requirements, for example, an applicant for a provisional or permanent certificate must pass designated examinations as part of the New York State Teacher Certification Examination program (NYSTCE) (8 NYCRR §§ 80.2(q); 80.16(a)(2); 80.16(b)(2)). The NYSTCE includes the Liberal Arts and Science Test (LAST), the Written Assessment of Teaching Skills (ATS-W), the Content Specialty Tests (CSTs), and the Performance Assessment of Teaching Skills (ATS-P).

While the NYSTCE testing program is being phased in, satisfactory performance on the NTE Core Battery tests is sufficient to receive certification for a limited number of teaching certificate titles. The LAST and ATS-W may also be acceptable alternatives. Since the regulations are complex and exceptions may apply to individuals in certain circumstances, specific information on certification requirements can be obtained from the New York State Education Department, Office of Teaching, Albany, N.Y. 12234; telephone 518-474-3901. Information is also available through the Office of Teaching's World Wide Web site: http://www.nysed.gov/tcert/homepage.htm.

8:30. Is there an application fee for a teacher's certificate?

Yes. The fee for a teacher's certificate based on completion of a New York State teachers' education program is $50, and the fee for a certificate based on education or experience completed in other than a New York State teaching program is $100 (§ 3006).

8:31. Are persons with disabilities entitled to teacher certification?

Yes. The commissioner of education and school districts cannot deny a teaching certificate to a teacher because of a disability, as long as that disability does not interfere with the performance of his or her teaching duties (§ 3004(1); see **8:6**).

8:32. What types of teaching certificates currently are issued by the State Education Department?

The State Education Department (SED) issues four types of teaching certificates: provisional certificates, permanent certificates, certificates of qualification and internship certificates. Most teachers hold either provisional or permanent certificates.

A *provisional certificate* allows an individual to teach in a public school for five years. Under certain circumstances, the provisional certificate may be extended by no more than two years or renewed for two periods of two years each (8 NYCRR § 80.2(f), (n)). A lapsed provisional certificate may also be renewed one time, for good cause subject to the approval of the commissioner, for a five-year period (8 NYCRR § 80.2(n); see **8:33**). The requirements for provisional certification vary, depending upon the area of teaching and the time the application is made. For detailed information about the requirements a person must meet to obtain a provisional certificate contact the New York State Education Department, Office of Teaching, Albany, N.Y. 12234.

The commissioner's regulations require teachers to replace their provisional certificates with a permanent certificate before the provisional certificate expires. To obtain *permanent certification,* teachers must complete one year of a supervised internship or two years of teaching experience in a public or nonpublic school and obtain a master's degree that is functionally relevant to the area in which they seek permanent certification. They also must pass a competency examination (see **8:29**; 8 NYCRR Part 80). As the name implies, a permanent certificate is valid for the life of a teacher unless revoked for cause.

Graduates of teachers' education programs and other qualified persons may receive *certificates of qualification* that indicate they are eligible for a provisional certificate. This certificate is valid for five years and would be considered proof of eligibility by prospective employers. The certificate of qualification provides a teacher with additional time to complete the requirements for obtaining permanent certification while unemployed. Upon accepting a part-time or full-time teaching position, the teacher must exchange the certificate of qualification for a provisional certificate. No certificates of qualification will be issued after September 2, 1998. Holders of certificates of qualification dated prior to this date may retain the certificate as evidence that the holder is eligible for a provisional certificate. After five years, the certificate of qualification must be exchanged for the provisional certificate (8 NYCRR § 80.2(l)).

Finally, an *internship certificate* is issued to a graduate student who will receive compensation for an internship with a school district. The internship certificate is issued without fee at the recommendation of a college or university that has an approved teachers' education program. It is valid only for two years and is restricted to use within a particular school district (8 NYCRR § 80.2(g)).

8:33. May a lapsed provisional certificate be renewed?

Yes. A provisional certificate that has lapsed may be renewed twice for two-year periods upon application to the commissioner of education (8 NYCRR § 80.2(n)). The applicant must show that he or she has completed the educational preparation requirements for permanent certification and has been offered a teaching position in the area of the provisional certificate. A lapsed provisional certificate may also be renewed one time, for good cause subject to the commissioner's approval, for a five year period (8 NYCRR § 80.2(n)).

8:34. Are there specific classifications in which teaching certificates are issued?

Yes. The State Education Department (SED) issues teaching certificates in the following classifications: lower and upper elementary grades pre-K–6 (prekindergarten through sixth grade) and 7–12 (seventh through 12th grade) in academic subjects (8 NYCRR §§ 80.15, 80.16). There is also an extension of the pre-K–6 certificate to teach academic subjects in grades 7-9, and an extension of the 7-12 certificate to teach academic subjects in grades 5-6 (8 NYCRR §§ 80.15(d); 80.16(d)). SED also grants a provisional and permanent annotation to indicate special preparation in early childhood education.

SED also grants special teachers' certificates in a number of areas, including career occupational subjects (8 NYCRR § 80.5); special education, the deaf and hearing impaired, the blind and partially sighted, and students with speech and hearing disabilities (8 NYCRR § 80.6); reading teacher (8 NYCRR § 80.7); school media specialist (8 NYCRR § 80.8); bilingual education (8 NYCRR § 80.9); English as a second language (8 NYCRR § 80.10); teachers of adult, community and continuing education (8 NYCRR § 80.11); and certification to teach in nonregistered evening schools (8 NYCRR § 80.23). Specific requirements must be met to qualify for these special area certificates. However, it should be noted that the commissioner's regulations do not provide for an extension of the tenure areas in experimental programs. Involuntary assignments outside of a teacher's tenure area for more than 40 percent of his or her time is prohibited (8 NYCRR § 30.9(b)).

8:35. What certification is required for teachers in a middle school?

Certification regulations pose problems for educators in middle schools because teachers' certificates are issued either for prekindergarten through sixth grade (elementary) or seventh through 12th grade (secondary). Thus, grade-level organizational patterns that combine students from both traditional elementary and secondary levels create situations that require variances from the standard certification categories. For this reason, the commissioner's regulations provide for an extension of certificate validity to meet the needs of experimentation in grade-level organization (8 NYCRR § 80.2(h)).

However, it should be noted that the commissioner's regulations do not provide for an extension of the tenure areas in experimental programs. Involuntary assignments outside of a teacher's tenure area for more than 40 percent of his or her time is prohibited (8 NYCRR § 30.9(b)).

A school district must apply for approval for an experiment in school organization where a teacher's certification must be extended to additional grade levels. The commissioner of education is authorized to grant approval to the district to employ a certified teacher in any teaching assignment within the scope of the experiment for a five-year period. The district must declare the teacher is qualified by education and experience for the position. Additionally, the experiment with grade-level organization must include procedures for evaluation of the program and must meet the approval of the school board and the commissioner.

The extension of teacher certification validity to additional grades may be renewed for additional five-year periods upon submission of evidence of instructional benefit to students to the commissioner of education.

8:36. Do state certification requirements apply to teachers in private and parochial schools of New York State?

No. They apply only to teachers in public schools (§ 3001).

8:37. What is a temporary license?

A *temporary license* is issued to a school district to legalize the employment of uncertified teachers (§ 3006; 8 NYCRR § 80.18; see **8:3**). It is granted only when the district is unable to employ a certified and qualified teacher for the position in question, despite extensive recruitment (8 NYCRR § 80.18(a)(1)). To obtain a temporary license, a district must submit to the State Education Department an application that describes, among other things, the justification for issuing the license, the qualifications of the prospective teacher and the district's plans to supervise the uncertified teacher (8 NYCRR § 80.18(a)(2)).

No uncertified person may receive more than four temporary licenses unless such person is making substantial progress toward certification following initial employment (8 NYCRR § 80.18(h)). They also must have the requisite undergraduate degree required by the regulations and be given the assistance and support of a mentor teacher permanently certified in that subject. Finally, they must be matriculated in a college program to fulfill the certificate requirements (8 NYCRR § 80.18 (a)(2)(iii)).

8:38. What rules apply to student teachers?

Students enrolled in a teachers' education program may teach a class without the presence of a certified teacher in the classroom, provided the classroom teacher is available at all times and retains supervision of the student teacher. However, the number of certified teachers employed in the district must not be reduced because of the presence of student teachers (§ 3001).

8:39. Must substitute teachers have a New York State teaching certificate?

Not always. There are three types of substitute teachers: those with certification or certificates of qualification; those without certification, who are completing college study at the rate of at least six semester hours annually; and those without certification who are not working toward certification. Substitutes may be employed on an itinerant, per diem basis on the occasional days when a teacher calls in sick, or on a regular basis when a teacher is absent for an extended period of time but will return at the end of a planned leave (8 NYCRR § 80.36).

Uncertified individuals who are not working toward certification may be employed legally on an itinerant basis for not more than 40 days in any one school year. This means public schools are free to use someone who is not certified as an itinerant substitute. This same uncertified person likewise could be employed for 40 days the following year (8 NYCRR § 80.36(c)(3)).

An uncertified individual who is attending college to become eligible for certification may be employed on either an itinerant or a regular basis. No limitations are placed on the number of days a district can employ this person; however, if the teacher serves as a regular substitute, he or she must be employed in an area where he or she is seeking certification (8 NYCRR § 80.36(c)(2)).

A certified teacher or a person with a certificate of qualification may serve as a substitute in any capacity for any length of time (8 NYCRR § 80.36(c)(1)). However, if employed as a regular substitute, the teacher must be employed in the area of certification. Thus, a district may use a teacher who is certified in one area to serve as an itinerant substitute teacher in another. For example, a teacher certified in high school business education could teach as an itinerant substitute in the elementary grades (8 NYCRR § 80.36(c)).

8:40. Must a teaching assistant be certified?

Yes. A teaching assistant must possess either a temporary license or a continuing certificate (8 NYCRR § 80.33(b)(3)). A high school graduate who has training and experience appropriate for the position is eligible for a temporary license. The temporary license is valid for one year and may be renewed once (8 NYCRR § 80.33(b)(3)(i)). A continuing certificate remains valid continuously, except when the person does not remain continuously employed as a teaching assistant in a New York State public school for a period of five consecutive years, the certificate lapses. An applicant for a continuing certificate must have completed six college credits in the field of education and one year of experience as a licensed teaching assistant or as a certified teacher in order to be eligible (8 NYCRR § 80.33(b)(3)(ii)).

A teaching assistant must serve under the general supervision of a licensed or certified teacher and may perform the following functions:

- Work with individual students or groups of students on special instructional projects.
- Provide the teacher with general information about students to aid the teacher in the development of appropriate learning experience.
- Assist students in the use of instructional resources and assist in the development of instructional materials.
- Utilize his or her own special skills and abilities in such areas as foreign language, arts, crafts, music and similar subjects.
- Assist in related instructional work as required (8 NYCRR § 80.33(b)(2)).

8:41. Must teachers' aides be certified?

No. Individuals appointed to teacher's aide positions are governed by civil service rules and regulations. They are classified in the noncompetitive class of the civil service (*Appeal of Latorre*, 27 Educ. Dep't Rep. 366 (1988)).

A teacher's aide assists in noninstructional duties such as managing records, materials and equipment; attending to the physical needs of students; supervising students; and performing other services under the supervision of a teacher (8 NYCRR § 80.33(a)).

8:42. Is a teacher's certificate required to coach interscholastic sports?

In most instances, a coach must be a certified teacher. A certified physical education teacher may coach any sport in any school. A teacher certified in an area other than physical education may coach any sport in any school, provided he or she has been trained in first aid; completes an education program for coaches within three years of appointment; completes an approved child abuse identification and reporting workshop within one year and an approved course in philosophy, principles and organization of athletics within two years after initial appointment (§ 3004(2); 8 NYCRR § 135.4(c)(7)).

A school district may employ an uncertified person as a temporary coach only when there are no certified teachers with coaching qualifications and experience available. However, this does not mean, according to the commissioner, that a school board can hire a person without a temporary coaching license over a certified teacher solely because of that teacher's unsuccessful coaching record (*Appeal of Canastota CSD*, 36 Educ. Dep't Rep. 508 (1997)).

An uncertified person must obtain a temporary coaching license from the commissioner of education, must be trained in first aid, and have coaching qualifications and experience which satisfy the school board. Although not specifically required by statute or regulation, the State Education Department also requires uncertified individuals who apply for a temporary coaching license to complete a workshop in the identification and reporting of child abuse and maltreatment.

The temporary license is valid for one year but may be renewed once upon the enrollment in or completion of an approved course in philosophy, principles and organization of athletics, and renewed subsequently upon completion of an education program for coaches (8 NYCRR § 135.4(c)(7)(i)(c)(3)).

All coaches must hold valid certification in first aid or meet equivalent requirements of the commissioner of education. This must include instruction in the administration of adult cardiopulmonary resuscitation (CPR). In addition, prior to the beginning of each sports season, coaches must provide valid evidence to the superintendent that their first aid and adult CPR knowledge and skills are current under the requirements established by the American Red Cross or equivalent requirements certified by the commissioner of education (§ 3001–b; 8 NYCRR § 135.5).

8:43. Must school administrators, guidance counselors, school psychologists and school librarians be certified?

Yes. The commissioner of education issues certificates for those in pupil personnel service, such as school psychologists and guidance counselors (8 NYCRR § 80.3); for those in administrative and supervisory service, such as school administrators (8 NYCRR § 80.4; see **7:2**); and for school media specialists, such as school librarians (8 NYCRR § 80.8). Only fully certified persons can be employed in these areas. However, school district administrators, such as superintendents, may be employed without certification through the exceptionally qualified person procedure (§ 3003(3); 8 NYCRR § 80.4; see also **7:3**).

8:44. May a certified teacher employed by a public school teach outside his or her certification area in that school?

Ordinarily, no. However, a superintendent of schools, with the approval of the commissioner of education, may assign a teacher to instruct a subject outside his or her certification area for no more than five classroom hours a week, when no certified or qualified teacher is available for the position, despite extensive recruitment efforts (8 NYCRR § 80.2(c)). This commonly is referred to as *incidental teaching*. The commissioner's approval must be sought in accordance with the requirements in section 80.2(c) of the commissioner's regulations.

The commissioner's regulations authorize school boards, for the school years 1997-98 and 1998-99 to assign a teacher to instruct a subject for no more than five classroom hours a week outside his or her certification area without obtaining prior approval of the commissioner of education (8 NYCRR § 80.2(c)(7)). In order to do this, the superintendent must:

• Determine that the teacher being assigned on an incidental basis has sufficient teaching experience and knowledge of the subject to teach it in a competent manner.
• Submit a list of all teachers assigned on an incidental basis, including the course assigned and the certification area of the teacher so assigned, to the school board at a public meeting by October 1 of each year, or at the next regularly scheduled public board meeting for assignments made after October 1.
• Submit the same list to the State Education Department.

In addition, the school district must establish a policy on incidental teaching that provides a process for informing parents about incidental teaching assignments and a process allowing parents to appeal the assignment (8 NYCRR § 80.2(c)(7)(iii)).

8:45. Is a teacher who is certified in New York State also certified to teach in other states?

Not automatically. However, New York State has entered into a joint agreement with nine northeast certifying jurisdictions which establishes a Northeast Regional Credential that allows a teacher certified in any of the participating jurisdictions to teach in the area of certification in another of these states (8 NYCRR § 80.2(s)). Regional credentials are valid for two years, except in Maine, where they are good for one year, and the teacher must take all necessary steps to qualify for certification in the new state within that time. Besides New York, northeast regional credentials are valid in Connecticut, the District of Columbia, Maine, Massachusetts, New Hampshire, Rhode Island, Pennsylvania and Vermont.

In addition, if a teacher has at least three years of experience in New York State or is a graduate of an approved course of study, he or she may qualify for a license from certain states that participate with New York in the Interstate Agreement on Qualification of Educational Personnel (§ 3030).

For more information, write to the New York State Education Department, Office of Teaching, Albany, N.Y. 12334, or check the Office of Teaching's World Wide Web site: http://www.nysed.gov/tcert/homepage.htm.

8:46. How are exchange teachers certified in New York State?

An exchange teacher from a foreign country whose qualifications are approved by the commissioner of education will be issued a two-year permit, at no cost, that will qualify that person to teach (§ 3005). Approval of the exchange teacher's qualifications will be based on that teacher's application for certification, which identifies the position to be filled and the education completed by that teacher. The citizenship of the foreign teacher would not bar him or her from certification for this purpose (see **8:4**).

8:47. Who enforces the teacher certification law?

It is the State Education Department's (SED) responsibility to enforce the law and regulations concerning teacher certification. SED's Office of Teaching, with assistance from superintendents and district superintendents, oversees compliance with these rules.

When matters arise that cast doubt on an applicant's or a teacher's moral character, and may warrant suspension or revocation of his or her certification, hearings are held under Part 83 of the commissioner's regulations (see **8:48-52**). This type of investigation of moral character to determine fitness for certification is different from discipline by an employing district under section 3020–a of the Education Law (see **8:104-120**).

8:48. May a teacher's certificate be revoked or suspended?

Yes. The commissioner of education is authorized to revoke, or where appropriate suspend, a teacher's certification after a hearing where it has been determined that the teacher lacks good moral character (§ 305(7); 8 NYCRR §§ 83.4; 83.5(c)).

Additionally, although this authority is seldom used, a district (BOCES) superintendent may revoke a teacher's certificate, following a hearing, for lack of good moral character (§ 3018).

8:49. Does a teacher's conviction of a crime constitute grounds for automatic revocation of his or her certification?

No. However, a conviction of drug-related crimes, crimes involving the physical or sexual abuse of minors or students, or crimes committed while on school property or while in the performance of teaching duties creates a "rebuttable presumption" that the teacher lacks the necessary good moral character to retain a teaching certificate (8 NYCRR § 83.4(d)). In other words, after the state has introduced evidence of a teacher's conviction of one of these crimes at a hearing, the teacher must demonstrate that he or she continues to have a good moral character in order to keep his or her license to teach.

8:50. What are some other potential grounds for revoking a teacher's certification?

A teacher's failure to complete a contract of employment for a school year without good reason may be sufficient grounds for the revocation of his or her certificate (§ 3019). In addition, a teacher must give written notice to the school district of his or her intention to resign at least 30 days prior to the termination date (§ 3019–a).

8:51. How are teacher certification hearings commenced?

The school superintendent must, and other individuals may, refer information of a criminal conviction or other act that raises a reasonable question as to the moral character of a certified teacher to the professional conduct officer of the State Education Department (SED). The state must review the findings and recommendations of 3020-a hearing officers or panels to consider whether or not teachers subject to such local disciplinary charges should retain their teaching certificates (8 NYCRR § 83.1).

Any individual may refer information of a criminal conviction or other act that raises a reasonable question as to the moral character of an applicant for teacher's certification to the executive coordinator for the teaching professions (8 NYCRR § 83.1(c)).

Once information is referred to SED, the professional conduct officer then conducts an investigation and reports the findings from the investigation and recommendations for action to the Teacher Professional Standards and Practices Board or a subcommittee of that body (8 NYCRR § 83.2). The board or subcommittee reviews the case to determine whether a substantial question about the moral character of the certified teacher or applicant exists and notifies the teacher of its decision (8 NYCRR § 83.3). If the board or subcommittee finds that a substantial question does exist, the teacher or applicant is entitled to request a hearing before either a hearing officer or a hearing officer and three panel members selected from the section 3020–a list maintained by the commissioner (8 NYCRR § 83.4(a)).

8:52. What are the procedures at hearings to revoke or suspend a teacher's certification for lack of good moral character?

Although both the commissioner of education and district (BOCES) superintendents are vested with the statutory authority to revoke a teacher's certification (see **8:48**), the procedures generally followed are in Part 83 of the commissioner's regulations (§§ 305(7); 3018; 8 NYCRR § 83).

The Office of Teaching must prove at a hearing that the teacher or applicant lacks good moral character. The teacher or applicant is entitled to be represented by an attorney at the hearing and may call witnesses and introduce other evidence of his or her good moral character. The hearing officer may issue subpoenas at the request of a party.

At the end of the hearing, the hearing officer or hearing panel issues a decision on whether the teacher's certification should be revoked or suspended or whether an applicant's request for certification should be denied. The hearing officer must notify the commissioner and the teacher or applicant, who may appeal the decision to the commissioner within 30 days. The commissioner is authorized to appeal only in cases involving a teacher convicted of drug-related crimes, crimes involving the physical or sexual abuse of minors or students, or crimes committed while on school property or while in the performance of teaching duties (8 NYCRR § 83.5).

8:53. Where can additional information about teacher certification be obtained?

Additional information about teacher certification is available from the State Education Department, Office of Teaching, Albany, N.Y. 12234; telephone 518-474-3901, or on the Office of Teaching's World Wide Web site: http://www.nysed.gov/tcert/homepage.htm.

Tenure and Tenure Areas

8:54. What is tenure?

Tenure is an employment status a teacher may earn by successfully completing a period of probationary employment and then, upon the superintendent's recommendation, being granted this status by the school board (§§ 2509; 2573; 3012; 3014). A teacher who has received tenure has earned the right to keep his or her job; in other words, to be free from discipline or dismissal, except for just cause to be proven by school officials in a due process hearing under section 3020-a of the Education Law.

A teacher's tenure status will not be affected by accepting a part-time position with the district (*Tadken v. Board of Education*, 65 A.D.2d 820 (2nd Dep't 1978)). However, upon submission of a resignation, a teacher relinquishes any tenure or seniority rights even if the teacher subsequently accepts a part-time position (*Matter of Middleton*, 16 Educ. Dep't Rep. 50 (1976).

8:55. Are teachers employed by a board of cooperative educational services (BOCES) eligible for tenure?

Yes. Probationary appointments and tenure at a BOCES are provided for by section 3014 of the Education Law.

8:56. May a teacher transfer his or her tenure when accepting a position in a different school district?

No. Tenure is not transferrable from one school district to another. Each school district is independent, and a teacher must serve a new probationary period whenever he or she moves to a different school district. However, a teacher who has acquired tenure in one district or BOCES in New York State and moves to another district or BOCES serves a probationary period of two years rather than the usual three (§§ 3012; 3014). Teachers who are transferred to a different school within the same district do not lose any tenure rights within that district.

Teachers who are transferred as a result of a BOCES takeover of services or a district takeover of BOCES services are entitled to full recognition of the tenure rights they previously held (§§ 3014-a; 3014-b). A comparable provision applies when teachers are transferred because a school district takes tuitioned-out students from another district or takes back students who were previously tuitioned out (§§ 3014-c; 3014-d).

8:57. What is the difference between tenure and tenure areas?

Tenure is a classification of employment granted to teachers who have completed a probationary period of satisfactory service with a school district (see **8:54**). *Tenure areas* are subject areas of teaching positions that are established by the Board of Regents (see **8:58**).

Teachers are granted tenure in the specific tenure areas established by the Board of Regents.

8:58. What is the legal definition of a tenure area?

A *tenure area* is defined as "the administrative subdivision within the organizational structure of a school district in which a professional educator is deemed to serve" (8 NYCRR § 30.1(h)). When a teacher is hired for a teaching position, he or she is appointed to a position in one of the tenure areas, or subject areas, established by law (8 NYCRR § 30.2).

Part 30 of the Rules of the Board of Regents establishes the various "vertical" or subject tenure areas that must be used for teachers hired after August 1, 1975. The tenure areas under Part 30 include, for example, elementary education, mathematics, English, science and art.

Teachers who were hired before August 1, 1975 are governed by the old tenure areas that were established by each district before the enactment of Part 30 (*Baer v. Nyquist*, 34 N.Y.2d 291 (1974)). Tenure areas often were established by grade level and not by subject area under this "horizontal" system, where, for example, an English teacher and a science teacher teaching at the secondary grade level may be in the same tenure area.

As a result of this, a dual system of tenure areas will exist for many years, with one set of tenure area rules applying to persons appointed before August 1, 1975 and another set of rules governing those appointed after that date (*Rippe v. Board of Educ.*, 64 N.Y.2d 281 (1985); *Matter of Platania*, 20 Educ. Dep't Rep. 670 (1981)).

8:59. What tenure areas are recognized by part 30 of the Rules of the Board of Regents?

The tenure areas for teachers hired after August 1, 1975 include elementary, middle grades, academic and special subject areas (8 NYCRR §§ 30.5; 30.6; 30.7; 30.8). The *elementary tenure area* encompasses prekindergarten through sixth grade (8 NYCRR § 30.5). The *middle grades tenure area* applies when the instruction of seventh and eighth grades is not departmentalized by academic area (8 NYCRR § 30.6).

Teachers at or above the seventh-grade level, where instruction in the core academic subjects is departmentalized, are placed into the *academic tenure areas* of English, social studies, mathematics, science and foreign languages (8 NYCRR § 30.7). *Special subject tenure areas* encompass 15 academic areas, six career education subject areas, nine supportive educational services, and one teaching assistant area (8 NYCRR § 30.8; see **8:60**).

These tenure areas apply to all school districts except those in the cities of New York and Buffalo or to those employing fewer than eight teachers. They are not retroactive and apply only to teachers appointed to probationary teaching positions on or after August 1, 1975 (8 NYCRR § 30.2).

The commissioner of education has ruled that districts may only appoint teachers to those tenure areas designated in Part 30 and may not create new tenure areas for teaching positions, such as a gifted and talented teacher, that do not easily fit within those areas (*Appeal of Bales*,

32 Educ. Dep't Rep. 559 (1993)). If a district should appoint a teacher to an unauthorized tenure area, the teacher will be deemed to actually serve within the authorized tenure area which encompasses the teacher's actual duties *(Abrantes v. Bd. of Educ. of the Norwood-Norfolk CSD*, 233 A.D.2d 718, *appeal denied*, 89 N.Y.2d 812 (1997); *Herbert-Glover v. Board of Educ. of Wantagh UFSD*, 213 A.D.2d 404 (2nd Dep't 1995); *Appeal of Lessing*, 34 Educ. Dep't Rep. 451 (1995)).

8:60. What are special subject tenure areas under Part 30 of the Rules of the Board of Regents?

Special subject tenure areas are specific topical areas the Regents have designated as being tenure areas. There are four general types of special-subject tenure areas: academic areas, career education subject areas, supportive educational services, and a teaching assistant area.

The *academic areas* include such subjects as art, music, driver education, business education, health, home economics, industrial arts, physical education, remedial reading, remedial speech, English as a second language, and four branches of education for the disabled (8 NYCRR § 30.8(a)).

Career education subject areas in which the tenure area is coextensive with the certification possessed by the teacher, such as, for example, agriculture, health occupations, home economics, technical subjects and trade subjects, are also special subject tenure areas (8 NYCRR § 30.8(c)).

Positions in *supportive educational services* include guidance counselor, school media specialist, school library media specialist, school education communications media specialist, school psychologist, school social worker, school nurse teacher, school dental hygienist and school attendance teacher (8 NYCRR § 30.8(b)).

8:61. What tenure areas are recognized under the horizontal tenure practices?

Teachers hired before August 1, 1975 are subject to the old horizontal tenure areas plus several special subject areas *(Baer v. Nyquist*, 34 N.Y.2d 291 (1974)). Those teachers who serve at a given horizontal level, such as elementary, middle school, junior high or high school, frequently serve in a single grade-level tenure area, regardless of the subject they teach (such as English, mathematics, social studies, science and foreign languages). The courts and the commissioner of education also have recognized certain permissible special subject tenure areas for teachers hired before August 1, 1975 such as guidance counselor *(Steele v. Board of Education*, 40 N.Y.2d 456 (1976); *Matter of Glowacki*, 14 Educ. Dep't Rep. 122 (1974)) and music and physical education (*Baer v. Nyquist*).

Part 30 of the Rules of the Board of Regents may be used as a guideline in determining whether a subject may be considered a traditional special subject tenure area under horizontal tenure practices *(Steele v. Board of Education; Mitchell v. Board of Education,* 40 N.Y.2d 904 (1976)). In a case where it is unclear whether a teacher has served in a separate tenure area, resolution of the dispute depends on whether the district has treated the subject as being separate (*Hicksville Congress of Teachers v. Hicksville UFSD,* 118 A.D.2d 623 (2nd Dep't 1986)). Separate tenure areas may have been created by school policy, board resolution or regulation (*Matter of Muzante,* 16 Educ. Dep't Rep. 149 (1976)), as well as by tenure appointment resolutions, schedules of appointment or employment records (*Matter of Zappulla,* 25 Educ. Dep't Rep. 54 (1985); *Matter of Platania,* 20 Educ. Dep't Rep. 670 (1981)).

Teachers and administrators must be notified that they are serving in a separate tenure area (*Waiters v. Board of Education,* 46 N.Y.2d 885 (1979); *Mitchell v. Board of Education*). When a district creates a separate tenure area, it cannot affect a teacher's seniority rights by eliminating that tenure area from the tenure structure (*Baer v. Nyquist*).

8:62. May a teacher with tenure or in a probationary status be transferred to a position in a different tenure area?

A teacher with tenure or in a probationary status may not be assigned without his or her consent to devote a substantial portion of his or her time outside his or her existing tenure area (8 NYCRR § 30.9(b); *Matter of Zamek,* 19 Educ. Dep't Rep. 77 (1979)). If transferred to a new tenure area with the teacher's consent, the teacher begins a new probationary period in a new tenure area (8 NYCRR § 30.9(d)). However, the teacher does not lose any previously earned tenure or seniority in the former area.

The general rule is that if a teacher is transferred to service in another tenure area without his or her consent, all service in that other area is deemed, as a matter of law, to constitute service for purposes of seniority in the teacher's prior tenure area *(Appeal of Lawrence,* 32 Educ. Dep't Rep. 398 (1992)).

However, the New York State Court of Appeals has ruled that a teacher who is transferred to another tenure area without his or her consent may knowingly and voluntarily waive his or her right to have his or her service in the later tenure area credited for purposes of seniority, in the teacher's prior tenure area. Under such circumstances, a district may grant seniority credit for such service to the teacher in the second tenure area *(Kaufman v. Fallsburg CSD,* 91 N.Y. 2d 57 (1997)).

A teacher who is certified in several subjects may be assigned to serve in another tenure area for less than 40 percent of the time without being deemed to work in a different tenure area (8 NYCRR §§ 30.1(g), 30.9(a); **8:63**).

8:63. May a teacher serve in more than one tenure area at the same time?
Yes. Under Part 30 of the commissioner's regulations, teachers are deemed to serve in any tenure area in which they spend at least 40 percent of their time. Teachers serving in more than one tenure area at the same time gain seniority credit under both tenure areas (8 NYCRR § 30.9(c)).

A teacher assigned to spend 40 percent or more of his or her time in a second tenure area may acquire tenure by estoppel (see **8:87**) in that area despite the district's failure to give him or her a formal probationary appointment *(Matter of Freeman v. Board of Educ.*, 205 A.D.2d 38 (2nd Dep't 1994)).

On the other hand, a teacher assigned to spend more than 40 percent of his or her time in a second area without the knowledge or consent of the district is not eligible for tenure. For example, in *Mack v. Board of Educ.*, 209 A.D.2d 416 (2nd Dep't 1994), a state Appellate Court ruled that a driver education teacher who had also taught physical education for 14 years had not acquired tenure because he had been assigned to that area by the director of health without the knowledge and consent of the district.

8:64. In what tenure areas do teachers who also perform administrative functions serve?
In determining whether particular employees serve in an administrative tenure area or a teacher tenure area, the courts and the commissioner of education have applied what is commonly known as the 50 percent rule: if at least 50 percent or more of an employee's duties are administrative in nature, he or she will be deemed to serve in an administrative tenure area *(Coates v. Ambach*, 52 A.D.2d 261, *aff'd,* 42 N.Y.2d 846 (1977); see **7:7**).

Prior to the enactment of Part 30, an individual who served in an administrative rather than a teacher tenure area under the 50 percent rule was not eligible for seniority credit in the teacher tenure area. Subsequent to the enactment of Part 30, however, teachers are deemed to serve in any tenure area in which they serve at least 40 percent of their time (see **8:63**; *Sapphire v. Board of Education*, 96 A.D.2d 1033 (2nd Dep't 1983)). Therefore, teachers serving in Part 30 tenure areas would be eligible to receive seniority credit in both the administrative and Part 30 teacher tenure areas under the 40 percent rule (see **8:63**). Accordingly, an employee who spends 45 percent of his or her time in a Part 30 tenure area and 55 percent of his or her time in an administrative tenure area may be entitled to seniority credit in both tenure areas.

8:65. What is the difference between tenure rights and seniority rights?

Tenure rights are those rights and privileges enjoyed by tenured teachers, the most important of which is the limitations surrounding employment disciplinary proceedings (see **8:104-106**).

Seniority rights are those rights to job security and priority based on appointment to a tenure area (see **8:88-94**). Seniority rights apply to both tenured and probationary teachers, while tenure rights apply only to tenured teachers. (For more information on seniority see **8:88-103**.)

8:66. Does a teacher acquire seniority in a definite subject or specific grade as a result of an appointment in a grade-level tenure area?

No. Staff assignments are within the discretion of the school authorities as long as the assignments are within the proper tenure area (*Mishkoff v. Nyquist*, 57 A.D.2d 649 (3rd Dep't 1977); *Matter of Gould*, 17 Educ. Dep't Rep. 283 (1978)).

Probationary Teachers and the Granting of Tenure

8:67. What is a probationary teacher?

A *probationary teacher* is a teacher employed by a school district during a period of probation, which usually lasts three years. The probationary appointment allows districts to evaluate the competency of a teacher prior to making an appointment to tenure (see **8:74**).

8:68. How are teachers appointed to probation?

Teachers are appointed to full-time teaching positions for a probationary period by majority vote of the school board upon recommendation of the superintendent of schools (§§ 2509; 2573; 3012(1)(a)).

For each probationary appointment, the board must indicate in its resolution the name of the appointee, the tenure area of the teaching position, the certification status of the teacher and the date of the beginning and end of the probationary appointment (8 NYCRR § 30.3).

Each tenure area that makes up 40 percent or more of a teacher's total instructional course load requires a separate probationary appointment (8 NYCRR § 30.9(c)). Thus, a teacher hired to divide his or her time equally between mathematics and science would need two separate probationary appointments. Likewise, a tenured teacher whose duties are reassigned to include instruction in a new tenure area for more than 40 percent of his or her work load is also entitled to a probationary appointment in the new tenure area (8 NYCRR § 30.9(d)).

Even in the absence of a probationary appointment, if a teacher is serving 40 percent or more of his or her time in multiple separate tenure areas, the teacher is deemed as having received a probationary appointment in each such area, notwithstanding the absence of a formal probationary appointment (*Freeman v. Bd. of Educ.*, 205 A.D.2d 38 (2nd Dep't 1994)).

8:69. How is a teacher informed of a probationary appointment?

Usually the district sends a letter or a notice to the teacher, which indicates the appointment, the duration of the probationary period and the salary that is sufficient to inform a teacher of a probationary appointment. The teacher should acknowledge the receipt of the notice and accept or reject the appointment.

Both the courts and the commissioner of education have emphasized the importance of clear and explicit notice to both probationary and tenured employees of the tenure area to which they have been appointed. Teachers must be alerted sufficiently when they are entering a different tenure area by board action (*Mitchell v. Board of Education*, 40 N.Y.2d 904 (1976); *Matter of Keeney*, 17 Educ. Dep't Rep. 314 (1978)).

8:70. Are contracts with individual teachers used to employ probationary teachers?

Because probationary teachers are appointed by the school board, a contract of employment technically is not required. However, most districts enter into collective bargaining agreements with teachers, including probationary teachers, which describe the terms and conditions of employment (see **10:1-5**).

8:71. What type of teaching position requires a probationary appointment?

A probationary appointment must be made when filling any vacant, unencumbered, full-time teaching position. There is no legal authority for a temporary appointment to evade the provisions of the tenure laws (*Board of Education of Oneida CSD v. Nyquist*, 59 A.D.2d 76 (3rd Dep't 1977), *rev'd*, 45 N.Y.2d 975 (1978)). Additionally, a school district may not assign substitute teachers to temporarily fill vacant positions, even during the pendency of negotiations over the possible transfer of the duties of the vacant positions (*DiPiazza v. Board of Educ.*, 214 A.D.2d 729 (1995)).

When a teacher is granted a leave of absence, the position is encumbered by that leave and is not considered vacant (*Brewer v. Board of Education*, 51 N.Y.2d 855 (1980)). Thus, a vacancy is not created when the district contracts with a regular substitute teacher, even when the incumbent resigns before the leave has ended (*Eisenstadt v. Ambach*, 79 A.D.2d 839 (3rd Dep't 1980)).

8:72. May a prospective teacher waive his or her right to a probationary appointment in a tenure-bearing position?

Yes, under certain circumstances. The New York State Court of Appeals has held that a teacher's right to receive a probationary appointment and consideration for tenure may be waived through an agreement in certain cases. A teacher can be held to the terms of such waiver only as long as he or she freely, knowingly and voluntarily accepts them (*Feinerman v. Board of Cooperative Educational Services*, 48 N.Y.2d 491 (1979); *Yastion v. Mills*, 229 A.D.2d 775 (3rd Dep't, 1996)).

However, some courts have ruled that a district may not require all prospective teachers in a district to sign a waiver of their tenure rights as a condition to being hired by the district (*Costello v. Bd. of Educ. of East Islip*, 673 N.Y.S. 2d 468 (2nd Dep't 1998); *Lambert v. Middle Country CSD*, 174 Misc. 2d 487 (Sup. Ct., Nassau County 1997)).

8:73. Do part-time teachers receive probationary appointments?

Normally, part-time teachers do not receive probationary appointments or credit toward tenure (*Ceparano v. Ambach*, 53 N.Y.2d 873 (1981)). A school board may, however, extend credit to a part-time teacher either by a board resolution (*Moritz v. Board of Education*, 60 A.D.2d 161 (4th Dep't 1977)) or by a provision in a collective bargaining agreement (*Schlosser v. Board of Education*, 62 A.D.2d 207, *aff'd*, 47 N.Y.2d 811 (1979)).

The one exception to the general rule is kindergarten teaching, where the commissioner of education has construed the tenure statutes as encompassing both full-time (two sessions) and part-time (one session) positions (*Ablondi v. Commissioner of Education*, 54 A.D.2d 507 (3rd Dep't 1976); *Matter of Clark*, 17 Educ. Dep't Rep. 311 (1978)). Consequently, even where a district uses a combination of full-time and part-time teachers to meet its kindergarten needs, the part-time teachers still will receive credit toward tenure.

8:74. What is the length of the probationary period?

The probationary period is three years for most teachers (§§ 2509(1)(a); 2573(1)(a); 3012(1)(a); 3014(1)(a)). However, there are two exceptions to the general rule. First, a teacher who has received tenure in another school district or BOCES, or in another tenure area within the same district or

BOCES, is entitled to a shortened two-year probationary period (§§ 2509(1)(a); 2573(1)(a); 3012(1)(a); 3014(1)(a)).

Second, a teacher who serves as a regular substitute for one or more semesters immediately preceding an appointment to a probationary position in the same tenure area is entitled to have up to two years of the prior substitute service applied toward completion of the probationary period (§ 2509(1)(a); *Robins v. Blaney*, 59 N.Y.2d 393 (1983); *Appeal of Negii*, 19 Educ. Dep't Rep. 35 (1979)). This exception is sometimes referred to as *Jarema credit.* (See **8:92**; for information on Jarema credit for probationary administrators, see **7:8**.) A school district is only required to grant Jarema credit to an individual who is employed as a regular substitute for a full semester or more. Where the period of service as a regular substitute is for less than a full semester, the individual is not entitled to any credit toward his or her probationary period (*Lifson v. Board of Education of the Nanuet Public Schools*, 109 A.D.2d 743 (2nd Dep't 1985), *aff'd,* 66 N.Y.2d 896 (1985); *Appeal of Czajkowski,* 34 Educ. Dep't Rep. 589 (1995)).

The two exceptions cannot be combined to allow a teacher who previously held tenure and two years of substitute service to earn tenure without completing an additional probationary period (*Carpenter v. Board of Education,* 71 N.Y.2d 832 (1988)). A teacher with prior tenure and substitute service would therefore get the benefit of whichever exception would provide the most credit, but not both.

Part-time service does not count as part of the probationary period toward tenure (*Appeal of Mau,* 35 Educ. Dep't Rep. 275 (1996)).

8:75. What is the definition of "regular substitute" for purposes of determining Jarema credit?

There is no definition provided within the law. However, the New York State Court of Appeals has ruled that the term is defined by the actual nature and continuity of the substitute service, not by the anticipated duration of the replaced teacher's absence. In one case, a teacher who served as a "per diem substitute" in place of another teacher on leave for an indefinite time, and who taught continuously every school day for at least one full semester before her formal appointment to a probationary term, was entitled to Jarema credit for that time period (*Speichler v. Board of Cooperative Educational Services, Second Supervisory District,* 90 N.Y.2d 110 (1997)).

In another case, a teacher who served as a "permanent" substitute, but served all of the functions of a "regular" substitute was entitled to Jarema credit (*Hudson v. Bd. of Educ. of the Hempstead Public School District* (Sup. Ct., Nassau County, 1997)).

8:76. Can a teacher be granted tenure prior to the expiration of the probationary period?

Yes, although it is not clear exactly how much before the expiration of the probationary period it is permissible to grant tenure. In *Weinbrown v. Board of Education*, 28 N.Y.2d 474 (1971), the New York State Court of Appeals ruled a school district could offer tenure to a teacher in the spring immediately preceding the expiration of the probationary period. In that case, the court found that since school districts must make tenure decisions at least 60 days prior to the expiration of the probationary period, there was "no purpose in requiring the district to withhold its favorable determinations until the last day."

The commissioner of education, on the other hand, ruled that a school board can confer early tenure in a case where the employee had only served two out of three years in the probationary period at the time tenure was granted (*Appeal of Sullivan*, 33 Educ. Dep't Rep. 566 (1994)). However, this decision contradicts an earlier opinion of the Westchester County Supreme Court, which had found that public policy, as embodied in section 3012 of the Education Law, precluded a school district from conferring tenure after two years (*Matter of Altamura*, Sup. Ct. Westchester County, Pirro, J.S.C. (Dec. 30, 1992)).

8:77. May the district and a teacher agree to extend a probationary appointment for an additional year?

Yes. A district and a teacher may enter into an agreement to extend a probationary appointment for an additional year when the teacher will not be recommended for tenure (*Juul v. Board of Educ. of Hempstead UFSD*, 76 A.D.2d 837 (2nd Dep't 1980), *aff'd*, 55 N.Y.2d 648 (1981)). Under such an agreement, called a *Juul agreement*, the district waives its right to dismiss the teacher at the end of the probationary period, and the teacher waives any claim of tenure by estoppel (see also **8:87**). The teacher is given a second chance to prove his or her worth and the district is free to grant or withhold tenure at the end of the fourth year (see *Appeal of Fink*, 33 Educ. Dep't Rep. 340 (1993)). Juul agreements are valid as long as they are entered into freely, with full knowledge of their consequences.

In addition, a district can enter into a collective bargaining agreement that permits an arbitrator to review procedural aspects of the tenure determination, but not a substantive review of the board's decision (*Vestal CSD v. Vestal Teachers Ass'n*, 60 A.D.2d 720 (3rd Dep't 1977), *aff'd*, 46 N.Y.2d 746 (1978); *Board of Education v. Elwood Teachers' Alliance*, 94 A.D.2d 692 (2nd Dep't 1983)).

8:78. Can a school district dismiss a teacher during his or her probationary period?

Yes. A teacher's probationary appointment may be terminated at any time on the recommendation of the superintendent, provided the dismissal is approved by a majority vote of the school board (§§ 2509(1)(a); 2573(1)(a); 3012(1); 3014(1)(a)). However, a teacher cannot be terminated for an illegal or unconstitutional reason. Although the law does not require a hearing to effect a termination, the district must meet certain notice requirements in order to fire a teacher during his or her probationary period (§ 3019-a).

Some collective bargaining agreements place further restrictions on the discharge of probationary teachers. Therefore, school officials should refer to those agreements before taking action against a probationary teacher.

8:79. What notice must be given to a probationary teacher who is dismissed during his or her probationary period?

The superintendent of schools must give the probationary teacher notice that he or she will be recommending to the board that the teacher be dismissed at least 30 days prior to the board meeting at which such recommendation will be considered (§ 3031).

In all districts except New York City, if requested by the teacher no later than 21 days before the board meeting at which the recommendation will be considered, the superintendent of schools must provide the reason(s) for the proposed dismissal recommendation within seven days after the request. The teacher may file a written response with the clerk of the board seven days before the board meets to consider the recommendation for dismissal (§ 3031).

The law does not require that the teacher be given an opportunity to speak or present evidence at the board meeting. Failure to provide the requisite notice under section 3031 does not entitle the teacher to automatic reinstatement or back pay. The remedy is for the board to reconsider the termination recommendation with proper notice to the teacher and an opportunity for him or her to respond (*Appeal of Gold*, 34 Educ. Dep't Rep. 372 (1995)).

If a majority of the board accepts the recommendation and votes to dismiss, the teacher must then be given a 30-day written notice of termination (§ 3019-a). Failure to provide the termination notice required by section 3019-a entitles a dismissed teacher to back pay and not reinstatement (*Appeal of Madden-Lynch*, 31 Educ. Dep't Rep. 411 (1992)). Back pay was not available, however, to a probationary teacher who was dismissed for lack of certification without proper notice because the Education Law precludes school districts from paying a teacher who is uncertified at the time of initial hiring (*Sullivan v. Windham-Ashland-Jewett CSD*, 212 A.D.2d 63 (3rd Dep't 1995)).

The two notification periods do not run concurrently (*Appeal of Madden-Lynch*).

8:80. Is a school district required to provide a terminated teacher with a name-clearing hearing?

A terminated teacher is not entitled to a name-clearing hearing unless the district's reasons for the termination have a stigmatizing affect upon the teacher and the district disseminates those reasons (*Appeal of Federico*, 35 Educ. Dep't Rep. 269 (1996)).

The United States Court of Appeals for the Second Circuit has ruled that a name-clearing hearing will be required when the reasons for termination "denigrate the employee's competence as a professional and impugn the employee's professional reputation in such a fashion as to effectively put a significant roadblock in that employee's continued ability to practice his or her profession."

According to the court, the disclosure requirement was met in this case when the reasons for termination were placed in the discharged employee's personnel file and were likely to be disclosed to prospective employers (*Donato v. Plainview-Old Bethpage CSD*, 96 F.3d 623 (2nd Cir.), *cert. denied*, 117 U.S. 1083 (1997)).

8:81. For what reasons may a probationary teacher be denied tenure?

Although a school district generally has the "unfettered right" to terminate probationary teachers and deny tenure, the denial of tenure is invalid if the reason for the termination is unconstitutional or in violation of the law (*James v. Board of Educ.*, 37 N.Y.2d 891 (1975)). Therefore, unless a teacher demonstrates that the reasons given for the denial of tenure lack a rational basis, the courts will not find the district acted in bad faith in denying tenure (*Matter of Altamura*, Sup. Ct. Westchester County, Pirro, J.S.C. (Dec. 30, 1992)).

In one case, the commissioner found a school district could deny tenure to a teacher who had been excessively absent, even though the absences did not exceed the number of sick days under the teachers' collective bargaining agreement (*Appeal of Toma*, 31 Educ. Dep't Rep. 477 (1992)).

A school district may not deny a teacher tenure based upon the school board's philosophical objection to the tenure system (*Conetta v. Board of Educ.*, 165 Misc.2d 329 (1995)). In addition, a school board member may not abstain from voting on whether to grant tenure to an employee based upon a philosophical objection to the state's tenure system (*Appeal of Craft & Dworkin*, 36 Educ. Dep't Rep. 314 (1997)).

8:82. What notice must be given to a probationary teacher who is being denied tenure?

The superintendent of schools must notify the teacher in writing at least 60 days prior to the expiration of the probationary period that an affirmative recommendation for appointment on tenure will not be made. Notice must also be given that the board of education will review the failure to recommend for appointment on tenure at a board meeting to be held at least 30 days after the notice is given. Both notices may be contained within the same written statement, or they may be transmitted separately (§§ 2509(1)(a); 2573(1)(a); 3012(2); 3031).

In all districts except New York City, if requested by the teacher no later than 21 days before the board meeting at which the recommendation will be considered, the school superintendent must provide the reason(s) for the recommendation to deny tenure in writing seven days after the request (§ 3031). The teacher may file a written response with the clerk seven days before the board meets to consider the recommendation for dismissal (§ 3031). The law does not require that the teacher be given an opportunity to speak or to present evidence at the board meeting.

If a district fails to provide the required notice for denial of tenure, the teacher is not entitled to automatic reinstatement or salary beyond the last day he or she rendered service. The remedy is for the board to reconsider the recommendation against tenure with notice to the teacher and an opportunity for him or her to respond (*Appeal of Gold*, 34 Educ. Dep't Rep. 372 (1995)).

In a case in which a district learned of inappropriate conduct by a probationary teacher 22 days before the end of the probationary period, the New York State Court of Appeals ruled the district could deny tenure to the teacher even though it was impossible for the district to comply with the notice requirements of section 2573(1) (*Tucker v. Community School Dist. No. 10*, 82 N.Y.2d 274 (1993)). However, the court did require the district to pay back wages to the teacher to ensure she had the required notice prior to termination.

A district need not provide such notices to part-time employees who are not eligible for tenure in the district (*Appeal of Longshore*, 32 Educ. Dep't Rep. 311 (1992)). The notice procedures also are not applicable in the case of probationary teachers who resign voluntarily to prevent any reference of the discharge in their personnel file (*Biegel v. Board of Educ.*, 211 A.D.2d 969 (3rd Dep't 1995)).

8:83. When is a decision to deny tenure final?

A superintendent's recommendation to deny tenure must be reviewed by the board of education (§ 3031). Except for instances in which the teacher acquires tenure by estoppel (see **8:87**), tenure may only be bestowed upon a teacher with the superintendent's affirmative recommendation to grant tenure and the school board's acceptance of that recommendation (§§ 3012(2); 2509(2)).

When a school board votes to deny a tenure appointment despite the superintendent's recommendation to grant tenure, such a vote is considered advisory in nature and the school board must reconsider the issue at a second meeting. At least 30 days before final consideration of the recommendation, the board must notify the teacher of its intention to deny tenure and the date of the board meeting when it will take final action. No later than 21 days before the board meeting, the teacher may request a written statement giving the board's reasons for denial which must be provided by the district within seven days of the request, and may file a written response with the district clerk seven days before the board meeting when final consideration will take place (§ 3031(b)).

8:84. Does a teacher who resigns rather than be denied tenure have any rights?

A teacher who resigns rather than be denied tenure may be eligible for unemployment insurance benefits. A New York State Appellate Court held that the teacher's "resignation" under such circumstances is not voluntary and therefore, he or she is eligible for unemployment benefits (*In re the Claim of Harp*, 202 A.D.2d 876 (3rd Dep't 1994)).

8:85. What is the procedure for granting a teacher tenure at the end of his or her probationary period?

Before the end of a teacher's probationary period, the superintendent recommends those teachers for tenure who are found competent, efficient and satisfactory. This recommendation is made in writing to the school board. The board may then appoint to tenure, by majority vote, any or all of the teachers recommended (§§ 2509(2); 3012(2)).

A tenure appointment must be considered separately for each tenure area that requires more than 40 percent of a teacher's instructional time (8 NYCRR § 30.9(c); see **8:63**). Thus, a teacher who had two probationary appointments in separate tenure areas may be granted tenure in one, both or neither.

8:86. Who has the final authority to appoint a teacher to tenure?

The school board by majority vote may appoint to tenure any or all of the persons recommended by the superintendent (§§ 2509(2); 3012(2)). Additionally, school boards, except for those in New York City and Buffalo, may reject any recommendation in favor of tenure from the superintendent and deny tenure despite that recommendation (§§ 2573(6); 3031); see *Caraballo v. Community School Board*, 49 N.Y.2d 488 (1980)).

However, the board has no power to make a tenure appointment without the recommendation of the superintendent (*Anderson v. Board of Education*, 46 A.D.2d 360 (2nd Dep't 1974); *Matter of Burke*, 11 Educ. Dep't Rep. 231 (1972)).

The power to grant or deny tenure may not be impaired by a collective bargaining agreement because the Education Law vests authority to make tenure decisions in the board of education (*Cohoes City School District v. Cohoes Teachers Association*, 40 N.Y.2d 774 (1976); see **10:37** regarding prohibited subjects of bargaining). However, an arbitrator may direct a school district to extend the probationary period of a teacher and to re-evaluate the teacher at the end of the extended probationary period (*Cohoes City School District*). The Public Employment Relations Board (PERB) has imposed similar orders (see *Sag Harbor UFSD*, 8 PERB ¶4524, *aff'd*, 54 A.D.2d 391 (3rd Dep't 1976)).

8:87. May a teacher be granted tenure in the absence of a school board's action?

Yes. Courts have granted tenure appointments to teachers when school boards do not act but allow the probationary period to expire while continuing the teachers' employment (*Lindsey v. Board of Education*, 72 A.D.2d 185 (4th Dep't 1980)). This is known as *tenure by estoppel* or *tenure by acquiescence*.

Tenure by estoppel or acquiescence will occur only when the district "with full knowledge and consent" allows the teacher to continue to teach after the probationary period has expired (*Lindsey*). In essence, tenure is imposed on the district because it acquiesced or consented to the employment of the teacher under conditions that implied the granting of tenure.

The New York State Court of Appeals ruled a school district must permit a tenured teacher to rescind her resignation when she resigned under the mistaken belief that she had not yet acquired tenure and was going to be denied tenure (*Gould v. Board of Educ.*, 81 N.Y.2d 446 (1993)). The teacher had obtained tenure by estoppel because her probationary period was two rather than three years and she was employed as a "probationary teacher" for three years because neither she nor the district had noticed that she was entitled to a shortened probationary period.

Seniority Rights and Excessing

8:88. What are seniority rights?

Seniority rights are those rights to job security and priority within a school district based on length of actual paid service in a specific tenure area. Seniority rights are different from tenure rights because they apply to both tenured and probationary teachers (see **8:65**).

The Education Law does not provide a definition of the term *seniority*, but it does require that seniority be used in determining the order in which teachers are dismissed in the event that teaching positions are abolished (§§ 2510(2); 2585(3); 3013(2)). Seniority is the sole criterion districts may use to decide which teacher will be excessed — tenured status may not be a consideration (*Matter of Fallick*, 18 Educ. Dep't Rep. 586 (1979), *aff'd*, Sup. Ct. Albany County, Hughes, J.S.C. (Feb. 11, 1980)). Likewise, certification may not be used as a factor in determining seniority (*Lynch v. Nyquist*, 41 A.D.2d 363, *aff'd*, 34 N.Y.2d 588 (1974); *Silver v. Board of Education*, 46 A.D.2d 427 (4th Dep't 1975)).

8:89. Can seniority rights be waived or altered by a written agreement?

Seniority rights may be waived but cannot be altered by a written agreement. In a case upheld by the Albany County Supreme Court, the commissioner of education ruled that a business education teacher was not entitled to continue to accrue seniority in a teaching tenure area while placed on special assignment in the district's business office, even though the district, the teachers' union and the teacher signed a written agreement that the teacher would continue to accrue such seniority (*Appeal of Tropia*, 32 Educ. Dep't Rep 606 (1993), *aff'd*, *Matter of Camden CSD*, Sup. Ct. Albany County, Keegan, J.S.C. (Jan. 11, 1994)).

Even though a school district cannot enter into an agreement to extend seniority rights, it can enter into an agreement whereby a teacher waives his or her seniority rights (*Matter of Cesaratto*, 17 Educ. Dep't Rep. 23 (1977)). A waiver is effective only if it is clearly evidenced and given with knowledge and consent (*Feinerman v. Board of Cooperative Educational Services*, 48 N.Y.2d 491 (1979); *Ambramovich v. Board of Education*, 46 N.Y.2d 450 (1979)).

8:90. How is seniority calculated?

The courts and the commissioner of education have defined seniority in terms of length of actual paid service within a tenure area to a school district (*Dreyfuss v. Board of Education*, 76 Misc. 2d 479 (1973), *aff'd*, 45 A.D.2d 988 (2nd Dep't 1974); *Matter of Halayko*, 23 Educ. Dep't Rep. 384 (1984)).

The first criterion for determining seniority is the actual full-time service rendered within the tenure area. If such full-time service is equal, the teachers' respective appointment dates are to be used for determining seniority. When two teachers have equal seniority and the same appointment date, a school district may use any reasonable method to establish seniority, including the dates on which an employment agreement was signed or returned, and the district may consider the salaries of the employees (*Matter of Sommers*, 19 Educ. Dep't Rep. 99 (1979); *Appeal of Kiernan*, 32 Educ. Dep't Rep. 618 (1993)).

School districts are required to comply with the requirements of section 30.1 (which is applicable to all probationary appointments made after August 1, 1975) which mandate that seniority "need not have been consecutive but shall, during each term for which seniority credit is sought, have constituted a substantial portion of the time of the professional educator" (i.e., equaling 40 percent or more of the total time spent by the professional educator in the performance of his or her duties (8 NYCRR § 30.1(f),(g)). Thus, the commissioner has held that years of regular full-time substitute teaching service, which was interrupted by periods of part-time substitute service and ultimately led to a probationary appointment should count for purposes of seniority by virtue of section 30.1(f) (*Appeal of Carey*, 31 Educ. Dep't Rep. 394 (1992)).

Days spent on unpaid leave of absence may not be included in determining seniority (*Matter of Halayko*). A district is not obliged to grant credit for interrupted service when the teacher has not obtained a leave of absence. However, a district may choose to grant credit for interrupted service pursuant to a collective bargaining agreement with its teachers (*Board of Education v. Lakeland Federation of Teachers*, 51 A.D.2d 1033 (2nd Dep't 1976)).

8:91. Do part-time teachers receive seniority credit for part-time service?

Generally, part-time service does not qualify a teacher for any seniority rights except in the case of part-time kindergarten teachers (see **8:73**). However, part-time service rendered after a full-time probationary appointment is included in calculation of seniority if the change in position is requested by the district (*Matter of Oursler*, 15 Educ. Dep't Rep. 258 (1975); *Matter of Blanchard*, 14 Educ. Dep't Rep. 260 (1975)), but not if the reduction to part-time status is at the request of the teacher. Seniority is "frozen" at this point (*Matter of Walsh*, 17 Educ. Dep't Rep. 434 (1978)). A collective bargaining agreement or board policy may oblige a school district to give seniority credit for part-time service (*Garcia v. Board of Education*, 100 A.D.2d 967 (2nd Dep't 1984); *Schlosser v. Board of Education*, 62 A.D.2d 207, *aff'd*, 47 N.Y.2d 811 (1979)).

A teacher who has served full time does not lose existing seniority upon accepting or requesting a part-time position with a school district (*Matter of Bellarosa*, 20 Educ. Dep't Rep. 252 (1980); *Matter of Walsh; Matter of Blanchard*).

8:92. Is service as a regular substitute teacher considered when calculating seniority?

Yes. Jarema credit, which reduces the probationary period of a teacher under certain circumstances, limits credit toward tenure for substitute service to two years (§§ 2509(1)(a); 2573(1)(a); 3012(1)(a); see **8:74**). However, no such limitation exists when calculating length of service for purposes of seniority. Thus, a teacher must be given seniority credit for regular substitute service rendered any time prior to a probationary appointment, even if the substitute service is longer than two years (*Kransdorf v. Board of Educ. of Northport-East Northport UFSD*, 81 N.Y.2d 871 (1993); *Appeal of Carey*, 31 Educ. Dep't Rep. 394 (1992)).

Despite contrary decisions in the past, the New York State Court of Appeals and the commissioner of education have ruled that the regular substitute service need not immediately precede the probationary appointment (*Kransdorf; Carey*).

8:93. What are a teacher's seniority rights when another school district or board of cooperative educational services (BOCES) takes over a program formerly provided by his or her employer?

A teacher who will be excessed because of a takeover by another school district or a BOCES must be employed by the district taking over the program (§§ 3014–a(1); 3014–b(1)). The teacher maintains the same tenure and seniority status he or she enjoyed before the takeover. The law applies to school district teachers when a program is contracted out to a BOCES and to BOCES teachers when a district no longer contracts for a program by a BOCES. The teacher may also be entitled to retain the salary step and sick days credited to him or her prior to the takeover (*Appeal of Adler*, 37 Educ. Dep't Rep. 95 (1997)).

The new program provider must continue the employment of the teachers of the former provider of the program (§§ 3014–a(1); 3014–b(1)). If the new program provider cannot employ all of the teachers, it must hire those teachers with the greatest seniority to fill the teaching positions for the program (§§ 3014–a(2); 3014–b(2); *Buenzow v. Lewiston-Porter CSD*, 101 A.D.2d 30 (4th Dep't 1984), *aff'd*, 64 N.Y.2d 676 (1984); *Acinapuro v. Board of Cooperative Educational Services*, 89 A.D.2d 329 (2nd Dep't 1982)).

However, the law cannot be used by teachers who are not excessed by the change to obtain a superior placement with the new provider (*Buenzow*).

The former program provider must place all excessed teachers who cannot be employed on its preferred eligible list for similar positions (§§ 3014-a(2); 3014-b(2); *Acinapuro*).

A similar law provides the same rights to teachers whose positions are excessed as a result of tuitioning out students to another district or taking back tuitioned-out students (§§ 3014-c; 3014-d). However, the two provisions may not be combined to require a component district to employ BOCES teachers excessed when a district takes back a student from a BOCES program and tuitions the students out to another component district (*Herrman v. Board of Educ.*, 194 A.D.2d 673 (2nd Dep't 1993)).

8:94. How do tenure areas affect seniority rights?

Seniority within a specific tenure area is the determining factor in establishing seniority credit prior to excessing a teacher (*Lynch v. Nyquist*, 41 A.D.2d 363, *aff'd*, 34 N.Y.2d 588 (1974); *Matter of Daly*, 23 Educ. Dep't Rep. 147 (1983)). Thus, a teacher's seniority rights are tied directly to tenure areas.

A teacher who has several probationary or tenure appointments in separate tenure areas accrues seniority separately in each area, depending on the actual service performed. For example, if a teacher serves as a mathematics teacher and a science teacher for five years and then teaches only mathematics for two years, that teacher has seven years of seniority credit in mathematics and five years of seniority credit in science.

Once a teacher is placed on a preferred eligible list, however, seniority is determined by length of service within the district rather than service in a tenure area (*Mahony v. Board of Education*, 140 A.D.2d 33 (2nd Dep't 1988)). Thus, the same teacher described above would have seven years of seniority for purposes of reappointment to either a mathematics or science position.

8:95. May a school board abolish a teaching position?

Yes, if the position is no longer necessary to the school system. Traditionally, both the courts and the commissioner of education have given school boards broad latitude to abolish, reorganize or consolidate positions (*Zurlo v. Ambach*, 53 N.Y.2d 1035 (1981); *Young v. Board of Education*, 35 N.Y.2d 31 (1974); *Currier v. Tompkins-Seneca-Tioga Board of Cooperative Educational Services*, 80 A.D.2d 979 (3rd Dep't 1981)). However, there should be a bona fide reason for abolition or reorganization.

Before a teaching position is abolished, school districts must consider adjusting teaching schedules in order to continue the services of a teacher within his or her certification (*Steele v. Board of Education*, 53 A.D.2d 674 (2nd Dep't 1976), *aff'd*, 42 N.Y.2d 840 (1977); *Amos v. Board of Education*, 54 A.D.2d 297 (4th Dep't 1976), *aff'd*, 43 N.Y.2d 706 (1977)).

When teachers challenge the abolition of positions in cases where schedule shuffling has taken place, districts must demonstrate the impossibility of retaining the teachers through adjustment of schedules. A board can meet this burden by demonstrating that the educational and financial impact of the teaching assignment will be detrimental *(Chambers v. Board of Education*, 47 N.Y.2d 279 (1979)). A school district has no obligation to shuffle the schedules of teachers outside the tenure area of the particular teacher whose position is being abolished (Appeal of Chaney, 33 Educ. Dep't Rep. 12 (1993)).

A school must adopt a formal resolution abolishing a particular position and provide notice to a teacher that his or her position is being abolished. The board's resolution must identify the tenure area in which a position is to be abolished (*Appeal of Lessing*, 34 Educ. Dep't Rep. 451 (1995)).

Where a school board appointed a teacher to a nonexistent tenure area, the court ruled the board could not abolish the position and terminate the teacher without first reclassifying the teacher's tenure area. The board was ordered to determine the teacher's proper tenure area based upon the work she actually performed *(Abrantes v. Board of Educ. of the Norwood-Norfolk Central School District*, 233 A.D.2d 718 (3rd Dep't 1996), *appeal denied*, 89 N.Y.2d 812 (1997)). School districts may only appoint teachers to the tenure areas designated in Part 30 of the commissioner's regulations and may not create their own tenure areas for teaching positions (8 NYCRR Part 30).

8:96. May a district abolish a position rather than fire a teacher?

No. Abolishing a position may not be used as a way to fire a teacher or an administrator (*Young v. Board of Education*, 35 N.Y.2d 31 (1974); *Weimer v. Board of Education*, 76 A.D.2d 1046 (2nd Dep't 1980); *Board of Education v. Niagara-Wheatfield Teachers' Assoc.*, 54 A.D.2d 281 (4th Dep't 1976)).

However, the commissioner of education has held that in a 3020–a proceeding involving a "schedule shuffling" question, a hearing panel cannot require a district to show why it abolished positions in one subject rather than another (*Rappold v. Board of Education*, 20 Educ. Dep't Rep. 664 (1981), *aff'd*, 95 A.D.2d 890 (3rd Dep't 1983)).

8:97. Does a teacher whose position is being abolished have the right to take the job of another teacher?

Yes. If a position is abolished, the teacher with the least seniority within the tenure area of that position in that school district must be the person dismissed (§§ 2510(2); 2583(3); 3013(2)). Although this is sometimes incorrectly referred to as "bumping" the junior teacher, the more senior teacher need not take over the assignment of the excessed teacher. The district retains the authority to make all teaching assignments.

True bumping rights are available only to teachers appointed under Part 30 of the Rules of the Board of Regents. These rights allow a teacher whose position is eliminated in one area and who accrued seniority based on prior service in a different tenure area to claim the position of another teacher serving in that previous tenure area, provided the first teacher has more seniority in the tenure area than other teachers (8 NYCRR § 30.13).

In addition, if a district creates a new position at the same time that it abolishes an existing position, the teacher who would be excessed must be hired at his or her existing salary for the new position if the duties performed under both positions are similar and the record of the person has been one of faithful, competent service in the position (§§ 2510(1); 2585(2); 3013(1)). The two positions are considered similar if more than 50 percent of the functions to be performed in the new position are the same as those performed under the old position (*Coates v. Ambach*, 52 A.D.2d 261 (3rd Dep't 1976), *aff'd*, 42 N.Y.2d 846 (1977)). The 50 percent rule should not be applied rigidly, and the emphasis should be on the type of duties the employee could have been expected to perform in the old position.

8:98. What rights of reappointment do excessed teachers have?

A teacher who is excessed because a teaching position has been abolished has the right to be placed on a preferred eligible list (PEL) of candidates for appointment to a similar position for seven years after the position is abolished (§§ 2510(3)(a); 2585(4); 3013(3)(a); *Brewer v. Board of Education*, 51 N.Y.2d 855 (1980); *Jester v. Board of Education*, 109 A.D.2d 1004 (3rd Dep't 1985)). According to the New York State Appellate Division for the Third Department, two positions will not be deemed "similar" if they are in different tenure areas and require different certification (*Brown v. Board of Education*, 211 A.D.2d 887 (3rd Dep't 1995)). However, the Second Department ruled there is no provision in the Education Law which requires that to be "similar," the vacant position exist within the excessed teacher's area (*Leggio v. Oglesby*, 69 A.D.2d 446 (2nd Dep't 1979)).

Teachers are only entitled to reappointment within the tenure area in which they served, even if they hold certification or positions in other tenure areas *(Board of Education v. Barker Teachers Union,* 209 A.D.2d 945 (1994), *appeal denied,* 85 N.Y.2d 807 (1995); *Appeal of Moravus,* 32 Educ. Dep't Rep. 419 (1992)). A collective bargaining agreement may not require that a teacher whose position has been abolished be appointed to any job opening in his or her tenure area or any position for which that teacher is certified *(Barker)*.

A teacher who retired under the disability retirement provisions of the Education Law is entitled to be placed on the PEL if that teacher recovers from the disability (§ 2510(3)(a)).

Teachers on the PEL also must be offered regular substitute positions of at least a five-month duration (§§ 2510(3)(b); 3013(3)(b)), as well as a part-time teaching position of shorter duration if one becomes available *(Abrams v. Ambach,* 43 A.D.2d 883 (3rd Dep't 1974)). A teacher recalled from the PEL and placed in a part-time position after being excessed from a full-time position is entitled to a new seven-year period on the PEL from the date the school district abolishes his or her part-time position *(Avila v. Bd. of Educ. of the North Babylon UFSD,* 240 A.D.2d 661 (2nd Dep't 1997), *appeal denied,* 91 N.Y.2d 801 (1997)).

A teacher who is reappointed to a similar position within the district must receive the same pay as what that teacher received before the layoff (§ 2510(3)).

8:99. Is there any particular order for recalling excessed teachers?

When several different teachers have been excessed, they must be offered reappointment in order of seniority (§§ 2510(3); 2585(4); 3013(3)). For purposes of determining seniority of teachers on preferred eligible lists, the length of service in the system, not length of service within a particular tenure area, is used *(Mahony v. Board of Education,* 140 A.D.2d 33 (2nd Dep't 1988); see **8:94**).

8:100. Do teachers lose their rights under the preferred eligible list (PEL) if they accept a position in a different tenure area?

No. A teacher does not waive any right to reappointment within his or her tenure area by accepting a position in another tenure area in the district *(Matter of Mead,* 23 Educ. Dep't Rep. 101 (1983)). A teacher does not waive any right to reappointment from the PEL for refusing an offer of reemployment. A teacher who refuses an offer of reemployment because of a short-term commitment to another employer does not waive his or her seniority rights *(Lewis v. Cleveland Hill UFSD,* 119 A.D.2d 263 (4th Dep't 1986)).

8:101. What are the rights of an improperly excessed teacher?

Such a teacher is entitled to reinstatement and back pay less any earnings from jobs worked at during normal school hours (*Matter of Lezette v. Board of Education*, 35 N.Y.2d 272 (1974); *Appeal of Lessing*, 34 Educ. Dep't Rep. 451 (1995); see **8:102**). In addition, the district may not offset the back pay it owes a reinstated teacher by the amount of unemployment benefits the teacher received. All or part of the unemployment benefits received by the teacher might be recovered by the Labor Department (*Appeal of Lessing*, 35 Educ. Dep't Rep. 116 (1995)).

8:102. Does an improperly excessed teacher have a duty to mitigate (lessen) any damages during the pendency of proceedings brought to review the abolition of his or her position?

Yes. The New York State Court of Appeals held that an improperly excessed teacher may not collect damages from his or her former employing school district to cover periods during which he or she refuses to accept comparable work (*Gross v. Board of Educ. of Elmsford UFSD*, 78 N.Y.2d 13 (1991)).

8:103. Must a district pay the full salary of a teacher assigned from the preferred eligible list (PEL) to teach a subject in which he or she is not certified during the pendency of 3020-a proceedings brought against that teacher on grounds of lack of certification?

Yes. When a district reduces its workforce and later recalls a teacher from the PEL to teach a subject within that teacher's tenure area but outside his or her certification area, it must continue to pay the teacher's full salary during the pendency of section 3020-a charges brought to remove that teacher for lack of certification (**8:114**).

In *Winter v. Board of Educ. for Rhinebeck CSD*, 79 N.Y.2d 1 (1992), the New York State Court of Appeals dismissed the district's argument that a teacher who was not certified to teach in the particular subject area she was recalled for from the PEL was not qualified under the Education Law. Therefore, she was not entitled to receive a salary, pursuant to sections 3009(1) and 3010, which prohibits school districts from paying unqualified teachers. According to the court, teachers certified on the day they are initially hired by the district are qualified under the Education Law for purposes of receiving a salary when they are called back from the PEL (see **8:98**) to teach outside their area of certification.

In *Winter*, the court also rejected the district's argument that it was required to reassign excessed teachers to subjects for which they are uncertified, under section 2510 of the Education Law. The court found "no support in the statute" and, therefore, no authority for the practice of reassigning a teacher to teach in an area in which he or she is uncertified and then terminating that teacher's services. This decision casts uncertainty as to future district obligations under this section of the Education Law.

Disciplining Tenured Teachers

8:104. May a school district fire a teacher?

A probationary teacher may be fired at any time, on the recommendation of the superintendent of schools, by a majority vote of the school board (§§ 2509(1)(a); 2573(1)(a); 3012(1)) subject to certain restrictions (see **8:78-79**).

A tenured teacher may not be fired unless the school district follows certain rules under section 3020–a of the Education Law. The procedures for a tenured teacher disciplinary hearing were altered substantially from prior procedures under this section as a result of amendments adopted in 1994.

8:105. Under what circumstances may a tenured teacher be disciplined?

Tenured teachers have the right to retain their teaching positions as long as they exhibit good behavior and competent and efficient service (§§ 2509(2); 2573(5); 3012(2)). A tenured teacher may only be disciplined or discharged for "just cause" (§ 3020(1)).

Before a teacher is disciplined, that teacher is entitled to a hearing, often called a section 3020–a hearing, on the charges brought by the district. All school districts, including New York City, follow the disciplinary procedures established in section 3020–a, or alternative procedures contained within a negotiated collective bargaining agreement. (§ 3020(1); see **8:107; 8:120**).

The New York State Court of Appeals has ruled that section 3020–a is constitutional (*Board of Education v. Gootnick*, 49 N.Y.2d 683 (1980)).

8:106. What is the procedure for removing or otherwise disciplining tenured teachers?

The procedure for removing or otherwise disciplining tenured teachers is mandated by section 3020–a of the Education Law. Any person, but usually the superintendent, files written charges and the school board votes to prefer charges against the teacher (*Matter of Van Dame* 15 Educ. Dep't Rep. 63 (1975)). The teacher is notified of the charges and is entitled to request a hearing on the charges (§ 3020-a(2)(a),(c)). A pre-hearing conference must be held prior to the hearing (§ 3020-a(3)(c)(ii)).

The 3020-a hearing is usually conducted before a single hearing officer who determines the guilt or innocence of the teacher and orders any penalty to be imposed. However, when the charges against the teacher concern pedagogical incompetence or issues involving pedagogical judgment, the teacher has his or her choice of either a single hearing officer or a three-member panel, often called a 3020-a panel (3020-a(2)(c)).

A teacher's resignation after the conclusion of a hearing but prior to the hearing officer's decision does not preclude a school district from continuing the disciplinary proceedings and placing a record of the final determination in the teacher's personnel file (*Folta v. Sobol*, 210 A.D.2d 857 (3rd Dep't 1994)).

8:107. May a tenured teacher waive his or her rights, such as the right to a hearing, under section 3020-a?

Yes. A teacher may waive his or her right to a hearing under the law as part of a stipulation of settlement in a 3020–a case, provided the waiver is made knowingly and freely (*Abramovich v. Board of Education*, 46 N.Y.2d 450 (1979), *cert. denied*, 444 U.S. 845 (1979)).

A teacher may also choose, under the law, to proceed under alternative disciplinary procedures contained within a negotiated collective bargaining agreement. Any such negotiated alternative must also result in a disposition of the charges within the same time frame established under section 3020-a (§§ 3020(1); 3020-a).

The state Court of Appeals has upheld a decision by the commissioner of education that a provision in a collective bargaining agreement for suspension without pay is permissible and enforceable (*Board of Education v. Nyquist*, 48 N.Y.2d 97 (1979)).

In addition, a tenured teacher who fails to appear at a scheduled 3020–a hearing waives the right to a hearing on the merits of his or her case. The school board then is free to vote on the charges as if the teacher had never requested a hearing (*Matter of Syracuse City School Dist.*, 21 Educ. Dep't Rep. 461 (1982)).

8:108. How are section 3020–a charges filed?

Detailed charges specifying the grounds for discipline must be filed in writing with the school district clerk (§ 3020–a(1)). Although any individual may file charges, the charges usually are filed by the superintendent of schools (see **8:106**). Charges must be brought during the school year during which the employee is normally required to serve (§ 3020–a(1)).

Charges may not be brought more than three years after the occurrence of the alleged misconduct, unless it constitutes a crime when committed

(3020–a(1); 2590–j(7)(c)). In one case, a federal district court in New York upheld the termination of a teacher found guilty of engaging in illegal sexual misconduct with two of his former students over 20 years earlier (*DeMichele v. Greenburgh Central School District 7 and Arnold B. Green,* United States District Court, S.D.N.Y, 1997).

Upon receiving the charges, the school board must vote to determine whether there is probable cause to bring the charges. The vote must be conducted in executive session within five days of submission of the charges and must be carried by a majority of the membership of the board (§ 3020-a(2)(a)).

The teacher must be notified by certified mail, registered mail or personal service of the charges filed against him or her, the maximum penalty that would be imposed by the school board if a hearing is not requested or that will be sought by the board if the teacher is found guilty of the charges after a hearing, and the teacher's rights under the law (§ 3020-a(2)(a)). The teacher has 10 days to request a hearing and, if the charge concerns pedagogical incompetence or issues of pedagogical judgment, whether a hearing before a single hearing officer or three-member panel is preferred (§ 3020-a(2)(c).

If no hearing is requested, the board decides the guilt or innocence of the teacher within 15 days and determines the penalty to be imposed. If the teacher requests a hearing, the district must forward the charges to the commissioner of education within three working days of receipt of the request (§ 3020-a(2)(d)).

8:109. How is the hearing officer selected?

Once the hearing is requested and the charges have been forwarded to the commissioner of education, the commissioner contacts the American Arbitration Association (AAA) to obtain a list of eligible labor arbitrators to conduct the hearing (§ 3020–a(3)(a)). The school board and the employee jointly must agree on a hearing officer from the list provided by AAA within 10 days or, in the event they cannot agree, the commissioner will request AAA to select the hearing officer.

The hearing officer may not be a resident of the school district, except in New York City, and may not be currently serving as a mediator or fact finder in the school district. Additionally, the hearing officer may not be an agent or employee of the school board or of the teachers' union, or have served as an agent or employee in the last two years (§ 3020-a(3)(b)).

Hearing officers are paid the customary AAA fee (§ 3020–a(3)(b)(i)). However, where a hearing is conducted under a contractual alternative procedure which alters the way hearing officers are selected but otherwise provides the hearing be conducted in accordance with the provisions of section 3020-a, the fees paid a hearing officer may not exceed $200 (Laws of 1996, Ch. 474 § 134).

8:110. May 3020-a charges be heard by a three-member panel instead of a single hearing officer?

Teachers charged with pedagogical incompetence or issues involving pedagogical judgment can choose to have 3020-a hearings before a three-member panel rather than a single hearing officer.

Under the current law, the panel chairperson is selected in the same manner as a single hearing officer, and the school board and teacher each chooses one panel member from a list of hearing panelists maintained by the commissioner (§ 3020-a(3)(b)(iv)). The commissioner establishes the hearing panel list from names submitted by statewide organizations, including the New York State School Boards Association.

In a hearing before a three-member panel, the panelists selected by the board and the teacher each receives $100 per day plus expenses for service on the panel. Parties may not supplement a panelist's $100 per diem compensation with extra money because these additional payments would give the appearance of bias (*Syquia v. Board of Education of Harpursville CSD*, 80 N.Y.2d 531 (1992)). Where a panel is appointed under a contractual alternative procedure which alters the way panel members are selected, the fee paid a panel chairperson may not exceed $200. The other panelists are to be paid the same as additional panel members in all other school districts (Laws of 1996, Ch. 474 § 134).

A panel hearing may not proceed without all three members present (8 NYCRR § 82-1.10(d)).

8:111. Must the 3020-a hearing officer or panel conduct a pre-hearing conference?

Yes. The pre-hearing conference must take place within 10 to 15 days of the hearing officer's agreement to serve (§ 3020-a(3)(c)(ii)). The hearing officer at the pre-hearing conference issues subpoenas; rules on all motions by the district and the teacher, including motions to dismiss the charges; and rules on requests for bills of particulars or other requests for materials and documents by the parties (§ 3020-a(3)(c)(iii)).

The hearing officer at that time also determines the number of days required for the hearing and schedules the hearing dates. Any hearing dates must be scheduled on consecutive days. The law requires the final hearing to be completed no later than 60 days after the pre-hearing conference has concluded, unless the hearing officer determines that extraordinary circumstances warrant a limited extension (§ 3020–a(3)(c)(vi)).

If the school district presents evidence at the pre-hearing conference that the teacher's certification has been revoked, the hearing officer must conduct an expedited hearing within seven days (§ 3020-a(3)(c)(v)).

8:112. Is a school district required to disclose to the teacher in a 3020-a proceeding the nature of its case and the evidence against the teacher?

Yes. The teacher must be given the opportunity to defend himself or herself and the district must fully and fairly disclose the nature of its case and the evidence it will use against the teacher (§ 3020-a(3)(c)(i)).

In addition, some hearing officers have ruled that the hearing officer may grant limited disclosure rights to school districts in 3020-a proceedings *(Board of Education, Abbott Union Free School District v. Walthall,* Howard C. Edelman, Hearing Officer (1997); *Board of Education of the City of New York v. Midy,* Arthur A. Riegel, Hearing Officer (1996); see § 3020-a(3)(c)(iii)). However, other hearing officers have held that only the teacher has the right to disclosure *(Marcus Whitman Central School District v. Kevin L.F.,* Douglas J. Bantle, Hearing Officer (1996)).

8:113. How is a section 3020–a hearing conducted?

The hearing officer or panel presides over the hearing. The rules of procedure and evidence used in a 3020–a hearing are not as strict as those followed in a court. The district and the teacher have the right to call witnesses to testify at the hearing, to issue subpoenas and to have an attorney present at the hearing. The teacher must be given an opportunity to testify but may not be required to do so (§ 3020-a(3)(c)(i); 8 NYCRR § 82-1.10).

In presenting its evidence, a school district may not access court records of a teacher who has been acquitted of misdemeanor charges even if the disciplinary hearing charges the teacher with the same conduct *(In re Joseph M.,* 82 N.Y.2d 128 (1993)). Taped telephone conversations between a student and a teacher charged with maintaining an inappropriately close relationship with the student have been ruled admissible by the commissioner if the tape is authentic and unaltered *(Appeal of Malone CSD,* 33 Educ. Dep't Rep. 108 (1993)).

A transcript of the hearing must be made and a copy provided free of charge to the teacher and the board, upon request (§ 3020–a(3)(c)(i)).

Within 30 days of the last day of the hearing, or within 10 days of an expedited hearing of a teacher charged with a revoked certification, the hearing officer must issue a written decision. The decision must include whether the teacher is guilty or innocent of each charge and what penalty or other action, if any, should be taken by the board (§ 3020-a(4)(a)). If the hearing officer finds that any or all charges filed against the teacher were frivolous, he or she must order the school board to reimburse the State Education Department for all or a portion of the costs of the hearing, including the teacher's attorneys' fees (§ 3020–a(4)(c)).

8:114. May a teacher be suspended while a 3020–a charge is pending?

Yes. A teacher charged with misconduct under 3020-a may be suspended by the school board until the case is resolved (§ 3020–a(2)(b)). Generally, the teacher must be given full pay and benefits during suspension (§ 3020-a(2)(b); *Jerry v. Board of Education*, 35 N.Y.2d 534 (1974)). According to one court, such payments are not an unconstitutional gift of public funds (*Brady v. A Certain Teacher*, 166 Misc.2d 566 (1995)).

Under certain circumstances, suspension without pay is permissible. For example, a district need not pay a suspended teacher where a collective bargaining agreement provides for suspension without pay (*Romano v. Canuteson*, 11 F.3d 1140 (2nd Cir. 1993); *Board of Education v. Nyquist*, 48 N.Y.2d 97 (1979)); or where the teacher faces charges for lack of certification for the course he or she has been hired to teach (*Meliti v. Nyquist*, 41 N.Y.2d 183 (1976)). A district is not required to pay a suspended teacher who has pleaded guilty to or been found guilty of a felony drug crime or a felony crime involving the physical or sexual abuse of a minor or student (§ 3020–a(2)(b)).

A district cannot withhold a teacher's pay during the pendency of 3020–a charges when delays are caused by the teacher's good faith request for adjournments (*Derle v. North Bellmore UFSD*, 77 N.Y.2d 483 (1991)); or when a certified teacher is reassigned involuntarily to teach a course he or she is not certified to teach (*Winter v. Board of Educ. for Rhinebeck CSD*, 79 N.Y.2d 1 (1992); **8:103**).

A school district can reduce a teacher's pay during the pre-hearing suspension period by the amount of income the employee has earned in another job (*Jerry*). However, the teacher is not required to mitigate or reduce damages by seeking other employment (*Hawley v. South Orangetown CSD*, 67 N.Y.2d 796 (1986)).

8:115. How is the penalty determined when a teacher is found guilty of misconduct?

The hearing officer, or a three-member panel in cases of pedagogical incompetence, decides the appropriate penalty to be imposed if a teacher is found guilty of charges following a 3020–a hearing. At the request of the teacher, the hearing officer must consider the extent to which the school board has made efforts to correct the teacher's behavior, including remediation, peer intervention or an employee assistance program (§ 3020–a(4)(a)).

The penalties authorized by the Education Law include a written reprimand, a fine, a suspension without pay for a specified period or dismissal. In addition, the hearing officer can order remedial action, such as continuing education, counseling or medical treatment, or leaves of absence with or without pay (§ 3020–a(4)(a)). The hearing panel may not impose more than one penalty at the same time (*Adrian v. Board of Education*, 60 A.D.2d 840 (2nd Dep't 1978)), although the law permits combinations of remedial actions to be imposed (§ 3020–a(4)(a)).

The school board must adopt the recommended penalty of the 3020–a panel within 15 days of receipt of the decision (§ 3020–a(4)(b)). If the board disagrees with the penalty imposed by the panel, its sole recourse is to appeal the decision (see **8:119**).

8:116. Is a teacher who was suspended with pay pending the outcome of a 3020-a disciplinary proceeding, and is subsequently discharged, entitled to unemployment insurance benefits?

To be eligible for unemployment insurance benefits, a discharged teacher must establish that he or she was employed for at least 20 weeks in the 52-week period prior to filing a claim (Lab. Law §527(1)(d)). In one case, the Appellate Division, Third Department upheld a determination of the unemployment insurance appeal board that a tenured teacher who was suspended with pay for one year during the pendency of a 3020-a proceeding, and who performed no work at all for the district during her suspension with pay, was not entitled to unemployment insurance benefits after the district discharged her (*Claim of Odell*, 233 A.D.2d 663 (3rd Dep't 1996)).

8:117. What happens if a teacher is acquitted of the 3020-a charges?

If acquitted, the teacher must be restored to his or her teaching position, with full pay for any period of suspension without pay, and the charges must be removed from the teacher's personnel record (§ 3020–a (4)(b)). If the hearing officer finds that any or all charges filed against the teacher were frivolous, he or she must order the school board to reimburse the State Education Department for all or a portion of the costs of the hearing, and to reimburse the teacher for all or a portion of the reasonable costs incurred in defending the charges (§ 3020–a(4)(c)).

8:118. Are 3020-a settlement agreements available to the public under the Freedom of Information Law (FOIL)?

Yes. Generally, agreements settling disciplinary charges are subject to disclosure under FOIL. However, certain portions of such agreements should be reviewed and edited before disclosure to the public in order to protect privacy, including charges that were denied and charges mentioning the names of other employees or students (*LaRocca v. Board of Educ. of Jericho Union Free School District.*, 220 A.D.2d 424 (2nd Dep't 1995); *Buffalo Evening News, Inc. v. Bd. of Educ. of the Hamburg CSD* (Sup. Ct. Erie County 1987); but see *Anonymous v. Board of Educ. for the Mexico CSD*, 162 Misc. 2d 300 (Sup. Ct. Oswego County 1994)).

8:119. Can either party appeal the 3020–a hearing officer or panel's decision?

A teacher or the school district may appeal the 3020–a hearing officer or panel's decision to the courts, under Article 75 of the Civil Practice Law and Rules (§ 3020–a(5)). Under this type of court review, the decision of the hearing officer would be reversed on narrow grounds; in other words, if it were proven there was corruption, fraud or misconduct in obtaining the decision, the hearing officer had exceeded his or her statutory power, or the hearing officer on a three-member panel had not been impartial. Since it is unusual for a court to reverse a decision under these standards, the decision of the hearing officer is likely to be final in most cases (Civ. Prac. L. & R. § 7511(b)).

Prior to the amendment of section 3020–a in 1994 and for cases commenced before September 1, 1994, the commissioner of education also had the authority to consider appeals of decisions of three-member panels. However, any charges brought after September 1, 1994 no longer have this venue for appeal.

8:120. What legal alternatives to section 3020–a may a district use to discipline teachers?

There are several available means of disciplining a teacher that do not violate the requirements of section 3020–a. For example, a counseling letter critical of a tenured teacher's performance may be placed in his or her personnel file (*Holt v. Board of Education*, 52 N.Y.2d 625 (1981)). A *Holt* letter, however, may not be used as a reprimand, which is one of the statutory penalties under Section 3020–a and as such requires a hearing.

Districts and their bargaining units may implement alternatives to the 3020–a process. However, any alternatives negotiated after September 1, 1994 must allow an employee to choose either those alternatives or the

3020–a process, as long as the charges are disposed of within the time constraints of 3020–a. Negotiated alternatives to 3020–a may remain in effect until they are changed by collective bargaining (§ 3020(1)).

Teachers' Compensation and Benefits

8:121. Are teachers guaranteed minimum salaries under state law?

No. There are no state-mandated minimum salaries for teachers. Often these are established locally by the school board after collective bargaining with the teachers' union. However, the Education Law does impose other requirements on the payment of teachers' salaries.

Except as otherwise provided by law, the school district must pay extra salary to teachers who work more than the regular 10-month school year (§ 3101(3)). For each summer month a teacher works, the school district must pay that teacher at least an additional 1/10th of his or her annual salary (§ 3101(3); *Matter of Walsh*, 21 Educ. Dep't Rep. 467 (1982)). If a teacher works additional days instead of a whole month, the extra salary is one 1/200th of the annual salary for each day (§ 3101(3)).

8:122. When are teachers entitled to be paid?

The salary of a teacher employed for a full school year must be paid in at least 10 installments (§ 3101(3); see *Matter of Schwartz*, 7 Educ. Dep't Rep. 130 (1968)). In addition, a school district must pay salaries at least once in each month that school is in session for those teachers who were employed before the end of the previous school year (§ 3101(3)).

A school district, however, cannot pay teachers in advance for service they have not yet rendered. For example, a school district cannot pay teachers returning to duty at the beginning of the school year two weeks' salary before they work for two weeks (*Board of Educ. v. Ramapo Teachers Ass'n*, 200 A.D.2d 62 (3rd Dep't 1994), *appeal denied*, 84 N.Y.2d 806 (1994)).

8:123. Are substitute teachers entitled to a minimum salary?

No. There is no state-mandated minimum salary for substitutes. Each school district establishes the salary for its own substitutes.

If a district has given substitutes reasonable assurance of continued employment, the substitutes can form a collective bargaining unit separate from the teachers' unit (Civ. Serv. Law § 201(7)(d)) and bargain over terms and conditions of employment including compensation.

A long-term substitute who is assigned to cover for a teacher who is on an extended leave may be considered part of the regular teachers' bargaining unit (*Weedsport CSD v. Weedsport Teachers' Ass'n*, 12 PERB ¶ 3004 (1979)). Thus, regular substitute teachers usually are compensated in the same manner as other teachers in the district.

On the other hand, itinerant substitutes who teach on an ad hoc basis are not a part of the teachers' collective bargaining unit (*Board of Educ., New York City School Dist. v. United Fed'n of Teachers*, 15 PERB ¶ 4004 (1982); *Levittown UFSD v. Levittown United Teachers*, 15 PERB ¶ 4039 (1982)). Most school districts formally adopt a separate salary schedule for itinerant substitutes. If these itinerant substitutes form a separate bargaining unit, their compensation would be a mandatory subject of bargaining with the district (see **10:36-37**).

8:124. What types of salary issues must be negotiated with a teachers' union?

A school board must negotiate terms and conditions of employment as noted in the Taylor Law (Civ. Serv. Law Art. 14; see chap. 10). Included salary issues may be increases in salaries (*Huntington UFSD v. Huntington Union Free School Dist. Clerical Unit*, 16 PERB ¶ 3061 (1983)) and/or decreases in salaries (*County of Monroe v. Local 381*, 10 PERB ¶ 3104 (1977)).

Additional salary issues that must be negotiated include incentive pay (*Volk v. Carle Place Teachers' Ass'n*, 6 PERB ¶ 7510 (1973)); longevity pay (*Town of Mamaroneck v. Town of Mamaroneck Police Benevolent Ass'n*, 16 PERB ¶ 3037 (1983), *aff'd*, 16 PERB ¶ 7022 (1983)); merit pay (*County of Ulster v. Ulster County Unit*, 14 PERB ¶ 3008 (1981)); overtime pay (*Spring Valley PBA v. Spring Valley*, 80 A.D.2d 910 (2nd Dep't 1981); pay for summer work (*Saugerties CSD v. Saugerties Teachers' Ass'n*, 10 PERB ¶ 4529 (1977)); and premium pay for extra work, such as teaching large classes (*West Irondequoit Teachers' Ass'n v. Helsby*, 35 N.Y.2d 46 (1974)).

Determining salaries for newly created positions that have not been filled is not a mandatory subject of bargaining and thus need not be bargained (*Churchville-Chili CSD v. Churchville-Chili Educ. Ass'n*, 17 PERB ¶ 3055 (1984); see **10:35-36**). However, once the two positions are filled, the salaries must be negotiated upon the union's demand (*New York City School Dist.*, 22 PERB ¶ 3011 (1989)).

8:125. May some teachers receive higher salaries based on their sex?

No. Federal and state laws prohibit employment discrimination on the basis of sex. The rights of teachers and other employees of both public and private educational institutions are protected by numerous state and federal laws that prohibit discrimination in employment practices on the basis of age, race, color, national origin, religion, creed, disability, sex and/or marital status (see **8:5-7**).

8:126. May teachers be required to sign a waiver or release as a condition of a salary payment?

No. Teachers and other employees of a school district may not be required or even requested to make a general release or waiver as a condition of any salary payment (§ 3108).

8:127. Must teachers' salaries be paid if a school is closed because of an emergency?

The usual practice is to pay salaries when schools are closed because of an emergency or inclement weather. However, in these cases, schools may require that teachers work additional school days, such as during vacation periods, for example.

A district's collective bargaining agreement may cover payment of teachers' salaries for periods when school is closed (see *Orchard Park Teachers' Assoc. v. Board of Education,* 71 A.D.2d 1 (4th Dep't 1979)).

8:128. Must a school board recognize teaching experience outside the school district when determining a new teacher's placement on a salary schedule or longevity increments under a collective bargaining agreement?

A school board may choose to recognize prior teaching experience outside the district, but it is not legally required to do so (§ 3101(4)). However, transfer credits granted to teachers before April 12, 1971, when a state law that required districts to recognize outside teaching experience was repealed, are irrevocable and must continue to be recognized *(Union Free School District v. Nyquist,* 38 N.Y.2d 137 (1975); § 3102(6), repealed by Laws of 1971, Ch. 123). Districts often recognize other experience, such as service in the armed forces or peace corps, depending on their teachers' collective bargaining agreement.

8:129. May a district reduce a teacher's salary to contribute to a tax-sheltered annuity plan, if the teacher so requests?

Yes. Any school district may include a provision in its teachers' collective bargaining agreement to reduce the annual salary of a teacher in order to invest in an annuity for that employee (§§ 3109; 3109-A). The annuity fund must meet specific requirements of the Internal Revenue Code (see 26 USC § 403(b)).

8:130. May a school district make salary adjustments when a teacher fails to provide services under a contract?

Yes. Salary adjustments are calculated based on section 3101(3) of the Education Law. For teachers who fail to render services during the school year, that law defines salary as being at least 1/10th of the annual salary for each full month of service and a daily rate of 1/200th of the salary.

The calculation of salary adjustments under this definition poses a problem of inequity when the number of work days in one month does not equal 20 days. For this reason, the commissioner of education has adopted the *Huntington formula* (*Matter of Swaim*, 9 Educ. Dep't Rep. 23 (1969)). This formula directs that salary adjustments for a teacher who has failed to serve at some time during the school year be calculated differently, depending on whether a teacher misses less than or more than half of the working days of the month (*Board of Education v. Ambach*, 97 A.D.2d 188 (3rd Dep't 1983), *aff'd*, 63 N.Y.2d 780 (1984)).

If a teacher works for more than half of the working days of the month, the district may deduct 1/200th of his or her annual salary for each day of unauthorized absence. If a teacher works for half of the working days of the month or less, the district need only pay the teacher 1/200th of the annual salary for each day of service rendered. These calculations apply regardless of the number of working days in the particular month.

8:131. May a teacher be reimbursed by a school board for work-related traveling expenses?

Yes. A school board is authorized to reimburse a teacher for work-related expenses and to make rules and regulations concerning expenses, including the establishment of a mileage rate (§ 1604(27)). The establishment of a mileage rate for reimbursement is a mandatory subject of collective bargaining (*Buffalo v. Buffalo Professional Fire-fighters Ass'n*, 17 PERB ¶3090 (1984); see **10:36**).

School districts also are authorized to pay for convention, conference and school expenses for teachers, including travel expenses (Gen. Mun. Law § 77–b).

8:132. Must school boards adopt rules and regulations governing leaves of absence for teachers and other school district employees?

Yes. School boards have both the authority and the obligation to adopt rules and regulations concerning excused absences and leaves of absences for teachers and other staff members (§ 1709(16)). School districts are required by the federal Family and Medical Leave Act to provide all employees, including teachers, with unpaid leave for medical or family care purposes, and to adopt policies concerning such leaves. Such family and medical leaves are limited to 12 weeks in duration and the district must provide health insurance coverage at the usual cost to the employee during the leave (see 29 USC § 2601 *et seq.;* **10:60-64**).

Generally, leaves of absences and other types of leaves are mandatory subjects of bargaining under the Taylor Law (*City of Albany v. Albany Police Officers' Union*, 7 PERB ¶ 3078 (1974); see **10:37**).

8:133. What are the legal requirements for sick leaves for teachers?

School districts, with the exception of New York City, must provide at least 10 sick days per year with pay for each teacher and any unused sick leave shall accumulate to at least 150 sick days (§ 3005–b).

In addition to sick leave authorized by section 3005-b, a teacher is entitled to medical leave under the federal Family and Medical Leave Act (FMLA) if he or she has a "serious health condition" that prevents the employee from performing his or her job, or to care for a spouse, child or parent who has a serious health condition (see 29 USC § 2611 *et seq.;* **10:60-64**).

Sick leave is a mandatory subject of bargaining, and the provisions of collective bargaining agreements are often more generous than those of section 3005–b or the FMLA (*Village of Spring Valley Policemen's Benevolent Ass'n v. Village of Spring Valley*, 14 PERB ¶ 3010 (1981); see **10:36-37**).

8:134. May a school district require a pregnant teacher to take sick leave?

No. The United States Supreme Court has rejected as unconstitutional school district rules that set cutoff dates, such as four or five months before the due date of birth, for the purpose of imposing mandatory sick leave for pregnant teachers *(Cleveland Bd. of Education v. La Fleur,* 414 U.S. 632 (1974)). In addition, the Executive Law prevents an employer from compelling a pregnant employee to take a leave of absence unless she cannot reasonably perform duties related to her job as a result of the pregnancy (Exec. Law § 296(1)(g)).

8:135. How can school districts handle maternity leaves?

School districts can treat maternity leaves in a number of ways, including as unpaid leaves under the federal Family and Medical Leave Act (FMLA) (29 CFR § 825.114(c); see **10:60-64**), unpaid leaves of absence for a fixed duration of more than 12 weeks, or paid leaves that last only for the actual period of disability. Under FMLA, an eligible teacher may elect, or the district may require the teacher to substitute his or her accrued vacation leave, personal leave or family leave for any part of the 12 weeks (29 USC § 2612(d)(2)).

The state Human Rights Law requires that a pregnant teacher who takes a maternity leave must be permitted to use her sick leave to the same extent as if she were suffering from some other physical disability (*Board of Educa-*

tion v. State Div. of Human Rights, 35 N.Y.2d 675 (1974)). In addition, a school district must treat sick or disability leave taken for pregnancy in the same manner as other leave in determining credit for time served by probationary teachers (*Schwabenbauer v. Board of Education*, 667 F.2d 305 (2nd Cir. 1981)). However, if no such credit is given to probationary teachers for any type of leave, those on maternity leave may not demand special treatment. FMLA provides that pregnancy is an authorized basis for medical leave.

Any personnel policy that singles out pregnancy, among all other physical conditions, as a category for special treatment in determining when a leave may commence violates the Human Rights Law (*Board of Education v. New York State Div. of Human Rights*, 35 N.Y.2d 674 (1974); *Union Free School Dist. v. New York State Human Rights Appeal Bd.*, 35 N.Y.2d 371 (1974)).

The district may not refuse to permit a teacher on FMLA leave from returning to the classroom except under limited circumstances which occur near the end of the semester (see 29 USC § 2611 *et seq.;* **10:63**). It may not establish a minimum time after birth, such as three months, before allowing a teacher to return. The district may require that a teacher provide a physician's statement that she is physically able to work and require a physical examination to ensure her fitness, but only if the district requires this for other types of temporary disabilities (*Cleveland Board of Educ. v. La Fleur*, 414 U.S. 632 (1974)).

8:136. What leave rights are afforded to adoptive parents?

Adoptive parents are entitled to take an unpaid child care leave under the Family and Medical Leave Act within one year of the adoption of a child under 18 years of age or the placement of a foster child in the home (see 29 USC § 2612; **10:61**).

Additionally, under the state Labor Law, any employer that permits an employee to take a leave of absence when a child is born must afford that same leave to an adoptive parent of a preschool child at the time the child is placed in the home by an authorized agency, or upon filing court papers for adoption if the adoption is not sponsored by an authorized agency (Lab. Law § 201–c).

8:137. Must school districts provide teachers leave to care for family members?

Yes. The Family and Medical Leave Act requires school districts to permit a parent to take an unpaid child care leave within one year of the birth, adoption or placement of a child. Additionally, employees are entitled to an unpaid leave to care for a sick spouse, parent or child. The district must provide health insurance to the employee at the employee's usual cost (see 29 USC §§ 2612; 2614(c); **10:61**).

8:138. Must a school district grant teachers time off or a leave of absence for purposes of commemorating religious holidays or observances?

A school district has the duty to make reasonable accommodations for teachers who desire time off for religious observance (*Ansonia Board of Educ. v. Philbrook*, 479 U.S. 60 (1986); *Sherbert v. Verner*, 374 U.S. 398 (1963)).

Although the district must make reasonable accommodations to allow employees time off for religious observances, it is not required to provide paid leave. It may treat the absence as an excused absence without pay or it may deduct the absence from vacation or personal time (*State Division of Human Rights v. Rochester Housing Authority*, 85 A.D.2d 897 (4th Dep't 1981)).

The Public Employment Relations Board (PERB) has ruled in two cases that a school district did not violate its duty to bargain in good faith by unilaterally rescinding a past practice of allowing employees to take extra paid leave for religious observances, finding that it was an unconstitutional practice and therefore not mandatorily negotiable (*CSEA v. Eastchester UFSD*, 29 PERB ¶3041 (1996); *Auburn Teachers' Association v. Auburn Enlarged City School District*, 30 PERB ¶3033 (1997)). However, one court has ruled that paid leave for religious observance is a permissive subject of bargaining (*Binghamton City School District v. Andreatta*, 30 PERB ¶7504 (Sup. Ct., Broome County, 1997)).

New York state law prohibits any employer, including school districts, from discriminating against an employee because of observance of a Sabbath or holy day (Exec. Law § 296(10)(a)). Except in emergencies, a district cannot require a teacher to work on a Sabbath or holy day and must allow the teacher time to travel to his or her home or places of a religious observance (Exec. Law § 296(10)(b)).

In one case, an administrative law judge ruled a school district violated the state human rights law when it refused to grant a teacher the district's perfect attendance award because she was absent from work to observe certain religious holidays (*Resnick v. Saranac Central School District*, State Division of Human Rights, Case No. 40E0C-89-137953E, Roberts, H. (1995)).

8:139. Is a school district required to give a teacher time off to vote?

Yes. A school district must allow up to two hours of paid time off from work for any employee who does not have sufficient time outside of work to vote (Elec. Law § 3–110(1)). This time must be taken at the beginning or the end of a shift. However, any employee who has four consecutive hours before or after work when the polls are open has sufficient time to vote and is not entitled to paid leave (Elec. Law § 3–110(2)).

A teacher who wants time off with pay to vote must notify the district at least two but not more than 10 days before Election Day (Elec. Law § 3–110(3)). Districts must post notices advising employees of their right to time off to vote (Elec. Law § 3–110(4)).

8:140. May a teacher be given a leave of absence to become an exchange teacher?

Yes. A teacher who has taught in the district for more than five years may be given up to two years' paid leave to serve as an exchange teacher in another state or foreign country, provided the state or country sends an exchange teacher with corresponding qualifications (§ 3005). Exchange teachers are paid by their employer; however, districts may supplement the income of foreign teachers (§ 3005). A teacher who is granted a leave of absence to serve as an exchange teacher must be granted the same compensation, retirement protection and seniority rights as if he or she had served within the district.

Although a teacher with less than five years of service with a district may serve as an exchange teacher, the provisions of section 3005 of the Education Law do not apply to that teacher (*Dreyfuss v. Board of Education*, 76 Misc.2d 479 (1973), *aff'd*, 45 A.D.2d 988 (2nd Dep't 1974)).

8:141. Must a district pay cash for unused leave time of teachers who resign?

A district is not required to provide employees with a cash payment for accumulated unused vacation, sick and other leave time. However, districts may adopt a resolution to grant cash payments for unused time (Gen. Mun. Law § 92). Payment for accumulated sick, vacation and leave time is a mandatory subject of collective bargaining (*Matter of Lynbrook*, 10 PERB ¶ 3065 (1977); see **10:37**). Many collective bargaining agreements oblige the employer to pay for unused leave time.

8:142. Is a teacher entitled to continued coverage in the district's group health plan if employment with the district is terminated?

Yes. Under most circumstances, an employee can continue coverage in a group health plan under the federal Comprehensive Omnibus Budget Reconciliation Act of 1985 (COBRA) (42 USC §§ 300-bb *et seq.*). This law requires school boards with 20 or more employees to offer participants in group health plans and their covered dependents an opportunity to buy back into continued coverage should they cease to be covered because of termination, reduced hours, retirement, resignation or when their dependents would otherwise cease to be covered because of the participants' death, divorce, legal separation, Medicare entitlement or ineligibility for dependent coverage under the group plan. This continued coverage must be offered for at least 18 months, in the case of termination or reduced hours, and up to 36 months in other instances.

In addition, the State Health Insurance Plan provides for continued health insurance coverage under certain circumstances such as when the employee is on authorized leave without pay, is suspended and placed upon a preferred list, up to a period of one year, or when an employee who was hired prior to April 1, 1975 retires after completion of at least five years of service with the employer and the employer elected to participate in the plan prior to March 1, 1972 (4 NYCRR § 73.2(a)(3); Civ. Serv. Law §§ 163, 165). However, an employer may elect not to provide continued coverage to retiring employees hired on or after April 1, 1977, if such a decision is applied to all employees who meet certain specified conditions upon retirement (4 NYCRR § 73.2(a)(3)(iv); Civ. Serv. Law § 163).

In some instances continued coverage may also be available to dependents upon the death of an employee or retiree (Civ. Serv. Law § 165–a; 4 NYCRR § 73.2(b)(1), (3)).

An employee on leave pursuant to the Family Medical Leave Act (FMLA) is entitled to coverage under COBRA when (1) the employee (spouse or dependent) is covered under an employer's group health plan on the day before the first day of FMLA leave or becomes covered during the FMLA leave; (2) the employee does not return to employment with the employer at the end of the FMLA leave; and (3) the employee (spouse or dependent) would in the absence of COBRA continuation coverage lose coverage under the employer's group health plan before the end of what would be the maximum coverage period.

In recent years, Congress has added several amendments to COBRA that have changed COBRA coverage rules significantly since the law was first enacted. Given the complexity and highly technical nature of this law, districts are encouraged to consult with their school attorneys or other COBRA advisers to better understand their obligations in applying these laws to specific situations.

9. Noninstructional Employees

The Civil Service

9:1. What is the civil service?

The civil service includes all offices and positions in the service of the state or any of its civil divisions (i.e., counties, cities, towns, villages and school districts), except offices or positions in the military departments. The civil service is divided into two broad categories: the unclassified service (§ 35) and the classified service (§ 40-44); (see Fig. 1 below).

The *unclassified* service comprises all positions in 11 categories listed in the Civil Service Law, including teachers and supervisory personnel in public schools, the State University and certain community colleges, elective offices, legislative officers and employees, and members and employees of boards of election (§ 35). If a position is not included in one of the enumerated categories of positions in the unclassified service, the position is, by definition, in the classified service (§ 40; see *Ficken v. Vocational Education and Extension Board of the County of Suffolk,* 201 A.D.2d 481 (2nd Dep't 1994)).

The *classified* service comprises all offices and positions not included in the unclassified service. The classified service is further divided into four subcategories or "jurisdictional" classes: the competitive class, the non-competitive class, the labor class and the exempt class (§ 40; see **9:6**).

Article 5, section 6, of the New York State Constitution provides that appointments and promotions in the classified civil service must be made according to merit and fitness to be determined by examination, which, as far as practicable, must be competitive. The New York State Civil Service Law was enacted to carry out this purpose.

Fig. 1

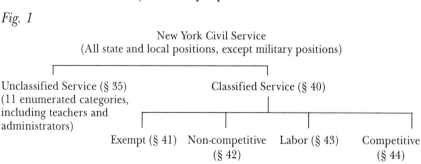

New York Civil Service
(All state and local positions, except military positions)

Unclassified Service (§ 35)
(11 enumerated categories,
including teachers and
administrators)

Classified Service (§ 40)

Exempt (§ 41)   Non-competitive   Labor (§ 43)   Competitive
                 (§ 42)   (§ 44)

All statutory references in this chapter are to the New York State Civil Service Law unless noted otherwise.

9:2. Who administers and enforces the Civil Service Law with respect to persons employed by local governments, including school districts, in the classified civil service?

The administration and enforcement of the civil service system for local governments in New York State is decentralized and is primarily the responsibility of local civil service agencies (§§ 15, 17). Every county, some cities and a few towns in the state have either a local civil service commission or a personnel officer. The county civil service commission or personnel officer is responsible for civil service administration with respect to all positions in the classified service of the county and all the local governments within the county, including school districts, except for cities that have elected to operate their own local civil service agency (§§ 15-18).

With respect to a BOCES or any school district which operates in more than one county, the provisions of Civil Service Law section 19 govern. As a general rule, the BOCES board or multi-county school board is responsible for deciding which county civil service agency will have jurisdiction over its employees. The board must make the decision within 90 days after the BOCES or multi-county district is established. If it fails to make a decision within that period, the BOCES or district will be subject to the jurisdiction of the local civil service agency in which the greatest territorial area of the BOCES or district is located. Once the designation is made it is final (§ 19).

Each local civil service agency is responsible for adopting rules that govern the administration of civil service (§ 20). As a general rule, the local rules cover matters such as how positions will be classified, examinations, appointments, promotions, transfers, resignations and reinstatements. The local rules frequently reflect issues and concerns unique to that area. Since they are not uniform, they should always be reviewed in connection with any civil service question involving a position under the jurisdiction of the local civil service agency.

The local rules also contain appendices which list all positions under the local civil service agency's jurisdiction that have been classified in other than the competitive class. Unless otherwise specifically designated by law or administrative action of the local civil service agency, all positions are automatically in the competitive class.

The adoption or modification of any local rules, except a modification required because of a change in statute, may occur only after a public hearing. Local rules, including those dealing with placing positions in other than the competitive class, are not effective until approved by the State Civil Service Commission and filed with the secretary of state (§ 20).

9:3. What is the school board's role in making appointments to positions in the classified service?

The school board is the entity within a school district that is legally responsible for making appointments to positions in the classified service (Educ. Law §§ 1709(15)(16); 1711(2)(e)). As the appointing authority, the school board is required to notify the local civil service agency of all classified service appointments on a form prescribed by the local agency (§ 97).

In addition, the school board is required to comply with all provisions of the Civil Service Law when making appointments to classified service positions. If the board fails to select or appoint classified service employees in accordance with the law, the board members may be personally responsible for paying that employee's salary (§ 95).

9:4. What kinds of positions in school districts are in the classified civil service?

In school districts, virtually all noninstructional support staff positions are in the classified service. Thus, non-teaching administrative positions such as school tax collector, district treasurer, internal auditor, business manager and labor relations director are generally in the classified service. So too are all clerical and noninstructional student-related positions, such as teacher aide and school monitor, as well as positions related to building maintenance, school security, school bus operation and the school lunch program. All local civil service agencies maintain an appendix to their local rules setting forth all positions under their jurisdiction that have been classified in other than the competitive class (see **9:2**).

9:5. Are teachers and administrators in the classified service?

No. Public employees whose principal functions are teaching or the supervision of teaching in a school district or board of cooperative educational services (BOCES) are in the unclassified service (§ 35(g), (j)). This includes instructional employees such as superintendents, principals, teachers and other positions that have been certified by the commissioner of education to the State Civil Service Commission. The employment of persons in these unclassified positions is governed by the Education Law, not the Civil Service Law.

9:6. How do the four subcategories (exempt, non-competitive, labor and competitive) within the classified service differ?

The *exempt* class includes all positions for which competitive or non-competitive examination is found to be not practicable (§ 41). As such, there is no examination for exempt class positions. Nor are there are any set minimum qualifications for such positions. Instead, the person or body having the power to make the appointment (in the case of school districts, the school board) determines the qualifications for the position and which person possesses such qualifications. Exempt class positions are so named because they are exempt from virtually all civil service limitations and restrictions. The school board making the appointment has complete discretion in filling such positions. An important factor to be considered in determining whether a civil service position should be classified as exempt is whether the position involves highly confidential duties. School district positions typically placed in the exempt class include the secretary to the superintendent of schools, school tax collector, school district treasurer, internal auditor and school district attorney.

The *non-competitive* class includes all positions for which a candidate's qualifications can be objectively assessed, but for which competitive (i.e., ranked) examinations are not practicable (§ 42). The non-competitive class consists primarily of skilled trade positions. It also includes certain positions of a high-level administrative, scientific or technical character involving a confidential relationship between the incumbent and the employer or which may require the performance of functions influencing policy. Candidates for appointment to positions in the non-competitive class need only meet the minimum qualifications for the position set by the local civil service agency. Generally, no written or oral examination is required. Instead, the local civil service agency simply compares the candidates qualifications to those which it has issued for the position. If the local civil service agency determines the candidate meets those qualifications, the employer is free to make the appointment. School district positions typically placed in the non-competitive class include school bus driver, teacher aide, custodial worker, building maintenance mechanic, grounds keeper, automotive mechanic, cook and baker.

The *labor* class includes unskilled positions, with no minimum qualifications, although applicants may be required to demonstrate their ability to do the job (§ 43). Typically, appointments to positions in the labor class simply require notification to the local civil service agency of the employment, unless it decides to impose additional requirements such as the filing of an application (§ 43). School district positions typically placed in the labor class include school monitor, cleaner and food service helper.

The *competitive* class includes all positions not in the exempt, non-competitive or labor classes (§ 44). Candidates for competitive class positions must meet minimum qualifications established by the local civil service agency and are subject to competitive (ranked) examination. Unless otherwise specifically designated by law or administrative action of the local civil service agency, all positions are automatically in the competitive class. School district positions typically found in the competitive class include business manager, safety officer, secretary, keyboard specialist, clerk, custodian, supervisor of building maintenance, director of transportation, head bus driver, bus dispatcher, and school lunch manager.

9:7. Can a school board create a new civil service position or reclassify an existing position for its school district?

Yes, but first the district must submit a proposal, including a statement of the duties of the position, to the local civil service agency (§ 22). The local civil service agency must furnish a certificate stating the appropriate civil service title for the position. Any such new position may be created or existing position reclassified only with the title approved and certified by the local civil service agency.

9:8. How are appointments or promotions to positions in the competitive class made?

An appointment or promotion to a position in the competitive class can be made only by selection of one of the three persons certified by the local civil service agency as standing highest on the appropriate eligible list who is willing to accept such an appointment or promotion (§ 61(1)). An eligible list is a list prepared by the local civil service agency (or in some cases by the State Civil Service Department) which lists in rank order the names of all persons who have passed the required civil service examination for the position to which an appointment is to be made.

Even though the Civil Service Law gives public employers the flexibility to appoint any one of the three highest scoring individuals on an eligible list, some public employers have, through collective bargaining, agreed to appoint the highest scoring individual, even though they are not required to enter into such negotiations (*Town of West Seneca*, 29 PERB ¶ 3024 (1996)). Such agreements have been upheld by the courts.

For example, in *Matter of Professional, Clerical, Technical Employees Ass'n (Buffalo Board of Education)*, 90 N.Y.2d 364 (1997)), the state Court of Appeals held that "there is nothing in our state's constitution, the Civil Service Law or decisional law that prohibits an appointing authority from agreeing, through collective bargaining negotiations, on the manner in which it will select one of the top three candidates from an eligible list for promotion." The court noted that the appointment of the highest scoring candidate, where compelled by a collective bargaining agreement, does not violate public policy, since appointees are required to serve a probationary term before their appointments become permanent, during which time the appointing authority has the ability to assess other traits not measurable by competitive examination.

9:9. What are provisional appointments to competitive class positions?

A *provisional* appointment is an appointment made to a competitive class position when there is no eligible list available (either because an examination has not been given or the eligible list expired), or the existing eligible list contains fewer than three names *(Davey v. Department of Civil Service,* 60 A.D.2d 998 (4th Dep't 1978)).

To be appointed provisionally to a competitive class position, the candidate need only demonstrate to the local civil service agency, by way of an application, that he or she meets the established minimum qualifications for the position (§ 65(1)). The duration of a provisional appointment is limited to nine months (§ 65(2)); however, under extenuating circumstances it may be extended, provided there is no valid eligible list available (§ 65(4)). Once a provisional appointment is made, the local civil service agency must order a competitive examination within one month or as soon as practicable to ensure that the provisional appointment does not exceed nine months (§ 65(2)). Notwithstanding the specific statutory mandate, provisional appointments regularly exceed nine months.

Provisional appointments can never ripen into a permanent appointment, no matter how long they exist, and the appointee can be terminated at any time for any reason. In addition, provisional appointees must be terminated within two months after the establishment of an appropriate eligible list, unless there is a large number of persons in a particular title serving on a provisional basis. In this case, the appointment can continue, with the approval of the local civil service agency, for an additional two months to a maximum of four months to avoid programmatic disruption (§ 65(3)).

9:10. What are temporary appointments to competitive class positions and when may they be made?

A *temporary* appointment is a short-term appointment to a competitive class position specifically authorized by the Civil Service Law (§ 64). A temporary appointment may be made (1) on an emergency basis for a period not exceeding three months; (2) to replace a permanent appointee who is on leave of absence for the duration of the leave; or (3) when a position is expected to exist for less than six months (§ 64(1)).

In addition, a local civil service agency can authorize a temporary appointment, without examination, when the person appointed will render professional, scientific, technical or other expert services on either an occasional basis or on a full-time or regular part-time basis in a temporary position established to conduct a special study or project for not longer than 18 months (§ 64(3)).

9:11. Must an employer use the appropriate eligible list when making a temporary appointment?

The answer depends on how long the temporary appointment is to last. If the appointment is to be for three months or less, use of an eligible list is not required. If the appointment is to last between three and six months, the appointment must be made from the eligible list, but the appointee does not have to be among the top three on the list. If the appointment is to last for six months or longer, the appointee must be among the three highest scoring candidates on the list willing to accept the appointment (§ 64(2)).

Irrespective of the duration of the position to which a temporary appointment is made, the candidate must meet the stated minimum qualifications for the position and file an application with the local civil service agency.

9:12. Does a person appointed to a competitive class position from an eligible list automatically attain permanent status?

No. Permanent appointments to positions in the competitive class require satisfactory completion of a probationary term. The probationary term is established by the local civil service agency and is included in the local civil service rules (§ 63). Because the length of the probationary term may vary from one jurisdiction to another, the local civil service agency should be contacted for specific information. Typically, the probationary period for a person appointed from an open competitive list (as opposed to a promotion list) has both a minimum and maximum period, while the probationary period for a person appointed from a promotion list is generally for a fixed period of time (see, e.g., 4 NYCRR § 4.5 (a)(1)).

In general, a probationary employee whose conduct or performance is not satisfactory may be terminated at any time after completion of the minimum period and before completion of the maximum period without a hearing so long as the decision is not made in bad faith (see *Matter of Albano v. Kirby*, 36 N.Y.2d 526, 533 (1975); *Macklin v. Powell*, 107 A.D.2d 964 (1985)). However, local civil service rules may impose certain requirements, such as minimum notice and the opportunity to be heard (see *Saulpaugh v. Diehl*, 148 A.D.2d 928 (4th Dep't 1989)).

At the expiration of the minimum probationary period, the probationary appointment becomes permanent unless the probationer has been given notice that the probationary term will be continued (*Marlow v. Tully*, 100 A.D.2d 786 (1st Dep't 1984), *aff'd*, 63 N.Y.2d 918, *reargument denied*, 64 N.Y.2d 755, cert. denied 472 U.S. 1010, *rehearing denied*, 473 U.S. 924). Once a probationary employee attains permanent status, he or she can be terminated only for cause, after a hearing held in accordance with section 75 (see **9:24**).

9:13. Are veterans entitled to preference in appointment or promotion to a competitive class position?

Yes. The New York State Constitution authorizes a preference for veterans as an exception to the rule that appointments and promotions be made on the basis of merit and fitness (Art. V, § 6; § 85). Disabled veterans, as defined by the Civil Service Law, are entitled to 10 additional points on competitive examinations for original appointment and five points for promotion. Veterans who are not disabled are entitled to five additional points on a competitive examination for original appointment and two-and-one-half points for promotion (§ 85(2)(a)).

To be eligible for the preference, the veteran must have been a member of the armed forces of the United States who served in time of war and was honorably discharged or released under honorable circumstances from such service. He or she also must be a citizen of the United States or an alien lawfully admitted for permanent residence in the United States and a resident of the state of New York when applying for preference (§ 85(1)(a)).

Before additional credits can be added to a veteran's grade, the veteran must have obtained a passing grade on the examination. In other words, additional credits may not be used to change a veteran's rating from failing to passing (§ 85(2)(b)).

Veteran's credit may only be used once to obtain an appointment or promotion. Thus, if a veteran has been permanently appointed or promoted to a position by means of additional credits which affected his or her position on the appropriate eligible list, he or she is not entitled to receive any additional credit in future examinations (§ 85(4)).

9:14. May a school board require that candidates for a noninstructional position be residents of the local school district?

No, a school board may not require that candidates for a noninstructional position be residents of the local school district, but the local civil service agency may establish residency requirements, even over the objection of a local school board (§ 23(4-a); see *Buffet v. Municipal Civ. Serv. Com.*, 58 A.D.2d 362, *aff'd*, 45 N.Y.2d 1003 (1978)).

A school district may, however, require that district residents be certified for hiring from an eligible list before nonresidents (§ 23(4-a)). Once the district makes an appointment from among certified residents, it must continue to do so until the list of residents is exhausted. After exhausting the list of district residents, selection must be made from the entire eligible list without regard to residency.

9:15. Can a competitive class employee in one school district transfer to another school district without further examination?

Yes. Most local civil service agencies have rules that permit transfers to similar positions in other school districts or other units of government. Requests for transfer should be referred to the local civil service agency for approval (§ 70).

9:16. May a school district assign an employee hired to perform services in one title of the classified service to the duties of another position?

Generally, no. Except in cases of short-term emergency, it is improper for an employer to assign an employee hired to perform services in one title of the classified service to the duties appropriate to another position (§ 61(2)).

For example, requiring a school nurse to be responsible for allowing persons into the school has been found not to fall within the general statement of duties of a registered professional school nurse and therefore violative of Civil Service Law §61 (*CSEA v. New Hyde Park/Garden City Park UFSD*, 230 A.D.2d 702 (2nd Dep't 1996)). Further, assigning an employee duties beyond the inherent nature of the position is a mandatory subject of negotiations (*Village of Scarsdale*, 8 PERB ¶ 3075 (1975)).

9:17. Are noninstructional employees in the classified service required to file a constitutional oath of office?

Yes. Every person employed by a school district, except employees in the labor class, must take an oath of affirmation in support of the United States and New York State constitutions before he or she starts work. However, a Native American Indian enrolled in or affiliated with an Indian nation recognized by the United States or State of New York may choose to affirm that he or she will perform his or her duties in a manner consistent with the United States and New York constitutions, rather than declaring his or her support of these constitutions (§ 62).

9:18. Must school district noninstructional employees be paid minimum wage and overtime?

School district employees are covered by the federal minimum wage and overtime standards in the Fair Labor Standards Act (FLSA) (29 USC

§§ 206, 207; *Garcia v. San Antonio Metropolitan Transportation Authority,* 469 U.S. 528, 533 (1985)). They are also covered by the New York State Minimum Wage Act (Lab. Law, Art. 19). As of September 1, 1997, the minimum wage under both New York State and federal law is $5.15 per hour (Lab. Law § 652 and 29 USC § 206).

FLSA requires employers to pay their employees overtime wages of one-and-one-half times the employees' regular rates of compensation for each hour they work in excess of 40 hours per week (29 USC § 207). However, public employers may provide for compensatory time off in lieu of over-time compensation, so long as the benefit is equal to one-and-one-half hours off for each hour over 40 worked in a week (see 29 USC § 207(o)). No more than 240 hours of compensatory time off may be accrued, and employees must be allowed to use this time off on request within a reasonable period, as long as the employer's operations will not be unduly disrupted.

9:19. Must school districts submit payrolls of employees to the local civil service agency?

Yes, for employees in the classified civil service. The local civil service agency having jurisdiction must certify at least annually that each person on the payroll list has been employed in accordance with law (§ 100). Additionally, each person who is hired or whose payroll status changes must be certified (§ 100(2)). It is a misdemeanor for any school officer to willfully pay or authorize the payment of salary to any person in the classified service if he or she knows that the local civil service commission has refused to certify the payroll because the individual in question has been appointed, employed, transferred, assigned to perform duties or reinstated in violation of the Civil Service Law (§ 101; see also **9:3**).

9:20. Is there any set time period which a noninstructional employee of a school district must be given for lunch?

A noninstructional employee working more than six hours in a day must receive at least 45 minutes for a lunch period. However, the state commis-sioner of labor may permit a shorter meal period to be fixed (Lab. Law § 162(5)). Moreover, while school districts and their employees cannot completely bargain away the lunch period, the 45-minute period may be modified in a collective bargaining agreement (see *American Broadcasting Cos, Inc. v. Roberts,* 61 N.Y.2d 244 (1984)). However, school districts may not unilaterally change the duration of meal breaks (*County of Nassau,* 24 PERB ¶ 3029 (1991); *Hammondsport CSD,* 18 PERB ¶ 4647 (1985)).

9:21. Are noninstructional school employees entitled to leave under the federal Family and Medical Leave Act?

Yes. Under the federal Family and Medical Leave Act (FMLA) (29 USC §§ 2601-2654; 29 CFR Part 825), all employers with more than 50 employees must provide up to 12 weeks of unpaid leave after the first year of employment to any employee who works more than 1,250 hours a year, as needed for personal or family illness, or for the birth or adoption of a child (29 USC § 2612). The law also requires the employer to continue any health insurance it provides to employees during the period of leave, and prohibits any collective bargaining agreement from reducing this benefit. Upon return from FMLA leave, the employee must be restored to the same position he or she held prior to the absence, or one equivalent to it (see 29 USC § 2614(a)(1)).

The law allows employers to designate periods of paid leave as FMLA leave if employees are properly informed (see 29 USC § 2612(d); 29 CFR § 829.208).

Because employers are prohibited from reducing the rights granted by this law (see 29 USC § 2652), a school district should consult with its school attorney to ensure that its leave policies meet the requirements of the law.

School districts should also afford the appropriate employee organization the opportunity to negotiate over specific issues relating to FMLA leave, such as substitution of paid leave for FMLA leave and procedures for applying for FMLA leave. Although FMLA prohibits the negotiation of leave benefits which would be less than those mandated by FMLA, any leave benefit that is more generous than that mandated by FMLA, as well as procedures regarding leave that are not mandated by the statute or its regulations, must be negotiated at the option of the appropriate employee organization (see *Rome Hospital*, 27 PERB ¶ 4575 (1994)).

For more information on FMLA, see **10:60-64.**

9:22. Are noninstructional employees of school districts entitled to military leaves of absence?

Yes. Under section 242 of the Military Law, all public employees who are required to perform ordered military duty are entitled to take a leave of absence from work for the duration of their military duty.

An employee absent from regular duties at a school district because of ordered military duty is entitled to be paid his or her usual pay for 30 calendar days, or 22 working days, whichever is greater, per calendar year (Mil. Law § 242(5)).

All such service, even if beyond the period of mandated paid leave, is to be treated as regular service with the school district and counted as time served towards completion of a probationary period (Mil. Law § 242(4)). Any leave in excess of the statutorily mandated leave is a mandatory subject of bargaining (*State v. New York State Public Employment Relations Board*, 187 A.D.2d 78 (3rd Dep't 1993)).

Federal law also requires all employers to allow employees to be absent for up to five years to serve in the military (see 38 USC §§ 4301-4318).

Discipline of Noninstructional Employees

9:23. Are classified service employees entitled to due process protection prior to being disciplined?

Yes, but only certain employees in the classified service are entitled to such protection. The following types of classified service employees are entitled to protection: (1) persons holding a position by permanent appointment (as opposed to provisional or temporary appointment) in the competitive class (§ 75(1)(a)); (2) honorably discharged war veterans and exempt volunteer firefighters (as defined in the General Municipal Law) employed permanently in the classified service, regardless of the employee's jurisdictional classification, except for persons holding the positions of private secretary, cashier or deputy of any official or department (§ 75(1)(b)); and (3) employees holding positions in the noncompetitive class who have completed at least five years of continuous service in the noncompetitive class, provided the employee's position has not been designated as confidential or policy making by the local civil service agency (§ 75(1)(c)).

9:24. What is the procedure for removing or otherwise disciplining a covered classified service employee?

Persons entitled to protection under section 75 of the Civil Service Law (i.e., persons holding the types of positions identified in **9:23**) have the right to notice of any charges against them and a hearing prior to discipline and may not be removed or otherwise disciplined except for incompetency or misconduct.

The protected employee is entitled to at least eight days to respond to the charges in writing (§ 75(2)).

At the hearing, the employee may be represented by counsel or by a representative of a recognized or certified employee organization and may present witnesses on his or her behalf. The burden of proving incompetency or misconduct by the employee is on the district (§ 75(2)).

The required hearing is conducted by the school board or a designated hearing officer having the power to remove the person against whom the charges are lodged. The hearing officer and the person who makes the final determination of guilt or innocence and sets the penalty must be unbiased; in other words, they should have no personal knowledge of the events surrounding the charge and should not have brought or prosecuted the charges (see *Memmelaar v. Straub*, 181 A.D.2d 980 (3rd Dep't 1992)). A departure from this standard violates the employee's right to due process.

9:25. Is an employee covered by section 75 entitled to notice and a hearing before his or her position is abolished?

As a general rule, no (see **9:24**). Under the Civil Service Law, a public employer may abolish civil service positions for purposes of economy or efficiency so long as the abolition is not a "subterfuge to avoid the statutory protections afforded to civil servants before they are discharged." (*Cifarelli v. Village of Babylon*, 93 F.3d 47 (2nd Cir. 1996); *Dwyer v. Regan*, 777 F.2d 825 (2nd Cir. 1985), *modified*, 793 F.2d 457 (2nd Cir. 1986); *Matter of Aldazabal v. Carey*, 44 N.Y.2d 787 (1978); *Bianco v. Pitts*, 200 A.D.2d 741 (2nd Dep't 1994); §§ 80, 81). Simply stated, a school district can lay off an employee entitled to the protection of section 75 without giving that employee notice and a hearing (see **9:23**).

There is, however, a exception to the general rule. Where a public employer abolishes an employee's position and there is no indication that the employer acted for reasons of economy or efficiency but rather it is alleged that the employer targeted the employee for termination, the employer has an obligation to provide the employee a hearing prior to removing the employee from his position, provided the employee requests such a hearing (*Cifarelli v. Village of Babylon; Dwyer v. Regan*). Such a hearing must be held before a neutral fact finder, not the employer (*Dwyer v. Regan*). The burden is on the employee to prove that the abolition was done in bad faith (*Bianco v. Pitts*).

9:26. Must a school district afford an employee covered by section 75 any special rights *before* bringing disciplinary charges?

Yes. A noninstructional employee with section 75 protection is entitled to union representation when questioned by a supervisor if it appears that the employee may be the subject of disciplinary action. The affected employee must be notified in advance, in writing, of that right (§ 75(2)).

The United States Supreme Court has ruled that public employees who lie in the course of an investigation into alleged misconduct cannot rely on the federal constitutional protection of due process to shield them from additional discipline based upon having lied (*LaChance v. Erickson, et al.*, 118 S.Ct. 753 (1998)).

9:27. Is Civil Service Law section 75 the only source of due process protection available to employees in the classified service?

No. While school districts must comply with the procedures specified in this section to discipline or discharge employees covered by the law, they may also collectively negotiate alternative disciplinary procedures with the union representing employees in recognized bargaining units (§ 76(4)). If separate contractual procedures exist, they should be consulted prior to the discipline of any employee in the bargaining unit. However, the right to a hearing may not be waived by the provisions of a negotiated collective bargaining agreement (see *Romano v. Canuteson*, 11 F.3d 1140 (2nd Cir. 1993)).

9:28. Is there any time limit for bringing disciplinary charges against an employee under section 75?

Yes. No removal or disciplinary proceeding may be commenced more than 18 months after the occurrence of the misconduct or incompetency alleged in the charge. However, this limitation does not apply where the charges would, if proved in the appropriate court, constitute a crime (§ 75(4)).

9:29. May an employee facing discipline under section 75 be suspended without pay pending the outcome of the hearing?

Yes. The Civil Service Law allows for the suspension without pay of an employee for up to 30 days pending the hearing and determination of charges (§ 75(3)). If the employee is acquitted at the hearing or later reinstated after appeal to the local civil service agency or to the courts, that employee is entitled to back pay for the period during which he or she was off the payroll, less the amount of any unemployment benefits he or she may have received during such period (§§ 75(3), 76(3), 77). The right to paid suspensions during the pendency of disciplinary actions under section 75 may be waived by provisions in a negotiated collective bargaining agreement (*Romano v. Canuteson*, 11 F.3d 1140 (2nd Cir. 1993)).

9:30. What penalty or punishment may be imposed after a section 75 hearing?

The penalty or punishment imposed after a section 75 hearing may consist of: (1) a reprimand; (2) a fine not to exceed $100 to be deducted from the employee's wages; (3) suspension without pay for a period not exceeding two months; (4) demotion in grade and title; or (5) dismissal (§ 75(3)).

9:31. May an employee who has been disciplined under section 75 file an appeal?

Yes. An appeal may be made to the local civil service agency having jurisdiction or to the courts (§ 76(1)). The commissioner of education has no jurisdiction over this type of case (*Appeal of McGregor*, 35 Educ. Dep't Rep. 363 (1996)).

An employee may appeal any penalty except an official reprimand that is accompanied by a remittance of compensation lost during suspension. An employee wishing to appeal a discharge following a section 75 hearing to the courts in an Article 78 proceeding must serve a notice of claim upon the school district within three months of the discharge, and not within four months as is usually the case with Article 78 proceedings (*Harder v. Board of Educ. Binghamton City Sch. Dist.*, 188 A.D.2d 783 (3rd Dep't 1992), citing Educ. Law § 3813(1)).

9:32. What procedures must be observed to either discipline or discharge a noninstructional employee who does not have section 75 protection?

Such employees may have job protections under a collective bargaining agreement. Employees who do not have section 75 or collective bargaining agreement protections are "at will" employees, meaning that they can be discharged without cause and without a hearing. Simply stated, such employees can be disciplined or discharged for any reason, except an illegal reason (e.g., because of race, religion, sex, disability). Nonetheless, a school district's decision to discipline or discharge such an employee should be supported by evidence rationally related to its action in the disciplinary action or discharge.

The discipline or discharge may be reversed in court if it was done in bad faith or for a legally impermissible reason, such as retaliation for the exercise of a protected right or with reckless disregard for the truth of the charges.

9:33. Under what circumstances are noninstructional employees entitled to a name-clearing hearing?

Any public employee, regardless of whether the employee is entitled to the protection of Civil Service Law section 75, is entitled to a hearing to challenge his or her dismissal if the alleged reason for the dismissal puts the employee's good name, reputation, honor or honesty in question.

Such a hearing is referred to as a "name-clearing" hearing *(Board of Regents v. Roth,* 408 U.S. 564 (1972); *Wisconsin v. Constantineau,* 400 U.S. 433 (1971); *Marzullo v. Suffolk County,* 97 A.D.2d 789 (2nd Dep't 1983)).

Allegations of professional incompetence will support a right to a name-clearing hearing only when they denigrate the employee's competence as a professional and impugn his or her reputation to the point of significantly hampering the employee's continued ability to practice his or her profession *(Donato v. Plainview-Old Bethpage CSD,* 96 F.3d 623 (2nd Cir. 1996)).

In order to be entitled to a name-clearing hearing, the employee must establish that the stigmatizing statements made by the public employer have been publicly disclosed (see *Bishop v. Wood,* 426 U.S. 341 (1976)). The disclosure requirement can be satisfied where the stigmatizing charges are placed in the discharged employee's personnel file and are likely to be disclosed to prospective employers *(Donato v. Plainview-Old Bethpage CSD).*

The right to a meaningful opportunity to refute charges in a name-clearing hearing does not require a full, formal proceeding. However, rights and procedures such as the right to secure counsel, to call witnesses on the employee's behalf, and to confront and cross examine witnesses supporting the allegations, may be granted or agreed to (see *Goss v. Lopez,* 419 U.S. 565 (1975)).

At the hearing, the employee has the burden of proving that the charges are false *(Marzullo v. Suffolk County).*

Following the hearing, the employer need not rehire the employee even if the employee can prove the inaccuracy of the stigmatizing allegations. If the charges are proven false, the employer may be liable to the employee for damages *(Donato v. Plainview-Old Bethpage CSD).*

9:34. Does the placement of a critical letter in the file of a noninstructional employee who is entitled to section 75 protection constitute discipline that would require a hearing as described in 9:24?

No. Civil Service Law section 75 does not insulate noninstructional school district personnel from all written critical comments from their supervisors. Documents such as critical administrative evaluations or admonitions which are intended to warn or instruct a given employee may be placed in an employee's file without resort to a formal hearing *(CSEA v. Southhold UFSD,* 204 A.D.2d 445 (2nd Dep't 1994); *Tomaka v. Evans-Brant CSD,* 107 A.D.2d 1078, *aff'd,* 65 N.Y.2d 1048 (1985)).

However, a letter which addresses more serious allegations may be treated as a disciplinary reprimand, requiring a hearing conducted under section 75 *(CSEA v. Southhold UFSD)*. In deciding whether a particular written communication constitutes a reprimand which will require a hearing, no single factor will be determinative. A court will likely consider the identity of the author, the subject matter of the document, the tenor of the document, the employer's characterization of the document, and whether the document's focus is on punishment or warning and instruction *(CSEA v. Southhold UFSD)*.

9:35. What is the so-called "whistle-blower law"?

Section 75-b of the Civil Service Law, the so-called "whistle-blower law," prohibits a public employer from taking retaliatory personnel action against an employee who discloses to a governmental body information concerning either a violation of law, rule or regulation which creates a substantial and specific danger to the public health or safety, or that the employee reasonably believes to be true and reasonably believes constitutes an improper governmental action (§ 75-b(2)(a)).

If disciplinary action is brought under section 75 of the Civil Service Law or under a collective bargaining agreement against an employee who reveals such information, the employee may assert a defense based on this statute in the disciplinary proceedings, which must be addressed by the hearing officer or arbitrator (§ 75-b(3)). Employees who do not have the right to such procedures may instead bring an action in court within one year after the alleged retaliatory action using the procedures set forth in section 740 of the Labor Law (§ 75-b(3)(c); see *Hanley v. New York State Executive Department, Division for Youth*, 182 A.D.2d 317 (3rd Dep't 1992)).

9:36. Where may additional information about civil service matters affecting schools be obtained?

Contact the city or county civil service commission or personnel officer in the city or county in which your school district is located.

Security Guards

9:37. Is a school district required to comply with the requirements of the Security Guard Act of 1992?

Yes. If a school district employs at least one security guard, then the district is subject to the Security Guard Act of 1992 (Gen. Bus. Law § 89-f(5), (7)). Under section 89-o of the General Business Law, the secretary of state is empowered to adopt rules and regulations implementing the provisions of this article.

Any security guard employed by a school district must be registered by the Department of State (Gen. Bus. Law § 89-g(1)(b)). Registration for a security guard is effective for two years

A district employing a security guard must provide proof of self-insurance or liability insurance coverage to the Department of State in the amount of $100,000 per occurrence and $300,000 in the aggregate (Gen. Bus. Law § 89-g(6)).

9:38. Whom should a school district contact for additional information or with questions regarding the Security Guard Act of 1992?

Questions about the Security Guard Act of 1992 should be directed to the state Division of Criminal Justice Services at 518-457-4135, or the Department of State at 518-474-4429.

10. Employee Relations

Contracts of Employment

10:1. What is an individual contract of employment?

An *individual contract of employment* is an agreement, usually in writing, that contains a set of promises between an employer and an employee. Contracts of employment typically set forth terms of employment, duties of the position, salary and employment benefits such as health insurance, retirement benefits, paid vacation and sick leave.

10:2. How are individual contracts of employment formed?

Following a period of negotiation during which an agreement is reached, a contract usually is executed or formed when both parties sign the written document. Although the school board is the entity that appoints all district personnel (see, for example, Educ. Law §§ 1604(8), 1709(16), 1950(4)(e), 2503(5); 2509(3); 2573), a common practice in many districts is for the board to approve the contract by resolution and to specify in that resolution the individual authorized to sign the contract on the board's behalf, such as the board president or the superintendent.

10:3. What is the difference between an individual contract of employment and a collective bargaining agreement?

An *individual contract of employment* is an agreement between the school district and an individual employee. A *collective bargaining agreement* is a contract between the school district, executed by the superintendent acting as the chief executive officer of the school district, and an employee organization (or union) that represents a group of employees included within a bargaining unit (see § 201(12); **10:15**).

Employees who are covered by the terms of a collective bargaining agreement are appointed to their positions by resolution of the board, and the agreement serves to describe the terms and conditions of that employment. However, employees covered by a contract of employment derive the right to the appointment to their positions from the contract itself.

All statutory references in this chapter are to the New York State Civil Service Law unless noted otherwise.

10:4. Must all employees have individual contracts of employment?

No. Most school district employees do not have individual contracts of employment with the district but instead are covered by a collective bargaining agreement.

Some employees, such as the superintendent of schools, have individual employment contracts specifying their terms and conditions of employment.

Employees who are designated as either "managerial" or "confidential" employees under the Taylor Law (§ 201(7)(a)) are precluded from being members of a bargaining unit and therefore not covered by a collective bargaining agreement. Still others who are not protected by the provisions of Civil Service Law section 75 or Education Law section 3020-a and who serve without contracts of employment are employed in accordance with such school board policies as may apply to their positions. These employees are known as "at-will" employees, meaning that they can be discharged without cause and without a hearing. Simply stated, these employees can be disciplined or discharged for any reason, except an illegal reason (e.g., because of race, religion, sex, disability, etc.) (**9:32**). There are very few school district employees who fall in this category. Those that do may include members of the district's managerial staff, confidential clerks and secretaries.

Board policies, as well as employee manuals or handbooks, may, however, give even at-will employees specific protections and assurances regarding their terms and conditions of employment, including rights regarding discipline and discharge. Such rights may be enforceable as contracts, or create other grounds for challenging an employment decision in court. Districts should therefore exercise care and consult with their school attorneys to avoid unintentionally creating such rights.

10:5. What powers do school boards have in connection with collective bargaining agreements?

Under the Taylor Law, it is the superintendent, as chief executive officer of the school district (§ 201(10)), and not the board, as the district's legislative body, who is technically responsible for negotiating and executing collective bargaining agreements (§ 201(12)). However, as a practical matter, given the employment relationship between the board and the superintendent (a relationship that does not exist between most chief executives and legislative bodies) school boards frequently play an active role in the negotiations process.

In addition, the school board also plays two distinct roles in the conclusion of the negotiations process. One, the board may ratify a tentative agreement reached by the district and the union before execution of the agreement (provided the right has been reserved to the board by the district's negotiator), and two, a board has the right to legislatively approve certain provisions of the executed agreement (§§ 201(12), 204-a; *Jamesville-DeWitt CSD*, 22 PERB ¶ 3048 (1989); *Town of Dresden*, 17 PERB ¶ 3096 (1984); *Harpursville CSD*, 14 PERB ¶ 3003 (1980)). Contract ratification and legislative approval are two related concepts that are often confused (*Glen Cove City SD*, 6 PERB ¶ 3004 (1973)).

Contract ratification is a voluntary process under which a tentative agreement is submitted to a school board or a union for a vote to accept or reject the tentative agreement. School boards do not have an inherent or automatic right of ratification (see *Town of Dresden*, 17 PERB ¶ 3096 (1984)). The right of ratification is created by agreement or through understanding between the parties' negotiators. It is not a right that a school board or any other party may unilaterally reserve to itself. (See, for example, *Town of Dresden*, 17 PERB ¶ 3096 (1984); *Falconer CSD*, 6 PERB ¶ 3029 (1973); *Jamestown Teachers' Ass'n*, 6 PERB ¶ 3075 (1973)).

Legislative approval is a right and duty of the board created by statute (§§ 201(12), 204-a(1)). Unlike the negotiated right of ratification which allows the board to approve or reject the entire tentative agreement, the statutory right of legislative approval only allows the board to act on those contract provisions which require an amendment of board policy or additional funding. As a general rule, those provisions of an executed agreement do not become binding on the school district until the board has given its approval (§ 210(12)).

Provisions requiring legislative approval in a multi-year agreement may not be conditioned upon or subject to annual appropriations. Once there has been legislative approval of a multi-year agreement, the school district is bound by the agreement for its full specified term (*Association of Surrogates and Supreme Court Reporters v. State of New York*, 78 N.Y.2d 143 (1991)).

10:6. Must an agreement reached by negotiators at the bargaining table be ratified by the school board?

No. However, the negotiators for both the district and the employee organization may agree to require ratification by the school board and/or union membership in the ground rules established for negotiation of a collective bargaining agreement or within the collective bargaining agreement itself (see **10:34**). This is commonly done. It is important for the right to be reserved explicitly, however, because the Public Employment Relations Board (PERB) has held that it is an improper practice for either the school board or the employee organization to attempt to reject the agreement after the negotiator has given assent, unless the parties have agreed that the board or employee organization's members have reserved the right to ratify or reject the terms of a tentative agreement (see *Harpursville CSD*, 14 PERB ¶ 3003 (1980); *Falconer CSD*, 6 PERB ¶ 3029 (1973)).

The ratification process involves at least the following elements. First, the ratifying body (that is, the school board) must be aware that negotiations have been completed and that its negotiators have reached an agreement subject only to ratification. Second, while the members of the ratifying body may differ on reasons for ratifying or rejecting the agreement, the agreement should be ratified or rejected as a whole and not on a piecemeal basis. Third, the negotiators must affirmatively support ratification, unless they have made the other party aware of their opposition to the tentative agreement. Finally, a decision to ratify must be clearly and unequivocally made and communicated (*Jamesville-DeWitt CSD*, 22 PERB ¶ 3048 (1989)).

10:7. Can a school board lose its properly reserved right to ratify an agreement?

Yes. The right of a school board to ratify an agreement, even though properly reserved, can nonetheless be lost by the conduct of the district's negotiators. All members of the district's negotiating team have a duty to support and affirmatively seek ratification of a tentative agreement, unless a team member has explicitly given advance notice to the union that he or she does not intend to support it (*Copiague UFSD*, 23 PERB ¶ 3046 (1990)). This is considered an indication of good faith at the bargaining table. Failure to perform this duty will result in the loss of an employer's right to ratify the agreement.

In addition, the affirmative duty to support a tentative agreement requires all members of the negotiating team to actively advocate for ratification of the contract. PERB has held that this duty may be breached simply by silence on the part of a negotiating team member in the face of opposition to the tentative agreement or by neutrality during the ratification process (see *Copiague UFSD*, 23 PERB ¶ 3046 (1990); *Jeffersonville-Youngsville CSD*, 16 PERB ¶ 3106 (1983)).

When a negotiator improperly fails to affirmatively support ratification of an agreement, the superintendent can be required to execute that agreement. This situation occurred in a case where one of the district's negotiators distributed material to certain members of the school board in opposition to a tentatively reached agreement on the settlement of a new contract. PERB considered this evidence of failure to negotiate in good faith, which is an improper practice (see **10:47-49**), and directed the superintendent to execute the agreement without the board's ratification

(Buffalo Teachers Federation v. Buffalo City School Dist., 24 PERB ¶ 3033 (1991), *aff'd*, 191 A.D.2d 985 (4th Dep't 1993), *motion for leave to appeal denied*, 82 N.Y.2d 656 (1993)).

In addition, a school board can lose a properly reserved authority to ratify an agreement if it fails to conduct a ratification vote. Failure to conduct a ratification vote, at which the tentative agreement is either approved or disapproved, is a violation of the district's duty to negotiate in good faith. A failure to make a ratification decision in accordance with ground rules results in a waiver of the right to ratify. From this result a district can be directed by PERB to execute the agreement (*Utica City School Dist.*, 27 PERB ¶ 3023 (1994); see **10:14** in regard to powers and duties of PERB).

10:8. Can a school board's statutory right to legislatively approve a contract be lost through prior board action?

Yes. For example, in one case, PERB determined that a school board had exercised its right of legislative approval when all the members of the board served on the negotiating team which came to an agreement with the union (*Sylvan-Verona Beach CSD*, 15 PERB ¶ 3067 (1982)). In another case, the state Court of Appeals ruled that a school board, which had reluctantly directed, by resolution, the superintendent to execute a contract after PERB and the courts ruled that the right of ratification had been lost due to a failure on the part of one of the district's negotiators to support ratification, did not have a separate right to legislatively approve the funding provisions of the agreement (*Board of Educ. v. Buffalo Teachers Fed'n*, 89 N.Y.2d 370 (1996), *motion for reargument denied*, 89 N.Y.2d 983 (1997); see also **10:5**).

10:9. Can changes be made in the terms of a contract of employment or a collective bargaining agreement during the period of the contract or agreement?

Generally, the parties to a contract of employment or a collective bargaining agreement must adhere to all the specifications contained therein for the duration of the contract or agreement, unless the parties agree mutually to changes in such terms. A board may change the terms of a contract of employment or a collective bargaining agreement only with the consent of the employee or the employee organization, respectively; that is, by renegotiating the terms of the contract or agreement (see generally, *Village of Endicott*, 23 PERB ¶ 3053 (1990)).

Additionally, all the terms of an expired collective bargaining agreement must be continued until a new agreement is negotiated pursuant to the Triborough Amendment to the Taylor Law (§ 209–a(1)(e); see **10:46**).

10:10. What employee relations and negotiation services are available through the New York State School Boards Association?

The State School Boards Association provides a variety of employee relations services.

Association attorneys can perform analyses of existing collective bargaining agreements and meet with school boards, superintendents and administrators to assist in analyzing current contracts and developing goals for negotiations.

Association staff members are also available to assist in on-going negotiations and in fact finding by gathering, analyzing and developing information and issues for further use.

Through the use of its computerized arbitration and 3020-a databases, the Association can help a school district select the best available arbitrator for an arbitration proceeding, or for cases brought pursuant to section 3020-a of the Education Law or section 75 of the Civil Service Law. These databases also can be used for research of grievance and 3020-a issues.

The Association also has compiled extensive information from annual, statewide surveys and directly from collective bargaining agreements. This information may be helpful to identify goals and priorities in collective bargaining by providing additional points of comparison on a regional or statewide basis.

The Association's staff is available for consultation on a wide variety of other labor issues, including arbitration, tenure and seniority. Association attorneys also are available to assist with legal work on employee relations issues.

The Taylor Law

10:11. What is the Taylor Law?

The Taylor Law, officially entitled the Public Employees' Fair Employment Act, is article 14 of the Civil Service Law. Enacted in 1967, the Taylor Law governs labor relations between public employers and public employees in New York State. The law is named after Prof. George W. Taylor of the University of Pennsylvania, chairman of Gov. Nelson Rockefeller's Committee on Public Employee Relations (also known as the Taylor Committee), whose report and recommendations formed the basis for the law.

The Taylor Law's purpose is to foster harmonious and cooperative labor relations in the public sector and to avoid strikes (§ 200; *City of Newburgh v. Newman*, 69 N.Y.2d 166 (1987)).

10:12. What rights are given to public employees under the Taylor Law?

Under the Taylor Law, public employees are guaranteed the rights of self-organization and representation for collective negotiations (§§ 202, 203). Self-organization rights enable public employees to join or refrain from joining unions (referred to in the Taylor Law as "employee organizations") of their choice (§ 202). Representation rights enable employees to designate an employee organization as their representative in collective negotiations with their public employer over terms and conditions of employment, and in the administration of grievances arising from their negotiated agreements (§ 203).

The rights given to employees under the Taylor Law do not extend to all persons employed by a public employer. Classes of employees to whom the law does not extend include managerial or confidential employees (§ 201(7)(a)) or to "casual" employees and per diem substitute teachers who have not been given a reasonable assurance of continued employment by the district (§ 201(7)(d) and (f)) (see **10:19, 10:22**).

10:13. What are the rights of a school district as a public employer under the Taylor Law?

As a public employer, a school district has the right to recognize (or withhold recognition of) employee organizations for the purpose of negotiating collectively and entering into collective bargaining agreements (§ 204(1); see **10:17**).

In addition, while a school district is required to negotiate collectively with a certified or recognized employee organization (see **10:30, 10:33**), the district has the right to insist that the employee organization participate in good-faith bargaining with the district (§§ 204(2), 209–a(2)(b)). Although a school district must engage in negotiations over mandatory subjects of bargaining, negotiations cannot be conditioned on negotiating nonmandatory or permissive subjects (see *Seneca Falls CSD*, 23 PERB ¶ 4518 (1990)).

A district also has the right to negotiate free from strike activities or threats of strikes, and the right and the obligation to invoke the Taylor Law's procedures concerning strikes if a strike or strike activity occurs (§ 210; see **10:51**)).

10:14. Who administers the Taylor Law?

The Taylor Law is administered by the Public Employment Relations Board (PERB) (§ 205). The PERB Board consists of three members appointed by the governor and confirmed by the New York State Senate, one of whom serves as the chairperson of the board (§ 205(1)). In addition, PERB has a staff consisting of administrators, attorneys, administrative law judges (ALJs), mediators and fact-finders.

PERB's powers and duties include establishing bargaining units, certifying employee organizations as the exclusive representatives of such units, remedying improper practices by employers and employee organizations (including obtaining injunctions, when appropriate), administering some strike penalty provisions, presiding over hearings, assigning mediators and fact-finders to help resolve negotiation impasses, conducting research, and establishing a staff to assist in all of these powers and duties (§§ 205, 207, 209, 210). PERB, however, generally has no authority to enforce a school district's collective bargaining agreement, unless an alleged contract violation would also constitute an improper practice (§ 205(5)(d)).

To help administer the Taylor Law, PERB employs administrative law judges to consider charges of improper practices by employee organizations or employers, to certify bargaining units and to enforce other provisions of the Taylor Law. PERB considers appeals (called "exceptions") from the decisions of administrative law judges (§ 205).

PERB's decisions are reviewable pursuant to article 78 of the Civil Practice Law and Rules (CPLR), which authorizes judicial review of determinations of administrative boards. Final orders of PERB are enforceable by the state supreme court upon petition by PERB in a special proceeding. An order by PERB which determines whether an employer or employee is subject to the Taylor Law may be deemed final when made (§ 213; CPLR § 7803). An article 78 proceeding to challenge a PERB order must be filed within 30 days after service of the order (§ 213(a); *PERB v. Bd. of Educ. of City of Buffalo*, 46 A.D.2d 509, *aff'd*, 39 N.Y.2d 86 (1976)).

Employee Representation Under the Taylor Law

10:15. What is a bargaining unit and how is its composition determined?

A *bargaining unit, or negotiating unit*, is a group of employees organized for the purpose of collective negotiations and represented by an employee organization. A unit may consist of all the employees in a locality, all the employees in a department or agency, or all the employees in a certain occupational category. Three typical bargaining units in schools would be for administrators and supervisors; teachers and other instructional staff; and noninstructional staff.

When defining a bargaining unit, the positions to be included in the unit must have a sufficient community of interest to enable the unit to effectively negotiate collectively through its representatives (§ 207(1)(a); *Dutchess County BOCES*, 25 PERB ¶ 3048 (1992)). The law also requires that the appropriate unit be defined or drawn along lines that permit public officials at the level of the unit to agree or to make effective recommendations with regard to the terms and conditions of employment to be negotiated (§ 207(1)(b)). Moreover, the unit must be compatible with the joint responsibilities of the public employer and the public employees to serve the public (§ 207(1)(c)).

There is no steadfast rule for the definition of an appropriate bargaining unit, although public policy is in favor of large rather than fragmented bargaining units (see *Committee of Interns & Residents v. New York State Public Employment Relations Board*, 78 A.D.2d 730 (3rd Dep't 1980)). It is important to examine the professional status of the employees to be included in the bargaining unit, the employer's organizational hierarchy, conflicting interests among the positions to be included, and the employer's administrative convenience (see *Altmar-Parish-Williamstown CSD*, 13 PERB ¶ 4029 (1980); *Whitesboro CSD*, 11 PERB ¶ 4043 (1978)). The inclusion of employees who function in a supervisory capacity in a unit with those who do not may or may not be acceptable, depending on the circumstances of the particular case (see, e.g., *East Greenbush CSD*, 17 PERB ¶ 3083 (1984); *Buffalo City School Dist.*, 16 PERB ¶ 3084 (1983)).

Employees need not be members of the union representing members of their bargaining unit (§ 202), but the union has the same duty of fair representation towards them as it has towards its members (§ 204(2); **10:21**).

10:16. What is an employee organization and how does an employee organization become the authorized representative of public employees?

An "employee organization" is a union. The Taylor Law, however, does not use the term "union" to refer to the entity authorized to represent a group of public employees in collective negotiations; instead, it uses the term "employee organization" (§ 201(5)).

There are basically two procedures by which an employee organization can become the authorized representative of a group of public employees: recognition by the employer upon agreement with the union over a unit definition, or certification by the Public Employment Relations Board (PERB) after determining the most appropriate unit (see **10:17-18**; §§ 204, 205(5), 206, 207).

10:17. How does the process of employer recognition work?

Recognition is the voluntary designation by the legislative body of a public employer of an employee organization as the negotiating representative of employees in an appropriate unit (4 NYCRR § 200.8). The process typically begins with a request for recognition by an employee organization to the public employer.

Once an employer receives a request for recognition, the first step in the employer's recognition process is to determine the appropriate bargaining unit (see **10:15**). The unit definition should be acceptable to employer and the employee organization.

After the unit has been defined, the unit employees will select an employee organization (a union) as their representative. Selection may be evidenced a number of different ways, including by employees' individual authorizations for the deduction of dues from their paychecks (called dues checkoff) (§ 207(2)).

Once the employer is convinced that the union represents a majority of the employees in the unit and the union affirms that it does not assert the right to strike against any government, to assist in any strike or to impose an obligation to conduct, assist or participate in a strike, the union is then designated by the employer as the exclusive negotiating representative of the employees in the unit (§ 207(3); *CSEA v. Helsby*, 1 PERB ¶ 702 (1968)).

PERB has issued regulations which set forth the procedures that an employer must comply with to voluntarily recognize a union (4 NYCRR § 201.6). An employer must:

1. Post a written notice of recognition in a conspicuous place at suitable offices of the public employer for not less than five working days.

2. Include the notice in a public advertisement of a newspaper of general circulation in the employer's area for not less than one day.

3. Send notification to any employee organizations that have, in a written communication within a year preceding the recognition, claimed to represent any of the employees in the unit.

The information published must include: the name of the union which has been recognized; the job titles included in the recognized unit; and the date of recognition.

An employer is not required to recognize any employee organization. However, if an employee organization requests recognition and that request is denied, the employee organization may seek certification from PERB (4 NYCRR § 201.3; **10:18**).

Following either certification or recognition, an employer must negotiate with the employee organization with respect to terms and conditions of employment (§ 204(2)).

10:18. How does the process of certification work?

If an employer refuses a request for recognition or does not respond to such a request, an employee organization may file a petition for certification with PERB within the time frame prescribed by PERB (4 NYCRR § 201.3). A petition for certification must be supported by a showing of interest of at least 30 percent of the employees within the unit alleged to be appropriate (4 NYCRR § 201.4(a)). An employee organization can establish a showing of interest with evidence of dues deduction authorizations from employees that have not been revoked, evidence of current membership, original designation cards which were signed and dated within six months of the petition, or a combination of the three (4 NYCRR § 201.4(b)).

If necessary, PERB will hold a hearing on the petition for certification (4 NYCRR § 201.9) and an election to determine the employees' choice of bargaining representative (4 NYCRR § 201.9(g)(1) and (2)).

Certification will not be issued to a union which has already been recognized because the same rights are acquired by either process (see *Village of Sloatsburg*, 20 PERB ¶ 3014 (1987)).

10:19. May substitute teachers be included in a bargaining unit under the Taylor Law?

Yes, if they are the type of substitutes considered to be public employees within the meaning of the Taylor Law. Specifically, the Taylor Law covers regular or long-term substitute teachers (see *Roosevelt Teachers' Ass'n*, 22 PERB ¶ 4052 (1989); *Weedsport CSD*, 12 PERB ¶ 3004 (1979)). Per diem substitute teachers who have received a "reasonable assurance of continued employment" so as to be disqualified from receiving unemployment insurance benefits during summer vacation periods may also be included in the teacher bargaining unit (§ 201(7)(d)).

Per diem substitutes who have not been given a reasonable assurance of continued employment from a district are not eligible for inclusion in a collective bargaining unit in that district.

10:20. Are employees who are hired after the recognition or certification of an employee organization included within the bargaining unit?

Generally, all employees whose positions fall within the unit's definition are considered to be members of the unit, regardless of when they are hired, and the school board must negotiate the terms and conditions of employment of all such employees with the appropriate employee organization (§ 204(2)).

However, a new position may be created which does not fall within the definition of the bargaining unit, in which case the district may not be required to negotiate the terms and conditions of employment with respect to that position with the union representing the particular bargaining unit in question (see *Merrick UFSD*, 16 PERB ¶ 4556 (1983); *Averill Park CSD*, 10 PERB ¶ 4560 (1977)). In such cases, the employee organization may petition PERB to add these positions to its existing bargaining unit (4 NYCRR § 201.2(b)).

10:21. May employees who are not members of the employee organization be excluded from the bargaining unit?

No. Nonmembership in the employee organization is not a basis for exclusion from the bargaining unit, or for nonrepresentation by the employee organization. Employees covered by the unit's definition who are not members of the union are still bound by and enjoy the benefits of the collective bargaining agreement.

10:22. When may an employee be excluded from coverage under the Taylor Law?

An employee may be excluded from a bargaining unit and excluded from coverage under the Taylor Law if he or she is properly designated as a managerial or confidential employee under the Taylor Law. Such a designation must be requested by the employer and granted by the Public Employment Relations Board (PERB) ((§ 201(7)(a)); see **10:23**).

In addition, some district employees, such as continuing education teachers, may not be entitled to representation under the Taylor Law because they are considered "casual employees" who lack the regular and continuing employment relationship required for covered public employee status under the Taylor Law (§ 201(7)(f); see *BOCES III Faculty Assoc. v. Public Employment Relations Board*, 92 A.D.2d 937 (2nd Dep't 1983)). However, "casual" employment cannot be claimed simply because a school employee provides services only during the school year (§ 201(7)(f)).

Most per diem substitute teachers are considered casual employees not entitled to representation (see **10:19**).

10:23. How are employees designated as managerial or confidential under the Taylor Law?

A school board must apply to the Public Employment Relations Board (PERB) for designation of employees as managerial or confidential (§ 201(7)(a)). School boards may not unilaterally make this designation (*Newburgh CSD*, 14 PERB ¶ 4582 (1981)).

Employers may file applications for designation of employees as managerial or confidential pursuant to PERB's rules of practice (4 NYCRR

§ 201.10). Applications may be filed at any time except for employees represented by a recognized or certified bargaining representative. Only one such application may be made during an employee organization's period of unchallenged representation (4 NYCRR § 201.10(b)).

Even after the designation is made, it does not take effect with respect to employees covered by a negotiated agreement until the termination of the period of unchallenged representation enjoyed by the employee organization (§ 201(7)(a)). Ordinarily the period of unchallenged representation status expires seven months prior to the expiration of the agreement (§ 208(2)).

10:24. What is the difference between a managerial and a confidential employee?

Persons designated as managerial or confidential are not "public employees" within the meaning of the Taylor Law and therefore are not entitled to union representation under the law. They are, however, subject to the law's prohibition against strike activity (§ 201(7)(a)); see *Owego-Apalachin CSD*, 28 PERB ¶ 4011 (1995)).

An employee may be designated as "managerial" only if he or she (1) formulates policy or (2) may reasonably be required on behalf of the school district to assist directly in the preparation for and conduct of collective negotiations or have a major role in the administration of collective bargaining agreements or in personnel administration, provided his or her role is not of a routine or clerical nature and requires the exercise of independent judgment (§ 201(7)(a)); see e.g., *Ellenville CSD*, 16 PERB ¶ 3066 (1983); *Board of Educ., City School District of the City of New York*, 6 PERB ¶ 3040, *aff'd*, 6 PERB ¶ 4017 (1973); *State of New York*, 5 PERB ¶ 3022 (1972)).

"Managerial" has been defined to be more than giving mere input. PERB has stated that "managerial status depends upon the exercise by the personnel involved of broad authority directly resultant from their intimate relationship 'to the top' (e.g., to a board of education or a superintendent of schools), while supervisory status is manifested by an individual's relationship to (and direct control over) 'rank and file' employees. The distinction is substantive, not semantic; those individuals who perform managerial functions will in all likelihood possess either direct or indirect supervisory authority, but the reverse is not true. And it is the Legislature's will that only those individuals whose authority in labor relations matters goes beyond traditional supervisory concerns are to be excluded from rights under the [Taylor Law]" (*Board of Educ., Beacon Enlarged City School Dist.*, 4 PERB ¶ 4024 (1971). Principals of schools may not be considered "managerial" unless they formulate policy or have a significant role in negotiations (see *McGraw CSD*, 21 PERB ¶ 3001 (1988)).

An employee may be designated "confidential" only if he or she serves in a confidential relationship to a managerial employee who directly assists in collective bargaining or has a major role in personnel administration (§ 201(7)(a)). According to PERB case law, "an employee is confidential . . . only when in the course of assisting a managerial employee who exercises labor relations responsibilities, that employee has access to or is privy to information related to collective bargaining, contract administration, or other aspects of labor-management relations on a regular basis which is not appropriate for the eyes and ears of rank and file personnel or their negotiating representative" (*Penfield CSD*, 14 PERB ¶4044 (1981)). Clerical staff may not be regarded as "confidential" unless they have regular access to information of serious importance in collective bargaining (see *South Colonie CSD*, 28 PERB ¶ 3022 (1995)).

10:25. What are the rights of a recognized or certified employee organization?

A recognized or certified employee organization is guaranteed the exclusive right to represent in collective bargaining the employees in the bargaining unit that it is designated to represent (§ 204(2)). The organization also has the right to represent those employees in grievance proceedings; to dues checkoff for those employees who authorize the dues checkoff; to agency shop fees from those employees who are included within the bargaining unit but who are not members of the union; and to unchallenged representation status during the term of the negotiated collective bargaining agreement up to seven months before its expiration, for up to three years (§ 208; see **10:28** for more information about agency shop fees).

10:26. May employees be forced to join an employee organization?

No. Section 202 of the Taylor Law guarantees public employees the right to join or refrain from joining employee organizations. However, amendments to the Taylor Law and the General Municipal Law give all public employee organizations the right to demand that bargaining unit members who are not also dues-paying members of that organization pay agency shop fees (§§ 201(2)(b), 208(3)(b); Gen. Mun. Law § 93-b(3); see **10:28** for more information about agency shop fees).

10:27. Is a recognized or certified employee organization entitled to dues deductions?

Yes. A public employer must deduct employee organization dues from employees' salaries upon the presentation of cards authorizing deduction of dues signed by the individual employees (§§ 201(2)(a), 208(1)(b)). Failure to deduct membership dues and transmit them to the union is a per se violation of the Taylor Law (*City of Troy*, 28 PERB ¶ 3027 (1995)).

Once the employer has received these cards, authorization to deduct dues may remain effective until withdrawn or changed by the employee in a written document presented to the employer (see Gen. Mun. Law § 93–b; *Erie County*, 5 PERB ¶ 3021 (1972)). This employee right of revocation cannot be restricted (see *Rochester City SD*, 10 PERB ¶ 3097 (1977)).

An employee organization may lose the right to dues checkoff if it is determined to have violated the Taylor Law's prohibition against strikes (§ 210(3); see **10:51**).

10:28. May employees included within a bargaining unit who are not members of the employee organization be required to pay fees to the organization?

Yes. Employees who are not members of the employee organization but whose positions are included in the bargaining unit may be required to pay agency shop fees according to the Taylor Law, on request of the union (§§ 201(2)(b), 208(3)(b); Gen. Mun. Law § 93-b(3)). Agency shop fees are representation fees deducted from the pay of nonunion members which are equivalent to the membership dues paid by members of the employee organization. The employer must collect the agency shop fees and pay them to the employee organization on its request (§§ 201(2)(b), 208(3)(b)).

The employee organization is entitled to that part of the agency fee that represents the nonmember's pro rata share of expenditures necessary or reasonably incurred by the employee organization in performing its duties as a representative of the employees in the bargaining unit (§ 208(3)(b); see also *Ellis v. Brotherhood of Railway, Airline and Steamship Clerks*, 466 U.S. 435(1984)).

Agency shop fee payers who object to any portion of their fees being spent "in aid of activities or causes of a political or ideological nature only incidentally related to terms and conditions of employment" are entitled to be refunded that portion of such fees (§ 208(3)(b)). The employee organization must maintain a refund procedure and, on request of such employees, it must provide the nonunion employee with financial information sufficient to determine whether a refund may be sought, and in what amount (see *Hampton Bays Teachers' Ass'n (Sullivan)*, 14 PERB ¶ 3018 (1981)). If the employee organization fails or refuses to do so, the fee payer may be entitled to a full refund of all agency shop fees he or she has paid (see *Marlboro Faculty Ass'n (Schanzenbach)*, 26 PERB ¶ 4672 (1993)).

This approach to agency shop fees has also been imposed on constitutional grounds by the United States Supreme Court (see *Lehnert v. Ferris Faculty Ass'n*, 500 U.S. 507 (1991)), which has ruled that agency shop fees cannot be used over the objection of the fee payer for purposes other than the collective bargaining addressed in the Taylor Law, including lobbying or other political activity; for union litigation that does not concern the employees' bargaining unit; or for public relations efforts to promote the teaching profession and public unionism in general. However, the court determined agency shop fees may be applied to the cost of a local union's affiliation with state and national union organizations, other than the pro rata share of the political or ideological expenditures of such affiliate, even over the objections of the nonunion members of the bargaining unit.

The Collective Bargaining Process

10:29. What is collective bargaining?

Collective bargaining, also known as *collective negotiations*, is the process of joint determination by employers and employee organizations of the wages, hours and other terms and conditions of employment of public employees.

10:30. Are public employers required to engage in collective bargaining?

Yes. A public employer must negotiate in good faith with an employee organization that has been recognized or certified as the exclusive representative of a bargaining unit of its public employees (§ 204(2)). This means the employer must meet at reasonable times to confer in good faith with respect to wages, hours and other terms and conditions of employment, with the aim of reaching an agreement that is to be incorporated into a written contract at the request of either party. Any action by either party that is intended to avoid meeting or reaching an agreement on one of these issues may be seen as not being in good faith. School districts may not refuse to negotiate, claiming that fiscal problems preclude meaningful negotiations (see *City of Fulton*, 27 PERB ¶ 4604) (1994)).

Under the Taylor Law, the obligation to bargain in good faith does not compel either party to agree to a proposal or require the making of a concession (§ 204(3); see **10:33**).

An employer's refusal to negotiate in good faith is an improper practice under the Taylor Law (§ 209–a(1)(d); see **10:48**).

10:31. Who participates in collective bargaining?

Collective bargaining generally is conducted by a negotiating team for the school district and a team for the employee organization. The school district's negotiating team typically consists of a chief spokesperson, a recorder to take notes, an individual who is familiar with the district's educational program and an individual who is familiar with the financial needs and resources of the district. The chief spokesperson, for example, could be an attorney, a labor relations specialist or a board of cooperative educational services (BOCES) negotiator.

10:32. May a school district choose anyone it wishes to negotiate its collective bargaining agreements?

Yes. Although the superintendent, as chief executive officer of the school district, is responsible for the collective bargaining agreement with the employee organization (§ 201(10),(12); *Utica City School Dist.*, 27 PERB ¶ 3023 (1994)), a district may generally choose whomever it pleases to serve on its negotiating team, so long as the selection is not intended to frustrate bargaining, either because of ill will or conflicting interest (*City of Newburgh*, 16 PERB ¶ 3081 (1983); *County of Nassau*, 12 PERB ¶ 3090 (1979)).

10:33. What are the obligations of negotiators of collective bargaining agreements?

The Taylor Law requires both public employers and employee organizations to negotiate "in good faith" (§ 204(3)). Although this does not require either party to agree to a proposal or to make a concession, the Public Employment Relations Board (PERB) has stated that good faith requires a party to actively participate in negotiations indicating a "present intent to find a basis for agreement" (*Deposit CSD*, 27 PERB ¶ 3020 (1994)).

Good faith negotiations does not mean that the parties are required to discuss issues in any particular order of priority or to negotiate any particular issue, such as wages, to the point of agreement before resolving other issues, but it does require them to be willing to discuss all issues (*Town of Haverstraw*, 9 PERB ¶3063 (1976)). PERB has held the good faith requirement, for example, to prohibit misrepresentations at the bargaining table (*County of Rockland*, 29 PERB ¶ 3009 (1996)); to require each party to listen to and respond to the other party's proposals (*Odessa-Montour CSD*, 28 PERB ¶ 4572 (1995)); and to require each party to give its negotiator sufficient authority to reach agreement on open issues (*County of Niagara*, 23 PERB ¶ 3003 (1990); *Sachem CSD No. 5*, 6 PERB ¶ 3014 (1973)).

PERB's decisions have also set the precedent that negotiators generally have an obligation to support a tentative agreement reached at the bargaining table unless they explicitly give notice to their opposition that they do not agree with certain proposals and do not intend to support those proposals at a ratification vote (see, for example, *Buffalo*

Teachers Federation v. Buffalo City School Dist., 24 PERB ¶ 3033 (1991), *aff'd*, 191 A.D.2d 985 (4th Dep't 1993); *Copiague UFSD*, 23 PERB ¶ 3046 (1990); see also **10:7**).

10:34. What are ground rules and negotiations procedures?

While ground rules and negotiations procedures are not mentioned specifically in the Taylor Law, they are intended by the parties to govern the negotiations process. The Public Employment Relations Board (PERB) has held that negotiations procedures and ground rules for the conduct of negotiations are nonmandatory subjects and that they are preliminary and subordinate to substantive negotiations and should not interfere with the commencement or progress of negotiations *(Madison Central School Noninstructional Employees' Asso.*, 22 PERB ¶ 3057 (1989)).

Examples of the issues that may be agreed to by the parties are the time and place for negotiating sessions, the length of sessions, the procedures for ratification of the agreement by one or both parties and the authority of the parties to reach an agreement (see *County of Niagara*, 23 PERB ¶ 3003 (1990); *Vestal Teachers Ass'n*, 3 PERB ¶ 3057 (1970)). Reserving the right of ratification may be important if a school board considers such final approval important before the contract becomes binding (see **10:5-7** for a detailed discussion of ratification).

Although ground rules and negotiations procedures can be very helpful in guiding the parties through the negotiations process, PERB may consider it an improper practice if a party insists on any ground rule at the expense of commencement or progress of substantive negotiations (see *Madison CSD*, 22 PERB ¶ 3057 (1989)). Violation of a ground rule is not an improper practice, as long as the two parties are able to continue negotiating in good faith (see *City of Batavia*, 16 PERB ¶ 4611 (1983)).

10:35. Can a school district set a deadline for an employee organization's submission of items to be negotiated?

No public employer has the power to unilaterally set a deadline for submission of the items to be negotiated. However, the employee organization and the district may agree in the collective bargaining agreement or in their ground rules for negotiations to establish a submission date for demands for future agreements. Such agreements are enforceable, and parties may waive their rights to make new demands if submitted after the date agreed upon (*Heuvelton CSD v. CSEA*, 12 PERB ¶ 3007 (1979)).

On the other hand, even absent such an agreement, it may be an improper practice for either party to submit new or previously withdrawn demands after impasse (see, e.g., *Schenectady County Community College*, 6 PERB ¶ 3027 (1973); see also **10:44**).

10:36. What subjects usually are negotiated in collective bargaining?

Subjects of collective bargaining negotiations may include salary and other wage issues, hours of employment, health insurance and other benefits, leaves of absence, grievance procedures, and other terms and conditions of employment.

Issues that may arise during collective bargaining can be categorized into three groups: mandatory subjects, over which both the employer and the union have an obligation to bargain in good faith to the point of impasse; permissive, or nonmandatory subjects, over which either party may, but is not obligated to negotiate; and prohibited subjects, about which neither party may lawfully negotiate (*Incorporated Village of Lynbrook v. New York State Public Employment Relations Board,* 48 N.Y.2d 398 (1979)). The Taylor Law does not delineate mandatory, nonmandatory or prohibited subjects of collective bargaining. Disputes about the "scope of bargaining" or whether a particular subject is a mandatory, nonmandatory or prohibited subject of bargaining are determined by the Public Employment Relations Board and the courts (§ 205).

10:37. How are mandatory, prohibited and permissive subjects of bargaining distinguished from one another?

A *mandatory* subject of bargaining is one which falls within section 201(4) of the Taylor Law which defines terms and conditions of employment as matters affecting "wages, hours . . . and other terms and conditions of employment." Examples of mandatory subjects of bargaining, other than those listed in section 201(4), include benefits, leave provisions, workload, disciplinary procedures and other related issues, such as the implementation of random drug test policies and the consequences thereof (*County of Nassau,* 27 PERB ¶ 3054 (1994); *Arlington CSD,* 25 PERB ¶ 3001 (1992)). Either party must negotiate with respect to mandatory subjects upon demand of the other party.

Any change to collective bargaining agreement provisions relating to mandatory subjects of bargaining must also be negotiated prior to the adoption of any such change. A willingness to negotiate after the change is immaterial (*Great Neck Water Pollution Control Dist.,* 28 PERB ¶ 3030 (1995)).

It is permissible, however, for an employee organization to waive the right to demand negotiations over changes in a mandatory subject of bargaining by agreeing to a "management rights" clause. Such language must clearly indicate the action allowed or the subject matter affected in order to be effective (see *Garden City UFSD,* 27 PERB ¶ 3029 (1994); *Sachem CSD,* 21 PERB ¶ 3021 (1988)).

Prohibited subjects of bargaining include subjects that are expressly prohibited by law or reserved to management by public policy. For instance, the Taylor Law specifically prohibits bargaining over retirement benefits to be provided by a public retirement system (§ 201(4)). New York State courts have held that law and/or public policy prohibit school districts from agreeing to delegate the board's power to grant or deny tenure *(Cohoes City School Dist. v. Cohoes Teachers' Ass'n,* 40 N.Y.2d 774 (1976); see also *Three Village Teachers Asso. v. Three Village CSD,* 128 A.D.2d 626 (2nd Dep't 1987)); to waive the right to enforce the Taylor Law's prohibition against strikes and the penalties mandated by that law *(Mineola UFSD v. Teachers,* 63 A.D.2d 965 (2nd Dep't 1978), *leave to appeal denied,* 45 N.Y.2d 713 (1978)); or to prepay the salaries of teachers on return to work in the fall in violation of provisions within the Education Law which prohibit the payment of teacher salaries in advance of the performance of services *(Board of Educ. v. Ramapo Teachers' Ass'n,* 200 A.D.2d 62 (3rd Dep't 1994)).

Also, because state and federal laws have made it illegal for employees to smoke in school buildings, in school district vehicles or on school grounds, such issues are subject to negotiations only to the extent that smoking is not prohibited by statute (see 20 USC § 6083; Educ. Law § 409(2); Pub. Health Law §§ 1399-n(9), 1399-o(8); *Newark Valley CSD v. Public Employment Relations Board,* 83 N.Y.2d 315 (1994); *County of Cayuga,* 26 PERB ¶ 4597 (1993)).

Unless the agreement would be in violation of a statute or a strong public policy, matters that are not terms and conditions of employment may be negotiated voluntarily *(Board of Education v. Yonkers Federation of Teachers,* 40 N.Y.2d 268 (1976)). Examples of such *permissive* or *nonmandatory* subjects of negotiation include transfer of programs to BOCES (see *Webster CSD v. Public Employment Relations Board,* 75 N.Y.2d 619 (1990); *Matter of Watkins Glen CSD v. Watkins Glen Faculty Ass'n,* 212 A.D.2d 34 (3rd Dep't 1995)); demands that merely duplicate a statutory benefit or requirement (see *City of Schenectady,* 21 PERB ¶ 3022 (1988)); demands regarding employees outside the bargaining unit, student scheduling, class size, hiring of substitutes, and staff reductions (see *Somers CSD,* 9 PERB ¶ 3014 (1976)); and demands affecting the determination of a school district's educational program (see *Yonkers City School Dist. v. Yonkers Federation of Teachers,* 129 A.D.2d 702 (2nd Dep't 1987)).

Nonmandatory subjects of negotiation do not become mandatory subjects by virtue of their incorporation in a collective bargaining agreement *(City of Glens Falls,* 30 PERB ¶ 3047 (1997)).

Some general subjects may fall into several categories. For example, determination of the criteria by which teachers are evaluated is a nonnegotiable prerogative of management, but procedures for evaluation of teachers are mandatory subjects of negotiations (see *Board of Education v. Newburgh Teachers' Asso.*, 146 A.D.2d 769, *motion for leave to appeal denied,* 74 N.Y.2d 608 (1989); *Somers CSD,* 9 PERB ¶ 3014 (1976); *Elwood UFSD,* 10 PERB ¶ 3107 (1977)).

Any single proposal that has both mandatory and nonmandatory aspects is considered a nonmandatory subject of bargaining in its entirety (see *Pearl River UFSD,* 11 PERB ¶ 3085 (1978)). For example, a proposal which would not only prohibit subcontracting, usually a mandatory subject of bargaining, but also the transfer of services to a BOCES provider, which is a nonmandatory subject of bargaining, is nonmandatory (*Remsen CSD,* 27 PERB ¶ 4650 (1994)).

10:38. Must a school board negotiate its decision to subcontract bargaining unit work to a private firm or individual?

The decision to transfer work from a bargaining unit to employees outside the bargaining unit or to subcontract work to outside employers generally is considered a mandatory subject of bargaining (see *Niagara Frontier Transportation Authority,* 18 PERB ¶ 3083 (1985)). Here, the Public Employment Relations Board (PERB) can order reinstatement of employees who were terminated as a result of a unilateral decision (as opposed to a negotiated agreement) (see *Saratoga Springs City School Dist. v. Public Employment Relations Board,* 68 A.D.2d 202 (3rd Dep't 1979), *appeal dismissed,* 47 N.Y.2d 711 (1979); *County of Onondaga,* 27 PERB ¶ 3048 (1994)).

However, a school district may not be required to negotiate a decision to transfer work under certain circumstances, such as where the decision to transfer unit work is directly related to a decision to alter the level of services provided (see *County of Erie,* 29 PERB ¶ 4520 (1995)); where there is a substantial change in the nature of the duties to be performed by the nonunit workers (see *Sidney CSD,* 29 PERB ¶ 4523 (1996); but see, *Hewlett-Woodmere UFSD,* 232 A.D.2d 560 (2nd Dep't 1996)); where there are significant changes in the qualifications of the workers necessary to perform the work (see *West Hempstead UFSD,* 14 PERB ¶ 3096 (1981)); where the work had been performed by non-unit employees in the past (see *Hammondsport CSD,* 28 PERB ¶ 3059 (1995)); or where the employee organization has agreed to language authorizing the district to subcontract unit work (see *Garden City UFSD,* 27 PERB ¶ 3029 (1994)).

Subcontracting may also be permitted without negotiation where the action is indicated by law. For example, the Education Law prohibits school districts from operating a school at a deficit when a district is on a contingency budget. In one case, a district was forced to end its cafeteria program after a budget defeat by voters caused the board to adopt a contingency budget. The district hired a contractor to provide lunches on a self-sustaining financial basis, without district funding. An appellate court ruled that subcontracting was permissible without negotiations because the budget defeat had caused the loss of union members' jobs, not the decision to hire a contractor. In so ruling, the court reversed a prior PERB decision to the contrary (see *Germantown CSD v. Public Employment Relations Board*, 205 A.D.2d 961 (3rd Dep't 1994)).

The decision of a school district to have a board of cooperative educational services (BOCES) take over academic programs pursuant to section 1950(4)(bb) of the Education Law is not a mandatory subject of bargaining (*Webster CSD v. Public Employment Relations Board*, 75 N.Y.2d 619 (1990)). Similarly, a district's transfer of printing services pursuant to a contract with the local BOCES has been found to be a nonmandatory subject of negotiation *(Vestal Education Assn. v. Vestal CSD*, 30 PERB ¶ 3029 (1997)). Because the legislative intent of the statute was not to require bargaining over the decision to subcontract work to the BOCES, districts need only negotiate over the impact of the decision and not the decision itself (see **10:40**).

10:39. What is coordinated bargaining?

Coordinated bargaining is a practice in which several school districts or several local unions form a committee to share information and develop common objectives to be obtained during negotiations, while still retaining independent decision-making authority at the bargaining table (see *County of Nassau*, 12 PERB ¶ 3090 (1979)). Similarly situated districts can get together to identify common problems, share common experiences and consider possible solutions to problems before they actually sit down at the bargaining table. To avoid an improper practice charge, each district must remain completely free to conduct its own negotiations and reach a settlement independent of the other districts, and may not bind itself to the other districts to achieve any particular proposals.

10:40. What are impact negotiations?

Although school districts need not bargain over managerial decisions involving permissive or nonmandatory subjects of bargaining (see **10:37**), they are required to negotiate over the impact of such decisions on the terms and conditions of employment (*County of Nassau*, 27 PERB ¶3054 (1994); see *West Irondequoit Teachers Asso. v. Helsby*, 35 N.Y.2d 46 (1974)). PERB has stated: "A demand for impact bargaining permits negotiation about those mandatorily negotiable effects which are inevitably or necessarily caused by an employer's exercise of a managerial prerogative" (*County of Nassau*). This requirement most often is triggered by unilateral action taken by the board which indirectly affects terms or conditions of employment, such as elimination of positions (see *City of Troy*, 28 PERB ¶ 4657 (1995); *New Rochelle City School Dist.*, 4 PERB ¶ 3060 (1970)).

Once a public employer offers to bargain over impact, the failure of the union to respond will relieve the district of any further obligation to negotiate on the issue (see *Wappingers CSD v. PERB*, 627 N.Y.S.2d 701 (2nd Dep't 1995).

A union's demand to negotiate impact must be "clearly made, and cannot be inferred from a demand to negotiate a decision" (*Lackawanna City School Dist.*, 28 PERB ¶ 3023 (1995)).

The requirement that a school district negotiate impact does not mean that the district is prevented from initiating its decision unless and until an agreement is reached on the terms and conditions of employment actually or potentially affected by those decisions *(Town of Oyster Bay, 12 PERB ¶ 3086 (1979))*.

10:41. What is a past practice and how does it impact collective bargaining?

A past practice involves a subject of bargaining which has not been included in a written agreement but which is unambiguous and has continued without interruption for a sufficient period of time under the circumstances that affected employees may have a reasonable expectation that the practice would continue (see *County of Nassau*, 24 PERB ¶ 3029 (1991)). Examples of past practices include the use of unused emergency days *(New Berlin CSD*, 25 PERB ¶ 3060 (1992)); waiver of tuition for students of staff living outside the school district (*Carle Place UFSD*, 28 PERB ¶ 4667 (1995)); and procedures for applying for unpaid leaves of absence (*Marcus Whitman CSD*, 27 PERB ¶ 4601 (1994)).

A change in an established past practice relating to a mandatory subject of bargaining must be agreed to by the employee organization representing affected employees (*East Ramapo CSD*, 17 PERB ¶ 3001(1984); **10:48**).

10:42. What is an impasse?

Impasse is a stalemate or deadlock in collective bargaining. It is the point at which either or both parties to the negotiation determine that no further progress toward settlement can be made through direct negotiation (see *Newburgh*, 15 PERB ¶ 3116 (1982), *aff'd as City of Newburgh v. Newman*, 117 A.D.2d 965 (3rd Dep't 1986), *aff'd*, 69 N.Y.2d 166 (1987)). Impasse may be declared if, despite efforts to bargain in good faith, the parties fail to reach an agreement at least 120 days prior to the end of the school district's fiscal year (§ 209(1)), which is commonly the final effective date of a collective bargaining agreement, or at any time after that date. Impasse cannot be declared if there are open issues which have not yet been discussed (see *Town of Haverstraw*, 9 PERB ¶ 3063 (1976)).

10:43. What happens when a school district and an employee organization reach an impasse?

Districts and employee organizations may agree to procedures on resolution of impasses, such as submission of open issues to impartial arbitration (§ 209(2); see *Newburgh v. Newman*, 69 N.Y.2d 166 (1987)). Such procedures, once agreed upon, must be followed.

In the absence of such agreed-upon impasse procedures or in the event that these procedures are unsuccessful, either party may request assistance from the Public Employment Relations Board (PERB), or PERB may render such assistance on its own (§ 209(2), (3); see **10:14, 10:44**).

The obligation to negotiate in good faith extends to participation in the mediation and fact-finding process. As such, refusal to participate in the fact-finding process constitutes an improper practice (*Pine Plains CSD*, 28 PERB ¶ 4574 (1995); *Poughkeepsie City School Dist.*, 27 PERB ¶ 3079 (1994); see **10:47**).

10:44. What role does the Public Employment Relations Board have in settling an impasse?

If there is no agreement on procedures to resolve an impasse in collective bargaining, or these procedures fail, either party may formally request PERB, or PERB on its own may determine, to assist in resolving the impasse (§ 209(3)). Such assistance may include the services of a mediator, and if mediation fails, the services of a fact-finder. The fact-finder's report of recommendations must be released to the public five days after the report is given to the school superintendent and employee organization (§ 209(3)(b) and (c)). Either party may accept or reject any or all of the fact-finder's recommendations. If the impasse continues, additional mediation, called "conciliation," may be provided.

There are no charges to either the employer or the employees for these PERB services.

10:45. Can a school district require an employee organization to pay for part of the costs of procedures that may be invoked in the event of an impasse?

The Public Employment Relations Board (PERB) pays for the mediator and fact-finder when it appoints them. If there is no provision in the current agreement regarding the costs of the agreed-upon impasse procedures, then neither party can require the other to share in the expenses it incurs (see **10:44**). However, if the agreement includes an impasse procedure, it usually specifies that both parties will share the costs of a mediator or arbitrator.

10:46. What happens if the current collective bargaining agreement expires before a successor agreement is negotiated?

In such situations, all the provisions of the expired agreement continue in full force and effect until the parties agree to a new agreement. This is because section 209–a(1)(e) of the Civil Service Law, commonly referred to as the Triborough Amendment, makes it an improper practice for an employer to refuse to continue all the terms of an expired agreement until a new agreement is negotiated.

This obligation ends, however, if the employee organization has violated section 210(1) of the Civil Service Law by striking or by causing, instigating, encouraging or condoning a strike. In case of such a violation, the district may not be required to refrain from unilaterally changing certain policies and practices (see **10:51**).

The New York State Court of Appeals has found that the Triborough Amendment has the effect of extending the term of the agreement until a new agreement is reached *(Association of Surrogates & Supreme Court Reporters v. State of New York*, 79 N.Y.2d 39 (1992)). However, despite this decision, PERB has ruled that collective bargaining agreements actually do expire for purposes of the Taylor Law, since to conclude otherwise would make it impossible for any union to ever establish the element of an "expired contract" which is necessary to state a claim for relief under the Triborough Amendment and thus, would effectively repeal the Triborough Amendment (*State of New York (Office of Parks and Recreation)*, 27 PERB ¶ 3001 (1994)).

Certain obligations contained in a collective bargaining agreement may be made to end with the contract's expiration even under the Triborough Amendment by use of what is known as a *sunset clause* (see *Waterford-Halfmoon UFSD*, 27 PERB ¶ 3070 (1994)). Such a clause simply attaches a final effective date to a specific provision in the contract, such as one which determines the conditions upon which salary increments or step advances are to take place (see *Schuylerville CSD*, 29 PERB ¶ 3029 (1997); *County of St. Lawrence*, 28 PERB ¶ 4521 (1995); *Waterford-Halfmoon*). The effectiveness of these clauses is based on the idea that the Triborough Amendment requires only that the contract, as written, continue in effect until a new contract is negotiated (§ 209-a (1)(e)).

It is important to remember that school districts must still provide education to their students, and that employees must continue to work in spite of the lack of agreement on a new contract because the law, in essence, ignores the expiration date of the agreement and continues the force and effect of the agreement's terms.

Improper Practices

10:47. What is an improper practice?

An *improper practice* is an action by either an employee organization or a public employer that is prohibited by section 209–a of the Civil Service Law. Most improper practices infringe on another party's ability to exercise rights granted by law (see **10:48-49**).

For an improper practice charge to be timely, it must be filed within four months of either the date when the decision to take the action complained of is announced or the date when the action is implemented (4 NYCRR § 204.1(a)(1)). However, if the relief sought is fundamentally private and the issue does not have significant public policy implications, the school district must be served a notice of claim within three months after the basis for the claim arose (Educ. Law § 3813(1); *Board of Educ. v. New York State Public Employment Relations Board*, 197 A.D.2d 276 (3rd Dep't 1994), appeal denied, 84 N.Y.2d 803 (1994); *Sidney Teachers Ass'n*, 28 PERB ¶ 3066 (1995); *Deposit CSD v. PERB*, 214 A.D.2d 288 (3rd Dep't 1995), *motion for leave to appeal denied*, 88 N.Y.2d 866 (1996); compare, *Mahopac CSD*, 28 PERB ¶ 3045 (1995), where an improper practice charge that the district intentionally interfered with its employees' right to representation was ruled not subject to the notice of claim requirements).

The improper practice charge itself provides sufficient notice to meet this requirement if it is actually served within the three-month period. A school district does not waive a notice of claim defense if it fails to raise it in its original answer to the improper practice charge, as long as it raises the issue before PERB (*Deposit CSD v. PERB*).

If an improper practice is found, PERB is authorized to order the offending party to cease and desist from that improper practice and to "take such affirmative action as will effectuate the policies" of the Taylor Law, including ordering payment of lost wages with interest and reinstatement of employees with or without back pay (§ 205(5)(d)). Punitive damages are not authorized, although under "extraordinary circumstances," attorney fees may be awarded (see *City of Troy*, 28 PERB ¶ 3027 (1995), *Town of Henrietta*, 28 PERB ¶ 3079 (1995)).

10:48. What types of improper practices might a public employer commit?

An employer commits an improper practice when it:

- Fails to negotiate collectively in good faith (see §§ 204(3); 209-a(1)(d); see **10:33**). Any long-standing practice on a mandatory subject of bargaining by an employer that is not incorporated in a contract is a term and condition of employment that cannot be altered unilaterally (*Town of Oyster Bay*, 9 PERB ¶ 3004 (1976); see **10:41**).

- Fails to continue all the terms of an expired agreement until a new one is negotiated, unless the employee organization has engaged in, caused, instigated, encouraged or condoned a strike (§ 209-a(1)(e)).

- Interferes with the rights of public employees to participate in or refrain from participating in employee organizations of their own choosing (see §§ 202; 209-a(1)(a)).

- Interferes with the formation or administration of employee organizations (§ 209-a(1)(b)).

- Discriminates against any employee for the purpose of encouraging or discouraging membership or participation in an employee organization (§ 209-a(1)(c)).

10:49. What are some examples of possible employee organization-initiated improper practices?

An employee organization commits an improper practice when it interferes with the right of public employees to participate in or refrain from participating in employee organizations of their own choosing (see §§ 202, 209-a(2)), when it refuses to negotiate collectively in good faith with a public employer as it is required to do (see §§ 204, 209-a(2)), or when it breaches its duty of fair representation to public employees under the Taylor Law.

For example, it is an improper practice for an employee organization to make a credible threat of a strike in order to create pressure in negotiations (see *East Meadow UFSD*, 16 PERB ¶ 3086 (1983)), or to threaten to "work to rule," which is a concerted refusal to participate in "voluntary" activities, such as escorting students on field trips, writing recommendation letters for students or attending faculty meetings, where the school district has a reasonable expectation of participation (see *Haverling CSD*, 22 PERB ¶ 4554 (1989); **10:50**).

It is also an improper practice for an employee organization to fail or refuse to provide to an agency shop fee payer an audited statement of its expenses and those of its affiliates to enable the filing of a request for rebate of non-chargeable expenses (see § 208(3)(b); *Public Employees*

Federation v. Public Employment Relations Board, 93 A.D.2d 910 (3rd Dep't 1983); *United University Professions v. Newman,* 146 A.D.2d 273 (3rd Dep't 1989), *appeal denied,* 74 N.Y.2d 614 (1989); *Marlboro Faculty Ass'n,* 26 PERB ¶ 4672 (1993); **10:28**).

10:50. What types of activities constitute a prohibited strike?

Any strike activity is prohibited activity. Specifically, the Taylor Law defines prohibited strike activity as "any strike or other concerted stoppage of work or slowdown by public employees" (§ 201(9)). It also states that "an employee who is absent from work without permission, or who abstains wholly or in part from the full performance of his duties in his normal manner without permission, on the date or dates when a strike occurs, shall be presumed to have engaged in such strike on such date or dates" (§ 210(2)(b)). For instance, an abnormally high absentee rate among employees may be deemed a strike *(Orleans-Niagara BOCES Teachers Ass'n,* 28 PERB ¶ 3050 (1995); *CSEA of Yonkers,* 13 PERB ¶ 3026 (1980)).

A violation of this prohibition can be found in many forms of conduct, including a boycott of voluntary assignments or other work, such as field trips and parent orientation sessions (see *Horseheads Teachers Ass'n and New York State United Teachers,* 15 PERB ¶ 3110 (1982); *Pearl River UFSD,* 11 PERB ¶ 4530, *aff'd,* 11 PERB ¶ 3085 (1978)); a boycott of faculty meetings (see *Webutuck Teachers Ass'n,* 13 PERB ¶ 3041 (1980)); refusal to help students or volunteer for extracurricular assignments (see *Baylis v. Seaford UFSD,* 22 PERB ¶ 7533 (Sup. Ct. Nassau County 1989)); or even to threaten to "work to rule," which is a boycott of "voluntary" activities (see **10:49**).

A union's responsibility for an unlawful strike can be established through circumstantial evidence (*Orleans-Niagara BOCES Teachers Ass'n*).

10:51. What types of sanctions and penalties may be imposed against employees and employee organizations in the event of a strike?

There are court-imposed, Public Employment Relations Board (PERB) administered, and school district-imposed sanctions and penalties against striking employees and their employee organizations. A court may issue an injunction against a strike, and if the injunction is violated, impose penalties for contempt (§ 211; Jud. Law §§ 750-751). PERB may determine that the employee organization will lose its automatic dues checkoff and any negotiated agency shop fee checkoff privileges (§§ 210(3)(a), (f); 208(1)(b); 208(3); see, for example, *Yonkers Council of Administrators,* 24 PERB ¶ 3005 (1991)). The school district is required to make certain deductions from the pay of each violating employee (§ 210(2)(f); also see **10:52**). Specifically, employees who strike are to be penalized twice their daily rate of pay for each day they are engaged in the strike (see § 210(2)(e), (f); *Plainview-Old Bethpage Congress of Teachers v. Plainview-Old Bethpage CSD,* 63 N.Y.2d 921 (1984)), as well as being subject to disciplinary action and penalties for misconduct (§ 210(2)(a)).

Furthermore, when an employee organization engages in prohibited strike activities, the district is no longer obligated to comply with the Triborough Amendment, which otherwise requires the continuation of the terms of an expired agreement until a new agreement is reached (§ 209–a(1)(e); see also **10:46**). The employee organization also may lose its right to charge an employer with an improper practice for making unilateral changes in mandatory subjects of bargaining (*Somers CSD,* 9 PERB ¶ 3061 (1976)).

10:52. What are a school district's responsibilities in the event of a strike by school district employees?

Section 211 of the Civil Service Law provides that when it appears public employees are threatening to strike, are about to strike, or have gone out on strike, the public employer, through its chief legal officer, must immediately apply to the New York State Supreme Court for an injunction against the strike. A temporary restraining order forbidding the strike may be issued by the court immediately. Those who continue to strike despite the restraining order are in contempt of court and subject to penalties of up to $1,000 and/or 30 days' imprisonment, at the discretion of the court (Jud. Law §§ 750-751).

Furthermore, school officials must impose the "two-for-one" payroll penalty on strikers. This penalty is a loss of twice the daily rate of pay for every day the employee strikes (§ 210(2)(f)). If the strike involved only limited activities, such as extra-curricular and coaching activities, the district may be limited to withholding compensation for those activities only (see *Baylis v. Seaford UFSD,* 22 PERB ¶ 7533 (Sup. Ct. Nassau County, 1989)).

These deductions must be made between 30 and 90 days after the determination that employees have violated the law prohibiting strikes, and cannot be made outside this statutory time period (see *King v. Carey,* 57 N.Y.2d 505 (1982); *Swital v. Board of Educ.,* 93 A.D.2d 839 (2nd Dep't 1983)).

Separate from the imposition of the payroll penalty, the Taylor Law prohibits the payment by the employer of any compensation to a public employee for any day or any part of a day in which he or she engages in such prohibited activities (§ 210(3)(h)).

Finally, the school district is responsible for notifying and providing information to the Public Employment Relations Board (PERB) concerning the strike violations (§ 210(3)(b)). School officials also should give PERB's Office of Counsel sufficient information so that it may begin proceedings to revoke the offending employee organization's dues checkoff and agency shop fee deduction privileges (§ 210(3)(a), (f)).

10:53. May school district employees who have participated in a strike be placed on probationary status?

No. While earlier versions of the Taylor Law allowed this penalty, currently there is no legal authority for placing tenured school district employees on probationary status for striking.

Grievances

10:54. What is a grievance?

Generally, a *grievance* is a claim that a specific provision or provisions of a collective bargaining agreement have been violated (see Gen. Mun. Law § 682(4)). However, contractual grievance procedures may be extended by mutual agreement to apply to a broad range of actions and decisions outside the contract, such as the application of district policies (see, e.g., *City of Schenectady*, 21 PERB ¶ 3022 (1988); *Pearl River UFSD*, 11 PERB ¶ 3085 (1978)).

The grievant, the party bringing the grievance, seeks a determination that the other party has violated the contract and that specific remedial action should be taken.

10:55. How are grievances resolved?

In most cases, procedures for resolutions of grievances, or grievance procedures, are provided in school district collective bargaining agreements. The Taylor Law provides that a certified or recognized employee organization has the right to represent employees in the settlement of grievances (§ 208(1)(a)). Most grievance procedures involve several different levels or steps that are progressively invoked to satisfy both parties. If a grievance cannot be resolved internally between the parties, such agreements usually provide for a final settlement by either advisory or binding arbitration.

In addition, article 15-C of the General Municipal Law (which pre-dates the Taylor Law) specifies rules regarding grievance procedures. Specifically, any political subdivision of the state, including school districts, that has 100 or more full-time employees, except the city of New York, must establish certain minimal grievance procedures (Gen. Mun. Law §§ 682(1), 684)). These mandated grievance procedures must cover any grievance relating to employees' health or safety, physical facilities, materials or equipment furnished to employees or supervision of employees (Gen. Mun. Law § 682(4)). The law does not require that grievance procedures address issues of an employee's rate of compensation, retirement benefits, disciplinary proceeding or other matters that can be appealed to the commissioner of education or through a contractual grievance procedure (see Gen. Mun. Law § 682(4); Educ. Law § 310; §§ 201(4), 203).

The General Municipal Law requires a grievance procedure to consist of at least two stages and an appellate stage (§ 684). If a school district does not adopt a grievance procedure, the procedure established by section 684 goes into effect automatically under the law's requirement. The law calls for final resolution of grievances by advisory arbitration by a grievance board appointed by the superintendent. Because the arbitration is advisory, the school board either may accept or reject the grievance board's recommendations.

10:56. May a school board agree to arbitration for the resolution of grievances?

Yes, absent clear prohibitions from the constitution, statute or common law principles, arbitration under the terms of a collective bargaining agreement is a permissible form of resolving disputes between a board of education and its employees (*Port Jefferson Station Teachers Assn. v. Brookhaven-Comsewogue UFSD*, 45 N.Y.2d 898 (1978); *Board of Education v. Associated Teachers of Huntington*, 30 N.Y.2d 122 (1972)). There are, however, some duties or responsibilities so important that a school district will not be permitted to delegate them or to bargain them away. For example, a school board cannot surrender its statutory obligations and allow an arbitrator to determine whether a teacher is to be granted tenure (see *Cohoes CSD v. Cohoes Teachers Asso.*, 40 N.Y.2d 774 (1976); *Three Village Teachers Asso. v. Three Village CSD*, 128 A.D.2d 626 (2nd Dep't 1987), *appeal denied*, 70 N.Y.2d 608 (1987)); or be divested of its right to inspect teacher personnel files (*Board of Education v. Areman*, 41 N.Y.2d 527 (1977)); or be bound by contractual provisions that interfere with a school board's responsibility to maintain adequate classroom standards (see *Honeoye Falls-Lima CSD v. Honeoye Falls-Lima Educ. Ass'n*, 49 N.Y.2d 732 (1980)).

10:57. Is arbitration of a grievance dispute binding or advisory?

The parties involved in a grievance may agree that arbitration either will be advisory, where the arbitrator's decision has limited legal effect, or binding, where the arbitrator's decision will be final and binding and can be appealed only under certain limited circumstances (see **10:58**).

10:58. May grievance decisions rendered after binding or advisory arbitration be appealed in court?

Yes. An arbitrator's award may be challenged in court. However, the standard by which a court will overturn or reject a decision rendered after arbitration is difficult to meet.

In a review of a binding arbitration decision, errors of law or fact are generally not grounds to vacate the arbitrator's award, and courts will grant a petition to vacate the award only in cases where the arbitrator's interpretation of the agreement is "completely irrational" (Civ. Prac. L. & R. § 7511; see *Silverman v. Benmor Coats, Inc.*, 61 N.Y.2d 299 (1984); *Rochester City School Dist. v. Rochester Teachers' Asso.*, 41 N.Y.2d 578, 582 (1977)).

As a general rule, a court will not confirm an award issued following advisory arbitration (*Benjamin Rush Employees United v. McCarthy*, 76 N.Y.2d 781 (1990)). However, in certain circumstances, the parties may, by their conduct, convert an arbitration award issued pursuant to an agreement providing for advisory arbitration into a binding determination (*Board of Education v. Yonkers Federation of Teachers*, 46 N.Y.2d 727 (1978); *Matter of Hempstead Classroom Teachers Assn v. Board of Education*, 79 A.D.2d 709 (2nd Dep't 1980)).

10:59. How are arbitrators selected?

Arbitration clauses usually designate one of a number of organizations, usually the Public Employment Relations Board (PERB) or the American Arbitration Association (AAA), as the administrator of an arbitration agreement. Thereafter, the organization may do most of the selection and scheduling work, including sending the parties one or more lists of names of arbitrators for each party to rank or veto, and appointing the highest-ranking arbitrator who was not vetoed by either party (see, for example, 4 NYCRR § 207.7).

In addition, before making such a selection, school districts may contact the New York State School Boards Association, which maintains a computerized database that contains biographical and other information about arbitrators.

Family and Medical Leave Act

10:60. What is the Family and Medical Leave Act?

The Family and Medical Leave Act (FMLA) is a federal law that requires school districts with more than 50 employees within 75 miles of their work site (see 29 USC §§ 203(x); 2611(2)(B)(ii),(4)(A)(iii); 2618(a)(1); 29 CFR §§ 825.104(a); 825.110(a)(3); 825.600(b)) to provide up to 12 weeks of unpaid leave to eligible employees for medical or child-care purposes during a designated 12-month period (see 29 USC § 2612(a)(1)). The 12-month period during which 12 weeks of leave may be taken is measured either against the calendar year, any fixed 12-month "leave year" (such as a fiscal year), or a rolling 12-month period measured either forward from the date of an employee's first FMLA leave or backwards from the date an employee uses FMLA leave (29 CFR § 825.200(b)). Failure by the employer to select any one of these methods allows employees to use the most beneficial method for them until the employer designates the appropriate measure (see 29 CFR § 825.200(e)).

An employee is eligible under the law to take family and medical leave if he or she has been employed for at least 12 months and has worked at least 1,250 hours in the 12 months immediately preceding commencement of leave (see 29 USC § 2611(2)(A); 29 CFR § 825.110(a)). When the need for family or medical leave is foreseeable, the employee must give 30 days' notice of his or her intention to take the leave (29 USC § 2612(e); 29 CFR §825.302(a)). Although the family and medical leave is generally unpaid (see 29 USC § 2612(c),(d); 29 CFR § 825.207(a); **10:62**), school districts must continue normal health insurance benefits during the leave except as otherwise provided by law and regulations (see 29 USC § 2614(c)(1); 29 CFR § 825.209).

Absences of one or more weeks when school is closed and employees are not expected to report to work do not count against FMLA leave entitlements. However, when a particular holiday falls during a week taken as FMLA leave, the entire week is counted as FMLA leave (see 29 CFR § 825.200(f)).

All school districts, regardless of the number of people they employ, are required to post notices on FMLA and include information about FMLA in any written policy or employee handbook on employee benefits and leave rights (29 USC § 2619; 29 CFR § 825.300(a), 825.301(a)(1)). In addition, districts must provide information on FMLA whenever an employee requests a FMLA-qualified leave, whether or not the employee actually requests FMLA leave (29 CFR § 825.301(b),(c); 825.302(c)).

An employee may sue a school district in state or federal court, or file a complaint in an administrative proceeding for violations of the law (29 USC § 2617(a)(2),(b)(1); 29 CFR § 825.400(a)). If the court rules in favor of the employee, that employee may recover wages, salary and benefits as well as attorney's fees (29 USC § 2617(a)(1),(3); 29 CFR § 825.400(c)).

10:61. What is the difference between family leave and medical leave under FMLA?

Family leave is available for the birth and care of an infant, adoption and care of a child, and the placement with the employee of a child in foster care (29 USC § 2612(a)(1)(A),(B); 29 CFR § 825.112(a)(1),(2); see also **8:132-137**). An employee may only take family leave during the 12-month period beginning with the birth or placement of a child (29 USC § 2612(a)(2); 29 CFR 825.201). Employees are not entitled to take intermittent leave for family leaves (29 USC § 2612(b)(1); 29 CFR § 825.203(b)).

Medical leave is available to an employee who has a serious health condition that prevents the employee from performing his or her job, or to care for a spouse, dependent child or parent who has a serious health condition (29 USC § 2612(a)(1)(C),(D); 29 CFR §§ 825.112 (a)(3), (4); 825.113). A serious health condition is defined generally by FMLA as "an illness, injury, impairment, or physical or mental condition" that involves hospitalization or other inpatient care or continuing treatment by a health care provider (29 USC § 2611(11)), and in more detail in FMLA's implementing regulations (see 29 CFR §§ 825.114; 825.800).

Unlike family leave, medical leave may be taken on an intermittent basis (29 USC § 2612(b)(1); 29 CFR § 825.203(c)). The district may temporarily transfer the employee to a position with equal pay and benefits if the intermittent leave is foreseeable and the position better accommodates recurring periods of leave (29 USC § 2612(b)(2); 29 CFR § 825.204). Additionally, for instructional employees whose absences due to foreseeable medical treatment will exceed 20 percent of the working days of the period over which that leave will occur, the district can require the employee either to take a block leave (take the time all at once) or accept a temporary transfer to another position with equal pay and benefits which better accommodates recurring periods of leave and for which the employee is qualified (29 USC § 2618(c); 29 CFR § 825.601).

A district can require an employee requesting a medical leave to produce a certificate from his or her doctor that gives the basis for and anticipated duration of the medical leave (29 USC § 2613(a),(b); 29 CFR §§ 825.305(a); 825.306(b)(1),(2)). If the district doubts the validity of the doctor's certification, the law provides a method for obtaining a second and, if necessary, a third medical opinion (29 USC § 2613(c),(d); 29 CFR § 825.307(a)(2),(c)).

10:62. Can a school district require an employee to use accrued paid leave time under a collective bargaining agreement rather than take an unpaid FMLA leave?

Yes. An employee may choose or a school district may require an employee to use accrued paid vacation, personal or family leave for purposes of a family leave or a medical leave to care for a spouse, dependent child or parent with a serious health condition (29 USC § 2612(d)(2)(A); 29 CFR § 825.207(b)). Although leave under a disability plan may count as FMLA leave, paid leave may not be substituted if the employee is receiving workers' compensation (see 29 CFR § 825.207(d)).

Additionally, an employee may choose or a district can require an employee to use accrued paid vacation, personal, or medical/sick leave for purposes of a medical leave (29 USC § 2612(d)(2)(B); 29 CFR § 825.207(a)).

Under FMLA, an employee cannot use accrued family or sick leave when he or she would not otherwise be able to use such leave under the terms of a collective bargaining agreement or board policy (see 29 USC §2612(d)(2)(B); 29 CFR § 825.207(b),(c)).

10:63. Does an employee who takes a FMLA leave have the right to return to his or her job after the leave is over?

Yes. At the end of the leave the employee is entitled to return to the position he or she held when the leave commenced or to an equivalent position (see 29 USC § 2614(a); 29 CFR § 82.214(a)). For school district employees, the determination of how an employee will be restored to an equivalent position must be made on the basis of established school board policies and practices and the collective bargaining agreement (29 USC § 2618(e); 29 CFR § 825.604). For example, school districts are free under the law to assign a returning elementary teacher to a different grade from the class he or she taught prior to the leave.

Generally, employers may not require employees to take more FMLA leave than necessary, and employees may return to work earlier than anticipated (29 CFR § 825.309(c)). However, special limitations apply with respect to instructional employees returning from leave near the conclusion of an academic term (see 29 USC § 2618(d); 29 CFR § 825.602(a)). Depending on the duration of the leave and the length of time remaining until the end of the school term, the district can require the employee to wait until the next term to return. The additional time is not counted as FMLA leave (see 29 CFR § 825.603(b)).

An employee does not lose any accrued employment benefits as a result of the leave, but he or she is not entitled to accrue seniority for the period of the leave (29 USC § 2614(a)(2),(3)).

10:64. What are the collective bargaining implications of FMLA?

The leave entitlements established by FMLA do not diminish any employee benefits established in a collective bargaining agreement (29 USC § 2652(a)). Thus, if a contract provides greater leave benefits, the provisions of the contract apply.

Conversely, no collective bargaining agreement may diminish the benefits provided by FMLA (29 USC § 2652(b)). Thus, FMLA provides a minimum floor of benefits for all eligible employees, even if a collective bargaining agreement provides lesser benefits.

Any decision on the implementation of FMLA which is not already determined in the statute and its implementing regulations is a mandatory subject of bargaining (see *Rome Hospital*, 27 PERB ¶ 4575 (1994)).

11. Retirement

11:1. Is there a mandatory retirement age for school district employees?
No. There is no mandatory retirement age for most public employees in New York State (§ 530; Exec. Law § 296(3–a)(a)).

11:2. Under what circumstances are school district employees entitled to health benefits when they retire?
Employees retiring under an existing contract that obligates the district to contribute to the health insurance of a retiree are entitled to those benefits for the life of the contract. Any changes must be negotiated during the life of the contract.

Once the contract has expired, the district may unilaterally change its obligations, unless the successor contract provides for these benefits for retirees. Therefore, employees who retired under a now-expired contract may not negotiate any changes the district may want to make in the new contract, and may receive only benefits the district wishes to continue to provide or provides pursuant to the successor agreement.

Employees retiring under a present contract that does not address the issue of retirees' health benefits must look to the school district's policy. If the district's policy or practice is to provide retirees' health benefits, any changes in future retirees' benefits must be negotiated with their union.

Once an employee has retired, the school board may unilaterally change the policy (*Lippman v. Board of Education*, 66 N.Y.2d 313 (1985)). However, Chapter 68 of the Laws of 1998 prohibits a school district or BOCES from diminishing the health insurance benefits provided to retirees and their dependents unless a corresponding decrease from the present level is made to the corresponding group of active employees through May 15, 1999 (Laws of 1998, Ch. 68).

If, by some other representation, the district promises to provide benefits to an employee, the courts may find that the employee is entitled to these benefits based on his or her reliance on the district's representations (*Allen v. Board of Educ. of Union Free School Dist.*, 168 A.D.2d 403 (2nd Dep't 1990), *appeal dismissed without opinion*, 77 N.Y.2d 939 (1991)).

All statutory references in this chapter are to the Retirement and Social Security Law unless noted otherwise.

11:3. Can retired school district employees have the costs of participating in benefit plans deducted from their retirement allowance?

Yes. The Education Law allows such employees to have the cost of participating in union employee benefit plans automatically deducted from their retirement allowance (Educ. Law § 536).

General Provisions

11:4. What state retirement plans are available for school district employees?

Outside New York City, noninstructional employees participate in the New York State Employees' Retirement System (ERS), while teachers participate in the New York State Teachers' Retirement System (TRS). Public school employees in New York City are covered by the New York City Teachers' Retirement System or the Board of Education Retirement System of the City of New York (BERS).

11:5. Do all members of state retirement plans have the same obligations and benefits?

No. The obligations and benefits of members of the Teachers' Retirement System and the Employees' Retirement System vary, depending on the tier in which an employee belongs. For convenience, the systems use a tier concept to distinguish these groups. Participation in a particular tier is based on the date the employee joined the system. The same tier structure is used for members in all state retirement plans. Tiers are established to ensure that members' benefits are not reduced or impaired, since the New York State Constitution prohibits diminishment of benefits (see **11:11**).

Members in *Tier I* include employees who joined one of the systems before July 1, 1973 (2 NYCRR § 325.2(a)).

Tier II members include those employees who joined the systems on or after July 1, 1973 through July 26, 1976 (2 NYCRR § 325.2(b)). Although Tier II expired on June 30, 1976 (see § 451), anyone becoming a member between July 1 and July 27, 1976 became a member in Tier II, because Chapter 890 of the Laws of 1976, which created Tier III, was not signed into law until July 27, 1976 (*Oliver v. County of Broome*, 113 A.D.2d 239 (3rd Dep't 1985), *appeal denied*, 67 N.Y.2d 607 (1986)).

Members in *Tier III* include those employees who became members of one of the systems on or after July 27, 1976, but before September 1, 1983 (2 NYCRR § 325.2(c)).

Members in *Tier IV* include those employees who joined one of the systems on or after September 1, 1983 (2 NYCRR § 325.2(d)).

11:6. What are the requirements for service retirement for members in Tier I?

Tier I TRS members may retire at any age with 35 years of total credited service. Tier I TRS and ERS members may retire after age 55 with the equivalent of 10 or more years of credited service.

11:7. What are the requirements for service retirement for members in Tier II?

The normal retirement age for members in Tier II is 62 years.

Retirement is permitted between the ages of 55 and 62, but with a reduction in benefits according to the following formula:

- One-half of 1 percent per month for each of the first 24 full months by which retirement predates age 62.
- One-quarter of 1 percent per month for each full month by which retirement predates age 60. In no event is retirement allowed before age 55 (§ 442(a)).

A Tier II member, however, may retire without reduction in benefits if he or she is at least 55 years old and has completed 30 or more years of service (§ 442(b)).

11:8. What are the requirements for service retirement and benefits available to members in Tier III?

Members in Tier III are covered by the provisions of the Coordinated-Escalator Retirement Plan (CO-ESC), as set forth in Article 14 of the Retirement and Social Security Law, or the Coordinated Retirement Plan, as set forth in Article 15. The Article 14 plan integrates Social Security benefits with service retirement. Members must contribute 3 percent of their wages (§§ 517(a); 613(a)). Members must render at least 10 years of credited service and attain age 62 to be eligible for normal retirement (§§ 503(a); 516(a)).

Members who retire between the ages of 55 and 62 with less than 30 years of credited service have their benefits reduced based on their age at retirement. A member's retirement benefits commencing at or before age 62 will be reduced by 50 percent of the primary Social Security benefit when he or she reaches age 62, or leaves service after age 62. Members may retire and be eligible for benefits at age 70 with a minimum of five years of creditable service (§§ 502–511).

In addition, the benefits afforded to Tier IV members are also available to Tier III members.

11:9. What are the requirements for service retirement and benefits available to members in Tier IV?

Members in Tier IV are covered by the provisions of the Coordinated Retirement Plan, as set forth in Article 15 of the Retirement and Social Security Law. Members in Tier IV must contribute 3 percent of their wages. Members will be eligible for a normal retirement benefit at age 62, if they have a minimum of 10 years of credited New York State service, or at age 55, if credited with 30 years of service. At age 70 they may retire with a minimum of five years of credited New York State service (§§ 602, 603, 613).

Members may retire at age 55 with less than 30 years of service, with a reduced retirement allowance (§ 603(i)).

11:10. How do early retirement incentives offered by the state affect the age requirements for retirements in the various tiers?

Periodically, the state offers early retirement incentive plans that allow public employees to retire at an earlier age than at which they would normally be allowed to retire. For example, Chapter 47 of the Laws of 1998 allows employees who are at least 50 years of age with at least 10 years of service to take advantage of an incentive. However, there are penalties which vary by tier and which are also affected by factors such as age and years of service (see also Laws of 1998, Ch. 109).

A teacher who submits his or her resignation prior to a district's decision to participate in a state early retirement incentive program is not entitled to participate in the program (*Dodge v. Board of Educ.*, 655 N.Y.S.2d 123 (3rd Dep't 1997)).

11:11. Can the benefits of a member of a state retirement plan be changed to the member's disadvantage?

No. The state constitution makes membership in any pension or retirement system of the state or a civil division a contractual relationship and, thus, the system's benefits may not be diminished or impaired by the Legislature (NYS Const. Art. 5, § 7).

The New York State Court of Appeals has invalidated any reductions in Tier III benefits that purportedly were made by Chapter 414 of the Laws of 1983. The 1983 law attempted to alter previous benefits by preventing members from withdrawing their contributions to the system until age 62, even if they left service earlier (*Public Employees' Federation v. Cuomo*, 62 N.Y.2d 450 (1984)).

This constitutional provision also has been held to require that the mortality table in effect on the date a member joins the Teachers'

Retirement System is guaranteed to the member in the calculation of her or his benefits and may not be changed *(Birnbaum v. New York State Teachers' Retirement System,* 5 N.Y.2d 1 (1958)).

11:12. Are there any noncontributory retirement plans, and, if so, to whom are they available?

Yes. There are four noncontributory retirement plans and they are available to members in Tier I and Tier II. Employees enrolled in any one of these plans are not required to contribute to it (§ 75-b) .

The Noncontributory Plan (1/60th Plan). At retirement, a member will receive a pension equal to 1/60th of his or her final average salary for each year of service rendered as a member on and after April 1, 1960, plus 1/120th of final average salary for each year of service rendered as a member before April 1, 1960, plus an annuity from any accumulated contributions left on deposit with the system. Each year of prior service (up to a maximum of 35 years) will increase the pension by 1/60th of the member's final average salary (§ 75-c).

The Noncontributory Plan with Guaranteed Benefits (Improved 1/60th Plan). At retirement, a member will receive a pension equal to 1/60th of his or her final average salary for each year of service since April 1, 1960, plus a pension that will produce, when added to the annuity purchasable by required member contributions, a retirement allowance of 1/60th of his or her final average salary for each year of service between April 1, 1938 and April 1, 1960. All members' contributions since April 1, 1960, and those in excess of the contributions required under the Age 60 Plan for the years between 1938 and 1960 will, if left in the system, purchase additional annuity. Service before April 1, 1938 is credited in the same manner for the Improved 1/60th Plan as it is for the 1/60th Plan. Each year of prior service (to a maximum of 35 years) will increase the pension portion of the retirement allowance by 1/60th of final average salary (§ 75-e).

The Career Plan (25 years). A member retiring with at least 25 years of total service (that is, service while a member plus prior service) will receive a retirement allowance of 1/50th of final average salary for each of the first 25 years of service, plus 1/60th of final average salary for each year in excess of 25, provided that required contributions are on deposit. Members retiring with fewer than 25 years of service will receive the Improved 1/60th Plan benefit (§ 75-g).

The Improved Career Plan. The employer may elect to reduce the number of years of total service required for career retirement benefits to 20, and the employee will receive a retirement allowance of 1/50th of the member's final average salary for each year of service, provided that the maximum pension payable does not exceed three-quarters of final average salary (§ 75-i).

If a member's employer has not elected a noncontributory plan, the employee has a choice between the Age 55 Plan and the Age 60 Plan, both of which require an employee's contribution.

The Age 60 Plan. A member in Tier I may retire at or after age 60, regardless of length of service, with a pension of 1/140th of final average salary for each year of his or her service as a member, plus 1/70th of final average salary for each year of prior service (to a maximum of 35 years), plus an annuity purchased by his or her contributions. The same benefit formula applies to members in Tier II, but those members must meet the criteria described in **11:7.** Rate of contribution is based on occupation, sex and age at entry into membership (§ 75).

The Age 55 Plan. A member in Tier I may retire at or after age 55, regardless of length of service, with a pension of 1/120th of final average salary for each year of service as a member, plus 1/60th of final average salary for each year of prior service (to a maximum of 35 years), plus an annuity purchased by member contributions. The same benefit formula applies to members in Tier II, but those members must meet the criteria described in **11:7.** The contribution rate for this plan is greater than that for the Age 60 Plan (§ 75).

11:13. Are Tier III and Tier IV member contributions subject to taxation?

Under section 414(h) of the Internal Revenue Code as implemented by sections 517(f) and 613(d) of the Retirement and Social Security Law, the 3 percent contribution made by Tier III and Tier IV members is not subject to federal income tax. Those contributions are still subject to New York State taxation. The 3 percent contributions are included in gross income for federal income tax purposes when they are distributed at retirement or upon withdrawal from a retirement system.

11:14. Can a member of a retirement system buy credit for prior public service?

Generally, members in Tiers II, III and IV can buy credit for prior public service if they have completed five years of current service and if a public retirement system in this state previously credited the service or it was rendered by an employee during which employment he or she became a member of the retirement system. Members in Tiers III and IV cannot get credit for prior service out of state.

Members in Tier I who joined before July 1, 1973, can buy prior in-state public service without limit and in many cases members of TRS Tier I can buy up to 10 years of out-of-state service in a public school on a matching basis with their credited New York State service.

Members of the Teachers' Retirement System who joined on or after July 1, 1973 may purchase prior service credit for services rendered as a New York State public school teacher prior to January 1, 1986, and prior to when the teacher last became a member of the system. To be eligible, the member must have five years' service credit when the prior service credit is granted and must have filed the claim by July 1, 1998 (Laws of 1997, Ch. 639).

11:15. Can a member of a public retirement system transfer membership between retirement systems?

Yes. Members who joined a public retirement system prior to April 1, 1993 who, because of simultaneous membership in two public retirement systems, were entitled to transfer membership to a public retirement system, but failed to do so in a timely manner, may be entitled to transfer that membership. A written notice to transfer must have been filed by January 1, 1998 (§ 801).

11:16. Can a member receive credit for previously credited service that was not transferred?

Yes. The Retirement and Social Security Law allows a member who has rendered five years of credited service since last joining a public retirement system to obtain prior credit, even though that person may have had the right to transfer and failed to do so. The granting of previous service credit will not affect the individual's date of membership or tier status. To be eligible, a member must file a written request before the effective date of retirement. The member must also deposit the amount required to obtain previous service credit under his or her current membership (§ 802).

11:17. What is meant by vesting?

Vesting occurs when an employee is legally entitled to receive retirement benefits without the need to render additional service (see §§ 516(a), 612(a)). Generally, employees become vested after five years of service in one of the retirement systems (Laws of 1998, Ch. 389). Once vested, an employee may receive benefits under one of the retirement systems upon retiring at the statutorily specified age, depending on the tier to which he or she belongs.

11:18. Is the retirement income of a retired school district employee subject to federal and New York State income tax?

There is no New York State income tax on any part of the retirement allowance. There is federal income tax on the amount contributed by school districts on interest on the annuity part of the retirement allowance. When the employee retires, a statement is furnished giving the necessary data for income tax purposes. In January of each year, a W–2P statement is sent to each retiree. For those who retired on or after January 1, 1974, the W–2P gives the taxable portion of the allowance received during the previous year. Check with the United States Internal Revenue Service for information about other changes.

11:19. Can a school district employee increase his or her retirement income by using a tax-sheltered annuity plan?

Yes. Such a plan, however, is external to the system. Employees are qualified because they are employed by an organization that is eligible, under section 403(b) of the Internal Revenue Code. Approval of this plan has to be given by the local school board, pursuant to a written agreement (usually the collective bargaining agreement between the employee's union and the district) by which the district reduces the employee's annual salary for the purpose of purchasing the annuity (Educ. Law §§ 3109, 3109–A; see **8:129**).

11:20. Can a school district employee who is retired from service return to public employment without the loss of his or her retirement allowance?

Yes, under specified conditions. Commencing with the calendar year in which he or she reaches 70, a member retired from service is not subject to restrictions on his or her earnings. Any retiree under 70 can earn up to $14,500 in calendar year 1998 and $15,500 in calendar year 1999 without prior approval from the appropriate state official and without loss or suspension of his or her retirement allowance. Otherwise, retired teachers must obtain approval from the commissioner of education, and noninstructional employees must obtain approval from the state civil service commission, the respective appropriate official.

If the retiree works for an employer from whom he or she received no pay during the two years of his or her employment preceding retirement, the retiree may earn any amount without loss or suspension of his or her allowance, provided his or her employment has had prior approval by the appropriate state official as set forth above (§§ 211-212).

If a retiree works for a former employer by whom the retiree was paid any amount during the two years preceding his or her retirement, his or her earnings in a calendar year cannot exceed the next multiple of $500 higher than the difference between the sum of his or her annual retirement allowance computed without optional modification and annual supplemental payments to him or her, if any, and the greater of the final average salary on which his or her retirement allowance is based or the salary he or she now would be receiving had he or she not retired from his or her original position. Prior approval must be obtained by the employer as set forth above (§ 211).

The formula works this way: Ms. Smith retires on a final average salary of $18,000. Her retirement allowance, without modification by option, is $10,000. The difference is $8,000. Her salary now, had he or she not retired, would have been $19,600. The difference is $9,600. The next multiple of $500 higher than the larger of the differences is $10,000. That is the limit on her earnings for the calendar year.

11:21. What happens if a retiree returning to public employment earns more than the maximum amount permitted?

A retired member of the system who accepts employment under the applicable regulation outlined above, and who earns, as the result of such employment in any calendar year, an amount in excess of the maximum earnings permitted, is subject to suspension of his or her retirement allowance until the total amount suspended equals the amount of the excess (§ 211(3)).

11:22. Can a retired school district employee who returns to public employment rejoin a state retirement system?

Yes. However, the retirement allowance is stopped during work periods (§101).

11:23. What happens if a retiree returns to work for a private employer?

Work for a private employer, an out-of-state employer (public or private) or the federal government does not affect a service retiree's retirement allowance.

Teachers' Retirement System

11:24. Who is covered by the Teachers' Retirement System?

The Teachers' Retirement System (TRS) includes teachers in public schools of New York State, except New York City teachers, and some members of the State University of New York teaching staff (Educ. Law § 501(4)). New York City teachers are covered by the New York City

Teachers' Retirement System.

The term *teacher* is defined broadly in the law to include regular teachers, special teachers, superintendents, principals, school librarians and other members of the teaching and professional staff of public schools (Educ. Law § 501(4).

11:25. May substitute or other part-time teachers join the Teachers' Retirement System (TRS)?

Yes. Membership for substitute or other part-time teachers is at the individual employee's option. Employers must notify part-time teachers in writing of their right to membership in the system (Educ. Law § 520(2)(b)).

11:26. Who is responsible for operating the Teachers' Retirement System (TRS)?

Primary responsibility for the proper operation of the TRS rests with its board and staff (Educ. Law § 504(1)). Additional supervision is provided by the New York State Department of Insurance. TRS funds may be invested only in accordance with statutory specifications. An actuarial valuation is made each year to determine whether the system has the resources to meet its obligations. Any deficiency must be made up by increasing the contributions made by the school districts (Educ. Law §§ 508; 521).

11:27. How many members are on the Teachers' Retirement System's (TRS) board, and how are they chosen?

The TRS board has 10 members. Three of them are elected by the New York State Board of Regents. One of those members must be or have been an executive officer of a bank authorized to do business in the state and may not be an employee of the state. Two of those members must be current or former trustees or board members of a school district who have experience in finance and investment. Neither may be an employee of the state. One of those members must also be or have been an executive officer of an insurance company. These two members are chosen from a list of five presented to the Board of Regents by the New York State School Boards Association.

Two administrative officers from New York State's public school system are chosen by the commissioner of education. The state comptroller or his appointee also sits on the board. Three members are elected from among TRS's members, and one member, who must be a retired teacher, is elected from among the retired members of the retirement system (Educ. Law § 504; 505-a).

All members, with the exception of the comptroller or his appointee, serve for a term of three years (Educ. Law § 504(2)).

11:28. How is the Teachers' Retirement System (TRS) funded?

The TRS is funded through members' contributions, school district employers' contributions and investment income.

11:29. How much money do the Teachers' Retirement System's (TRS) members contribute?

Members' contributions to the TRS vary depending on their tier. Members in tiers III and IV must contribute 3 percent of their salaries toward their pensions. Except to purchase prior service, Tier I and II teachers who joined the system on or after July 1, 1970 through July 26, 1976 cannot contribute to the retirement system. Teachers who joined before July 1, 1970 may continue to contribute at their present rate or discontinue making contributions. Once they have ceased making regular contributions, they may not start again (Educ. Law § 516).

11:30. How much do school districts contribute to the Teachers' Retirement System (TRS)?

The amount a school district contributes to the TRS varies from year to year, depending on actuarial analysis. The employer's contribution rate payable by school districts was 1.25 percent of a member district's payroll for the 1997-98 school year and 1.42 percent during 1998-99. TRS's board sets the rate annually, based on the recommendations of the system's actuary.

11:31. When are school districts' contribution payments to the Teachers' Retirement System (TRS) due?

Pursuant to changes made in the payment schedule for employer contributions during the 1990 state budget, school districts' payments to the TRS are made in the fall for salaries paid during the previous school year (Educ. Law § 521).

11:32. How are payments made to the Teachers' Retirement System (TRS)?

Payments are credited directly to the pension fund by the state comptroller in three equal installments due on September 15, October 15, and November 15 of each fiscal year. The funds are deducted from each district's state aid apportionment (Educ. Law § 3609-a(1)(a)(1)). Employers who receive no state aid or whose state aid payments are insufficient to pay the amount due the system are billed directly by the system (Educ. Law § 521; see also **21:3**).

11:33. What happens if an employer underpays its obligation to the Teachers' Retirement System (TRS)?

The amount of the underpayment is deducted from the employer's state aid apportionment for the following year, on April 15 (Educ. Law § 521(2)(h)). Employers whose payments from such appropriation are insufficient to pay the amount due, or who do not receive such payments, will be billed by the system for the underpayment. Payments that are not made within 30 days will accrue interest (Educ. Law § 521).

11:34. How long may teachers leave their own contributions in the Teachers' Retirement System (TRS) after they cease to teach in a New York state public school?

There is no limit on the length of time a teacher may leave his or her contributions in the TRS, but no interest is credited on contributions after membership ceases. The law also provides that seven years after a member ceases to be a teacher for cause other than death or retirement, his or her unclaimed contributions may be declared abandoned (Educ. Law § 531(1)). Unclaimed contributions may be reclaimed upon presentation of a valid claim by the former member or his estate (Educ. Law §§ 512, 531; see **11:39** in reference to a member borrowing against his or her contributions to TRS).

11:35. May a member of the Teachers' Retirement System receive a lump sum retirement payment?

Yes. A member of TRS who is entitled to receive a retirement allowance, other than for disability, may elect at retirement to receive, in lieu of a retirement allowance, a lump sum payment which is the actuarial equivalent to the retirement allowance if the allowance is less than $1,000 per year. Payment of the lump sum would complete the retirement system's obligation to the member (Educ. Law § 537).

11:36. Are some retired teachers entitled to supplemental pensions?

Yes. A cost-of-living supplemental retirement allowance program is provided to all who retired because of disabilities, recipients of an accidental death benefit, as well as to those who retired from service before January 1, 1994, who have reached age 62 or have reached the age of 55 and have been retired for 10 or more years.

The supplemental allowance is computed as a percentage of the first $14,000 of the member's maximum retirement allowance, excluding return on voluntary contributions, without optional modification, and is based on a schedule contained in section 532 of the Education Law.

There is also a minimum supplemental allowance for persons who retired before July 1, 1970, the amount of which is the lessor of $10,500 or the number of years of credited service up to 35, multiplied by $300 (Laws of 1998, Ch. 390).

Members receiving supplemental allowances under earlier provisions of the law receive the greater of the supplemental benefits to which they may be entitled under the old or new laws (Laws of 1984, ch. 658; Educ. Law § 532. Chapter 8 of the Laws of 1988 provides for a further pension supplementation over and above the one granted in 1984).

11:37. Is an in-service death benefit available to a teacher member of the Teachers' Retirement System?

Yes. The benefit depends on the member's date of membership and length of service (Educ. Law § 512(2)).

In addition, a pre-retirement death benefit is available to members of the state retirement systems who are out of public service and who die on or after January 1, 1997 but prior to retirement, having at least 10 years of credited service at the time of death. The death benefit is equal to one-half of the benefit payable if the member had died in active service on the last date of employment (Laws of 1998, Ch. 388).

11:38. Can teachers who are members of the Teachers' Retirement System retire on disability?

Yes. To be considered for a disability allowance, members must be credited with 10 years of service with New York State, except for members in Tier III, who need only five years of service if they are eligible for a primary Social Security disability benefit. Members in Tier III and Tier IV who become disabled through job-related accidents may be eligible, under certain conditions, for accidental disability benefits (Educ. Law § 511; Retire. & Soc. Sec. Law §§ 506-507).

The TRS Board may approve the disability retirement application of an eligible member who would have been entitled to retire for disability, but died before the application could become effective. The eligible member's death must be as a result of the disability (Educ. Law § 511(8)).

11:39. May a teacher borrow from his or her accumulated deposits in the Teachers' Retirement System (TRS)?

TRS members who are in Tiers III and IV can borrow up to 75 percent of their accumulated contributions. The loan may not be less than $1,000, and must be repaid in equal installments that are at least 2 percent of the member's contract salary, and sufficient to repay the total amount due together with interest paid on the unpaid balance within five years (§§ 517(e), 517–b, 613–a).

Any member who has credit for at least one year of service may borrow from their contributions. The loan may not be less than $300 or exceed three-fourths of the member's accumulated contributions. The amount, together with interest on any unpaid balance, must be paid in equal installments that are at least 2 percent of the member's contract salary, and sufficient to pay the interest on any unpaid balance (Educ. Law § 512-b).

The legislature has authorized TRS to adopt rules and regulations permitting a loan at any time prior to retirement to a teacher who is not in active service or on a leave of absence (Educ. Law § 512-b)).

11:40. Does the Teachers' Retirement System (TRS) include bonus termination pay in computing a member's retirement benefit?

Not usually. A bonus is included in computation of retirement benefits only if the member joined the TRS before June 17, 1971, and a five-year final average salary, including termination pay, is higher than the three-year final average salary, excluding termination pay (§ 431).

11:41. Where can further information about the Teachers' Retirement System (TRS) be obtained?

For more information about the TRS, contact the system's offices at 10 Corporate Woods Drive, Albany, N.Y. 12211; telephone 518-447-2900 or 1-800-348-7298; website at http://www.nystrs.albany.ny.us.

Employees' Retirement System

11:42. What retirement benefits are available to noninstructional employees?

A school board may elect to provide retirement coverage to noninstructional employees by participating in the New York State Employees' Retirement System (ERS). There is no law that requires them to do so; however, participation by an employer, once made, may not be revoked (§ 30(a)). The law likewise precludes the establishment of any retirement system for a civil service employee other than the Employees' Retirement System (§ 113(a)).

11:43. If a school board elects to participate in the Employees' Retirement System, must all noninstructional employees become members?

No. Any such person in the service of the district on the date the system is adopted may or may not elect to become a member (§ 40(c)).

11:44. Once a school district starts participating in the Employees' Retirement System (ERS), must new employees join the system?

Yes. All persons appointed to service on and after the date of adoption whose positions are in the competitive or noncompetitive class of the civil service must become members of the ERS as of their dates of appointment. The only exception to this occurs when a person is appointed to a competitive-class position on a temporary or provisional basis, pending the results of an examination. That person may join immediately if desired, but cannot be required to join the system until his or her appointment becomes permanent (§ 40(b)(1)).

11:45. Who is responsible for operating the Employees' Retirement System (ERS)?

The state comptroller serves as the sole trustee and administrative head of the ERS (§ 13).

11:46. How is the Employees' Retirement System (ERS) funded?

Funding for the ERS is accomplished through member and employer contributions, as determined by the Retirement and Social Security Law, and investment income. Until 1990, the system was funded by the aggregate method, which based employer contributions on estimated future costs to the retirement system. As a result, payments were relatively level.

In 1990, the governor and the state Legislature instituted a new method of calculating contributions, known as the projected unit credit (PUC) system. This system essentially postponed payments due to the retirement system from the state and local governments. In 1993, the state's highest court declared invalid the 1990 funding method, and the state comptroller developed a plan to return to the aggregate method and make up for contributions lost during that period (*McDermott v. Regan*, 82 N.Y.2d 354 (1993). The system has returned to the aggregate cost method.

11:47. How are payments made to the Employees' Retirement System (ERS)?

Employees' contributions are paid into ERS by payroll deductions each payroll period (§ 517(a))

Employers' contributions to ERS are paid once each year upon receipt of a bill from the Comptroller (§ 17). Payment cannot be required before December 15 of the calendar year in which the statement is received (§ 17(c)).

11:48. What happens if an employer underpays its obligation to the Employees' Retirement System (ERS)?

Payment must be made within 30 days after receipt of a statement from the system. Interest is added to the amount on the first day after the date that the payment is required to be paid (§17(c), (d)). The state comptroller has the authority to bring suit in a state supreme court against any participating employer to recover any sum due the system (§ 17(e)).

11:49. Are the rights of members of the Employees' Retirement System (ERS) affected by leave taken under workers' compensation?

Tier III and Tier IV members of ERS are not penalized for any period of leave taken under workers' compensation provisions. Their leave is credited for purposes of calculating retirement service, retirement contributions and the final average salary (§§ 513(4), 609(a)(3)).

11:50. Where can more information about the Employees' Retirement System (ERS) be obtained?

More information about the ERS can be obtained by contacting the New York State Employees' Retirement System, Gov. A. E. Smith State Office Building, Albany, N.Y. 12244, telephone 518-474-7736. Retirement-related information may also be found at the Office of the State Comptroller's homepage at www.osc.state.ny.us/.

Social Security

11:51. Are teachers in New York State covered by Social Security?

Yes. Almost all teachers in New York State now have Social Security coverage. The few exceptions are:
- Teachers who were members of the New York State Teachers' Retirement System before the Social Security referendum on December 12, 1957, and who rejected coverage or who did not sign a declaration accepting coverage before the referendum, and who did not accept Social Security during the 1959 or 1961-62 reopenings.
- Teachers whose employment began after December 31, 1957, who are eligible to become retirement system members and who have not done so.

All newly employed teachers must participate (§ 138–a).

11:52. Are noninstructional employees of school districts covered by Social Security?

Yes. Almost all noninstructional employees of school districts are covered by Social Security. Exceptions are:

- Employees who were members of the Employees' Retirement System before the Social Security referendum on December 2, 1957, and either rejected coverage or failed to accept it before the referendum and did not accept Social Security during the 1959 or 1961-62 reopening.
- Employees whose employment began after December 31, 1957, other than those in positions that exclude them from membership in a retirement system and who are provided with Social Security as the result of action completed before December 1957, who are eligible to become members of ERS, but whose positions do not require membership and who have not filed a membership application.

11:53. Can a school district withdraw entirely from the Social Security system?

No. Chapter 837 of the Laws of 1977 prohibits an employer from discontinuing coverage of its employees by the Social Security system.

Also, state and local governments whose coverage had been terminated may now be covered again. In the past, the law had prohibited a terminated group from being covered again.

11:54. Are there limits on earnings, after retirement, for Social Security benefits?

Yes. In 1998, an individual 65 to 69 years old could earn $14,500 ($15,500 beginning in 1999) and, if under 65, $9,120, without loss of Social Security benefits. If the person is 65 to 69 years old, the reduction is one dollar for every three dollars earned over the earnings limitation during the year. If the person is under 65, benefits are reduced one dollar for every two dollars earned over the earnings limitation during the year (see Social Security Update – 1998, United States Department of Health and Human Services, Social Security Administration).

There is no reduction of benefits for earnings once a person reaches age 70 (42 USC § 403).

11:55. Should employees who intend to work beyond age 65 contact the Social Security Administration?

Yes. To enroll in Medicare, these individuals should contact the Social Security Administration, even though no retirement benefits will be paid until actual retirement.

11:56. Where can further information about Social Security be obtained?

More information about Social Security can be obtaining by calling the Social Security Administration at 1-800-772-1213 or http://www.ssa.gov.

12. Students

School Attendance

12:1. At what age must children in New York State receive instruction?

Minors who turn six years old on or before December 1 in any school year must receive full-time instruction from the first day school is in session in September of such school year. Minors who turn six years old after December 1 of a school year must receive full-time instruction from the first day of school in the following September. All children must remain in attendance until the last day of the school year in which they reach the age of 16 (§ 3205(1)(c)).

In each city and union free school district of more than 4,500 inhabitants that employs a superintendent of schools, the school board has the authority to require minors from ages 16 through 17 who are not employed to attend school until the last day of the school year in which they become 17 years of age (§ 3205(3)).

Instruction may take place in a public, private or parochial school, or at home (§§ 3202; 3204(1),(2); 3210(2)). A minor who has completed a four-year high school course of study is not required to attend school (§ 3205(2)(a)).

12:2. Are there any exemptions from the compulsory education requirements?

The landmark case regarding exemption from compulsory school requirements is *Wisconsin v. Yoder*, 406 U.S. 205 (1972), where the United States Supreme Court permitted an exemption from compulsory school attendance for Amish children after the eighth-grade level. However, the exemption was granted, based exclusively on the recognition that the preservation of Amish society depended on its children learning how to maintain an agrarian way of life that was free from modern technology.

According to the court, the accommodation afforded the Amish did not contravene the principles of public education; rather, it allowed Amish children to be educated in the ways necessary to preserve the Amish way of life.

12:3. Is a student under 16 or 17 years of age who marries subject to the compulsory education law?

Yes. Attendance is compulsory for minors (see **12:1**). There is no exception for students under the ages of 16 or 17 who are married. However, 16- or 17-year-old students who have a certificate of full-time employment may attend school not less than 20 hours per week instead of full time (§ 3205(2)(b); for more detail on employment of students, see **12:127-134**).

12:4. May a student from the ages of six to 16 or 17 attend a school other than a public school?

Yes. However, the compulsory attendance law requires that instruction given to a minor elsewhere than a public school must be "at least substantially equivalent to the instruction given to minors of like age and attainments at the public schools of the city or district where the minor resides" (§ 3204(2)).

12:5. At what age may children attend a prekindergarten program?

Under the universal prekindergarten legislation, school boards may, but are not required to, adopt a plan to provide prekindergarten services to resident children (§ 3602-e(4)). If such a plan is adopted by the school board and approved by the commissioner of education, resident children who are four years of age on or before December 1 of the year in which they are enrolled or who will otherwise be first eligible to enter public school kindergarten commencing with the following year will be eligible to receive pre-kindergarten services (§ 3602-e(1)(c)). Once a child is enrolled in a prekindergarten program, an attendance policy must be applied to the child (8 NYCRR § 151-1.2(d)).

12:6. Is a child five years of age entitled to go to public school?

Yes. The law provides that a person over five and under 21 years of age who does not possess a high school diploma is entitled to attend the public schools maintained in the district where he or she resides (§ 3202(1); see **12:1** for compulsory education age requirements). A child over five years of age is entitled to attend the public schools in the district regardless of whether or not the district maintains a kindergarten program. That child would be entitled to be admitted to the first grade (*Appeal of Carney*, 15 Educ. Dep't Rep. 325 (1976); Formal Opinion of Counsel No. 75, 1 Educ. Dep't Rep. 775 (1952)).

The law does not require a school district to admit a child who becomes five years old after the school year has commenced unless his or her birthday occurs on or before December 1. School boards may, at their discretion, admit children at an earlier age (§ 3202(1)).

If a school district maintains a policy that would delay the admission to kindergarten of any child who becomes five after December 1, it need not alter such policy on an individual basis for particular students

(*Frost v. Yerazunis*, 53 A.D.2d 15 (3rd Dep't 1976); *Appeal of Sollitto*, 31 Educ. Dep't Rep. 138 (1991)).

In *Matter of Benjamin*, 26 Educ. Dep't Rep. 533 (1987), the commissioner of education held that a school district may not enact a policy requiring that a child be at least five years of age by September 1 of the school year he or she begins school.

12:7. Are all children who attend public schools required to go to kindergarten?

No. Transfer students to upper grades may avoid kindergarten. However, within certain legal limitations, the age of entrance and the grade placement of children are matters for the local education authorities to decide. A local school board may:

- Require any child entering school under the age of six to attend and complete a year of kindergarten, provided that the child has not already done so in another kindergarten, such as a private one, substantially equivalent to that of the local public school. Even in such a case, a school board can require the child to be tested and evaluated before making any determination with respect to placement. If the testing indicates that the child will be unable to perform at a first-grade level, the board may require the child to remain in kindergarten (*Matter of Pleener*, 30 Educ. Dep't Rep. 55 (1990); *Matter of Kitchen*, 12 Educ. Dep't Rep. 20 (1972)).
- Delay until the following September the admission of any child who becomes five after December 1 (§ 3202(1)).
- Base the initial entrance of children into kindergarten on chronological age within the statutory limitations.
- Decide the date and place of enrollment of children in school.

A nonpublic school kindergarten may not admit a child who is younger than the age of entrance into the public schools established by the district in which the child resides (8 NYCRR § 125.9).

12:8. May a child who attended kindergarten elsewhere be denied admission to a public school first grade class, based solely on that child's age?

No. The commissioner of education has held that a school board policy that uses age as the sole criterion for admission of kindergarten students into the first grade contravenes the legal right of a child to be graded in the school system in accordance with ability. However, a school board may require testing and evaluation of the child before making any determination with respect to placement (*Matter of Kitchen*, 12 Educ. Dep't Rep. 20 (1972); *Matter of Lazar*, 6 Educ. Dep't Rep. 7 (1966)).

12:9. May individuals who have obtained a high school diploma attend public school?

Yes. A school board must admit an individual who has received a high school diploma and is under 21 years of age to classes in the district, provided that person pays the stated tuition. The school board may waive this tuition. However, if this is done, the student may not be counted for state aid purposes (§ 3202(1); *Matter of Brown*, 15 Educ. Dep't Rep. 79 (1975)).

12:10. May individuals who have obtained a high school equivalency diploma, but not a high school diploma, attend public school?

Yes. According to the State Education Department, an otherwise qualified individual who has received a high school equivalency diploma, but not a high school diploma, remains entitled to attend the public schools in his or her district of residence, without the payment of tuition, until the age of 21, or until that person has obtained a high school diploma (see "School Executive's Bulletin," Office of Elementary, Middle and Secondary Education, State Education Department, June 1989).

12:11. How may an adult over 21 years of age secure a high school diploma?

Section 100.7 of the commissioner's regulations provides that an adult may secure a high school equivalency diploma by achieving an acceptable score on the comprehensive examinations under the New York State Equivalency Diploma program. Inmates of a state correctional institution also may take these examinations (8 NYCRR § 100.7(a)(1)(ii)(c)).

Additionally, as an alternative to the comprehensive examinations, candidates may qualify by completion of 24 college credits at an approved institution of higher education (8 NYCRR § 100.7(a)(2)(iii)).

12:12. Must districts maintain accurate school attendance registers for students?

Yes. School attendance records must be kept for use in the enforcement of the Education Law (§§ 3024, 3211(1)), and as the source for the average daily attendance used to help determine a district's state aid allocation (§ 3025(1)). In addition, school attendance records may be subpoenaed as legal evidence.

Keeping and verifying school attendance records, formerly a teacher's task, can be done by others in the school system, although a teacher must be assigned to supervise those employees (§ 3211(1); 8 NYCRR § 104.1(e)).

The commissioner of education can prescribe the form and manner of keeping such records (§§ 3024, 3025(1), 3211(1); 8 NYCRR § 104.1(b)). The purpose of this is to facilitate electronic attendance and other record keeping.

12:13. What school attendance is prescribed for minors who are required to attend school?

Minors who are required to attend school must do so regularly, as prescribed by the school board where the student resides or is employed, for the entire time the appropriate public schools or classes are in session (§ 3210(1)).

12:14. May parents home-instruct students?

Yes. A student who is instructed at home must be provided with a substantially equivalent education to that of the public schools where he or she resides, with instruction by a competent instructor (§ 3204(2)). Instructors need not be certified teachers (see 8 NYCRR § 100.10; see **24:18-33**).

12:15. Can students attend public school part time and receive home instruction for the balance of the school day?

No. According to the commissioner of education, the Legislature has not authorized partial attendance at a public school except under certain specified circumstances (*Matter of Mayshark*, 17 Educ. Dep't Rep. 82 (1977)). One of those circumstances is detailed in section 3602-c of the Education Law, commonly referred to as the dual-enrollment law, which permits instruction in the areas of career education, gifted and talented education, education for students with disabilities, and counseling, psychological and social work services related to instruction (see "Revised Questions and Answers on Home Instruction," Nonpublic School Services Team, NY State Education Department, December 1996).

12:16. Does a parent have the right to refuse to send his or her child to a specified school on the grounds that the parent considers it unfit and unsafe?

No. The school board has the power to assign students to a particular school, to prescribe their courses of study and to regulate their transfer from one class or department to another (§ 1709(3)).

12:17. May a student be absent from school for observance of religious occasions?

Yes. The Education Law recognizes school days missed for religious observance or any other reason as "absences" (§ 3210(1)(b)). The commissioner's regulations provide that the absence of a student from school during school hours for religious observance outside the school building and grounds will be excused upon a written request signed by his or her parent or guardian (8 NYCRR § 109.2(a)).

The commissioner of education has upheld a school board's policy requiring completion of compensatory work when a student exceeded seven absences in any quarter, when applied to a student whose eighth absence was due to the student's observance of a religious holiday (*Matter of Hegarty*, 31 Educ. Dep't Rep. 232 (1992)).

12:18. May a student be released for religious instruction?

Yes. A student may be released during school hours for religious instruction upon a written request by his or her parent or guardian (8 NYCRR § 109.2(a)). The courses in religious education must be maintained and operated by or under the control of duly constituted religious bodies (8 NYCRR § 109.2(b)). Students must be registered for the courses and a copy of the registration must be filed with the local public school authorities (8 NYCRR § 109.2(c)). The attendance of students enrolled in such religious classes must be reported to the public school principal at the end of each semester (8 NYCRR § 109.2(d)).

Absence for release-time programs for kindergarten through 12th grade cannot be for more than one hour each week at the close of either the morning or afternoon session, or both, at a time to be fixed by the local school authorities. The time designated for each separate unit – the primary grades (kindergarten through third grade), intermediate grades (fourth through sixth grades), junior high school grades (seventh through ninth grades), and senior high school grades (10th through 12th grades) – must be the same for all students in that unit in each separate school (8 NYCRR § 109.2(e)).

If there is more than one school offering religious education within the district, the hours for absence from each particular public elementary or secondary school in that district must be the same for all such religious schools (8 NYCRR § 109.2(e)).

A school board may establish an optional program for high school students in grades 9 through 12, permitting them to enroll in a course in religion in a registered nonpublic high school, with the written approval of the student's parent or guardian. This is subject to prior approval of the public high school principal with respect to course schedule, student attendance and reporting of student achievement. Absence to attend such a course may be excused for the number of periods per week that the course is scheduled in the nonpublic school, provided that the excused absences must be at the beginning or close of the public school session and are mutually agreed upon by the school officials (8 NYCRR § 109.2(f)).

12:19. What is truancy?

Truancy is the willful violation by a student of the compulsory attendance provisions in Article 65 of the Education Law, which require minors from six to 16 or 17 years of age to attend school full time (§ 3205).

12:20. Is truancy a violation of law?

Yes. An attendance officer may arrest a truant without a warrant (§ 3213(2)(a)). Habitual truancy is grounds for a person in need of supervision (PINS) petition in family court (Family Court Act §§ 712(a), 732).

Section 3213(2)(c) of the Education Law requires that an attendance officer or other person authorized by the school district to notify the parent of an elementary-grade student of his or her child's absence from school, if the parent so requests. The obligation to notify a parent arises only after a parent has submitted a request to be notified.

The commissioner has ruled that school authorities may not suspend students from school for truancy (*Appeal of Ackert*, 30 Educ. Dep't Rep. 31 (1990); see **12:97**).

12:21. May a student be absent from school, in violation of the school district's attendance policy, if that student's parent consents to such an absence?

No. The commissioner of education has ruled that parental consent to a student's absence does not preclude the school district from taking disciplinary action against the student for violating the district's attendance policy (*Matter of Auch*, 33 Educ. Dep't Rep. 84 (1993)). A school board can establish rules concerning the order and discipline of the schools, as it may deem necessary (§ 1709(2)). These rules are not subject to parental consent (*Matter of Auch*).

12:22. May a school board adopt a minimum attendance policy for students to receive academic credit?

Yes. The commissioner of education has upheld the adoption and implementation of minimum attendance policies for students to receive academic credit (*Appeal of Hansen*, 34 Educ. Dep't Rep. 235 (1994); *Appeal of Peter C.*, 34 Educ. Dep't Rep. 171 (1994)). However, the policy may not deny credit to a student who has taken all tests and secured a passing grade, but has exceeded the allowable number of absences for that course (*Matter of Shepard*, 31 Educ. Dep't Rep. 315 (1992); *Matter of Burns*, 29 Educ. Dep't Rep. 103 (1989)).

Minimum attendance policies may not distinguish between excused and unexcused absences for denying course credit (*Appeal of Pasquale,* 36 Educ. Dep't Rep. 290 (1997); *Appeal of Hansen*). However, these policies may contain an appeal process which is available to challenge the number of absences on record, ensure that no violation of the federal Individuals with Disabilities Education Act (IDEA) or section 504 of the Rehabilitation Act has occurred, and to provide an opportunity to waive the maximum allowable absence limit for "extenuating circumstances" – without regard to whether the absences were excused or unexcused. Such an appeal process must be administered in a neutral manner and comply with applicable law (*Appeal of Ehnot,* 37 Educ. Dep't Rep. 648 (1998)).

12:23. May a school district count the days when a student is suspended from school as absences?

No. A school may not count days when a student is suspended from school as absences, unless the student is offered alternative instruction and fails to attend such instruction (*Appeal of Shepard,* 31 Educ. Dep't Rep. 315 (1992)).

12:24. Can students be transferred involuntarily from one school to another in the same district?

Yes. The school board, the superintendent of schools or the district superintendent may transfer a student from regular classroom instruction to an appropriate educational setting in another school on the written recommendation of the school principal and following an independent review (§ 3214(5)(a)).

Before the school principal may initiate an involuntary transfer, he or she must provide the student and his or her parents with written notification of the consideration of transfer recommendation. The notice must set forth the time and place for an informal conference with the principal, and specify their right to be accompanied by an attorney or an individual of their choice (§ 3214(5)(b)).

After the conference is held, and if the principal believes the student would benefit from the transfer or receive an adequate and appropriate education in another school program or facility, the principal may recommend that course of action to the superintendent. These transfers are usually recommended because of behavior or academic problems. The recommendation must include reasons indicating the need for transfer and other supporting information. A copy must be sent to the parent and the student (§ 3214(5)(c)).

Once the superintendent receives the recommendation, he or she must notify the parents and the student of the proposed transfer, their right to a fair hearing on the issue, and other procedural rights. The written notice must include a statement that the student or parents have 10 days to request a hearing (§ 3214(5)(d)).

A hearing to determine whether a student should be transferred is not the same as a hearing for disciplinary reasons. While the purpose of a disciplinary hearing is to punish a student for wrong-doing, the purpose of a transfer hearing is to determine what educational setting would be most beneficial for the student (*Appeal of Reeves*, 37 Educ. Dep't Rep. 271, (1998); see § 3214(5)).

Unless the parents consent to the transfer, the proposed transfer may not take place until the 10-day period to request a hearing has elapsed, or a formal decision is rendered following a hearing, whichever is later (§ 3214(5)(d)). Ultimate responsibility for the assignment of students rests with the school board (§ 1709(3)).

Students with disabilities may not be involuntarily transferred without the participation of the committee on special education (CSE) (*Appeal of Wanda D.*, 34 Educ. Dep't Rep. 556 (1995)).

Involuntary transfers, for the purposes of this question, do not include transfers made to reduce racial imbalance or to change attendance zones (§ 3214(5)(a)).

12:25. May a student who is over the compulsory school attendance age and who does not possess a high school diploma be dropped from school enrollment?

Yes. Students over the age of compulsory school attendance in the school district may be dropped from enrollment if they have been absent 20 consecutive school days and the district has complied with the following procedure:

The principal or superintendent must schedule an informal conference and notify both the student and parent or guardian of this situation in writing at their last known address. At that conference, the principal or superintendent must determine the reasons for the student's absence and whether reasonable changes in the student's educational program would encourage and facilitate his or her continuance of study. The student and parent or guardian must be informed orally and in writing of the student's right to re-enroll at any time in the school maintained in the district of residence, as long as the student remains qualified to attend.

If, after reasonable notice, the student and parent or guardian fail to attend the informal conference, the student may be dropped from enrollment, provided there is notification in writing of the right to reenter at any time, as long as the student is qualified for attendance (§ 3202(1-a)).

12:26. Are public schools required to provide educational services to youths who are incarcerated in county correctional facilities?

Yes. The Education Law and the commissioner's regulations require school districts to provide educational services to youths under age 21 who do not have high school diplomas and who are incarcerated in county correctional facilities located within their districts (§ 3202(7)(a); 8 NYCRR Part 118). These districts receive state aid for such programs (§ 3602(35)).

12:27. Must school districts provide pregnant students with educational opportunities equal to those provided to students who are not pregnant?

Yes. Schools may not discriminate against students based on their parental and/or marital status (Title IX of the Educ. Amendments of 1972, 20 USC § 1681; 45 CFR § 86.40). Pregnant students should be encouraged to remain in school and to participate in programs designed especially for them. All programs for pregnant students should be developed in cooperation with the school physician and student personnel staff to best provide for each individual. Homebound instruction should be made available to pregnant students when necessary.

12:28. May school districts preclude students from attending district schools on the basis of race, creed, color or national origin?

No. No person may be refused admission to or be excluded from any public school in New York State because of race, creed, color or national origin (§ 3201(1)). In addition, segregation of students by race is prohibited by the federal constitution (*Brown v. Board of Educ.*, 347 U.S. 483 (1954); *Lee v. Nyquist*, 318 F.Supp. 710, *aff'd*, 402 U.S. 935 (1971)).

In *Brown*, the United States Supreme Court held that statutorily imposed separate school facilities for blacks and whites were unconstitutional. However, the mere existence of racially segregated schools does not constitute a federal constitutional or statutory violation (*U.S. v. Yonkers Board of Education*, 624 F.Supp. 1276, *aff'd* 837 F.2d 1181 (2nd Cir. 1987); *cert. denied* 486 U.S. 1055 (1988)).

De facto segregation is segregation that is inadvertent and without assistance of school authorities and not caused by any state action but rather by social, economic and other factors (*Hart v. Community School Board of Education*, 512 F.2d 37 (2nd Cir. 1975)). Since the *Brown* decision, New

York State courts and the commissioner have held that, although alleged de facto racial segregation does not constitute a sufficient basis for a court to order a racial integration plan, school officials can adopt voluntary plans to remedy the effects of de facto segregation (see *Balaban v. Rubin*, 14 N.Y.2d 193 (1964), *cert. denied*, 379 U.S. 881 (1964); *Van Blerkom v. Donovan*, 15 N.Y.2d 399 (1965); *Matter of Barnhart*, 21 Educ. Dep't Rep. 126 (1981); see also, *U.S. v. Yonkers Board of Education*, 624 F.Supp. 1276, *aff'd*, 837 F.2d 1181 (2nd Cir. 1987), *cert. denied*, 486 U.S. 1055 (1988)).

However, in some circumstances the commissioner of education may require districts to take action to counteract de facto racial imbalance (*Matter of Fishburne*, 12 Educ. Dep't Rep. 5 (1972)).

Student Residency

12:29. May school districts preclude students from attending district schools on the basis of residency?

Yes. School districts are required to admit only district residents who are over five and under 21 years of age who have not received a high school diploma (§ 3202(1)). A school district may, however, accept nonresidents on terms prescribed by the school board (§ 3202(2); see **12:35-36**).

12:30. May a school district refuse to admit nonresident students?

Section 3202(2) of the Education Law provides that nonresidents of a district may be admitted into its schools on terms prescribed by the school board. But where a district has contracted with another district to receive that district's students under section 2045 of the Education Law, it may not refuse to receive nonresident students without demonstrating valid and sufficient reasons (*Matter of Board of Education of South Manor UFSD*, 14 Educ. Dep't Rep. 412 (1975); *Matter of Brunswick CSD*, 14 Educ. Dep't Rep. 33 (1974)).

School districts that admit nonresident students may not exclude students with disabilities. Such an action would be a violation of section 504 of the Rehabilitation Act and the Americans with Disabilities Act, which prohibit discrimination on the basis of disability (29 USC § 794; 42 USC § 12132; see **12:36**).

12:31. How is a student's legal school district of residence determined?

Generally, a student's legal school district residence is presumed to be that of his or her parents or legal guardian (*Appeal of Reynolds*, 37 Educ. Dep't Rep. 58 (1997)). If a student does not live with a parent or legal guardian but there has been no surrender of parental control, that student's legal residence still may be that of the parent or guardian, depending on the particular set of circumstances.

In making residency determinations, the commissioner and the courts have considered financial support, the child's day-to-day care, delegation of parental authority and whether it may be revoked at will (*Catlin v. Sobol*, 77 N.Y.2d 552 (1991); see also, *Catlin v. Sobol*, 93 F.3d 1112 (2nd Cir. 1996) (presumption of residence with parents not unconstitutional)). Physical presence alone is insufficient to establish residence for purposes of attending the school in that district on a tuition-free basis (see *Catlin v. Sobol*; *Appeal of Ritter*, 31 Educ. Dep't Rep. 24 (1991); *Matter of Bunk*, 22 Educ. Dep't Rep. 38 (1982); *Matter of Van Curran*, 18 Educ. Dep't Rep. 523 (1979)).

Students may also rebut the presumption that their residence is with their parents by establishing their emancipated minor status. A student is considered emancipated if he or she is beyond the compulsory school age, is living separate and apart from his or her parents in a manner inconsistent with parental custody and control, is not receiving financial support from his or her parents, and has no intent to return home (*Appeal of Kehoe*, 37 Educ. Dep't Rep. 14 (1997)).

A student's living in a district solely for the purpose of attending a particular school has been rejected as a basis for establishing residency in such district (*Appeal of Ritter*).

12:32. What is the legal school district of residence for students of divorced parents?

Where a child's parents are divorced and a court awards custody to one parent, the child's residence is presumed to be that of the custodial parent (*Appeal of Forde*, 29 Educ. Dep't Rep. 359 (1990)). This presumption is rebuttable. In determining whether that presumption is rebutted, a school board must consider several factors, including the extent of the time the child actually lives in the district and the intent of family members to have the child reside in the district (*Appeal of O'Brien*, 35 Educ. Dep't Rep. 46 (1995)).

Where a child's parents are divorced and the child's time is divided between the households of the parents, the determination of the child's residence ultimately rests with the family (*Matter of Juracka*, 31 Educ. Dep't Rep. 282 (1992)). In such cases, the custodial parent may designate the child's residence (*Appeal of Forde*).

12:33. May a parent who has more than one residence choose either as his or her legal residence for purposes of securing a child's attendance in a particular school district?

No. Residence in this context means permanent domicile, as distinguished from a temporary abode.

When a person claims legal residency in a place where he or she does not remain all year, it becomes necessary to look for some overt act that indicates the individual has made a choice to consider this his or her domicile, such as whether or not the parent registers and votes from that place or whether that parent uses it as his or her residence on income tax reports.

The payment of school taxes does not necessarily make a person a legal resident of that district. Any such amount, however, must be deducted from the tuition charged to a nonresident student (§ 3202(3)).

A person does not lose his or her legal residence or domicile until another residence is established through both intent and action expressing such intent (*Appeal of Reifler*, 31 Educ. Dep't Rep. 235 (1992); *Matter of Aufiero*, 26 Educ. Dep't Rep. 406 (1987)). A temporary absence does not constitute the abandonment of a permanent residence (*Matter of Richards*, 25 Educ. Dep't Rep. 38 (1985); *Matter of Aufiero*).

12:34. What procedures must be observed during a determination of a child's entitlement to attend the schools of a particular district?

The school board or its designee will determine whether a child is entitled to attend the schools of the district. Any decision by a school official, other than the board or its designee, that a child is not entitled to attend the schools of the district must include notification of the procedures to obtain review of the decision within the district.

Prior to reaching such a decision, the board or its designee must allow the parent or guardian the opportunity to submit information concerning the child's right to attend school in the district. If the board determines that the child is not entitled to attend its schools, it must, within two business days, provide written notice of its decision to the child's parent, person in parental relation, or to the child as appropriate (8 NYCRR § 100.2(y)). The written notice must state the following:

- The child is not entitled to attend the public schools of the district.
- The basis for the determination that the child is neither a resident of the district nor entitled to attend its schools as a homeless child.
- The date as of which the child will be excluded from school.
- The board's determination may be appealed to the commissioner of education, in accordance with section 310 of the Education Law, within 30 days of the date of the determination, and that the procedure for taking such an appeal may be obtained from the Office of Counsel, New York State Education Department, State Education Building, Albany, N.Y., 12234, or by calling 518- 474-5807 (8 NYCRR § 100.2(y)).

12:35. Under what circumstances may a school district charge tuition?

A school district may charge tuition for nonresident students attending public schools in the school district (§ 3202(2); see 8 NYCRR § 174.2).

A nonveteran under 21 years of age who has received a high school diploma who is permitted to attend classes in the schools of the district in which he or she resides or in a board of cooperative educational services (BOCES) must also pay tuition (§ 3202(1); see 8 NYCRR § 174.3).

In the case of a nonresident student placed in a family home by a social services district or a state department or agency, the cost of instruction must be paid by the district in which the student resided at the time the agency assumed responsibility for the student's support (§ 3202(4)(a)). However, when the home is the actual and only residence of the student and the student is not supported and maintained by the agency, the student is considered a resident of the district in which the family home is located and no tuition may be charged (§ 3202(4)(b)).

A foreign student who attends a public secondary school under an F-1 visa must reimburse the school district for the full unsubsidized per capita cost of providing education at the school during the student's attendance (8 USC § 1184(l)(1)(b)(ii)).

12:36. How is tuition determined for the instruction of nonresident students?

Tuition is computed according to a formula established by the commissioner of education (8 NYCRR Part 174). School districts may not charge different tuition rates to nonresident students with disabilities. Any such differentiation would be a violation of section 504 of the Rehabilitation Act (Letter from the Assistant Secretary for Civil Rights, United States Department of Education, Office for Civil Rights, Aug. 10, 1994).

The Education Law also provides that the school tax payments of nonresidents who own assessable property in the school district must be deducted from any tuition charges levied against any such nonresident (§ 3202(3)).

Districts that contract with other districts to provide education for some of their students must designate the receiving district by April 1 (8 NYCRR § 174.4). Tuition becomes due at the completion of each school year (*Appeal of the Board of Educ. of the Marcellus CSD*, 26 Educ. Dep't Rep. 510 (1987)).

12:37. Is a school district required to pay the tuition for a high school student who elects to go to a vocational high school if the district of residence does not have vocational courses?

Yes. If a student resides in a district where high school courses are offered but no vocational high school is available, or if vocational high school courses are not available in the academic school or schools designated by the district, the student may select and attend any other academic school within the state in which vocational courses are available. The tuition charge, if any, in excess of the difference between the cost of educating the student and the apportionment of public monies on account of the attendance of such student, is charged to the district in which the student resides. The cost of transporting that student need not be paid by the district of the student's residence (§ 2045(2)).

12:38. May students be charged fees such as textbook fees, yearbook fees or locker fees in New York State's public schools?

Yes. As a general rule, no fee or charge may be required as a condition of school attendance, credit in a required course, or for materials or activities that are part of a course requirement. However, school districts may rent, sell or loan supplies to students attending the public schools on such terms and under such rules and regulations as may be prescribed by the school board (§ 701(5)). Thus, a school board may require students who are financially able to pay a fee for supplies provided by the school (*Matter of Posman*, 12 Educ. Dep't Rep. 51 (1972)).

A school district operating under a contingency budget is not required to furnish instructional supplies to the district's school children free of charge (*Sodus Central School v. Rhine*, 63 A.D.2d 820 (4th Dep't 1978); *Reiss v. Abramowitz*, 39 A.D.2d 916 (2nd Dep't 1972)).

Homeless Children

12:39. What is the definition of a homeless child within the Education Law?

Except as otherwise provided by law, a *homeless child* is a child who does not have a fixed, regular and adequate nighttime residence or whose primary nighttime location is in a public or private shelter designed to provide temporary living accommodations or a place not designed for, or ordinarily used as, a regular sleeping accommodation for human beings (§ 3209(1)(a); 8 NYCRR § 100.2(x)(1)(i)).

12:40. Where may a homeless child attend school?

A homeless child may attend either the school district in his or her current location, the school district of origin, or a school district participating in a regional placement plan without payment of tuition (§§ 3202(8); 3209(2)(a),(b)(1); 8 NYCRR § 100.2(x)(2)(i)). Any such designation is made by the parent or guardian of a homeless child, the homeless child, if no parent or guardian is available, or the director of a residential program for runaway and homeless youth, where applicable, in consultation with the homeless child (§ 3209(1)(b); 8 NYCRR § 100.2(x)(1)(ii)).

The school district of origin is the district within New York State in which the homeless child was attending a public school on a tuition-free basis or was entitled to attend when circumstances arose which caused the child to become homeless, which is different from the school district of current location (§ 3209(1)(c); 8 NYCRR § 100.2(x)(1)(iii)).

The school district of current location is the district within New York State in which the temporary housing arrangement or the residential program for a homeless or runaway child is located, which is different from the school district of origin (§ 3209(1)(d); 8 NYCRR § 100.2(x)(1)(iv)).

A regional placement plan is a comprehensive regional approach to the provision of educational placements for homeless children which must be approved by the commissioner of education (§ 3209(1)(e); 8 NYCRR § 100.2(x)(1)(v)).

12:41. Once a district is designated as the district of attendance for a homeless child, may it subsequently be changed?

Yes. The homeless child's district of attendance may be changed if the person so deciding (see **12:40**) finds that the original designation to be educationally unsound. The change must be made before the end of the first semester of attendance or within 60 days after commencing attendance at a school (8 NYCRR § 100.2(x)(2)(vi)).

12:42. Is a homeless child who previously resided in a school district outside New York State entitled to enroll in a public school in New York State on a tuition-free basis?

Yes. The homeless child is a resident of the district where the temporary housing arrangement is located and is entitled to attend school on a tuition-free basis (§ 3209(2)(b)(2); 8 NYCRR § 100.2(x)(2)(iv)).

12:43. What procedures must be followed for securing the admission of homeless children into the designated school district?

A designation form provided by the commissioner of education must be completed by the person responsible for designating a homeless child's district of attendance (§ 3209(2)(d); 8 NYCRR § 100.2(x)(3)). All school districts must provide a form to any homeless child or parent or guardian who seeks to enroll a child in school (8 NYCRR § 100.2(x)(3)).

The school district must immediately review the designation form to assure that it has been completed, admit the homeless child and provide the child with access to all of its programs, activities and services to the same extent as they are provided to resident students. The designated district must also make a written request to the school district where the child's records are located for a copy of such records. The district must then forward the designation form to the commissioner of education, and the school district of origin, where applicable (§ 3209(2)(e); 8 NYCRR § 100.2(x)(4)).

The district where the child's records are located must forward a complete copy of the homeless child's records, including, but not limited to, proof of age, academic records, evaluations, immunization records, and guardianship papers, if applicable, within five days of receiving a written request (§ 3209(f); 8 NYCRR § 100.2(x)(5)).

12:44. Who is responsible for the payment of a homeless child's tuition?

If the parent or guardian of the homeless child, or the homeless child, if no parent or guardian is available, designates a school district other than that of the child's last residence, that district will be eligible for reimbursement by the State Education Department (SED) (§ 3209(3)(a)). The district where the child last attended school then must reimburse SED for its expenditure for educational services on behalf of that child. Reimbursement will be equal to the school district's basic contribution, pro-rated for the period of time for which the services are provided by a school district other than the one in which the child last attended school (§ 3209(3)(b)).

12:45. May a homeless child attend any school within the school district he or she chooses to go to?

If the homeless child attends school in the district of origin, the child may choose to attend the school building in the attendance zone where the child is temporarily located, or the child may choose to remain in the public school building he or she previously attended until the end of the school year. The homeless child may attend the same school building for an additional year if that year constitutes the child's last year in such a building (§§ 3209(1)(c), 3209(2)(b)(1); 8 NYCRR § 100.2(x)(2)(ii),(v)).

If the child goes to school in the district of current location, that child may attend the school in the zone of his or her temporary location or any other school that nonhomeless students who live in the same attendance zone may attend (§ 3209(1)(d); 8 NYCRR § 100.2(x)(2)(v)).

12:46. What happens when a homeless child who attends school in the district of current location is subsequently relocated to a different temporary housing arrangement outside that district, or to a different attendance zone within that district?

The homeless child may continue to attend the same school building until the end of the school year and for one additional year if that year constitutes the child's last year in such building (§ 3209(2)(c); 8 NYCRR § 100.2(x)(2)(iii)).

12:47. Are homeless children entitled to receive school transportation services?

Yes. When a homeless child designates the school district of current location to attend school, that district must provide transportation to the child on the same basis as it is provided to resident students (§ 3209(4)(d); 8 NYCRR § 100.2(x)(6)(iii)).

If the child attends the school district of origin or a school district participating in a regional placement plan, that district must provide transportation to and from the child's temporary housing and school (§ 3209(4)(c)).

If a homeless child attends the public school building where he or she previously attended, that district must provide transportation to and from the temporary housing location and the school the child legally attends if the temporary housing location is located in a different attendance zone or community school district within such district (§ 3209(4)(e); 8 NYCRR § 100.2(x)(6)(iv)).

However, a social services district is responsible for providing transportation to homeless children who are eligible for benefits under section 350-j of the Social Services Law and who are placed in temporary housing arrangements outside their designated districts. To the extent funds are available, the state Division for Youth must provide transportation for each homeless child who lives in a residential program for runaway and homeless youth located outside the designated district. The social services district or division of youth may contract with a school district or BOCES to provide such transportation services (§ 3209(4)(a),(b)).

Any homeless child not entitled to receive transportation from the Department of Social Services or the Division for Youth must be transported by the designated school district (§ 3209(4)(c); 8 NYCRR § 100.2(x)(6)).

12:48. Are there any mileage limitations that apply to the provision of transportation to homeless children?

Yes. A designated school district that must provide transportation to a homeless child may not provide transportation in excess of 50 miles one way, unless the commissioner determines that it is in the best interest of the child (§ 3209(4)(c); 8 NYCRR § 100.2(x)(6)(ii)).

12:49. Is state aid available for districts that provide transportation to homeless children?

Yes. A school district may receive state aid to offset expenditures incurred by the district for the transportation of homeless children under certain circumstances (§ 3209(4)(c)).

Student Health and Welfare

12:50. Are school districts required to provide a health service program?

Yes. According to the commissioner's regulations, all school districts must provide a health service program (8 NYCRR §§ 136.2(a), 136.3; see also article 19), although these programs are not intended to supplant the provision of medical services from the student's primary physician (see Opn. Counsel No. 98, 1 Educ. Dep't Rep. 824 (1961); Opn. Counsel No. 67, 1 Educ. Dep't Rep. 766 (1952)).

Each child enrolled in a school (except in Buffalo, New York City and Rochester) must have a satisfactory health examination as required under law and regulations (§§ 903-905) and any special health examinations "as may be essential" (8 NYCRR § 136.3(a)(2)). Districts are authorized to conduct physical examinations of students (§ 903; 8 NYCRR § 136.3(a)(2)) except in Buffalo, New York City and Rochester, which have their health services provided by county health departments.

Every district is required to provide approved and adequate personnel and facilities, maintain for each child cumulative records covering the essential features of the health service program, and make reports to the State Education Department on forms prescribed by the commissioner of education (8 NYCRR § 136.2(d)).

12:51. Are school districts required to employ a school physician or school nurse?

Each district must employ a competent physician as a medical inspector to make inspections of students attending the public schools in the city or district (§ 902(1); 8 NYCRR § 136.2(c)).

However, there is no requirement that schools employ nurses. The only requirement is that if a school chooses to hire a nurse, the nurse must be a registered nurse, graduated from a school of nursing registered by the Regents, and authorized to practice as such (§ 902(1)).

Additionally, the state has no requirement mandating schools to employ the services of school nurse-teachers. A school nurse-teacher is a registered nurse who is a certified teacher or teaching assistant, qualified and trained to perform, in addition to nursing services, other educational services in the classroom (*Bork v. North Tonawanda City School Dist.*, 60 A.D.2d 13 (4th Dep't 1977), *appeal denied*, 44 N.Y.2d 647 (1978); *Matter of Festa*, 21 Educ. Dep't Rep. 374 (1982)).

12:52. What requirements must school districts comply with when providing health service programs?

The Education Law and the commissioner's regulations require, among other things, that each district do the following:

- Record the results of the health examinations (the dental inspection and/or screening, hearing, vision and scoliosis screening) on approved forms that will be kept on file in the school.
- Require the physician making the examination to sign the health record card and make approved recommendations.
- Advise, in writing, the parent or guardian of each child in whom any aspect of the total school health service program indicates a defect, disability or other condition that may require professional attention with regard to health.
- Keep confidential health records of children except when the records must be used by approved school personnel and, with the consent of the parents or guardians, for use by appropriate health personnel of cooperating agencies.
- Require adequate health inspections of students by teachers, school nurse-teachers and other approved school personnel.
- Maintain a suitable program of education to inform school personnel, parents, nonschool health agencies, welfare agencies and the general public regarding school health conditions, services and factors relating to children's health.
- Provide adequate guidance to parents, children and teachers in procedures for preventing and correcting defects and diseases and in the general improvement of children's health.
- Furnish appropriate instruction to school personnel in procedures to follow in case of accident or illness.
- Provide suitable inspections and supervision of the health and safety aspects of the school building.
- Provide adequate health examinations before student participation in strenuous physical activity and periodically throughout the season.
- Provide health examinations necessary for issuing employment certificates, vacation work permits, newspaper carrier certificates and street trades badges.

• Provide scoliosis screening for each child between the ages of eight and 16 years of age, regardless of the child's grade, at least once each school year (8 NYCRR § 136.3; see article 19 and **12:56**).

School districts must permit students who have been diagnosed by a physician with a severe asthmatic condition to use a prescribed inhaler during the school day, with the written permission of a physician and parental consent. The diagnosis of a severe asthmatic condition must be based on the physician's determination that the student is subject to sudden asthmatic attacks severe enough to debilitate the student. A record of this permission must be maintained in the school office (§ 916).

12:53. Is a school board required to provide health and welfare services to students attending private schools?

At the request of a private school, a school board is required to provide any or all of the health and welfare services and facilities available to students attending the public schools. Services may include those performed by a physician, dentist, dental hygienist, nurse, school psychologist, school social worker or school speech therapist. They may also include dental prophylaxis, vision and hearing tests, the taking of medical histories and the administration of health-screening tests, the maintenance of cumulative health records and the administration of emergency-care programs for ill or injured students (§ 912; see **12:50**).

These services are mandatory only for residents of the district (§ 912). The district where the nonpublic school is located, however, must contract with the district(s) where the nonresident students of such school reside for payment of the agreed-upon amount for health services (§ 912). Provision for this expenditure must be included in the annual budget.

While the law requires school districts to provide health services to nonpublic school students which are equivalent to the public schools, it does not require a school district to provide full-time nursing services for a nonpublic school (*Appeal of Burke*, 34 Educ. Dep't Rep. 3 (1994)).

12:54. Are students required to furnish certificates of health in New York State public schools?

Yes. Every student who initially enters school, and thereafter begins the first, third, seventh and 10th grades, except in Buffalo, New York City and Rochester, is required to present a health certificate signed by a duly licensed physician authorized to practice medicine in New York State (§ 903; 8 NYCRR § 136.3(a)(2)).

For students who attend a city school district, the examination for a certificate must include a one-time test for sickle-cell anemia. In all other school districts, the test for sickle-cell anemia is performed in the discretion of the physician. This testing requirement does not apply to students who refuse to take the test because of religious beliefs (§ 903).

The certificate, which must state whether or not the student's condition of bodily health is fit enough to permit his or her attendance in the public schools, must be submitted to the principal or teacher in charge of the school within 15 days of entrance to the school or the grades cited above. This certificate then is filed with the clerk of the district (§ 903).

If a student does not present a health certificate, a notice must be sent to the student's parents or guardian stating that, if the required health certificate is not furnished within 15 days from the date of that notice, the student will be given a medical examination (§ 903).

Parents do not have the right to withhold a student from all school medical examinations (including those testing sight, hearing, etc.) *and* to refuse to transmit certificates from their family physician in these cases (Opn. Counsel No. 54, 1 Educ. Dep't Rep. 750 (1952)). The student must either submit to the exam or provide a health certificate from his or her family physician.

12:55. Must school districts conduct medical examinations of students who have not furnished certificates of health?

Yes. Except in the Buffalo, New York City and Rochester schools, the school district's physician must examine all students who have not furnished certificates, or who are disabled, to determine whether they have defective sight or hearing or any other disability that might prevent them from doing well in school. This is also done to determine whether a possible condition might require modification of the student's education program to prevent possible injury or to ensure that student does well in school (§ 904; 8 NYCRR §§ 136.2(b), 136.3(a)(2)).

For students who attend a city school district, the examination must include a one-time test of all students between the ages of four and nine to determine the presence of sickle-cell anemia. In all other school districts, the test for sickle-cell anemia is performed in the discretion of the school district's physician. This testing requirement does not apply to students who refuse to take the test because of religious beliefs (§ 904).

Parents or guardians must be notified of the existence of defective sight or hearing or other physical disability. If a student's parent or guardian is unable or unwilling to provide the necessary relief and treatment for a student's condition, this must be reported by the principal or teacher to the school district's physician, whose duty it will be to provide the relief (§ 904).

12:56. What other medical tests must be performed by school districts?

Student hearing tests must be performed once a year in grades seven and below, in grade 10, and at other times deemed necessary by the school physician, principal or teachers (§ 905(1)).

Student eye tests must be performed once a year for students between the ages of eight and 16 (§ 905(1)). In addition, all students, regardless of grade level, must be tested for color perception, distance acuity and near vision, within six months of admission to school. Students whose parents or guardians object to these eye tests on the grounds that they conflict with their sincerely held religious beliefs are exempt from these requirements (§ 905(4)). These test results must be made available to the students' parents and teachers within that school and kept in a permanent file for at least as long as the student is enrolled in the school (§ 905(4)).

Student scoliosis examinations must be performed once a year for students between the ages of eight and 16, except those students whose parents or guardians are bona fide members of a recognized religious organization whose teachings are contrary to this requirement (§ 905(1)). These results must be provided in writing to a parent or person in parental relation within 90 days if a finding of the presence of scoliosis is made (§ 905(2)).

An examination of any child may be required by the local school authorities at any time, at their discretion, to promote that child's educational interest (§ 903).

12:57. What are the pertinent drug- and alcohol-abuse laws concerning students?

Probably the most important statute concerning drug and alcohol abuse for school districts is the federal Safe and Drug-Free Schools and Communities Act (SDFSCA, 20 USC §§ 7101 *et seq.*). The act contains information about how state education departments and local educational agencies, such as school districts, can gain access to federal funds for use to provide programs offering drug-abuse prevention to students of school age.

School districts which receive funds under the SDFSCA must adopt and carry out a comprehensive drug and violence prevention program which shall be designed to:
- prevent the use, possession and distribution of tobacco, alcohol, and illegal drugs by students;
- prevent violence and promote school safety; and
- create a disciplined environment conducive to learning (20 USC § 7116(a)(1)).

The district program must include activities to promote the involvement of parents and coordination with community groups and agencies, including the distribution of information about the district's needs, goals and programs. The district program may contain the following activities:
- Age-appropriate, developmentally-based drug and alcohol education and prevention programs for all students, from preschool level through grade 12, that address the legal, social, personal and health consequences of the use of illegal drugs, promote a sense of individual responsibility, and provide information about effective techniques for resisting peer pressure to use illegal drugs.
- Programs of drug prevention, comprehensive health education, early intervention, pupil services, mentoring or rehabilitation referral which emphasize students' sense of responsibility.
- Dissemination of information about drug prevention.
- Professional development of school personnel, parents, students, law enforcement officials, judicial officials, health service providers and community leaders in prevention, education, early intervention, pupil services or rehabilitation referral.
- Strategies to integrate the delivery of services from a variety of providers, to combat illegal alcohol, tobacco and drug use, such as family counseling, early intervention activities that prevent family dysfunction, enhance school performance, and boost attachment to school and family, and activities, such as community service and service-learning projects, that are designed to increase students' sense of community.
- "Safe zones of passage" for students between home and school through such measures as Drug-Free School Zones, enhanced law enforcement, and neighborhood patrols.
- Before-and-after school recreational, instructional, cultural and artistic programs in supervised community settings.
- Drug abuse resistance education programs, designed to teach students to recognize and resist pressures to use alcohol or other drugs, which may include activities such as classroom instruction by uniformed law enforcement officers, resistance techniques, resistance to peer pressure and gang pressure, and provision for parental involvement.
- Evaluation of any of the activities listed above. (20 USC § 7116(b)).

New York's Education Law also authorizes school districts to take supervised urine samples of students in grades seven through 12, with written parental consent, to determine whether they are using dangerous drugs. (§ 912-a; see **12:90**).

12:58. Must children be immunized in order to attend the public schools?

Yes. Children must be immunized against poliomyelitis, mumps, measles, diphtheria, rubella, Haemophilus influenzae type b (Hib) and hepatitis B (Pub. Health Law § 2164(2), (7)(a)).

If there is no proof or record of a child's immunization, the principal or teacher must direct the child's parent or person in parental authority to have the child immunized by any health practitioner. The child may also be immunized without charge by the county health officer, if the parent or guardian consents (Pub. Health Law § 2164(6); see **12:59** for exceptions).

The immunizing physician must provide an immunization certificate to the person in parental relation to the child (Pub. Health Law § 2164(5)).

No child may be admitted to school or allowed to attend school for more than 14 days without an appropriate immunization certificate or acceptable evidence of immunization. This period may be extended to 30 days on a case-by-case basis by the principal if a student has transferred from another state or country and can show a good faith effort to get the necessary certification or other evidence of immunization (Pub. Health Law § 2164(7)(a)).

The principal must forward a report to the local health authority and to the parent, and notify the parent to have the child immunized in a case where a student is refused admission to or continued attendance at a school for failure to provide appropriate proof of immunization (Pub. Health Law § 2164(8-a)(a)). In addition, the principal must send an immunization consent form to the parent and cooperate with the local health authority in scheduling a time and place for immunizing a child for whom consent has been obtained.

A student may appeal a denial of admission to or continued attendance at school to the commissioner of education (Pub. Health Law § 2164(7)(b)).

12:59. Are there any exceptions to the immunization requirements?

Yes. Students may be admitted to school or continue attendance without a certificate or proof of immunization if:

- A physician will testify or certify that administering a vaccine to a specific student will be detrimental to that student's health (Pub. Health Law § 2164(8)), or
- The student, or the student's parents or guardian, hold genuine and sincere religious beliefs which prohibit immunization (Pub. Health Law § 2164(9)).

Parents may oppose immunizations on religious grounds without belonging to an organized religion (*Lewis v. Sobol*, 710 F.Supp. 506 (S.D.N.Y. 1989); *Sherr v. Northport-East Northport UFSD*, 672 F.Supp. 81 (E.D.N.Y. 1987)).

12:60. Must school districts participate in surveys on student immunizations directed by the state commissioner of health?

Yes. Each school district must participate in surveys directed by the state commissioner of health and provide any records or reports so requested (§ 914(3)). Furthermore, the commissioner of health must conduct an annual audit of the immunization level of children attending schools (Pub. Health Law § 613(2)).

12:61. May the commissioner of health develop an educational program of inoculation to improve the immunity of the children in the state?

Yes. The commissioner of health may develop and supervise such an educational program and may encourage the local municipalities to develop and implement local programs of inoculation. The commissioner also may invite the assistance and cooperation of medical societies, organizations of other licensed health personnel, hospitals, corporations, trade unions and associations, parents and teachers and their associations, and voluntary groups in these educational activities (Pub. Health Law § 613(1)).

12:62. Must students who have contracted contagious diseases be prohibited from attending school?

Yes. Whenever a student in a public school shows symptoms of any contagious or infectious disease, as defined in section 2(1)(l) of the Public Health Law, he or she must be sent home immediately. Before that student is allowed to return to school, he or she must either present a certificate from the city or town health officer or family physician, or be examined by the district medical officer (§ 906).

A district may be obligated to provide temporary home instruction for a student suffering from a short-term physical disability (§ 1709(24); *Appeal of Douglas and Barbara K.*, 34 Educ. Dep't Rep. 214 (1994); *Appeal of Anthony M. and D. M.*, 30 Educ. Dep't Rep. 269 (1991)). However, the commissioner has ruled that a district was not obligated to provide home instruction to students who missed approximately one and one half months of school because of head lice, a condition that could normally be alleviated in one or two days, because the students' parent contributed to the excessive absence by failing to follow the recommended course of treatment to rid her children of the lice (*Appeal of Douglas and Barbara K.*).

12:63. Does New York State regard acquired immune deficiency syndrome (AIDS) as a contagious, communicable or infectious disease?

No. Acquired immune deficiency syndrome (AIDS) has not been defined in the regulations of the New York State Department of Health as a contagious, communicable or infectious disease, and its exclusion from this category has been upheld by the New York State Court of Appeals (*New York State Soc. of Surgeons v. Axelrod*, 77 N.Y.2d 677 (1991)).

12:64. May a student with AIDS or any other human immunodeficiency virus (HIV)-related illness be prohibited from attending public school solely because he or she has an HIV-related illness?

No. A student with AIDS or another HIV-related illness cannot be denied the opportunity to attend school, continue his or her education, or take part in school-related activities, solely on the basis of having been diagnosed with AIDS or becoming infected with HIV. Automatic exclusion from school of children infected with HIV or who have contracted AIDS would violate those students' rights under section 504 of the Federal Rehabilitation Act of 1973 (*District 27 Community School Board v. Board of Education*, 130 Misc.2d 398 (Sup. Ct. Queens County 1986); see 29 USC § 794).

Several federal courts with jurisdiction outside of New York have held that children infected with HIV are disabled for purposes of the Rehabilitation Act and otherwise are qualified to attend classes in the absence of evidence that they pose a significant risk of harm to classmates or teachers (see *Martinez v. School Board of Hillsborough County*, 861 F.2d 1502 (11th Cir. 1988); *Thomas v. Atascadero Unified School District*, 662 F.Supp. 376 (C.D. Cal. 1987)).

The Americans with Disabilities Act (ADA) also prohibits school districts from denying students with disabilities the benefits of or participation in the services, programs and activities of the district on the basis of disability (42 USC § 12132). The United States Supreme Court has ruled that asymptomatic HIV infection is a disability under the ADA (*Bragdon v. Abbott*, 118 S.Ct. 2196 (1998)).

The regulations implementing the ADA also state that HIV, whether symptomatic or asymptomatic, is included in the definition of "disability" (28 CFR § 35.104). The regulations prohibit discrimination in the provision of educational and other services against individuals infected with HIV (see 28 CFR § 35.130(a)).

12:65. Must information concerning HIV and/or AIDS be kept confidential?

Yes. Current law and regulations strictly limit the disclosure of confidential information about HIV or AIDS (Pub. Health Law article 27-F; 10

NYCRR Part 63). In most circumstances, disclosure of such information concerning a student is contingent on obtaining an authorization for release form signed by the student, or if the student lacks the "capacity to consent," by a person legally authorized to consent on behalf of the student (Pub. Health Law § 2782; 10 NYCRR § 63.4(a)).

Disclosure of such information also is permitted if a court order has been issued requiring its release because of the presence of a clear and imminent danger to another person who unknowingly may be at significant risk as a result of contact with the student (Pub. Health Law § 2785(2); 10 NYCRR § 63.5(a)(12),(b)(4)). This information can be given only to persons identified on the form or in the court order, only for the reasons provided in the form, and only for the length of time stated on the form (Pub. Health Law § 2785(6)).

12:66. Are there any precautions school districts are required to observe to prevent the spread of HIV and other diseases communicable through contact with blood and other bodily fluids?

Yes. School districts must have a written "exposure control plan." The plan must provide for employee training on how to deal with body fluids and other materials, and the keeping of accurate medical and training records. The plan must also identify positions, such as nurses, coaches and custodians, and tasks likely to come into contact with blood and other bodily fluids. In addition, it must set forth the procedures to be followed, including "universal precautions" which require, for instance, that all bodily fluids and material be treated as infectious, and the wearing of protective equipment (29 CFR § 1910.1030(c)(1)).

12:67. Are safety glasses required in school shops or lab courses?

Yes. School boards must provide that students and teachers participating in certain vocational, shop and laboratory courses wear eye safety devices (§ 409-a(1); 8 NYCRR § 141.10(a)). This requirement also extends to visitors to such courses (§ 409-a(3); 8 NYCRR § 141.10(a)).

12:68. Are public schools required to maintain home telephone numbers of each student?

Yes. The Education Law requires each school to maintain the telephone numbers of each student enrolled, and of their parent or guardian, including both residential and business telephone numbers, for emergency notification purposes (§ 3212-a(1)). The law allows parents and students to refuse to supply their telephone numbers, and exempts those districts whose school boards adopt resolutions providing these records need not be maintained (§ 3212-a(1),(2)).

12:69. What can be done for children who are absent from school because of lack of suitable clothing, food and other necessities?

Public welfare officials, except as otherwise provided by law, must furnish indigent children with suitable clothing, shoes, books, food, transportation and other necessities to enable them to attend upon instruction required by law (§ 3209(6)).

Missing and Abused Children

12:70. What is a school district's responsibility in relation to the identification and finding of missing children?

The commissioner of the Division of Criminal Justice Services (CJS) is required to disseminate regularly a bulletin with information about the children listed in the statewide register to the State Education Department (SED). SED then must forward this bulletin to every public and private school where parents, guardians or others legally responsible for such children have given consent (Exec. Law § 837-f(10)).

The CJS commissioner also must cooperate with public and private schools to develop education and prevention programs concerning child safety; to operate a toll-free, 24-hour hotline for the public to use to relay information concerning missing children; and to provide other assistance to local agencies in the investigation of these cases (Exec. Law § 837-f(5),(8),(11)).

A school district which is notified by CJS that a child has been listed as missing must flag the schooling record of the child in such a manner that whenever a copy of or information concerning that record is requested, the person authorized to issue such record is alerted to the fact that the child has been reported as a missing child. The school then must immediately report any such requests to the local law enforcement authority and CJS (§ 3222(4)).

A superintendent of schools or an authorized representative may make inquiries to determine if any entries in the State Register or in the National Crime Information Center register could match the subject of the inquiry. Once CJS has notified the school that a reported missing child has been recovered, the school must remove the flag from the child's schooling record (§ 3222(4)).

A school which discovers that a child, who is reported missing by the division, but is currently enrolled in that school, must immediately notify CJS (§ 3222(5)).

12:71. To whom may a student be released from school?

Section 3210(1)(c) of the Education Law provides that a person who requests the release of a student from school must be identified against a list of names provided by the student's parent or guardian at the time of the child's enrollment in the school.

A school district may adopt procedures for submitting a list of names at a later date or updating the list of names provided by the person or persons in parental relation to the student. If someone whose name is not on the list attempts to obtain the release of a student, that student may not be released. There is an exception for an emergency release, provided that the student's parent or guardian agrees.

12:72. What is the school's responsibility concerning a child's release from school in cases where the child's parents are separated or divorced?

A school district may presume that either parent of a child has authority to obtain the child's release, unless the district has been provided with a certified copy of a legally binding instrument, such as a court order or decree of divorce, separation or custody, that indicates the noncustodial parent does not have the right to obtain such release (§ 3210(1)(c)).

12:73. Is a school district required to provide instruction to prevent the abduction of children?

Yes. All students in kindergarten through eighth grade must receive instruction designed to prevent the abduction of children. Such instruction must be provided either by a regular classroom teacher or be under the teacher's direct supervision, if it is provided by a public or private agency (§ 803-a(1)).

In providing for a course of study, the school board may establish a local advisory council or use the school-based shared-decision-making committee to recommend the content and implementation of such courses. Alternately, school districts may use courses of instruction developed by others, such as other school districts, BOCES, or any other public or private agency. Advisory councils shall consist of, but not be limited to, parents, school board members and trustees, appropriate school personnel, business and community representatives, and law enforcement personnel having experience in the prevention of child abduction (§ 803-a(3)).

School districts must provide appropriate training and curriculum materials for those teachers who provide the instruction (§ 803-a(4)).

12:74. What is a school district's responsibility to report abused or maltreated school children?

School officials must make a report to child protective services when they have reasonable cause to suspect a student is abused or maltreated. If the person who suspects abuse or maltreatment is a school staff member, he or she must notify the head of the school immediately, who must then make the report (Soc. Serv. Law § 413(1)).

The law also states that, in addition to those persons legally required to report suspected child abuse or maltreatment, any person who has reasonable cause to suspect child abuse or maltreatment may make such a report (Soc. Serv. Law § 414).

Reports of child abuse or maltreatment must be made immediately by telephone or fax on a form supplied by the commissioner of social services. An oral report must be followed by a written report within 48 hours. Oral reports must be made to the statewide central register of child abuse and maltreatment, unless an appropriate local plan provides these reports should be made to the local child protective service. Except in specified instances, written reports also must be made to the local child protective service (Soc. Serv. Law § 415).

The Social Services Law provides legal penalties for failure to report cases of suspected child abuse, including liability for damages proximately caused by such failure (Soc. Serv. Law § 420). The law also provides immunity from liability for the school official making such a report in good faith (Soc. Serv. Law § 419).

The hotline telephone number to report a case of suspected abuse or maltreatment is 1-800-342-3720. An additional hotline telephone number for school administrators and teachers to report suspected abuse or maltreatment is 1-800-635-1522.

The Education Law requires that school districts develop, maintain and disseminate written policies and procedures on reporting child abuse, pursuant to the Social Services Law and the Family Court Act. These must include procedures for mandatory reporting of child abuse or neglect; obligations of persons required to report; taking a child into protective custody; mandatory reporting of deaths; a statement of immunity from liability; penalties for failure to report; and providing services and procedures necessary to safeguard the life or health of a child. In addition, every board must establish and maintain a training program for all current and new school employees regarding these policies and procedures (§ 3209-a).

Sex Offender Registration Act
("Megan's Law")

12:75. What is the Sex Offender Registration Act?

The Sex Offender Registration Act (commonly referred to as "Megan's Law") is a law which requires convicted sex offenders to register with the Division of Criminal Justice Services (CJS) upon discharge, parole or release (Correct. Law § 168 *et seq.*). Based on the recommendations of a Board of Examiners of Sex Offenders, convicted sex offenders will be designated either as "sex offenders" or the more serious "sexually violent predators," and assigned to one of three risk classifications, which will determine the extent of public notification of their return to the community (Correct. Law § 168-l(6)).

Public notification ranges from notification to law enforcement agencies only, to authorizing the law enforcement agencies to disseminate such information as address, photograph, modus of operation and the crime for which the offender was convicted. School districts are not automatically notified. However, local law enforcement agencies are given authority, at their discretion, to release information on a sex offender related to the nature of the offense committed to any community with vulnerable populations (Correct. Law § 168-l(6)).

The United States Court of Appeals for the Second Circuit has upheld the community notification provisions of the Sex Offender Registration Act (*Doe v. Pataki*, 120 F.3d 1263 (2nd Cir. 1997), *cert. denied*, 118 Ct. 1066 (1998)). However, a lower federal court has issued an injunction which has the effect of preventing the implementation of the notification provisions of the law for individuals convicted before January 21, 1996. Nonetheless, sex offenders are required to register with law enforcement authorities.

12:76. May a school district disclose information it receives under the Sex Offender Registration Act to members of the public?

Under the law, any entity, including a school district, receiving information on a sex offender may disclose or further disseminate such information at their discretion (Correct. Law § 168-l(6)(b),(c)). However, under an injunction issued by the United States District Court for the Southern District of New York, school districts may not disseminate information received concerning individuals convicted before January 21, 1996 (see **12:75**).

An agency, its officials and employees will be immune from civil or criminal liability for any decision on their part to release what they believe to be relevant and necessary information, unless it is proven they acted with gross negligence or in bad faith. The law further provides that no civil or criminal liability will be imposed against any agency, official or employee for failing to release the information unless it is shown that they acted with gross negligence or in bad faith (Correct. Law § 168-r).

Students' Constitutional Rights

12:77. What constitutional rights do students enjoy while they attend public school?

Certain constitutional rights, as set forth in the Bill of Rights of the United States Constitution, and listed below, are of special importance to students who attend public schools.

The *First Amendment* provides, in part, that Congress will make no law prohibiting the free exercise of religion, freedom of speech, the right of people to assemble peaceably and to petition the government for a redress of grievances.

The *Fourth Amendment* guarantees in part the right of people to be secure in their persons, houses, papers and effects against unreasonable searches and seizures.

The *Fifth Amendment* maintains that no person shall be compelled in any criminal case to be a witness against himself or herself, nor be deprived of life, liberty or property without due process of law.

The questions that follow illustrate the impact of these constitutional rights in the day-to-day activities of a public school system. (See chapter 23 for more information on the role of religion in the schools.)

12:78. Can public school students protest or demonstrate peacefully during school hours?

Yes. The United States Supreme Court has ruled that students have a constitutional right to demonstrate peacefully during school hours, as long as there is no disruption of the educational process of the school.

In the landmark case in this area, the court upheld the right of three students who were suspended from school in 1965 to wear black arm bands as a protest against the Vietnam War. The court stressed that the demonstration did not disrupt regular school work or intrude on the rights of others. It suggested that the decision could not be applied to aggressive, disruptive action. The court decided the armbands were "the type of symbolic act" protected by the constitutional guarantees of free speech and that an "apprehension of disturbance is not enough to overcome the right to freedom of expression" (*Tinker v. Des Moines Independent Community School Dist.*, 393 U.S. 503 (1969)).

12:79. Can a school district ban student speech that is not religious or political in nature?

Yes. The United States Supreme Court has upheld the right of a school district to discipline a student who gave a nominating speech containing sexual innuendos in support of a fellow student's candidacy for a school office. The student speaker was suspended by the school for violating its rule against disruptive conduct. In upholding the suspension, the court held that the penalties imposed in this case, in contrast to *Tinker*, were unrelated to any political point of view. The court also held that the First Amendment does not prevent school officials from determining that the use of vulgar and lewd speech would undermine the school's basic educational mission (*Bethel School Dist. v. Fraser*, 478 U.S. 675 (1986)).

In *Poling v. Murphy*, 872 F.2d 757 (6th Cir. 1989), *cert. denied*, 493 U.S. 1021 (1990), a federal court of appeals held that school officials did not violate the constitutional rights of a student when they disqualified him from a student council election for making discourteous and rude remarks about an assistant principal at a school assembly.

12:80. Can a school district censor or curtail student publications?

Yes, if they are school sponsored. In *Hazelwood School District v. Kuhlmeier*, 484 U.S. 260 (1988), the United States Supreme Court held that a school need not tolerate student speech that is inconsistent with its "basic educational mission." Such a determination rests with its school board and is supported by the distinction between "a student's personal expression that happens to occur on school premises" and a school's "authority over school-sponsored publications, theatrical productions, and other expressive activities" that are viewed by students, parents and the community, and could reasonably be considered part of the school curriculum. According to the court, educators may constitutionally exercise "editorial control over the style and content of student speech in school-sponsored expressive activities so long as their actions are reasonably related to legitimate pedagogical concerns" (484 U.S. at 273, 274).

Based on the rationale in *Hazelwood*, a school district could reject an advertisement from a family-planning group in school district newspapers, yearbooks and programs for athletic events (*Planned Parenthood of Southern Nevada, Inc. v. Clark County School District*, 941 F.2d 817 (9th Cir. 1991)).

On the other hand, a school district may establish a policy granting students broader protection for free speech than required, which then becomes the standard to be applied. A board policy, for instance, may limit the school district's authority to censor a school-sponsored student publication to those situations where there is an imminent threat to disrupt the education process or where the literary work is libelous or obscene (*Matter of Brenner*, 28 Educ. Dep't Rep. 402 (1989)).

12:81. Can students wear or display armbands, buttons or other badges of symbolic personal expression in school buildings?

Yes. Students may wear or display buttons, armbands, flags, decals or other badges symbolic of personal expression, where the manner of expression does not materially intrude on the orderly process of the school or the rights of others. The buttons, armbands and other badges of personal expression must not contain obscene or libelous material or material that advocates racial or religious prejudice (*Tinker v. Des Moines Independent Community School Dist.*, 393 U.S. 503 (1969); *Frasca v. Andrews*, 463 F.Supp. 1043 (E.D.N.Y. 1979); *Appeal of Parsons*, 32 Educ. Dep't Rep. 672 (1993)).

12:82. May a school district prescribe the way students must dress while they attend school?

Generally, a principal or a school board may not prescribe students' dress while they attend school in cases where fashion or taste is the sole criterion; however, a dress code may be adopted when there are legitimate educational concerns (*Appeal of Pintka*, 33 Educ. Dep't Rep. 228 (1993)).

According to decisions of the courts and the commissioner of education, however, a dress code may not be vague, subjective or overly broad (*Appeal of Parsons*, 32 Educ. Dep't Rep. 672 (1993)). It should be developed in consultation with teachers, administrators, other school service professionals, students and parents (8 NYCRR § 100.2(l)(1)) to ensure that it reflects "current community standards" or "proper decorum and deportment" (*Appeal of Pintka*). Districts may regulate students' dress when such rules relate to a specific educational purpose such as health, safety, or full participation in school activities, such as in science laboratories and physical education classes (*Matter of Scally*, 16 Educ. Dep't Rep. 243 (1977)). However, clothing worn to make a religious or political statement cannot be banned, unless it is disruptive of the educational process, lewd or offensive (*Tinker v. Des Moines Independent School District*, 393 U.S. 503 (1969)).

Accordingly, the commissioner of education has ruled that the wearing of hats cannot be prohibited in school hallways unless the display is vulgar and indecent, imposes a health risk, is disruptive or implicates other compelling educational concerns. Hats may be banned in the classroom for the same reasons, and also if they are considered disrespectful and improper under community standards (*Appeal of Pintka*). An unwritten policy prohibiting the wearing of vests and outerwear by students was found not to violate student First Amendment rights where there was no evidence that a student's vest was protected as symbolic speech of either political or religious expression (*Appeal of Mangaroo*, 33 Educ. Dep't Rep. 286 (1993)).

12:83. Do students have the right to distribute literature on school grounds?

Yes. School authorities, however, may regulate the time, manner, place and duration for distributing literature on school grounds. They may regulate the content of literature to be distributed on school grounds only to the extent necessary to avoid material and substantial interference with the requirements of appropriate discipline in the operation of the school (*Eisner v. Stamford Board of Educ.*, 440 F.2d 803 (2nd Cir. 1971); see also **12:80** on a school district's right to control school-sponsored expressive activities).

Guidelines for the distribution of literature on school grounds should specify the time, place and duration of distribution, and provide a method of distribution that will not interfere with normal school procedures. For example, it should be made clear that those individuals who distribute literature may not block pedestrian traffic or the entrance to a building, and must remove any litter they create. The guidelines also may provide for sanctions against those who violate the prescribed procedures.

The guidelines may establish procedures for the submission of literature to the district for prior approval. These procedures should identify to whom the material is to be submitted, the criteria by which the material is to be evaluated and a limitation on the time within which a decision must be made (see *Eisner*).

In addition, school officials may not punish students for the publication and distribution of student magazines or papers produced off school property (*Thomas v. Board of Education*, 607 F.2d 1043 (2nd Cir. 1979), *cert. denied*, 444 U.S. 1081 (1980)).

Although there are no New York cases with respect to whether students have a right to distribute written religious materials in school, federal courts in other jurisdictions have concluded that the same constitutional standards apply to student distribution of religious and nonreligious literature (*Hedges v. Wauconda Community Unit School Dist. No. 118*, 9 F.3d 1295 (7th Cir. 1993); *Hemry v. School Board of Colorado Springs School Dist. No. 11.*, 760 F.Supp. 856 (D. Colo. 1991)).

12:84. Can school districts ban fraternities or sororities from public schools?

Yes. Under the Education Law, school boards may adopt rules and regulations to abolish and/or prohibit any fraternity, sorority or secret society in any secondary school under their jurisdiction (§§ 1709-a(1), 2503-a(1), 2554-a(1)).

Before taking such action, a board must find that the group has, by virtue of its activities, caused or created a disruption of or interference with the academic processes of any secondary school, or caused or created such interference with the progress of any student or students in any secondary school within the district's jurisdiction (§§ 1709-a(1(a)), 2503-a(2), 2554-a(2)).

Such groups are defined as those where the decision to accept new members is made by a decision of the membership of the group rather than by the free choice of the student who wishes to enter. Certain organizations, such as the Boy Scouts and the Girl Scouts, are exempt from this definition (§§ 1709-a(2), 2503-a(3), 2554-a(3)).

After such a regulation has been adopted and disseminated, the board may discipline any student who promises to join, becomes a member of, remains a member of, or solicits any person to join the group in question (§§ 1709-a(3), 2503-a(4), 2554-a(4); for information on fraternity initiations, see sections 120.16 and 120.17 of the Penal Law, which concern hazing).

12:85. Can school authorities confiscate dangerous and illegal weapons, such as knives and guns, brought to school by students?

Yes. If possible, these articles should be taken from students, and the police and parents should be notified. School authorities have the same responsibility as every other citizen to report violations of law. A school official has the right to search a student based on a reasonable suspicion that he or she has a gun (*In re Ronald B.*, 61 A.D.2d 204 (2nd Dep't 1978); see also *New Jersey v. TLO*, 469 U.S. 325 (1985)).

12:86. May public school officials search a student's belongings while in attendance at school?

Yes. In *New Jersey v. TLO*, 469 U.S. 325 (1985), the United States Supreme Court held that a student may be searched by a school official if the official has "reasonable suspicion" to believe that a search of that student will result in evidence that the student violated the law or a school rule. In that case, the court upheld a search of a student's purse after she denied smoking at school in violation of school policy. The court ruled that the principal had reasonable cause to search the student's purse based on a teacher's report that the student was smoking in the bathroom. The court also upheld an extended search of the pocketbook for drugs, after the principal found rolling papers in the student's purse.

In addition, the New York State Court of Appeals held that a less intrusive search conducted by school officials, such as the touching of the outside of a book bag, requires a less strict justification than that of reasonable suspicion (*In re Gregory M.*, 82 N.Y.2d 588 (1993)).

12:87. May public school officials search a student's person while in attendance at school?

Yes. In *People v. Scott D.*, 34 N.Y.2d 483 (1974), the New York State Court of Appeals held that school authorities could conduct a search of a student's person, but only when "sufficient cause" for such a search exists, and that "the special responsibilities of the teachers in charge of students permit a wider latitude for finding cause for [a] search than would be applied to an adult."

The court stated that factors to be considered include the child's age, his or her school record, the seriousness of the problem in the school to which the search is directed and the need to make the search without delay.

In *People v. Scott D.*, a high school student's drug possession conviction was reversed because the court determined that the drugs were found as a result of an illegal search conducted by school officials. According to the court, the school officials did not have sufficient facts to justify the search.

It must be noted as well that, as the level of the intrusiveness of the search increases, a higher standard of suspicion is required. For example, the United States Court of Appeals for the Second Circuit held that a teacher who conducts a strip search must have probable cause (*M. M. v. Anker*, 607 F.2d 588 (2nd Cir. 1979)).

12:88. May school officials search student lockers?

Yes. The New York State Court of Appeals held that although a student may have exclusive use of a locker as far as other students are concerned, he or she "does not have such exclusivity over the locker as against the school authorities" (*People v. Overton*, 20 N.Y.2d 360, *aff'd on reh'g*, 24 N.Y.2d 522 (1969)).

School authorities should include in their student handbooks a provision that states that lockers, desks and other such storage spaces remain the exclusive property of the school, and that students have no expectation of privacy with respect to these areas.

12:89. May a school district use trained narcotics dogs to search for drugs in school buildings?

The use of scent dogs to detect the scent of drugs, alcohol or other contraband in public schools is still an open question in New York State. But in one federal-level case outside New York, the United States Court of Appeals for the Fifth Circuit upheld a school district's use of trained dogs to sniff students' lockers and cars for drugs or alcohol by ruling this type of action did not constitute a search under the Fourth Amendment (*Horton v. Goose Creek Independent School District*, 690 F.2d 470

(5th Cir. 1982), *cert. denied*, 463 U.S. 1207 (1983)).

However, courts differ on the use of scent dogs to sniff students. In *Horton*, the court ruled that the district's use of scent dogs to sniff students was a search under the Fourth Amendment and therefore, dog sniffing of a student without a reasonable suspicion that the student possessed drugs violated the Fourth Amendment.

In contrast, the Seventh Circuit Court of Appeals ruled that sniffing of students by scent dogs is not a "search" under the Fourth Amendment and upheld the sniffing of students without individualized suspicion that a particular student possessed drugs (*Doe v. Renfrow*, 475 F.Supp. 1012, *aff'd*, 631 F.2d 91 (7th Cir. 1980), *cert. denied*, 451 U.S. 1022 (1981)).

12:90. May public school students be tested for the use of illegal drugs?

Yes. The Education Law permits urine testing of students in grades seven through 12 for detection of use of "dangerous drugs" (§ 912-a(1)). These tests must be conducted upon the written request or consent of a parent or legal guardian, without notice to the student (§ 912-a(2)). If the test result indicates that the student is using dangerous drugs, the district must report such information to the local social services department and to the parent or legal guardian, including a statement as to available programs and facilities to combat dangerous drug usage (§ 912-a(2)).

The test results may not be used for law enforcement purposes and must be kept confidential (§ 912-a(3)). The law also contains an exemption from testing based on religious considerations (§ 912-a(4)).

12:91. May a school district require students to submit to mandatory drug testing without reasonable suspicion that a particular student is using illegal drugs?

In *Vernonia School District 47J v. Acton*, 515 U.S. 646 (1995), the United States Supreme Court upheld an Oregon school district's policy that authorized random urinalysis drug testing of student athletes. The policy required students and their parents to sign a form consenting to the testing in order to participate in the district's sports program. The students were tested at the beginning of each sport season and 10 percent would be selected at random to be tested each week of the season.

The Supreme Court addressed the question of whether school districts may enact policies requiring student athletes to submit to mandatory drug testing, without having "reasonable suspicion" that a particular student is engaging in illegal drug use. The court determined that student athletes have a lesser expectation of privacy than other students and that the privacy interests compromised by the process of obtaining urine samples under the school district's policy were negligible, since the conditions of collection are nearly identical to those typically encountered in public restrooms.

The court recognized the nature and immediacy of the district's concern for eradicating illegal drug use in athletic competition where the risk of physical harm to the user and other players is high. Significant to the court's decision was the fact that the district was able to demonstrate that it had a severe problem with illegal drug use by student athletes and that they had attempted lesser intrusive means prior to implementing the drug-testing policy.

The court did not address the issue of whether a school district may conduct random drug testing of all of its students. Commentators have cautioned that the *Vernonia* decision should be read as permitting random drug testing only for student athletes because the court was clear that its opinion was based on the nature and immediacy of the district's concern for eradicating illegal use in athletic competition where the risk of physical harm to the user and other players is high, and where a student's expectation of privacy is low.

12:92. Are school administrators required to give "Miranda" warnings before questioning a student?

No. There is no requirement for any sort of "Miranda"-type warning during informal, noncustodial discussions with administrators (*Pollnow v. Glennon*, 594 F.Supp. 220, *aff'd*, 757 F.2d 496 (2nd Cir. 1985)). In addition, neither the Education Law nor the federal constitution requires school officials to contact the parents of a student before questioning him or her concerning an alleged infraction of a school rule (*Appeal of Pronti*, 31 Educ. Dep't Rep. 259 (1992)).

12:93. Do police have the right to enter schools?

Yes. Police can enter schools if a crime has been committed, if they have a warrant for arrest or search, or if they have been invited by school officials.

However, counsel for the State Education Department has indicated that police authorities have no power to interview children in schools or to use school facilities in connection with police department work, and that a school board has no right to make children available for such purposes. Law enforcement officers do not have a legal right to interrogate a student in the school without the permission of the parents, nor, of course, would any officers or employee of the school have the right to authorize this, since custody of the child by the school is limited to education purposes (Opinion of Counsel, 1 Educ. Dep't Rep. 800 (1959)).

12:94. Are school districts prohibited from requiring students to perform community service as a requirement for graduation?

No. In *Immediato v. Rye Neck School Dist.*, 73 F.3d 454 (2nd Cir. 1996), *cert. denied*, 117 S.Ct. 60 (1996)), a board of education established a requirement that students complete 40 hours of community service for an organization of their choice over four years of high school and participate in a classroom discussion of their projects in order to graduate from high school. The United States Court of Appeals for the Second Circuit, in reviewing a student's challenge of the graduation requirement, held that the service mandated by the district did not violate the Thirteenth Amendment to the federal constitution (which bans slavery and involuntary servitude). The court also ruled that the graduation requirement did not violate any constitutional liberty, parental, or privacy rights protected by the Fourteenth Amendment to the federal constitution (see **12:114**).

Student Discipline

12:95. Must a school district adopt a school conduct and discipline policy?

Yes. The commissioner's regulations require school districts to adopt and implement a written policy on school conduct and discipline. This policy must be developed locally, in consultation with teachers, administrators, school service professionals, students and parents. Included in the policy must be:

- A bill of rights and responsibilities of students that emphasizes positive student behavior which shall be publicized and explained to all students on an annual basis.
- A code of discipline for student behavior setting forth prohibited student conduct and the range of penalties that may be imposed for violation of the code. It must be publicized and explained to all students, and provided to all parents on an annual basis.
- Strategies and procedures for the maintenance and enforcement of public order on school property.
- Procedures within each building to involve pupil service personnel, administrators, teachers, parents and students in the early identification and resolution of discipline problems. For students with disabilities, the policy must include procedures for determining when a student's conduct becomes a reason for referral to the committee on special education (CSE) for review and modification, if appropriate, of the individualized education program (IEP); (see chap. 13).
- Alternative educational programs appropriate to individual student needs.

- Disciplinary measures for violations of school policies that are appropriate to the seriousness of the offense and, where applicable, to the previous disciplinary record of the student in question.
- Guidelines and programs for in-service education for all district staff members to ensure effective implementation of the policy (8 NYCRR § 100.2(l)(1)).

School boards must review the policy annually and file it in all school buildings, and make it available as public information (8 NYCRR § 100.2(l)(2)).

12:96. What types of discipline may be imposed upon students for violations of student disciplinary codes?

The following are among the types of discipline that may be imposed:
- Verbal warning.
- Written warning.
- Written notification to parents or guardians.
- Probation.
- Reprimand.
- Detention.
- Suspension from transportation.
- Suspension from participation in athletic events.
- Suspension from social or extracurricular activities.
- Suspension from other privileges.
- Exclusion from a particular class.
- In-school suspension.
- Suspension not in excess of five days.
- Suspension in excess of five days.

The commissioner of education has ruled that a student behavior code that imposed an automatic suspension on a student for certain behavior without regard to the circumstances giving rise to the offense was invalid (*Appeal of Nuttall,* 30 Educ. Dep't Rep. 351 (1991); 8 NYCRR § 100.2(l)(1)(vi)).

12:97. May a student be suspended from school for truancy?

No. According to the commissioner of education, while a properly implemented school board policy that provides for a loss of credit for nonattendance is appropriate, a school district may not suspend a student for truancy. According to the commissioner, suspending a student for truancy is inconsistent with the educational goal of encouraging children to regularly attend and participate fully in school (*Appeal of Ackert,* 30 Educ. Dep't Rep. 31 (1990)).

12:98. Under what conditions may a student be suspended from school?

A student may be suspended from required attendance for the following reasons:

- Insubordination or disorderly student conduct that otherwise endangers the safety, morals, health or welfare of others (§ 3214(3)(a)(1)).
- A student's physical or mental condition that endangers the health, safety or morals of himself or herself or of other students (§ 3214(3)(a)(2); see **13:38-44** concerning the suspension of students with disabilities).

A student who permanently withdraws from school may not later be suspended for conduct which occurred before the withdrawal because there is no longer any relationship between the former student and the school district (*Appeal of Rosenkranz,* 37 Educ. Dep't Rep. 330 (1998)).

12:99. Who may suspend a student?

The school board, the superintendent of schools or the board of cooperative educational services (BOCES) district superintendent of schools may suspend a student (§ 3214(3)(a)).

A building principal may suspend a student only if the school board adopts a policy delegating that power to the principal. However, in no case may a principal suspend a student for a period exceeding five school days (§ 3214(3)(b)).

Other school officials, such as teachers and assistant principals, do not have the legal authority to suspend a student (*Application of a Child Suspected of Having a Handicapping Condition,* 31 Educ. Dep't Rep. 42 (1991); *Matter of Henderson,* 11 Educ. Dep't Rep. 3 (1971)).

12:100. Are there any limitations on the duration of a student's suspension?

No. However, the commissioner of education has ruled that permanent suspensions (expulsions) should be reserved for extraordinary circumstances such as where the student's behavior poses a danger to the safety and well-being of other students (*Appeal of Osoris,* 35 Educ. Dep't Rep. 250 (1996); *Appeal of Sole,* 34 Educ. Dep't Rep. 270 (1994); *Matter of McDonald,* 8 Educ. Dep't Rep. 32 (1968)). For example, in one case, the commissioner stated the general rule that a single fight, without more, is an insufficient basis to permanently suspend a student from school (*Appeal of Khan,* 35 Educ. Dep't Rep. 322 (1996)).

Although a student may be permanently suspended under certain circumstances, there is no authority under the Education Law to permanently banish a student from school grounds (*Appeal of MacNamara,* 37 Educ. Dep't Rep. 326 (1998)).

12:101. Are students entitled to due process when suspended from school?

In *Goss v. Lopez*, 419 U.S. 565 (1975), the United States Supreme Court held that once a state provides public schools and requires its children to attend, this right may not be taken away without at least some minimal due process.

Due process requires that a student be given oral or written notice of the charges against him or her, and, if the charges are denied, an explanation of the evidence the authorities have and an opportunity to present the student's side of the story. In the majority of cases, the school administrator may be able to discuss the alleged misconduct with the student informally minutes after it has occurred. In being given an opportunity to explain his or her version of the facts at this discussion, the student must first be told what he or she is accused of and the basis of the accusation.

12:102. What due process rights do students have when they are suspended from a particular class?

District administrators who suspend students from a particular class must provide the same due process rights as would be provided if the student was being suspended from school (*Appeal of Trombly*, 26 Educ. Dep't Rep. 214 (1986); but see *Mazevski v. Horseheads CSD*, 950 F.Supp. 69 (W.D.N.Y. 1997)).

12:103. What procedures must be followed to suspend a student for five days or less?

For suspensions of five days or less, a school district must notify the student's parent or guardian immediately when their child is suspended. Districts must deliver written notice by personal messenger, express mail or an "equivalent means reasonably calculated to assure receipt" within 24 hours. In addition, districts must provide notification of the suspension where possible by telephone if the parent or guardian has provided the district with their telephone number. Such notice shall provide a description of the incident(s) which resulted in suspension and shall inform the parents or guardians of their right to request an immediate informal conference with the principal. The notification must be in the parent's dominant language or mode of communication (8 NYCRR § 100.2(l)(4)).

12:104. What procedures must be followed in order to suspend a student in excess of five days?

No student may be suspended in excess of five school days unless the student and his or her parent or guardian have had an opportunity for a hearing on reasonable notice (§ 3214(3)(c)).

While the law does not define "reasonable notice," the commissioner has held that a single day's notice of a suspension hearing was unreasonable (*Appeal of Eisenhauer*, 33 Educ. Dep't Rep. 604 (1994)). In another case, three days' verbal notice prior to the hearing was found to be sufficient (*Appeal of DeRosa*, 36 Educ. Dep't Rep. 336 (1997)).

Students are entitled to fair notice of the charges against them so that they can prepare and present an adequate defense. Notice which repeats the general statutory language of section 3214 of the Education Law, which contains the bases upon which a student may be suspended, or merely sets forth a statement that a student violated school rules or disrupted school activities, is not "reasonable" because it fails to provide the student with enough information to prepare an effective defense. However, the charges in a student disciplinary hearing need only be sufficiently specific to advise the student and his or her counsel of the activities or incidents which have given rise to the proceeding and which will form the basis for the hearing (*Board of Education v. Commissioner of Education*, 91 N.Y.2d 133 (1997)).

The student may bring his or her parents or guardians to the hearing and has the right to be represented by an attorney, to testify on his or her own behalf, to present witnesses and other evidence on his or her own behalf, and to cross-examine witnesses against him or her (§ 3214(3)(c); *Appeal of Johnson*, 34 Educ. Dep't Rep. 62 (1994)).

The decision to suspend a student from school must be based on competent and substantial evidence that the student participated in the objectionable conduct (*Appeal of Timothy R. and Janice A. Blake*, 37 Educ. Dep't Rep. 250 (1997)).

At the hearing, persons having personal knowledge of the facts should be called to testify. There must be some direct evidence of guilt of the charges. Hearsay evidence alone is not sufficient, notwithstanding the administrative nature of the proceeding (see *Appeal of Parker*, 34 Educ. Dep't Rep. 379 (1995); *Appeal of Swingle*, 32 Educ. Dep't Rep. 245 (1992); *Appeal of Normand*, 26 Educ. Dep't Rep. 389 (1987); *Matter of Dennis*, 19 Educ. Dep't Rep. 235 (1979); but see *Appeal of Hamet*, 36 Educ. Dep't Rep. 174 (1996)).

In one case, the New York State Court of Appeals ruled that a determination by a judge that certain evidence could not be used against a student in a family court proceeding, because it was obtained as a result of an illegal search, was not binding in a student disciplinary proceeding (*Matter of Juan C. v. Cortines*, 89 N.Y.2d 659 (1997)).

As in a court of law, the burden of proof rests on the person making the charge against the student, and the student is entitled to a presumption of innocence of wrongdoing unless otherwise proven (*Matter of Montero,* 10 Educ. Dep't Rep. 49 (1970)).

Both the superintendent and the school board are authorized to appoint a hearing officer to conduct student disciplinary hearings. The hearing officer's report is advisory only, and the superintendent or board may accept or reject all or any part of it (§ 3214(3)(c)).

12:105. What happens if a student is suspended for more than five days without a hearing?

A student who is suspended more than five days without a hearing may request an order of the commissioner of education directing reinstatement, pending a hearing and a determination of the charges (*Appeal of Knispel,* 35 Educ. Dep't Rep. 145 (1995)).

In addition, the United States Supreme Court, in *Carey v. Piphus,* 435 U.S. 247 (1978), determined that public school students who are suspended without a hearing can collect damages from school officials for the violation of their constitutional rights. Even if school officials can demonstrate that their suspensions were justified, students deprived of their due process rights are entitled to recover nominal damages not to exceed one dollar without proof of actual injury. The court also held that school districts may be liable for other damages if students suspended without a hearing can prove actual injury derived from the denial of due process.

12:106. May a student's suspension be revoked?

Yes. Where a student has been suspended for cause, the suspension may be revoked whenever it appears to be in the best interests of the school and the student to do so (§ 3214(3)(e)).

12:107. What are a school district's responsibilities after a student has been suspended?

In the case of a student of compulsory attendance age who has been suspended after a hearing for insubordination or disorderly conduct, immediate steps must be taken for his or her supervision or detention as provided by the Family Court Act, or for his or her attendance for instruction elsewhere (§ 3214(3)(e)).

The Education Law requires school boards to furnish alternative education to students under the age of 16 who have been suspended (§ 3214(3)(e)). Alternative instruction need not match in every respect the instructional program previously offered to the student; however, it must be sufficient so that the student can complete the required course work (*Matter of Malpica,* 20 Educ. Dep't Rep. 365 (1981); *Matter of Gesner,*

20 Educ. Dep't Rep. 326 (1980)). For example, a study hall does not satisfy the obligation to provide alternative instruction (*Appeal of Forster,* 31 Educ. Dep't Rep. 443 (1992); *Appeal of Ackert,* 30 Educ. Dep't Rep. 31 (1990)).

A district is not required to provide instruction for a suspended student over the age of 16 (*Matter of Reid v. Nyquist,* 65 Misc.2d 718 (1971); *Matter of Chipman,* 10 Educ. Dep't Rep. 224 (1971)).

12:108. How soon after a student is suspended must a district provide alternative instruction?

A school district is required to take immediate steps to provide the required alternative instruction (§ 3214(3)(e)). The term *immediately* does not mean *instantaneously,* but it does mean that the district should act promptly, with due regard for the nature and circumstances of the particular case (*Turner v. Kowalski,* 49 A.D.2d 943 (2nd Dep't 1975); *Appeal of Benkelman,* 34 Educ. Dep't Rep. 250 (1994)).

For example, a school district policy which stated that the district would not provide alternative instruction for students suspended for five days or less was ruled invalid (*Turner v. Kowalski*). In *Appeal of Bridges,* 34 Educ. Dep't Rep. 232 (1994), the commissioner also admonished a district for having a policy which stated that the district would not provide alternative instruction if the period of suspension was for less than three days.

12:109. What is in-school suspension, and what procedures are required for its implementation?

In-school suspension is the temporary removal of a student from the classroom and his or her placement in another area in the school building designated for such a suspension where that student will receive substantially equivalent, alternative education. A study hall does not satisfy the obligation to provide alternative instruction (*Appeal of Forster,* 31 Educ. Dep't Rep. 443 (1992); *Appeal of Ackert,* 30 Educ. Dep't Rep. 31 (1990)).

This kind of suspension does not require the more formal procedures required for out-of-school suspensions. However, with an in-school suspension, the student and his or her parents must be provided with a reasonable opportunity for an informal conference with the individual who imposed the suspension in order to discuss the conduct and the penalty involved (*Appeal of Gaslow,* 34 Educ. Dep't Rep. 293 (1994); *Matter of Danison,* 31 Educ. Dep't Rep. 169 (1991); *Matter of Watts,* 23 Educ. Dep't Rep. 459 (1984)).

12:110. May a district suspend a student from school transportation?

Yes. A suspension from transportation services does not require the prior safeguard of a full, formal hearing as required in section 3214 of the Education Law because such a suspension does not, per se, affect a student's right to attend school. All that is required is an opportunity to discuss the facts underlying the threatened discipline (*Appeal of Hale*, 30 Educ. Dep't Rep. 26 (1990)).

However, the commissioner of education has held that where suspending a student from school transportation amounts to a suspension from attending school because of the distance between home and school, and the absence of alternative public or private means of transportation, the school district must make "appropriate arrangements" to provide for the student's education (*Matter of Stewart*, 21 Educ. Dep't Rep. 654 (1982)).

12:111. May a district suspend or exclude a student from extracurricular activities for disciplinary reasons?

Yes. Under the Education Law, a school board has the authority to establish reasonable academic standards as prerequisites for eligibility for extracurricular activities (§ 1709(3); *Matter of Clark*, 21 Educ. Dep't Rep. 542 (1982)). School boards also have the authority to establish reasonable standards of conduct for participation in extracurricular activities (*Appeal of Douglas and Judy H.*, 36 Educ. Dep't Rep. 224 (1996)).

A full due process hearing does not apply to the exclusion or suspension of a student from extracurricular activities. However, the student and his or her parents must be given an opportunity to discuss the factual situation informally with the district official in charge (*Matter of Clark*).

In lieu of a suspension from extracurricular activities, the commissioner of education has upheld a board policy which required attendance at 10 "insight" classes for students who consumed alcohol during an extracurricular activity (*Appeal of Douglas and Judy H.*).

12:112. May a district use detention as a penalty?

Yes. A district may use detention as a penalty for certain student conduct when suspension would be inappropriate. Teachers and administrators may keep a student after school, provided there is no parental objection and the student has appropriate transportation home (State Education Department Memorandum on Detention to District Superintendents, April 28, 1995). They may also have the authority to prohibit students from participating in such activities as recess, interscholastic athletics and field trips (*Matter of Kubinski*, 26 Educ. Dep't Rep. 348 (1987)).

12:113. May a district involuntarily transfer a student from one school to another as a penalty in a student disciplinary proceeding?

No. Involuntary transfers may not be imposed as a penalty in a student disciplinary proceeding because the purpose of the procedure for involuntarily transferring a student is to determine whether the proposed transfer would be beneficial to the student (*Matter of Reeves*, 37 Educ. Dep't Rep. 271 (1998); see § 3214(5); see **12:24**).

12:114. May a district use community service as a penalty in a student disciplinary proceeding?

No. A school district has no authority to impose a community service requirement as a penalty under section 3214 of the Education Law (*Appeal of Eddy*, 36 Educ. Dep't Rep. 359 (1997); *Appeal of Alexander*, 36 Educ. Dep't Rep. 160 (1996); see **12:94**).

12:115. May a school district require counseling as a penalty in a student disciplinary proceeding?

No. A school district has no authority to condition a student's return to school from a suspension on participation in counseling services. Districts, however, are not precluded from recommending counseling in circumstances where a student may benefit from such services (*Appeal of Alexander*, 36 Educ. Dep't Rep. 160 (1996); see **12:111**).

12:116. Can a school board lower a student's grade as a disciplinary measure?

No. A student may not be disciplined by having his or her grades lowered, unless the student's misconduct is related to his or her academic performance, such as cheating on an examination or being illegally absent to avoid taking a test (*Matter of Augustine*, 30 Educ. Dep't Rep. 13 (1990); *Matter of Caskey*, 21 Educ. Dep't Rep. 138 (1981); *Matter of MacWhinnie*, 20 Educ. Dep't Rep. 145 (1980)).

12:117. Is corporal punishment forbidden in schools?

Yes. *Corporal punishment* is any act of physical force upon a student for the purpose of punishing that student (8 NYCRR §§ 19.5(b), 100.2(l)(3)(i)). The Rules of the Board of Regents specify that no teacher, administrator, officer, employee or agent of a school district may use corporal punishment against a student (8 NYCRR § 19.5(a)).

However, in situations where alternative procedures and methods not involving the use of force cannot reasonably be employed, the use of reasonable physical force is permissible to:

• Protect oneself, another student, teacher or any person(s) from physical injury.

- Protect the property of the school or others.
- Restrain or remove a student whose behavior interferes with the orderly exercise and performance of school district functions, powers and duties, if that student has refused to refrain from further disruptive acts (8 NYCRR §§ 19.5(c); 100.2(l)(3)(ii)).

12:118. Must a school district submit a report if a complaint about corporal punishment has been filed?

Yes. The commissioner's regulations require every school board to submit a written report to the commissioner on complaints about corporal punishment by January 15 and July 15 each year. The report must include the substance of each complaint about the use of corporal punishment received by local school authorities during the reporting period, the results of each investigation, and the action, if any, taken by the school authorities in each case (8 NYCRR § 100.2(l)(3)(ii)).

12:119. What is the Gun-Free Schools Act?

The Gun-Free Schools Act is a federal law which requires that all states receiving funds under the Elementary and Secondary Education Act of 1965 to have a law which requires school districts to suspend students who bring weapons to school for a minimum of one calendar year (20 USC § 8921(b)(1); U.S. Department of Education Guidance Concerning State and Local Responsibilities Under the Gun-Free Schools Act of 1994; see 25:9). The term *weapon* means a firearm as such term is defined by federal law (18 USC § 921(a)(3); 20 USC § 8921(b)(4); see 12:121).

The New York State Legislature has amended the Education Law to comply with the Gun-Free Schools Act (§ 3214(3)(d)). The United States Department of Education has issued guidelines on the application of the Gun-Free Schools Act.

12:120. Does the suspension requirement of the Gun-Free Schools Act apply only to violations occurring within school buildings?

No. The one-year suspension requirement applies to students who bring weapons to any setting that is under the control and supervision of the school district (U.S. Department of Education Guidance Concerning State and Local Responsibilities Under the Gun-Free Schools Act of 1994).

12:121. What is a weapon under the Gun-Free Schools Act?

For the purposes of the Gun-Free Schools Act, a *weapon* means a firearm as defined in section 921 of Title 18 of the United States Code

(20 USC § 8921(b)(4)). The following are *included* within the definition:

- Any weapon (including a starter gun) which will or is designed to or may readily be converted to expel a projectile by the action of an explosive.
- The frame or receiver of any weapon described above.
- Any firearm muffler or firearm silencer.
- Any destructive device, which is defined as, any explosive, incendiary, or poison gas, such as a bomb, grenade, rocket having a propellant charge of more than four ounces, a missile having an explosive or incendiary charge of more than one-quarter ounce, a mine, or other similar device.
- Any weapon which will, or which may be readily converted to, expel a projectile by the action of an explosive or other propellant, and which has any barrel with a bore of more than one-half inch in diameter.
- Any combination of parts either designed or intended for use in converting any device into any destructive device described in the two immediately preceding examples, and from which a destructive device may be readily assembled.

The following are *not included* in the definition:

- An antique firearm.
- A rifle which the owner intends to use solely for sporting, recreational, or cultural purposes.
- Any device which is neither designed nor redesigned for use as a weapon.
- Any device, although originally designed for use as a weapon, which is redesigned for use as a signaling, pyrotechnic, line-throwing, safety or similar device.
- Surplus ordnance sold, loaned, or given by the Secretary of the Army pursuant to the provisions of sections 4684(2), 4685, or 4686 of Title 10 of the United States Code (18 USC § 921(a)(3),(4)).

Neither class-c common fireworks nor knives are included in the definition of weapon. However, according to the U.S. Department of Education, a school district may decide to broaden its own definition of weapon to include knives (U.S. Department of Education Guidance Concerning State and Local Responsibilities Under the Gun-Free Schools Act of 1994).

The commissioner of education has ruled that a BB gun is not a weapon within the meaning of the Gun-Free Schools Act because the gun uses a spring mechanism to propel the projectile instead of an explosive charge (*Appeal of Eddy*, 36 Educ. Dep't Rep. 359 (1997)).

12:122. What are a school district's responsibilities under the Gun-Free Schools Act?

All school districts must suspend a student who brings a weapon to school for a period of not less than one calendar year. The superintendent of schools, district superintendent of schools or community superintendent may modify the suspension requirement on a case-by-case basis. A superintendent's determination may be appealed to the school board and the commissioner of education (20 USC § 8921; § 3214(3)(d)).

All school districts must have a policy which requires superintendents to refer students under the age of 16 who have been determined to have brought a firearm to school to the county attorney for a juvenile delinquency preceding, and students 16 years of age or older to the appropriate law enforcement officials (§ 3214(3)(d); 20 USC § 8922).

In addition, each school district that receives state funding must provide an assurance within its application for state aid that it is in compliance with section 3214(3)(d) of the Education Law (20 USC § 8921(d)(1)). The application must include a description of the circumstances surrounding any suspension imposed under the state law implementing the Gun-Free Schools Act, including the name of the school concerned, the number of students suspended from school, and the types of weapons concerned (20 USC § 8921(d)(2)).

12:123. Is a student entitled to due process before a school district may impose the one-year suspension required under the Gun-Free Schools Act?

Yes. A student charged with bringing a weapon to school is entitled to the same due process protection afforded to other students who have been suspended in excess of five days (see **12:104**).

12:124. Are school districts required to provide alternative educational services to students who have been suspended for bringing a weapon to school?

Yes. While the Gun-Free Schools Act neither requires nor prohibits the provision of alternative educational services to students that have been suspended, under state law, school boards are required to furnish alternative education to students under the age of 16 who have been suspended (§ 3214(3)(e); 20 USC § 8921(b)(2); see **12:107**).

12:125. Does the Gun-Free Schools Act apply to students with disabilities?

Yes. However, the Gun-Free Schools Act must be construed to be consistent with the Individuals with Disabilities Education Act (IDEA) and section 504 of the Rehabilitation Act (20 USC § 8921(c); § 3214(3)(d); for further information on the discipline of students with disabilities, see **13:38-44**).

12:126. May a school board offer a reward for information related to vandalism of school property?

Yes. School boards may offer monetary rewards in sums not to exceed $1,000 for information leading to the arrest and conviction of persons who have committed felonious or misdemeanor acts of vandalism of school district property (§ 1709(38)).

Student Employment

12:127. May students work while they attend school?

Yes. Students may work while they attend school, provided they obtain a valid employment certificate and do not work in excess of the number of hours prescribed by law.

12:128. Under what circumstances may students be issued employment certificates?

Minors who are 14 or 15 years old may secure employment permits and may work while school is in session or when school is not in session, but not in factories (§ 3216(1); Lab. Law § 131(1),(2)).

Minors who are 14 to 16 years of age must have a farm work permit for employment on a farm operated by an individual other than their parents or guardians (§ 3226(1); Lab. Law § 131(3)(f)). To obtain a farm work permit, a child must present evidence of age, written consent of a parent or guardian, and a certificate of fitness (§ 3226(3)(a)-(c)). A farm work permit is only valid when signed by an employer (§ 3226(4)). A child over the age of 12 may obtain a farm work permit to assist in the harvest of berries and fruits by hand under certain circumstances (§ 3226(2); Lab. Law § 130(2)(e)).

An employment certificate is not required for baby-sitting, caddying, shoveling snow or other so-called casual employment (§ 3215(4); Lab. Law § 131(3)(a); 8 NYCRR § 191.1).

The minimum age for a newspaper carrier is 11 (§ 3228(1); Lab. Law § 130(2)(c)). A newspaper carrier must possess a newspaper carrier permit issued by the commissioner of education or school physician (§ 3228(2),(3)).

Under certain conditions, a minor who is 15 years old, such as a child performer or a model, may secure a special employment certificate and leave school to work (§§ 3216(5), 3225(1); 8 NYCRR § 190.2; see also, Lab. Law §§ 130(2)(a),(b); 131(3)(b),(c); Arts & Cult. Aff. Law §§ 35.01, 35.05; see **12:142** for information about student employment in school lunch programs).

12:129. Do 16- and 17-year-old students need employment certificates?

Yes. Standard employment certificates may be secured by minors who have already reached age 16. These certificates are valid for work in factories or any other trade, business or service (§ 3216(2); Lab. Law § 132(2)).

12:130. Who issues employment certificates in New York State?

Employment certificates and vacation work permits are issued by the superintendent of schools, or his or her designee. In New York City, employment certificates or permits are issued by the chancellor of the City School District of New York City or his or her designee. In registered nonpublic secondary schools, the principal may issue these certificates (§ 3215-a(1)).

12:131. Must a student be issued an employment certificate for each new job?

No. An employment certificate is valid not only for initial employment but also for subsequent employment in work permitted by the particular type of certificate (§ 3216(6)).

12:132. What is the maximum number of hours 14- and 15-year-old students are legally allowed to work?

When school is in session, 14- and 15-year-old minors may not work more than three hours on any school day, more than eight hours on any day when school is not in session, more than 18 hours per week, more than six days per week, or after 7:00 p.m. or before 7:00 a.m. (Lab. Law § 142(1)).

12:133. What hours are 16- and 17-year-old students legally allowed to work?

The general rule is that when school is in session, 16- and 17-year-old minors may not be employed more than four hours on any day preceding a school day other than on a Sunday or a holiday; more than eight hours on a Friday, Saturday, Sunday or holiday; more than 28 hours per week; more than six days a week and before 6:00 a.m. (Lab. Law § 143(1)).

Employers who schedule minors who are 16 or 17 years old to work between 10:00 p.m. and midnight on any day preceding a school day must obtain written permission from the student's parent or guardian and a certificate from the school at the end of each marking period that indicates the student's academic performance is satisfactory, as measured by district standards (Lab. Law § 143(1)(e)). Employers who employ 16- and 17-year-olds between 10:00 p.m. and midnight on any day preceding a nonschool day need only secure written permission from the student's parent or guardian (Lab. Law § 143(1)(f)).

Before processing requests for students' certificates of academic standing, districts should make certain that students are afforded all of the rights and consent they would receive for any other requests for disclosures of information from their student records, under the federal Family Educational Rights and Privacy Act (FERPA) (see **2:70; 25:1**).

12:134. Are illegally employed students and their beneficiaries entitled to workers' compensation and death benefits?

Yes. Section 14-a of the Workers' Compensation Law provides double compensation and death benefits for illegally employed minors and their beneficiaries. The employer alone, not the insurance carrier, is liable for the increased compensation or increased death benefits provided for by this section.

School Lunch and Breakfast Programs

12:135. May school districts operate and maintain a school lunch program?

Yes. School districts may operate and maintain a school lunch program pursuant to the National School Lunch Act of 1946, as amended (42 USC § 1751 *et seq.*).

In addition, school districts can provide, maintain and operate a cafeteria or restaurant for the use of students and teachers while they are at school (§ 1709(22)). Districts operating under a contingency budget and conducting a food service program under contract with a food service management company may continue the program if the school cafeteria or restaurant service requires no tax levy (see 8 NYCRR § 114.2(f)).

The Child Nutrition Act of 1966, as amended (see 42 USC § 1772), and section 1709(23) of the Education Law also authorize school districts to provide milk for students within the limitations of the congressional budget appropriation made for such purpose.

12:136. May school districts operate and maintain a school breakfast program?

Yes. School districts may operate and maintain breakfast programs pursuant to the Child Nutrition Act of 1966 (42 USC §§ 1771 *et seq.*), and part 114 of the commissioner's regulations. Districts must submit an application to the commissioner of education before establishing this type of program (8 NYCRR § 114.1(c),(e)). Approval may be granted for selected schools rather than an entire district (8 NYCRR § 114.1(c)).

State law and regulations require school districts which provide a school lunch program on or after January 1, 1993 to establish and maintain school breakfast programs in public elementary schools (Laws of 1976, Ch. 537, as amended by Laws of 1993, Ch. 614 § 1 and Ch. 615 §§ 1,3; 8 NYCRR § 114.1(a)(5),(i)(2)). Annual exemptions to this requirement may be granted by the commissioner because a school district lacks a need for such a program due to low school enrollment or participation in the program, because of economic hardship, or for other good cause that makes the establishment of a breakfast program impractical (Laws of 1980 Ch. 798; Laws of 1993, Ch. 57 § 389, Ch. 614 § 3, and Ch. 615 § 3; 8 NYCRR § 114.1(i)(4)).

To the extent that state and federal funds are available, school districts eligible to participate in breakfast programs are reimbursed monthly for breakfasts served that meet meal pattern requirements and for their first year of operation for approved expenses exceeding revenues, subject to the commissioner's approval. Claims for reimbursement will be made on the basis of claims submitted to the commissioner in the form he requires (Laws of 1980, Ch. 798, § 4; 8 NYCRR § 114.1(g),(j)).

12:137. May a school district be exempted from or terminate a school breakfast program?

Yes. A school district which is required to establish a school breakfast program may seek an exemption from participation or may terminate the program under certain circumstances by applying to the commissioner of education for an annual exemption (Laws of 1980, Ch. 798 § 4 and Laws of 1993, Ch. 615 § 4; see 8 NYCRR § 114.1(i)(3)-(7)). Parents and taxpayers must be made aware of the district's intent to request an exemption by May 1 of each year and be offered an opportunity to share their concerns with school officials (8 NYCRR § 114.1(i)(8); see also Laws of 1980, Ch. 798 § 4, as amended by Laws of 1993, Ch. 615 § 4).

A school district which is not required to establish a school breakfast program may terminate its participation in the program by majority vote of the school board. A resolution to terminate the program is not effective prior to June 30 of the school year within which the vote was taken (Laws of 1980, Ch. 798 § 4, amended by Laws of 1993, Ch. 615 § 4).

In addition, no school district is required to operate a school breakfast program if the state elects to terminate participation in the National School Breakfast Program, the corresponding federal program ceases to exist, or if federal funding for the program is withdrawn for any reason whatsoever (Laws of 1976, Ch. 537 § 1(g)).

12:138. How is a student's eligibility to participate in a school district's breakfast program on a free or reduced-price basis determined?

A student's eligibility to participate in a school district's breakfast program on a free or reduced-price basis is determined according to income eligibility guidelines issued annually by the State Education Department and sent to school superintendents (Laws of 1976, Ch. 537 § 1(e); 8 NYCRR § 114.1(d)).

12:139. Are school meals subject to sales tax?

Sale of food and drink to students on the school premises are exempt from taxation. However, sale of food and drink to adults is subject to sales tax (Tax Law § 1105(d)(ii)(B)).

12:140. May school districts employ a food-service management company to operate their breakfast and lunch programs?

Yes. School districts may contract with a private food-service management company for the purpose of managing and operating, in whole or in part, its food-service program (7 CFR § 210.16(a); 8 NYCRR § 114.2). However, the food service program remains the legal responsibility of the school district, in accordance with the written agreement required by federal regulations (8 NYCRR § 114.2(a); 7 CFR § 210.9). This agreement is available from the State Education Department (8 NYCRR § 114.2(a)(1)).

Any contract with a food-service management company may not exceed one year and must conform to the commissioner's regulations (8 NYCRR § 114.2(c),(d)). In addition, the contract must be awarded to the lowest responsible bidder. Under certain circumstances, the competitive bidding requirement does not apply to annual, biennial, or triennial extensions of a contract (§ 305(14)(a); 8 NYCRR § 114.2(c),(g)). Furthermore, all food-service management company contracts must be reviewed and approved by the commissioner of education, including annual extensions of contracts (§ 305(14)(a); 8 NYCRR § 114.2(d)(1),(g)).

If contracting is being considered and the school district is subject to the terms of a collective bargaining agreement, the proposal may have to be negotiated with the bargaining unit (see **10:38**).

12:141. Do school districts contracting with a food-service management company remain eligible for reimbursement of funds expended in their breakfast and lunch programs?

Yes. Where a school district contracts with a private food-service management company, it nonetheless remains eligible to receive both federal and state reimbursement and food, in the same way it does for school-operated programs, provided the requirements in the commissioner's regulations are observed (8 NYCRR § 114.2).

12:142. May a school district employ students to work in its food-service program?

Yes. Children at least 14 years old may be employed in a school's food-service program if the student presents a valid employment certificate (Lab. Law §§ 131(3)(g), 132(3)(c)).

12:143. Are school districts eligible to receive federally donated surplus foods and price-support commodities for their breakfast and lunch programs?

Yes. Schools participating in the National School Lunch and Breakfast programs are eligible to receive such food available for distribution (42 USC § 1777; 7 USC § 1431). However, schools must pay the transportation costs for trucking the goods from the district warehouse to the school. In addition, the cost of warehousing is prorated on the basis of the number of case lots allocated to the school. This charge is made once a year and deducted from the claim for reimbursement. Operation of the Commodity Distribution Program is handled by the New York State Office of General Services, Bureau of Government Donated Foods.

12:144. Can school districts be reimbursed for meals served to preschool students?

Yes. School districts are eligible to be reimbursed for meals that meet the standards of the lunch meal pattern served to preschool children in school-sponsored classes, just as they are for meals provided to other school children, provided funds are not available from other sources to meet this need (see Laws of 1976, Ch. 537 § 1(a),(d)).

12:145. May a school district make its cafeteria facilities available for meals to community groups such as parent-teacher associations?

Yes, if permission is granted by the school board. In addition, it is recommended that a school cafeteria employee be available to ensure that facilities and equipment are used properly. This employee should be compensated by the agency or group using the facilities.

School districts should establish rules and regulations concerning, for example, the personnel to be involved, the number of activities during the year it is permissible for personnel to be involved in, and other pertinent matters (§ 414).

12:146. Are a school district's cafeteria and food-service programs subject to sanitation rules and regulations?

Yes. Federal regulations require all schools to abide by all state and local laws and regulations for proper sanitation and health (7 CFR § 210.13(a); see 10 NYCRR Subpart 14-1).

13. Students with Disabilities

Editor's Note: At press time, the United States Department of Education was in the process of drafting final regulations to implement the 1997 Reauthorization to the Individuals with Disabilities Education Act (IDEA). In addition, the New York State Legislature had not yet passed legislation to bring the state into compliance with IDEA. It is anticipated that the state Legislature will address special education reform during the 1999 legislative session. Therefore, readers should be cautioned that some of the material in this chapter may possibly change because of new federal regulations or state statutes.

Basic Definitions and Applicable Laws

13:1. What laws govern the education of children with disabilities?

The education of children with disabilities is governed by the following statutes and their accompanying regulations:

- The Individuals with Disabilities Education Act (IDEA), formerly known as the Education of Handicapped Children Act (EHA), which imposes on school districts an obligation to provide all children with disabilities, including children with disabilities who have been suspended or expelled from school, with a free, appropriate public education in the least restrictive environment. IDEA was amended and reauthorized on June 4, 1997 (20 USC §§ 1400-1487).
- Section 504 of the Rehabilitation Act of 1973 and the Americans with Disabilities Act of 1990, which prohibit discrimination on the basis of disability (29 USC §§ 706; 794-794(a); 42 USC §§ 12101- 12213).
- Article 89 of the New York State Education Law and part 200 of the commissioner's regulations, which are also the vehicles that implement federal law governing the rights of children with disabilities in New York State.

On occasion, there is a lag between changes in the federal statutes and the incorporation of those changes into state law. During such lags, school districts nonetheless are bound by the new federal requirements. In addition, New York State law may at times confer greater rights on students with disabilities than the federal statutes. In such cases, New York State law must be followed. Therefore, it is important for school districts to be familiar with all of the applicable laws.

The New York State Education Law and the commissioner's regulations still contain references to children with *handicapping conditions*, but pursuant to federal law, references in this chapter will be to children with *disabilities*.

13:2. What is the definition of children with disabilities applicable to the provision of education to such children?

Generally, *children with disabilities* are those who fall within one of the classifications set forth in the Individuals with Disabilities Education Act (IDEA) and section 200.1(mm) of the commissioner's regulations and who, because of this, need special education and related services (20 USC § 1401(3)(A); 8 NYCRR § 200.1(mm); see also Educ. Law § 4401(1)).

These classifications include children who suffer from mental retardation; hearing impairment, including deafness, speech or language impairment; visual impairment, including blindness; emotional disturbance; orthopedic impairment; autism; traumatic brain injury; other health impairments; or specific learning disabilities (20 USC § 1401(3)(A)(i); 8 NYCRR § 200.1(mm); see also § 4401(1)).

However, under section 504 of the Rehabilitation Act of 1973, an individual with a disability is defined as "any person who has a physical or mental impairment which substantially limits one or more of such person's major life activities, has a record of such an impairment, or is regarded as having such an impairment" (29 USC § 706(8)(B); see also Educ. Law § 4401(1)).

Similarly, the Americans with Disabilities Act (ADA) extends its benefits to disabled individuals "who, with or without reasonable modifications to rules, policies or practices, the removal of architectural, communication or transportation barriers, or the provision of auxiliary aids and services, meets the essential eligibility requirements for the receipt of services or the participation in programs or activities provided by a public entity" (42 USC § 12131(2)).

It is important for school districts to be aware of this broader definition of individuals with disabilities because section 504 and the ADA prohibit discrimination solely on the basis of disability.

In addition, under section 504 and the ADA, school districts may be responsible for providing education and related services to children with disabilities who do not fall under any of the classifications set forth in the IDEA or the commissioner's regulations (*Appeal of a Child with a Handicapping Condition*, 32 Educ. Dep't Rep. 56 (1992); *Application of a Child Suspected of Having a Handicapping Condition*, SRO dec. no. 92-12 (1992)). For example, according to the United States Department of Education's Office of Civil Rights, all students infected with HIV or who have HIV-related conditions, including those who are currently asymptomatic, are handicapped within the definition of section 504. School districts must provide for proper procedures in the evaluation and placement of these students, as well as for proper procedural safeguards *(Fairfax County (Va.) Public Schools,* 19 IDELR 649 (1992)).

13:3. What is meant by a "free appropriate public education," which school districts must provide to children with disabilities?

A *free appropriate public education* consists of special education and related services provided at public expense in conformity with an individualized education program (IEP), which is tailored to meet the unique needs of a student with a disability (20 USC § 1401(8)).

However, school districts are not required to maximize the potential of each disabled child. Districts must provide each child with a disability with a "basic floor of opportunity" consisting of "personalized instruction with sufficient support services to permit the child to benefit educationally from that instruction" *(Board of Education v. Rowley,* 458 U.S. 176 (1982); *Walczak v. Florida UFSD,* 142 F.3d 119 (2nd Cir. 1998)). The educational benefit afforded a disabled student must be more than minimal *(Polk v. Central Susquehanna Intermediate Unit 16,* 853 F.2d 171 (3rd Cir. 1988), cert. denied, 488 U.S. 1030 (1989)).

In addition, a school district is not obligated to provide an optional program or to match or surpass a program offered by a private school *(Matter of a Handicapped Child,* 26 Educ. Dep't Rep. 70 (1986)).

13:4. What is an individualized education program (IEP)?

An *individualized education program (IEP)* is a written statement outlining the plan for providing an educational program for a disabled student based on the unique needs of that student. It must include, for example:
- The classification of the student's disability.
- The present levels of educational performance of a disabled child indicating the individual needs of the student according to the level of academic or educational achievement and learning characteristics, levels of social and physical development, and management needs.
- The recommended special education program; the class size, if appropriate; and the extent to which the student will participate in regular education programs and an explanation of the extent to which the child will not participate with nondisabled children in the regular class and in extracurricular and nonacademic activities.
- The measurable annual goals, including benchmarks or short-term objectives, related to involving the child in the general curriculum.

- A statement of how the child's progress toward the annual goals will be measured and how the child's parents will be regularly informed of the child's progress.
- The special education, related services and supplementary aids and services to be provided to the child, or on behalf of the child.
- The program modifications or supports for school personnel provided for the child.
- The individual modifications in the administration of state or district-wide assessments of student achievement that are needed in order for the child to participate in such assessment.
- The projected date the student will begin receiving special education and related services, the frequency, location and amount of time per day he or she will receive services, whether the student is eligible for a 12-month educational program (and the name of the service provider for July and August), and a projected date to review his or her need for these services.
- Beginning at age 14 and updated annually, a statement of the transition services needs of the child under the applicable components of the child's IEP that focuses on the child's course of study.
- Any necessary transition services beginning at age 15 (or younger, if appropriate).
- Beginning at least one year before the child reaches age 18, a statement that the child has been informed of his or her rights under IDEA, if any, that will transfer to the child on reaching 18.
- The student's recommended placement (20 USC § 1414(d)(1)(A); 8 NYCRR §§ 200.1(t), 200.4(c)).

13:5. What is meant by the term "least restrictive environment" in which federal and state laws require students with disabilities be educated?

The requirement that students with disabilities be educated in the *"least restrictive environment"* appropriate to their individual needs means that to the maximum extent appropriate, children with disabilities must be educated with children who are not disabled, as close as possible to their home. Children with disabilities are not to be removed from regular classroom instruction unless it is determined that they cannot be educated satisfactorily in that environment, even with the use of supplementary aids and services (20 USC §§ 1412(a)(5)(A); 8 NYCRR § 200.1(x); *Oberti v. Board of Educ. of the Borough of Clementon School Dist.*, 995 F.2d 1204 (3rd Cir. 1993); *Greer v. Rome City School Dist.*, 950 F.2d 688 (11th Cir. 1991);

Daniel R.R. v. State Board of Educ., 874 F.2d 1036 (5th Cir. 1989); *Mavis v. Sobol*, 839 F.Supp. 968 (N.D.N.Y. 1993)).

Supplementary aids and services means aids, services and other supports that are provided in regular education classes or other education-related settings to enable children with disabilities to be educated with nondisabled children to the maximum extent appropriate, in accordance with the least restrictive environment requirement (20 USC § 1401(29)).

Students who must be removed from regular classroom instruction must be provided services within a "continuum of alternative placements" including, for example, the use of services such as resource rooms, related services or itinerant instruction in conjunction with regular class placement, and instruction in regular classes and special classes (8 NYCRR § 200.6). They also must be educated in public school buildings so they may interact with children who are not disabled in nonacademic areas such as music, art, gym, recess and lunch (see *Application of a Child with a Handicapping Condition*, 30 Educ. Dep't Rep. 108 (1990); *Application of a Child with a Handicapping Condition*, 30 Educ. Dep't Rep. 64 (1990); *Application of a Child with a Handicapping Condition*, 29 Educ. Dep't Rep. 223 (1990); *Application of a Child with a Handicapping Condition*, 29 Educ. Dep't Rep. 1 (1989)).

13:6. What are related services?

Related services consist of transportation and such developmental, corrective and other supportive services as may be required to assist a child with a disability to benefit from special education, and includes the early identification and assessment of disabling conditions in children. These services include, for example, speech-language pathology and audiology; psychological services; physical and occupational therapy; recreation, including therapeutic recreation; social work services; counseling services, including rehabilitation counseling; orientation and mobility services and medical services for diagnostic and evaluation purposes only (20 USC § 1401(22); 8 NYCRR § 200.1(gg)).

They also include "assistive technology services" defined as "any service that directly assists a child with a disability in the selection, acquisition, or use of an assistive technology device" (20 USC § 1401(2)). "Assistive technology device" means "any item, piece of equipment, or product system, whether acquired commercially off the shelf, modified, or customized, that is used to increase, maintain, or improve functional capabilities of a child with a disability" (20 USC § 1401(1)).

The School District's Responsibilities

13:7. What are the school district's basic responsibilities in providing services to children with disabilities?

School districts must provide all children with disabilities a free, appropriate education in the least restrictive environment, including children with disabilities who have been suspended or expelled from school, regardless of the severity of their disabilities (20 USC §§ 1412(a)(1)(A); 1412(a)(5)(A); *Board of Education v. Rowley*, 458 U.S. 176 (1982); *Timothy W. v. Rochester School District*, 875 F.2d 954 (1st Cir. 1989), *cert. denied*, 493 U.S. 983 (1989); *Application of a Child with a Handicapping Condition*, 30 Educ. Dep't Rep. 64 (1990); see **13:3, 13:5**), or their ability to benefit from special education *(Timothy W. v. Rochester School District)*.

In addition, school boards must:

- Provide for the identification and maintenance of information about children with disabilities residing in their districts, including children with disabilities attending private schools (20 USC § 1412(a)(3)(A); 8 NYCRR § 200.2(a); see **13:8**).
- Develop and adopt a written policy to ensure that children with disabilities have the opportunity to participate in programs to which they are entitled (20 USC § 1413(a)(1); 20 USC § 1412; 8 NYCRR § 200.2(b)), and have an appropriate amount of space to meet their needs (8 NYCRR § 200.2(c)(2)(iv), (v)).
- Ensure testing and evaluation materials and procedures for identifying and placing of children with disabilities are neither racially nor culturally discriminatory (20 USC § 1412(a)(6)(B); 8 NYCRR § 200.4(b)(4)(d)).
- Prepare plans by September 1 of every other year which outline the district's special education programs and services, as required by commissioner's regulations in order to receive state aid (8 NYCRR § 200.2(c)).
- Establish practices and procedures for appointing and training appropriately qualified personnel, including members and chairpersons of the committee on special education (CSE) and committee on preschool special education (CPSE) (20 USC § 1413(a)(3); 8 NYCRR § 200.2(b)(3)).
- Establish a committee and subcommittees on special education (CSE) and a committee on preschool special education (CPSE) (20 USC § 1414(b)(4)(A); 20 USC § 1414(d)(1)(B)).

- Arrange for the appropriate special education programs and services upon completion of a student's IEP and the recommendation of the CSE or CPSE (8 NYCRR § 200.2(d); 200.4(c)(5), (d)).
- Appoint impartial hearing officers to hear appeals over the school district's actions concerning the identification, evaluation and placement of students with disabilities (§ 4404(1); 8 NYCRR §§ 200.1(s), 200.2(e), 200.4(a)(8), 200.5(b)(2),(3), 200.5(c)).
- Establish procedures to ensure the observance of procedural safeguards afforded students with disabilities and their parents (20 USC §§ 1415; see 8 NYCRR § 200.5; **13:16**).
- Establish practices and procedures that ensure the confidentiality of personally identifiable data, information or records pertaining to students with disabilities (8 NYCRR § 200.2(b)(6)).

13:8. What specific responsibilities does a school board have for identifying and maintaining data on children with disabilities?

Each school board must locate and identify all children with disabilities who reside in the district, including children with disabilities enrolled in private schools, whether they are of preschool or school age (20 USC § 1412(a)(3)(A)). A register of such children must be maintained and revised annually by the district's committee on special education (CSE) for school-age children or the committee on preschool special education (CPSE) for younger children (Educ. Law § 4402(1)(a); 8 NYCRR § 200.2(a)).

Procedures must be implemented to ensure the availability of statistical data to determine the status of each child with a disability in the identification, location, evaluation, placement and program review process. Data must be reported by October 1 to the CSE or CPSE (8 NYCRR § 200.2(a)).

Procedures must be designed to record data on each child with a disability and shall include at least the following types of data:
- The child's name, address and birth date.
- The child's parents' names and address or addresses and the dominant language spoken in the child's home.
- The child's suspected disability.
- The dates of referral and evaluation, recommendations of the CSE or CPSE, actual placement and annual program reviews.
- The site where the child currently is receiving an educational program.
- In certain instances, any reasons why the child is not receiving an appropriate public education.

This data must be organized so that it can be determined readily whether the child is receiving an appropriate public education, a partial education or no education at all (8 NYCRR § 200.2(a)(2)).

Anyone who collects this data must receive training and written information on the procedures for collecting the data (8 NYCRR § 200.2(a)(3)).

13:9. Must school districts report the data collected on children with disabilities?

Yes. Data on children with disabilities must be reported according to the following rules:

- School districts must prepare and keep on file summary reports of data on students and preschool children, including the number of children who were served, the number of those who were not served and the reasons why they were not served.
- School districts must submit a summary report of the children they served to the State Education Department (SED) on prescribed forms.

Each year the school board or trustees of each school district, with the exception of cities with 125,000 or more inhabitants, must report the register of children who are under the age of 21 with disabilities to the superintendent of the board of cooperative educational services (BOCES) of which the district may be a part. In addition, the data must be reported to the district's committee on special education (CSE) or committee on preschool special education (CPSE), as appropriate, by October 1 of each year (see **13:8**). The regular census must be filed on or before October 15 of each year (see **2:16**). The register also must be available to representatives from SED (Educ. Law §§ 3241, 3242; 8 NYCRR § 200.2(a)(4)).

13:10. Are school districts responsible for providing medical services to students with disabilities?

School districts are not required to provide medical services except for diagnostic and evaluative purposes (20 USC § 1401(22); 8 NYCRR § 200.1(y), (gg)). However, courts have looked at a variety of factors to determine whether a particular procedure is indeed a medical service which school districts are not required to provide. The United States Supreme Court, for instance, ruled that clean intermittent catheterization, a mechanical process to empty the kidneys, did not fall within the medical services exclusion because the procedure did not have to be performed by a licensed physician, and in time could be performed by the student herself (*Irving Independent School Dist. v. Tatro,* 468 U.S. 883 (1984)).

In *Detsel v. Board of Educ. of Auburn Enlarged City School Dist.* (820 F.2d 587 (2nd Cir. 1987), *cert. denied,* 484 U.S. 981 (1987)), the federal Court of Appeals with jurisdiction over New York State ruled a school district did not have to provide constant in-school nursing care to a student who required constant respirator assistance and a continuous supply of oxygen. Considering the nature and extent of the services which were required to protect the student's life, the court explained that even though the services did not have to be performed by a licensed physician, they nonetheless more closely resembled medical services a school district is not required to provide under the federal Individuals with Disabilities Education Act (IDEA).

Similarly, a New York appellate court ruled that a school district was not required to provide a specially trained nurse in order to assist a respirator-dependent student paralyzed from the neck down (*Ellison v. Board of Educ. of the Three Village Central School Dist.,* 189 A.D.2d 518 (3rd Dep't 1993)). According to the court, the services required were not "simple school nursing services" but were more akin to "medical services" school districts are not required to furnish.

In the meantime, the United States Supreme Court has agreed to revisit this issue (see *Cedar Rapids Community School Dist. v. Garret F.,* 106 F. 3d 822 (8th Cir. 1997), *cert. granted,* 118 S.Ct. 1793 (1998)).

13:11. Are school districts required to provide year-round services to disabled students?

Yes, to students whose disabilities require a structured learning environment of up to 12 months' duration to prevent "substantial regression." This means the inability to maintain developmental levels due to a loss of skill or knowledge, during the months of July and August, severe enough to require an inordinate period of review at the beginning of the school year to reestablish and maintain the individualized education program's (IEP) goals and objectives mastered at the end of the previous school year (8 NYCRR § 200.1(nn); *Appeal of a Child with a Handicapping Condition,* 31 Educ. Dep't Rep. 17 (1991)). This standard does not require that children with disabilities actually regress in their skills before they are eligible for summer programs and services; what is required is a "reasonable basis" for concluding that regression would occur without these services (*Application of a Child with a Disability,* SRO dec. no. 93-28 (1993)).

Programs providing services during the months of July and August must operate at least 30 days. However, programs providing only related services must be provided with the frequency and duration specified in the IEP (8 NYCRR § 200.1(qq)).

13:12. Must school districts provide services to students with disabilities beyond the maximum statutory age for receiving special education services?

The general rule is that school districts must provide special education services to students with disabilities until the end of the school year in which the child turns 21 (20 USC § 1412(a)(1)(A); 8 NYCRR § 200.1(mm)).

However, courts have ordered school districts to provide compensatory education to disabled students beyond the statutory age in cases where the district has failed to provide a free appropriate public education when they were entitled to receive it *(Application of a Child with a Handicapping Condition,* SRO dec. no. 91-6 (1991); *Chester Upland School v. Lester H.,* 916 F.2d 865 (3rd Cir. 1990); *cert. denied,* 499 U.S. 923 (1991); *Cocores v. Portsmouth, N. H., School District,* 18 IDELR 461 (1991)).

13:13. Must school districts ensure that students with disabilities have an opportunity to participate in extracurricular activities?

Yes. School districts must adopt and implement procedures for ensuring that students with disabilities can participate in extracurricular activities, including, for example, providing a speech interpreter to enable a student to participate in athletics (8 NYCRR §200.2(b)(1)) .

Actual knowledge by the disabled students' parents of school district extracurricular programs and activities does not relieve the school district of its obligation to notify students with disabilities and their parents of these activities *(Application of a Child with a Handicapping Condition,* 30 Educ. Dep't Rep. 293 (1991)).

School districts, however, are not obligated to ensure that disabled children participate in all extracurricular activities which the parents or the child choose *(Application of the Board of Educ. of the East Syracuse-Minoa Central School Dist.,* SRO dec. no. 92-11 (1992)).

Districts may make an individual determination concerning the qualifications of a student with a disability to participate in an extracurricular athletic activity. If refused participation, the student then may commence a special court proceeding to prevent the district from prohibiting participation (§ 3208-a(1)). If, as a result, the court mandates participation, the law absolves the district from liability under certain circumstances (§§ 3208-a(9), 3208-a(4)).

13:14. Must school districts provide special education and related services to students with disabilities who are placed by their parents in private schools?

Yes. Under the dual-enrollment provisions of the state Education Law, districts must provide special education and related services to private school students with disabilities (§ 3602-c; *Application of a Child with a Handicapping Condition*, SRO dec. no. 91-13 (1991); see *Benjamin P. v. City of Lackawanna*, 23 IDELR 430 (W.D.N.Y. 1995)).

A school district, however, is not responsible for the student's tuition at the private school unless the parents have placed the student at the private school because they disagree with the program or placement recommended by the district, and they meet certain other conditions (see **13:36**).

13:15. May school districts provide on-site special education and related services to students with disabilities who attend private schools, including parochial schools?

Yes. Under the federal Individuals with Disabilities Education Act (IDEA), special education services may be provided to students with disabilities on the premises of private schools, including parochial schools, to the extent consistent with law (20 USC § 1412(a)(10)(A)(i)). The United States Supreme Court has ruled that the federal constitution does not prevent a school district from providing services to students on-site at the premises of their parochial school (*Agostini v. Felton*, 117 S.Ct. 1997 (1997)).

A school district is not required under federal law to provide on-site special education services to children with disabilities voluntarily enrolled in private schools. However, it is still an open question as to whether state law requires public school districts to provide such on-site services. (*Russman by Russman v. Mills*, 1998 WL 417452 (2nd Cir. 1998) see **13:14**).

In an earlier case, the New York State Court of Appeals ruled that a public school district was not required to provide special education services to students voluntarily enrolled in a private school on the private school premises (*Board of Educ. of Monroe-Woodbury CSD v. Wieder*, 72 N.Y.2d 174 (1988)).

13:16. What procedural safeguards must a school district provide to parents of a student with a disability?

The procedural safeguards provided include the parents' right to:

- Receive prior written notice whenever the district proposes or refuses to initiate or change the identification, evaluation, educational placement or provision of a free appropriate education.
- Examine all records pertaining to the child.
- Give parental consent for evaluations and reevaluations.
- Participate in committee on special education (CSE) and committee on preschool special education (CPSE) meetings with respect to the identification, evaluation and educational placement of the child.
- Obtain an independent evaluation of the child.
- Present complaints to the school district over the identification, evaluation or educational placement of a disabled child, or the provision of a free appropriate public education.
- Appeal adverse findings and decisions in an impartial hearing, including the right to disclosure of evaluation results and recommendations.
- Have the student remain in his or her then current educational placement during the pendency of due process proceedings, subject to certain exceptions.
- An explanation of the procedures for students who are subject to placement in an interim alternative educational setting.
- An explanation of the requirements for unilateral placement by parents in private schools at public expense.
- Mediation.
- Attorneys' fees.
- Request a school physician to participate in committee meetings.
- Request an interpreter, translator or reader for the meeting and be accompanied at such meetings by such individuals as the parent may desire.
- A list of free or low-cost legal assistance (20 USC § 1415(d); 8 NYCRR § 200.5).

13:17. Must a school district provide written notice of the procedural safeguards?

Yes. A school district must give parents written notice of the procedural safeguards upon:

- A child's referral for evaluation.
- Reevaluation.
- Each notification of an individualized education program (IEP) meeting.

- Each registration of a parental complaint relating to the identification, evaluation, or educational placement of the child, or the provision of a free appropriate public education.
- Each notification of a decision to place a child with a disability in an interim alternative placement as permitted by law, or take disciplinary action which involves a change in placement for more than 10 days (20 USC §§ 1415(d)(2); 1415(k)(4)(A)(i); 8 NYCRR § 200.5); see "Guidelines on Implementation of the Reauthorization of the Individuals with Disabilities Education Act," State Education Department, January 1998, for the required contents of the notice).

The Committee on Special Education

13:18. What is the function of a school district's committee on special education?

The primary function of the committee on special education (CSE) is to identify, evaluate, review the status of, and make recommendations concerning the appropriate educational placement of each school-age child with a disability, or thought to have a disability, who resides within the school district (8 NYCRR §§ 200.3; 200.4).

The CSE must also make an annual report to the school board on the status of services and facilities made available by the district for children with disabilities (Educ. Law § 4402(1)(b)(3)((f)). The CSE is also responsible for maintaining and annually revising the register of children with disabilities who are entitled to attend public school during the next school year or those referred to the committee (8 NYCRR § 200.2(a)).

13:19. Who are the members of a school district's committee on special education?

A committee on special education (CSE) must include the following members:

- The parent of the child with a disability.
- A regular education teacher (if the child is, or may be, participating in the regular education environment).
- A representative of the school district who is:
    (1) qualified to provide or supervise the provision of specifically-designed instruction to meet the unique needs of children with disabilities;
    (2) knowledgeable about the general curriculum, and
    (3) knowledgeable about the availability of resources of the district.

- A special education teacher, or where appropriate, a special education provider of such child.
- An individual who can interpret the instructional implications of evaluation results (may also be one of the above district team members).
- At the discretion of the parent or the district, other individuals who have knowledge or special expertise regarding the child, including related services personnel.
- A school psychologist.
- A school physician, if requested by the parents or the school district 72 hours before a meeting
- A parent of a child with a disability residing in the district, provided that parent is not employed by or under contract with the school district.
- Where appropriate, the child with a disability (20 USC § 1414(d)(1)(B); (Educ. Law § 4402(1)(b)(1)).

13:20. May a school district have more than one committee on special education (CSE)?

Yes. Buffalo, New York City, Rochester, Syracuse and Yonkers must establish CSE subcommittees to the extent necessary to ensure the timely evaluation and placement of students with disabilities. Other school districts also may establish CSE subcommittees but are not required to do so (Educ. Law § 4402(1); 8 NYCRR § 200.3(c)). The CSE, however, remains responsible for overseeing and monitoring the activities of each subcommittee to assure compliance with the requirements of applicable law and regulations (§ 4402(1)(b)(1)(b)).

13:21. Who are the members of a CSE subcommittee?

A CSE subcommittee must include the following members:
- The parent of the child with a disability.
- A regular education teacher (if the child is, or may be, participating in the regular education environment).
- A representative of the school district who is:
  (1) qualified to provide or supervise the provision of specifically designed instruction to meet the unique needs of children with disabilities,
  (2) knowledgeable about the general curriculum, and
  (3) knowledgeable about the availability of resources of the district.
- A special education teacher, or where appropriate, a special education provider of such child.

- An individual who can interpret the instructional implications of evaluation results (may also be one of the above district team members).
- At the discretion of the parent or the district, other individuals who have knowledge or special expertise regarding the child, including related services personnel.
- A school psychologist, whenever a new psychological evaluation is reviewed or a change to a program option with a more intensive staff/student ratio, as set forth in part 200.6(f)(4) of the commissioner's regulations, is required.
- Where appropriate, the child with a disability (20 USC § 1414(d)(1)(B); (Educ. Law § 4402(1)(b)(1); 8 NYCRR § 200.3(c)).

13:22. Is there any difference in function between a committee on special education (CSE) and a CSE subcommittee?

A CSE subcommittee performs the same functions as a CSE, except that the CSE remains responsible for deciding cases concerning the initial placement of a student in a special class, the initial placement of a student in a special class outside of the student's school of attendance and the placement of a student in a school primarily serving children with disabilities or a school outside the student's district (Educ. Law § 4402; 8 NYCRR § 200.3(c)(4)).

In addition, a CSE subcommittee must report to the CSE annually on the status of each student with a disability under its jurisdiction (8 NYCRR § 200.3(c)(6)). Upon written parental request, the CSE subcommittee also must refer to the CSE for review any of its recommendations not acceptable to the parent (8 NYCRR § 200.3(c)(5)).

13:23. What happens if the school board disagrees with the recommendation of the committee on special education or the subcommittee on special education?

If a school board disagrees with either committee's recommendation, it may follow one of the following procedures:
- Return the recommendation to the committee with a statement of the board's objections or concerns. The committee must then consider the board's objections or concerns, revise the individualized education program (IEP) where appropriate, and resubmit a recommendation to the board. If the board continues to disagree with the recommendation, it may either continue to return the recommendation to the original committee for additional review or establish a second committee to develop a new recommendation.

• Establish a second committee to develop a new recommendation. If the board disagrees with the recommendation of the second committee, it may return the recommendation to the second committee with a statement of its objections or concerns. The second committee then must consider the board's objections or concerns, revise the IEP where appropriate and resubmit a recommendation to the board. If the board continues to disagree with the revised recommendation, it may continue to return the recommendation to the second committee for additional review.

Once a school board establishes a second CSE, the board may not select the recommendation of the initial CSE.

Under either procedure, the school board must arrange for the programs and services in accordance with an IEP within 60 days of receiving the consent to evaluate a student not previously identified as a student with a disability, or within 60 days of the referral for review of the child with a disability (8 NYCRR § 200.4(d)).

13:24. Is a school district required to notify parents of its proposal or refusal to initiate or change the identification, evaluation or placement of a child with a disability?

Yes. A school district is required to give parents written notice of its proposal or refusal to initiate or change the identification, evaluation or placement of a child with a disability, along with a description of:

• An explanation of its decision.
• Other options considered and why they were rejected.
• Each evaluation procedure, test, record, or report used as a basis for its action, as well as other factors relevant to the district's decision.

The notice must also include a statement that parents of a student with a disability have procedural protections under the Individuals with Disabilities Education Act (IDEA). Additionally, if the notice is not an initial referral for evaluation, it must also inform the parent how to obtain a copy of the procedural safeguards, and where to obtain assistance in understanding parental rights under IDEA (20 USC § 1415(c)).

13:25. How often must a school district's committee on special education (CSE) review a student's individualized education program (IEP)?

Each student's IEP must be reviewed and, if appropriate, revised periodically, but it must be done at least annually. The review must be based on an assessment of the IEP and other current information pertaining to the student's performance. The review must consider the educational progress and achievement of the student with a disability and the student's ability to participate in instructional programs in regular education (20 USC § 1414(d)(4); 8 NYCRR § 200.4(e)).

In addition, the CSE must arrange for an appropriate reevaluation of each student with a disability if conditions warrant a reevaluation or if the child's parent or teacher requests a reevaluation, and at least every three years (20 USC § 1414(a)(2); 8 NYCRR § 200.4(e)(4)).

A school district may continue to develop and review a student's IEP and placement during the pendency of litigation concerning a prior IEP or placement. According to one federal court, to prohibit such efforts would require school districts to violate their statutory duties under the Individuals with Disabilities Education Act (*Norma P. v. Pelham School Dist.*, 19 IDELR 938 (1993)).

13:26. Is parental consent required before the committee on special education conducts an initial evaluation of a child suspected of having a disability or for any reevaluation of a child with a disability?

Yes. Informed parental consent is necessary for both an initial evaluation of a child suspected of having a disability, and for any reevaluation of a child with a disability before the initial evaluation or reevaluation is conducted (20 USC §§ 1414(a)(1)(C); 1414(c)(3)).

If a parent fails to give consent for an initial evaluation, a school district may go to mediation and/or due process (20 USC §§ 1414(a)(C)(ii); 1415).

Parental consent for a reevaluation is not necessary if a school district has taken reasonable measures to obtain such consent and the child's parent has failed to respond (20 USC § 1414(c)(3)).

13:27. Must a parent of a disabled student be present at the committee on special education (CSE) or CSE subcommittee meeting where his or her child is being discussed?

A parent of a child with a disability is a mandated member of the CSE or the CSE subcommittee and should be present at all meetings of the committee in which his or her child is being discussed (20 USC § 1414(d)(1)(B)). According to the State Education Department, a telephone conference involving the parent is a permissible strategy to involve the parent in the individualized education program (IEP) development process.

However, a meeting may be conducted without the parent in attendance, if the school district is unable to convince the parent that he or she should attend. The district must have a record of the attempts it made to arrange for a mutually agreed on time and place for the meeting, such as detailed records of phone calls, copies of correspondence and detailed records of visits to the parent "Guidance on Implementation of the Reauthorization of the Individuals with Disabilities Education Act," State Education Department, January 1998, pp. 16-17)).

13:28. May a parent tape-record his or her child's committee on special education (CSE) or CSE subcommittee meeting?

Yes. A parent may tape-record his or her own child's CSE or CSE sub-committee meeting without approval by the CSE, CSE subcommittee or school board. However, the parent may forfeit the right to tape-record future proceedings if there are circumstances that indicate this right is being abused. A school district also must be permitted to tape-record CSE or CSE subcommittee meetings at its option *(Application of a Child with a Handicapping Condition,* 30 Educ. Dep't Rep. 178 (1990)).

13:29. May the school attorney attend a school district's committee on special education (CSE) or CSE subcommittee meetings?

Yes. However, school attorneys should attend CSE or CSE subcommittee meetings only on those rare occasions when the committee's ability to perform its functions depends on the immediate resolution of critical legal issues. The school attorney should not become a listening post for the school board, nor may he or she attend CSE or CSE subcommittee meetings to intimidate parents or undermine the decision-making process *(Application of a Child with a Handicapping Condition,* 30 Educ. Dep't Rep. 286 (1991)).

Parental Challenges

13:30. May the parents of a disabled student challenge the actions taken by the committee on special education (CSE), CSE subcommittee or the school board regarding the classification, evaluation or placement of the student?

Yes. Parents who disagree with the actions taken by either the committee on special education (CSE), CSE subcommittee, and/or the school board concerning the classification, evaluation or placement of their child may request, in writing, an impartial due process hearing. The school board then must appoint an impartial hearing officer to hear the appeal and make appropriate recommendations to resolve the issue (Educ. Law § 4404(1); 8 NYCRR § 200.5(c)).

13:31. How are impartial hearing officers selected?

School districts appoint impartial hearing officers on a rotation basis, according to a selection process established by the commissioner of education. Individuals employed by a school district, school, or program serving disabled students placed by a CSE may not serve as impartial hearing officers while employed as such and for a period of two years after they cease working for these employers (Educ. Law § 4404(1); 8 NYCRR §§ 200.1(s), 200.5(c); 200.21; *Application of a Child with a Disability (Canastota CSD)*, SRO dec. no. 96-84 (1996)).

13:32. May an impartial hearing officer's determination be appealed?

Yes. The hearing officer's decision may be appealed to the state review officer at the State Education Department (§ 4404(2); 8 NYCRR § 200.5(d)).

The state review officer's decision may, in turn, be appealed to the New York State Supreme Court or federal district court (20 USC § 1415(i)(2); § 4404(3); 8 NYCRR § 200.5(d)).

13:33. Are school districts liable for the cost of attorneys' fees and expert witnesses incurred by the parents of a child with a disability during an appeal of the district's determination regarding the classification, evaluation or placement of the student?

Yes, if the parents are the prevailing party (20 USC § 1415(i)(3); *Aranow v. District of Columbia*, 18 IDELR 962 (1992)). To successfully claim prevailing party status, the parents must show that they obtained a decision which altered the legal relationship between the school district and the disabled student, and that the decision fosters the provision of a free, appropriate public education to students with disabilities (see *Angela L. v. Pasadena Independent School District*, 918 F.2d 1188 (5th Cir. 1990)).

Attorneys' fees may not be awarded for an attorney's attendance at an individualized education program (IEP) meeting, unless the meeting is convened as a result of an administrative proceeding or judicial action, or at the discretion of the state, for mediation that is conducted prior to the filing of a complaint (20 USC § 1415(i)(3)(D)(ii)). Attorneys' fees may not be awarded under certain circumstances for services performed after a written offer of settlement is made to a parent (20 USC § 1415(i)(3)(D)(i),(E)). In addition, attorneys' fees may be reduced under certain circumstances (20 USC §1415(i)(3)(F),(G)).

Courts have refused to award attorneys' fees to pro se litigants (litigants who represent themselves) even when the litigant is an attorney (*Rappaport v. Vance*, 19 IDELR 770 (1993)). However, attorneys' fees may be awarded despite the fact that the parents were represented by a publicly-funded attorney (*Yankton School Dist. v. Schramm*, 93 F.3d 1369 (1996)).

13:34. What happens to a student with a disability while proceedings regarding his or her classification, evaluation or academic placement take place?

With the exception of certain disciplinary proceedings, during the pendency of any proceedings challenging the classification, evaluation and placement of a student with a disability, that student must remain in his or her current educational placement unless the school district and the parent agree otherwise. This is what is referred to as the "stay-put" requirement. A student applying for initial admission to a public school must be placed in the public school program until all such proceedings have been completed (20 USC § 1415(j); Educ. Law § 4404(4); 8 NYCRR §200.5(a)(2)(iii); see **13:39**).

13:35. Do parents of a child with a disability have a right to an independent educational evaluation (IEE) of their child at public expense?

Yes, if they disagree with the evaluation obtained by the school district. However, the district may initiate a hearing to show that its evaluation is appropriate. If the hearing officer finds the school district's evaluation is appropriate, the parents still may obtain an IEE but not at public expense (20 USC § 1415(d)(2)(A); 8 NYCRR § 200.5(a)(1)(vi)(a); *Application of a Child with a Handicapping Condition,* 30 Educ. Dep't Rep. 108 (1990)).

Independent educational evaluations obtained by the parent at public expense must be subject to the same criteria which the school district uses when it initiates an evaluation, including the location of the evaluation and the qualifications of the examiner (8 NYCRR §§ 200.1(u); 200.5(a)(1)(vi)(a)). Upper limits on the costs of particular tests may not simply be an average of fees customarily charged by professionals in the area, but must permit parents to choose from among qualified individuals in the area *(Application of a Child with a Handicapping Condition,* SRO dec. no. 92-35 (1992); 93-26 (1993)).

13:36. May parents unilaterally place their child with a disability in a private school, if they disagree with the school district's determination concerning their child, and be reimbursed by the district for the cost of the placement?

Yes, subject to certain conditions. Under the Individuals with Disabilities Education Act (IDEA), a parent who disagrees with a school district's placement and proceeds to enroll his or her child in a private school may be entitled to tuition reimbursement if a court or hearing officer determines that the school district did not make a free appropriate public education available to the child in a timely manner (20 USC § 1412(a)(10)(C)(ii)).

However, tuition reimbursement may be denied or reduced if the parents failed to give the school district notice at the most recent individualized education program (IEP) meeting that they were rejecting the proposed placement, stating their concerns, and their intent to enroll the child in a private school at public expense, or failed to provide 10 business days (including any holidays that occur on a business day) written notice to the district prior to removing the child (20 USC § 1412(a)(10)(C)(iii)(I)).

Parental notice will be excused if the parent is illiterate and cannot write English, if compliance would likely result in physical or serious emotional harm to the child, if the school prevented the parent from providing such notice or if the parents were not notified of the notice requirement (20 USC § 1412(a)(10(C)(iv)).

In addition, tuition reimbursement may be reduced or denied if the school district gave the parents written notice of its intent to evaluate the child and the reasons for the evaluation prior to the parents' removal of the child, but the parents failed to make the child available for the evaluation (20 USC § 1412(a)(10)(C)(iii)(II)).

According to the United States Supreme Court, the parents of a student with a disability may be awarded reimbursement for private school placement, even though the private school does not meet state educational agency standards. Courts, however, may consider whether the private school costs are reasonable *(Florence County School District Four v. Carter,* 510 U.S. 7 (1993)). Further ruling that parents are not required to place their children at state-approved schools, the United States Supreme Court in *Carter* explained that parents cannot be held to the same standards as public school districts when arranging for the placement of their children.

13:37. May parents unilaterally place their child with a disability in another public school district, if they disagree with the school district's determination concerning their child, and be reimbursed by the school district of residence for the cost of the placement?

Yes. Parents may be entitled to reimbursement for tuition paid to another public school district and for reasonable transportation costs after the parents remove their child from the school district of residence because they are dissatisfied with the special education services provided to their child *(Northeast CSD v. Sobol,* 79 N.Y.2d 598 (1992)).

Disciplining Students with Disabilities

13:38. May a student with a disability be suspended from school?

Yes. The general rule is that a disciplinary suspension of a student with a disability for more than 10 days under federal law constitutes a change in placement. This action requires compliance with the procedural safeguards afforded students with disabilities, including referral to the committee on special education (CSE), and the right of the disabled student to remain in the "current educational placement" pending all appeals, unless the student's parent agrees to an interim placement (20 USC §§ 1415(j); 1415(k)(1)(A)(i); *Honig v. Doe*, 484 U.S. 305 (1988); see Educ. Law § 3214).

In addition, under New York law, all students are entitled to certain other procedural safeguards for suspensions beyond five days, whether or not they are disabled (see **12:104**). The school district must conduct a disciplinary hearing to determine if the student is guilty of the misconduct before a suspension penalty beyond five days can be imposed (§ 3214(3)(c)). In the case of students with disabilities, consistent with federal law, upon a finding of guilt, a determination must also be made as to whether the student's misconduct was related to his or her disability. If a connection exists, no further penalty may be imposed. The student must be referred to the CSE for possible program modification. If no connection is found, the student is still entitled to due process protection regarding any change in placement, discussed above *(Appeal of a Student with a Disability,* 35 Educ. Dep't Rep. 22 (1995)). The same applies to declassified students and to certain students suspected of being disabled (20 USC § 1415(k)(8)(A)); *Appeal of a Student Suspected of Having a Disability,* 35 Educ. Dep't Rep. 492 (1996); see **13:42**).

13:39. Under what circumstances may a school district remove a student with disabilities from school beyond 10 days without parental consent?

A school district may place a student in an interim alternative placement for up to 45 days under the following circumstances:

- The child carries a weapon to school, or a school function.
- The child knowingly possesses or uses illegal drugs or sells or solicits the sale of a controlled substance while at school or a school function.

In addition, the school district can seek permission to place a child in an interim alternative placement if it can demonstrate to an impartial hearing officer by substantial evidence that maintaining the current placement of such child is substantially likely to result in injury to the child or others, and the district has taken steps to minimize the risk of harm in the child's current placement (20 USC § 1415(k)(1)(A); 1415(k)(2)).

The committee on special education (CSE) determines the interim alternative setting (20 USC § 1415(k)(3)).

13:40. What constitutes an appropriate interim alternative placement for a student with a disability who is removed from his or her current placement for more than 10 days?

An interim alternative setting is appropriate if it enables the student to continue to participate in the general curriculum, although in another setting, and to receive services and modifications, including those in his or her current individualized education program (IEP), that will allow the child to meet the goals of the IEP. The interim alternative setting must include services and modifications designed to address the behavior so that it does not reoccur (20 USC § 1415(k)(3)(B)(ii)).

While a school district is not required to conduct a manifestation determination as to whether the student's misconduct was related to his or her disability for suspensions for five days or less, only those records of the student's behavior which have been found not to have a nexus with the student's disability may be considered in imposing a disciplinary penalty. In addition, a penalty may not be based on behavior for which no nexus determination was made. Thus, it is inappropriate for a hearing officer in a disciplinary proceeding to consider short-term suspensions for which there is no determination as to whether the student's behavior was disability-related (*Appeal of a Student with a Disability*, 36 Educ. Dep't Rep. 273 (1996)).

13:41. Are there any special procedures which a school district must follow when removing a student from school beyond 10 days without parental consent?

Yes. The committee on special education (CSE) must make a manifestation determination as to the relationship between the child's disability and his or her behavior whenever a school district contemplates placing the child in an interim alternative setting for misconduct involving weapons, drugs or controlled substances, or for any other violation of a school rule or code of conduct where disciplinary action involves a change in placement for more than 10 days, immediately if possible, but no later than 10 days after the date on which the decision to take action is made (20 USC § 1415(k)(4)).

In addition, the CSE, either before or not later than 10 days after placing a child with a disability in an interim alternative setting, must develop an assessment plan to address the behavior if it had not conducted a functional behavioral assessment and implemented a behavioral intervention plan for such a child before the behavior occurred, or review and modify the plan, as necessary, to address the behavior if the child already has a behavioral intervention plan (20 USC § 1415(k)(1)(B)).

13:42. Are the due process safeguards governing the discipline of disabled students applicable to short-term suspensions lasting less than 10 days?

No, except for suspensions of more than five days under New York state law (see **13:38**) and successive short-term suspensions totaling more than 10 days over a short period of time *(Application of a Child with a Handicapping Condition,* 28 Educ. Dep't Rep. 342 (1989)).

While an isolated short-term suspension is not a change in placement requiring compliance with procedural safeguards, such as referral to the committee on special education (CSE), successive short-term suspensions over a brief period of time are equivalent to a change of placement. The CSE then must follow the procedures established under article 89 of the Education Law, including maintaining the "current educational placement" while appeals are pending *(Application of a Child with a Handicapping Condition).*

13:43. Are due process safeguards concerning the discipline of disabled students applicable to students who have not been classified as students with disabilities?

Yes, under certain circumstances. The procedural safeguards which apply to students with disabilities apply equally to children who have not been determined to be eligible for special education and related services if the school district has knowledge, as defined by statute, that the child was a child with a disability before the misconduct occurred (20 USC § 1415(k)(8)(A)).

In addition, certain due process safeguards apply to students who have been declassified but later exhibit behavioral problems *(Appeal of a Student Suspected of Having a Disability (South Country CSD),* 35 Educ. Dep't Rep. 492 (1996)).

13:44. Are students with disabilities subject to a school district's attendance policy?

Yes. However, a school district may not apply its attendance policy to a student with disabilities in order to deny the student course credit where the absences are related to the student's disability or to a medical condition which would constitute a handicap under section 504 of the Rehabilitation Act (*Appeal of a Child with a Handicapping Condition*, 32 Educ. Dep't Rep. 56 (1992)).

Preschool Children with Disabilities

13:45. What are the school districts' responsibilities in regard to preschool special education?

School boards must adopt a written policy that establishes administrative practices and procedures to ensure that each preschool child with a disability can participate in preschool programs approved by the commissioner of education (8 NYCRR § 200.2(b)(2)). School districts, for instance, must identify, evaluate, refer, place and review the placement of preschool children (age three and four) with disabilities, including children enrolled in Head Start programs (20 USC § 1400 *et seq;* Educ. Law § 4410; 8 NYCRR §§ 200.2(a)(1), 200.16; OSEP Response to Inquiry, 18 IDELR 596 (1992)).

Every school board also must appoint and train qualified personnel to a committee on preschool special education (CPSE), which makes recommendations on the identification, evaluation, and appropriate services for these children (20 USC § 1413(a)(3); § 4410(3); 8 NYCRR §§ 200.2(b)(3), 200.3(a)(2), 200.16), and ensure the allocation of appropriate space within the district for special education programs that meet the needs of preschool students with disabilities (Educ. Law § 4410; 8 NYCRR §§ 200.1, 200.2(c)(2)(v), 200.7, 216).

13:46. What types of services and programs must school districts provide to preschool children with disabilities?

Preschool children with disabilities are entitled, for example, to special education itinerant services and to the same type of related services available to school-age children with disabilities (Educ. Law § 4410(1)(j),(k)). Special education itinerant services may be provided as part of an approved program given by a certified special education teacher in accordance with the regulations of the commissioner of education, at sites determined in the same way as for the provision of related services (§ 4410(1)(k)).

Related services need not be provided in conjunction with a program at a facility approved or licensed by a government agency. They can be provided at a site determined by the school board, including, but not limited to, an approved or licensed prekindergarten or Head Start program, the work site of the provider, a hospital, a state facility, or a child-care location, including the child's home or a place where care for less than 24 hours a day is provided on a regular basis, such as day care centers, family day care homes and in-home care by persons other than parents. A preschool child with disabilities is entitled to receive services at home if the documented medical or special needs indicate the child should not be transported to another site (§ 4410(1)(j)).

Prior to recommending any program, the CPSE should consider the appropriateness of providing related services or special education itinerant services only, related services in coordination with special education itinerant services, and a half-day or full-day program. Special education services must be provided consistent with least restricted environment requirements (§ 4410(5)(b)(i)). Whenever possible, school districts should select related service providers employed by a single agency (8 NYCRR § 200.16(e)(2)).

13:47. Who is responsible for coordinating the provision of related and itinerant special education services to preschool children with disabilities?

When the committee on preschool special education (CPSE) recommends two or more related services, the school board designates one of the providers as coordinator. When special education itinerant services are provided in conjunction with one or more related services, the special education itinerant service provider must serve as the coordinator (8 NYCRR § 200.16(e)(2)).

13:48. What is the difference between a committee on special education (CSE) and a committee on preschool special education (CPSE)?

Generally, the CSE addresses the needs of school-age children with disabilities, while the CPSE focuses on the needs of preschool children with disabilities. However, generally speaking, parental rights and district responsibilities governing the CSE also apply to the CPSE.

A CSE and a CPSE also are made up of different members. The CPSE must include the following members:

- The parent of the child with a disability.
- A regular education teacher (if the child is, or may be, participating in the regular education environment).
- A representative of the school district who
    (1) is qualified to provide or supervise the provision of specifically designed instruction to meet the unique needs of children with disabilities;

(2) is knowledgeable about the general curriculum; and

(3) is knowledgeable about the availability of resources of the district. This individual serves as the chairperson of the committee.

- A special education teacher, or where appropriate, a special education provider of such child.
- An individual who can interpret the instructional implications of evaluation results (may also be one of the above district team members).
- At the discretion of the parent or the district, other individuals who have knowledge or special expertise regarding the child, including related services personnel.
- A parent of a child with disabilities who resides in the district and whose child is enrolled in a preschool or elementary-level education program, as long as that parent is not employed by the school district or municipality responsible for the child.
- For a child evaluated for the first time, the CPSE must also include a professional who has evaluated the child or an appropriate professional employed by the school district who is knowledgeable about the evaluation procedures used with the child and familiar with the results of the evaluation. This individual must be someone other than the CPSE chairperson, the child's teacher or other person present at the meeting.
- For a child in transition from early intervention programs and services (infant and toddler programs), the appropriately licensed or certified professional from the Department of Health's Early Intervention Program. This professional must attend all meetings of the CPSE conducted prior to the child's initial receipt of services.
- Whenever appropriate, the student with a disability.

An appropriately certified or licensed professional from the municipality should also attend; however, attendance of the appointee of the municipality is not required for a quorum. Parents have the right, however, to invite the child's evaluator to attend and participate at the CPSE meeting. No approved evaluator shall vote on a CPSE recommendation (Educ. Law § 4410(3)(a), (f); see **13:19; 13:21** for the membership of the CSE).

Specific responsibilities for each committee are set forth in the Education Law sections 4402 and 4410; and part 200 of the commissioner's regulations.

14. Instruction and Curricula

14:1. How is a school district's instructional plan organized?

A school district's instructional plan is organized around the school calendar, which indicates the number of days school will be in session, holidays, vacation, snow days and other pertinent information.

14:2. Is there an official school year?

The Education Law defines the school year as the period commencing on the first day of July in each year and ending on June 30 of the next year (§ 2(15)). However, court decisions have recognized that the normal instructional year extends from September through June (see *Schneps v. Nyquist*, 58 A.D.2d 151 (3rd Dep't), *appeal denied*, 42 N.Y.2d 808 (1977)).

14:3. Who determines the exact length of a school district's school year?

Local school districts determine the number of days that their schools will be in session and when personnel must report for duty (*City School Dist. v. Helsby*, 42 A.D.2d 262 (3rd Dep't 1973)). The State Education Department does not determine the local school year.

Additionally, school boards have discretion in dividing the school year into semesters and marking periods and, following negotiation with the appropriate bargaining units, to expand the number of instructional days for their districts.

14:4. Is there a minimum number of school days in a school year?

Yes. Section 3204(4) of the Education Law provides that school must be in session 190 days each year for instructional purposes, inclusive of legal holidays that occur during the school term and exclusive of Saturdays. The law also requires 180 days of instruction for state aid purposes (§ 3604(7)).

In general, no school may be in session on a Saturday or a legal holiday, except Election Day and Washington's and Lincoln's birthdays. However, driver education classes may be held on Saturdays (§ 3604(8)). Also, school authorities in a district having fewer than 600 students may provide classes for the disadvantaged on any day of the week, including Saturday and Sunday (§ 3604(8-b)).

The financial apportionment from the state will be reduced by 1/180th for each day less than 180 days the school actually is in session. However, the commissioner of education may disregard this reduction for up to five days for certain reasons, such as adverse weather or a break-down of school facilities, where it is demonstrated that the district cannot make up such lost days of instruction during the school year (§ 3604(7)).

For further information concerning the length of the school year, see the "School Executive's Bulletin" (State Education Department, February/March 1998).

14:5. What are the public holidays in New York State?

Section 24 of the General Construction Law lists the following public holidays in New York:

- New Year's Day (January 1)
- Dr. Martin Luther King, Jr. Day (third Monday in January)
- Lincoln's Birthday (February 12)
- Washington's Birthday (third Monday in February)
- Memorial Day (last Monday in May)
- Independence Day (July 4)
- Flag Day (second Sunday in June)
- Labor Day (first Monday in September)
- Columbus Day (second Monday in October)
- Veterans Day (November 11)
- Thanksgiving Day (fourth Thursday in November)
- Christmas Day (December 25)

In addition, each general election day and any day appointed by the president of the United States or by the governor of New York State "as a day of general thanksgiving, general fasting and prayer, or for other general religious observances" may be declared public holidays (Gen. Constr. Law § 24; see also **14:4**). This generally has been interpreted to include Sundays.

14:6. Is there a minimum number of hours in a school day for public schools in New York State?

Yes. Section 175.5 of the commissioner's regulations lists the minimum daily session lengths for students. To qualify for apportionment of state aid, schools must be in session as follows:

- The daily sessions for students in half-day kindergarten must be a minimum of two-and-one-half hours.
- The daily sessions for students in full-day kindergarten and grades one through six must be a minimum of five hours, exclusive of the time allowed for lunch.
- The daily sessions for students in grades seven through 12 must be

a minimum of five-and-one-half hours, exclusive of the time allowed for lunch (8 NYCRR § 175.5(a)).

There is no maximum number of hours in a school day and there is no requirement in law concerning the time of day classes must be held.

14:7. What are the minimum school-day hours for schools that operate on double or overlapping (split) sessions?

To qualify for apportionment of state aid, schools that operate on double or overlapping (split) sessions, provided the written approval of the commissioner of education to operate such sessions has been obtained before the scheduling of such sessions for any school year, must meet the following minimum-hours requirements:

- The daily sessions for students in half-day kindergarten must be a minimum of two hours.
- The daily sessions for students in full-day kindergarten and grades one through six must be a minimum of four hours, exclusive of the time allowed for lunch.
- The daily sessions for students in grades seven through 12 must be a minimum of four-and-one-half hours, exclusive of the time allowed for lunch (8 NYCRR § 175.5(c)).

14:8. Are school districts required to offer a kindergarten program?

No. It is within the discretion of the school board to offer a kindergarten program to students between the ages of four and six years old. The school board may fix a higher minimum age for admission to kindergarten (§ 1712).

However, children over the age of five years are entitled to attend the public schools in the district, regardless of whether or not the district maintains a kindergarten program. These children would be entitled to be admitted to the first grade. A board is not required to admit a child who becomes five after the school year has commenced unless the child's birthday occurs on or before December 1 (§ 3202(1); *Appeal of Carney*, 15 Educ. Dep't Rep. 325 (1976); Formal Opinion of Counsel 75, 1 Educ. Dep't Rep. 775 (1952); see **12:6**)).

14:9. Are school districts required to offer a prekindergarten program?

No. It is up to each local school board to decide whether or not to offer a prekindergarten program. Some school districts qualify for the New York State Experimental Pre-kindergarten Program, created to provide early intervention services related to school preparation to disadvantaged or at-risk children (§ 3602-a(15)). This program still operates in approximately 99 school districts and BOCES throughout the state.

In addition, Chapter 436 of the Laws of 1998 established a universal prekindergarten program, which is eventually intended to serve those four-year-olds who are not served by the experimental prekindergarten program or a full-day special education prekindergarten program. The program is optional at the discretion of the school board and not all school districts in the state are eligible to participate. In the 1998-99 school year approximately 125 school districts qualified under the law and were therefore eligible to receive between $2,700 and $4,000 per pupil in state grant moneys (§ 3609).

The program is expected to be fully phased in by the 2002-03 school year when all school districts in the state will be eligible to participate (§ 3602-e).

Further information on this program may be obtained from the State Education Department's Child, Family and Community Services Team at 518-474-5807 or at http://www.nysed.gov.

14:10. Who determines whether or not a school district will offer a prekindergarten program?

The school board is ultimately responsible for determining whether or not to offer a prekindergarten program. However, under the law, all eligible districts must form a prekindergarten policy advisory board appointed by the superintendent which must include members of the school board, teachers employed by the district as selected by their respective collective bargaining unit, parents of children who attend the district's schools, community leaders and child care and early education providers (§ 3602-e(3)).

14:11. When must an eligible school district form a prekindergarten policy advisory board?

School districts are not required to form the advisory board until the school year immediately preceding the school year in which funds will first become available to the district (Memorandum from James Kadamus, Deputy Commissioner for Elementary, Middle, Secondary and Continuing Education, State Education Department, March 1998). The commissioner of education will notify eligible districts by November 15 of each year.

14:12. What is the role of the prekindergarten policy advisory board?

The advisory board must submit a recommendation to the school board as to whether or not the district should offer a prekindergarten program. Prior to reaching its determination, the advisory board must hold at least one public hearing to provide an opportunity for input from parents, school personnel, child-care providers and other interested members of the community. In reaching its recommendation, the advisory board must consider a number of factors set forth in the statute (§ 3602-e(3)(b)).

If the advisory board determines that it will recommend the implementation of a prekindergarten program, it must develop a prekindergarten plan and submit the same to the school board by a date determined by the commissioner of education (§ 3602-e(3)(c)).

14:13. Is a school board required to accept the recommendation of the prekindergarten policy advisory board?

No. The school board has 30 days from receiving such recommendation to adopt, reject or modify the recommendation and/or plan. However, if the board is considering modifying or rejecting the advisory board's recommendation and/or plan, it must hold a public meeting with the advisory board to discuss it (§ 3602-e).

If the board adopts a plan to implement a prekindergarten program, it must submit an application pursuant to the rules and regulations of the Board of Regents and the commissioner of education (§ 3602-e (5)).

Curriculum

Editor's Note: At press time, the State Education Department was in the process of revising part 100 of the commissioner's regulations which governs curriculum in public schools in the state. According to the State Education Department, the final regulations are not expected to be issued until February 1999. Therefore, readers should be cautioned that some of the material set forth in this section may be changed through new regulations introduced at that time.

14:14. Are there state-mandated learning standards?

Yes. The Education Law and the commissioner's regulations set forth specific subject areas in which instruction must be offered at the elementary and secondary school levels and the minimum units of study required in each of these areas for graduation (Educ. Law, Art. 17 and Art. 65; 8 NYCRR Part 100). While the State Education Department refers to them as learning standards, they are also commonly referred to as curricula, syllabi or courses of instruction.

School boards, however, are empowered to authorize the general courses of study offered in the schools and may exceed the state minimum requirements, provided these new course requirements are not arbitrary, capricious nor unreasonable, and do not supplant the state-mandated minimum units of study (*Appeal of O'Neill*, 29 Educ. Dep't Rep. 297 (1990); see **14:16-21**). The authority of school boards to determine what instructional programs will be offered is not subject to a public vote (*Appeal of Brush*, 34 Educ. Dep't Rep 274 (1994)).

14:15. What are the new learning standards?

The Board of Regents has adopted 28 learning standards to guide the development of local school curricula in the following areas: health, physical education, and family and consumer sciences; mathematics, science and technology; the arts; career development and occupational studies; English/language arts; languages other than English; and social studies.

In addition, the Regents have adopted new graduation standards and assessments correlated to the new learning standards. Once the new graduation requirements are fully phased in, Regents competency tests will be eliminated and all students will be required to pass Regents exams in English, science, mathematics, U.S. history and government, and global history. Successfully completed additional Regents exams will result in an advanced designation on a student's high school diploma (see **14:65-66**).

The Regents have endeavored to set higher standards of achievement by adopting these learning standards to make the curriculum more demanding. For example, the mathematics standards will require students to progress through algebra, geometry, trigonometry, mathematical reasoning, and statistics.

Toward this end, the Regents have endorsed more accurate measures of student achievement, such as performance-based assessments which include the maintenance of portfolios of students' work, and examinations which contain multiple-step questions that require students to demonstrate how they arrived at their answers.

14:16. What are the program requirements for students in grades prekindergarten and kindergarten?

Each school operating a prekindergarten and kindergarten program must provide an education program based on and adapted to the ages, interests and needs of the children. Required learning activities in such programs include development of communication skills and exposure to literature; dramatic play, creative art and music activities; participation in group projects, discussion and games; science and mathematical experiences; large-muscle activities in prekindergarten and instruction in physical education in kindergarten; and instruction in health education for students in kindergarten.

School districts must also develop procedures that invite the active participation of each child's parents or guardians in these programs (8 NYCRR § 100.3(a)).

14:17. What are the program requirements for students in grades one through six?

All students in grades one through six must receive instruction in arithmetic, reading, spelling, writing, the English language, geography, United States history, science, health education, music, visual arts, physical education, and bilingual education and/or English as a second language where student need is established (8 NYCRR §100.3(b)).

14:18. What are the program requirements for students in grades seven and eight?

By the end of the eighth grade, students must complete two years of English, social studies, science and mathematics; one year (one-half unit each) of art and music; one year of technology education; health education (one-half unit); physical education (not less than three times per week in one semester and two times per week in the other semester); three-quarters of a unit in home and career skills; and the equivalent of one period a week in library and information skills (8 NYCRR § 100.4; see **14:20-21** for foreign language and remediation requirements).

14:19. What are the graduation requirements for students in grades nine through 12?

All students are required to earn 18.5 units of credit for a local or Regents diploma (8 NYCRR § 100.5(a)(2)).

Core requirements for both diplomas include four units of English, four units of social studies, two units of science, two units of mathematics, one-half unit of health education and one unit of art or music. For a local diploma, the balance of units will be met through electives taken to fulfill sequence requirements (8 NYCRR § 100.5(c)(2)). For a Regents diploma, a student must complete three years of a second language in addition to sequence requirements (8 NYCRR § 100.5(b)(2)(i),(ii)). All students must earn the equivalent of two units of physical education, which do not count toward the required units of credit (8 NYCRR § 100.5(a)(3); see **14:20-21** for foreign language and remediation requirements).

In November of 1997, the Board of Regents approved a proposal to revise graduation requirements and directed the State Education Department to promulgate regulations accordingly. According to the State Education Department, the regulations are expected to be issued in February 1999. For the most current information on this subject, contact the State Education Department.

14:20. Are school districts required to provide instruction in a foreign language?

Yes. Currently, all districts are required to offer instruction in at least one foreign language in grades eight through 12. All public school students are required to complete two units of study in foreign language instruction by the end of the ninth grade. A student with a disability may be exempted by his or her individualized education program (IEP). Students who pass an approved proficiency examination by the end of the ninth grade will be awarded the first unit of academic credit in foreign language instruction (8 NYCRR § 100.2(d)). These requirements may be subject to change in light of the new learning standards (see **14:15; 14:19**).

14:21. Are school districts required to provide remediation?

Yes. The individual instructional needs of students scoring below the statewide reference points on standardized tests or failing required tests as described in the commissioner's regulations must be met through planned remedial course work. To facilitate remediation in grades seven and eight, instructional time in other required subjects may be reduced but not eliminated (8 NYCRR §§ 100.3(b)(3), 100.4(b)(5), 100.5(a)(4)(iii)).

14:22. May school districts establish curriculum requirements for a diploma above and beyond the minimum units of study required by the state for graduation?

Yes. School districts may impose, as part of a credit-bearing course of study, requirements that exceed the state's minimum requirements, provided the additional requirements are not arbitrary, capricious or unreasonable (*Appeal of O'Neill*, 29 Educ. Dep't Rep. 297 (1990)).

For example, in *Immediato v. Rye Neck Central School District*, 73 F.3d 454 (2nd Cir. 1996), *cert denied*, 117 S. Ct. 60 (1996)), the United States Court of Appeals for the Second Circuit upheld a district's community service program which required students to complete 40 hours of community service sometime during their four high-school years and to participate in corresponding classroom discussion about their service in order to earn a high school diploma. The program had no exceptions or opt-out provisions for students who objected to performing community service. The court recognized the district's interest in teaching students the values and habits of good citizenship, and introducing them to their social responsibilities as citizens.

The commissioner of education had reached a similar conclusion previously in *O'Neill*. However, the *Immediato* court cautioned that if students were required to wash their teachers' cars, paint their houses or weed their gardens, the extent, nature and conditions of "service" and the more exploitive purpose of the program might warrant a finding of involuntary servitude in violation of the 13th Amendment of the United States Constitution.

14:23. What authority does the State Education Department hold over the local school district in the matter of curriculum?

Before a district is entitled to receive state aid, the commissioner of education must be satisfied that proper instruction is given by qualified teachers for the required time (§ 3604(7)).

The Rules of the Board of Regents also state that no school district will receive any apportionment unless it submits all required reports, maintains an approved course of study, provides a school building and site that are in conformity with the Education Law, the commissioner's regulations and the Regents' rules, and meets all other requirements of law (8 NYCRR § 3.35). Lack of compliance also may result in loss of a school's charter or registration.

14:24. Are public schools required to follow specific state syllabi?

Generally, no. However, schools must make use of state syllabi in certain circumstances in mathematics, science and occupational education in grades nine through 12 (8 NYCRR §§ 100.5(a)(7), (8); 100.5(b)(6); 100.5(d)(3)(ii)). State syllabi provide a more detailed specification of course content.

In addition, the use of state syllabi may be required for individual schools identified as in need of improvement pursuant to section 100.2(m)(3) of the commissioner's regulations (8 NYCRR § 100.2(b); see 100.2(p)(5)).

For further information on state syllabi, contact the Office of Curriculum and Instruction, EBA Room 681 State Education Department, Albany, N.Y. 12234.

14:25. Are there any legal requirements concerning homework in the instructional programs of schools?

No. Although homework generally is considered an important part of a student's education because of the knowledge of subject matter gained, the reinforcement of school learning, and the development of independent thinking and good work habits, there are no state requirements concerning the assignment or completion of homework by students. A school board may establish a policy providing that homework be assigned to students for the purpose of reinforcing, preparing, supplementing and reviewing concepts that have been or will be taught.

14:26. Can districts limit student participation in academic programs and other school activities on the basis of sex?

No. Title IX of the Federal Educational Amendment of 1972 (20 USC § 1681 *et seq.*) and regulations that went into effect in July of 1975 forbid sexual discrimination in any activity or program receiving federal funds, including all of the operations of a local educational agency, vocational school system or any other type of school system that receives federal aid (see 20 USC § 1687).

With respect to school athletes, the U. S. Department of Education in 1979 issued "Intercollegiate Athletics Policy Interpretation" and a further clarification in 1996, the general principles of which also apply to elementary and secondary interscholastic athletic programs. The Policy Interpretation and subsequent clarification provide a three-part test to assess whether an institution is violating Title IX in the area of interscholastic sports. A school district need only pass one part to be in compliance. The three parts are:

1. Whether interscholastic level participation opportunities for male and female students are provided in numbers substantially proportionate to their respective enrollments.

2. Where the members of one sex have been and are underrepresented among interscholastic athletes, whether the institution can show a history and continuing practice of program expansion which is demonstrably responsive to the developing interests and abilities of the members of that sex.

3. Where the members of one sex are underrepresented among

interscholastic athletes, and the institution cannot show a history and continuing practice of program expansion, as described above, whether it can be demonstrated that the interest and abilities of the members of that sex have been fully and effectively accommodated by the present program (44 CFR § 71413 *et seq.;* "Clarification of Intercollegiate Athletics Policy Guidance: The Three-Part Test" (1996)).

In New York, the Education Law also provides that no person may be excluded from any course of instruction in the public schools by reason of that person's sex (§ 3201-a). Additionally, section 135.4(c)(7)(ii)(c) of the commissioner's regulations requires that boys and girls be given equal opportunity to participate in interscholastic competition, either on separate teams or in mixed competition. When a school provides separate teams, the superintendent of schools may permit girls to participate on boys' teams. However, when a school provides a team for girls, the superintendent has the discretion to determine whether to allow one or more boys to participate on the girls' team, based on whether such participation would have a significantly adverse effect on the opportunity for girls to participate successfully in interscholastic competition (8 NYCRR § 135.4(c)(4); *Lantz v. Ambach,* 620 F.Supp. 663 (S.D.N.Y. 1985)).

14:27. Can a high school principal or guidance director prevent a student from taking a high school course because, in that person's judgment, the student could not pass the course?

Ordinarily, no. School authorities do not have the legal authority to prevent students from taking a specific subject when the students maintained passing grades in any earlier courses that may be viewed as prerequisites. The commissioner of education has held, however, that a school board may require completion of a certain curriculum in order for a student to be eligible for admission to a BOCES vocational program (*Matter of Tripi,* 21 Educ. Dep't Rep. 349 (1981)).

Also, no legal basis exists for denying a student admission to a particular subject course on the basis of test results, other than tests for preceding courses.

14:28. May students be excused from courses or lessons that conflict with the religion of their parents or guardian?

Students may be excused from courses or lessons only in accordance with the rules and regulations of the Board of Regents and the commissioner's regulations.

A student may be excused, consistent with the requirements of public education and public health, from any study of health and hygiene that conflicts with the religion of his or her parents or guardian. While the Education Law and the Regents rules specifically require parents to submit a petition certified by a proper representative as defined by section 2 of the Religious Corporation Law, this requirement has been determined in another context to be unconstitutional (§ 3204(5); 8 NYCRR § 16.2; see generally *Sherr v. Northport-East Northport U.F.S.D.*, 672 F.Supp. 81 (E.D.N.Y. 1987); *Lewis v. Sobol*, 710 F. Supp. 506 (S.D.N.Y. 1989)).

Students also may be excused from instruction concerning the methods of preventing contraction of the acquired immune deficiency syndrome (AIDS), if the parent or guardian has filed with the school principal a written request that includes an assurance that the student will receive AIDS instruction at home (8 NYCRR § 135.3(b)(2); see also *Ware v. Valley Stream High School District*, 75 N.Y.2d 114 (1989)).

However, it should be noted that the right to exercise one's religion freely is not burdened simply by mandating one to be exposed to ideas with which the person disagrees, and that this is not a violation of the Free Exercise Clause of the First Amendment of the United States Constitution (*Mozert v. Hawkins County Bd. of Education*, 827 F.2d 1058 (6th Cir. 1987), *cert. denied*, 484 U.S. 1066 (1988); **23:3**).

14:29. What are 21st Century Schools?

Designation as a 21st Century School permits a school, group of schools or even an entire district to be relieved from compliance with many of the state regulations pertaining to schools. Schools so designated still must comply with mandates that relate to the health, safety and civil rights of students, as well as those regulations derived from federal law or regulation. Selected schools could also not be exempt from Title II of the Education Law which pertains to school organization and Title IV, which pertains to teachers, supervisors, administrative staff, compulsory education and school census requirements.

A school seeking to be designated a 21st Century School must submit a five-year plan outlining how it will achieve high academic standards for all students by implementing innovative instructional strategies and the restructuring of school management and programs. The applications must be submitted by April 1 preceding the school year for which the designation would commence. The applications will first be considered by a 21st Century Schools Committee comprised of appointees of the governor, the commissioner of education and the legislative leadership. The commissioner then reviews the committee's recommendations before making the final designations.

A 21st Century School must submit to the commissioner annual reports evaluating its effectiveness in improving student performance. Prior to the start of a school's third year of designation as a 21st Century School, the school and the commissioner jointly review its operation. If the commissioner deems the review unsatisfactory, he may begin proceedings to revoke the 21st Century School designation. He may also revoke the designation at any time for good cause.

14:30. Must school districts provide bilingual education or English as a Second Language (ESL) programs?

No. However, every district must screen all new students for proficiency in the English language as part of their overall diagnostic evaluation (8 NYCRR §§ 117.2(b), 117.3).

In addition, all school districts must have a policy setting forth how students with limited English proficiency (LEP) will be educated (8 NYCRR § 154.4). This policy must include:

- The district's philosophy for the education of LEP students.
- Administrative practices and procedures to screen students diagnostically for LEP, to identify LEP students and to evaluate each such student annually, including his or her performance in content areas to measure academic progress.
- An assurance of access to appropriate instructional and support services for such students, including guidance programs.
- An assurance that each LEP student has equal opportunities to participate in all school programs and extracurricular activities as non-LEP students.

School districts must provide the commissioner of education with a copy of their written policy, along with a report by building principals on students initially identified and annually evaluated as being limited English proficient in the preceding school year, a report by building principals on the number of teachers and support personnel providing services to LEP students, and a description by building principals of the curricular and extracurricular services provided to LEP students. For information pertaining to state aid for LEP programs, see **21:12**.

14:31. Must school districts provide programs for the education of gifted and talented students?

No. Article 90 of the Education Law and part 142 of the commissioner's regulations contain guidelines for the education of gifted and talented students in districts that provide this kind of education. However, there is no state mandate requiring that such education be provided. Nevertheless, the commissioner's regulations provide for screening of students entering the public schools for gifted abilities as well as for disabilities and limited English proficiency, and require a student identified as possibly gifted to be reported to the superintendent no later than 15 calendar days after completion of the screening (8 NYCRR § 117.3(c)(3),(f)). Beyond these requisites, school districts have considerable discretion as to the scope and content of programs for gifted and talented students.

In the event a school district offers a gifted program, it must obtain the consent of a student's parents before conducting any tests or evaluations to determine the student's eligibility in the program. If the parents do not grant their consent, the child may not be tested or evaluated and may not participate in the program. In addition, the district may not impose a fee for the administration of such tests or evaluations (§ 4452(1)(e)).

14:32. Are school districts required to provide instruction on acquired immune deficiency syndrome (AIDS)?

Yes. Section 135.3 of the commissioner's regulations includes provisions for mandated instruction about acquired immune deficiency syndrome (AIDS) in kindergarten through 12th grade. This instruction must be designed in an age-appropriate manner and provide accurate information to students on the nature of the disease, methods of transmission and methods of prevention.

In public schools, the school board is required to establish an advisory council to be responsible for making recommendations concerning content, implementation and evaluation of an AIDS instructional program. The council must consist of parents, school board members, appropriate school personnel and community representatives, including representatives from religious organizations (8 NYCRR § 135.3(b)(2)). The requirement for participation of representatives of religious organizations on the council has been upheld by the New York State Court of Appeals (*New York State School Bds. Ass'n vs. Sobol*, 79 N.Y.2d 333 (1992), *cert. denied*, 506 U.S. 909 (1992)). However, the commissioner has upheld a district's decision to deny a member of its AIDS advisory council access to observe health education classes because the presence of a noninstructional adult could stifle open classroom discussion. The advisory council member's role does not entitle him or her to "unfettered access" to district classrooms (*Appeal of Canazon*, 33 Educ. Dep't Rep. 124 (1993)).

Recommended guidelines for HIV/AIDS instruction are available from the State Education Department. According to the commissioner of education, "peer" teaching may be used to present AIDS education, but if it is to be incorporated into the district's curriculum, it should first be reviewed by the district's advisory council and be implemented consistent with the commissioner's regulations (*Appeal of Akshar*, 35 Educ. Dep't. Rep. 424 (1996)).

In addition, a student may be excused from instruction concerning the methods of preventing contraction of AIDS if the parent or guardian has filed with the school principal a written request that includes an assurance that the student will receive AIDS instruction at home (8 NYCRR § 135.3(b)(2); see also *Ware v. Valley Stream High School District*, 75 N.Y.2d 114 (1989); **14:28**).

14:33. May school districts distribute condoms to students as part of the AIDS instruction curriculum?

No. A state appellate court ruled that a school district policy or regulation which directs schools to make condoms available upon a student's request violates Public Health Law section 2504, which requires parental consent for children's health services. Such a policy or regulation would also deny parents their constitutional rights "to influence and guide the sexual activity of their children without state interference." But in making this ruling, the court also rejected the parents' claim that condom distribution should be prohibited because it violated their religious beliefs (*Alfonso v. Fernandez*, 195 A.D.2d 46 (2nd Dep't 1993), *appeal dismissed without opinion*, 83 N.Y.2d 906 (1994)).

14:34. May school districts conduct demonstrations on the use of condoms as part of the AIDS instruction curriculum?

Yes. The commissioner of education has explained that school boards may exercise considerable discretion in prescribing an AIDS curriculum, in consultation with its AIDS advisory council, in a case where extensive public comment was solicited as well. However, the opt-out provision, which requires the parent or guardian to assure that their child will receive AIDS instruction at home (see **14:32**) does not dictate that the parent must provide a condom demonstration at home (*Appeal of O'Shaughnessy*, 35 Educ. Dep't Rep. 57 (1995)).

14:35. May schools teach about religion?

Yes. Although the federal and state constitutions forbid the teaching of religion in the public schools, they do not prevent teaching about religion.

The schools have a responsibility to teach about religion and its place in civilization, which may be a positive force in the inculcation of moral values in youths and in the development of a respect for religion and for religious beliefs (*Matter of Rubinstein*, 2 Educ. Dep't Rep. 299 (1962); see chapter 23).

School districts may not require that creation science be taught as a counterbalance to the teaching of evolution (*Edwards v. Aguillard*, 482 U.S. 578 (1987)). Evolution science may not be taught as a religion either, to counterbalance the religious doctrine of creationism (*Peloza v. Capistrano Unified Sch. Dist.*, 37 F.3d 517 (9th Cir. 1994), *cert. denied*, 515 U.S. 1173 (1995)).

14:36. Are schools required to provide instruction on drug, alcohol and tobacco abuse?

Yes. The Education Law and the commissioner's regulations mandate a program of instruction regarding the misuse and abuse of alcohol, tobacco and other drugs for all students in kindergarten through 12th grade (§§ 804, 806-a, 3028-a; 8 NYCRR §§ 100.2(c)(3), 135.3(a)).

The State Education Department has developed an integrated health-education curriculum for kindergarten through 12th grade that includes instruction on the physical and psychological impact of substance abuse, with an emphasis on nonuse as a means of avoiding health problems. Districts may choose to develop local syllabi that incorporate state and local criteria.

14:37. May schools offer instruction in parenting skills?

Yes. All school districts are authorized, at their discretion, to include as an integral part of family and consumer sciences or health education, instruction regarding child development and parental skills and responsibility.

The State Education Department has been charged to establish a curriculum for parenting skills. Until the curriculum is available, school authorities are authorized to vary the course contents to meet the needs of their particular districts (§ 804-b).

14:38. Must instruction and training in fire drills be given to students in public schools in New York State?

Instruction and training in fire drills must be provided in all public and private schools. These fire drills must be held at least 12 times in each school year, and eight of the drills must be held between September 1 and December 1 of each year. Two additional drills during summer school must be held in buildings where summer school is conducted. One of these must be held during the first week of summer school. Students also must be instructed at one of the drills about procedures to be followed if a fire occurs during a lunch period (§ 807).

Every school year, three fire drills must also be held on each school bus, and include practice and instruction in the location, use and operation of the emergency door, fire extinguishers, first-aid equipment, and windows as a means of escape in case of fire or accident (8 NYCRR § 156.3(h); see **22:41**).

In addition, instruction in fire and arson prevention must be given to all students for at least 45 minutes in each month school is in session. The course of instruction must relate to the protection of life and property against loss or damage as a result of criminally initiated or other preventable fires (§ 808).

14:39. Is instruction on the use of firearms permitted in the public schools?

Yes. School boards may authorize instruction within their schools on the safe and proper use of firearms that are allowed by law to be used in hunting wild game, and on the study of game laws and proper hunting and conservation practices. However, this course of instruction must be approved by both the State Education Department and the Department of Environmental Conservation (§ 809–a).

Although the federal Gun-Free Schools Act of 1994 and the state law which implements it (§ 3214(3)) both mandate an automatic one-year suspension for possession on school grounds of a weapon (see **12:119-125**), U.S. Department of Education guidelines clarify that the act does not apply to firearms or rifles which the owner intends to use solely for sporting, recreational or cultural purposes. Neither the Gun-Free Schools Act nor state law preclude hunting or rifle clubs which may involve the handling or use of weapons (U.S. Department of Education's Guidance Concerning State and Local Responsibilities under the Gun-Free Schools Act of 1994).

14:40. Is instruction about the environment required in the public schools?

Yes. Section 810 of the Education Law requires that all public school students receive instruction relating to the conservation of the natural resources of the state on Conservation Day, which is the last Friday of April of each year. The commissioner of education may prescribe a course of exercises and instruction which must be adopted and observed by school authorities on Conservation Day.

14:41. Are schools required to provide instruction about human rights issues?

Yes. Section 801 of the Education Law requires courses of instruction in human rights issues, with particular attention to the study of the inhumanity of genocide, slavery, including the freedom trail and the underground railroad, the Holocaust, and the mass starvation in Ireland from 1845 to 1850.

14:42. Are schools required to provide instruction about the prevention of child abduction?

Yes. Section 803-a of the Education Law requires that all students in grades kindergarten through eight in all public schools receive instruction designed to prevent the abduction of children. The instruction must be provided under the direct supervision of regular classroom teachers, provided, however, that it may be given by any other agency, be it public or private. In developing and implementing these courses of study, a school board may establish local advisory councils or employ the school-based shared-decision-making teams to make recommendations to the board.

14:43. Are schools required to provide instruction in the humane treatment of animals?

Yes. Students in elementary school must receive instruction in the humane treatment and protection of animals and the importance of the part they play in the "economy of nature" as well as the necessity of controlling the proliferation of animals which are subsequently abandoned and caused to suffer extreme cruelty. This instruction may be joined with work in literature, reading, language, nature study or ethnology (§ 809(1)).

14:44. Must students participate in dissections of animals that are part of the curriculum?

No. Any student expressing a moral or religious objection, substantiated in writing by his or her parent or guardian, to the performance or witnessing of the dissection of an animal must be allowed to complete an alternative project approved by the student's teacher. Students who perform alternative projects shall not be penalized (§ 809(4)).

14:45. Is military instruction permitted in the public schools?

Yes. School boards may offer, during school hours, a junior reserve officer training program in conjunction with the United States Department of Defense to students in grades nine through 12 who are at least 14 years of age. Enrollment and participation in such a program must be voluntary on the part of the student, and written consent of a parent or guardian must be submitted by each student. However, instruction in or the presence within any school of any type of current or future weaponry as part of such a program is prohibited (§ 802(3)).

14:46. What opportunities for training in health care services may a school provide?

The Education Law authorizes the commissioner of education, in cooperation with the Board of Regents, to establish a program of credit for health care service training for those secondary school students interested in such a career. The program may be instituted by any school district seeking to provide its secondary school students with an opportunity to participate in a health care facility or agency training program. Students receive academic credit for work-related training received at the health care facilities or agencies (§ 812).

14:47. Are school districts required to provide school-to-work programs?

No. School districts are not required to offer students opportunities for work-based learning experiences. However, the federal School-to-Work Opportunities Act of 1994 has made federal funding available to qualifying states, including New York, for the creation of local school-to-work partnerships. These partnerships bring together schools, public and private employers, community-based organizations, higher education institutions, and training and human services agencies in collaborative efforts to link the worlds of school and work (see **25:13**).

New York is in the fourth year of an anticipated five-year federal funding cycle which provides money for planning grants, to assist in the development of partnerships, and implementation grants, to help fund the operation of these programs. Any questions regarding participation in the school-to-work initiative should be directed to the State Education Department, Office of Workforce Preparation and Continuing Education, EBA Room 319, Albany, N.Y. 12234.

14:48. May high schools offer automobile driver education and training courses for credit towards a diploma?

Yes. Authority for this is granted under section 507(1) of the Vehicle and Traffic Law. Any vehicle used for driver training must bear identification indicating that the car is driven by a student driver (see also Veh. & Traf. Law § 375(44)).

The Education Law requires all schools that offer driver education courses to include a driver safety component, based on curriculum established by the commissioner of education. The safety component should emphasize the effects of drug and alcohol use (§ 806-a).

A school district may also offer driver education courses outside of the regular school day which are supplemental and not part of the regular school curriculum, and do not count as credit towards a diploma. In addition, if such a course is not offered as part of an adult or continuing education program, the district may charge a fee, provided no student is denied access if he or she cannot pay the fee. Certified teachers must be used as instructors for such a course (§ 3604(8); State Education Department Memorandum from Terry Schwartz, dated June, 1992).

14:49. Must students take physical education?

Yes. Education Law and the commissioner's regulations require that all students receive physical training as part of the required course of study each year they attend school, from kindergarten through grade 12 (§§ 803, 3204(3)(a)(1); 8 NYCRR § 135.4; however, see **14:50** for alternatives to regularly scheduled physical education classes). The commissioner's regulations specify that the frequency of such required physical education classes varies based on grade level (8 NYCRR § 135.4(c)(2)).

Students who are temporarily or permanently unable to participate in the regular physical education program must be provided with adapted activities that may be vigorous, moderate or restful, depending on the needs of the student. Temporary or short-term adaptations should be made by the physical education teacher in consultation with appropriate medical personnel. Permanent or long-term program adaptations should be based on the recommendation of the student's family physician (8 NYCRR § 135.4 (c)(1)(iv)).

Students classified by the committee on special education (CSE) may not be able to participate safely or successfully in the activities of the regular physical education program and must be provided with adaptive physical education. A written individualized education plan (IEP) must include a prescriptive physical education program for a student in need of special education. The physical education teacher should be involved in the development of the IEP (8 NYCRR § 200.4(c)(2)(iv)(a); see also chap.13).

14:50. May districts offer their students alternatives to regularly scheduled physical education classes?

Yes. Districts may offer such alternatives only to students in grades seven through 12. Students in grades 10 through 12, for example, may be permitted to use an "extra-class" athletic program for physical education credit. However, before using this option, students must be scheduled into the regular physical education classes and demonstrate they have achieved acceptable levels of physical fitness and have acquired the skills and knowledge of the instructional activities of the class (8 NYCRR § 135.4(c)(2)(ii)(c)). Once the extra-class athletic program has ceased, the students must return to class. Program options other than those set forth in the commissioner's regulations must be approved by the commissioner of education (8 NYCRR § 135.4(c)(2)).

14:51. Is physical education a requirement for receiving a high school diploma?

Yes. Under the approved proposal for new graduation requirements, two units of physical education will be required as part of the 18.5 core credits required for a high school diploma.

A student who graduates in fewer than eight semesters is not required to continue enrollment in high school for the sole purpose of completing the physical education requirement; however, he or she must have fulfilled the physical education requirement successfully each semester up to that time (8 NYCRR § 100.5 (a)(3)).

If a student does not meet the physical education requirement, he or she should be given an incomplete until the requirement is fulfilled. A school district should offer reasonable makeup opportunities to complete the requirement. Students may not be dropped from their regular physical education program (8 NYCRR § 135.4(a)(3)(ii)).

14:52. Are school districts required to provide instruction relating to the flag?

Yes. School districts must provide instruction regarding respect for the flag of the United States of America, including its display and use (§ 802; 8 NYCRR § 108.4; 36 USC §§ 170-177; see **16:50-51**).

Instructional Resources

14:53. What is a textbook?

A *textbook* is defined as a "book, or a book substitute, which shall include hard covered or paperback books, workbooks or manuals which a pupil is required to use as a text, or a text-substitute in a particular class or program in the school he [or she] legally attends" (§ 701(2)).

14:54. Can New York State dictate the use of certain textbooks?

No. The school board, or whatever body or officer that performs the function of the board, designates the textbooks to be used (Educ. Law § 701; Opn. Att'y Gen. 1919, 18 St. Dep't Rep. 456 (1919)).

14:55. Does the school have a duty to provide free textbooks to students?

Yes. School boards have the power and duty to purchase and to loan, upon individual requests, textbooks to all children residing in the district enrolled in kindergarten through 12th grade. These textbooks are to be loaned free to such students, subject to rules and regulations that are or may be prescribed by the Board of Regents and the school board (§ 701(3)). For information on the purchase and loan of textbooks for nonpublic school students, see **24:14.**

14:56. Is there any limitation on how frequently textbooks may be changed in a school system?

Yes. After a textbook has been designated for use, the district is prohibited from replacing it with any other book within a period of five years from the time of its designation, except upon a three-fourths vote of the school board or whatever body or officer that performs the function of such board (§ 702).

14:57. Do parents have a right to inspect classroom material?

Under the Hatch Amendment (20 USC § 1232h), parents have the right to inspect classroom materials used "in connection with any [federally funded] survey, analysis, or evaluation." However, the Hatch Amendment does not give parents the right to inspect course materials because they find such materials offensive or just because the school receives federal aid.

Additionally, students may not be required to submit to a survey, analysis or evaluation which reveals information regarding the following: political affiliation; mental or psychological problems potentially embarrassing to the student or his or her family; sex behavior and attitudes; illegal, anti-social, self-incriminating and demeaning behavior; critical appraisals of other individuals with close family relationship, legally recognized or analogous privileged relationship or income (20 USC § 1232h(b)). Participation in survey instruments soliciting such information requires the consent of the student, or his or her parent, if the student is a minor. School districts must give parents and students notice of this right (20 USC § 1232h(c)).

14:58. Do parents have the right to require that certain alleged controversial books or other curricular materials not be used or given to their child?

No. The school board has broad authority to determine what books will be used in its courses, and parents of a student cannot compel a board to use a particular textbook or to discontinue the use of one (*Appeal of*

Smith, 34 Educ. Dep't Rep. 346 (1994)). The only exceptions are for students who may be excused from that part of the study of health that conflicts with their religious beliefs, and from instruction about AIDS (§ 3204(5); 8 NYCRR §§ 16.2, 135.3(b)(2); see also **14:28; 14:32**).

The courts have also upheld the broad discretion of school boards in selecting instructional materials against parental challenges that the use of particular materials violates the First Amendment rights of both them and their children. For example, despite the claim by parents in two separate cases that the use of the "Impressions" reading series fostered a pagan belief in the occult, in direct opposition to their Christian beliefs, two federal appellate courts have ruled that the school districts' use of the book did not violate either the Establishment or Free Exercise Clause of the First Amendment *(Brown v. Woodland Joint Unified Sch. Dist.,* 27 F.3d 1373 (9th Cir. 1994); *Fleischfresser v. Directors of Sch. Dist. 200,* 15 F.3d 680 (7th Cir. 1994)).

14:59. May a school board remove a previously approved textbook because of objections to the material contained in it, without violating the First Amendment?

Yes. However, according to a decision from the United States Court of Appeals for the Eleventh Circuit, the removal and the methods used must be "reasonably related to legitimate pedagogical concerns." In *Virgil v. School Bd.,* 862 F.2d 1517 (11th Cir. 1989), the court reviewed the removal of a textbook used in an elective humanities course designed for 11th- and 12th-grade students because of the explicit sexuality and excessively vulgar language and subject matter contained in selections within the textbook of Aristophane's "Lysistrata" and Chaucer's "The Miller's Tale." Neither of these selections was required or assigned during the course. The book remained available in the school library for students' use, along with other adaptations and translations of "Lysistrata" and "The Miller's Tale."

In upholding the removal, the court applied the standard set by the United States Supreme Court in *Hazelwood School District v. Kuhlmeier,* 484 U.S. 260 (1988), concerning a permissible school board regulation of expression that "may fairly be characterized as part of the school curriculum," provided such regulation is "reasonably related to legitimate pedagogical concerns." (The *Hazelwood* case had involved school censorship of a school-sponsored student newspaper.) In *Virgil,* the court found that the selections were part of the school curriculum because it may be reasonable to think that the public may perceive them to bear the school's imprimatur, and that the motivation for the removal presented a legitimate concern regarding the appropriateness of the selections for the student audience in question.

Although New York State is under the jurisdiction of the Second Circuit, the case may have some persuasive value in New York.

14:60. Are schools required to have a library?

Yes. Commissioner's regulations require each school to maintain a library that meets the needs of students and serves as an adequate complement to the instructional program in the various areas of the curriculum.

The commissioner's regulations also provide the following direction as to the number of holdings that junior and senior high schools of different sizes must maintain:

- The library of a junior high school with fewer than 200 students must contain at least 1,000 titles.
- The library of a high school with fewer than 200 students must contain at least 1,000 titles.
- The library of a junior-senior high school with fewer than 200 students must contain at least 2,000 titles.
- The library of a secondary school in which the average daily attendance is more than 200 but fewer than 500 students must contain at least 3,000 titles.
- The library of a secondary school in which the average daily attendance is more than 500 but fewer than 1,000 students must contain at least 5,000 titles.
- The library of a secondary school in which the average daily attendance is more than 1,000 students must contain at least 8,000 titles (8 NYCRR § 91.1).

14:61. Are schools required to have a school librarian?

Yes. Each school district must employ a certified school library-media specialist, unless equivalent service is provided by an alternative arrangement approved by the commissioner of education, in accordance with specified standards contained in the commissioner's regulations (8 NYCRR § 91.2).

14:62. May a school board remove books from the school library without violating the First Amendment?

The constitutional issues in the removal of books from a school library are focused on the school board's motivations in taking such action. In

Board of Education v. Pico, 457 U.S. 853 (1982), the United States Supreme Court held that although a school board has the authority to remove certain books it deems inappropriate from the school library, the school board may not remove such books for purposes of restricting access to certain social, political and moral ideas of which the school board simply disapproves. In its decision, the court said that the school board would have been within its rights to remove the books if they contained vulgar language or if the school board had established a policy setting forth criteria, such as "educational suitability," for keeping books in the district's libraries.

In a similar case, the United States Court of Appeals for the Second Circuit (which includes New York State) dismissed a student's complaint that the school board had violated the First Amendment by removing certain library books because of their vulgar and obscene language (*Bicknell v. Vergennes Union High School Bd. of Directors,* 638 F.2d 438 (2nd Cir. 1980)). Here there was no dispute that the board had not removed the books in question simply because of the ideas they contained or that there was any political motivation on the part of the board. Rather, the court stated the school board had the right to remove those books because of their vulgar and sexually explicit content.

14:63. Do teachers have the right to duplicate copyrighted material in books or musical compositions for their classes or student groups without prior permission?

With certain restrictions, yes. Federal law prohibits any "infringing use" of copyrighted works, that is, the use of copyrighted works without the consent of the author or owner of the copyright (see 17 USC §§ 101, 106, 107, 117).

The law specifically states, however, that the "fair use" of such works for teaching purposes, including making "multiple copies for classroom use," as well as for criticism, comment, scholarship or research, is not an infringing use. Fair use is not a rigidly defined term, but rather is based on a number of factors, including the purpose and character of the use, including whether such use is of a commercial nature or is for non-profit educational purposes, the nature of the original work, the size of the portion used, and the effect on the value or market of the original work (see *Basic Books, Inc., v. Kinko's Graphics Corp.,* 758 F.Supp. 1522 (S.D.N.Y. 1991); Notes of Committee on the Judiciary, House Report No. 94-1476, in note following 17 USC § 107).

Based on guidelines for classroom copying by the House Judiciary

Subcommittee, teachers may reproduce materials if four tests are passed: brevity (a single poem, story, essay or illustration, or a short excerpt of a larger work); spontaneity (a decision made by the teacher making the copy close to the time the material is to be used); cumulative use (generally no more than nine occasions per teacher per term); and notice (the name of the copyright owner, year of publication and a © or ® symbol).

Copyrighted, or "proprietary," computer software and documentation may not be reproduced other than to make archival back-ups (see 17 USC § 117). "Shareware," which is software in the public domain, is not subject to this restriction (37 CFR § 201.26).

It is important to note that classroom and instructional fair use for plays and musical numbers does not include public performances, especially if an admission fee is charged (17 USC § 110).

Violation of copyright may result in fines and injunctive actions against a school district. Particularly in the case of computer software, violation of a license agreement may void any applicable warranty or continued service arrangement, even if the copyright laws have not been violated (17 USC §§ 501-505).

14:64. What is the law regarding use and possession of hypodermic syringes for instructional purposes?

In accordance with section 811 of the Education Law and part 137 of the commissioner's regulations, school personnel may procure, use and possess hypodermic syringes and needles for educational purposes, provided school authorities file a certificate of need for such equipment with the commissioner of education and the New York State Department of Health.

Authorized use of hypodermic syringes and needles by school districts is limited to actual educational demonstrations or other educational purposes designated in the certificate of need. Any other use is unauthorized and prohibited.

A certificate of need designates the individuals responsible for the custody of hypodermic syringes and needles used in the institution, the names of individuals designated as responsible for supervising the use of such hypodermic syringes and needles, and the safeguards to be taken to prevent such instruments from falling into the hands of unauthorized persons (§ 811; 8 NYCRR §137.1).

A record of all hypodermic syringes and needles purchased, lost, stolen or destroyed must be maintained and kept for a period of two years (8 NYCRR § 137.3).

Academic Achievement

14:65. Are New York State public high schools required to use Regents examinations?

Yes. Rules of the Board of Regents pertaining to apportionment provide, in part, that secondary schools receiving state aid must use Regents examinations or approved equivalent examinations in the senior high school grades (8 NYCRR § 3.35). As the state moves toward an all-Regents curriculum and the new graduation requirements are fully phased in, all students will be required to take the Regents exams in English language arts, mathematics, global history, U.S. History and Government and science. The Board of Regents has established a statewide testing council to evaluate alternative testing instruments. If these tests are deemed to be at least as rigorous as the Regents exams, districts may receive a variance to use them instead of the Regents in fulfillment of the state requirements for higher standards.

14:66. What examinations are all students required to take?

As part of the transition to higher standards, the Regents have approved plans for new assessments to ensure congruity between the standards and assessments. According to the approved plan, the following tests will be phased out and replaced with new ones:

- Pupil Evaluation Program (PEP) tests in mathematics and reading for grades three and six (May 1998 last administration), and in writing for grade five (May 1999 last administration).
- Preliminary competency test for grades eight and nine (May 1998 last administration).
- Program Evaluation Test (PET) in social studies for grades six and eight.
- Regents competency tests (between 1999-2004).

New tests are being developed to replace these phased-out exams. They include:

- New exams for mathematics, science and English/language arts, which will incorporate reading, writing, and listening, will be administered to students in grades four and eight.
- A new social studies exam will be given to students in grades five and eight.
- Regents examinations are being modified to meet the new learning standards and will be required for all students entering the ninth grade in 2001 in English/language arts, mathematics, global history, U.S. history and government, and science.

• Extended tasks are being developed to supplement the above examinations and ensure that students can demonstrate critical thinking skills applied to what they have learned.

If the district so requests, the commissioner may approve alternative testing procedures for all the above tests for students identified by the committee on special education (CSE) as having a handicapping condition, and students whose native language is not English (8 NYCRR § 100.2(g)).

The Regents have approved eliminating the less challenging Regents competency tests for high school students and requiring them to take courses leading to Regents examinations. In order to provide a transition for students currently in non-Regents examination courses, students will be required to fulfill these requirements according to the following schedule:

REGENTS EXAM SCHEDULE

Students Entering 9th Grade in 1996	Students Entering 9th Grade in 1997	Students Entering 9th Grade in 1998	Students Entering 9th Grade in 1999	Students Entering 9th Grade in 2000	Students Entering 9th Grade in 2001
English/ Lang. Arts*	English/ Lang. Arts*	English/ Lang. Arts*	English/ Lang. Arts*	English/ Lang. Arts	English/ Lang. Arts
	Math *	Math *	Math *	Math *	Math
		Global History*	Global History*	Global History	Global History
		U.S. History and Gov't *	U.S. History and Gov't*	U.S. History and Gov't	U.S. History and Gov't
			Science*	Science*	Science

Regents exams marked above with an asterisk may be successfully completed with a modified passing score as these exams are phased in over the next several years. The modified score is determined by the school board and may range from 55 to 64. Students who pass the exams with a modified score will receive a local diploma.

Students entering ninth grade in 2001 must pass all exams with a minimum score of 65 and must fulfill all of the Regents new graduation requirements to receive their diplomas (8 NYCRR § 100.5(a)).

Students with disabilities must take all of the required Regents examinations, with certain modifications. This requirement may be subject to change. For more information, contact the State Education Department's Office of Curriculum, at 518-473-4698.

14:67. Who may be admitted to Regents examinations?

All students who have studied a subject at an approved school for a period of time not less than what has been prescribed by the commissioner of education has the right to take a Regents examination at the school they attend. However, students taking the Regents science examination must have satisfactorily met the laboratory requirements as stated in the state syllabus for that science (8 NYCRR § 8.2(a)(c)).

Students who wish to demonstrate academic proficiency acquired through independent, out-of-school or other study may also be admitted to a Regents examination, but only at the discretion of the principal of the school administering the examination (8 NYCRR § 8.2(b)).

14:68. May a student be prohibited from taking a Regents examination because of a failure to pass a local qualifying examination?

No. While school boards may set requirements for admissions and for high school graduation that are more stringent than those prescribed by the state, they may not prohibit a student who has not met those requirements from taking a Regents examination, provided that student meets the requirements set by the Board of Regents (8 NYCRR § 8.2).

14:69. What procedure should be followed in applying penalties for fraud in Regents examinations?

The commissioner's regulations allow full discretion and latitude to local school administrators when fraud is found in regard to a Regents examination. If a local administrator responsible for giving the examination concludes there is sufficient evidence of fraud, he or she may find a student guilty of cheating and cancel that student's examination, and exclude that student from further exams until the student has demonstrated to the administrator's satisfaction that the student is entitled to the restoration of this privilege.

In each instance where fraud has been established, the administrator promptly must file a brief report with the commissioner of education, giving the name of the student and describing the circumstances and the action taken. A student accused of fraud should have a full opportunity for a hearing before the local school administrator, if requested, and in the presence of his or her parents and legal counsel, if desired (8 NYCRR § 102.4; see *Matter of Pellinger*, 20 Educ. Dep't Rep. 53 (1980), in regard to "substantial evidence" needed in such cases).

14:70. Are school districts required to issue student progress reports, in the form of report cards, to parents or guardians?

No. However, most school districts provide parents or guardians with progress reports, generally prepared by the students' teachers, which provide information on grades, attendance, conduct and other relevant data. Report cards are issued each quarter in most districts.

Districts also may send out additional information on student progress or lack of progress in the form of interim reports when a student is failing a course or has attained a noteworthy achievement.

14:71. Must school districts report the results of state tests?

Yes. As part of the district's school report card, each school building and school district must provide to the State Education Department the results of state tests for the three school years immediately preceding the school year in which the report is issued (8 NYCRR § 100.2(m)(1)(i); see **14:72**).

In addition, section 3211–a of the Education Law requires that schools must report the standardized reading test result of any student scoring at or below the 23rd percentile to his or her parents or guardian. School districts also must provide either a certified teacher of reading or other appropriate school district personnel to interpret the score of a child whose parents have requested an interpretation of such test results.

14:72. What is the school report card?

The state issues an annual report card for each school to measure students' progress in each school building in a district. This practice began in December of 1996. The State Education Department (SED) annually receives information on educational programs and services, student performance and fiscal data from each public school district and each nonpublic school.

Each school board, and in New York City, the board of education and each community school board, must prepare a school district report card pursuant to commissioner's regulations. The report card must include measures of academic performance, on a school-by-school basis, on state evaluation tests in reading, writing, mathematics, science and vocational education, as well as performance on Regents exams in English, and languages other than English, mathematics, science and social studies.

The school report card must compare such measures of academic performance to statewide averages for all public schools and statewide averages for public schools of comparable wealth and need, as developed and distributed by the commissioner. It must also include measures of fiscal performance for the district such as expenditures per pupil in regular and special education and compare this data to statewide averages for all districts and those of comparable wealth and need.

The report card must also contain the number and percentage of students in special education by placement, including both public and private placements, and a comparison of such percentages to the statewide average. It must also include other measures such as the graduation and college-going rates, and attendance, suspension and dropout rates (8 NYCRR § 100.2(bb)).

The report cards must be distributed to local newspapers of general circulation, appended to the proposed school budget and available for distribution to the public at least 14 days before the budget vote (§§ 1716(6); 2254(24); 2590-e(8); 2601-a(7); see **4:13**).

14:73. Are BOCES required to prepare a report card?

Yes. BOCES are required to prepare a BOCES report card. The BOCES report card must include measures of academic performance by students on a school-by-school or program-by-program basis in the following:

- Measures of program participation, completion and placement in areas including, but not limited to, special education, occupational education, alternative education and adult and continuing education.
- The aggregate performance of students of component school districts on statewide evaluation tests in reading, mathematics, science and vocational courses, and Regents exams in English, mathematics, science and social studies.
- The percentage of students in the BOCES region who graduate with Regents and other diplomas.
- A comparison of such measures of academic performance to statewide averages for all BOCES.
- Other measures that support the achievement of higher standards, such as curriculum and staff development activities, and a comparison of the same to statewide averages for all BOCES.

The report card must also include measures of fiscal performance of the supervisory district, including expenditures per pupil and a summary of BOCES expenditures for administration, program and capital. These fiscal measures shall also be compared to statewide averages across BOCES.

The BOCES report card must be transmitted to newspapers of general circulation, be appended to copies of the administrative budget made publicly available, and copies must be available for distribution at the annual meeting (§ 1950(4)(kk); 8 NYCRR § 100.2(cc)).

14:74. Can a school be designated as low-performing and monitored by the State Education Department because of the failure of its students on state tests?

Yes. If a school scores below performance criteria approved by the Board of Regents in September of 1996, and is identified by the commissioner of education as most in need of improvement, it is designated a school under registration review (SURR).

The new performance criteria require at least 90 percent of a school's students to achieve the state performance benchmarks, formerly known as standard reference points, for minimum competency on the following tests: pupil evaluation program tests, preliminary competency tests, Regents competency tests, and Regents examinations. The dropout rate standard, formerly 10 percent, has been revised to 5 percent. Students with individualized education programs (IEPs) who take state tests must be included in reports of achievement, as do limited English proficiency (LEP) students, with certain exceptions (8 NYCRR §100.2(7)(ii)).

The school boards of those schools identified by the commissioner as failing to meet the criteria will be required to develop and adopt "local assistance plans" in order to improve the schools' performance. Of those schools, the commissioner shall determine, based on local assessment, which schools are most in need of improvement and must be placed under registration review. Parents must be informed annually of a school's registration review status, and the status must be reported at the next public board meeting after notification.

Upon identification as a SURR, a school must undergo a state-conducted resource planning and program audit. Based on the audit, the school superintendent must develop a "corrective action plan" to be approved by the school board before it is submitted to the commissioner for review and approval.

A school has three academic years to demonstrate improvement, although the commissioner may modify that period of time. If improvement is not met, the commissioner shall recommend that the Board of Regents revoke the school's registration.

Without registration, a school may not provide public education services. For schools that have their registration revoked, the commissioner must develop a plan to protect the educational welfare of the students and require the school board to implement the plan (8 NYCRR § 100.2(m),(p)).

School Assistance to College-bound Students

14:75. May school districts restrict the number of college applications students may submit for processing by their high schools?

No. School districts may, however, establish rules of procedures for submission of such requests (§ 209–a).

14:76. What funds are available for college scholarships for New York State high school graduates?

The Tuition Assistance Program (TAP) is a state grant. It is based on a family's taxable income balance, adjusted to take into account other family members attending college, tuition costs and the receipt of other financial aid. Neither a qualifying examination nor repayment is required. Awards are made to all eligible applicants. Students who are in an approved postsecondary program are eligible to receive annual TAP grants for up to eight years of combined undergraduate and graduate study. For more information about TAP, please consult the Higher Education Services Corporation, 99 Washington Avenue, Albany, N.Y. 12210; telephone 518-474-1688.

The Pell Grant is a federal aid program for undergraduates. It is the "floor" of the aid package, designed to be combined with other aid sources. Like TAP, it is based on a family's resources, is noncompetitive and does not need to be repaid.

The New York State Higher Education Services Corporation's Guaranteed Student Loan Program enables students to borrow money from New York State lending institutions at a low interest rate.

For information about state-supported scholarship assistance programs and/or medical, dental and veterinary loan programs, please consult the Higher Education Services Corporation, 99 Washington Avenue, Albany, N.Y. 12210; telephone 518-474-5642.

15. School District Reorganization

15:1. What is school district reorganization?

School district reorganization is the term used to define the statutory processes by which two or more school districts are merged into a single district or a school district is dissolved. The various methods of school district reorganization include centralization, annexation, consolidation and dissolution, each of which has a different purpose and implication. Each reorganization procedure is limited in its application to one or more of the organizational types of school districts: for example, union free, central, common and city school districts (see *A Guide to the Reorganization of School Districts in New York State,* Albany, N.Y.: State Education Department, 1993).

15:2. What is centralization?

Centralization is the most common form of reorganization. A new central school district is created by the merger of two or more contiguous districts, with a new school board and boundaries that encompass the area of the districts being reorganized. Under the Education Law, city school districts are not eligible for centralization (§§ 1801(2), 1804(2)).

15:3. What is annexation?

Annexation is a reorganization procedure whereby any school district, other than a city school district, is dissolved and its territory annexed to a contiguous central school district (§ 1802(2)) or to a union free school district (§ 1705). The dissolution of the annexed district is a part of the annexation process and is different from the dissolution of a school district ordered by the district superintendent (§ 1505; see **15:15**).

Unlike in centralization, a new district is not created, nor is a new school board elected. The operation of the annexing school district remains basically the same before and after the annexation. Residents of the annexed district become eligible to vote and may be elected to the school board of the annexing district in subsequent elections (see *A Guide to the Reorganization of School Districts in New York State,* Albany, N.Y.: State Education Department, 1993; § 1803(9)).

15:4. What is consolidation?

Consolidation is a reorganization procedure which may involve the merger of any combination of common or union free school districts to form a new common or union free school district (§ 1510). Central and city school districts may not participate in the consolidation of union free and/or common school districts.

However, consolidation may also involve the incorporation of districts contiguous to city school districts of cities with populations of less than 125,000 residents into the city school district. The resulting school district becomes known as an enlarged city school district (§§ 1524, 1526).

15:5. What is dissolution?

Dissolution is a seldom-used form of reorganization in which a district superintendent of schools dissolves a district by order and unites the territory with an adjoining district or districts, other than a city school district (§ 1505(1)).

15:6. Is there a legal procedure by which a school district can be broken up and divided into two or more smaller districts?

No. The only example of this was the creation of community school districts in New York City, which was a change in the Education Law that required enactment of a specific law by the state Legislature (see Art. 52-A).

15:7. What is the Master Plan and its impact on school district reorganization?

The Master Plan, codified in 1972 in section 314 of the Education Law under the name State Plan, is an administrative and statutory effort intended to advance school district reorganization so as to provide education facilities in the most efficient and economical manner, while also serving the best interests of children. It originally was adopted by the State Education Department in 1947, and was designed to encourage consolidation, annexation and centralization, in order to improve the functioning of public schools. The result was massive reorganization of districts, a reduction in the number of school districts in the state, and the creation of larger districts.

15:8. What is the role of the commissioner of education in school district reorganizations?

The commissioner of education is not authorized to compel a reorganization of school districts without voter approval. However, the commissioner does play a pivotal role in school district reorganization, including preliminary activities conducted prior to voter consideration of district reorganization.

In most circumstances, the process of district reorganization begins with the issuance of an order by the commissioner. For example, the commissioner issues an order laying out the new district boundaries for a centralization (§ 1801). The order laying out the new school district does not constitute the establishment of a new district, but, rather, constitutes a proposal made by the commissioner to the residents of the new proposed district.

In an annexation, for example, the commissioner issues an order dissolving one or more common, union free, or central school districts and annexing the territory of such district, or portion thereof, to one or more adjoining central or union free school districts, subject to the approval of the voters of each affected district (§§ 1705(1)(a), 1801(2)).

Although the commissioner has the statutory authority to independently issue orders concerning reorganization, the practice has been that he will not issue these orders until an adequate feasibility study is available to indicate that the proposal is desirable, the people in the district have been informed of the potential reorganization, and there is evidence that the majority of the voters in the affected district or districts support the proposal (see *A Guide to the Reorganization of School Districts in New York State*, Albany, N.Y.: State Education Department, 1993).

Reorganization Procedures

15:9. Are there any preliminary steps school districts must take before they can reorganize?

Yes. There must be a feasibility study, also known as an efficiency study, which is a written report commissioned by a school district considering reorganization. Its purpose is to describe how a specific combination of districts may operate if reorganization were to be implemented.

The commissioner of education has ruled that the authority to order a feasibility study rests solely with the school board; district voters may not compel the board to conduct a feasibility study (*Appeal of Leman*, 32 Educ. Dep't Rep. 579 (1993)).

A feasibility study should cover several areas, including:
- Current and projected student enrollments.
- Current and projected professional staffing plans.
- Current and projected housing plans.
- A plan for educational programs and curricula in the proposed district.
- A plan for transportation in the proposed district.
- Fiscal implications of the reorganization, including changes in state

aid, expenditures and local tax effort (see *A Guide to the Reorganization of School Districts in New York State,* Albany, N.Y.:   State Education Department, 1993).

15:10. Is state aid available to school districts that conduct a feasibility study?

Yes. The commissioner of education is authorized to award a grant of up to $50,000 for a school board to study reorganization of the district with one or more school districts, to explore the sharing of programs between school districts, or to conduct a district-wide administrative and operational efficiency study and review to identify ways to improve the delivery of educational services and reduce district costs.

In evaluating grant proposals, the commissioner may give preference to proposals to study reorganization or sharing of programs between districts (§ 3602(14)(h)(1), (h)(4)). Grants of up to $20,000 are also available for efficiency studies between one or more school districts, or a BOCES and a county or other municipality, to study a collaborative service delivery system for school aged at-risk youth and their families, including training.

In addition, an efficiency grant may be awarded for: collaboration with human service agencies, such as a county department of social services; consolidation of services in such areas as health, youth or other human services; transportation; facilities, bidding and purchasing, equipment, insurance, maintenance and communications (§ 3602(14)(h)(2), (h)(4)).

15:11. What are the procedures involved in centralization?

After an adequate study is performed indicating that the proposed centralization is desirable and that a majority of the voters in the affected districts support the proposed centralization, the commissioner of education may issue an order laying out the new central school district (§ 1801(1); see *A Guide to the Reorganization of School Districts in New York State,* Albany, N.Y.: State Education Department, 1993). The clerk of each affected district must post a certified copy of the commissioner's order in five conspicuous places within each district within five days of receiving the certified copy of the order (§ 1801(3)).

A petition requesting the commissioner to call a special meeting must then be filed. The petition must be signed by at least 100 voters or by the number of voters equal to at least 10 percent of the student population of the combined districts, whichever is less (§ 1802(1)). The commissioner may then call a special meeting to allow the qualified voters in the affected districts to determine whether or not the new district will be created

(§§ 1801(4), 1802(1)(b)).

The Education Law establishes a special meeting in which either votes of all districts are combined, or an alternative procedure by which the votes of each district are separately tabulated, to determine if voter approval exists (§§ 1803, 1803-a).

15:12. What are the procedures involved in annexation?

After an adequate study is performed indicating that the proposed annexation is desirable and that a majority of the voters in the affected districts support the proposed annexation, in a central school district, the commissioner of education may issue an order annexing an existing school district to a central school district, which becomes effective in 60 days, unless the voters submit a petition requesting a referendum on the annexation (§§ 1801; 1802(2)). The clerk of each affected district must post a certified copy of the commissioner's order in five conspicuous places within each district within five days of receiving the certified copy of the order (§ 1801(3)).

The voters of any school district affected by the proposed annexation may submit a petition requesting a referendum, signed by at least 100 qualified voters or by the number of voters equal to at least 10 percent of the student population in the district, whichever is less (§ 1802(2)(b)). The commissioner may then schedule a referendum and provide notice of the referendum in each district which has requested one to determine whether or not the annexation will occur (§ 1802(2)(b)). A majority of the voters in each district must vote in favor of the annexation in order for it to be valid (§ 1803(1)).

In an annexation to a union free school district, voter approval of the commissioner's order proposing the annexation is required in order for the reorganization to become effective (§ 1705(1)(a)). In an annexation to a union free school district, no petition by the voters is necessary since a vote is required by statute (§ 1705(1)(b)).

15:13. What are the procedures involved in the consolidation of union free and/or common school districts?

After an adequate study is performed indicating that the proposed consolidation is desirable and that a majority of the voters in the affected districts support the proposed consolidation, a petition must be submitted by at least 10 qualified voters of each affected school district requesting a meeting to consider the consolidation of one or more school districts (§ 1511). Each district submits the consolidation plan to the commissioner of education and, upon his or her approval, a special meeting is called in each district to gain the approval for the consolidation by the qualified voters of each district (§§ 1511, 1512). If the consolidation is approved, a new district is created and a new school board is elected (§§ 1512, 1513, 1702).

15:14. What are the procedures for consolidations involving city school districts?

In this form of reorganization, after an adequate study is performed indicating that the proposed consolidation is desirable and that a majority of the voters in the affected districts support the proposed consolidation, the consolidation must be approved by the school board of the city district and the qualified voters of the adjoining district (§§ 1524(1), 1526). If so approved, the adjoining district is dissolved and the territory is added to the city school district. A new district is not created, nor is a new school board elected (§ 1524(1)).

15:15. What are the procedures for the dissolution of a district?

After an adequate study is performed indicating that the proposed dissolution is desirable and that a majority of the voters in the affected districts support the proposed consolidation, the district superintendent issues an order dissolving one district and annexing the territory to an adjoining district (§ 1505(1)). If the territory of more than one district superintendent is affected by the dissolution, approval by the majority of the district superintendents is required (§ 1505(1)).

Dissolution is the only reorganization process that does not specifically provide an opportunity for the qualified voters of the district or districts affected to make the final determination as to whether or not a reorganization will be implemented. However, the Education Law establishes a process by which voters may contest the dissolution by filing their objections with the local county court judge, who then appoints a committee to determine whether the dissolution should occur (§ 1505(2)).

15:16. Is there a limit to the number of times a proposal to reorganize may be submitted to the voters within a given time period?

Yes. If a reorganization proposition is defeated by the voters, a revote on the same proposal cannot be called within one year after the original vote (§§ 1512(1), 1705(2)(b), 1803(8), 1803-a(6)). Additionally, the commissioner's order for reorganization is deemed null and void if a second special meeting is not called within two years of the original meeting at which the voters rejected the reorganization, or if a second meeting is held and the proposal is again defeated (§§ 1705(2), 1803(8), 1803-a(6)).

Impact of Reorganization

15:17. How is the name of a newly created central school district selected?

The name of a centralized district is designated by the commissioner of education in the centralization order (§ 1801(2)). Subject to the commissioner's approval, school boards of new or reorganized central school districts may select a different name if a written request for a name change is filed with the commissioner no later than 14 days before the centralization order is to become effective (§ 315). Reorganized districts must comply with the commissioner's regulations concerning the use of simplified names by school districts (see 8 NYCRR Part 240).

15:18. What happens to the property and debts of former school districts after a reorganization?

Under all forms of reorganization, the debts of the former school district, such as bonds or notes or those relating to school building construction, are assumed by the newly reorganized district (§§ 1517, 1705(3), 1804(5)(b)). Any other debts of the defunct district must be paid off out of that district's assets (§§ 1518, 1705(3), 1804(5)(a)).

In a centralization or annexation, the new central school district or annexing district "shall succeed to all the property rights" of the defunct district (§§ 1705(3), 1804(5)).

In a dissolution, under section 1505 of the Education Law, the dissolved school district's property must be sold and the net proceeds of the sale are apportioned to the taxpayers of the dissolved district based on the latest assessment roll (§ 1520).

15:19. How does a school district reorganization affect employment contracts?

If a teacher has an employment contract with a school district, that contract is a property right subject to the normal rules of property distribution in a reorganization (*Barringer v. Powell*, 230 N.Y. 37 (1920)). For example, in a centralization, the employment contract would be an obligation assumed by the new district.

However, one court has ruled a collective bargaining agreement is not a contract assumed by an annexing district in an annexation. The teachers from the annexed district become covered by the collective bargaining agreement between the teachers and the annexing district and the contract between the annexed district and its union is not enforceable against the annexing district (*Cuba-Rushford CSD v. Rushford Faculty Ass'n.*, 182 A.D.2d 127 (4th Dep't 1992)).

15:20. What employment rights are provided to employees of districts that have been dissolved or reorganized pursuant to annexation to a union free school district?

The Education Law only specifies the employment rights of employees in cases of dissolution of a school district and annexation to a union free school district. Employment rights in other forms of reorganization are less clear (see **15:21**).

In an annexation to a union free school district, the employees of the annexed district become employees of the annexing district and retain their tenure status and seniority (§ 1705(4)). If fewer teaching positions are necessary following the annexation, the teachers from both districts with the greatest seniority within each tenure area are retained in positions in the annexing district, and excessed teachers from both districts are placed on preferred eligible lists based on seniority (§ 1705(4)). To determine "salary, sick leave and any other purpose" in the annexing district, service in the annexed district will be credited as service in the annexing district (§ 1705(4)).

In a dissolution of a school district, where the district is dissolved and added to more than one school district, the teachers of the dissolved district are entitled to select the district where they desire to be employed. They will be appointed to positions in the newly created district based on their preferences and seniority (§ 1505-a(1)). A district that employs teachers from dissolved districts is required to transfer the seniority credit acquired in the dissolved district and credit such seniority as if the teacher had served in the annexing district, to determine "salary, sick leave and any other purpose" (§ 1505-a(3)).

In a dissolution in which no new positions are created, the teachers of the dissolved district are entitled to be placed on the preferred eligible list of the district that has added the dissolved district, in order of seniority acquired in the dissolved district. The teachers would fill any future vacancies in that annexing district at the payment schedule set by that district (§ 1505-a(2),(3)).

15:21. What employment rights exist for employees of districts that have been reorganized pursuant to centralization, consolidation or annexation to a central school district?

Although the Education Law does not specify the employment rights of employees in school district reorganizations other than annexation to a union free school district or dissolution of a district, the State Education

Department (SED) has clarified the employment rights applicable under the various forms of reorganization (*A Guide to the Reorganization of School Districts in New York State,* Albany, N.Y.: State Education Department, 1993). SED asserts that in a centralization or consolidation, teachers in the former school district become employees of the newly created district. Thus, the teachers from both districts with the greatest seniority within each tenure area are retained in positions in the new district and teachers from both districts are placed on preferred eligible lists based on seniority.

In an annexation to a central school district, according to SED, teachers in the annexing district are not displaced by more senior teachers from the annexed district. However, teachers from the annexed district are entitled to fill any new positions created by the annexation in the annexing district based on the seniority credit earned at the annexed district. Former teachers of the annexed district not employed by the annexing district are entitled to be placed on the preferred eligible list of the annexing district. According to SED, similar rights are applicable in a consolidation with a city school district.

15:22. How are superintendents affected by reorganization?

A superintendent under contract, other than one in an annexing district, does not have employment rights in the reorganized district. However, that superintendent's employment contract is considered a property right and becomes an obligation of the reorganized school district (*Matter of Foster,* 28 Educ. Dep't Rep. 29 (1988); § 1804(5)(b)). Thus, the reorganized district must pay that superintendent's salary and benefits under his or her contract.

A superintendent of a district that is consolidated with a city school district has no right to the superintendent's position in the city district. If that superintendent is serving under a contract, the contract is considered a property right and becomes an obligation upon the city school district as a successor in interest, and the superintendent must be paid for the duration of the contract (see *A Guide to the Reorganization of School Districts in New York State,* Albany, N.Y.: State Education Department, 1993).

15:23. Is state aid available to school districts which reorganize?

Yes. Additional operating aid and building aid is available to certain school districts that reorganize and comply with particular requirements of the Education Law (§ 3602(14)).

15:24. Where can more information be obtained about reorganization?

Information about reorganization can be obtained by contacting the State Education Department, Office of Educational Management Services: School District Organization and BOCES, EBA, Room 876, Albany, New York 12234; or by calling the office at 518-474-3936. See also *A Guide to the Reorganization of School Districts in New York State* (Albany, N.Y.: State Education Department, 1993).

16. School Buildings, Grounds and Equipment

16:1. Are school districts required to prepare long-range plans on educational facilities?

Yes. Section 155.1 of the commissioner's regulations requires each school district to prepare and keep on file a comprehensive long-range plan pertaining to educational facilities.

The plan must be reevaluated and updated at least annually. It must include an appraisal of the following: the educational philosophy of the district with resulting administrative organization and program requirements; current and projected student enrollments; use of space and state-rated student capacity of existing facilities, priority of need of maintenance, repair or modernization of existing facilities, including consideration of the retirement of certain facilities; and the provision of additional facilities.

A copy of this plan must be submitted to the State Education Department's Bureau of Facilities Planning in Albany, along with any preliminary applications and plans for a new school, addition or reconstruction project (see also **16:23**).

In addition, the Capital Assets Preservation Program (CAPP) requires districts to develop a five-year facilities preservation plan, including the estimated expense by school building of facility needs for current or proposed construction, additions, alterations, reconstruction, major repairs, operations and maintenance and energy consumption (§ 3641(1)(4); see 8 NYCRR § 155.1 (a)(4)).

16:2. Is the school board required to send a committee to visit each of the schools in the district?

Yes. Section 1708(2) of the Education Law requires at least an annual visit to every school by a committee appointed by the school board. This committee must report on the conditions of the schools at the next regular board meeting. This inspection by the committee is different than the structural inspection, which is also required (see **17:10**).

16:3. Do individual school board members have the right to visit schools?

Yes. Every school board member has the same right as other parents or residents of the district to visit the schools in accordance with whatever procedures apply to the public in general. However, individual board members may visit schools for official purposes, such as for building inspection, interviewing staff or inspection of personnel records, only with authorization of the board (*Matter of Bruno*, 4 Educ. Dep't Rep. 14 (1964)).

Acquisition and Disposal of School Property

16:4. Must the voters approve the designation of a site for a new school building?

No, unless it is a common school district or a union free school district that has a population of less than 5,000 (§§ 401(2); 2512(1); 2556(2)). However, although certain districts are not required to get voter approval for site selection, the board may still submit the issue of site selection to the voters (*Matter of Albanese*, 11 Educ. Dep't Rep. 166 (1972)).

16:5. Must the commissioner of education approve the site for construction and enlargement of facilities?

Yes. Section 155.1(c) of the commissioner's regulations requires that sites for the construction or enlargement of facilities be approved by the commissioner. This regulation also requires the district take the following factors into consideration when selecting a site:

- The size and location of a site must be consistent with the long-term building plans of the district (8 NYCRR § 155.1(c)(1)).
- The educational adaptability of the site must take into account the placement of the building and development of the grounds for outdoor educational programs and related activities, without excessive initial or development costs. Sites must also include the following minimum usable acres (8 NYCRR § 155.1(c)(2)), unless otherwise approved by the commissioner: elementary school (kindergarten through sixth grade)—a three-acre base plus one acre for each 100 students, or fraction thereof; and secondary schools (seventh through 12th grade)—a 10-acre base plus one acre for each 100 students, or fraction thereof.
- Sites must be developed to conserve natural resources and avoid environmental problems within the limits of the educational program. Care must be taken to ensure that the site and facilities are consistent with and contribute to the school and community environment and provide for the health and safety of occupants (8 NYCRR § 155.1(c)(3)).

The Association recommends that a district considering a site contact both the State Education Department's Facilities Planning and Construction Projects departments, prior to purchase, to ensure that the site or sites will meet the requirements of the State Environmental Quality Review Act (see also **16:25**).

16:6. How may a school district acquire real property for school purposes?

A school district may acquire real property for school purposes by gift, grant, devise (a clause in a will disposing of real property) or purchase; and by involuntary acquisition under some circumstances if an agreement cannot be made with the owner for the purchase (§ 404).

Title to real property is held by the school board as a corporate body (§§ 406, 1603). In city school districts with fewer than 125,000 inhabitants, the school district holds title to real property purchased by it in the name of the school district. In a Big 5 city school district, the school board takes title to real property in the name of the city, which holds the property in trust for use by the school district (§ 2557).

Special provisions regarding purchase and sale of real and personal property apply to large city school districts, as indicated in section 2556 of the Education Law.

16:7. Once a site has been properly selected, must the voters approve the purchase of real property?

Yes, except in city school districts with a population over 125,000 inhabitants, the purchase of real property is subject to the approval of the voters (§§ 416(1); 2511(1); 2556(1); see **16:16**).

16:8. If a school district is given a site as a gift, must the district still get the voters' approval to accept it?

No. The voters' approval is not necessary to accept the property as a gift. However, when the board decides to erect a school building on it there must be a district vote, except in large city school districts (§ 404).

16:9. Can a school board enter into an option agreement for the purchase of a school site without the voters' authorization or consent?

Yes, provided that the amount paid for the option is reasonable (Op. of Counsel No. 65, 1 Educ. Dep't Rep. 764 (1952)). In such instances, the district is purchasing the option to buy the site at a later date, and not the site itself.

16:10. Can a district enter into a lease for a school building?

Yes. The school board in any union free, central or city school district may authorize the lease of a school building from either another school district or from any person, partnership or corporation (§§ 403-b(1); 1726; 2503(8); 2554(6)).

If the lease is between two school districts, the leased building must be within a reasonable distance of the leasing district, as determined by the commissioner of education (§ 403-b(1)). If the lease is between a school district and a non-school entity, the leased building or facility must be located within the school district (§ 403-b(1)).

All leases and leased facilities must meet the following requirements:

1. No lease shall become effective until approved by the commissioner of education (§ 403-b(1)(c)).
2. The lease may not exceed five years unless the district voters have approved a longer term. The initial term of lease, however, cannot exceed the period of probable usefulness as prescribed by law (Local Fin. Law §11.00(a)(2)).
3. The voters of the lessee district must approve any renewal of the lease, except for those leases made by a large city school district (§§ 403-b(1)(d); 2503(8); 2554(6)).
4. The voters in the lessee district must approve any capital project to be undertaken in a leased building or facility during the term of the lease subject to prior approval by the commissioner after the need for such project has been established, except for those leases made by a large city school district (§§ 403-b(1)(b); 2503(8); 2554(6)).
5. The leased facility must meet all applicable standards for the health, safety and comfort of its occupants.
6. The leased facility must be educationally adequate.
7. The school district must have a current five-year facilities plan, or other applicable long-range facilities plan, that includes such lease.
8. To be eligible for state aid, any leased facility must meet the requirements for access by individuals with disabilities (§§ 403-b(1)(e); 2503(8); 2554(6)).

16:11. May a school district enter into a lease-purchase agreement for the purchase of school buildings?

Yes. A school board may enter into agreements for the lease-purchase of buildings for school purposes, either to be placed or erected on a district-owned site. Such an agreement is subject to the requirements in section 1726 of the Education Law. Approval by the district voters and the commissioner of education is also required (§§ 1726; 2503(8); Local Fin. Law § 11.00(a)(2); Gen. Mun. Law § 101; *Appeal of Brousseau*, 37 Educ. Dep't Rep. 295 (1998)).

16:12. May a school district sell its property?

Yes. A school board may, as prescribed by law, sell the real and personal property owned by the school district (§§ 1604(36); 1709(11); 1804(6)(a), (c); 2511; 2554(5); 2557).

In union free and small city school districts, voter approval is required to sell real property (§§ 1709(11); 2511). In central school districts that have been centralized for at least seven years voter approval is not necessary unless a petition requesting a vote is submitted to the board, signed by at least 10 percent of the voters (§ 1804(6)(c)). Large city school districts do not need voter approval to sell real property (§ 2557).

With respect to the sale of unneeded personal property, such as a used station wagon, the sale must be bona fide and for adequate consideration. Bids at a public auction are not required (Opn. St. Comp. 58-120).

According to the commissioner of education, school boards have a fiduciary responsibility to obtain the best price possible when selling or disposing of school district property *(Matter of Baker,* 14 Educ. Dep't Rep. 5 (1974)). However, the board may exercise its judgment and discretion in good faith concerning the method of sale that will bring the best price. Equipment that has no appreciable market value may be discarded, destroyed or donated to a not-for-profit organization (Opn. St. Comp. 82-232). It may not be given away to private individuals (NYS Const., Art. VIII, § 1).

Private sale of surplus equipment to a school board member or other school official or employee who is involved in the purchasing function is generally prohibited (Gen. Mun. Law Art. 18; Opn. St. Comp. 58-120).

16:13. May a school district donate its property as a gift?

Yes. The Education Law authorizes a school district to donate unused school buildings and sites, but only to a public corporation for its use. The gift may be made on terms and conditions determined by the school board, and may or may not involve a money transaction. Except in large city school districts, voter approval is required (§ 405).

The term *public corporation* includes counties, cities, towns, villages, district corporations (territorial divisions of the state with the power to issue obligations and levy taxes or require the levy of taxes) and public-benefit corporations. This last category includes such units as the various bridge and housing authorities (General Const. Law § 66).

16:14. Can a school board rent out a school building or other school property?

Yes. A school board may adopt a resolution which states that the real property to be leased is not currently needed for school district purposes and that the leasing of such real property is in the best interest of the school district (see § 403-a(1); see also *Camillus v. West Side Gymnastics School,*

Inc., 109 Misc.2d 609 (Sup. Ct. Onondaga County, 1981)).

The terms of the lease must reflect a fair market rental value as determined by the school board; a term not to exceed 10 years; and require the lessee to restore the real property to its original condition, less ordinary depreciation, upon termination of the lease. The lease may be renewed for a period up to 10 years, upon approval of the commissioner of education (§ 403-a).

There is no requirement for voter approval of lease terms once the district has properly complied with the requirements of 403-a of the Education Law (*Matter of Hollister*, 33 Educ. Dep't Rep. 294 (1993)). However, voter approval must be sought for any proposed lease agreement that will exceed 10 years in length (§ 403-a(5)).

In addition, school boards and BOCES, without voter approval, may convey a right-of-way over school property for public utilities services to any municipality, municipal district, authority or public utility. This is known as granting an easement (§ 405).

Construction and Renovation of Facilities

16:15. Is a school district subject to zoning regulations with regard to its buildings or proposed buildings?

No. School districts are not subject to town, city or village zoning provisions regulating setback, selection of a school building site, school building construction and the size of the open areas surrounding school buildings. A district is not required to obtain a municipal building permit (Opn. St. Comp. 68-426). It also is relieved of compliance with the provisions of a town building code (*Board of Educ. v. Buffalo*, 32 A.D.2d 98 (4th Dep't 1969); *Camillus v. West Side Gymnastics School, Inc.*, 109 Misc.2d 609 (Sup. Ct. Onondaga County 1981); see also **16:21**).

16:16. Must the district voters approve the construction of new facilities?

Yes. A majority of the voters of any school district, except for a large city school district, who are voting at any annual or special district meeting must authorize and approve taxes for the addition, alteration, repair or improvement to the sites or buildings belonging to the district (§ 416(1), (7)).

In addition, the Education Law prohibits resubmission of propositions for construction of new school buildings (or additions at the same site) more than twice in a one-year period and prohibits the resubmission of the same or similar proposition within 90 days. However, if the proposition is to approve an additional amount necessary to carry out an already approved building project, this restriction does not apply (§ 416(6)).

16:17. May a school district contract with an architect for the preparation of preliminary plans and specifications for a school building construction project before submitting the building project to the voters?

Yes. The school board may so contract with an architect, whose fee may legitimately be paid by the district. However, before an architect prepares final plans, voter approval must be obtained at a school district meeting, except in large city school districts (Formal Opn. of Counsel No. 1, 1 Educ. Dep't Rep. 701 (1951)).

16:18. Can a school board print and distribute to the voters an informational brochure relating to a bond issue for a new school building to be approved at a district election?

Yes. However, the New York State Court of Appeals held that although a school board may use public funds to pay for an advertisement or newsletter to explain a proposed district budget or bond issue, it may not include subjective statements in such publications that, for example, urge district residents to vote "yes" because the board believes that particular budget or bond issue to be in the best interest of the school district (*Phillips v. Maurer*, 67 N.Y.2d 672 (1986)).

In order to avoid any appearance of impropriety, any informational materials sent to district voters should be kept strictly factual and impartial (*Appeal of Friedman*, 37 Educ. Dep't Rep. 363 (1998); *Appeal of Moessinger*, 33 Educ. Dep't Rep. 487 (1994)).

16:19. Can the cost of construction of a new public school building exceed the amount authorized by the school district's voters?

No. Where the voters of a school district have approved a maximum expenditure for the construction of a school, the district may not exceed the maximum amount authorized (Local Fin. Law § 37.00; 12 Opn. St. Comp. 4 (1956)).

Additional funds may be authorized only with the voters' approval either in a regular budget vote or by special referendum. If the school board deems it an emergency situation, then, within certain restrictions, a budget note can be issued to cover the excess cost (Local Fin. Law § 29).

16:20. Is the Board of Regents' approval required for a school district to undertake a construction project?

Yes, under certain circumstances. Regents' approval is required when the net bonded indebtedness, including the proposed issue, exceeds 5 percent of the average full valuation of the district for those districts wholly or partly within cities with a population of less than 125,000, or the net bonded indebtedness exceeds 10 percent of the full valuation of the district for all other districts (Local Fin. Law § 104.00(b)(8), (d)).

Net bonded indebtedness, in the case of noncity school districts, means gross indebtedness less any aid provided by the state in the form of building aid. In city school districts, no deduction can be made for state aid; here also, the approval of the comptroller is needed (Local Fin. Law § 104.00).

When Regents' approval is required, districts should consider working with the State Education Department's Bureau of Management Services in preparing a long-term financial study.

16:21. Are there required specifications on the construction of school buildings in New York State?

Yes. Details on construction of public school buildings may be found in Part 155 of the commissioner's regulations and in the "Manual of Planning Standards and Guide to Administrative Procedures." Both of these publications are available from the State Education Department's Bureau of Facilities Planning in Albany. Construction information is also available from the Department of Education's web page at http://www.nysed.gov.

16:22. Must plans and specifications for school buildings be approved by the commissioner of education?

Yes. Plans and specifications for the construction, enlargement, repair or remodeling of school facilities, other than in a city school district having a million or more residents or a BOCES district, must be submitted for the commissioner's approval when the construction cost of the work is contemplated to be at least $10,000, and for all projects that affect the health and safety of students (§ 408(1); 8 NYCRR § 155.2(a)). Plans and specifications must show detailed requirements of design and construction, space layout, circulation and exits, smoke and fire control, accident protection, visual and thermal environment and related electrical and mechanical work, sanitation features and related plumbing work (8 NYCRR § 155.2(a)(1)(i)).

The commissioner's approval of school building plans signifies only that the plans and specifications meet the minimum requirements of sections 408 and 409 of the Education Law, the commissioner's regulations and policies of the Bureau of Facilities Planning relating to educational requirements, heating, ventilation, lighting, sanitation and health, and fire and accident protection. It does not signify approval of architectural or structural design, choice of building materials, any contracts that may be awarded or executed, or any features that will go beyond the minimum requirements. Additionally, this approval gives no assurance that this project qualifies for state aid for education in accordance with the provisions of section 3602 of the Education Law.

In addition, any construction or remodeling project costing $5,000 or more must comply with the state Uniform Fire Prevention and Building Code, and Part 155 of the commissioner's regulations, and the district must procure the services of an architect or engineer licensed to practice in New York State (8 NYCRR § 155.2(b)).

16:23. How does a school district obtain the commissioner of education's approval and a building permit for a building project?

Approval of building projects is the responsibility of the State Education Department (SED), which is the lead agency for building projects. Receipt of a building permit from SED is evidence of official approval of a building project and is obtained according to the following procedure:

- A district sends a letter of intent to SED's Bureau of Facilities Planning. The letter informs the bureau that the district is planning a building project.
- The bureau sends a letter to the district acknowledging receipt of the letter of intent and informing the district what procedures must be followed and what information must be submitted. A project manager is assigned to each project. The project manager coordinates all aspects of the project and serves as the district's contact with SED. The district submits a project description form, used to determine whether an environmental impact statement (EIS) is required, as explained in **16:25**; a copy of its long-range facilities plan (see **16:1**); and the preliminary plans for the project, usually two to three pages in length.
- The bureau sends the district a notice informing it whether an EIS is needed. The bureau reviews the preliminary plans and informs the district of the approximate amount of state aid it will receive for the project.
- The bureau sends notification of preliminary approval on a form that also describes any revisions needed to be made in the plans before final plans are submitted.
- Final plans are submitted and reviewed again by bureau staff, architects and engineers. The state building aid to be received by the district is recalculated based on the final plans.
- Pending approval of the final plans, the district receives a building permit and bond certification if the project is to be funded with a bond issue (see the "Reference Guide to Capital Construction," available from SED's Bureau of Facilities Planning in Albany).

16:24. Must districts advertise for bids for construction projects?

Yes. In addition, section 101 of the General Municipal Law, more commonly referred to as the Wicks Law, requires that school districts bid out separate specifications for plumbing and gas fitting, steam heating, hot water, ventilating and air conditioning apparatus; and electrical wiring and standard illuminating fixtures on any construction program exceeding $50,000. Separate contracts must be awarded in these areas in accordance with the competitive bidding requirements of the General Municipal Law (see **19:45; 19:47**).

However, districts may not advertise bids for school building construction projects that exceed $10,000 until the plans and specifications have been submitted to and approved by the commissioner of education. There is an exception for city districts with populations of one million or more, or a BOCES district (§ 408(1); 8 NYCRR § 155.2(a)).

16:25. Are school districts required to submit a draft of an environmental impact statement to the commissioner of education when a building project is being planned?

The State Education Department assumes lead-agency status for administration of the State Environmental Quality Review Act (SEQRA) for those capital construction projects undertaken by school districts and BOCES that require the approval of the commissioner of education. The project manager will review the narrative description on the project description form submitted by the district to determine the proper course of the State Environmental Quality Review process (SEQRA Process Reference Guide, State Education Department; 6 NYCRR § 617 *et seq.;* 8 NYCRR § 155.5; see also **16:23**).

16:26. May new school buildings be occupied before they are completely finished?

Yes, but be aware that conditions may exist that could compromise the health and safety of students when new schools are occupied before they are completed.

At the time of substantial completion of the project (when the work is sufficiently complete for occupancy of the building for its intended use), the architect or engineer must submit a certification of substantial completion form to the commissioner of education (8 NYCRR § 155.2(a)(6)). The district also must have an inspection of the building conducted to ensure that the building is suitable for occupancy and free of violations of the State Uniform Fire Prevention and Building Code and the commissioner's regulations. A satisfactory report will result in a certificate of occupancy (8 NYCRR § 155.4(e)). Following receipt and posting of the certificate of occupancy, the building can be fully used (see the "Reference Guide to Capital Construction," available from SED's Bureau of Facilities Planning in Albany).

16:27. Must school buildings be accessible to persons with disabilities?

Yes. Under the federal Americans with Disabilities Act (ADA), school districts must ensure that all new construction or alterations to existing facilities are accessible to persons with disabilities. However, districts are not required to make structural changes to existing facilities if other methods would make their programs accessible to individuals with disabilities (42 USC § 12101 *et seq.*).

16:28. Are there legal restrictions in determining wages for workers on school construction contracts?

Yes. The state Labor Law requires that the "prevailing rate of wages" be paid to all workers on public school building projects in the state. This includes construction, alterations and repairs (Lab. Law § 220(3)), even when the work is performed by staff from a board of cooperative educational services (BOCES) *(Cayuga-Onondaga Counties Bd. of Co-op. Educational Services v. Sweeney*, 89 N.Y.2d 395 (1996)).

The determination of prevailing wages must be made in accordance with the rates of wages paid pursuant to collective bargaining agreements in the locality in which the work is done (Lab. Law § 220(5)(a)).

16:29. Can districts receive state aid for a portion of the approved expenditures associated with a building project?

Yes. State building aid is available to reimburse school districts for portions of the costs of borrowing to fund building programs. The amount of building aid is determined by an aid ratio based on district property wealth per pupil. Property-poor districts are reimbursed for a greater portion of their building expenditures than property-wealthy districts (§ 3602(6)).

In addition, if school districts have expenditures for site purchase, grading or improvement of the site, original furnishings, equipment, machinery or apparatus, professional fees or other incidental costs with the commissioner of education's approval, the cost allowances for new construction and the purchase of existing structures can be increased by the actual expenditures for such purposes up to 20 percent for school buildings or additions housing kindergarten through grade six, or 25 percent for school buildings or additions housing grades seven through 12 and special education programs (§ 3602 (6)(a)(2)).

According to section 3602(6-b) of the Education Law, building aid is also available for the construction of joint facilities by two or more school districts that are eligible for building aid, with the exception of the Big 5 city school districts. To be eligible for this aid, the general contracts for the project must have been awarded on or after July 1, 1993 and the project and joint agreement must have been approved by the commissioner. For participating school districts in which the school budget is subject to voter approval, the joint agreement is subject to voter approval.

16:30. Can a district receive building aid for a leased building?

Yes. A district can receive building aid if the leased school or facility meets requirements for access by individuals with disabilities to both facilities and programs, as defined in the commissioner's regulations (§ 403-b(1)(e); 8 NYCRR § 155.8(b)(6)(i)). The leased space must be used to house programs for students in grades prekindergarten through 12, with minimal associated administrative and support services space, as approved by the commissioner of education (§§ 3602(6); 2503(8)).

16:31. May a public school rent highway equipment from a county highway department to construct or repair school roads or for snow removal?

Yes, as provided in section 133-a of the Highway Law. The state comptroller has indicated that loaning an operator for the equipment is also an implied authorization (Opn. St. Comp. 58-328).

Closing of School Buildings

16:32. Can certain areas of a school building be declared unsafe and unusable?

Yes. If the commissioner of education judges the general condition of a school building, or any part or area, would be detrimental to the health and safety of its occupants, he may designate an area or areas of the building as unusable or may limit the number of occupants allowed in that area (8 NYCRR § 155.3(j)).

16:33. Does a school board have the right to close school buildings and create new attendance zones without voter approval?

Yes. Decisions about the assignment of students and the establishment of reasonable methods of zoning for the purpose of school attendance rest with the school board under section 1709 of the Education Law (see *Matter of Lanfear*, 31 Educ. Dep't Rep. 340 (1992); *Matter of Furman*, 15 Educ. Dep't Rep. 70 (1975)).

16:34. Are there any specific procedures a school board must follow before closing down a school building?

Yes. As indicated by section 402-a of the Education Law, a notice of the proposed closing must be published in a newspaper in the community, posted conspicuously in the affected school district, and circulated to elected state and local public officials who represent the affected communities. The board must also hold a public hearing to evaluate the impact of the proposed closing on the affected district before rendering a decision (§ 402-a).

In addition, a district may establish an advisory committee on school building utilization to investigate the educational impact of the closing six months prior to the scheduled closing. The Education Law indicates the following factors must be reviewed as the committee makes its findings. These include, but are not limited to, the following:

- The current and projected pupil enrollment, the prospective need for such a building, the ramifications of such closing upon the community, initial costs and savings resulting from such closing, and the potential disposability of the closed school.
- The possible use of the school building for other educational programs or administrative services.
- The effect of the closing on personnel needs, and on the costs of instruction, administration, transportation and other support services.
- The type, age and physical condition of the building, outstanding indebtedness, maintenance and energy costs, recent or planned improvements for the building, and such building's special features.
- The ability of the other schools in the affected district to accommodate students if the school building closes.
- The possible shared utilization of space in such school building during or after regular school hours, pursuant to the Education Law.

The committee's educational impact statement findings must be filed with the school board (§ 402-a).

Use of Public School Buildings, Grounds and Equipment

16:35. What uses of school buildings may be permitted by a school board under the Education Law?

Section 414(1) of the Education Law sets forth the permissible uses of school buildings. As long as the school board determines that the particular use will not disrupt normal school operations, school buildings and grounds and other property of the district may be used for the following:

- Instruction in any branch of education, learning or the arts.
- Public libraries or stations of public libraries.
- Social, civic and recreational meetings and entertainments and other uses pertaining to the welfare of the community that are nonexclusive and open to the general public.
- Meetings, entertainments and occasions where admission fees are

charged, when the proceeds are to be expended for an educational or charitable purpose. However, these uses are not permitted if they are under exclusive control and the proceeds are to be applied for the benefit of a society, association or organization of a religious sect or denomination, or of a fraternal, secret or exclusive society or organization other than organizations of veterans of the military, naval and marine service of the United States and organizations of volunteer fire fighters or volunteer ambulance workers.

- Polling places for holding primaries and elections, for the registration of voters and for holding political meetings. However, no meetings sponsored by political organizations are permitted unless authorized by the voters' approval, or, in cities, approved by the school board. Except in cities, it is the school board's duty to call a special meeting for these purposes upon the petition of at least 10 percent of the qualified electors of the district (see § 414 (1)(e); Elec. Law § 4-104).
- Civic forums and community centers (see § 414(1)(f)).
- Classes of instruction for mentally retarded minors operated by a private organization that is approved by the commissioner of education.
- Recreation, physical training and athletics, including competitive athletic contests of children attending a private, nonprofit school.
- Child-care programs when school is not in session, or when school is in session for the children of students attending schools of the district and, if there is additional space available, for children of employees of the district, to be determined by the school board.
- Graduation exercises held by not-for-profit elementary and secondary schools, provided that no religious service is performed.

16:36. Who has the final authority in granting use of a public school building?

Section 414 of the Education Law gives a school board the authority to adopt reasonable regulations with regard to granting the use of school buildings to outside organizations. In New York City, each community school board is authorized to prohibit any uses of school buildings and grounds within its district which is otherwise granted by section 414 of the Education Law (§ 414(1)).

No association or organization has the right to use a school building without the express permission of the board. For example, local teachers' associations or organizations are not entitled as a matter of right to use a school building for meetings *(Matter of Charlotte Valley*, 18 PERB ¶ 3010 (1985)).

The board has the authority to prescribe the terms of use of a school building and may also refuse to grant an organization's request for use. For example, if it can be proven that a "clear and present danger" of possible damage to the building exists, the board can deny access to the organization (*Matter of Ellis*, 77 St. Dep't Rep. 32 (1956)).

16:37. Can private or restricted meetings be held in a public school building?

No. Meetings, entertainment and other uses of a public school building cannot be restricted and must be open to the general public (§ 414(1)(c)). School districts permitting community use of school property for after-school programs are required to ensure such programs are open to all school districts' children, regardless of whether they attend public or private school (see § 414(2)).

16:38. Can a school building be used as a polling place in a general election?

Yes. A school building can be designated as a registration and polling place, if this use of the building will not interfere with its customary use, and if it is conveniently situated for the voters residing in the election district. Any expense incurred as a result of this use must be paid like the expenses of other registration and polling places (§ 414).

If an election board selects a public school as a polling place, school officials are required to make available a room suitable for registration and voting as close as possible to the main entrance (Elec. Law § 4-104).

16:39. May school property be used to provide child-care services?

Yes. Section 410-c(5) of the Social Services Law and section 414 of the Education Law authorizes child-care programs for school-age children during hours school is not in session and permits school buildings to be used for this purpose. In addition, section 414(1)(i) of the Education Law authorizes the use of school facilities for child-care services during school hours for children of students attending school. These services may also be made available to school employees, depending on space availability and as determined by the school board.

16:40. Can a district conduct bingo or similar games in a school building?

Only in very limited circumstances. According to article 1, section 9 of the New York State Constitution, any city, town or village may authorize bingo or similar games within the municipality. Only bona fide religious, charitable or nonprofit organizations are permitted to conduct these games, and the entire net proceeds must be devoted to the lawful purposes of the organization. However, section 414 of the Education Law prohibits the use of a school building by exclusionary groups.

Therefore, the only types of outside groups that could use a school building for this purpose would be charitable or nonprofit organizations, such as PTAs, veterans, volunteer fire fighters or volunteer ambulance workers. Proceeds from the games would go to benefit these groups, and only after the city, town or village approved the games.

16:41. May the military use school facilities to recruit students?

Yes. Section 2-a of the Education Law provides such authority. However, in *Lloyd v. Grella*, 83 N.Y.2d 537 (1994), the New York State Court of Appeals upheld a school policy barring groups access to school facilities if such groups had engaged in discriminatory practices. The district had barred the military from access to school facilities, basing its action upon its belief that the military discriminated against homosexuals. The court held that no special status set forth in section 2-a was granted to the military, and, therefore, the school district's policy was not illegal so long as all groups with discriminatory policies were equally barred from access on that basis.

16:42. May a school building be used by an outside religious organization?

Yes. A school building may be used by an outside religious organization just like any other community group. However, a school building may not be used by such an organization if a meeting, entertainment or occasion sponsored by such an organization is under its exclusive control and any proceeds from its activity are to be applied for the benefit of the religious organization (§ 414(1)(d)).

The United States Supreme Court has ruled that school districts cannot deny access to religious organizations solely on the basis that they would present a religious perspective, where the school would permit other groups to present their views on the same topic *(Lamb's Chapel v. Center Moriches UFSD*, 508 U.S. 384 (1993)).

Applying this precedent, the United States Court of Appeals for the Eighth Circuit ruled a school district acted unconstitutionally when it closed its facilities between 3 p.m. and 6 p.m. to all community groups except the Boy Scouts, thereby depriving other groups from expressing their views on morals and character development from a religious perspective, even though the Boy Scouts were allowed to address such issues *(Good News/Good Sports Club v. School Dist.*, 28 F.3d 1501 (8th Cir. 1994), *cert. denied*, 115 S.Ct. 2640 (1995)). While not binding on New York State school districts, courts in the state may consider the Eighth Circuit's decision.

However, a district may enact a policy that prohibits any organization from using school facilities for lectures, presentations, demonstrations, political events or seminars. The key requirement is that such a restriction be applied uniformly to all applicants, regardless of their viewpoints (*Saratoga Bible Institute, Inc. v. Schuylerville Central School District*, __ F.Supp. __ (N.D.N.Y. 1998)).

16:43. Are school districts authorized to permit outside religious groups to use school facilities for purposes of conducting religious worship services or to conduct religious instruction?

No. The use of school property for religious worship or instruction is not among the uses in the Education Law (§ 414). In addition, the United States Court of Appeals for the Second Circuit upheld a school district's policy and regulation, based on section 414 of the Education Law, which prohibited an outside organization or group from conducting religious services or religious instruction on school premises (*Bronx Household of Faith v. Community School District No. 10*, 127 F.3d 207 (2nd Cir. 1997), *cert. denied*, 1998 WL 85986).

At press time there was a case pending before the United States Court of Appeals for the Second Circuit which raises the issue as to whether a school district which had erroneously allowed an outside organization to use school facilities for conducting religious worship services in the past, is required to permit future use of school facilities for such purpose. In that case, the lower court ruled that the school district was not required to grant such access *(Full Gospel Tabernacle v. Community School District 27*, 97 F. Supp. 214 (S.D.N.Y. 1997); compare with *Liberty Christian Center, Inc. v. Watertown School District*, 1998 WL 328378 (N.D.N.Y.)).

16:44. May students use a school building for Bible study meetings?

Yes. The Federal Equal Access Act (20 USC § 4071) requires that public secondary schools that receive federal financial assistance must provide students equal access to the forum and not deny them use of school facilities on the basis of the religious, political, philosophical or other content of the speech that can be expected to take place at the meeting if it permits student groups to use school premises for any noncurriculum-related purpose. The United States Supreme Court held the act is constitutional in *Board of Educ. of Westside Community Schools v. Mergens*, 496 U.S. 226 (1990).

The act requires that:
• Meetings be voluntary and initiated by the students.
• There be no sponsorship of the meeting by the school, the government, or its agents or employees.

- Employees or agents of the school or government attend only in a nonparticipatory capacity.
- Meetings do not interfere materially and substantially with the orderly conduct of educational activities within the school.
- Nonschool people do not direct, conduct, control or regularly attend activities of student groups.

The United States Court of Appeals for the Second Circuit ruled that a school district may not preclude a student Bible club from meeting on school premises by claiming that the club violated the district's non-discrimination policy because the club's constitution required that only Christians could serve as officers of the club (*Hsu by & Through Hsu v. Roslyn Union Free Sch. Dist. No. 3*, 85 F.3d 839 (2nd Cir. 1996), *cert. denied*, 117 S.Ct. 608 (1996)).

16:45. May a school building be used for religious instruction during school hours?

No. The use of a school building for religious instruction is prohibited by article 11 of the New York State Constitution (see *Illinois ex. rel. McCollum v. Board of Education*, 333 U.S. 203 (1948); see also **23:1**). However, schools may offer comparative religion courses so long as such courses teach *about* religion as opposed to proselytizing religious messages.

16:46. May a school district charge for the use of its facilities by outside organizations?

Yes. The Education Law provides that a school board may adopt reasonable regulations for the use of its buildings and grounds, including a schedule of fees as prescribed by law (§ 414). For instance, a school district is authorized to charge for the cost of maintaining its facility or property (i.e., heat, electricity, custodian/maintenance costs). Although this issue has not yet come before the courts, failure to charge for such costs might be deemed to violate the state constitutional prohibition against gifts of public funds.

A school board may also charge a nonresident for the use of district property (e.g., jogging track), since the commissioner of education has interpreted the Education Law to require that any meeting, entertainment or other use for the benefit of the community be non-exclusive and open only to the general public of the school district, i.e., to the residents of the school district (*Matter of Emilio*, 33 Educ. Dep't Rep. 75 (1993)). According to the commissioner, it would be highly unusual to interpret the language of section 414(1)(c) as compelling school districts to open up the uses of its property intended to promote the welfare of the community served by the school district to those who did not reside in the community.

16:47. May a school district charge churches higher fees than other non-profit organizations for the use of school facilities?

No. To charge churches higher fees than other nonprofit organizations would discriminate against religious speech and interfere with or burden the church's right to speak and practice religion as protected by the free exercise clause *(Fairfax Covenant Church v. Fairfax County Sch. Bd.,* 17 F.3d 703 (4th Cir. 1994), *cert. denied,* 511 U.S. 1143 (1994)).

16:48. May a school district allow admission fees to be charged to school-sponsored athletic events held on school grounds and permit the broadcasting of such events?

Yes. A school board may allow admission fees to be charged to school-sponsored athletic events held on school grounds as long as the proceeds are expended for school purposes (§ 414(1)(d); Opn. St. Comp. 81-18). A board also may allow radio and television stations to broadcast reports on high school games and other events, even though the broadcasts may be commercially sponsored (Arts & Cult. Aff. Law § 61.09).

16:49. Do school districts have the authority to loan school equipment, such as trucks or tools, to members of their communities?

No. This would likely constitute a gift or loan of public property, which is unconstitutional under article 8, section 1 of the state constitution. However, school districts can provide equipment when permitting use of school buildings or grounds, under section 414 of the Education Law.

16:50. Must school districts display the American flag?

Yes. The Education and Executive Laws require that a district purchase and display the American flag on or near the public school building during school hours every school day (§ 418; Exec. Law § 403(5)). However, the flag may not be displayed in inclement weather, in which case it is to be displayed in the "principal room of the schoolhouse" (§ 420; Exec. Law § 403(3)). Outside display, except on special occasions for patriotic effects, is limited to the hours from sunrise to sunset (Exec. Law § 403(1)).

In addition, the Executive Law further requires that the flag be displayed, weather permitting, on holidays, including:

- New Year's Day (January 1)
- Dr. Martin Luther King, Jr., Day (third Monday in January)
- Lincoln's Birthday (February 12)
- Washington's Birthday (third Monday in February)
- Memorial Day (last Monday in May)
- Flag Day (second Sunday in June)

- Independence Day (July 4)
- Labor Day (first Monday in September)
- POW/MIA Recognition Day (third Friday in September, or if this is in conflict with a religious observance, the second Friday in September)
- Columbus Day (second Monday in October)
- Veterans Day (November 11)
- Thanksgiving Day (fourth Thursday in November)
- Pearl Harbor Day (December 7)
- Christmas Day (December 25)

If any of these holidays fall on a Sunday (except for Flag Day), the flag should be displayed the next day. In addition, the flag must be displayed on any general election day and on any day designated by the president of the United States or the governor of New York State as a day of general thanksgiving or for displaying the flag (Exec. Law § 403(2)).

The flag is to be displayed at full staff except that it must be flown at half-mast on December 7 (Pearl Harbor Day); on days commemorating the death of a personage of national or state standing, of a local service-man, or of an official or public servant who, in the opinion of the school district, contributed to the community; and it may be flown at half-mast on days designated by the president of the United States or the governor of New York State as special periods of mourning (Exec. Law § 403(21)). One court has held, however, that it is improper for a district to fly its flag at half-mast as an expression of political dissent *(Lapolla v. Dullaghan, 63 Misc.2d 157 (1970))*.

In addition, the flag must be displayed in all assembly rooms of the school, (i.e. the auditorium) pursuant to the regulations of the commissioner of education (§ 419; 8 NYCRR §§ 108.1-108.3). The willful failure to comply with § 419 is a misdemeanor.

The Education Law also requires that school authorities establish rules and regulations governing the proper care, custody and display of the flag (§ 420). Both the United States Code and the Executive Law provide guidance regarding the proper display and care of the flag (36 USC §§ 171-178; Exec. Law § 403). In addition, the commissioner's regulations provide the requirements for the material and size of the flag, care of the flag, and for its display in assembly rooms (8 NYCRR Part 108).

16:51. Must the salute to the flag and the pledge of allegiance to the flag be recited daily in school?

Yes. Section 802 of the Education Law requires that the commissioner of education prepare a program for public schools that provides for the salute to the flag and a daily pledge of allegiance to the flag, and for instruction in its correct use and display (§ 802; 8 NYCRR § 108).

However, students have the right to abstain from reciting the pledge, and teachers have the right to stand silently during the daily recitation of the pledge. In *West Virginia State Bd. of Educ. v. Barnette*, 319 U.S. 624 (1943), the United States Supreme Court ruled that requiring teachers and students to stand in salute of the flag and recite the pledge of allegiance against their religious beliefs constituted a violation of their rights under the Free Exercise Clause of the First Amendment to the U.S. Constitution (see also *Russo v. CSD No. 1*, 469 F.2d 623 (2nd Cir. 1972), *cert. denied, CSD No. 1 v. Russo*, 411 U.S. 932 (1973)).

In addition, those refusing to salute the flag may not be required to either stand or leave the room, according to the United States Court of Appeals for the Second Circuit, which has jurisdiction over New York State. According to the court, the act of standing itself is a "gesture of acceptance"; the option of leaving the room, "punishment [for] nonparticipation" (*Goetz v. Ansell*, 477 F.2d 636 (2nd Cir. 1973)).

The official text of the pledge and the manner in which it must be recited is contained in the commissioner's regulations. The text is: "I pledge allegiance to the Flag of the United States of America and to the Republic for which it stands, one Nation, under God, indivisible, with liberty and justice for all" (8 NYCRR § 108.5).

Conduct on School Property

16:52. Is the school board responsible for regulating conduct on school district property?

Yes. School boards must adopt rules and regulations for the maintenance of public order on school property and ensure they are enforced (§ 2801). These rules and regulations must govern the conduct of students, teachers and other staff, as well as visitors and other licensees and invitees. They must be filed with the Board of Regents and the commissioner of education. This requirement also applies to any amendments, which must be filed no later than 10 days after their adoption. If a board fails to follow these filing requirements, the district may not be eligible to receive any state aid or assistance until the regulations are filed. The penalties for violations must be clearly set forth and must include provisions for ejecting a person from school property, and, in the case of a student or teacher, his or her suspension, or other appropriate disciplinary action. The law states that this section of the Education Law is not intended to limit or restrict anyone's freedom of speech or right to peaceful assembly (§ 2801).

However, the Federal District Court for the Northern District of New York found that a school district which barred a reporter from school grounds did not violate the reporter's First Amendment rights to freedom of the press, speech or association, where the reporter had attempted to initiate personal contacts of a sexual nature with two female coaches and then failed to stop at the district's directive. The court found the district's order to bar the reporter from attending athletic events and restricting his contact with coaches to written and telephone contact through the main office or athletic office was a reasonably tailored time, place and manner regulation that did not restrict all forms of news gathering access (*Hone v. Cortland City School District,* 985 F.Supp. 262 (N.D.N.Y. 1998)).

16:53. Is it unlawful to loiter on school grounds?

Yes. To loiter has been interpreted to mean to be slow in moving, to delay, to be dilatory, to saunter or to lag behind. Section 240.35(5) of the Penal Law states that any person who is not a parent or legal guardian of a student in regular attendance, who loiters on or about any school building or grounds, public or private, without written permission or in violation of posted rules, is guilty of violating the law. That person also may be charged with criminal trespass (Penal Law § 140.00).

16:54. Is it unlawful to draw graffiti upon school property?

Yes. Sections 145.60 and 145.65 of the state Penal Law establish the making of graffiti as a class A misdemeanor and the possession of graffiti instruments a class B misdemeanor. The Education Law states that school districts may offer monetary rewards of no more than $1,000 to individuals for information leading to the arrest and conviction of any person or persons for felonies or misdemeanors directly connected to vandalism of district property (§ 1604(38)).

16:55. Are there funds available to help school districts prevent violence and drug abuse within the community?

Yes. Under the Safe and Drug-Free Schools and Communities Act (SDFSCA, 20 USC § 7101 *et seq.*), local school districts are eligible to receive funds to develop comprehensive drug and violence prevention programs which are designed to:

- Prevent the use, possession, and distribution of tobacco, alcohol, and illegal drugs by students.

• Prevent violence and promote school safety.

• Create a disciplined environment conducive to learning (20 USC § 7116(a)(1); see also **12:57**).

To further these goals, the act provides funds for a number of initiatives, including "safe zones of passage" for students between home and school through such measures as drug-free school zones, enhanced law enforcement and neighborhood patrols (20 USC § 7116(b)(5)).

16:56. What are drug-free school zones?

A *drug-free school zone* is an area within 1,000 feet of a school. Signs designating the drug-free school zone may be erected upon the request of a school district and in cooperation with those entities having jurisdiction over the highways (Highway Law § 317).

In addition, the New York State Penal Law defines as a felony the criminal sale of drugs within any building, structure, athletic playing field, playground or land contained within the real property boundary line of a public or private child day care center or nursery, prekindergarten, kindergarten, elementary, parochial, intermediate, junior high, vocational, or high school, or any area accessible to the public or any parked vehicle located within 1,000 feet of the real property line comprising any such school (Penal Law §§ 220.00; 220.34; 220.44).

16:57. May a school district establish its own traffic and parking regulations on school property?

Yes. Local authorities, including school districts, have the power to regulate, restrict, or prohibit parking or standing and to regulate the direction of traffic. They also may regulate the speed of motor vehicles and motorcycles. In addition, they may restrict or prohibit the movement of motor vehicles and motorcycles on any parking fields, driveways or public ways accessory to any school, playground, park, municipal building, installation or facility under the jurisdiction of the school district or local authorities for general regulatory or custodial purposes (Veh. and Traf. Law § 1670; see also chap. 22 for further details).

16:58. Can a school district prohibit the sale of sweetened foods to students in school?

Yes. Section 915 of the Education Law prohibits the sale of certain sweetened foods, including, but not limited to, soda, chewing gum and candy, from the beginning of the school day until the end of the last scheduled meal period.

Commercialism in the Public Schools

16:59. Can a school district allow commercial television or radio programming in its schools?

No. Part 23 of the Rules of the Board of Regents prohibits a school district from entering into a contract that, in whole or in part, promises the district will permit commercial promotional activity on school premises through electronic media, such as the promotion or sale of products and services on television or radio (8 NYCRR § 23.2). However, the rules state that this should not be construed as prohibiting commercial sponsorship of school activities.

16:60. Can a school district allow the sale of student photographs by a private business firm on school grounds?

Ordinarily, no, because this action would violate the New York State Constitution (Art. 8, § 1). However, where photographs are taken "for a valid school purpose," such as for the school yearbook, they may be taken on school premises during school hours. But school personnel may not solicit or collect money for this purpose (*Matter of Fusare*, 20 Educ. Dep't Rep. 14 (1980); *Matter of Hoyt*, 17 Educ. Dep't Rep. 173 (1977); *Matter of Albert*, 7 Educ. Dep't Rep. 7 (1967); see also memo of August 27, 1974, from Counsel for State Educ. Dep't: "Sale of School Photographs").

School rings may be sold on the school premises if certain specific conditions are met (*Matter of Gary Credit Corp.*, 26 Educ. Dep't Rep. 414 (1987)).

16:61. Can a school district allow the collection of money from students for charitable donations in the schools?

No. Section 19.6 of the Rules of the Board of Regents prohibits the direct solicitation of charitable donations from children in the public schools during the school day. However, there are three types of activities which this section does not proscribe:

- Fund-raising activities which take place off school premises or outside of the regular school day. Thus, recruiting children during the school day for participation in fund-raising activities is permissible as long as the activities themselves occur off school premises or outside of the school day.
- Arms-length transactions where the contributor receives something for his or her donation. Thus, this rule does not prohibit the sale of goods or tickets for concerts or admission to social events where the proceeds go to charity, because the purchaser receives a con-

sideration — the concert or admission to a social event — for the funds expended.

• Indirect forms of charitable solicitation on school premises that do not involve coercion, such as having a bin or collection box in a hallway or other common area for the donation of food, clothing or money. In these instances, the collection activity is passive, and no pressure is exerted upon students to participate.

What the rule does prohibit is approaching students in their classrooms or homerooms and asking them directly to donate money or goods to charity (see "Guidelines Relating to Solicitation of Charitable Donations from School Children," State Education Department, January, 1994).

17. School Building Safety

Emergency Management

17:1. Must school districts have emergency-management plans?

Yes. Except for New York City, each school district and board of cooperative educational services (BOCES) must have an emergency-management plan which must be updated by October 1 every year (8 NYCRR § 155.13). This plan is intended to insure the safety and health of children and staff, and must be designed to "prevent or minimize the effects of emergencies and to coordinate the use of resources" (8 NYCRR § 155.13 (b)) with emergency planning at the state, county and municipal levels (8 NYCRR § 155.13).

Emergencies include natural and human disasters, such as extreme weather conditions (snow, ice storms, hurricanes, tornadoes and earthquakes), technological failures (power failures, chemical and radiological accidents, fires and explosions), bomb and hostage threats, fuel and water shortages, and epidemics.

The emergency-management plan must include:

- Identification of sites of potential emergencies.
- Identification of appropriate responses to emergencies.
- Arrangements for obtaining assistance from emergency-services organizations and local government agencies.
- Procedures for coordinating the use of district resources and personnel during emergencies.
- Identification of district resources available during emergencies.
- A system for informing all schools within the district of emergencies.
- Plans for school cancellation, early dismissal, evacuation and sheltering.
- Pertinent information about each school, such as population, number of staff and transportation needs.
- Procedures for obtaining advice and assistance from local government officials (8 NYCRR § 155.13 (b)).

During the occurrence of a local or state emergency, the district superintendent serves as a communications liaison to notify all public and nonpublic schools within his or her supervisory district. The superintendents of schools in the Big 5 city school districts of Buffalo, New York City, Rochester, Syracuse and Yonkers perform this function for all educational agencies within their city districts (8 NYCRR § 155.13(d)).

Local county emergency-management or civil defense offices are available to help school officials coordinate their plan for disasters. These offices are located in each county and a number of cities. School officials should make sure their district's disaster plans are coordinated with local disaster-preparedness plans (Unconsol. Laws § 9121(3); see also Exec. Law § 20). Planning assistance also is available from the State Education Department's Facilities Planning Office, EBA, Room 1069, Albany, N.Y. 12234.

17:2. Are school districts required to conduct emergency management drills?

Yes. Each school district and BOCES annually must conduct an emergency management plan drill, including sheltering and early dismissal (at a time no earlier than 15 minutes before normal dismissal), in coopera-tion with local county emergency-preparedness-plan officials if possible. Parents or guardians must be notified of the drill at least one week in advance (8 NYCRR § 155.13(g)).

School officials also are required to hold bus emergency drills (§ 3623(2); 8 NYCRR § 156.3(h); see **22:41**)).

17:3. Are school districts required to conduct fire drills?

Yes. School districts must conduct fire drills to ensure that, in the event of an emergency, students will be "able to leave the school building in the shortest possible time and without confusion or panic" (§ 807; see **14:38**).

In addition, school officials must provide students with fire and arson prevention instruction. This instruction must be at least 45 minutes a month when school is in session (§ 808; see **14:38**).

17:4. Are school districts required to hold emergency drills for after-school programs?

No. However, a principal or other person in charge of the school building during an after-school program, event or performance must notify the participants who are not regular occupants of the building of the procedures to be followed, should an emergency occur (§ 807(1-a)).

17:5. What should a district do if it receives a bomb threat?

In addition to following its emergency management plan, the district should notify the local police immediately. Section 240.55 of the Penal Law states that any person who knowingly reports false information or initiates or circulates a false warning of an impending occurrence of a fire or explosion to an official or quasi-official agency that deals with emergencies is guilty of a misdemeanor.

For more information, see "New York State Education Department School Emergency Management Planning Bomb Threat Standards: Law, Regulation, and Policy Requirements."

17:6. Who makes the decision to close schools because of an emergency?

Schools may be closed by the local school board, which frequently delegates this authority to the superintendent of schools (see **21:19** for the effect of closing the schools on state aid payments).

Building Structure Safety

17:7. Who promulgates health and safety regulations for public school buildings in New York State?

The commissioner of education is authorized to promulgate health and safety regulations for all educational facilities. These regulations apply to all public school districts other than city school districts in cities of 125,000 or more residents (§ 409; 8 NYCRR Part 155).

For example, the commissioner must approve all plans and specifications for newly constructed school buildings when the project costs are $10,000 or greater, and for all projects affecting the health and safety of students (8 NYCRR § 155.2(a)) . Likewise, the commissioner must approve plans and specifications for the enlargement, repair or remodeling of existing buildings for the same project costs. Additionally, when approving new lease agreements by school districts, the commissioner must determine whether the leased facility meets "all applicable standards for the health, safety and comfort of occupants" (§ 403-b(1)(c)).

The commissioner also has the power to designate a school building or a particular area within a school building as "unusable for pupil occupancy" when, based on these regulations, the general conditions of the building indicate it would be detrimental to the health and safety of its occupants (8 NYCRR § 155.3(j)).

17:8. What subjects are covered by the commissioner's regulations on school building safety?

The commissioner's regulations detail safety requirements for a broad range of subjects, such as building exits (8 NYCRR § 155.3(a)); fire and smoke control (8 NYCRR §155.3(b)); accident protection (8 NYCRR § 155.3(c)); mechanical equipment, including heating, ventilation and air conditioning (HVAC) systems (8 NYCRR § 155.3(d)); water and sanitation systems (8 NYCRR § 155.3(e)); natural gas (8 NYCRR § 155.3(f)); and electrical systems (8 NYCRR § 155.3(g)). For example, the regulations forbid the obstruction of emergency exits and mandate that safety glass be used in certain areas of school buildings.

The regulations also cover structural inspections of school buildings (8 NYCRR § 155.1(d), see **17:10**); fire and building safety inspections

(8 NYCRR§ 155.4; see **17:11**); and school emergency-management plans (8 NYCRR § 155.13; see **17:1**).

17:9. Are electronically-operated doors covered by safety rules?

Yes. School districts which have electronically-operated doors or partitions must post notices concerning their safe operation, and adopt a policy concerning notification to employees and others of proper procedures for their operation (§ 409-d).

17:10. Are school building structural inspections required?

Yes. Under Chapter 56 of the Laws of 1998, the commissioner of education is directed to establish, develop and monitor a comprehensive public school building safety program, including a uniform inspection, safety rating and monitoring system. According to this legislation, the program will require an annual inspection of all public school buildings throughout the state. In addition, each school district will be required to develop a building condition survey and a five-year capital facilities plan.

At press time, the State Education Department (SED) had not yet adopted the necessary regulations to implement the legislation. Therefore, SED recommends that school districts continue to perform structural inspections as previously required until the new regulations are adopted (§ 409-d).

17:11. Are fire-safety inspections required for school buildings?

Yes. Annual inspections are required at least once a year for fire and safety hazards that may endanger the lives of students, teachers and other employees. BOCES and school districts, except for the Big 5, must have all their school buildings inspected by a qualified inspector under procedures established by the State Fire Administrator. This inspection report must be filed in the district offices and with the commissioner of education. A school administrator has the right to be present during this inspection (§ 807-a). The annual inspection must be conducted in accordance with a schedule established by the commissioner of education. All buildings, including those owned, leased or used in any manner by the district, must have a separate fire-safety inspection (§ 807-a; see also 8 NYCRR § 155.4(a)).

In addition, the commissioner of education may order a fire-safety inspection at any reasonable time. School authorities may not refuse the inspector access to the school building. In addition, any public school building may be inspected at any reasonable time by the local fire chief or a fire fighter assigned to do so by the fire chief (§ 807-a(6), (7)).

17:12. Who is responsible for enforcing fire-safety requirements in the public schools?

The commissioner of education has the responsibility to administer and enforce the New York State Uniform Fire Prevention and Building Code (see 9 NYCRR Parts 600–1250) with respect to buildings, premises and equipment in the custody of school districts and boards of cooperative educational services (BOCES) (8 NYCRR § 155.4 (a)-(c)).

The commissioner has the authority to issue a certificate of occupancy to public school districts which indicates that a school building is in compliance with part 155 of the commissioner's regulations and with the New York State Uniform Fire Prevention and Building Code (8 NYCRR § 155.4 (e)(1)). The commissioner also has the power to issue temporary certificates of occupancy, and to deny or revoke certificates of occupancy to school districts that fail to comply with these standards (8 NYCRR § 155.4(e)(2),(3)).

17:13. What happens if a public school building does not pass a fire inspection?

If a school building fails to pass a fire inspection, the school board must adopt a plan, approved by the commissioner, to correct all violations. The commissioner may issue a temporary certificate of occupancy pending these corrections and, particularly when the building is not suitable for occupancy or intended use, he may refuse to issue or revoke an existing certificate of occupancy (8 NYCRR § 155.4(e)).

17:14. Must the school district inform the public of the results of fire-safety inspections?

Yes. Fire inspection reports must be filed in the school district and with the commisisoner of education (see **17:11**). All such reports shall be retained as public record for at least three years. Within 20 days, school districts must also publish a notice in a local newspaper stating the report has been filed.

17:15. Must a school's fire alarm system be connected with the community's fire departments?

Yes, wherever practical. The school's fire alarm system must be connected if the school building is located in a fire district that has an electrically-operated, general municipal fire alarm box system so that sounding the school-building fire alarm system automatically relays the alarm to the fire department (8 NYCRR § 155.3(g)(4)). Additionally, wherever practical, a fire alarm box compatible with the municipal system must be located and accessible on the site or in the school building.

In a case where a fire district may not have an electrically-operated, general municipal fire alarm system, it is up to the district to decide whether to connect the school building to the fire department (§ 807-c; see also 8 NYCRR § 155.3(g)(4)).

17:16. What authority does the local fire department have if a school building fire alarm is activated?

If a school building's fire alarm goes off, the fire department has the authority to enter the school building to determine whether the fire is out and whether the building is safe for occupancy, even in the event of a false alarm (Gen. Mun. Law § 204–d). School officials may not deny fire fighters access to the school building or order them to leave (Inf. Opn. Att'y Gen. 81–13).

If a school building's fire alarm sounds, students may not reenter the building until the fire department determines the building is safe for occupancy. Only the fire department, not the police department or school district, has the authority to order students back into the building (Inf. Opn. Att'y Gen. 83–67, 81–13).

Workplace Safety

17:17. Are school districts required to provide a safe workplace for school employees?

Yes. However, while the employer is required to furnish a workplace that is free from recognized hazards to employees, employees also must comply with safety and health standards and other regulations that are applicable to their own actions and conduct (Lab. Law § 27-a; see also Lab. Law § 884 for information on workplace safety training and education programs).

17:18. Who is responsible for enforcing workplace safety requirements?

Schools are governed by the Public Employees' Safety and Health (PESH) Bureau of the New York State Department of Labor, which was established by the State Occupational Safety and Health Act (SOSHA) (Lab. Law § 27-a), to protect public employees from hazards in their workplaces. PESH's jurisdiction covers public employers and employees, including both instructional and noninstructional employees of school districts.

17:19. What does the Public Employees' Safety and Health (PESH) Bureau require of school districts with regard to worker safety rules?

School districts must comply with worker safety rules adopted by PESH that run the gamut from very general to explicitly precise. In general, districts are required to maintain a safe workplace under what is known as the "general duty clause" (Lab. Law § 27-a(3)(a)(1)). Other PESH rules are more detailed and precise, such as the Hazard Communication Standard (see **17:25-27**) and the chemical laboratory safety rules (see **17:30**).

17:20. Must school districts comply with workers' safety rules established by the federal Occupational Safety and Health Administration (OSHA)?

Yes. The Public Employees' Safety and Health (PESH) Bureau adopts all OSHA regulations through state rule-making procedures (Lab. Law § 27-a(4); 12 NYCRR § 800.3), even though OSHA itself has jurisdiction only over private employers. School districts must comply with PESH regulations; therefore, indirectly they are complying with OSHA regulations. Thus, PESH is responsible for enforcement and interpretation of these rules.

17:21. What happens if a school district violates a workers' safety rule established by the Public Employees' Safety and Health (PESH) Bureau?

PESH is authorized to issue stringent monetary penalties for safety violations committed by public employers. However, the procedures adopted by PESH permit school districts to correct their mistakes before fines are imposed (Lab. Law § 27-a(6)).

Initially, an employer is cited by a PESH safety inspector for a safety violation that is labeled at the time of the citation as either "serious" or "nonserious." Then the employer is given a certain period of time to correct the violation. If the employer fails to correct this problem by a set deadline, then PESH can assess a fine.

The fine for a nonserious violation can be up to $50 per day beyond the deadline; for a serious violation, it could be as high as $200 per day. A state formula for calculating penalties also takes into account other mitigating factors, such as the district's good faith efforts to remediate (Lab. Law § 27-a(6); Department of Labor Field Operations Manual for Penalty Guidelines; see also *Matter of New York City Transit Authority v. NYS Dep't of Labor*, 88 N.Y.2d 225 (1996)).

The seriousness of a violation is decided in part by a determination of the extent of injury that could occur to workers exposed to the hazard in question (Lab. Law § 27-a(6)). Because a majority of hazards could result in injury, many violations may be considered serious by PESH.

17:22. Is financial assistance available to comply with a citation from the Public Employees' Safety and Health (PESH) Bureau?

Yes. Section 27-a of the state Labor Law provides grants under certain circumstances in conjunction with the State Occupational Safety and Health Act (SOSHA). Under this section, the state Department of Labor is authorized to provide school districts with a percentage of the cost of capital abatement projects incurred in order to comply with a SOSHA citation (Lab. Law § 27-a(16)(A)).

17:23. Do worker safety rules apply to shop classes and other instructional locations?

Yes. Under the federal Occupational Safety and Health Administration (OSHA) rules adopted by PESH, school districts must ensure that teachers and other instructional employees in shop classes and other instructional locations are protected by fundamental safety measures. In machine technology or shop classes, these safety measures include, for example, adequate guards for radial-arm saws and grinders (see 29 CFR §§ 1910.213, 1910.215).

School districts must also implement a chemical hygiene plan for all chemical laboratories (29 CFR §1910.1450(b),(e); see **17:30**).

In addition, school districts must perform a survey in order to determine what other personal protective equipment may be necessary for their employees (29 CFR §§ 1910.132(d); 1910.1001(h)).

17:24. What is a school district's responsibility for protecting employees from exposure to the human immunodeficiency virus (HIV) and hepatitis infections?

The Public Employees' Safety and Health (PESH) Bureau has adopted federal Occupational Safety and Health Administration (OSHA) regulations concerning workers' protection from exposure to blood-borne pathogens such as the human immunodeficiency virus (HIV) and hepatitis B. These require public employers, including school districts, to adopt exposure-control plans to eliminate or minimize employees' exposure to blood-borne diseases, and to use various methods of compliance to protect workers. Methods of compliance include requiring employees to wash their hands, handle needles properly, use plastic gloves made available by the employer in the workplace, and ensure work areas contaminated by blood or body fluids are properly decontaminated.

Employers must provide additional protection to certain employees who encounter "occupational exposure" to blood-borne pathogens. These include participation in special training programs and free hepatitis B vaccinations for employees who choose to be vaccinated. Employees are "occupationally exposed" to blood-borne pathogens if "reasonably anticipated" skin, eye, mucous membrane or parenteral contact with blood or body fluid "may result" from an employee's performance of his or her duties. Under these regulations, school nurses are probably occupationally exposed, and other school employees, such as special education teachers and coaches, may be exposed (see 29 CFR § 1910.1030).

Hazardous Materials and Toxic Substances

17:25. What are a school district's responsibilities regarding the presence of hazardous materials and toxic substances on school premises?

Districts must comply with the federal Occupational and Safety Health Administration (OSHA) Hazard Communication Standard (29 CFR § 1910.1200), adopted by the Public Employees' Safety and Health (PESH) Bureau, concerning hazardous substances, and New York State's Right-to-Know Law concerning toxic substances (Lab. Law §§ 875-883; Pub. Health Law §§ 4800-4808).

Both laws require school districts to develop and maintain a written hazard-communication program that includes information and training about materials that pose potential health and/or safety hazards. Both also apply to materials commonly used by employees as part of a daily occupational routine, such as cleaning fluids, photocopier toner, glues and photographic developing fluids.

The hazard-communication program must ensure containers that hold hazardous materials are properly labeled to identify their contents and warn of any hazards that may be related to their use. It must also provide for the maintenance of material safety data sheets at the work site, as well as employee training at the work site. In addition, school districts must make available for inspection a list of all hazardous chemicals to which employees might be exposed and document employee training in hazardous-materials management and protection, as well as any incident that involves an employee's exposure to hazardous materials (29 CFR § 1910.1200(e)(1)).

Under OSHA regulations, school districts must also report the exposure of any employee to any of 13 listed carcinogens. Incidents that result in the release of any of these carcinogens into areas where employees may be potentially exposed must be reported to the nearest OSHA area director within 24 hours. This report must state what happened and include information on any medical treatment of affected employees. A more detailed written report must be filed within 15 days (29 CFR §1910.1003(f))(2)).

In addition, OSHA regulations require school districts to adopt and implement a written respiratory protection program (29 CFR § 1910.134(a)(2),(b)), which includes effective engineering control methods to prevent employee breathing of contaminated air, and provisions for employee use of respirators, if necessary, to protect health and safety.

17:26. What type of information must be included in the material safety data sheet school districts must maintain under the Hazard Communication Standard?

The Hazard Communication Standard requires a material safety data sheet (MSDS) for each known hazardous material on school district property, which includes information such as the name of the chemical or compound, any possible ill effects a worker may experience from exposure to it and instructions on how to handle a related hazard, should one occur.

An MSDS is usually provided by the supplier or manufacturer of a chemical or compound. MSDSs also are available through the New York State Department of Health. However, it is the district's responsibility to obtain an MSDS for each chemical or compound if one has not been automatically supplied (Lab. Law. § 876; 29 CFR § 1900.1200(g)).

The state Right-to-Know Law requires that information about known hazardous materials in the workplace, such as an MSDS, be provided to an employee requesting such information within 72 hours, excluding weekends and public holidays, of the district's receipt of the request (Lab. Law § 876(7)).

17:27. What happens if a district fails to comply with the Hazard Communication Standard or Right-to-Know Law?

Employers that violate the Hazard Communication Standard are subject to fines imposed by the Public Employees' Safety and Health (PESH) Bureau for violation of state regulations (Lab. Law § 27-a(6); *New York City Transit Authority v. NYS Dep't of Labor*, 88 N.Y.2d 225 (1996); **17:18**; see also Department of Labor Field Operations Manual for the state penalty guidelines).

In addition, if a school district fails to provide timely information on known hazardous materials (see **17:25-26**), the employee is permitted under the state's Right-to-Know Law to refuse to work with the material until the information is furnished (Lab. Law § 876(7)). This provision is known as the right-to-strike provision.

17:28. What are a school district's responsibilities regarding the use of pesticides on school premises?

The State Education Department recommends that school districts notify parents, students and staff prior to any pesticide application.

In addition, the state Department of Environmental Conservation (DEC) has issued regulations regarding the use of pesticides that are applicable to school districts (6 NYCRR Part 325). These regulations require the following:

- A copy of the label of each indoor or outdoor pesticide must be available at the facility where it is being used. This information must be made available to anyone who requests it.
- Contracts with contractors taking care of the grounds must state which chemicals are going to be used.
- Contractors must post on the grounds visible five-by-eight-inch signs during a 24-hour period warning that pesticides were used.
- School district employees applying pesticides do not have to post signs unless the grounds on which the pesticides have been applied are within a park or within 100 feet of any building.

In addition, at press time DEC was in the process of adopting regulations on indoor pesticide application, notification and certification. For more information, refer to 6 NYCRR Part 325, or contact the nearest regional office of the Department of Environmental Conservation.

17:29. Are school districts required to use integrated pest management?

No. Integrated pest management (IPM), which is a practice that emphasizes the use of the least toxic method to control pests, including, when feasible, the elimination of the use of pesticides, is not mandated. However, given the hazards associated with the use of and misapplication of pesticides, the state attorney general has recommended all school districts adopt IPM (see "Pesticides in Schools: Reducing the Risks" (Albany, N.Y.: State Attorney General's Office, 1995)).

IPM is offered as a state contract under the state Office of General Services. The State Education Department recommends the use of IPM and can provide information to school districts on pesticide applicator certification and pesticide management.

17:30. What rules apply to the use of chemicals in school laboratories by district employees?

Districts must comply with federal Occupational Health and Safety Administration (OSHA) regulations governing the use of certain hazardous chemicals in school laboratories (29 CFR § 1910.1450). The state Public Employees' Safety and Health (PESH) Bureau has interpreted these regulations to be applicable only to chemicals used in science laboratories and not to the use of compounds in industrial arts and other school subjects (see 29 CFR § 1910.1450(a)(3)).

Under the regulation, school districts must adopt a chemical hygiene plan that includes practices, policies and procedures to ensure that employees are protected from all potentially hazardous chemicals in their work areas (29 CFR § 1910.1450(e)). In addition, the school district must:

- Monitor employees' exposure to chemicals (29 CFR §1910.1450(d)).
- Provide permanent and temporary employees with training and information (29 CFR § 1910.1450(f)).
- Provide updated training when a new toxic substance is introduced into the workplace (29 CFR § 1910.1450(f)).
- Provide employees with medical consultations and examinations under certain circumstances (29 CFR § 1910.1450(g)).
- Identify hazards of chemicals used in the workplace, including the maintenance of labels and material safety data sheets (MSDSs) of chemicals (29 CFR § 1910.1450(h)).
- Provide employees with respirators when required (29 CFR § 1910.1450(i)).
- Maintain certain records proving compliance with the regulation (29 CFR § 1910.1450(j)).

In addition, section 305(19) of the Education Law requires school districts to follow certain procedures to ensure safety in school science laboratories and directs the commissioner of education to adopt regulations on chemical laboratory safety. It requires that all schools must store chemicals in locked, secure rooms and cabinets, and provides for the arrangement, ventilation and fire protection of chemicals in accordance with guidelines issued by the commissioner.

School districts must also take an annual inventory of all chemicals used in their science laboratories, including specific information on each substance, and must retain the inventory and make it available to the commissioner for inspection (§ 305(19); 29 CFR § 1910.1200(e)(1)(i)).

17:31. What are a school district's responsibilities over the presence of radon in schools?

Radon is a naturally occurring colorless, odorless, tasteless gas in the ground and atmosphere created by the natural breakdown (radioactive decay) of uranium deposits in the earth. When it is present in the air, it causes ionization (or splitting) of the molecules that make up the air. This ionization process results in the release of uranium, lead and other substances in the environment, often called radon progeny or radon's daughters.

Based upon current scientific studies, radon and its progeny can affect cell development adversely in humans and exposure can lead to cancer. Some scientists believe radon is the leading cause of lung cancer among nonsmokers. Children would be particularly susceptible to damage from radon because their cells are developing and reproducing at a much more rapid rate than adults' cells.

Although there are no laws or regulations that require schools to be tested for radon, both the federal Environmental Protection Agency (EPA) and the State Education Department (SED) recommend radon testing of school buildings in locations designated by the state Department of Health as having high concentrations. Testing methods that can measure the presence of radon include charcoal canisters, alpha-track detectors and electrets. SED's Bureau of Facilities Planning advises school districts to call them before conducting any testing to prevent districts from incurring any unnecessary expenses.

SED has issued a program guideline for radon detection and control which includes recommendations to school districts, although districts are not required to follow them. These recommendations concern testing for radon in school buildings, devices used during testing, training for school district personnel conducting testing, and response actions to testing results. SED recommends against the use of charcoal canisters to test for radon; instead it supports the use of an electret, a small air chamber encompassed by an electromagnetic field, or alpha-tract detectors, to conduct radon testing.

For more information, see "Radon Detection and Control in New York State Schools: An Interim Program Guideline" (Albany, N.Y.: State Education Department, 1990) and "Environmental Quality in Schools" (Albany, N.Y.: State Education Department, 1994). Or contact SED's Bureau of Facilities Planning, Room 1069, Education Building Annex, Albany, N.Y. 12234, or the New York State Department of Health's Bureau of Environmental Radiation Protection, Room 380, 2 University Place, Albany, New York 12203.

17:32. What are a school district's responsibilities over the presence of lead in the schools?

Lead is a naturally occurring toxic metal that is harmful to health and can cause damage to the brain and nervous system resulting in reduced attention span, behavioral problems, impaired hearing and a lowered IQ. Lead is especially dangerous to young children, pregnant women and fetuses. Lead enters the human body through inhalation (by breathing particles of lead-contaminated dust) and by ingestion (by drinking lead-contaminated water). Common sources of exposure to lead include paint chips and dust from paint that contains lead, and lead leached in water from lead solder or pipes.

The State Education Department has included recommendations concerning lead in its report, "Environmental Quality in Schools" (Albany, N.Y.: State Education Department, 1994).

17:33. What are a school district's responsibilities over the presence of lead in its water supply?

A school district that supplies its own water from wells it owns must test for lead under the federal Safe Drinking Water Act of 1974, which limits lead content to five parts per billion or less (42 USC § 300f *et seq.*).

Districts connected to a public water system need not test for lead in the drinking water. However, the federal Environmental Protection Agency (EPA) has issued a guidance document that recommends school districts do a plumbing profile to test for lead, and describes appropriate response actions (see "Lead in School Drinking Water: A Manual for School Officials to Detect, Reduce or Eliminate Lead in School Drinking Water" (Washington, D.C.: EPA, 1989)).

17:34. What is the law concerning water coolers with lead-lined tanks in school buildings?

Under the United States Lead Contamination Control Act of 1988, the Consumer Product Safety Commission is directed to recall water coolers with lead-lined tanks; manufacturers must repair, replace or refund the cost of the tanks (42 USC § 300j-22). The Environmental Protection Agency (EPA) is directed to publish a list of manufacturers of lead-containing water coolers (42 USC § 300j-23(a)). The sale of lead-containing water coolers is banned (42 USC § 300j-23(b)). School districts must disseminate to staff, students and parents the results of any tests conducted (42 USC § 300j-24(d)(2)).

17:35. What are a school district's responsibilities regarding the disposal of hazardous waste?

A school district has an obligation to properly dispose of hazardous waste (42 USC § 9601 *et seq.*; Envtl. Conserv. Law § 27-0900 *et seq.*). A district's liability for the disposal of hazardous waste is far-reaching. Under federal "cradle-to-grave" liability policies, one who arranges for the disposal of hazardous wastes may be liable for the cost of cleaning up those substances forever, even though the person or entity lawfully disposed of the waste with a licensed waste hauler. Continuing liability stems from the interwoven obligations created by numerous federal hazardous waste laws and regulations, including the Resource Conservation and Recovery Act (RCRA) (42 USC § 6901 *et seq.*), and the Comprehensive Environmental Response, Compensation, and Liability Act (CERCLA), (42 USC § 9601 *et seq.*).

17:36. What are a school district's responsibilities for underground storage tanks for petroleum?

The state Department of Environmental Conservation (DEC) has adopted regulations applicable to owners of both underground and above-ground storage tanks for petroleum to prevent and/or minimize damage from leaks and spills from tanks. The federal Resource Conservation and Recovery Act (RCRA) and the Environmental Protection Agency (EPA), the federal agency that enforces RCRA, impose additional requirements on owners of underground storage tanks.

The regulations adopted by DEC require school districts that own underground and above-ground storage tanks containing petroleum to register and pay a registration fee for storage tanks (6 NYCRR §§ 612.2; 613.3). In addition, owners of tanks must:

- Install overfill protection and secondary containment systems.
- Test underground storage tanks for leaking and damage when the tank is 10 to 15 years old, depending on the type of tank.
- Retest underground storage tanks every five years from the date of the last test.
- Inspect above-ground storage tanks for leakage and damage each month.
- Conduct an extensive inspection of above-ground storage tanks when the tank is 10 years old, or by 1990.
- Conduct an extensive reinspection of above ground storage tanks every 10 years from the date of the last test (6 NYCRR Part 613).

The regulations also contain record-keeping and reporting requirements in the event of a spill or leak from a tank (6 NYCRR § 613.8). Finally, strict requirements are imposed for new underground storage tanks, new above-ground tanks and for closing out-of-service tanks (6 NYCRR § 613.9 and Part 614).

The federal law and regulations require owners of underground storage tanks to meet strict standards designed to prevent leaks and to ensure financial responsibility for clean-up costs and third-party damage claims (40 CFR Part 280). The financial responsibility requirement of the

EPA regulation requires school districts and other owners of underground storage tanks to demonstrate their ability to pay for site clean-up and any liability to others for leak damage (40 CFR § 280.93). The regulations relieve a district of the obligation to carry special insurance policies for such coverage if it can meet one of two alternative requirements: a bond-rating test or a worksheet test. The bond-rating test requires the district to have $1,000,000 or more of general obligation bonds of investment grade or better outstanding. The worksheet test involves the calculation of nine financial ratios (40 CFR § 280.95).

In addition, federal regulations require that bare steel tanks of 110 gallons or larger (except on-site heating tanks) be upgraded by December 22, 1998. To upgrade the tank means essentially that the old system must be either retrofitted or closed, or a new system installed (40 CFR § 280.21).

Indoor Air Quality

17:37. What is indoor air quality?

Indoor air quality refers to the numerous environmental elements that affect the purity of air within enclosed structures. Materials that negatively influence indoor air quality include substances such as tobacco smoke, fumes from paints, cleaning materials and formaldehyde. The heat, ventilation and air-conditioning (HVAC) system in a school building may affect its indoor air quality under certain circumstances. The State Education Department encourages school districts to periodically clean their ducts and filters.

17:38. What laws apply to indoor air quality?

Indoor air quality is not highly regulated on either the state or federal level. Other than provisions concerning asbestos (see **17:41-62**), state and federal no-smoking laws impose one of the few legal restrictions specifically intended to address indoor air quality (see **17:39**).

Although the commissioner of education has not adopted regulations concerning indoor air quality, in the past he has ordered a school district to monitor students' physical symptoms when the air quality of a school building allegedly caused health problems *(Appeal of Anibaldi*, 33 Educ. Dep't Rep. 166 (1993)).

A 1994 report by the Regents Advisory Committee on Environmental Quality in Schools recommends that the simplest and most effective way to avoid potential indoor air quality problems is to isolate work areas, ensure that renovation work is scheduled when the school building is not occupied and increase ventilation. According to the report, the number of schools reporting indoor air quality problems has steadily increased over the past few years. Schools with concerns should survey students and staff, and, if necessary, report any potential problems to the State Education Department or the state Department of Health.

The New York State Energy Research and Development Authority (NYSERDA) offers technical assistance to help school districts address their indoor air-quality problems. For more information, contact NYSERDA at 518-862-1090.

17:39. Is smoking permitted in school buildings?

No. The federal Pro-Children Act of 1994 prohibits smoking tobacco in an indoor facility used for the routine provision of education or library services for students in schools receiving federal education aid. This prohibition extends to the entire school building, not just the classrooms used for instruction (20 USC § 6083(a)). For example, teachers' lounges located in elementary school buildings must be smoke-free.

The Education Law further restricts smoking in schools by prohibiting smoking in school buildings and on school grounds during school hours, meaning whenever there is a student activity that is supervised by faculty or staff, or any officially school-sanctioned event taking place (§ 409(2)). The law defines *school grounds* as any buildings and land "contained within legally-defined property boundaries as registered in a county clerk's office."

The provisions of the state law do not supersede any collective bargaining agreement, during its term, in existence on the effective date of the act, August 25, 1994 (Laws of 1994, Ch. 565, § 8).

The state law does permit smoking by adult faculty and staff members in a designated smoking area during non-school hours. However, the state law, read in conjunction with the federal prohibition on smoking in instructional buildings at all times, means that the designated smoking area during nonschool hours would have to be located in a bus garage or administration building where instruction does not take place or on school grounds outside school buildings during nonschool hours.

In addition to federal and state laws specifically addressing smoking in school settings, New York's Clean Indoor Air Act prohibits smoking in certain workplaces and some specific areas in buildings open to the public, such as elevators and any "indoor area open to the public" in buildings (Pub. Health Law § 1399-o(1), (2)). Under this law, employers must adopt a written policy on smoking in the workplace, prominently post the policy, and designate an agent, such as a staff member, to enforce the policy. The law mandates that no smoking be permitted in an area where an employee who requests a nonsmoking environment is routinely assigned. It also mandates a smoke-free area be established in an employees' cafeteria (Pub. Health Law § 1399-o(6)).

17:40. Must a district negotiate with its employees over rules concerning smoking in the workplace?

Not in most circumstances. A school district has no obligation to bargain over a ban on smoking in any area where smoking is prohibited under either the federal or the state law. However, any attempt by an employer to unilaterally impose restrictions greater than those required by the law, such as imposing an absolute ban on smoking in a school building not used for instruction, and that are inconsistent with the district's past practice concerning smoking, may constitute an improper practice by the school district *(Oneonta City School District,* 24 PERB ¶ 3025 (1991); see **10:37, 10:41**).

Asbestos

17:41. What is asbestos?

Asbestos is a naturally occurring mineral silicate, which may be present in the air in the form of invisible fibers not readily identifiable to the naked eye and which may cause several medical problems, including cancer and lung damage. However, its presence can be detected through the use of special techniques.

Asbestos-containing materials (ACM) were used widely in school building construction from the 1940s to the 1970s. They commonly included acoustical material, wall board, sprayed-on fireproofing, air cell pipe wrap, and floor and ceiling tiles. ACM may be potentially harmful if it is sanded, sawed or subjected to any action that would release asbestos fibers and render them airborne.

17:42. What is friable asbestos?

Under New York State law, *friable asbestos* is a "condition of crumbled, pulverized, powdered, crushed or exposed asbestos which is capable of being released into the air by hand pressure" (Lab. Law § 901(11)).

In its rule entitled "Damaged Friable Surfacing ACM" (asbestos-containing material), the federal Environmental Protection Agency (EPA) defines friable asbestos to include the following: deteriorated or physically injured material such that the internal structure of the material is inadequate; or the bond of the lamination to its substrate is inadequate; or a lack of fiber cohesion or adhesion qualities; flaking, blistering, or crumbling; water damage, significant water stain, scraped, gouged, marred or other signs of physical injury (see 40 CFR § 763.83).

17:43. What laws govern a school district's obligations regarding asbestos-containing material?

Requirements regarding asbestos management for school districts are governed by the federal Asbestos Hazard Emergency Response Act (AHERA) and Article 30 of the New York State Labor Law.

AHERA is administered by the federal Environmental Protection Agency (EPA). The EPA has adopted regulations concerning asbestos-containing material (ACM) in schools (see 40 CFR Part 763, Subpart E; see **17:44-45** for more information about AHERA). The State Education Department is the AHERA designee for New York State's schools and, thus, serves a role in providing information to schools and collecting information, such as asbestos-management plans.

The Labor Law is administered by the state Department of Labor, which has adopted work rules concerning asbestos known as Industrial Code Rule 56 (see 12 NYCRR Part 56; see also **17:44** and **17:55** for more information about Industrial Code Rule 56).

AHERA and the EPA regulations describe requirements concerning inspection and management of asbestos-containing material in school buildings, while the Labor Law and Industrial Code Rule 56 control work practices for interaction with asbestos-containing material. The asbestos laws and regulations seek to reduce or eliminate the potential risks associated with asbestos fibers.

17:44. What are some of the specific requirements school districts must comply with regarding asbestos-containing materials (ACM)?

The federal Asbestos Hazard Emergency Response Act (AHERA) requires that school districts:

- Identify all friable and nonfriable asbestos-containing material (ACM) in school buildings (40 CFR §§ 763.85-763.88).
- Appoint an individual as asbestos designee (40 CFR § 763.84 (g)(1)).
- Conduct an initial inspection and subsequent reinspection once every three years (40 CFR § 763.85).
- Conduct a "periodic asbestos surveillance" in each building at least once every six months (40 CFR § 763.92 (b).
- Prepare, administer and maintain an asbestos-management plan.
- Adopt and execute appropriate response actions (40 CFR § 763.90).
- Notify workers and building occupants or their legal guardians about inspections, response actions and post-response actions (40 CFR § 763.84 (c); § 763.93 (e)(10)) at least once each school year.

State aid is not available for costs incurred after July 1, 1989 for the completion of asbestos inspections and management plans (see 8 NYCRR § 155.14(a)).

In addition, AHERA requires that school districts post warning labels in maintenance and custodial locations (29 CFR § 1910.1001(j)(3),(4); 40 CFR § 763.95), and properly train all custodial and maintenance employees annually (29 CFR § 1910.1001(j)(7); 40 CFR §§ 763.92(a)(1); 763.84(b)). Two hours of asbestos awareness training must be provided for new employees (29 CFR § 1910.1001(j)(7); 40 CFR § 763.92(a)(1)).

In addition, school districts must provide personal protective equipment, including the use of respirators where necessary, for housekeeping employees who are exposed to dangerous levels of ACM (29 CFR § 1910.1001(g),(h)).

School districts must also ensure that the various records required under AHERA regulations are properly maintained and distributed as required by law. For example, school officials must keep a copy of the asbestos management plan in the district's administrative office. Each building also must have a copy of that building's asbestos management plan in its administrative office.

The management plan must be made available without cost for inspection by the Environmental Protection Agency (EPA) and state representatives, as well as to workers before work begins in any area of a school building. It also must be made available to the public, school personnel and their representatives, and parents or legal guardians; in this case, the district may charge a reasonable fee for copying the plan. Except for requests for inspection from workers, the district must provide the copy of a management plan within five working days after receipt of the request for inspection of the plan (40 CFR § 763.93(g)(3)). In addition, school districts are required to keep AHERA asbestos records for at least three years after the last required inspection (40 CFR § 763.94(a)).

New York State Industrial Code Rule 56, which is in conformity with AHERA, requires that persons employed in any aspect of an asbestos project, as well as those who supervise them, be trained appropriately and certified. In addition, Industrial Code Rule 56 sets standards and procedures for the removal, enclosure, application, encapsulation or disturbance of friable asbestos and the handling of asbestos or asbestos-containing material (ACM) in a manner that prevents the release of asbestos fibers (see **17:47**). For example, school districts must conduct an asbestos survey and removal project of all asbestos identified when a school building is scheduled for demolition. This rule also establishes an inspection and enforcement program administered by the New York State Department of Labor and sets forth record-keeping, reporting and retention requirements for asbestos contractors (12 NYCRR Part 56).

17:45. Are school districts responsible for conducting ongoing asbestos reinspections?

Yes. The asbestos management plans required by the Asbestos Hazard Emergency Response Act (AHERA) (see 17:44) should contain a time schedule for the reinspection and periodic surveillance of school buildings. The buildings must be physically and visually reinspected in all areas that contain either known or assumed asbestos-containing material (ACM) by a certified inspector or management planner. With each reinspection, the district's asbestos designee should visually inspect material that was previously considered nonfriable and determine whether it has become friable since the last inspection(40 CFR § 763.85(b)(3)(ii)). The asbestos designee must be satisfied that the reported information is accurate and complete and must sign a statement to that effect (40 CFR § 763.85(b)).

The management plan's time schedule should outline surveillance of all friable and nonfriable known or assumed ACM every six months (40 CFR § 763.92(b)). This surveillance need not be performed by a certified inspector, but the person who performs the surveillance must have undergone at least two hours of asbestos-awareness training. Since this is a visual inspection, no additional training is necessary (only required for handling ACM) (40 CFR § 763.92 (a)(1)).

Although not required to do so, school districts may require that all district staff members participate in regular surveillance of ACM. They should be instructed to report immediately any change in the condition of ACM to the person designated to receive such reports (40 CFR § 763.93(b)(2)(iii)).

17:46. Are school officials required by law to remove all asbestos-containing material to make a school safe?

No. In fact, an asbestos-removal project may, on occasion, increase the amount of airborne asbestos fibers in a building if it is not conducted and monitored properly. Therefore, removal should be considered only as a last resort.

17:47. What response actions may school districts take regarding the presence of asbestos in the schools?

There are five federally-approved response actions or methods of responding to the presence of asbestos from which school officials may choose: removal, encapsulation, enclosure, repair, and operations and maintenance (40 CFR §§ 763.90, 763.91).

- Removal involves taking out or stripping of any asbestos-containing materials (ACM) from an area in a school building (40 CFR § 763.83; see 12 NYCRR § 56-1.4(bm)).
- Encapsulation is the application of either a penetrating material that penetrates the ACM and binds the components together or a bridging agent that surrounds the asbestos fibers or embeds them in an adhesive matrix, creating a membrane over the surface of the ACM (40 CFR § 763.83; see 12 NYCRR § 56-1.4(ag)).
- Enclosure involves the construction of airtight walls, ceilings and floors between the ACM and the facility's environment, or around surfaces coated with asbestos material or any other appropriate procedure that prevents the release of asbestos fiber (40 CFR § 763.83; 12 NYCRR § 56-1.4(ah)). The goal of enclosure is to create an airtight, impermeable, permanent barrier around the ACM to prevent release of asbestos fibers into the air (see 40 CFR § 763.83).
- Repair consists of returning damaged ACM to an undamaged condition or an intact state to prevent the release of asbestos fibers (40 CFR § 763.83). The state Department of Labor defines *repair* as corrective action using required work practices to control the release of asbestos fiber from damaged ACM (12 NYCRR § 56–1.4(bn)).
- Operation and maintenance is a program of work practices to maintain friable ACM in good condition, ensure cleanup of asbestos fibers previously released, and prevent further release by minimizing and controlling friable ACM disturbance or damage (40 CFR § 763.83).

The Environmental Protection Agency (EPA) requires school districts to select from these options a response action that protects human health and the environment and is the "least burdensome method" (40 CFR § 763.90(a)). Currently, the EPA suggests that the safest and most cost-effective response action is to manage the asbestos in place.

The state Labor Law and Industrial Code Rule 56 also authorizes asbestos projects to be undertaken by a contractor, which involves any aspect of the removal, encapsulation, enclosure or disturbance of friable asbestos or any handling of asbestos material that may result in the release of asbestos fiber (Lab. Law § 901(7); 12 NYCRR § 56-1.4(o)). The contractor's obligations may depend on the amount of square and/or linear feet of asbestos or ACM, and whether the asbestos project is defined as a large, small or minor asbestos project (12 NYCRR § 56-1.4(au), (bs), (aw); see **17:55**). In addition, certain asbestos projects may qualify as "emergency asbestos projects" or a "repair," resulting in slight variance from some of the general rules concerning asbestos projects (12 NYCRR § 56-1.4(ae), (bn)).

17:48. Once asbestos has been removed from a school district, does all liability cease?

No. A school district still must concern itself with how the material is handled, where it is to be stored, how it is to be transported and whether it is transported to an approved dumping site. If the abatement contractor violates any of the rules regarding these matters, the school district may share liability for an Environmental Protection Agency (EPA) fine.

Additionally, diseases attributed to exposure to asbestos have long periods of latency, perhaps as much as 40 years. Under the current statute of limitations on certain personal injury lawsuits, injured persons now have up to three years after they discover they have an asbestos-related disease to bring a lawsuit against a school district or other party that they allege has wrongfully exposed them to asbestos (Civ. Prac. L. & R. § 214-c).

17:49. Who is responsible for ensuring a school district's compliance with the asbestos laws?

An asbestos designee appointed by the school district is responsible for coordinating the asbestos program in the district and for keeping the district in compliance with all asbestos mandates (see 40 CFR § 763.84(g)). The asbestos designee must be knowledgeable about the federal, state and local laws and regulations concerning asbestos.

The asbestos designee need not be a separate position within the district, but may be added to the responsibilities of an existing position. The overall size of the district and the size of its asbestos project or projects should determine whether the school board should create a separate position to perform these duties.

17:50. What are some of the responsibilities of a school district's asbestos designee?

Generally, an asbestos designee is responsible to ensure that the requirements of the federal regulations pertaining to asbestos-containing materials (ACM) in schools are properly implemented (40 CFR § 763.84(g)(1)). Specifically, the asbestos designee must:

- Ensure that mandatory periodic inspections, reinspections, and surveillances comply with federal regulations (40 CFR § 763.84(a)).

- Ensure that the district's asbestos management plan conforms to federal regulations (40 CFR § 763.84(a)). The asbestos designee must include reports of all training, inspections, reinspections, analysis of ACM, inspector assessments, recommendations for response actions, and periodic surveillance into the asbestos management plan (40 CFR §§ 763.84(a),(g)(2); 763.85(a)(4)(vi),(b)(3)(viii); 763.87(d); 763.88(a)(2),(d); 763.92(b)(2)(iii)). The asbestos management plan must include a certification by the asbestos designee that the school district is in compliance or will be in compliance with the federal regulations pertaining to ACM in schools (40 CFR § 763.93(i)). The asbestos designee must also ensure the asbestos management plan is available for inspection and that notice of its availability is provided in accordance with federal regulations (40 CFR § 763.84(f); see 40 CFR § 763.93(g)).

- Ensure that training programs for staff, students, custodians and other maintenance personnel, including substitute custodial and/or maintenance workers or part-time workers, are provided (40 CFR § 763.84(b),(d),(g)(1)).

- Ensure that district employees, students (or legal guardians) and other building occupants are informed about inspections in progress at least once each school year (40 CFR § 763.84(c)).

- Ensure that proper asbestos warning signs remain posted (40 CFR § 763.84(f); see 40 CFR § 763.95).

17:51. Who may conduct asbestos inspections, develop asbestos management plans and effectuate response actions on behalf of a school district?

Inspections, management plans and response actions may be conducted by school district employees, or by a person or company from outside the school district. If a district uses a member of its own staff to perform these duties, it must obtain a New York State contractor's license, and the person who reinspects a school building or performs a response action must obtain the appropriate certification from the state Department of Labor. This certification requires special training that may be available through a board of cooperative educational services (BOCES) health and safety office or through a private organization whose courses have been approved by the state Department of Health.

If a district employs outside personnel to perform these duties, school officials must take special care to be sure that the outside company's certification is valid in New York State; the laboratories used for testing purposes are certified and approved by the state Department of Health's Environmental Laboratory Approval Program; and the company has adequate facilities and properly trained, certified personnel to fulfill the requirements of all laws and regulations pertaining to the potential disturbance of asbestos (see 12 NYCRR §§ 56-2.1; 56-2.2).

17:52. Is an asbestos-abatement project a capitol project for which school districts can receive building aid?

Yes. A public school district can apply for state aid at its building aid ratio to help finance an asbestos project that is part of an approved capital building project.

17:53. Can a school district proceed on an asbestos-abatement project if it has underestimated the cost and does not have voter approval for the project?

Yes. Asbestos abatement for all hazardous asbestos material is an ordinary contingent expense, if undertaken pursuant to a formal resolution of the school board that will enable the district to proceed with and comply with the expeditious containment or removal of asbestos materials. This work can proceed without voter approval as long as no building alteration is involved in the process (see chap. 19 and Opn. of Counsel, 1 Educ. Dep't Rep. 792 (1954), which held that expenditures in the name of safety are ordinary contingent expenses).

17:54. How can a school district finance an unanticipated asbestos-abatement project?

There are several ways to finance an asbestos-abatement project. The school board first must declare, by resolution, the project's costs to be a contingent expense. By a second resolution, the board may assign the balance of any unappropriated funds for this purpose (see 8 NYCRR § 170.2(l)). Any remaining debt that ensues could be financed in the subsequent year by increasing taxes (see § 2023).

Another way the board may finance a large-scale asbestos project is to request the voter approval of a bond issue for asbestos abatement. Voters would actually decide on the bond, not the project itself. If the voters approve the bond issue, then the district could finance the project over a period of years (see § 416). If the voters determine not to approve the bond issue, however, the entire sum would be taxable on the next tax roll.

17:55. Are there any notice requirements that must be met before an asbestos project begins?

Yes. In a large asbestos project, defined as one involving more than 260 linear feet or 160 square feet of material, the contractor must notify both the Environmental Protection Agency (EPA) and the New York State Department of Labor at least 10 days before beginning the project (Lab. Law § 904(2); 12 NYCRR § 56-1.6(b)(1)). If an asbestos hazard is present that requires immediate attention, or if emergency conditions make it impossible to give 10 days' notice, the owner, owners agent, consultant or contractor must notify the program manager's office at the Asbestos Control Bureau in Albany by telephone at 518-457-2072 or in person prior to beginning the project (12 NYCRR § 56-1.7(a)).

In addition, Industrial Code Rule 56 requires all contractors, in both large and smaller projects, to provide "business occupants" written notice 10 days prior to beginning any work on any asbestos project in a building. With regard to projects being conducted in school buildings, the faculty, staff and students attending such school shall be considered "business occupants". (Lab. Law § 904(4); 12 NYCRR § 56-1.8(a)). If the contract is signed less than 10 days prior to scheduled work, contractors are required to give three-days notice (12 NYCRR § 56-1.8 (b)). In an emergency, notice to business occupants must be given as soon as practicable (12 NYCRR § 56-1.8 (c)).

17:56. Must air sampling be performed during an asbestos-abatement project?

Yes. Air sampling is the process of measuring the asbestos fiber content of a known volume of air collected during a specific period of time (12 NYCRR § 56-1.4(f)). Air sampling is performed in conjunction with an abatement project in order to determine the asbestos fiber content in the air in the vicinity of the project. The size of the abatement project, as defined under Industrial Code Rule 56, determines when air sampling must be performed (12 NYCRR § 56-17.1).

Amendments to Industrial Code Rule 56 adopted by the Department of Labor in 1991 strictly limit the performance of air sampling and analysis by parties otherwise involved with an asbestos project (12 NYCRR § 56-17.4). In addition, the technological method used to analyze the final-clearance air sample is transmission electron microscopy (TEM) (12 NYCRR § 56-17.1).

17:57. How is a containment area formed around an asbestos-abatement project?

There are extensive rules and regulations about the type and quantity of plastic to be used in an asbestos-abatement project and the number of layers of plastic to be placed on floors, walls, ceilings and other surfaces to prevent any possible release of asbestos fibers from the containment area. Negative air pressure helps to ensure that air from inside the containment area flows through high-efficiency particulate air (HEPA) filters before being discharged back into the air as clean air. In addition, workers leaving the work area must comply with detailed procedures to prevent contamination outside the project area (see 12 NYCRR subparts 56-4 through 56-11).

17:58. Who qualifies as an asbestos contractor on an asbestos project?

State Labor Law defines an *asbestos contractor* to include the state, any political subdivision of the state, a public authority or any other governmental agency or instrumentality, a self-employed person, company, unincorporated association, firm, partnership or corporation, and any owner or operator who engages in an asbestos project or employs persons engaged in any phase of an asbestos project (Lab. Law § 901(9); 12 NYCRR § 56-1.4(z)). A school district is included within this definition and, thus, must comply with all requirements imposed on contractors.

17:59. Must an asbestos contractor and its employees be licensed and certified?

Yes. The state Department of Labor issues licenses to contractors who wish to conduct asbestos-abatement projects in this state. In addition, the department issues a variety of certificates for workers who wish to work for asbestos-abatement contractors (see 12 NYCRR § 56-2), which are valid for one year and cost from $30 to $150 (see Lab. Law § 903).

All contractors who engage in an asbestos project, as well as any business that provides management planning, project design, monitoring, inspection and/or air-monitoring services, must have an asbestos-handling license. This license costs $300 and must be renewed annually (Lab. Law § 902(1); 12 NYCRR § 56-2.1(a)).

Although the Department of Labor actually issues the license or certification, the state Department of Health has the responsibility for approving training programs (12 NYCRR § 56-2.2 (a)).

17:60. Must an asbestos contractor keep records on asbestos projects?

Yes. Every contractor must maintain, for at least 30 years, records on each asbestos project in which the contractor was engaged. These records must include the name, address and Social Security number of the supervisor of the project; the location and description of the asbestos project; the amount of asbestos material that was abated or disturbed; the starting and ending dates of the project; the name and address of each waste-disposal site where asbestos waste material was deposited; the name and address of any site used for interim storage of asbestos waste materials; the name and address of any transporter of asbestos waste material; and the names, addresses and Social Security numbers of all the people who worked on the project (Lab. Law § 904(1); 12 NYCRR § 56–1.6(a)(1)).

17:61. What is an asbestos handler?

An *asbestos handler* is a person who performs certain duties described in Industrial Code Rule 56 (12 NYCRR § 56-1.4(k)): specifically, the removal, encapsulation or disturbance of friable asbestos or handling of asbestos in any manner that may result in the release of asbestos fibers (12 NYCRR § 56-2.2(c)(1)).

Any person who is not required to obtain any other asbestos-related certification, but who removes, encapsulates or disturbs friable asbestos or who handles asbestos in any manner that may result in the release of asbestos fiber, must obtain an asbestos handler's certificate (12 NYCRR § 56-2.2(c)(1)). Handlers' certificates are required for school district personnel who perform tasks that disturb friable asbestos or that may result in the release of asbestos fibers.

17:62. What is a clerk of the works, and what is that person's role in an asbestos project?

A *clerk of the works* is a person, generally employed by the school district, who is in charge of seeing to it that all contractors hired by the district for a project adhere to the contracts, plans and specifications for the job. The clerk of the works must be certified by the Department of Labor as a project monitor if he or she oversees an asbestos-abatement project (12 NYCRR § 56-2.2(c)(8)). The clerk of the works need not be the same person who serves as a school district's asbestos designee.

18. School District Liability and School Insurance

18:1. Are school districts exempt from lawsuits?

No. The concept of sovereign immunity, which prevented lawsuits against the state and other governmental entities, has been abolished in New York State by virtue of the Court of Claims Act (Court of Claims Act § 8).

A school district may be liable as a corporate entity for its own negligence and other improper actions such as breach of contract, as well as the wrongful actions of school board members. It may also be liable for the negligence of its employees under the doctrine of *respondeat superior* which makes the master responsible for the negligence of its employees when the negligence occurs during the performance of their employment responsibilities and results in injury to others *(Shante D. by Ada D. v. City of New York*, 190 A.D.2d 356 (1993), *aff'd*, 83 N.Y.2d 948 (1994)).

Liability would entail the financial responsibility to pay a person or entity, or to otherwise remedy a wrong, when there is injury or damage to such person or entity due to the wrongful action or inaction of the school district, school board members or their employees.

School districts carrying liability insurance generally are protected to the limits of such insurance. Above these limits, and under any applicable deductible in the insurance policy, the responsibility to pay the claim rests with the school district.

18:2. Are school board members exempt from lawsuits brought against them personally?

No. However, there is immunity for school board members when they carry out official functions within the context of a school board meeting. For immunity to apply, these functions cannot be exclusively ministerial. They must involve the exercise of discretion or expert judgment in policy matters (see *Haddock v. City of New York*, 75 N.Y.2d 478, 484-85 (1990); see **18:19**).

18:3. Can a school district be sued for injuries occurring during the use of school facilities by an outside organization?

Yes, if it has been found that the school district was negligent in some manner. The requirement of some school boards that outside organizations carry liability insurance when they use school property does not necessarily relieve the school district from liability in the event of an accident to either a participant or a spectator. In most such cases, however, the district's liability insurance policy may cover this situation.

18:4. Is there a procedure for bringing a lawsuit against a school district?

Yes. The Education Law provides that no action or special proceeding relating to district property or claim against the district or involving the rights or interests of the district may be brought unless the claimant files a written verified claim, or notice of claim, that describes the basis of the lawsuit within three months after the incident on which the claim is based occurred (§ 3813(1)). The three-month period also applies to certain improper practice proceedings under the Taylor Law (see **10:47**) even where the claimant has complied with the four-month statute of limitations under PERB rules (see 4 NYCRR § 204.1(a)(1); *Board of Educ. v. New York State Pub. Employment Relations Bd.,* 197 A.D.2d 276 (3rd Dep't 1994), *leave to app. den.,* 84 N.Y.2d 803 (1994)).

Where the lawsuit involves a claim for the payment of money owed, the party bringing the lawsuit must serve a summons and complaint on the school district, indicating that a notice of claim was served and that the officer or body having the power to approve the payment of the claim refused to do so within 30 days of its receipt (§ 3813(1)). This 30-day waiting period has been found to extend the four-month statute of limitations for bringing an Article 78 proceeding (*Perlin v. South Orangetown Cent. Sch. Dist.,* 216 A.D.2d 397 (2nd Dep't 1995), *mot. for leave to app. dismissed,* 86 N.Y.2d 886 (1995)).

In order to bring tort claims for personal injury against school officials, teachers, or other employees, the claimant must comply with the provisions of the General Municipal Law. These require, for instance, that a notice of claim be made and served upon the school district within 90 days after the claim arose (Educ. Law § 3813(2); Gen. Mun. Law § 50-e).

18:5. Can a lawsuit against a school district proceed if the required notice of claim is not filed in a timely manner?

Yes. Upon application, a court, at its discretion, may extend the time to serve the notice of claim on the school district, but not beyond the statute of limitations for the bringing of the lawsuit, and never beyond one year (§ 3813(2–a), (2–b); Gen. Mun. Law § 50-e(5); *Bader v. Board of Educ.,* 216 A.D.2d 708 (3rd Dep't 1995)).

In granting an extension, a court will consider, for example, whether the district acquired knowledge of the facts of the claim within the three-month period, whether the claimant was a minor or incapacitated, or was operating under another hardship, and whether the delay prejudiced the district in maintaining its defense (§ 3813(2-a); Gen. Mun. Law §50-e(5)).

18:6. Can a lawsuit against a school district proceed without the filing of a notice of claim?

There are certain limited exceptions to the notice of claim requirement. For example, the notice of claim provisions of the Education Law do not apply to appeals to the commissioner of education (*Appeal of Shusterman,* 18 Educ. Dep't Rep. 516 (1979)) or to declaratory judgments (*Levert v. Central School Dist.,* 24 Misc.2d 832 (1960)). Also, one state appellate court has ruled that an action for employment discrimination brought under the state Human Rights Law (Exec. Law § 296) is not an action subject to the notice of claim provisions (*Lane-Weber v. Plainedge Cent. School Dist.,* 213 A.D.2d 515 (2nd Dep't 1995)).

A notice of claim is not necessary, either, where the action or proceeding against the district "seeks to vindicate a public interest" rather than a private right (*Board of Educ. v. New York State Public Employment Relations Bd.,* 197 A.D.2d 276 (3rd Dep't 1994), *mot. for leave to app. den.,* 84 N.Y.2d 803 (1994)); *Union Free School Dist. v. New York State Human Rights Appeal Bd.,* 35 N.Y.2d 371 (1974)).

In addition, in a case where a school district was served with an improper practice charge and answered the charge within the requisite three-month period, an appellate court ruled the union's failure to file a notice of claim was not fatal because the district had received constructive notice of the claim (*Deposit Cent. Sch. Dist. v. Public Employment Relations Bd.,* 214 A.D.2d 288 (3rd Dep't 1995), *appeal denied,* 88 N.Y.2d 866 (1996)).

Negligence

18:7. What is negligence?

Negligence is a legal principle which imposes liability on entities and individuals who breach a duty they owe to others thereby causing them injury (see *Prosser & Keaton on the Law of Torts* § 30 (5th ed. 1984)).

In general, school districts do have a general duty to supervise students in their care and to maintain the school premises and any equipment in a safe working condition. A school district has the duty to exercise the same degree of care toward its students as would a reasonable, prudent parent under comparable circumstances (*Mirand v. City of New York,* 84 N.Y.2d 44 (1994); *Shante D. by Ada D. v. City of New York,* 190 A.D.2d 356 (1st Dep't 1993), *aff'd,* 83 N.Y.2d 948 (1994); *Lawes v. Board of Educ.,* 16 N.Y.2d 302 (1965)). Should a breach of this duty by either the school system, board members or their employees result in an injury to a student, the school district may be held liable (see **18:1**).

For example, a school district was found negligent for its failure to protect two students, where school personnel had knowledge of threats against them and the potential for harm (*Mirand v. City of New York*). In another case, the school district was liable for the sexual assault of a third-grader who was allowed to go to the hallway bathroom alone although there was a bathroom in the classroom (*Shante D. by Ada D. v. City of New York*).

In addition, a school district may be held liable for harm to a student caused by a criminal act of a third party when the crime is a "reasonably foreseeable" consequence of circumstances created by the school district. For example, the New York State Court of Appeals upheld a jury verdict based on negligent supervision against a school district for injuries sustained by a student who was raped off school premises while on a school field trip (*Bell v. Board of Educ. of City of New York*, 90 N.Y.2d 944 (1997)).

In another case decided since *Bell*, the Appellate Division, Third Department ruled that a school district could not be held liable for a sexual assault by two male students against a female student that occurred on school grounds during the school day because the male students' actions were so "extraordinary and intervening" that they were not "foreseeable" by the district (*Schrader v. Board of Education of Taconic Hills Central School District*, 671 N.Y.S.2d 785 (3rd Dep't 1998)).

It is unlikely a school district could escape liability for its own negligence by requiring from parents or guardians a waiver of liability or a permission slip frequently used by schools when children participate in certain school-sponsored events. Although a signature on a permission slip indicates a parent or guardian is aware the student will participate in a particular activity, it may not release the school from liability. Liability will depend on whether there was negligent supervision by school personnel.

18:8. Can a school district be sued in negligence for educational malpractice?

No. The New York State Court of Appeals has held that actions for educational malpractice are barred by public policy considerations because the courts will not second-guess the professional judgments of school officials and educators in selecting and implementing educational programs and evaluating students (*Torres v. Little Flower Children's Servs.*, 64 N.Y.2d 119, 126-27 (1984), *cert. denied*, 474 U.S. 864 (1985); *Hoffman v. Board of Education*, 49 N.Y.2d 121 (1979); *Donohue v. Copiague Union Free School Dist.*, 47 N.Y.2d 440 (1979)).

For example, where a high school graduate who could not read or write sufficiently to complete a job application sued the district for its failure to provide him with adequate teachers, administrators and psychologists in order to evaluate his progress, the Court of Appeals explained it is not for the courts to make a judgment on the validity of school board policies or to review day-to-day implementation of these policies (*Donahue v. Copiague UFSD*).

On the other hand, where a principal willfully and intentionally falsified test scores as a result of which a student was denied remedial and special education, a state appellate court dismissed the educational malpractice claim against the school district, but gave permission to the student's parent to proceed against the principal on the basis of intentional wrongdoing as well as against the school district, under the doctrine of respondeat superior, in the event the principal's actions were reasonably foreseeable (*Helbig v. City of New York*, 212 A.D.2d 506 (2nd Dep't 1995)).

18:9. Can a school district be sued for negligence in its hiring or retention of staff?

A school district may be held liable for negligence in its hiring or retention of an employee if it fails to follow its own established procedures for making employment decisions, such as those which might require investigating the criminal history of new employees (*Haddock v. New York*, 75 N.Y.2d 478 (1990)). In *Haddock*, the City of New York failed to comply with its own policy of investigating employees with a known criminal record. Therefore, the city officials were not subject to a defense of immunity in their decision to hire and retain the employee.

Where there is no violation of internal procedures and policies, a school district enjoys immunity with respect to the exercise of discretion in deciding whether to hire a particular employee (*Mon v. New York*, 78 N.Y.2d 309 (1991); see **18:18**).

18:10. Can a school district which provides recommendations for former employees be held liable for injuries sustained by students in another district?

Maybe. In one case, California's highest state court ruled that school officials who provided misleading letters of recommendation on behalf of a former employee, which helped the employee obtain a job in another school district, may be held liable for injuries sustained by a student in the new school district. The letters of recommendation in that case highlighted the employee's favorable characteristics but did not disclose the fact that the employee had been the subject of sexual misconduct charges and complaints at his old district. The employee subsequently sexually assaulted a student in the new district (*Randi W. v. Muroc Joint Unified School Dist.*, 14 Cal.4th 1066 (1997)).

While this decision is not binding in New York State, districts should be alerted that it represents a new theory of liability in light of the fact that school administrators are routinely asked to provide letters of recommendation for former employees.

18:11. Can school districts be sued for negligence in failing to protect teachers who are assaulted by students?

In general, the courts have not held school districts liable for injury to teachers who are assaulted by students at school, ruling that districts do not owe a duty to teachers to protect them from harm by third parties (*Verra v. City of New York*, 217 A.D.2d 577 (2nd Dep't 1995), *appeal denied*, 86 N.Y.2d 710 (1995); *Krakower v. City of New York*, 217 A.D.2d 441 (1st Dep't 1995), *appeal denied*, 87 N.Y.2d 804 (1995)).

18:12. Can a school district be sued for the negligence of an independent contractor it hires?

The general rule is that an employer is not liable for the negligence of an independent contractor because in such an instance the employer has no control over how the independent contractor performs the work, and the independent contractor should be held accountable for its own improper actions. There are exceptions, however, such as when the employer owes a non-delegable duty to the individual harmed by the independent contractor or when such individual would be left without a remedy if the general rule was applied strictly *(Feliberty v. Damon*, 72 N.Y.2d 112 (1988); *Prosser & Keaton on the Law of Torts § 71* (5th ed. 1984)).

The New York State Court of Appeals applied the general rule in favor of school districts in a case where it ruled that a district was not liable for the negligent actions of a bus company with which it had contracted for the transportation of school children to and from school. In *Chainani by Chainani v. Board of Educ.*, 87 N.Y.2d 370 (1995), a student was injured by a school bus driven by the employee of an independent contractor, when the bus drove over the student after dropping her off at her stop. The parents sued the district for damages based on the negligence of the driver. The court ruled the parents could not recover damages from the district.

18:13. On what basis can school districts be found negligent when there is an accident involving children on their way to and from school?

In general, school districts have no legal responsibility for children before they arrive on school grounds at the start of the school day and after they leave school grounds at the end of the school day (*Chainani by Chainani v. Board of Educ.*, 87 N.Y.2d 370 (1995)), and therefore cannot be found negligent for any injuries sustained by students on their way to and from school.

However, where a district transports students to and from school, it may be liable for its own negligence in failing to provide a "reasonably safe mode of conveyance" (*Williams v. Board of Trustees*, 210 A.D. 161 (1924); see also *Blair v. Board of Education*, 86 A.D.2d 933 (3rd Dep't 1982)), even though generally it will not be liable for the negligent acts of an independent contractor hired to transport students to and from school (*Chainani by Chainani v. Board of Educ.*; see **18:12**).

The district's responsibility begins when a child is picked up and ends when he or she has been properly discharged from the bus (see *Pratt v. Robinson*, 39 N.Y.2d 554 (1976); *Fornaro v. Kerry*, 139 A.D.2d 561 (2nd Dep't 1988); *Sewar v. Gagliardi Bros. Service*, 69 A.D.2d 281, 286 (4th Dep't 1979), *aff'd*, 51 N.Y.2d 752 (1980); Veh. & Traf. Law § 1174(b); 8 NYCRR § 156.3(f)(4)).

A school district is not liable for injuries sustained by a student who leaves the custody of the district by exiting from a school bus prior to reaching school, or getting off before his or her regular bus stop at the end of the school day (*Bushnell v. Berne-Knox-Westerlo School Dist.*, 125 A.D.2d 859 (3rd Dep't 1986), *appeal denied*, 69 N.Y.2d 609 (1987)), even if that student's conduct violates school policy (*Hurlburt v. Noxon*, 149 Misc.2d 374 (Chenango County Sup. Ct. 1990)).

Similarly, a school district will not be found negligent where a student who fails to get on the school bus gets injured because there is no duty to assure that students get on the school bus. However, if school officials accede to a parental request and promise to see to it that a student takes the school bus, the school could be found negligent for any injuries sustained by the student as a result of its failure to do so. For example, a court refused to dismiss a claim against a district that failed to keep such a promise and the student was injured when riding home after school in a friend's car. According to the court, the district had undertaken a special duty when it promised the parent it would make sure his son took the bus home from school (*Wenger v. Goodell*, 220 A.D.2d 937 (3rd Dep't 1995)).

18:14. On what basis can school districts be found negligent when there is an accident involving students who leave school grounds during the school day?

Generally, the school district has no duty to supervise a student who leaves school grounds without permission, although the courts will examine all the circumstances, such as the student's age and whether school authorities provided or should have provided supervision.

For example, a court refused to find a school district negligent where a 14-year-old student was involved in a car accident at 5:00 p.m the same day he had left school without permission. The court rejected the parents' argument that the district had breached its duty of supervision, finding that "once a student is beyond its lawful control, the school district owes no legal duty to supervise the activities of a student." In addition, the court refused to rule that a school district must impose security measures to prevent students from leaving the premises (*Palella v. Ulmer*, 136 Misc.2d 34 (Rensselaer County Sup. Ct. 1987)).

In another case, a state appellate court found a school district was not negligent for injuries to third parties caused by a 10th-grade student who drove his own car from his home district to a BOCES in violation of school policy which required that he take the school bus (*Thompson v. Ange*, 83 A.D.2d 193 (4th Dep't 1981)). The court refused to find that the school district assumed a legal duty to prevent injury to the public by the mere adoption of its no-driving policy.

18:15. On what basis can school districts be found negligent when student participants at school-sponsored athletic events are injured?

With respect to student athletes, school districts must exercise "reasonable care" to protect them from injuries that may result from unassumed, concealed or unreasonably increased risks (see *Benitez v. Board of Educ.*, 73 N.Y.2d 650 (1989)). In *Benitez*, for example, a high school athlete who was paralyzed during a football game claimed that the district owed him the same duty of care as a prudent parent in warning him not to play because he was fatigued. The court found that "injury and fatigue are inherent in team competitive sports" and the student had assumed the risk of competition as he was properly equipped, well trained and had played voluntarily.

Similarly, a school was found not negligent for injuries to a varsity wrestler who was struck in the jaw by an opponent in a weight classification one category higher, because the student reasonably could be found to have assumed the risk (*Edelson v. Uniondale Union Free School Dist.*, 219 A.D.2d 614 (2nd Dep't 1995)).

By contrast, one appellate court refused to dismiss a lawsuit against a school district by an inexperienced student pole vaulter who injured his knee when he landed on a seam in the mat, and where the pole was placed six inches higher than he had ever cleared. According to the court, the student had not necessarily assumed the risk because the seam was concealed and the student was not used to attempting the sport at that level of difficulty (Laboy v. Wallkill Cent. Sch. Dist., 201 A.D.2d 780 (3rd Dep't 1994)). In another case, an appellate court refused to dismiss a lawsuit against a school district by a student who was injured when he did not wear a mouth guard during field hockey practice. According to the court, the district may have failed to assure adequate supervision of practice and warn students about the risk of injury (*Baker v. Briarcliff Sch. Dist.*, 205 A.D.2d 652 (2nd Dep't 1994)).

18:16. On what basis can school districts be found negligent when non-student participants at school-sponsored events are injured?

Assumption of risk principles applicable to student athletes (see **18:15**) apply also to non-student participants in school-sponsored athletic events. For example, in *Arbegast v. Board of Education*, 65 N.Y.2d 161 (1985), a student teacher was injured when the donkey she was riding in a donkey basketball game put its head down and she fell off. The participants had been told they might fall off and that they were participating at their own risk. The court held that the teacher had assumed the risk and found the school district not liable.

18:17. Are school districts liable for spectator injuries at school-sponsored events?

It depends. Generally, spectators are deemed to have assumed the normal risks associated with attendance at a game. For instance, in *Akins v. Glens Falls City School Dist.*, 53 N.Y.2d 325 (1981), a spectator sitting and watching a school's baseball game was injured. The court held the district was not liable, explaining that the owner of a baseball field is only required to exercise reasonable care and need only provide screening for the area of the field behind home plate, where the danger of getting hit by a ball is the greatest.

Civil Rights Liability

18:18. What does civil rights liability consist of and how do school districts become exposed to it?

Civil rights liability arises under section 1983 of the Civil Rights Act of 1876. Accordingly, a civil rights lawsuit is also referred to as a section 1983 action. Liability attaches to any person who, "acting under color of state law, custom or practice," deprives a person of his or her federal constitutional rights.

An individual bringing a section 1983 lawsuit against a school district must establish not that the district or its officials or employees were negligent, but rather that the individual enjoyed a protected federal right, a school district official or employee deprived him or her of that right, and the cause of that deprivation was a statute, official practice, policy or custom (42 USC § 1983; *Monell v. Department of Social Servs.*, 436 U.S. 658 (1978)). "Policy" includes policies and decisions officially adopted and promulgated by the school board; regulations and decisions adopted and promulgated by school officials to whom the board has delegated final policy-making authority in the particular area in question; and widespread practices of officials and employees which, although not authorized by adopted policy, are so common and well settled as to constitute a custom that fairly represents district policy (*St. Louis v. Praprotnik*, 485 U.S. 112 (1988)).

The United States Supreme Court has indicated that as a general rule, a single hiring decision by an employee of a municipality, which does not itself violate federal law, does not rise to the level of a municipal "policy" under which a municipality can be held liable under section 1983 (*Board of the County Commissioners of Bryan County, Oklahoma v. Brown*, 520 U.S. 397 (1997)).

18:19. May a school board member be held personally liable for the violation of an individual's civil rights when performing legislative activities?

No. The United States Supreme Court has recently ruled that local legislators, such as school board members, have absolute immunity from civil liability in connection with lawsuits arising out of their performance of legislative activities (*Bogan v. Scott-Harris*, 118 S.Ct. 966 (1998)). This case does not shield board members from lawsuits for actions which are not legislative in nature. For example, the court distinguished the abolition of a position, which it determined to be legislative, from the hiring or firing of a particular employee.

18:20. May school board members and district employees be held personally liable for the violation of an individual's civil rights?

Yes. School board members and other district employees may be individually liable in a civil rights action if they knew or should have known that their actions would violate the federal constitutional or federal statutory rights of a person (see **18:19** for exception pertaining to school board members and legislative activities). Government officials enjoy "qualified immunity" which protects them from liability only when their actions or their performance of "discretionary functions" "do not violate a clearly established constitutional or statutory right of which a reasonable person would have known" (*Davis v. Scherer*, 468 U.S. 183, 191

(1984); *Harlow v. Fitzgerald*, 457 U.S. 800, 818 (1982)).

For example, in *Spivey v. Elliott*, 41 F.3d 1497 (11th Cir. 1995), the United States Court of Appeals for the Eleventh Circuit ruled a school district was not responsible for the sexual abuse of a 13-year-old disabled student by a classmate at a state-operated residential facility because there was no clearly established constitutional duty to protect the student from this particular harm at the time of the assault. The court then refused to rule whether such a duty actually exists.

18:21. Are there any limitations on the scope of a civil rights lawsuit?

The United States Supreme Court has established two theories for imposing civil rights liability. The first of these requires a finding of governmental conduct that reflects a "deliberate" or "conscious" choice which can be deemed to amount to a deliberate indifference toward the constitutional or federal statutory rights of the individual injured. Deliberate indifference cases have involved, for example, the failure to properly train staff (*Canton v. Harris*, 489 U.S. 378 (1989)).

Deliberate indifference may be established through the existence of a continuing, widespread, persistent pattern of unconstitutional misconduct by government officials and employees; a deliberate indifference to or tacit authorization of such conduct by policy-making officials after notice to the officials of the misconduct; and evidence that the complaining party was injured by conduct undertaken pursuant to official policy or custom; in other words, the policy or custom was the moving force behind the constitutional violation (*Jane Doe "A". v. Special District*, 901 F.2d 642 (8th Cir. 1990); *Doe v. Taylor Indep. Sch. Dist.*, 15 F.3d 443 (5th Cir. 1994) *cert. denied sub nom, Lankford v. Doe*, 513 U.S. 815 (1994)).

The second theory of civil rights liability requires the existence of a special relationship which imposes on governmental authorities an affirmative duty of care and protection with respect to the individual injured (*DeShaney v. Winnebago County Dep't of Social Servs.*, 489 U.S. 189 (1989)). The courts have limited special relationship cases to situations where the government has deprived individuals of their liberty and ability to defend themselves as in the case of prisoners and involuntarily institutionalized patients (see, e.g. *DeShaney; Stoneking v. Bradford Area School Dist.*, 856 F.2d 594 (3rd Cir. 1988), *vacated sub nom, Smith v. Stoneking*, 489 U.S. 1062, *on remand*, 882 F.2d 720 (3rd Cir. 1989) *cert. denied*, 493 U.S. 1044 (1990)).

Courts have refused to consider state compulsory education laws as placing students in the "functional custody" of school authorities with a concurrent affirmative duty to protect students from injury (*Stoneking v. Bradford; Wright v. Lovin*, 32 F.3d 538 (11th Cir. 1994); *Johnson v. Dallas*

Indep. Sch. Dist., 38 F.3d 198 (5th Cir. 1994), *cert. denied*, 514 U.S. 1017 (1995); *Walton v. Alexander*, 44 F.3d 1297 (5th Cir. 1995)). In New York, however, there have been several federal district court decisions where school districts have been found to have a special relationship with students subject to civil rights liability, based on the state's compulsory education law (see, e.g., *Lichtler v. County of Orange*, 813 F.Supp. 1054 (S.D.N.Y. 1993); *Robert G. v. Newburgh City School Dist.*, 1990 WL 3210 (S.D.N.Y. Jan. 8, 1990 (unreported)); see also *Pagano v. Massapequa Public Schools*, 714 F.Supp 641 (E.D.N.Y. 1989)).

Employment Discrimination

18:22. What constitutes employment discrimination?

Generally, employment discrimination consists of practices which impair employment opportunities for individuals who meet certain protected characteristics such as race, sex or disability, in violation of federal and/or state law. For example, on the federal level, Title VII of the Civil Rights Act of 1964 (42 USC § 2000e-2) prohibits all employers with 15 or more employees from discriminating in the hiring, firing, demotion or promotion of employees on the basis of race, sex, religion and national origin.

The United States Supreme Court has expanded Title VII to protect former employees who have filed employment discrimination complaints from retaliation by their former employer. In one case, a former employee was permitted to sue his former employer for providing unfavorable job recommendations to prospective employers *(Robinson v. Shell Oil Company*, 117 S.Ct. 843 (1997)). Generally, an employee who prevails in a Title VII lawsuit is granted reinstatement and back pay. However, 1991 amendments to the act also permit a court to award compensatory and punitive damages and grant the right to a jury trial (*Landgraf v. USI Film Prod.*, 511 U.S. 244 (1994)).

The Pregnancy Discrimination Act of 1978 (PDA) (42 USC § 2000e(k)) amended Title VII to also prohibit discrimination in employment against pregnant women and to require that they be treated no differently than any other temporarily disabled employee. School districts and their attorneys must be sure to apply leave provisions and other terms and conditions of employment equally to all employees, with no greater burden on women who take leave in order to give birth.

In addition, the Age Discrimination in Employment Act (ADEA) (29 USC §§ 621 *et seq.*), applicable to employers with 20 employees or more, protects employees over the age of 40 from discrimination based on age. An employee alleging a violation of the ADEA must prove that the employee's age played a motivating role in, or contributed to, an employer's employment decision *(Rentz v. Grey Advertising*, 135 F.3d 217 (2nd Cir. 1997); *Gallo v. Prudential Residential Servs., Ltd. Partnership*, 22 F.3d 1219 (2nd Cir. 1994)). The ADEA may be violated even if the worker hired to replace an older employee is himself or herself over 40 (*O'Connor v. Consolidated Coin Caterers Corp.*, 517 U.S. 308 (1996)). One New York appellate court ruled the ADEA applied to a town assessor as well, even though that position is considered a public office (*Matter of Scopelliti v. Town of New Castle*, 210 A.D.2d 308 (2nd Dep't 1994)).

The Americans with Disabilities Act (ADA) (42 USC § 12102 et seq.) and section 504 of the Rehabilitation Act (29 USC § 794) prohibit discrimination on the basis of disability. The ADA, which applies to both private and public employers with more than 15 employees, prohibits discrimination in employment against a "qualified" disabled person, one who can perform the essential functions of the position with or without a "reasonable accommodation" unless offering the reasonable accommodation would impose an undue hardship (42 USC § 12111(9), (10)). In addition, the United States Supreme Court has ruled that the ADA applies to people infected with the human immunodeficiency virus (HIV) (*Bragdon v. Abbott*, 118 S.Ct. 2196 (1998)).

18:23. What state laws prohibit employment discrimination?

New York's Human Rights Law prohibits discrimination on the basis of age, race, creed, color, national origin, sex, marital status, disability, and prior arrest or conviction record (Exec. Law § 290 *et seq.*). It applies to all employers with four or more employees, and their unions. The statute is enforced either by filing an administrative complaint with the State Division of Human Rights or bringing a lawsuit directly in state court.

The state Whistle-blower Law prohibits public employers from retaliating against employees for disclosing to a governmental body information regarding a violation of a law, rule or regulation when the violation "creates and presents a substantial and specific danger to the public health or safety," or for disclosing to a governmental body information "which the employee reasonably believes to be true and reasonably believes constitutes an improper governmental action." However, unless there is imminent and serious danger to public health or safety, prior to disclosing such information, an employee must make a good faith effort to provide his or her employer with the information to be disclosed and must give the employer a reasonable time to take appropriate action. It provides for reinstatement and back pay if the employee can show that the employer retaliated illegally for the protected activity (Civil Service Law § 75-b).

By comparison, in the private sector, an employee may be fired for reporting "possible" violations of law, because the protections of the statute (Lab. Law § 740) only apply to reports of actual violations of law (*Bordell v. General Electric Co.*, 88 N.Y.2d 869 (1996)).

The state Legal Activities Law protects employees who engage in certain legal activities after work hours, such as consuming legal substances, recreational activities that do not involve compensation, and political activities (Lab. Law §201-d). According to one appellate court, dating does not fall within the scope of the definition of "recreational activity" under the law (*State v. Wal-Mart Stores*, 207 A.D.2d 150 (3rd Dep't 1995)). The *Wal-Mart* case involved the discharge of two employees for violating a "fraternization policy" when they dated each other even though they each were married to others.

18:24. Can individual employees be held personally liable for employment discrimination conduct?

In a sexual harassment case, the federal Court of Appeals for the Second Circuit with jurisdiction over New York ruled that employees may not be held individually liable for acts of discrimination under Title VII of the Civil Rights Act of 1964 (*Tomka v. Seiler Corp.*, 66 F.3d 1295 (2nd Cir. 1995)). Other federal circuit courts have taken the opposite view, however (see e.g., *Paroline v. Unisys Corp.*, 879 F.2d 100 (4th Cir. 1989)). Until the United States Supreme Court decides the issue, New York is bound by the *Tomka* decision.

Sexual Harassment

18:25. What is sexual harassment?

Sexual harassment is a form of sex discrimination or gender-based employment under Title VII of the federal Civil Rights Act of 1964 (42 USC § 2000e-z; *Meritor Savings Bank, FSB v. Vinson*, 477 U.S. 57 (1986)). It is also a form of sex discrimination under Title IX of the 1972 Educational Amendments (20 USC § 1681), which prohibits discrimination in educational programs and activities that receive federal funds (*Franklin v. Gwinnett County Pub. Sch.*, 503 U.S. 60 (1992); see *Davis v. Monroe County Board of Educ.*, 120 F.3d 1390 (11th Cir. 1997); *Bruneau v. South Kortright CSD*, 935 F.Supp. 162 (N.D.N.Y. 1996); compare *Rowinski v. Bryan Indep. Sch. Dist.*, 80 F.3d 1006 (5th Cir. 1996), *cert. denied*, 117 S.Ct. 165 (1996)).

In addition, sexual harassment is recognized as a form of sex discrimination under the New York State Human Rights Law, which prohibits discrimination in employment on the basis of certain immutable characteristics such as gender (Executive Law § 296 *et seq.;* see **18:23**). Damages for mental anguish may be awarded under state law if the complainant produces testimony as to hurt and humiliation derived from the acts of sex discrimination (*New York State Dep't of Correctional Servs. v. State Div. of Human Rights,* 215 A.D.2d 908 (3rd Dep't 1995); *Cornwell v. Robinson,* 23 F.3d 694 (2nd Cir. 1994)).

Men can be victims of sexual harassment by female supervisors (*Forte v. East Harlem Block Schools,* 1994 WL 265918, 65 Fair Empl. Prac. Case (BNA) 383 (S.D.N.Y. 1994)); *Goering v. NYNEX Info. Resources Co.,* 209 A.D.2d 834 (3rd Dep't 1994), and sexual harassment directed at members of the same sex has also been found to be actionable (*Oncale v. Sundowner Offshore Services, Incorporated,* 118 S.Ct. 998 (1998)).

18:26. What are the characteristics of sexual harassment?

Sexual harassment consists of "unwelcome sexual advances, requests for sexual favors, and verbal or physical conduct of a sexual nature" (29 CFR § 1604.11; 34 CFR § 106.8; 29 CFR § 1609.1(b)).

In the employment context, the United States Supreme Court has recognized two types of sexual harassment: quid pro quo and hostile environment sexual harassment (*Meritor Savings Bank, FSB v. Vinson,* 477 U.S. 57 (1986)).

Quid pro quo sexual harassment involves situations where an employee's submission to or rejection of unwelcome sexual conduct is used by an employer to determine that person's terms or conditions of employment. School districts would be vicariously liable when a member of their supervisory staff uses his or her authority to obtain sexual favors from another employee, meaning that the district would be held liable as an entity even if higher school authorities did not know about or condone the action. Examples of this kind of sexual harassment would include being given or denied a raise, transfer, or being disciplined for refusing to accede to the sexual advances of a supervisor.

Hostile environment sexual harassment, on the other hand, can take many forms. Usually, it is a pattern of unwelcome sexual conduct sufficiently severe to interfere with an individual's performance or to create an intimidating, hostile, or offensive working environment. Examples of this would include repeated sexual remarks aimed at an individual who finds the remarks offensive.

The U.S. Supreme Court has ruled that in both quid pro quo and hostile environment sexual harassment, an employer may be liable for the harassment of an employee by a supervisor even if the employer did not know that the harassment was taking place (*Burlington Industries v. Ellerth,* 118 S.Ct. 2257 (1998); *Faragher v. City of Boca Raton,* 118 S.Ct. 2275 (1998)).

If the sexual harassment is so pervasive that it is "calculated to drive someone out of the workplace," it may be a constitutional violation (*Annis v. County of Westchester,* 36 F.3d 251 (2nd Cir. 1994); see **18:29-30** for discussion on peer sexual harassment and teacher-student sexual harassment).

18:27. Is it necessary for an employee to show serious psychological harm or economic loss in order to prevail in a sexual harassment lawsuit?

No. In *Harris v. Forklift Sys.,* 510 U.S. 17 (1993), the United States Supreme Court ruled that an employee need not prove serious psychological harm in order to succeed in a sexual harassment lawsuit.

However, the Supreme Court has ruled that in cases where the complaining employee suffers no economic harm as a result of the harassment, employers can successfully defend themselves by proving that they exercised reasonable care to prevent and promptly correct sexually harassing behavior and that the employee unreasonably failed to take advantage of opportunities provided by the employer to report the harassment (*Faragher v. City of Boca Raton,* 118 S.Ct. 2275 (1998)).

18:28. What should a school district do to protect itself against claims of sexual harassment?

School districts should adopt comprehensive sexual harassment prevention programs that include the following elements: policies that condemn sexual harassment and which contain procedures for clearly and regularly communicating the district's strong disapproval of sexual misconduct; procedures for resolving complaints which encourage victims to come forward, and ensure their confidentiality and protect them against retaliation; and provisions for immediate and effective remedies. Districts should also take appropriate disciplinary action against offenders, and provide ongoing and comprehensive training for district employees and students.

In addition, school districts should be aware that Title IX of the 1972 Educational Amendments (20 USC § 1681) requires federal fund recipients not only to adopt a policy which condemns actions prohibited by the act but also to appoint an employee responsible for ensuring compliance with Title IX. This policy must be posted and disseminated to all students and employees, as well as to the parents of students.

Prior to adopting or revising a sexual harassment policy and procedures, school districts may have an obligation to negotiate certain aspects of the policy and procedures relating to employee discipline with employee organizations (unions) (*Patchogue-Medford Congress of Teachers v. Patchogue Medford Union Free School District*, 30 PERB ¶ 3041 (1997)).

18:29. May a school district be held liable when a teacher sexually harasses a student?

Yes. The United States Supreme Court has ruled that a school district may be held liable under Title IX for sexual harassment of a student by a teacher *(Franklin v. Gwinnett County Pub. Sch.,* 503 U.S. 60 (1992)). However, damages may not be recovered unless an official of the district who has authority to institute corrective measures on the district's behalf has actual notice of, and is deliberately indifferent to, the teacher's misconduct (*Gebser v. Lago Vista Independent School District,* 118 S.Ct. 1989 (1998)).

18:30. Can a school district be held liable when a student sexually harasses another student?

A federal district court in New York has ruled that to establish a claim for hostile learning environment created by peer-on-peer sexual harassment under Title IX, a student must demonstrate that the school or school board received actual notice of the sexually harassing conduct and failed to take action to remedy it *(Bruneau v. South Kortright Central School District,* 935 F.Supp. 162 (N.D.N.Y. 1996)).

However, the Eleventh Circuit Court of Appeals, which does not have jurisdiction over school districts in New York, has ruled that a school district cannot be held liable for student on student sexual harassment under Title IX. The student in that case has asked the United States Supreme Court to review that court's decision *(Davis v. Monroe County Board of Education,* 120 F.3d 1390 (11th Cir. 1997), *pet. for cert. filed,* 66 U.S.L.W. 3387 (1997)).

Defense and Indemnification

18:31. Must a school district retain an attorney?

No. Although most school districts retain counsel to provide legal advice to the school board and represent it in matters pending before the courts or administrative tribunals (*Yorktown Cent. School Dist. v. Yorktown Congress of Teachers,* 42 A.D.2d 422 (2nd Dep't 1973)), there is no requirement that every district retain counsel. Such a decision is within the discretion of the school board.

Some districts retain outside counsel for specific purposes, such as labor negotiations or disciplinary proceedings against tenured teachers;

others appoint attorneys to handle any legal matters that arise. Some districts have attorneys on staff serving in this capacity.

Outside attorneys may be employed by a retainer agreement, which is terminable at any time, or pursuant to a contract at a fixed salary (see *Harrison Cent. School Dist. v. Nyquist*, 59 A.D.2d 434 (3rd Dep't 1977)).

18:32. Do the bidding requirements of the General Municipal Law apply to the appointment of a school attorney?

No. Because the attorney's services require the use of professional skill, a district need not subject the selection of its attorney to a bidding process (see Gen. Mun. Law § 104-b; *People ex rel. Smith v. Flagg*, 17 N.Y. 584 (1858)).

Nonetheless, the General Municipal Law requires that school districts adopt internal policies and procedures governing procurement of professional services, such as those provided by a school attorney. The law requires that professional services must be "procured in a manner so as to assure the prudent and economical use of public moneys in the best interests of the taxpayer" (Gen. Mun. Law § 104–b).

18:33. Are school districts responsible for defending and indemnifying school board members and employees who are sued for negligence and other improper actions?

Section 3811 of the Education Law requires school districts (other than New York City) and boards of cooperative educational services (BOCES) to defend and indemnify any superintendent, principal, teacher, other member of the teaching and supervisory staff, noninstructional employee, any school board member, any member of the committee on special education (CSE) or committee on preschool special education (CPSE) or subcommittee thereof, or any person appointed to serve as a surrogate parent on local CSEs, for all reasonable costs and expenses, including awards resulting from any action or proceeding against him or her arising out of the exercise of his or her powers or the performance of his or her duties (other than one brought by a school district or a criminal action brought against the individual). Any such costs and expenses must be approved pursuant to board resolution, which also authorizes the levying of a tax for such purpose. Section 3812 provides for inclusion of these costs in the next annual budget so that they may be assessed against the school district.

With respect to New York City, section 2560 of the Education Law requires the New York City school district as well to provide legal representation and indemnification against claims to members of the school board, members of each community school board, employees, members of

CSEs, and authorized participants in school volunteer programs in the city, pursuant to section 50-k of the General Municipal Law.

In addition, section 3023 of the Education Law also requires school boards and BOCES boards to indemnify and provide legal representation to teachers, practice or cadet teachers, members of the supervisory and administrative staff, other employees and authorized participants in volunteer programs against lawsuits for negligence, accidental bodily injury or property damage, provided those persons were performing their duties within the scope of employment or their authorized volunteer duties and under the direction of the board. Section 3023 also permits school boards to arrange for and maintain appropriate insurance with any appropriate insurance company.

An additional indemnification provision applies specifically to teachers and volunteers who are sued as a result of taking disciplinary action against students. Section 3028 of the Education Law requires all school boards and BOCES boards to provide an attorney and to pay the attorneys' fees and expenses incurred in the defense of teachers or authorized volunteers who are sued either in a civil or criminal action arising out of disciplinary action taken against any student of the district. As with most indemnification provisions, the protection applies only if the teacher or volunteer was discharging his or her duties within the scope of employment or authorized volunteer duties when the disciplinary action took place.

Because the Board of Regents has strictly limited the circumstances under which teachers may use physical force against students legally (see **8:22**), the New York State Insurance Department has indicated that insurance carriers may limit their coverage to damages arising out of the use of physical force as permitted by the Regents while not providing coverage for unauthorized corporal punishment. However, the school district's duty to provide a legal defense and/or pay attorneys' fees is not affected by the availability of liability insurance.

18:34. Are there any procedures that school board members and employees must comply with before a school district can defend and indemnify them?

Pursuant to section 3811 of the Education Law, the board member or employee must notify the board in writing of the commencement of the proceeding against him or her within five days after service of process. Within 10 days, the school board has the right to designate and appoint legal counsel to represent the individual. In the absence of such a designation and appointment, the individual may select his or her own counsel.

Under sections 3023 and 3028, the teacher or other employee or volunteer must deliver a copy of the summons and complaint or demand or notice to the board within 10 days of the time the complaint is served upon that person.

In addition, either the courts or the commissioner of education must provide a certificate of good faith which certifies that the individual appeared to have acted in good faith with respect to the exercise of his or her powers or the performance of duties. If the amount of costs claimed by an individual is disputed by a district meeting or the school board, it may be adjusted by the county judge in the county in which the district or any part of it is located (§ 3811).

18:35. Are there any alternative provisions affecting a school district's responsibilities regarding indemnification and defense of school board members and district employees?

Yes. If a school board or BOCES board adopts a resolution as prescribed by section 18 of the Public Officers Law, board members, officers and employees acting within the scope of their employment or duties may be covered by this statute. This coverage may supplant or supplement the protection provided under the Education Law, depending on the language of the resolution passed by the board (see *Matter of Percy*, 31 Educ. Dep't Rep. 199 (1991)). In order to supplement the Education Law protection, the resolution must do so explicitly.

Section 18 also requires the district to pay for employees' legal defense costs and damages if the case is of the type covered by the statute, provided that the employee was acting within the scope of his or her duties when the allegedly wrongful act occurred. The employee must forward a copy of any summons or other court papers to the superintendent of schools or school attorney within 10 days after he or she was served in order to obtain protection under the statute, and must fully cooperate in his or her defense. It is not necessary for the employee to obtain a good faith certificate to be protected under the statute.

Insurance

18:36. Must a school board have insurance or other protection against damage to school property?

Yes. Section 1709(8) of the Education Law states that a school board must "insure the schoolhouses and their furniture, apparatus and appurtenances, and the school library." School districts may establish a liability and casualty reserve fund for self-insurance purposes (Gen. Mun. Law § 6-n; see **18:43**).

18:37. What other types of insurance are commonly purchased by school boards to protect their districts?

Many school districts purchase what is known as special multi-peril insurance policies. These are package policies designed to provide a combination of property and general liability coverages. Other coverages often purchased by districts are floater policies to protect district property that is taken off school grounds; automobile coverage, which protects against vehicular accidents; and school board members' errors and omissions coverage, also known as school board legal liability coverage (see **18:40** for more information about this type of policy).

School districts also may purchase catastrophe-umbrella or excess policies to protect the district against large losses. The school district's administrative staff and insurance professionals can help the school board determine an adequate amount of coverage for the types of insurance they choose to purchase.

18:38. Are school districts required to carry workers' compensation insurance?

Yes. School districts must provide workers' compensation coverage for all teachers and other employees for injuries incurred in the performance of their duties (§§ 1604(31), 1709(34), 2503(10)). The Workers' Compensation Law requires employers to provide benefits to employees for disability or death "arising out of and in the course of employment" (Work. Comp. Law § 10).

The courts have recognized a "special errand" exception for injuries that occur while the employee is on an errand to or from work and home. If the employer encouraged the errand and obtained a benefit as a result of its performance, the injury will be deemed to have occurred in the course of employment (*Neacosia v. New York Power Auth.*, 85 N.Y.2d 471 (1995); *Jennette v. MSC Canon*, 211 A.D.2d 943 (3rd Dep't 1995)).

Similarly, in a case where an employee was injured in an altercation with a co-worker in the stairwell of the employer's building, the court found that the conduct leading to the injury was tacitly condoned by the employer, and, therefore the injury arose from the course of employment (*Rosen v. First Manhattan Bank*, 84 N.Y.2d 856 (1994)).

The law establishes a complex plan to determine the amount of such benefits based upon the employee's average weekly wage and the extent and permanency of the injury (Work. Comp. Law §§ 14-15). The school district's workers' compensation protection can be obtained through the State Fund, a worker's compensation insurance carrier, a county self-insurance plan or by individual self-insurance (see Work. Comp. Law Arts. 4 and 5; practice commentary to Work. Comp. Law § 50).

In addition, section 212(2) of the Workers' Compensation Law provides that school districts may elect to cover their employees under the Disability Benefits Law. These benefits are provided to employees unable to work because of an injury unrelated to their employment.

18:39. Are school districts required to provide unemployment insurance?

Yes. The federal government requires that unemployment insurance be provided to all employees of state and local governments, including public school employees, for states to be in conformity with federal law (see 26 USC § 3304; *County of Los Angeles v. Marshall*, 442 F.Supp. 1186 (D.D.C. 1977), *aff'd*, 631 F.2d 767, *cert. denied*, 449 U.S. 837 (1980); Lab. Law §§ 512, 565).

The general rule is that employees of educational institutions are not allowed unemployment insurance benefits for periods between academic years or terms or vacation periods or holiday recess periods, provided an employee has a contract or a reasonable assurance that he or she will perform services in such capacity for both such academic years or terms or for the period immediately following such vacation period or holiday recess (Lab. Law § 590(10), (11); *In re Claim of Bicjan*, 219 A.D.2d 751 (3rd Dep't 1995)). However, at least one court has ruled that when a school district enters into a contract with an independent agency which is responsible for compiling a list of available substitute teachers and for selecting the teacher to be hired for each job, using the agency's own criteria to make the selection, the employee was eligible for unemployment insurance because the district could not give "reasonable assurance" of employment *(Makis v. Owego-Apalachin Central School Dist.*, 233 A.D.2d 743 (3rd Dep't 1996)).

The courts have held that individual notices taken together with their collective bargaining agreement constitute a contract within the meaning of section 590(11) of the Labor Law, resulting in the claimant's ineligibility for unemployment benefits over the summer vacation (*In re Claim of La Mountain*, 51 N.Y.2d 318 (1980)). However, federal law permits states to adopt legislation to permit noninstructional employees to receive unemployment benefits during the summer months (26 USC § 3304). New York has not adopted such legislation.

In the event that an employee successfully sues a district for reinstatement and back pay, a district may not deduct unemployment payments from the award of back pay, even where the district paid the unemployment tax directly to the state Labor Department's Unemployment Insurance Division on behalf of the employee (*Appeal of Lessing*, 35 Educ. Dep't Rep. 116 (1995)).

18:40. How much insurance should a school board maintain for its district?

Since the risks of liability differ in all districts, depending on such issues as the number of students and employees, programs operated and other factors, there is no simple answer to this question that is appropriate for all school boards. It is possible that a board could go many years without being sued, or it could face several lawsuits in a short span of time. In addition, the possible cost to a district of a lawsuit varies greatly, in part, depending upon the type of lawsuit and the damages the plaintiff is seeking. Predicting the outcome of multiple lawsuits is even more difficult.

Thus, the New York State School Boards Association recommends that the board examine the risks faced by the district and consult with its school attorney and professionals in the insurance field to determine appropriate coverage for itself.

In most situations where a school board and/or its employees are sued, the school district has an obligation to defend and indemnify the school board members as long as the lawsuit arose out of the exercise of its powers or the performance of its duties (see **18:33-35**).

Thus, if the district has an insurance policy for school board members, commonly referred to as an errors and omissions or school board legal liability policy, and the limit of the insurance policy is too low to cover the costs involved in the settlement or verdict, the district still will retain these obligations. The district will have to find the funds to pay, even if it means raising taxes. In such a situation, a school board member is not obligated to pay amounts, out of his or her own pocket, above the district's policy limits.

18:41. Do the legal requirements on competitive bidding apply to the purchase of school insurance?

No. Section 103 of the General Municipal Law does not cover service contracts, and a school district is not obligated to submit its insurance coverage to competitive public bidding (*Lynd v. Heffernan*, 286 A.D. 597 (1955); *Surdell v. Oswego*, 91 Misc.2d 1041 (1977); Opn. St. Compt. 61-233).

However, the General Municipal Law requires that school districts adopt internal policies and procedures governing the procurement of professional services, such as insurance, so they are procured "in a manner so as to assure the prudent and economical use of public moneys in the best interests of the taxpayer" (Gen. Mun. Law § 104-b).

18:42. How may a school board secure information on the reliability or financial status of an insurance company with whom it wishes to do business?

A school board can receive information that would be helpful in evaluating an insurance company by consulting an insurance reference such as Best's Key Rating Guide, or the New York State Insurance Department, 25 Beaver Street, New York, N.Y. 10004-2319, 212-480-6400, http://www.ins.state.ny.us.

18:43. May a school district act as a self-insurer for protection against claims?

Yes. A self-insurance fund may be established by any school district or board of cooperative educational services (BOCES) except one in a city with a population of 125,000 or more. This fund may be used to pay for almost any loss, claim, action or judgment for which the district is authorized or required to purchase or maintain insurance (Gen. Mun. Law § 6-n (1,2)). The amount paid into such fund may not exceed the greater of $33,000, or 5 percent of the total district budget for the fiscal year (Gen. Mun. Law § 6-n(4); see **19:24**).

The law provides for oversight and regulation of municipal cooperative health insurance plans and self-funded health insurance consortia by the State Insurance Department and provides legal and regulatory requirements, safeguards, and other conditions for the plans (Ins. Law Art. 47).

18:44. Are school districts permitted to arrange group insurance programs for district employees?

Yes. Sections 1604(31-a), 1709(34-a) and 2503(10-a) of the Education Law permit the establishment of group insurance programs applying to teachers and other employees on life insurance, accident and health insurance, medical and surgical benefits, and hospital benefits. These sections of the law make it permissible, at the discretion of the board, to pay a share of the cost (or the whole thereof) of group insurance on school employees.

For unionized employees, most changes in benefits first must be negotiated with their bargaining agent (*Genesee Valley BOCES School Related Personnel Assoc. v. Genessee-Livingston-Steuben-Wyoming BOCES,* 29 PERB ¶3065 (1996)).

Section 565(7) of the Labor Law states that any two or more school districts may form a joint account to pay unemployment insurance benefits, pursuant to the rules and regulations of the commissioner of labor. In addition, school districts and boards of cooperative educational services (BOCES), along with other municipal corporations, are specifically authorized to establish reserve funds for unemployment insurance payments (Gen. Mun. Law § 6–m; see **19:24**).

Additionally, there are other special rules related to state and local governments regarding their responsibilities under the Federal Unemployment Tax Act. For example, state and local governments are specifically granted the option to pay on the reimbursement method instead of being subject to federal unemployment payroll tax (26 USC § 3309(a)(2); see Lab. Law § 565(5)). Thus, districts pay for only the actual benefits sent to former employees, rather than the administrative costs of the program.

18:45. Can school boards legally withhold funds for the payment of various group insurance programs from employees' salaries?

Yes. School boards have the legal right to withhold, at the written request of individual employees, a portion of their salaries to pay group insurance premiums (§§ 1604(34-a), 1709(34–a), 2503(10-a)).

18:46. Are school board members permitted to participate in school employee hospitalization and medical service plans?

Yes. Section 92–a(4) of the General Municipal Law permits school board members to participate in hospitalization and medical service plans, but they must pay the total cost for both themselves and their family members.

Retired school board members with at least 20 years of service in such a position are also eligible for these plans, as long as they pay the total cost (Gen. Mun. Law § 92–a(1-a)).

18:47. May a school board insure its students against personal accidents regardless of whether or not the district is responsible for the accident?

Yes. School boards may, at their discretion, purchase insurance against accidents to students occurring in school; on school grounds; during physical education classes; during intramural and interscholastic sports activities, while students are being transported between home and school in a school bus; and during school-sponsored trips. The premiums may be paid from district funds (§§ 1604(7–a), (7–b); 1709(8–a), (8–b)).

18:48. May a school require students to purchase insurance as a pre-requisite for participation in a school program?

No. Although school boards are authorized to insure students against injuries sustained while participating in school programs, they may not lawfully pass on to their students the cost of such insurance or require the students to purchase it themselves. In addition, a school board may not use its staff to solicit the purchase of insurance, because this is considered an unconstitutional use of public moneys, property and services in aid of a private corporation (*Matter of Shapnek*, 3 Educ. Dep't Rep. 99 (1963); *Matter of Countryman*, 1 Educ. Dep't Rep. 538 (1960)).

18:49. Can a bidder on a school construction job be required to secure surety bonds from a particular insurance company or broker?

No. This would be a violation of section 2504 of the Insurance Law.

19. Fiscal Management

19:1. What is the fiscal year of a school district?

The fiscal year of a school district runs from July 1 to June 30.

19:2. Who is legally responsible for the fiscal management of a school district?

Although the Local Finance Law identifies the president of the school board as the chief financial and chief executive officer of the school district (Local Fin. Law § 2.00(5)(e); (5-a)(e)), as a general rule, legal responsibility for fiscal management of the school district rests with the school board itself. The board, however, may delegate fiscal responsibilities to an officer or officers of the district such as the treasurer, superintendent and/or business administrator (§ 2503(1), (2)).

19:3. What are some of a school board's primary fiscal responsibilities?

School boards must appoint a clerk of the board, a tax collector (in some cases), a treasurer and, at its discretion, an auditor (§§ 1709(20-a); 2130(1),(4); 2503(15); 2526; 8 NYCRR § 170.2(a)). The board must designate individuals to be responsible for purchasing and the certification of payrolls (8 NYCRR § 170.2 (b)).

It is also the board's responsibility to ensure that district expenditures do not exceed the budget approved by the voters and to require quarterly financial reports from the treasurer (monthly reports are required if budget transfers have been made since the last report) (§ 1718(1); 8 NYCRR § 170.2(k),(p)). The board must also take steps to ensure that transactions are recorded in accordance with the Uniform System of Accounts for School Districts (8 NYCRR § 170.2(f); see **19:12**).

19:4. Must a school district's treasurer, tax collector and auditor, if one is appointed, be bonded?

Yes. The Education Law and commissioner's regulations require that the school district treasurer, tax collector and auditor execute and deliver to the board an "official undertaking" (§ 2130(5); 8 NYCRR § 170.2(d)). In districts under the jurisdiction of a district superintendent, the district superintendent also must approve the bonds. Bonds must be received by the board within 10 days after each officer is notified of appointment and before each assumes his or her duties.

The bond required must be in an amount fixed and approved by the school board. There is no law that specifies the amount of each bond.

However, a frequently applied rule of thumb is that the collector's bond should be the full amount to be raised by taxation, and the treasurer's bond should be at least 15 percent of the amount of the annual school budget. Treasurers, collectors and certain other public officers may be covered by a blanket bond (Pub. Off. Law § 11(2); see also **3:21**).

19:5. Can a school board administer an endowment fund or scholarship fund of a public school?

Yes. Section 1709(12) of the Education Law authorizes a board "to take and hold for the use of the . . . schools . . . any gift, legacy or annuity, of whatever kind, given or bequeathed to the . . . board, and apply the same, or the interest and proceeds thereof, according to the instructions of the donor or testator."

The administration of the trust funds may be directed in detail by the donor's or testator's instructions or may be left to the discretion of the trustees by the donor or testator. In either case the applicable provision of the law relating to the handling and safeguarding of trust funds must be followed by the trustees.

School districts are cautioned, however, that any such gift must be free of any restrictions that might be contrary to law. They may accept a conditional gift with the understanding that the school board will honor the donor's wish if and only for so long as the board determines in its discretions that the inclusion or continuation of such a limitation is appropriate.

19:6. May a school district donate money to a scholarship fund?

No. This would violate the state constitutional prohibition against gifts of public funds (see 29 Opn. St. Comp. 154 (1973)). According to the comptroller, however, a school district may enter into an agreement, for instance, whereby the fee that would be payable to a school contractor may be paid to a student as a scholarship (see 26 Opn. St. Comp. 81 (1970)).

19:7. May a school board make contributions from school district funds to charitable organizations?

No. This would be considered an improper gift of public funds under article VIII, section 1 of the New York State Constitution which prohibits the disbursement, gift or loan of public moneys and resources for the benefit of private groups or individuals.

19:8. May school boards in New York State legally pay dues to the New York State School Boards Association?

Yes. This is authorized by section 1618 of the Education Law.

19:9. May a school district pay for the expenses incurred by members of its school board and district employees in attending a convention of the New York State School Boards Association or other conferences?

Yes. The General Municipal Law authorizes municipalities, including school districts, to permit and pay for the attendance of board members, officers and staff at conferences. The term *conference* includes conventions, conferences or schools for the benefit of the municipality (Gen. Mun. Law § 77-b(1)(c), (3)). The authorization must be by a board resolution adopted prior to attendance and entered in the board minutes, or the board may delegate the power to authorize attendance at conferences to any executive officer (Gen. Mun. Law § 77-b(2)).

19:10. May school board members carry and use school credit cards?

Yes. The comptroller has taken the position that municipalities, including school districts, may issue cards in their name for the use of their officers and employees for, among other things, reimbursable travel expenses incurred in the performance of their duties, provided that the claims submitted are paid within a reasonable period of time to avoid incurring unnecessary service charges (Opn. St. Comp. No. 79-202), and provided that certification of claim requirements are met by the companies involved (see § 1724; 23 Opn. St. Comp. 456 (1967)).

19:11. What is a school board's responsibility for the protection and supervision of the financial affairs of student clubs and extracurricular activities?

Part 172 of the commissioner's regulations provides that the school board of each school district outside New York City that has an educational program beyond grade six not only must make rules and regulations for the conduct, operation and maintenance of extra classroom activities, but also for the safeguarding, accounting and audit of all moneys received and derived from such activities (8 NYCRR § 172.2). An extra classroom activity encompasses any organization within the district that is conducted by students and received no financial support from district voters or the board (8 NYCRR § 172.1).

The board must direct that the moneys received from the conduct, operation or maintenance of any extracurricular activity be deposited with an official designated by the school board as the treasurer of extra-curricular activity funds (8 NYCRR § 172.4; "Safeguards, Accounting and Auditing of Extra Classroom Activity Funds," Albany, N.Y.: State Education Department, 1992).

Cash Management

19:12. Is a school district required to use a particular accounting system?

Yes. A school district must use the Uniform System of Accounts for School Districts prescribed by the state comptroller. Refusing or neglecting to comply with the comptroller's directive to keep accounts as prescribed within a reasonable time constitutes a misdemeanor (Gen. Mun. Law § 36).

19:13. What are the major accounting funds maintained by school districts as defined by the Uniform System of Accounts for School Districts?

The general fund is the principle fund of the school district and includes all operations not required to be recorded in other funds.

Special revenue funds include the following:

- **School store records** — transactions of stores maintained and operated by the school board for the sale of textbooks and other school supplies.
- **School lunch records** — transactions of the school district lunch and milk programs.
- **Insurance reserve** — used by districts that have established a self-insurance program and have established various reserves to fund that program.
- **Special aid** — provides accounts for special projects or programs supported in whole or in part by federal funds and/or state-funded grants, except capital projects.
- **Public library** — records transactions of a library established and sponsored by the school district. The Education Law requires that money received for library purposes must be kept in a separate fund (§ 259(1)).
- **Capital project fund** — accounts for capital improvements and acquisitions.
- **Debt-service fund** — accounts for the payment of interest and principal on long-term debt.
- **Trust and agency funds** — account for assets held in a trustee capacity and/or as agent for individuals, private organizations, other governmental units and/or other funds. These include agency funds, expendable trust funds and nonexpendable trust funds (principal must be preserved).

19:14. Must a school board designate a bank or trust company for the deposit of school funds?

Yes. The school board must designate at least one bank or trust company for the deposit of all funds received by the treasurer and collector, by a resolution adopted by a majority vote of the board (see § 2129; Gen. Mun. Law § 10(2-a); 8 NYCRR §§ 170.1(a), 170.2(c)).

19:15. Is a school board authorized to spend school district funds in excess of the budget appropriations approved by the voters?

Section 1718 (1) of the Education Law expressly provides that "no school board shall incur a district liability in excess of the amount appropriated by a district meeting unless the board is specially authorized by law to incur such liability." Section 2023 provides for exceptions in the case of ordinary contingent expenses such as teachers' salaries and the purchase of library books (see **19:37-44**).

19:16. Are vouchers required to be submitted with bills and invoices to a school board for approval before payment?

Yes. With few exceptions, a claim against a school district may not be paid unless an itemized voucher has been presented to the school board and audited and approved (§§ 1604(13); 1724; 1804(1); 2523(2)); 2524). Payment before board approval is permissible, however, under certain circumstances (see **19:18**).

In school districts with an internal auditor, the responsibility for auditing, rejecting or allowing any and all claims rests with the auditor (§§ 1709(20-a); 1804(1); 2526(2)).

19:17. May a school board authorize the payment of certain claims against the school district in advance of audit or board approval?

Yes. A school board may authorize, by resolution, the payment in advance of audit claims for public utility services, postage and freight, and express charges. All such claims must be presented at the next regular meeting for audit, and the claimant and the officer incurring or approving the claim are jointly and severally liable for any amount not allowed by the school board (§§ 1724(3); 2524(2)).

19:18. May a school district's treasurer ever issue a check for payment of an invoice before the board's approval?

Yes. The school board in a common or union free school district may designate school district officers and employees to pay out of a petty cash fund, in advance of the board's authorization, properly itemized bills for materials, supplies or services furnished to the school district under conditions calling for immediate payment to the vendor upon delivery of such materials, supplies or services (§§ 1604(26), 1709(29)). This would allow the school district, for instance, to take advantage of cash discounts.

19:19. May a school district's checks be signed with a facsimile signature, reproduced by a check signer or other machine?

Yes. Upon adopting of a board resolution, district checks may be signed by facsimile signature of the treasurer and other district officers whose signatures may be required (§§ 1720(2), 2523(2)).

19:20. Are school districts subject to financial audits?

Yes. There are three types of audits which are conducted in school districts:

- **Internal Audits**. The Education Law provides for the establishment of an Office of Internal Auditor and the appointment of such auditor. The auditor has the powers and duties of the school board with respect to allowing or rejecting all accounts, charges, claims or demands against the school district. The purpose is to detect and correct any errors at the time the transactions occur (§§ 1709(20-a); 2526; 8 NYCRR §§ 170.2(a)).
- **State or Federal Audits**. Governmental agencies may review the records of a school district. The purpose is usually to determine that legal provisions prescribed by the government agency are being followed. Section 34 of the General Municipal Law authorizes the state comptroller to examine the financial affairs of school districts.
- **Independent Audits**. The commissioner's regulations require that all school districts obtain an independent audit by an outside certified public accountant or public accountant. The purpose of this audit is to verify the accuracy of invoices, purchase orders, payroll, claims and contracts transacted by the school district during the school year. The independent auditor will review the documentary evidence and thus determine the district's compliance with all laws, policy, and rules and regulations regarding the expenditure of money. A copy of the certified audit in a form prescribed by the commissioner of education must be furnished to the State Education Department (SED). School districts with fewer than eight teachers are not included in this requirement. The audit must be carried out by the auditor in conformity with SED's audit

guidelines. The auditor's final report must be adopted by a board resolution, and a copy must be filed with the commissioner of education by October 1 of each year and by January 1 in large city school districts (§ 2116-a; 8 NYCRR § 170.2(r)).

19:21. Are school districts required to file financial reports with the state comptroller?

Yes. Each school district must make an annual report of its financial condition to the comptroller in forms prescribed by the comptroller. The comptroller, in turn, will examine these reports and issue a review to the school district (Gen. Mun. Law § 30). The school district must then give public notice of the examination report, as set forth in law (Gen. Mun. Law §§ 34-35).

19:22. May petty cash funds be established by a school board?

Yes. The Education Law and commissioner's regulations authorize the establishment of petty cash funds in school districts for the payment of certain specified items and upon the adoption of rules and regulations regarding the operation of such funds (§§ 1604(26); 1709(29); 1804(1)).

For example, whenever a petty cash fund is established, school authorities must designate the school district's officers and employees who will administer and be responsible for the petty cash fund and prescribe the method of record keeping (8 NYCRR § 170.4(a)(1), (3)).

In addition, no such fund may exceed $100 at any one time in school districts with eight or more teachers, or $5 in districts employing fewer than eight teachers. Deposits to petty cash funds may not exceed the amount paid out from the fund (8 NYCRR § 170.4(b),(c)).

Petty cash funds provided for buildings, cafeterias, school stores or other activities that do not operate during July and/or August must be closed out by June 30 (8 NYCRR § 170.4(e)).

Reserve Funds

19:23. What is a reserve fund?

A *reserve fund* is a separate account established by a school district to finance the cost of various objects or purposes of the school district (§ 3651). Reserve funds can be thought of as self-imposed savings accounts for particular purposes into which funds will be deposited over a period of time until the desired amount is accrued. Any interest earned or capital gains realized on the reserve fund deposits must accrue to the fund (§ 3651(2)).

19:24. What kinds of reserve funds are school districts authorized to establish?

The following are the kinds of reserve funds that school districts are authorized to establish, together with a summary of their characteristics:

Capital Reserve Fund (§ 3651)
- Pays the cost of any object or purpose for which bonds may be issued.
- Established through voter approval.
- Funds spent through voter approval.
- Accounted for in the capital project fund.

Repair Reserve Fund (Gen. Mun. Law § 6-d)
- Covers repair to capital improvements or equipment of a type not recurring annually or at shorter intervals (26 Opn. St. Comp. 225 (1970)). Expenditures from this fund, however, are not limited to cases of emergency (Opn. St. Comp. 85-20).
- Established without voter approval.
- Funds spent without voter approval. Expenditures in non-emergency situations require a public hearing. In emergency situations expenditures from the fund may be authorized without a public hearing by a two-thirds vote of the school board. The amount expended in an emergency situation must be repaid to the fund over the next two subsequent fiscal years (§ 3651; Gen. Mun. Law § 6-d(2), (3)).
- Accounted for in the general fund.

Workers' Compensation Reserve (Gen. Mun. Law §6-j)
- Pays for compensation benefits and other expenses authorized by article 2 of the Workers' Compensation Law and for payment of expenses of administrating this self-insurance program.
- Established without voter approval.
- Funds spent without voter approval.
- Accounted for in the general fund.

Unemployment Insurance Payment Reserve Fund (Gen. Mun. Law § 6-m)
- Pays for the cost of reimbursement to the State Unemployment Insurance Fund for payments made to claimants.
- Established without voter approval.
- Funds spent without voter approval.
- Accounted for in the general fund.

Reserve for Tax Reduction (§§ 1709(37), 1604(36))
- Provides for the return to taxpayers, for a period not to exceed 10

years, of the proceeds of the sale of school district real property, where the proceeds are not needed to pay any debts.
- Established without voter approval.
- Funds spent without voter approval.
- Accounted for in the general fund.

Mandatory Reserve for Debt Service (Gen. Mun. Law § 6-l)
- Used for retiring outstanding obligations remaining at the time of the sale of district property that was financed by obligations. The funding of the reserve is from the proceeds of the sale of district property or capital.
- Established without voter approval.
- Funds spent without voter approval.
- Accounted for in the debt service fund.

Insurance Reserve (Gen. Mun. Law § 6-n)
- Pays liability, casualty and other types of losses, except those incurred for which certain types of insurance may be purchased, such as life insurance, accident and health insurance.
- Established by board approval.
- Funds spent through board approval.
- Accounted for in the general fund.
- Funds do not have to be kept in a separate bank account.

Note: The annual contribution to the insurance reserve may not exceed $33,000 or 5 percent of the budget, whichever is greater. Settled or compromised claims up to $25,000 may be paid without judicial approval.

Property Loss and Liability Reserve (§ 1709(8-c))
- Pays for property loss and liability claims incurred.
- Established without voter approval.
- Funds may be spent without voter approval.
- Accounted for in the general fund.

Note: Total reserves of the property loss and liability reserve may not exceed 3 percent of the annual budget or $15,000, whichever is greater.

Tax Certiorari Reserve (§ 3651(1-a))
- Pays judgments and claims resulting from tax certiorari proceedings.
- Established without voter approval.
- Funds may be spent without voter approval.
- Accounted for in the general fund.
- Funds must be kept in a separate bank account.

Employee Benefit Accrued Liability Reserve Fund (Gen. Mun. Law § 6-p)
- Pays the cash payment of the monetary value of accrued and accumulated but unused sick leave, personal leave, holiday leave, vacation time, time allowances granted in lieu of overtime compensation and any other forms of payment of accrued but unliquidated time earned by employees.
- Established without voter approval.
- Funds may be spent without voter approval.
- Accounted for in the general fund.

Reserve Fund for Uncollected Taxes (§ 3651(1-b))
- Pays for uncollected taxes.
- Only applies to small city school districts.
- Established without voter approval.
- Funds may be spent without voter approval.
- Accounted for in the general fund.

19:25. Is voter approval required to establish and spend money from reserve funds?

Some reserve funds require voter approval to be established, and some require voter approval in order to spend money (see **19:24**). The proposition to establish a reserve fund must specify the purpose, the ultimate amount, the probable term and the source from which the funds will be obtained.

The following is a suggested resolution that may be used for a particular capital reserve fund:

RESOLVED, that the school board of the Blanktown Central School District hereby is authorized and directed to establish a reserve fund to be known as the Garage Construction Reserve Fund, which shall be for a part of the construction of a school bus garage. The ultimate amount of such fund shall be $25,000, of which amount there shall be raised annually by installments by taxes levied on the taxable property of the district the sum of $5,000 for five successive years.

The details of each resolution should be different in order to cover the particular items to be included in the establishment of each fund. A school district attorney should be consulted on the exact wording.

19:26. Are school districts authorized to transfer excess funds from certain reserve funds?

Yes. Money remaining in the workers' compensation, unemployment insurance reserve and insurance reserve funds after required payments are made may be transferred to certain reserve funds or applied to the budget appropriation for the next fiscal year (Gen. Mun. Law § 6-j(5); 6-m(5); 6-n(13)). Money remaining in a tax certiorari fund must be returned to the general fund under certain circumstances (§ 3651(1-a)).

Investment of School District Funds

19:27. May a school district invest the money it holds in its reserve fund?

Yes. A school district may temporarily invest its reserve funds in the following ways:

- In special time-deposit accounts or in certificates of deposit issued by a bank or trust company. However, these time-deposit accounts or certificates of deposit must be payable when the proceeds will be needed to meet expenditures for which the reserve was established. The time-deposit accounts or certificates of deposit must be secured by a pledge of obligations of the United States or obligations of New York State.
- In obligations of the United States, obligations of New York State or obligations of the school district that has established the fund. These obligations, unless registered or inscribed in the name of the school district, must be purchased through, delivered to and sold or presented for redemption or payment only by such bank or trust company upon receipt of written instructions from the governing board or the chief fiscal officer (school board president) if the governing board has delegated the duty of making investments to this officer.

These instruments may be purchased only if they are payable or redeemable at the option of the school district within such time as the proceeds will be needed to meet expenditures for which the reserve was established (Gen. Mun. Law § 11).

19:28. May the school board temporarily invest money from the school district's general fund?

Yes. Money may be invested in special time-deposit accounts or certificates of deposit; however, these must be made in the name of the school district and payable in time for the proceeds to be available to meet expenditures for which the money was obtained. Investments also may be made in obligations of the United States of America or in obligations of New York State or, with the approval of the state comptroller, in certain obligations of municipalities, school districts or district corporations other than the one investing the money (Gen. Mun. Law § 11).

Obligations can be sold or presented for redemption or payment only upon the receipt of written instructions from the district officer having custody of school district money (Gen. Mun. Law § 11(3)(b)). The proceeds of the obligations must be deposited to the credit of the school district (see **19:27** for information on the investment of reserve fund money).

19:29. What types of investments may a school district make?

In addition to the investments discussed in 19:27, a school district may make a variety of short-term investments that include the purchase of United States Treasury bills, United States Treasury certificates of indebtedness, or United States Treasury notes and bonds. It also may invest in negotiable certificates of deposit. However, school districts are cautioned to examine the terms and conditions of any investment agreement carefully and to seek legal advice before investing (Gen. Mun. Law §§ 10, 11).

19:30. Must the school board adopt a policy for the investment of school district funds?

Yes. Section 39 of the General Municipal Law requires a school board to adopt a comprehensive investment policy which sets forth both the district's general operative policy as well as instruction to its administrators and staff regarding the investing, monitoring and reporting of the district's investments. The investment policy must be annually reviewed by the district.

See the Association's *School Policy Encyclopedia (SPE)* policy number 6240 for a model investment policy.

The District Budget

19:31. Are school districts required to have a budget?

Yes. The Education Law requires that school districts other than large city school districts present an annual budget to the district voters for their approval and that the board adopt a contingency budget if the voters refuse to approve a budget (§§ 1608, 1716, 2022-a, 2601-a, 2023; see **4:1**; see also **19:37-38**). For more information on school district budget elections, see **4:13-30**).

19:32. May a school board include in its budget a contingent fund item to cover unanticipated expenses?

No, there is no authority that would allow a school board to include in its budget a contingent fund to be used for contingent purposes.

19:33. May school district residents delete budgetary items from the board's budget and call for a separate vote on the deleted items at a special meeting?

No. Section 2008 of the Education Law provides that the school district's residents may file a petition with the school board requesting a vote on one or more propositions regarding items that are within the powers of the voters to approve, such as transportation limitations. This section does not, however, include the right to delete corresponding items from the board's own proposed budget (*Matter of Amsel*, 28 Educ. Dep't Rep. 406 (1989)).

19:34. What is a fund balance?

A *fund balance* is the amount of unexpended funds at the end of the year. The law requires that the tax warrant state the amount of "unexpended surplus funds." The tax rate must reflect the return of all unexpended funds to the taxpayers, except for an amount equal to 2 percent of the current budget, which may be retained as surplus funds and used to meet contingent expenses (Real Prop. Tax Law § 1318).

19:35. May a school district levy a tax to create a planned balance?

Yes. With voter approval, school districts may levy funds in one fiscal year to be appropriated during the next fiscal year. The primary purpose of a planned balance is to avoid the cost of borrowing to meet expenses during the first part of the fiscal year, before state aid is received.

Section 2021(21) of the Education Law provides that the planned balance of the budget of a school district is limited to the amount necessary to meet expenses during the first 120 days of the fiscal year following the fiscal year in which such tax is collected.

School districts in Suffolk County should consult the Suffolk County Tax Act regarding different provisions in that area.

19:36. May a union free school district legally transfer funds between budget categories without voter approval?

Section 170.2(l) of the commissioner's regulations provide that "the board of education of every union free school district shall have the power and it shall be its duty: . . . (1) to make transfers between and within functional unit appropriations for teachers' salaries and ordinary contingent expenses. Boards of education may, by resolution, authorize the chief school officer to make transfers within limits as established by the board" (see also **19:44**).

19:37. What is a contingent or austerity budget?

A *contingent* or *austerity budget* is prepared and adopted by the school board when the board's proposed budget is rejected by the voters. The contingent budget funds only teachers' salaries and those items the board determines to be "ordinary contingent expenses."

The school board determines which items are to be included in a contingency budget subject to review by the commissioner of education if someone brings an appeal before him to challenge the board's decision.

The school board is authorized to levy a tax to fund these expenses if the proposed budget is defeated (§§ 2023, 2601-a(5)). When adopting a contingency budget, the board may still submit to the voters separate propositions on specific items that require their approval such as expanding the district's transportation mileage limitations. However, a board may not submit a proposition involving the expenditure of money more than twice (§ 2022(4); see **4:29**).

19:38. When must a district adopt a contingency budget?

A school board *must* adopt a contingency budget after the proposed budget has been defeated twice by the voters. A school board *may* adopt a contingency budget after the proposed budget has been defeated by the voters once (§§ 2022(4)(5); 2023(1-4); 2601-a(4)(5)).

19:39. Are there limitations imposed on a contingency budget?

Yes. A contingency budget may not result in a percentage increase in total spending over the district's total spending under the district budget for the prior year that exceeds the lesser of (1) the result obtained when computing 120 percent of the consumer price index, or (2) 4 percent over the prior year's budget.

However, the following types of expenditures may be excluded in determining total spending:
- Expenditures resulting from a tax certiorari proceeding.
- Expenditures resulting from a court order or judgment against the school district.
- Expenditures for emergency repairs that are certified by the commissioner as necessary as a result of damage to, or destruction of, a school building or school equipment.
- Capital expenditures, including debt service and leases resulting from projects approved by the voters.
- Expenditures attributable to projected increases in public school enrollment, including new prekindergarten enrollment.
- Non-recurring expenditures in the prior year's budget (§ 2023(4)(b)).

In addition, the administrative component of a contingency budget shall not comprise a greater percentage of the contingency budget, exclusive of the capital component, than the lesser of (1) the percentage the administrative component had composed in the prior year's budget exclusive of the capital component, or (2) the percentage the administrative component had comprised in the last proposed defeated budget, exclusive of the capital component (§§ 2023(3); 2601-a(5)).

19:40. How is an expense determined to be contingent for purposes of a school budget?

Generally, an expense is considered contingent if it is a legal obligation, specifically authorized by statute or necessary to maintain the educational program, or necessary to preserve property or ensure the health and safety of the students or staff (§ 2601-a (5); Formal Opn. of Counsel 213 (1967)).

The school board is responsible for initially determining what items constitute ordinary contingent expenses (*Matter of Gouverneur CSD*, 15 Educ. Dep't Rep. 468 (1976)).

While the board is the first authority in determining what are ordinary contingent budget items, any questions arising as to what are ordinary contingent expenses may be referred to the commissioner of education, and this referral must be made before judicial redress is sought (§§ 2024; 2601-a (6); *Board of Education of Freeport UFSD v. Nyquist*, 71 A.D.2d 757 (3rd Dep't 1979), *aff'd*, 50 N.Y.2d 889 (1980)).

19:41. What are some examples of ordinary contingent expenses?

Examples of ordinary contingent expenses include the following:

Legal obligations:
- Debt service (both principal and interest payments).
- Judgments from courts and orders of the commissioner of education.
- Social Security and retirement obligations, as well as other payroll taxes and assessments.
- Pre-existing contractual obligations.

(See Educ. Law § 2601-a(5)(c) with respect to small city school districts and Formal Opinion of Counsel 213, 7 Educ. Dep't Rep. 153 (1967) as to all other districts).

Expenditures specifically authorized by statute:
- Teachers' salaries (§§ 2023(1), 2601-a(5)(a)).
- Interschool athletics, field trips and other extracurricular activities (§§ 2023(1), 2601-a(5)(f)).
- Transportation within the state-mandated mileage limitations

(K-8 students: 2-15 miles, 9-12 students: 3-15 miles (§ 3635(1)), children with disabilities: up to 50 miles (§§ 4401(4), 4402(4)(d)).

- Transportation to and from school under the mileage limitations last approved by the voters if more generous than the minimum mileage limitations required under state law (§ 2023(2)).
- Transportation related to interschool athletics, field trips and extracurricular activities (§§ 2023(1)(2), 2601-a(5)(f)).
- Textbooks (§§ 701(3), 2601-a(5)(b)).
- Expenses in connection with membership in the New York State School Boards Association, Inc. (§ 1618).
- Convention and conference expenses (Gen. Mun. Law § 77-b(2),(3)).
- Under limited circumstances: youth bureaus, recreation and youth service projects, and other youth programs (Exec. Law §§ 422-423).
- The district's share of BOCES services (§§ 1950, 2601-a(5)(b)).
- Health and welfare services (§§ 912, 2601-a(5)(b)).
- Grants in aid received from either the state or federal government, other gifts, and insurance proceeds not involving the expenditure of local money (§ 1718(2)).
- Nursery school (§ 1712(2)).
- Prekindergarten, if the board chooses to offer a prekindergarten program (§ 3602-e(11)).
- Kindergarten, if the board chooses to offer a kindergarten program (§§ 1712(1), 2601-a(5)(b)).
- Accident insurance for students (§ 1709(8-a),(8-b)).
- In-service training for teachers (§ 1709(32)).
- Eye safety devices (§ 409-a).
- Library books and other instructional materials associated with a library (§§ 2023(1), 2601-a(5)(d)).

Other items necessary to maintain the educational program, preserve property and assure the health and safety of students and staff. The following is a partial list:

- Necessary travel expenses of board members and employees on official business.
- Amounts needed to pay for necessary legal services (§ 2601-a(5)(e)).
- "Teacher supplies" but not "student supplies."
- Salaries for necessary non-teaching employees (§ 2601-a(5)(e)).
- Utilities, including fuel, water, light, power, and telephone (§ 2601-a(5)(e)).
- Use of school buildings for teachers' meetings and PTA meetings with school-connected purposes. However, this does not include

programs of entertainment or of a social nature.
- Emergency repairs of school plant.
- Maintenance of necessary, sanitary facilities.
- Necessary expenditures for complying with the commissioner's regulation pertaining to such items as fire alarm systems and fire escapes.
- Rental of temporary classroom facilities with approval of the commissioner, in the case of an unforeseeable emergency (§§ 1726(5), 2601-a(5)(e)). But in the absence of an unforeseeable emergency, voter approval is required *(Appeal of Wiesen,* 35 Educ. Dep't Rep. 157 (1995)).
- Required civil defense equipment.
- Certain expenses, such as for emergency repairs, or to equip a classroom or classrooms where it is essential to house additional students. This does not include equipment.
- Materials used in classes by students where uniformity is essential to the program or to preserve health and safety.
- Newspapers and periodical subscriptions for libraries and classroom use where essential for instruction or to preserve continuity of sets.
- Expenditures necessary to advise district voters concerning school matters (§ 2601-a(5)(e)). However, hiring a public relations firm to assist the district in promoting its image to district residents is not an ordinary contingent expense *(Appeal of Nolan,* 35 Educ. Dep't Rep 139 (1995); see also *Appeal of Mitzner,* 31 Educ. Dep't Rep. 274 (1992), where the commissioner provided guidance on what is meant by "necessary" information)).
- Preliminary plans and specifications needed to submit propositions to voters.
- Options on land where the price of land is nominal.

19:42. Are increases in employee salaries an ordinary contingent expense?

Yes, in most cases. Increases in teachers' salaries are authorized by the Education Law (§§ 1709(16), 3108; *Matter of New Paltz CSD,* 30 Educ. Dep't Rep. 300 (1991); Formal Opn. of Counsel 213, 7 Educ. Dep't Rep. 153, 154 (1967)).

Increases in salaries for non-instructional employees who are subject to a collective bargaining agreement are authorized as a contractual obligation of the district *(Matter of Powell,* 22 Educ. Dep't Rep. 353 (1983)). However, non-instructional employees who are not members of a collective bargaining unit and employees designated by the Public Employment Relations Board (PERB) as management and confidential employees may not be given a salary increase during a contingency budget, "unless it is impossible to assure qualified personnel for the minimum service, in which case these employees may also be paid necessary amounts" (*Appeal of Lauterback*, 30 Educ. Dep't Rep. 223 (1990)). Additional pay to employees not covered by a collective bargaining agreement may be provided if they are assigned new duties (*Appeal of Parsons*, 32 Educ. Dep't Rep. 444 (1993)).

19:43. How does the adoption of a contingency budget affect a school district's transportation requirements?

The Education Law requires that school districts which adopt a contingency budget continue the mileage limitations for the transportation of students last approved by voters. The mileage limits can be changed only by a special proposition passed by a majority of voters (§§ 2023(2); 2503(12)). In addition, transportation to and from interscholastic athletic events, field trips and other extracurricular activities is permissible under a contingency budget (§§ 2023(1),(2); 2601-a (5)(f)).

19:44. Can a district on a contingency budget transfer money from a non-contingent fund to a contingent fund?

Yes. The commissioner of education has ruled that a district under a contingency budget may refuse to expend funds appropriated for voter approved non-contingent programs and may transfer monies intended for these programs to contingent accounts (*Appeal of Blizzard*, 35 Educ. Dep't Rep. 120 (1995)). However, any transfer causing the total budget cap and/or the administrative component cap to be exceeded cannot be made, even when the transfer is for an ordinary contingent expense.

Purchasing

19:45. Are school district purchases subject to competitive bidding?

Yes. All contracts for public works (for example, services, labor and construction) in excess of $20,000 and purchase contracts (for example, commodities, materials, supplies and equipment) in excess of $10,000 must be awarded, after advertising for bids, to the lowest responsible bidder. The board may not restrict its bids to residents of the school district (Gen. Mun. Law § 103(1),(2)).

School districts cannot avoid competitive bidding by signing a series of separate contracts for the same item, each for less than the $10,000 or $20,000 limit.

Special rules apply to competitive bidding on construction projects (see **16:24**).

19:46. Is the lease of personal property by a school district subject to competitive bidding?

Yes. Section 1725 of the Education Law requires that any agreement by a school board for the lease of personal property is subject to the bidding requirements of the General Municipal Law for purchase contracts.

19:47. What are some specific requirements regarding the bidding process?

School boards must advertise in a newspaper designated for such purpose. At least five days must elapse between the first publication of the advertisement and the date specified for the opening of bids (Gen. Mun. Law § 103(2)). The board may designate any officer or employee to open the bids at the time and place specified in the notice.

In cases where two or more responsible bidders furnishing the required security submit identical bids as to price, the contract may be awarded to any of the bidders.

The designated officer may, at his or her discretion, reject all bids and re-advertise for new bids (Gen. Mun. Law § 103(1)).

19:48. Are there any exceptions to the competitive bidding requirements?

Yes. The competitive bidding law need not be followed if there is an emergency, accident or unforeseen occurrence whereby the life, health, safety or property of the inhabitants of the school district require immediate action (Gen. Mun. Law 103(4); Opn. St. Comp. 71-543). Competitive bidding is not required either when there is only one possible supplier or source from which to procure goods or services, such as in the case of a public utility or patented item.

In addition, surplus and secondhand supplies, material or equipment may be purchased without competitive bidding from the federal government, New York State, or from any other political subdivision, district or public benefit corporation (Gen. Mun. Law § 103(6)). School districts also may make direct purchases of fresh farm products such as eggs, livestock, fish, dairy products, fresh fruit and vegetables without competitive bidding (Gen. Mun. Law § 103(9)(10); 8 NYCRR § 114.3) and milk in some instances (8 NYCRR § 114.4).

Competitive bidding is not required either with respect to contracts for professional services requiring, for example, special skill or training, legal services, medical services, property appraisals or insurance (*Trane Co. v. Broome County*, 76 A.D.2d 1015 (3rd Dep't 1980); *Matter of Mantler*, 18 Educ. Dep't Rep. 311 (1978)).

At the school board's discretion, contracts for the transportation of students which involve an annual expenditure in excess of $10,000 may be awarded through the competitive bidding process or through an evaluation of proposals process § 305(14)(a),(e); 8 NYCRR § 156.12; see **22:66-68**).

Districts also may extend contracts for the transportation of students, or for leasing mobile instructional units, for four or five years without using competitive bidding requirements (§ 305(14)).

19:49. Are there any alternative procedures a school district must follow when competitive bidding is not required?

Yes. Section 104-b of the General Municipal Law requires that districts procuring goods or services not subject to the requirements of the competitive bidding law must take measures to ensure the prudent and economical use of public moneys. Alternative proposals or quotations must be secured by requests for proposals (RFPs), written or verbal quotations, or other appropriate methods of procurement except for procurement under a county contract, under a state contract of items manufactured in state correctional institutions, or from agencies for the blind and severely disabled.

Districts must develop standards for the methods of competition to be used and the sources of documentation to be maintained in the most cost-effective manner possible when soliciting non-bid procurement. District purchasing policies and regulations must require adequate documentation of actions taken, particularly if contracts are awarded to an offerer other than the lowest responsible dollar offerer.

In addition, comments must be solicited from those administrators involved in the procurement process before enactment of a district's policies and regulations regarding purchasing, and from time to time thereafter. Such policies and regulations must then be adopted by a board resolution and reviewed by the school board at least annually.

An alternative to the competitive bidding process for contracts for the transportation of students which involve an annual expenditure in excess of $10,000 is the evaluation of proposals process (§ 305(14)(a),(e); 8 NYCRR § 156.12; see **22:66-68**).

19:50. Are there any procedures that must be followed for determining whether a particular purchase is subject to competitive bidding?

Section 104-b of the General Municipal Law requires that a district's policies set forth the procedures for determining whether a procurement is subject to competitive bidding. If a procurement is not subject to competitive bidding (see **19:48-49**), the district must document the basis for such determination.

19:51. May a school district enter into a cooperative purchasing agreement?

Yes. Legally, school districts may join together to purchase materials and supplies in bulk to get the benefit of lower prices. An agreement entered into by school districts for joint purchasing should contain provisions relative to the manner of making and awarding these contracts. This arrangement must conform with the competitive bidding law (Gen. Mun. Law § 119-o).

19:52. May a school district make purchases through the state Office of General Services?

Yes. Section 104 of the General Municipal Law authorizes school districts to purchase materials, equipment or supplies, except for printed materials, through the state Office of General Services, provided the purchase exceeds $500 and the school districts accept sole responsibility for any payment due the vendor. Where bids have been received by a district, however, no such purchase may be made through the Office of General Services unless it can be made on the same terms, conditions and specifications, but at a lower price.

19:53. Must school districts make purchases from correctional institutions of needed goods that are manufactured at these institutions?

Generally, yes. Under section 184 of the Correction Law, school districts are required to purchase goods manufactured in prisons from the Department of Correctional Services, unless the commissioner of corrections certifies that such goods are not available upon requisition. An application may be made to the department for a waiver which would permit the purchase to be made from other sources pursuant to normal bidding requirements (see the State Comptroller's Financial Management Guide 8.3020, updated annually).

19:54. Must school districts give preference to products and services offered by the blind, the mentally ill or individuals with severe disabilities?

Yes, as long as the products or services sought by the district are available from qualified, charitable, nonprofit agencies for the blind, the mentally ill and other severely disabled individuals approved by the commissioners of education and mental health. The prices of these products and services are determined by the commissioner of general services.

When products are purchased, priority must be given to agencies for the blind. As far as the procurement of services is concerned, equal priority is given to all three types of agencies.

If goods and services are available from another department or agency of the state, and state law requires school districts to purchase them from such department or agency, the preceding two paragraphs are superseded by the applicable law (State Fin. Law § 162).

19:55. May a school district award a paper products contact to a company that uses recycled paper, even if this company is not the lowest responsible bidder?

Yes, as long as the recycled product is reasonably competitive and costs no more than 10 percent more than the non-recycled product. Each document printed on recycled paper must include a printed statement or symbol indicating the document was printed on recycled paper (Gen. Mun. Law § 104-a).

19:56. May a school board enter into a lease-purchase agreement for instructional equipment?

Yes, for limited purposes. Section 1725-a of the Education Law permits school boards to enter into lease-purchase agreements for instructional equipment, with the payment to be applied against the purchase price of the equipment. These agreements must have the prior written approval of the commissioner of education and are subject to the bidding requirements of the General Municipal Law.

Under the commissioner's regulations, applications for approval of these agreements must be submitted no more than 90 days nor less than 30 days before the execution of the agreement. A variance can be granted upon a showing of good cause.

The regulations define *instructional equipment* to mean: instruments, machines, apparatus or other types of equipment that are used directly in the instruction of students and are not consumed in use and retain their original shape and appearance with use; are not expendable items, such as textbooks or supplies; are not capital improvements, as such term is defined in section 2(9) of the Local Finance Law; and do not lose their identity through incorporation into a different or more complex unit (8 NYCRR § 170.7).

19:57. May a school district enter into installment contracts to purchase equipment?

Yes. Under the conditions set forth in section 109-b of the General Municipal Law, districts can enter into installment contracts to purchase "equipment, machinery or apparatus." No payments may be financed by the proceeds of municipal bonds or bond anticipation notes (BANs), and the contract term may not exceed the useful life of the item or items purchased (subject to a maximum term of 30 years).

19:58. Does the state sales tax law apply to school districts?

School districts, in their role as purchasers, users or consumers, are exempt from sales tax, as they are when they sell services or property of a kind not ordinarily sold by private persons (Tax Law § 1116).

All school lunch fund sales to students are tax-exempt. All lunch sales to adults are subject to the sales tax (Tax Law § 1105).

Hotel or motel rooms and meal charges for school district officials and employees who are traveling on official business for their school districts and whose travel expenses are paid from or fully reimbursed from school district funds are exempt from state and local sales taxes (Tax Law § 1116).

19:59. Are school districts exempt from federal excise taxes?

Yes. School districts generally are exempt from federal excise taxes. School districts should so advise vendors of this and furnish a tax-exemption certificate, which may be duplicated.

For more information, see individual sections of the Internal Revenue Code for exemptions regarding specific excise taxes.

Borrowing

19:60. Can a school district borrow money?

Yes. School districts may issue long-term obligations, including serial bonds (§ 21.00) and statutory installment bonds (§ 62.10).

They may also issue short-term obligations, including bond anticipation notes (BANs) (§ 23.00), tax anticipation notes (TANs) (§ 24.00), revenue anticipation notes (RANs) (§ 25.00), capital notes (§ 28.00) and budget notes (§ 29.00).

In addition, school districts are authorized to issue zero coupons and capital appreciation bonds (§ 57(e)). They may also issue variable rate obligations up to July 15, 2000 (§ 54.90) and discounted bonds at negotiated sales through July 15, 2000, subject to rules and regulations promulgated by the state comptroller and the comptroller's prior approval except as provided in the rules and regulations.

All of the statutory references in the section "Borrowing" are to the New York State Local Finance Law unless noted otherwise.

19:61. Is there any limit to the amount of money that school districts may borrow?

Yes. In school districts that have a total assessed valuation of taxable real property of $100,000 or over, no bonds or bond anticipation notes (BANs) can be issued if the indebtedness of the school district will exceed 10 percent of the full valuation of the taxable real property in the district. Details of and exceptions to this rule, including computing the debt limit for city school districts, are found in section 104.00 of the Local Finance Law. Additional limitations applying to the issuance of budget notes are found in section 29.00(3).

19:62. What is the 50 percent rule and how does it affect a school district's ability to borrow money?

According to the 50 percent rule, no installment of a bond issue may be more than 50 percent in excess of the smallest previous installment. The purpose of this rule is to prevent the ballooning of bond issue installments close to the date of maturation, while earlier installments are minimized.

School districts may also use level debt financing as an alternative to the 50 percent rule for the purpose of retiring debt (NYS Const. Art. 8(2) and Local Fin. Law § 21.00(d)).

19:63. When are long-term borrowing instruments used?

Section 11.00 of the Local Finance Law describes approximately 80 purposes for which a district may issue long-term obligations. For each purpose listed, there is a period of probable usefulness, and districts may not borrow for longer than the period of probable usefulness of the objector purpose. For example, the period of probable usefulness for school buses is five years (§ 11(29)). School districts may use a "weighted average period of probable usefulness" for two or more objects or purposes under the same bond issue (§ 11).

Serial bonds are used primarily to finance capital projects and are issued in accordance with the provisions of section 11.00 of the Local Finance Law. A serial bond must mature in annual installments (§ 21.00(b)). The last installment of a serial bond must mature not later than the expiration of the period of probable usefulness of the object or purpose for which it was issued, as computed from its date of issue or the date of the earliest bond anticipation note if such a note has been issued (§ 21.00(c)). Districts are authorized to issue bonds or notes with a maximum maturity equal to the weighted average period of probable usefulness of all projects being financed in a multi-purpose issue (§ 11).

Statutory installment bonds are issued when the principal amount does not exceed $1,000,000 and may be used for the same purposes as a serial bond (§ 62.10).

19:64. When are short-term borrowing instruments used?

Short-term borrowing instruments, which include bond anticipation notes (BANs), capital notes, tax anticipation notes (TANs), revenue anticipation notes (RANs) and budget notes, are used as follows:

Bond anticipation notes (BANs) most commonly are used for temporary financing before the issuance of serial bonds. This gives the district flexibility in timing the actual bond sale. The adoption of a serial bond resolution is a prerequisite to issuing a BAN. The total amount of the note may not exceed the amount of the bond in anticipation of which it is issued.

A BAN may be renewed, but this note or renewal may not extend more than five years beyond the original date of issue. Section 23 of the Local Finance Law sets forth the method for redeeming BANS that are issued in anticipation of bonds having substantially level or declining debt service payments and are outstanding for more than two years.

Capital notes may be issued to finance all or part of the cost of the purposes listed in section 11.00 of the Local Finance Law. They must mature not later than the last day of the second fiscal year succeeding the fiscal year in which such notes are issued. However, an installment of not less than 50 percent of the amount of such notes must mature in the first fiscal year succeeding the fiscal year in which such notes are issued, unless such notes are authorized and issued during a fiscal year at a time subsequent to the date of the adoption of the annual budget for the next succeeding fiscal year (§ 28.00).

Tax anticipation notes (TANs) and *revenue anticipation notes (RANs)* are used, respectively, to borrow in anticipation of the collection of taxes and the receipt of revenues, other than real property taxes, by the school district. TANs and RANs must mature within one year from the date of their issuance. Although provision is made in the law for their renewal, in most school districts TANs and RANs would be retired within one year after their issuance because the anticipated taxes and revenues would have been received by the district. The law requires such taxes and revenues to be used to pay off a note (§§ 24.00, 25.00).

Budget notes may be issued during the last nine months of the fiscal year to finance required expenditures for which either no or insufficient provision was made in the annual budget or to provide temporary school buildings or facilities in a year when an unforeseeable public emergency, such as an epidemic, riot or storm, prevents the use of all or part of the district's buildings and facilities.

Budget notes may be renewed, but these notes, including renewals, may not mature later than the close of the fiscal year succeeding the fiscal year in which they are issued. However, if the notes are authorized and issued during the fiscal year at a time subsequent to the date of adoption of the annual budget for the next succeeding year, they may mature not later than the close of the second fiscal year succeeding the fiscal year in which they were issued (§ 29.00).

19:65. Are there any special rules regarding the finance of capital projects through bonds or bond anticipation notes (BANs)?

The Local Finance Law requires that at least 5 percent of the estimated cost of a capital improvement project or the acquisition of equipment be provided from current funds (§ 107.00(b)).

However, through July 15, 2000, districts may issue bonds or BANs for capital improvements or the acquisition of equipment or make expenditures from the proceeds of these instruments for capital improvements without complying with this "down payment" requirement (§ 107.00(d)(9)).

19:66. Are there any limits on the rates of interest for school borrowing?

In general, sections 57.00(b), 60.00(b) and 63.00(b) of the Local Finance Law authorize the sale of bonds and notes without limitation on the rate of interest.

19:67. Is the interest earned from temporary investments subject to the provisions of the Internal Revenue Code?

Yes. The Internal Revenue Code imposes rebate (return of investment profits to the federal government) requirements on income from arbitrage that relate to the time period during which all gross proceeds must be spent on the purpose for which the funds were borrowed. Districts that borrow less than $5 million annually are exempt from these requirements. For more information, contact a bond counsel, and/or consult the Internal Revenue Code of 1986, as amended.

19:68. Must a school board adopt a resolution to authorize the issuance of bonds and notes?

Yes, according to section 31.00 of the Local Finance Law.

19:69. Must the school district's voters approve the issuance of bonds and capital notes?

Yes. Before a school board can adopt a resolution authorizing the issuance of bonds or capital notes, voters must approve a tax to be collected in installments for the bonds which are to be issued (§ 37.00). Different restrictions can be found in sections 37.00 and 104.00 of the Local Finance Law.

19:70. Does a school district need the consent of the Board of Regents or the state comptroller to issue bonds?

The consent of the Board of Regents to issue bonds is necessary only when a district exceeds its 10 percent debt limit (§ 104(d); see **19:61** for an explanation of this limit). In certain school districts in the Adirondack Park, the consent of the state comptroller is also necessary to exceed this limit (§ 104(d)).

19:71. How are bonds bought and sold?

Generally, bonds must be sold at public sale (§ 57.00). Sections 57.00 (2 NYCRR Part 25), 58.00 and 59.00 of the Local Finance Law describe, respectively, the procedure for the public sale of bonds, requirements for notice of sale of bonds and bidding regulations related to the sale of bonds.

Bonds may be sold at private sale in the following instances:

- The bonds are sold to the United States government or to the New York State Municipal Bond Bank Agency or to certain sinking funds or pension funds (§ 57.00(a)).
- The bonds are issued in an amount not to exceed $1 million (§ 63.00). The total amount of bonds which may be sold at private sale in any one fiscal year of the school district is $1 million.
- The sale is of a statutory installment bond or bonds that does not exceed $1 million in the aggregate (unless sold to the United States government) and that may be issued for the full principal amount (§ 62.10).

All notes may be sold at either public or private sale without limitation on interest rates (§§ 60.00, 60.10).

19:72. Is a school district required to file a debt statement with the state comptroller before it issues bonds?

A school district must file a debt statement with the state comptroller before it sells any bonds that are required to be sold at public sale. A school district may file a debt statement in connection with the issuance of bond anticipation notes (BANs) (Local Finance Law §§ 109.00, 137.00).

19:73. May a school district combine a number of projects into a single bond issue?

Yes. Section 57.00(c) of the Local Finance Law permits a school district to combine a number of projects such as the purchase of a school bus, reconstruction of a school building or construction of another building into a single bond issue. By selling such a single issue, it is frequently possible to obtain a lower interest rate as well as save on legal expenses, printing and advertising.

19:74. May a school district sell bonds and notes to a bank where an officer or employee of the school district is also an officer, director or stockholder of that bank?

Yes. School district bonds and notes may be sold to a bank under these circumstances at private sale without limitation as to rate of interest, provided that at least two other banks are unwilling or unable to purchase the notes at a rate of interest equal to or less than that at which the bank in which the officer or employee has an interest proposes to purchase such notes.

However, under these circumstances, the aggregate principal amount of notes purchased or held by the bank and bonds held by the bank must be less than $100,000 (§ 60.10).

19:75. Must the money received from the sale of bonds and notes be deposited in a special bank account?

Yes. With the exception of the proceeds of capital notes issued in amounts of $100,000 or less and budget notes, all proceeds from the sale of bonds, bond anticipation notes (BANs), budget notes and capital notes must be deposited in a special account in the bank or trust company and may not be combined with the other funds of the district (§ 165.00(a)(1)).

The law does permit the deposit of proceeds from the sale of any two or more such obligations in a single special account; however, a separate accounting record must be maintained for each issue (§ 165.00(a)(2)).

19:76. May a school district temporarily invest the proceeds from the sale of bonds pending actual use of the money?

Yes. Section 165.00(b) of the Local Finance Law provides that the proceeds from the sale of bonds, bond anticipation notes (BANs) and capital notes may be invested in obligations of the United States and agencies of the United States where the principal and interest are guaranteed by the federal government; in obligations of New York State and special time-deposit accounts, or in certificates of deposit issued by a bank or trust company located and authorized to do business in this state. All these investments must be made in accordance with the specific requirements in section 165.00 of the Local Finance Law. This is known as arbitrage. Its purpose is to earn interest by temporarily investing the proceeds at a better rate than the rate at which the funds were borrowed.

19:77. What happens if the school district voters refuse or fail to appropriate the amount of money needed to pay the district's bonds and interest?

The state constitution requires school districts to appropriate the amount of their debt service requirements annually. If a district fails to appropriate the money, the constitution provides that upon the suit of a bondholder, the first revenues received by the district shall be "applied to such purposes" (NYS Const. Art. 8, § 2).

19:78. What is the role of the bond attorney when a school district plans to issue a bond?

A school district hires a bond attorney on a fee basis to obtain a professional opinion with respect to the legality of a bond issue. Such an opinion is required by dealers and investors. The attorney prepares papers and reviews procedures affecting the sale of the bonds, expedites borrowing, advises on meeting technicalities and furnishes appropriate forms. A careful distinction should be made between the functions of a bond attorney and those of local legal counsel.

19:79. From where may additional information about school district borrowing be obtained?

Additional information about school district borrowing may be obtained from the school district attorney, who should be consulted on all major borrowing proposals of the district; the State Education Department, Office of Counsel and Office of Management Services; and the Office of the State Comptroller. Also, consult the New York State Local Finance Law.

20. Assessment and Collection of Taxes

20:1. Are there state constitutional limits on taxes levied by school districts in New York State?

No. The constitutional limit on taxes levied by small city school districts was repealed in 1985 (NYS Const. Art. 8, §10).

20:2. Do all school districts assess and collect taxes?

No. Fiscally independent school districts levy taxes for school purposes. Fiscally dependent school districts do not.

Only the Big 5 city school districts are fiscally dependent. They are Buffalo, New York, Rochester, Syracuse and Yonkers. They are dependent on municipal tax revenue to fund education. A single real property tax is levied for school and nonschool purposes by municipal governments. They also may receive income from other local taxes, such as income taxes and sales taxes.

The remainder of the state's school districts are fiscally independent.

20:3. Are there any sources of tax revenue for school districts other than real property?

Yes. The Tax Law authorizes certain municipalities to levy non-realty taxes for both education and general purposes. These can be, for example, taxes on utilities, real estate sales, food and drinks in restaurants and bars, vending machines, and admissions to places of amusement and general sales taxes (Tax Law §§ 1200-1263).

20:4. May school districts receive a portion of the county sales tax?

Yes. The Tax Law authorizes counties to allocate a portion of their sales tax revenues to school districts and other localities (Tax Law § 1262). Seven counties in the state — Erie, Livingston, Monroe, Onondaga, Orleans, Wayne and Westchester — share a portion of their proceeds with their school districts ("Financial Data for School Districts," Office of the State Comptroller, p. 35).

All statutory references in this chapter are to the New York State Real Property Tax Law unless noted otherwise. The material in this chapter refers chiefly to school districts other than the Big 5 city school districts.

20:5. What does the New York State Board of Real Property Services do?

Formerly known as the State Board of Equalization and Assessment, the New York State Board of Real Property Services is the state oversight agency for the real property tax system. It assesses special franchises; establishes state equalization rates; approves assessments of taxable state lands; generally supervises the function of assessing throughout the state; and furnishes assessors with information, instructions and training (§§ 200-202).

20:6. What is the Board of Assessment Review?

The Board of Assessment Review is the body of officers empowered to hear and determine complaints about assessments. Members are appointed by the legislative body of the local government (§ 102(4)).

20:7. What are some key definitions related to the assessment and collection of school taxes?

Assessment is the determination of the valuation of real property, including exempt real property, by an authorized person, whether or not real property is subject to taxation or special levies (§ 102(2)).

The *assessment roll* is the list of each parcel of property in the municipality and its assessed value as it exists before a warrant for the collection of taxes is attached to it.

Real property is land, above and under water; buildings and other structures affixed to the land, including bridges and wharves; underground and elevated railroads and railroad structures; telephone and telegraph lines; mains, pipes and tanks; mobile homes and trailers; and other property (see § 102(12) for a complete definition).

The *state equalization rate* is the percentage of full value at which taxable real property in a county, city, town or village is assessed as determined by the Board of Real Property Services (§ 102(19)).

The *tax roll* is a final assessment roll to which tax amounts have been added and to which a warrant has been attached (§ 904(1)).

A *tax warrant* empowers the tax collector to collect the taxes (§ 904).

Assessment

20:8. Who conducts property assessments for tax purposes?

Property assessments for tax purposes are made by local municipal, town or county assessors, or boards of assessors charged with the duty of assessing real property within an assessing unit for purposes of taxation or special levies (§§ 102(3),1302(1)). All assessors must obtain state board certification of successful completion of the basic course of training prescribed by the New York State Board of Real Property Services (§ 310(5)).

Assessors may be appointed or elected (§§ 102(3), 310(1), 329). Appointed assessors serve for six years, except that they may serve an indefinite term if the office of assessor is a full-time position or has been classified in the competitive class of the civil service (§ 310).

Elected town assessors serve for six years unless the town retains a board of assessors, in which case the term of office for each is four years with no more than two assessors elected at the biennial election (Town Law § 24).

20:9. Who prepares a copy of the appropriate portion of the town or county assessment roll for school district tax-collection purposes?

Because municipalities usually are not contiguous with school districts, different portions of each municipality's tax roll contain properties that are attributed to different school districts. Therefore, once the assessment roll for town or county purposes has been completed, a duplicate assessment roll is prepared and a copy of the appropriate portion delivered by the assessor to the clerk, trustee or other proper official of each school district within five days after the completion and certification of the assessment roll. The expense of preparing this document is charged to the city, town or county except when prepared for a city school district, which must reimburse the municipality preparing the duplicate assessment role (§ 1302(2)).

20:10. Who is responsible for the accuracy of the assessment roll?

Each school district is responsible for determining whether certain parcels of real property are within its boundaries (§ 1302(2)). The district superintendent of a board of cooperative educational services (BOCES) district has the authority to determine the legal boundaries between adjoining school districts within his or her jurisdiction (Educ. Law § 2215; *Appeal of Shenendehowa*, 29 Educ. Dep't Rep. 355 (1990)).

20:11. What is the timetable for the administration of the assessment system?

January 1 is the valuation date, which is the date by which the value of the real property must be determined (§ 301).

March 1 is the taxable status date, which is the date by which assessors must complete an inventory of all real property in the community. The taxable status date in villages is usually January 1 (§ 302).

May 1 is the date by which the tentative assessment roll must be filed and made available for public inspection until the fourth Tuesday in May (§ 506).

The **fourth Tuesday in May**, also known as grievance day, is the date on which the Board of Assessment Review must begin hearing assessment complaints (§ 512(1)). The governing body of an assessing unit which employs an assessor who is at the same time employed by another assessing unit may set another date or dates for the meeting of the board of assessment review. The date, or the first date in cases where the board meets on more than one date, must be between the fourth Tuesday in May and the second Tuesday in June (§ 512(1-a)).

July 1 is the deadline for filing the final assessment roll (§ 516).

20:12. What is the law regarding the correction of assessment rolls and tax rolls?

Title 3 (Corrections of Assessment Rolls and Tax Rolls) of the Real Property Tax Law defines and describes the procedures for correcting clerical errors, unlawful entries, errors in essential fact, the assessment of omitted property and other errors (§§ 550-559).

A school board may authorize a designated official to approve the correction of the tax roll and tax bill where the correction does not exceed $2,500 (§ 554(9)).

20:13. What are the procedures for reviewing and changing assessments?

Complaints regarding assessments are filed with the assessor prior to a hearing of the Board of Assessment Review, or with the board at a hearing (§ 524(1)). Any complaint is timely if it is filed on or before the fourth Tuesday in May, or on or before a later date established by local law for the meeting of the board (§ 524(1)).

Where a complaint is filed within three business days preceding the hearing, the Board of Assessment Review must grant the assessor's request for an adjournment to permit the assessor to prepare a response to the complaint. During the adjournment, no new complaints may be filed (§ 524(1)). Once the response has been considered, the board makes a determination of the final assessed valuation and prepares a verified statement showing any changes (§ 525(3),(4)).

As soon as possible after receiving the statement from the Board of Assessment Review, the assessor makes the changes in the assessment on the assessment roll (§ 526(5)).

20:14. What are the procedures for challenging a board of assessment review's refusal to reduce a property tax assessment?

Property tax certiorari is a legal proceeding initiated by a taxpayer (a person — corporate or otherwise) who wishes to challenge his or her property tax assessment on the grounds of excessiveness, inequality, illegality or misclassification, and has been denied a reduction in assessment by a local assessment review board or the small claims procedure (§§ 700; 701; 706(1)).

Most requests by residential property owners for reductions in assessment are settled by local assessment review boards or in small claims courts. Generally, the minor reductions that result from these procedures are not problematic for school districts, but the large reductions in assessment granted to businesses, industries, multiple dwellings and other commercial property owners as a result of certiorari actions may present a problem for individual school districts. Procedural laws regarding certiorari actions are contained in Article 7 of the Real Property Tax Law.

20:15. May a school district become a party to a real property tax certiorari proceeding?

Yes, at the school board's discretion. Under the Real Property Tax Law, the superintendent will receive a copy of any petition concerning real property in the district (§ 708). This does not make the school district a party to the action. However, if a school board votes to become a party to the action, it must submit either an answer to the petition or a notice of appearance in the action within the time frame set by statute (§ 712).

Tax Exemptions

20:16. What kinds of property are wholly tax exempt from real property taxation?

Examples of property that is wholly exempt from real property taxation include:

- Real property of the United States, except by permission of Congress (§ 400).
- Real property of New York State other than property expressly subjected to taxation (§ 404).
- Real property of a municipal corporation held for public use (§ 406).

- Real property of a school district or a board of cooperative educational services (BOCES) (§ 408).
- Real property on American Indian reservations (§ 454).
- Real property owned by corporations or associations organized exclusively for religious, benevolent, charitable, hospital or educational purposes, for example, as specified by law (§ 420-a(1)). This property is exempt only to the extent of the value of the portion of the property so used (§ 420-a(2)).
- Real property of an agricultural society that permanently uses it for a meeting hall exhibition grounds (§ 450).
- Real property of a municipal corporation, not within the corporation, used as a public park, public aviation field, highway, or for flood control and soil conservation purposes, provided the school board agrees to the exemption in writing (§ 406(2)).
- Real property of a corporation, association or post composed of veterans of the Grand Army of the Republic, Veterans of Foreign Wars, Disabled American Veterans, the American Legion and other veteran organizations (§ 452).
- The homes of clergy owned by religious corporations (§ 462).
- Under certain conditions, improvements related to the accessibility of the property by an owner or member of the owner's household who is disabled (§§ 459; 459-b).
- Certain real property located on farms including: silos and farm feed storage bins, commodity sheds, bulk milk tanks and coolers, and manure storage and handling facilities (§ 483-a).

For a complete overview of exemptions, see sections 400-496 of the Real Property Tax Law.

20:17. What kinds of property are partially exempt from real property taxation?

Examples of property that is partially exempt from real property taxation includes:

- Real property of a minister, priest or rabbi under certain circumstances, and the property of his or her unremarried surviving spouse, up to $1,500 (§ 460).
- Real property owned by an industrial development agency (IDA) (§§ 412-a, 412-b).
- Under certain conditions, real property owned by a person who is 65 years old or older if authorized by the school board (§ 467; see **20:18**).

- Under certain conditions, real property constructed, altered, installed or improved for the purpose of commercial, business or industrial activity (§ 485-b).
- Under certain conditions, home improvements, if authorized by the school board, are partially exempt from real property taxes for a limited period (§ 421-f).
- Under certain conditions, and if authorized by the school board, real property altered, installed or improved subsequent to the Americans with Disabilities Act (ADA) for purposes of removing architectural barriers for persons with disabilities (§ 459-a).
- Under certain conditions, and if authorized by the school board, real property owned by one or more persons with disabilities, or real property owned by a husband, wife, or both, or by siblings, at least one of whom has a disability, with limited income as set forth in statute (§ 459-c).
- Certain property owners are entitled to a partial tax exemption under the New York State School Tax Relief Program (STAR) (see **20:22-29**).

For a complete overview of exemptions, see sections 400-496 of the Real Property Tax Law.

20:18. Are there any special rules pertaining to a real property tax exemption for persons age 65 or over?

Currently, the law enables school districts to grant, by board resolution, a 50 percent exemption to persons age 65 or over who have up to $18,500 in personal income, as defined by law (§ 467(3)). The law also enables school districts to offer an exemption of between 5 percent and 45 percent along a sliding scale for those persons age 65 and over whose income is above the income ceiling adopted by the school district, as set forth by statute. For example, if a district adopts the maximum income ceiling of $19,500 for the purpose of granting the 50 percent exemption, persons over age 65 whose personal income exceeds this amount, up to a maximum of $27,900, still will qualify for a partial exemption if the district also adopts the sliding scale exemption.

Any county, city, town, village or school district may adopt a local law, ordinance or resolution to grant up to a 50 percent tax exemption on the assessed value of real property owned by one or more persons age 65 or over, or real property owned by a husband and wife or siblings, one of whom is age 65 or over. A public hearing must be held prior to the adoption of such a resolution by a school board (§ 467(1)(a)). The board then must give a copy of the resolution to the assessor, who prepares the tax roll that will be affected by the tax exemption. The exemption cannot be granted under certain circumstances, for example, in the case of real property where a child resides if that child attends a public elementary or secondary school (§ 467(2)).

The board must also notify property owners of this resolution (§ 467(4)). Those who wish to take advantage of the exemption must file an application with the assessor on or before the appropriate taxable status date (§ 467(5)).

However, a person who purchases real property after the taxable status date and qualifies for an exemption may file a late application for an exemption with the assessor within 30 days of the transfer of title (§ 467(a)). Upon approval of the application, the new property owner may receive a pro rata exemption credit to reduce the amount of taxes due on the property for the following year. School districts which receive from the assessor notice of pro rata exemption credits must include such sums in the budget appropriations for the subsequent fiscal year (§ 467(9)(a)(iii)).

In addition, certain persons 65 years of age or older may also qualify for the enhanced STAR program tax exemption (see **20:23**).

20:19. Are there any special rules pertaining to exemptions from school taxes which apply to property owned by veterans?

Yes. They are found in Section 458 of the Real Property and Tax Law.

20:20. Is a municipality exempt from paying school taxes on real property it acquires on a tax foreclosure sale?

No. A municipality is liable for school taxes on real property it acquires by deed, a referee's deed in a tax foreclosure, or pursuant to a deed made in lieu of a tax foreclosure (§ 406(5); *Union Free School Dist. v. Steuben County*, 178 Misc. 415 (1942), *aff'd*, 264 A.D. 945 (1942)).

20:21. Is school district property located outside a city and village subject to special assessments or ad valorem taxes from that city or village?

No. Section 490 of the Real Property Tax Law exempts school district real property from certain special assessments and ad valorem levies (§§ 408, 490).

20:22. What is the New York State School Tax Relief Program (STAR)?

STAR is a state-funded exemption from school property taxes for owner-occupied, primary residences. To be eligible for the exemption, the property must be a one-, two-, or three-family residence, a mobile home, a farm home, or a residential condominium or cooperative apartment (§ 425(3)). The program has two components: the "enhanced" program for income-eligible senior citizens and the basic program for all other property owners (§ 425(3),(4)). The STAR exemption must be applied after any other applicable exemptions have been applied to the property's assessed value (§ 425(7)(b)).

20:23. What is the enhanced STAR program?

The enhanced STAR program is available to all eligible senior citizens beginning in the 1998-99 school year. The exemption will be $50,000 (§ 425(2)(b)).

To be eligible for the enhanced exemption, the property owners must all be at least 65 years of age, unless they are husband and wife, in which case only one need be at least 65 years of age. In addition, the combined annual income of all of the owners and their spouses residing in the premises must not exceed $60,000. Income is defined by law (§§ 425(4); 467).

20:24. What is the basic STAR program?

The basic STAR program applies to all primary-residence homeowners, regardless of age or income, starting with taxes for school year 1999-2000. The exemption will be phased in over a three-year period ($10,000 in the 1999-2000 school year; $20,000 in the 2000-01 school year; $30,000 in the 2001-02 school year) (§ 425(2)(b)). Senior citizens whose income exceeds $60,000 will be eligible for the basic STAR exemption (§ 425).

20:25. How do district residents obtain either the enhanced STAR program exemption or the basic STAR program exemption?

All owners of the property who primarily reside thereon must jointly file an application for the exemption with the assessor on or before the appropriate taxable status date (§425(6)). If the assessor is satisfied that the applicant(s) are entitled to an exemption, he or she will approve the application and such real property shall thereafter be partially exempt from school district taxation (§ 425(6)(b)). However, the enhanced program exemption only applies for one year; therefore, a renewal application must be submitted in subsequent years (§ 425(9)).

20:26. What are a school district's responsibilities under the STAR program?

School districts are required to provide information about the STAR exemption to each person who owns a residence in the school district. The statute provides a sample notice form which may be used by districts (§ 425(5)).

20:27. How do school districts set their tax rates under the STAR program?

The amount of taxes to be levied and the tax rate must be determined without regard to the STAR exemption (§ 1306-a(1)).

20:28. How will the state reimburse school districts for the tax shortfall attributable to the STAR exemption?

Under the law, the total tax savings from the STAR program must be incurred by the state. Each school district must submit an application to the State Board of Real Property Services, which after approving the application, certifies to the commissioner of education the amount of state aid payable to the district (§ 1306-a(3); Educ. Law § 3609-e(2)).

20:29. Where can further information about the STAR program be obtained?

For more information about STAR, contact the New York State Office of Real Property Services at 16 Sheridan Avenue, Albany, N.Y. 12210-2714; telephone 1-888-697-8275 or 518-473-1565, or http://www.orps.state.ny.us.

Determining the Tax Rate

20:30. How is the amount of tax to be imposed on each parcel of property in the school district determined?

There are three methods of determining the tax amount.

In a district that is completely within or coterminous with a single taxing jurisdiction, the amount of the tax is determined by multiplying the assessed value of the parcel by the tax rate per thousand dollars of assessed value. The school tax rate per thousand is determined by dividing the total amount of the tax levy by the total assessed value of the property in the town and multiplying that result by 1,000. For example, if the total amount of the levy is $8 million, and the total assessed value of all taxable property is $135 million, the tax rate per 1,000 is $59.25. The school tax on a parcel assessed at $50,000 is $2,962.96.

In a district that embraces two or more towns or other local taxing jurisdictions, the full value of assessed real property in each jurisdiction is calculated by dividing the assessed valuation determined by each local assessor by the equalization rate established by the State Board of Real Property Services for that locality (full value) (§ 1314(1)(a)).

Or the tax rate may be applied directly to the assessed value if the Board of Real Property Services determines that a majority of the taxing jurisdictions have reevaluated or updated their assessments at the same percentage of full value in the same town. For any taxing jurisdiction within the district that did not complete such a reevaluation, the equalization rate would need to be applied (§ 1315). The full values for each component town are then added together to produce the total full value for the school district (total full value). The portion of total full value that the full value in each town represents is expressed as a percentage (percent of full value). The total amount of the district tax levy is multiplied by the percent of full value for each town to determine the amount of tax levy to be raised in each town (tax levy per town). The tax rate per thousand in each town is calculated by dividing the tax levy per town by the total assessed value per town and multiplying that result by 1,000. Finally, the tax rate per 1,000 is applied to the assessed value of each parcel of real property to be taxed.

20:31. What is tax equalization, and what is its role in the process of setting tax rates?

Tax equalization, simply stated, is the ratio between the actual current market value of property and the assessed value of that property. Full value, or market value, is the price a piece of property would command if it were sold. Assessed value is the value of a piece of property established by taxing authorities on the basis of which the tax rate is applied. The assessed value is often a fraction of the actual market value (§ 305).

Tax equalization is a method of computation used with the aim of equitably apportioning the tax burden where a district encompasses parts of two or more tax districts that assess property at different fractions of full value. The end result of the use of the state equalization rate is supposed to be the determination of the full market value of property and tax rate on full value. (The method for computing the equalization is in section 1314 of the Real Property and Tax Law.)

20:32. Are residential and commercial properties taxed at the same rate?

Under the homestead/nonhomestead property-classification system, residential and commercial properties can be taxed at different rates in approved assessing units (those that have undergone reassessment of all parcels at full market value and have been approved by the State Board of Real Property Services). This ensures against a disproportionate tax burden for residential taxpayers by reducing tax rates on residential properties.

Section 1903 of the Real Property Tax Law regulates the adoption and implementation procedures of the homestead tax system.

20:33. How are school districts affected by the homestead/nonhomestead property-classification system?

If a locality elects this option, it must provide a copy of the local homestead classification system to the authorities of each school district located wholly or partially within that locality. When adopted by an approved assessing unit (a town, village or city), the homestead system applies to taxes levied on all real property by each school district wholly contained within the approved assessing unit (§ 1903(1)(a)(b)). However, an affected district may adopt a resolution rejecting this kind of property-classification system in its district (§ 1903(1)(a)).

20:34. Can the homestead/nonhomestead property-classification system apply to school districts located in more than one city or town?

Yes, if one or more cities or towns within the school district has adopted a homestead/nonhomestead property-classification system. A school board may, by resolution, adopt such a classification system, upon filing a notice of intent, as set forth in law (§ 1903-a(1)(b)), and following a public hearing to be held at any time prior to the levy of school taxes (§ 1903-a(3)).

School districts may cancel notice of intent to adopt such a system by filing a notice of cancellation, as set forth in law (§ 1903-a(1)(c)). They may also, by board resolution and without a public hearing, rescind any prior action adopting such a system at any time prior to the levy of taxes for the fiscal year to which the resolution is applicable. Any such rescission must also be filed in accordance with law (§ 1903-a(5)).

Tax Collection

20:35. Is there a procedure for authorizing the collection of taxes?

Yes. After the tax list has been prepared by applying the property tax rates against the properties assessed, the list must be confirmed by school board resolution. At the date and time at which this resolution is adopted, the school taxes become a lien on the properties (§ 1312).

The next step is to execute the warrant, which serves as a directive to the tax collector to collect taxes in accordance with the confirmed tax list and provides authorization for making collection (§ 1318(1)). The tax warrant must be affixed to the tax list on or before September 1 (§ 1306(1)). At least a majority of the school board is required to sign the warrant for the collection of taxes (§ 1318(1)).

The state does not fix a limit on the number of times a tax warrant may be renewed; however, warrants of school tax collectors must be returnable in time for the school authorities to transmit necessary information regarding unpaid taxes to the county treasurer by November 15 (§§ 1318(3), 1330(2)).

20:36. How are taxpayers notified of their school taxes?

Upon receipt of a warrant for the collection of taxes, the collecting officer must publish a notice in a newspaper, or two newspapers, if there are two, having general circulation in the school district, which states that the warrant has been received and all taxes due must be received within one month from the time of the first published notice.

The notice must be published at least twice and as many additional times as the school authorities may direct. If there is no newspaper having general circulation in the district, the notice must be posted immediately in at least 20 public places in the district.

In addition, the collecting officer also must mail a statement of taxes to each real property owner on the tax list. Where the school district has levied a tax for the purpose of a public library or on behalf of a library district, the amount of the taxes attributable to library purposes must be separately stated on each statement of taxes (§§ 1322(1); 1324; 922(1)).

The school board may, by resolution, require the collecting officer to enclose a copy of the adopted budget and an explanation of the computation of the tax rate (§§ 1322(1); 1324).

The tax collector also must give a like notice by mail or personally to all nonresident taxpayers whose post offices may be known or ascertained, and to all railroads and utility corporations. The notice should bear the date of the posting of the notice. The tax collector is required to give such notice at least 20 days prior to the expiration of the one-month period of tax collection (§ 1322(2)).

20:37. May residential taxpayers who are age 65 or over or disabled designate a third party to receive notification from the tax collector?

Yes. The tax collector must enclose with each statement of taxes a notice that residential taxpayers who are age 65 or over or disabled are eligible for the third-party notification procedure. This notice must explain the application procedure and other aspects of the provision (§ 1325(1)).

20:38. May school taxes be paid in installments?

Yes, but the law is different for city and non-city school districts.

City school districts may simply adopt a resolution stating that school taxes may be paid in installments. There cannot be more than six installments, the installments must be as equal as possible, and the resolution must state the number of installments and the dates on which installments are due to be paid (§ 1326).

Non-city school districts may adopt a resolution by a two-thirds vote allowing school taxes to be collected in three installments. The minimum amount per installment is set by statute and the due date for each installment must be specified in the school board's resolution. In addition, the school district may choose to limit the installment program to certain types of property as provided in the law (§ 1326-a).

20:39. Can a school board restrict the property tax installment payment option to senior citizens and/or disabled citizens?

Yes. A school board may limit installment payments of school property taxes to senior citizens that qualify for the senior citizen exemption and/or to those who are disabled as defined by law (§§ 467, 459, 1327, 1326-a(4)). In addition, non-city school districts can limit installment payments of school property taxes to one-, two- and three-family residential properties (§ 1326-a(4)(a)).

20:40. May the tax collector accept payment of taxes on only part of a parcel of real property?

Yes, provided the taxpayer furnishes certain specifications, including apportionment, regarding the assessment of the parcel (§ 932). Once a written request is submitted by a party interested in an affected property, an assessor must apportion an assessment under the law (9 Op. Counsel SBEA no. 13 (1990)).

20:41. What happens if school taxes are inadvertently paid to the wrong collector?

School taxes inadvertently paid to the collector of a district that does not include the assessed property within its boundaries should be refunded by the district (§ 556).

20:42. What happens if any taxes remain unpaid at the time the collecting officer is required to return a warrant to the school authorities?

The collecting officer must return the tax roll and warrant with a statement of the unpaid taxes and a description of the property upon which taxes remain unpaid (§ 1330(1)). When the school authorities receive this statement, they must compare it with the original tax roll. If it is correct, they must certify the statement as such (§ 1330(2)).

The school authorities then immediately transmit the statement and certificate to the county treasurer so that it is received by the treasurer no later than November 15 (§ 1330(2)).

On or before April 1 of the next year, the county treasurer must pay the school district the amount of unpaid school taxes (§ 1330(4); see § 1332 for city school districts; § 1342 relating to taxes paid in installments).

20:43. Does the return of unpaid school taxes by the county to the school district include any fees or penalties paid to the county by delinquent taxpayers?

Yes. School districts that have school tax collectors employed on a salary basis are entitled to receive, in addition to the unpaid taxes, interest at a rate set by the commissioner of taxation as set forth in law (§§ 942, 1328, 1330; see § 924-a).

If the school district's tax collector is compensated on a fee basis, the district receives no fees (§ 1328(1)).

20:44. What happens to the tax roll and warrant after they have been returned to the school authorities by the collecting officer?

The school authorities must deliver the tax roll and warrant to the school district clerk within 15 days (20 days in city school districts) of their return by the collecting officer. School districts under a district superintendent, however, deliver the tax list and warrant to the district superintendent who, in turn, delivers it to the school district clerk by July 1 (§§ 1330(3); 1332(4)).

20:45. How are tax collectors paid?

Some school districts employ tax collectors on a salary basis, with the salary determined at the school board's discretion (§ 1328(2); Educ. Law § 2130(4)). In other districts, the tax collector receives 1 percent of the amount of taxes collected during the first month after the publication of notice and not more than 5 percent of the amount collected after the first month (§ 1328(1)).

Industrial Development Agencies

20:46. What is an industrial development agency?

An *industrial development agency (IDA)* is an independent public benefit corporation created through state legislation at the request of one or more sponsoring municipalities. Article 18-A of the General Municipal Law sets forth powers, jurisdiction and requirements for IDAs. Legislation creating a specific IDA may contain provisions different from or in addition to the general legislation contained in the General Municipal Law. In 1998, there were 123 active IDAs in the state, according to the state comptroller's office.

20:47. May school board members serve on an IDA board?

Yes. The General Municipal Law states that school board members, municipal officials, and representatives of organized labor and business may serve on IDA governing boards (Gen. Mun. Law § 856(2)).

20:48. What is the taxable status of real property owned by industrial development agencies, mortgages on IDA projects and purchases made for IDA projects?

All property titled to an IDA is exempt from real property, sales and mortgage taxes (§ 412-a; Gen. Mun. Law § 874(1), (2)).

However, an IDA is authorized to negotiate payments in lieu of taxes (PILOTs) with the private developers participating in IDA projects (Gen. Mun. Law § 858(15)). PILOT moneys received from an IDA are to be included in the school budget as if they were tax dollars (Opn. St. Comp. 82-174). Furthermore, PILOTs must be included as estimated in the annual preparation of the school district's budget (Educ. Law §§ 1608(3); 1716(3); 2601-a) . PILOTs received by the IDA must be given to the school district within 30 days of receipt (Gen. Mun. Law § 874(3)).

In addition, all IDAs must adopt a uniform tax exemption policy with input from affected tax jurisdictions, including school districts, which states what tax exemptions are available to those interested in seeking IDA assistance for commercial enterprises. This policy must include guidelines for the claiming of real property, mortgage recording, and sales tax exemptions. The policy must also indicate the extent to which a proposed project will require additional educational services, and provide additional sources of revenue for school districts (Gen. Mun. Law § 874 (4)(a)).

20:49. Can IDAs distribute PILOT revenues as they see fit?

No. Unless otherwise agreed to by the school board and municipal governments affected by an IDA project, payments in lieu of taxes (PILOTS) must be distributed in proportion to the amount of real property and other taxes which would have been received had the project not been tax-exempt (Gen. Mun. Law § 858(15)).

20:50. What responsibilities do IDAs have with respect to notifying school districts about their IDA-assisted projects?

IDAs must notify school boards and municipalities within 15 days of an agreement reached for payments in lieu of taxes (PILOTS) on an IDA-assisted project (Gen. Mun. Law § 858(15)). IDAs also must notify school boards of pending projects which require more than $100,000 in IDA financial assistance, including the details of any tax exemptions and proposed PILOT agreements. This notice must also announce the schedule for a public hearing on a proposed project in writing at least 10 days prior to the hearing to enable boards to provide written and oral comments at that hearing (Gen. Mun. Law § 859-a)).

20:51. Where can more information about assessment and taxation be obtained?

Information about assessment and taxation may be obtained from the New York State Board of Real Property Services' Legal Services Department, 16 Sheridan Ave., Albany, N.Y. 12210; telephone 518-474-8821, or http://www.orps.state.ny.us.

21. State Aid

21:1. How is public elementary and secondary education financed in New York State?

Public education in New York State is funded through a combination of local tax revenues, aid from the state government and a small amount of assistance from the federal government. For the 1998-99 school year, it was estimated that local revenues provided approximately 56 percent of all school district revenues. The state share was approximately 40 percent and the federal share was approximately 4 percent.

21:2. What is the source of money used to pay state aid?

The bulk of the money used to pay state aid is derived from state tax revenues. These include the personal income tax, the sales and use tax, the corporate franchise tax, the motor fuel tax and corporation utility taxes.

In addition, the net proceeds of the state lottery are dedicated to state aid to education. Under the State Finance Law, all revenues from the state lottery, after prizes and the cost of administration have been accounted for, must be used for the support of education (State Fin. Law § 92-c). School districts receive a portion of their fall state aid payment in the form of a check directly from the lottery fund on September 1 (§ 3609-a (1)(a)(2)). A portion of the lottery funds ($15 per resident pupil) is added to regular textbook aid, which is included in the check districts receive from the lottery fund. Lottery aid also includes a $10 payment for each blind and deaf student attending state-supported schools for the blind and deaf (State Fin. Law § 92-c (4)(b)).

21:3. When is state aid actually paid to local schools districts?

The state aid payment schedule, as amended by Chapter 53 of the Laws of 1992, provides school districts with funds beginning in the fall of each year (§ 3609-a; see also **21:2**).

The payment schedule includes the following features:
- The state sends payments to the New York State Teachers' Retirement System (TRS) on behalf of districts in September, October and November. The relative amount of a district's TRS obligation does not affect monthly aid payment calculations (§ 3609-a (1)(a)(1)).
- Lottery aid is paid in full on September 1 (§ 3609-a (1)(a)(2)).
- Fixed payments are paid in the months of October, November and December. These payments guarantee a "fixed" percentage of a

district's total aid, after TRS payments, by a given date: 12.5 percent by October 15, 18.75 percent by November 15, and 25 percent by December 15 (§ 3609-a(1)(a)(4)).

• Individualized payments are paid during the months of January through June. These are calculated to guarantee that each district receives 50 percent of its state and local revenues by the first business day of January, 60 percent by February, 70 percent by March, 80 percent by April, 90 percent by May and 100 percent in the June payment. Any amount in excess of 100 percent of aid projections will be paid in September (§ 3609-a(1)(b)(2)).

• A June prepayment advances an estimated percentage of the June payment into the prior state fiscal year. This prepayment allows school districts to receive their aid earlier in the school year (§ 3609-a (1)(b)(5)).

• Boards of cooperative educational services (BOCES) aid is paid directly to the BOCES. After deducting payments due to TRS on behalf of BOCES, 25 percent of BOCES aid is paid on or before February 1, and 55 percent is paid in June, and the remainder in September (§ 3609-d(1)).

• Growth aid is paid in full in June (§ 3609-a(1)(b)(3)(v)).

• Public and private excess cost aid payments are separated from the general aid payment schedule. There are four guaranteed dates for reimbursement. The calculated sum of aids is apportioned according to the following schedule: by December—25 percent; by March—70 percent; by June—85 percent; by August—100 percent; by September — any amount in excess of 100 percent of aid projections (§ 3609-b(2)).

For districts that participate in the federal Medicaid reimbursement program, reimbursement for excess cost aids will be paid in conjunction with the scheduled payment of federal share monies for Medicaid reimbursement (§ 3609-b).

21:4. What is the process for school districts to submit claims for state aid?

Claims for aid are generally submitted by the superintendent of schools or district superintendent to the Office of Management Services of the State Education Department. That office and the New York State Department of Audit and Control process claims for payment (§ 3601).

21:5. Is state aid available to nonpublic schools in New York State?

Yes. In 1979, the United States Supreme Court upheld the constitutionality of Chapters 507 and 508 of New York State's Laws of 1974, the so-called mandated services law. This law requires payment of state financial aid to nonpublic schools for costs incurred by them in complying with certain state mandates such as testing, pupil evaluation, achievement tests and attendance records (*Committee for Pub. Educ. & Religious Liberty v. Regan*, 444 U.S. 646 (1980)).

Prior to that, the court had struck down such statutes as being violations of the Establishment Clause of the First Amendment (see *Levitt v. Committee for Public Education & Religious Liberty*, 413 U.S. 472 (1973)). The present laws provide a means by which payment of the state funds are audited, thus ensuring that state funds are used only for secular services.

Nonpublic schools also secure state aid in the form of services and equipment in the areas of school transportation, health services, remedial services, occupational and vocational education, services for children with disabilities, textbooks, computer software and library materials (§§ 3635; 3602-c; 912; 701(3); 752; 712).

Since April 1975, an office of nonpublic school services in the State Education Department has been dealing specifically with state services to nonpublic schools.

Types of State Aid

21:6. What types of state aid are available to school districts?

There are two basic types of state aid available to school districts. *Unrestricted (or general) aid* may be used by districts for any purpose as determined by local priorities and needs. *Comprehensive operating aid* is the major unrestricted aid (§ 3602(12); see **21:7, 21:10, 21:12**). Other types of unrestricted aid are the extraordinary needs component of comprehensive operating aid, growth aid, tax effort aid and tax equalization aid (§ 3602 (12)(e), (13), (16); see **21:11**).

Categorical aid is provided to districts for particular purposes and must be spent for the purpose specified. In 1998-99, over 40 categorical grants and aids were available to school districts; however, not all districts are eligible for all categorical aids. Some categorical aids are distributed according to formulas; others are awarded on a grant basis (see **21:12** for major aids, categorical aids and grant programs).

21:7. What is comprehensive operating aid and how is it calculated?

Comprehensive operating aid is unrestricted aid. It is spent according to a district's priorities as determined by the school board, not for specifically legislated purposes. It is also the largest single category of allocation. In 1998–99, this aid constituted approximately 60 percent of state funds allocated by formula for public schools.

Chapter 57 of the Laws of 1993 replaced eight school aid formulas with comprehensive operating aid and the extraordinary needs aid component of comprehensive operating aid (see **21:10**). For operating purposes, the state shares in allocating aid to the public schools through an aid-ratio formula. Comprehensive operating aid is generated up to a certain ceiling level per pupil in inverse proportion to a district's wealth, as represented by the value of its real property and adjusted gross income of the community. Districts with low wealth receive a relatively high amount of aid, while districts with high wealth receive a relatively low amount of aid. In 1998-99, the ceiling for the comprehensive operating aid formula was $3,900 per pupil. Above this ceiling, the state will provide at least 7.5 percent of the amount the district spends between $3,900 and $8,000, adjusted by the state sharing ratio (§ 3602(12)(d)).

Comprehensive operating aid is calculated and distributed in accordance with an equalized formula based on a district's selected operating aid ratio. The formula calls for a district's aid per pupil to be multiplied by the number of total aidable pupil units (TAPU) (§ 3602(8)), as defined in **21:9**. For those districts in which the formula generates less than $400 per pupil, the statute guarantees $400 per-pupil minimum comprehensive operating aid, often referred to as the flat grant (§ 3602(12)(c)).

21:8. How is operating aid actually calculated?

The formula for operating aid can be expressed mathematically.

The sum of .5 (full-value wealth ratio) and .5 (income-wealth ratio) = (CWR) (§ 3602(1)(l))

A district's selected operating aid ratio is the greatest of: 1.37-(1.23 x CWR), 1.00-(0.64 x CWR), 0.80-(0.39 x CWR), 0.51-(0.22 x CWR) (§ 3602(3)(b))

The maximum aid ratio is .90. Based on this model, for a district of average wealth (1.0 CWR), the aid ratio is 41 percent. Thus, the state share of the first $3,900 a district spends per pupil will be 41 percent.

Operating aid ratio x ceiling ($3,900) = formula aid per pupil (§ 3602(12)(d))

Approved operating expenses (up to $8,000) per pupil – $3,900 x 7.5 percent. This product x district aid ratio = aid ratio aid (§ 3602(12)(d))

The greater of formula aid per pupil plus aid ratio per pupil or per pupil flat grant ($400) = total operating aid per pupil

Total operating aid per pupil x selected TAPU (see **21:9**) = total operating aid

21:9. What is the pupil count used in computing comprehensive operating aid?

Comprehensive operating aid is determined by multiplying aid per pupil unit, as computed in the formula, by the total aidable pupil units (TAPU) (§ 3602(8); see **21:8**).

The base pupil count for TAPU is based on average daily attendance (ADA) (§ 3602(1)(d)). ADA is the average number of pupils served during the calendar year, determined by dividing the total number of attendance days of all pupils by the number of days school was in session for the previous year.

For any given school year, districts are permitted to use the higher of the previous year's (base year) TAPU or a two-year average of the base year and the year prior to the base year. The count chosen is called selected TAPU for payment. The average daily attendance used in the calculation of TAPU does not include pupils attending private schools for children with disabilities.

Table 1 shows how different students are weighted in the calculation of TAPU for payment. For the calculation of aid in the 1998-99 school year, ADA will be calculated using the year prior to the base year, plus an enrollment adjustment.

Table 1
Basic Pupil Weightings

Half-day Kindergarten	.50
ADA (K–6)	1.00
ADA (7–12)	1.00
Dual Enrollment*	1.00
Additional Weightings	
Secondary (including PSEN** but excluding certain students with disabilities)	.25
PSEN (K–12 including pupils with disabilities)	.25
Summer School	.12

*See **21:23** for information about dual enrollment
**Pupils with special educational needs; § 3602(1)(e)

21:10. What is the transition adjustment for purposes of calculating comprehensive operating aid?

A *positive transition adjustment* prevents districts from receiving less total operating aid in the current year than its total operating aid paid in the base year. A *negative transition adjustment* limits or caps allowable increases in total operating aid.

The group of aids that are subject to the transition adjustment include operating aid, tax effort aid and tax equalization aid. Under the Laws of 1998, the transition adjustment provides a minimum increase of between 1.8 percent and 2.5 percent, depending upon district wealth for districts that have a positive transition adjustment. For districts that are subject to the negative transition adjustment, total operating aids were allowed to increase by the greater of 5 percent over the base year or 17.6 percent of the increase in formula aids (§ 3602(18)).

21:11. What other unrestricted state aid may districts receive in addition to comprehensive operating aid and extraordinary needs aid?

Districts may receive tax equalization and tax effort aids, both of which replace high tax aid (§ 3602(16)). Tax equalization aid is based on a district's per pupil expense (up to $8,000), minus its comprehensive operating aid per pupil. If the difference between these two measures would require a full value tax rate greater than $19.50, equalization aid is provided, according to Chapter 53 of the Laws of 1994. Tax effort aid is based on residential property taxes and income, and measures the residential tax levy against the district's ability to raise revenue.

21:12. What are the major categorical aids available to school districts?

The major categorical aids are:

- **Boards of cooperative educational services (BOCES) aid,** provided to help school districts pay for the services they purchase from BOCES (§ 1950(5)).
- **Transportation aid,** provided to pay between 6.5 percent and 90 percent of districts' approved transportation expenditures, depending upon one of two aid ratios (one is derived from the operating aid ratio; the other is from the resident weighted average daily attendance ratio), adjusted by a "sparsity" factor (§ 3602(7)).
- **Building aid,** provided to districts for building purposes, except those districts scheduled for reorganization (§ 3602(6)). Stationary metal detectors and computer wiring are also aidable expenditures under Chapter 53 of the Laws of 1994.
- **Minor maintenance and repair aid,** provided to repair schools, based on their age, square footage, and a growth index (§ 3602(6-d)).
- **Gifted and talented aid,** provided to defray the cost of special programs to meet the learning needs of gifted and talented students (§ 3602(23)).

- **Limited English Proficiency (LEP) aid**, provided for students who cannot benefit from the regular instructional program because of their limited ability to speak, read and write English. These students must receive a program of either bilingual education or English as a second language (ESL) so that they master English as well as learn their academic subjects (§ 3602(22)).
- **Aid for children with disabilities**, provided to partially defray the excess cost involved in educating children with disabilities, both in public school-BOCES programs (public excess cost aid) and in programs in private schools (private excess cost aid) (§ 3602(19)).
- **Educationally-related support services aid**, provided to support services to nondisabled students in order to maintain their placement in a regular education program. Speech therapy aid, which provides speech and language improvement services for students with speech impairments, was combined with this aid in 1993-94 (§ 3602(32)).
- **Employment preparation education (EPE) aid**, used to fund adult education programs such as literacy, basic skills and high school equivalency programs (§ 3602(24)).
- **Reorganization incentive aid**, provided for both operating and building expenses incurred by those school districts scheduled for reorganization (§ 3602(14)).
- **Textbook aid**, provided to reimburse districts for the current-year costs of the purchase of textbooks and other approved instructional materials. All textbooks owned or acquired by a district must be loaned to all resident pupils enrolled in kindergarten through 12th grade in public and nonpublic schools on an equitable basis (§ 701(4),(6-7); see **14:55–56**).
- **Computer software aid**, provided for the purchase and loan of computer software. Software programs designed for use in public schools must be loaned on an equitable basis to nonpublic school students (§§ 751-752)).
- **Computer hardware and technology equipment aid**, apportioned to districts for the lease or purchase of mini- and microcomputers, computer terminals or certain other technology equipment, such as lasers, robotics equipment and solar energy equipment, for instructional purposes (§ 3602(26)).
- **Education technology incentive aid**, apportioned to districts to provide additional funding for acquisition and maintenance of education technology (§ 3602(26-a)).
- **Library materials aid**, allocated to districts to purchase library

materials, which must also be loaned on an equitable basis to nonpublic school students (§§ 711(4); 712).

- **Special services aid**, provided to the Big 5 city school districts for occupational education and computer services (§ 3602(17)).
- **Aid for incarcerated youths**, provided for educational services to youths detained in local correctional facilities (§ 3602(35)).
- **Prekindergarten expansion aid,** allocated to enhance existing programs and establish new prekindergarten programs (§ 3602-e).
- **Full-day kindergarten incentive aid,** provided to school districts which do not currently offer a full-day kindergarten program as an incentive to do so (§ 3602(12-a)).
- **State bilingual categorical funds**, provided to fund regional bilingual programs at BOCES and support innovative two-way bilingual education programs that employ two languages, one of which is English, to instruct students whose primary language is not English.
- **Breakfast/lunch programs**, appropriated to subsidize school breakfast and lunch programs that provide students with nutritious meals that meet federal standards.
- **Nonpublic school aid**, appropriated to reimburse nonpublic schools for those expenses incurred for specified state testing and data-collection activities.

21:13. How are approved expenditures for debt service eligible for building aid determined?

There are two forms of debt service expenditures eligible for capital notes. Approved expenditures for bond anticipation notes (BANS) will be limited to actual expenditures for principal and interest related to financing of a school construction project through BANS except that such expenditures may not include:

- Expenditures for the first 23 months after issuance.
- Expenditures on principal or interest on BANS issued after a certificate of substantial completion is issued.
- Expenditures on principal in excess of the minimum principal payment required under the Local Finance Law (Educ. Law § 3602(6)(i)(1)).

Approved expenditures for bond and capital notes shall be computed based on an amortization period of 15 years for new construction and 10 years for reconstruction projects. If the district does not use a bond issue of this length, the commissioner of education will compute the state aid payments as if the district had done so (§ 3602(6)(i)(2)).

Calculation and Distribution of State Aid

21:14. How relevant to the calculation of state aid is the school district code number that appears on the state income tax form?

The school district code identifies the school district to which the income of the taxpayer is attributed.

As explained in **21:17**, income is a major factor in the calculation of a district's wealth and, therefore, in the calculation of state aid to be received by a district. It is crucial that the school district code number be accurate so that the correct amount of total income can be assigned to each district. If more than the actual amount of income per pupil is attributed to a district, it appears wealthier on paper than it actually is and may get less state aid than it deserves. Conversely, if less than the actual amount of income per pupil is attributed to a district, the district may get more state aid than it deserves.

For the purposes of annual aid distribution, a computerized income verification process is used to verify the match between addresses and school district codes reported on income tax returns used to determine district wealth (§ 3602(1)(k)(2)).

21:15. On what basis is state aid distributed?

There are a number of different bases on which state aid is distributed, depending on the type of aid. Some aid is distributed according to wealth-equalizing formulas. This means that the wealthier a district is, in terms of the property value and adjusted gross income behind each pupil, the less aid per pupil it receives. The poorer a district is, the more aid per pupil it receives.

Other aid is allocated based on a certain amount per pupil. Grants are allocated in a variety of ways: for example, the aid may cover a specific portion of the district's budgeted program costs, or lump sum amounts may be awarded to a limited number of districts. The latter method of allocation is often used when a grant is available only to certain districts, such as the Big 5 city school districts (see **21:16**). Certain categories of aid, like transportation, boards of cooperative educational services (BOCES) and building aid, reimburse districts for a portion of these costs.

The pupil count used to distribute aid is based on each district's average daily attendance (ADA) (§ 3602(1)(d)). ADA represents the average number of pupils present on each regular school day in a given period. The average is determined by dividing the total number of attendance days of all pupils by the number of days school was in session for the previous year (see **21:9**).

21:16. On what basis is state aid distributed to the Big 5 city school districts?

Buffalo, New York City, Rochester, Syracuse and Yonkers, each with populations over 125,000, are the Big 5 city school districts. These city school districts do not levy taxes to raise revenues as do the rest of the state's school districts. They are dependent on the portion of the city budget devoted to education each year for the local share of their budgets (§ 2576). Each of these cities also receives state and federal aid. The categorical state aids are accounted for separately by the cities, and each aid must be used entirely for its designated categorical purpose. The same is true for nearly all federal aid, since it is also categorical.

General-purpose state education aid becomes city revenue and is used to fund the schools; however, the cities do not necessarily allocate to the schools the exact amount of this aid received from the state. The cities differ in the extent to which general-purpose state education aid is used to supplement the municipal contribution to the schools.

21:17. How is a school district's wealth measured for purposes of school aid?

A school district's wealth is measured by comparing its property value per pupil with the state average property value per pupil, and the district's adjusted gross income per pupil with the state average adjusted gross income per pupil. The ratios derived from these comparisons are multiplied by .5 and added together to form the combined-wealth ratio (CWR) (§ 3602(1)(l)).

For purposes of calculating 1998-99 state aid, district property value is defined as the 1995 Actual Valuation (§ 3602(1)(c)) and district income is defined as the 1995 Adjusted Gross Income (§ 3602(1)(k)(2)).

21:18. Can attendance for state aid purposes be excluded for days when the employees in a school district are on strike?

No. Occasionally, legislation has been enacted on a year-by-year basis that allows a district to exclude the attendance for days on which there was a strike or for days on which attendance was affected adversely because of a strike. By being able to exclude the generally lower attendance on these days, a district was not penalized on the computation of weighted average daily attendance (WADA) (§ 3602(2)(a)), upon which state aid is based (see **21:15**). This legislation has not been enacted in recent years.

21:19. Is a school penalized by the state aid formula for days on which it must be closed because of an emergency which results in the district providing less than 180 days of instruction?

Not necessarily. The commissioner of education is authorized to excuse a reduction of up to five days of instruction below 180 days for certain reasons, such as adverse weather or impairment of heating facilities, if the days cannot be made up by using scheduled vacation days. Ordinarily, the apportionment of operating aid must be reduced by 1/180th for each day less than the required 180 days of instruction (§ 3604(7)).

21:20. Do districts receive aid for increased student enrollments?

Yes. Growth aid is available to districts with growth exceeding 0.4 percent. Growth aid is paid in the spring, separately from the general aid payment schedule (§ 3602(13)(b)).

21:21. Does state aid distribution reflect the needs of disadvantaged students?

Yes. Chapter 57 of the Laws of 1993 enacted the extraordinary needs component of comprehensive operating aid. Extraordinary needs aid (ENA) is distributed on the basis of student need using measures of poverty, such as the number of students in kindergarten through grade six eligible for free and reduced priced lunch, the number of students who have limited English proficiency and the number of students in geographically sparse areas (§ 3602(12)(e)).

At-risk "set asides" have been built into the system to ensure that changing levels of pupil needs are met. For instance, if the number of at-risk students in a district increases, based on PEP (pupil evaluation program) tests and attendance rates, the district must increase the amount of funds set aside to meet these students' needs. A decreasing at-risk population decreases the amount to be set aside and increases the district's level of unrestricted aid (§ 3602(12)(f, g, h)).

21:22. Is there special financial aid for those public schools that incur increased costs because of nonpublic school closings in their district?

Yes. There are two types of relief for public school districts experiencing enrollment increases resulting from the closing of nonpublic schools. The first type of relief is an impact aid, which is paid for each of the first two years the new students are in a district's public schools (§ 3602(5)).

The second type of relief, which is more indirect, comes from an immediate inclusion of students who formerly attended nonpublic schools in the definitions of total wealth pupil units (TWPU) (§ 3602(2-b)) and resident weighted average daily attendance (RWADA) (§ 3602(2)). The addition of these new students normally would not be reflected in a district's computations of TWPU and RWADA until two years after they had begun attending public schools. However, this two-year lag has been eliminated (§§ 3602 (2-b)(c)). Since the addition of these students is more quickly recognized in pupil wealth measures used in calculating those aids that use these measures, these aids are more accurately distributed.

21:23. Can districts receive aid for providing services required by the dual enrollment provision in the Education Law?

Yes. The dual enrollment provision requires school boards to provide instruction in the areas of gifted students, career education, education for students with disabilities, and counseling, psychological and social work services related to such instruction to students who attend nonpublic schools, provided that such instruction is given to students enrolled in the public school district (§ 3602-c).

Students receiving gifted or career education must be transported between the nonpublic school they legally attend and the public school where these services are offered, if the distance exceeds a quarter of a mile. Students with disabilities must receive transportation in accordance with the needs of such students (§ 3602-c(4)).

State aid for operating expenses is based on a formula that reflects the portion of the school day a nonpublic school student spends in a public school program (§ 3602-c(1)(e)). Districts that contract for these services with a board of cooperative education services (BOCES) receive aid based on the BOCES aid formula (§ 3602-c(3)). In addition, districts are reimbursed for 6.5 percent to 90 percent of approved transportation expenditures, depending upon the selected aid ratios plus a sparsity adjustment (§§ 3602(7)); 3602-c(4)).

Districts providing services to nonresident students under this provision are entitled to recover tuition from the students' home districts, according to the commissioner of education.

21:24. Where can additional information about the distribution of state aid and details of aid formulas be found?

Descriptions of aid, formulas and dollar allocations can be obtained from the Education Unit of the New York State Division of the Budget.

For questions about individual districts and for references to other sources of information, contact the State Education Department's Office of Management Services at 518-473-8364 or at http://www.nysed.gov.

22. Transportation

22:1. Must a school district furnish school bus transportation for students residing within the district?

Yes. School districts, except city school districts, are required to transport all students, including those attending nonpublic schools (§ 3635).

City school districts may, but are not required to, provide transportation (§ 3635(1)(c)). If it is provided, the transportation must be based on a reasonable and consistent policy that treats all children in like circumstances in a similar manner; however, students in different grade levels are not considered to be in "like circumstances." Therefore, a city school district may, for instance, provide transportation to students in certain grades and not others, based on its policy (*Appeal of Cassin*, 32 Educ. Dep't Rep. 373 (1992)).

Similarly, students receiving transportation services under section 3635 do not stand in like circumstances to children transported to and from school under other statutes (*Appeal of Neubauer*, 32 Educ. Dep't Rep. 320 (1992)). For example, a school district which provides transportation to students with disabilities under the provisions of article 89 of the Education Law is not required to transport students attending regular education beyond the distance limitations of section 3635 (see **22:2-4**), even if students with disabilities are transported a longer distance (*Appeal of Guiney*, 34 Educ. Dep't Rep. 410 (1995)).

In enlarged city school districts, transportation is required only for students residing outside the city limits, but it also may be provided to children living within the city limits (§ 2503(12)). An enlarged city school district may distinguish, in its transportation policy, between students residing within the city limits and those residing in areas of the enlarged city school district outside of the corporate boundaries of the school district (*Matter of Collar*, 14 Educ. Dep't Rep. 327 (1975)).

A district may use private carriers and/or public transportation to transport students to and from school (see *Appeal of Bruner*, 32 Educ. Dep't Rep. 276 (1992); *Appeal of Lavin*, 32 Educ. Dep't Rep. 249 (1992)).

22:2. Are there any distance limitations for the transportation of students?

Yes. Door-to-door transportation is not required (*Matter of Boyar*, 21 Educ. Dep't Rep. 286 (1981)). A district may require children in grades kindergarten through eight to walk a distance of up to two miles, and children in grades nine through 12 to walk a distance of up to three miles from their homes to their schools. The district must provide bus transportation up to a distance of 15 miles (§ 3635(1)(a),(c)).

However, transportation for distances less than two miles in the case of children in kindergarten through the eighth grade, or less than three miles in the case of students in grades nine through 12, and for distances greater than 15 miles may be provided, if the voters approve (*Appeal of Wenger,* 37 Educ. Dep't Rep. 5 (1997); *Matter of Zakrzewski,* 22 Educ. Dep't Rep. 381 (1983); *Matter of Silver,* 1 Educ. Dep't Rep. 381 (1959)). If transportation is provided, it must be offered equally to all children in like circumstances residing in the district (§ 3635(1)(a)).

Where the distance exceeds 15 miles, the law does not require a district to provide transportation to or from a point 15 miles along the route from a student's home to the school legally attended (see *Matter of Wasserman,* 15 Educ. Dep't Rep. 278 (1978)).

The cost of providing transportation for distances more than two or three miles, as the case may be, and less than 15 miles, must be considered an ordinary contingent expense of the district (§§ 2503(12)(a); 3635(1)(a)). So is the cost of providing transportation beyond these distance limitations if approved by the voters (§§ 2023(2); 2503(12)(b)).

22:3. Can a school district provide transportation to students who reside at a lesser distance from school than the minimum limitations solely on the basis of a hazard?

Yes. The Child Safety Act of 1992, with voter approval, allows a district to establish a child safety zone and provide transportation to students who live less than two or three miles from school but must walk along hazardous zones (§ 3635-b). While the statute does not specifically include city school districts, the State Education Department has taken the position that the Legislature intended to include city school districts by devolution (see **2:11**).

A child safety zone is determined based on regulations established by the commissioner of transportation and in consultation with local law enforcement officials. Children living within this zone may be transported without regard for distance or the "like circumstances" requirement (see **22:1**) contained in section 3635(1)(a) of the Education Law.

The cost of providing transportation within a child safety zone is not state aidable. It is also not considered an ordinary contingent expense (§ 3635-b(10)).

22:4. How are transportation distance limitations measured?

Distances from home to school to determine eligibility for transportation must be measured by the nearest available publicly maintained route from home to school (§ 3635(1)(a); *Matter of Kluge*, 31 Educ. Dep't Rep. 107 (1991); *Matter of Nowak*, 22 Educ. Dep't Rep. 91 (1982)). For example, a district's use of a footpath through a publicly owned and maintained park for purposes of determining the distance from home to school has been upheld by the commissioner and at least one court (*Arlyn Oaks Civic Assn. v. Brucia*, 171 Misc.2d 634 (Sup. Ct. Nassau County 1997); *Appeal of Rosen*, 37 Educ. Dep't Rep. 107 (1997)).

A district's distance determination will be upheld so long as the means of measurement are reasonable. The use of an automobile odometer to measure distance is legally reasonable and sufficient. Proof of calibration is a reasonable response to a bona fide challenge to the accuracy of the odometer as a measuring device (*Appeal of Jagoda*, 34 Educ. Dep't Rep. 154 (1994)). In addition, a district's use of an aerial survey has also been viewed as reasonable by the commissioner (*Appeal of Canossa*, 37 Educ. Dep't Rep. 456 (1998)).

22:5. Are there any restrictions on the length of time a student should ride to or from school?

No. Neither the Education Law or the commissioner's regulations specify a maximum time limit for the transportation of students. The commissioner of education has ruled that, depending on the circumstances, one-way trips of up to one and one-half hours are not necessarily excessive (*Appeal of Devore*, 36 Educ. Dep't Rep. 326 (1997); *Matter of Capozza*, 25 Educ. Dep't Rep. 15 (1985); *Matter of Rouis*, 20 Educ. Dep't Rep. 493 (1981); *Appeal of Polifka*, 31 Educ. Dep't Rep. 61 (1991)).

According to the commissioner, the school board is legally responsible for determining transportation routes and modes of transportation. A school board's transportation determination will be upheld unless the board's actions can be proven to be arbitrary or unreasonable (*Devore; Polifka; Rouis; Matter of Lauth*, 2 Educ. Dep't Rep. 484 (1963)).

On the same basis, the commissioner ruled against a parent who argued the school district should adopt a "first on, first off" policy to prevent students who are picked up early in the morning from being the last to be dropped off in the afternoon (*Appeal of Byrne*, 34 Educ. Dep't Rep. 389 (1995)).

22:6. May a school district provide transportation between school and child-care centers?

Yes. A school board may provide, at its discretion, transportation to any child attending kindergarten through eighth grade between a child's school and before and/or after-school child-care locations in accordance with the district's general transportation mileage limitations. The cost of providing transportation between school and child care centers is state aidable.

The Education Law defines a child-care location as a place within the district, other than the child's home, where care for less than 24 hours a day is provided on a regular basis.

A school board may limit transportation to child-care locations located within the attendance zone of the school the child attends and anywhere within the district for child-care locations licensed pursuant to section 390 of the Social Services Law (*Appeal of Grove*, 33 Educ. Dep't Rep. 176 (1993)).

When a child receives transportation from a before-school child-care location to the school he or she attends, the child is entitled to be transported from the school to his or her home or to an after-school child-care location only if the distance from the school to such location is within the district's mileage limitations. Similarly, when a child receives transportation from school to an after-school child-care location, he or she is entitled to be transported from home to school only if the distance between home and school is within the district's mileage limitations.

The child's parents must request this service in writing no later than April 1 preceding the next school year, except where the family moves into the district later than April 1. In that case, the request must be made within 30 days of establishing residency in the district (§ 3635(1)(e)).

22:7. Must a school district transport children of divorced parents to different locations on different days of the week?

No. According to the commissioner of education, a student can only have a single residence for school purposes even when that student's parents are divorced (see **12:32**). There is no statutory or regulatory requirement that a district transport a student to different places on different days of the week (*Appeal of VanDerJagt*, 33 Educ. Dep't Rep. 517 (1994)).

22:8. Must a school district provide transportation to students who move to the district after the district budget has been passed and bus routes approved?

Yes, under certain circumstances. Transportation must be provided if the parents or guardians submit a written request within 30 days after establishing residency in the district. No late request may be denied if a reasonable explanation is provided for the delay. A statement by the parents that they were not aware of their obligation to submit a timely transportation request normally would not constitute a reasonable explanation for delay (§ 3635(2); see **22:82-83**).

22:9. May a school district use a public carrier for student transportation?

Yes. Occasionally some districts do this by providing the students with bus tickets, a bus pass or railroad tickets. However, they may not advance cash for this purpose (*Matter of Farrell,* 18 Educ. Dep't Rep. 506 (1979)).

22:10. Can a regional transportation system be organized and operated to cover a number of different school districts?

Yes. A regional transportation system may include transportation between home and school, as well as cooperative bus maintenance. These regional services may be conducted jointly with other school districts or boards of cooperative educational services (BOCES) (§§ 1709(25)(g), 1950(4)(q), 3621(8), (9)). BOCES are authorized to provide transportation to and from BOCES classes at a district's request (§ 1950(4)(q)).

22:11. May a student's transportation privileges be suspended?

Yes. The school board and/or the superintendent of schools, not the bus driver, has the authority to suspend the transportation privileges of children who are disorderly and insubordinate. Students' rights to minimal due process applicable in classroom situations are not necessarily applicable to such student transportation cases. However, a student and his or her parents or guardian must be granted an opportunity to appear informally before the person or body authorized to impose discipline to discuss the factual situation underlying the threatened suspension.

In disciplining such a student, a district must consider the effect of a suspension of transportation on the student's attendance and, in some cases, must make appropriate arrangements for the student's education. In such situations, the parents or guardian of the child involved becomes responsible for seeing that the child gets to and from school (*Matter of Stewart,* 21 Educ. Dep't Rep. 654 (1982); *Matter of Roach,* 19 Educ. Dep't Rep. 377 (1980)).

According to the U.S. Department of Education's Office of Civil Rights (OCR), revocation of transportation services for an unruly student with disabilities is subject to the same due process protection that applies to the discipline of disabled students in cases where transportation is a related service (OCR Response to Inquiry, 20 IDELR 864, 867 (1993)).

22:12. Can a school district charge a fee to transport students?

There is no statute that specifically authorizes the board to charge a fee for this purpose. However, a commissioner's decision that a school district may not charge a fee or require a donation as a condition for participation in interscholastic athletic activities implies that such a charge is not permissible (*Matter of Ambrosio,* 30 Educ. Dep't Rep. 387 (1991)).

22:13. May parents transport their own children and collect compensation from the school district for doing so?

Yes, under certain circumstances. Although a district legally can contract with a parent for a student's transportation, this contract may not exceed the actual cost of the services provided (*Matter of Antonette*, 18 Educ. Dep't Rep. 413 (1979)). It should be done only if the district, through competitive bidding or the request for proposal process, has been unable to secure a regular contractor. The child also must be within the required transportation mileage limits. Unless an exemption is granted, the parent must satisfy the requirements of Article 19-a of the Vehicle and Traffic Law and Part 156 of the commissioner's regulations.

According to the New York State Department of Transportation, parents' vehicles used in the transportation of their own children to and from school, and where the parents are being reimbursed accordingly, are not subject to a Department of Transportation inspection. However, if a parent's vehicle is used to transport his or her own children and other children to and from school, and the parent is being reimbursed for transporting other children, that vehicle is subject to a Department of Transportation inspection. Under either scenario, the vehicles will be subject to the Department of Motor Vehicles' inspection program.

Bus Routes

22:14. Must a school bus travel roads that may be impassable or unsafe?

The commissioner of education has held that a school board may refuse to use a public road to provide transportation to students if the board can establish its use would involve an "unreasonably hazardous condition" (*Matter of Clark*, 15 Educ. Dep't Rep. 260 (1976)).

In *Matter of McGibbon*, 14 Educ. Dep't Rep. 271 (1975), for example, the district verified that a road where a parent wanted her child to be picked up by district transportation was so narrow that a school bus and another vehicle could not pass each other, the road did not have safe shoulders, and it included steep grades that buses had been unable to negotiate without skidding into trees. Based on this information, the commissioner held that it was not unreasonable or illegal for the student to walk a mile to a pick-up point, rather than authorize the school bus to travel on an unsafe road.

22:15. May a school bus be routed on private roads?

The commissioner of education has held that a school district is not required to provide transportation to students over privately maintained roads (see *Matter of Cohen*, 21 Educ. Dep't Rep. 280 (1981)). However, a school district may provide transportation to students over privately maintained roads with the landowner's consent (*Appeal of Taylor*, 26 Educ. Dep't Rep. 255 (1986)).

22:16. May a school board designate pick-up points for school buses?

Yes. School districts are not required to provide transportation to students directly to and from home (§ 3635(1)(d)).

A school board is authorized to exercise its discretion in designating pick-up points after considering and balancing issues of student safety, convenience, routing efficiency and cost (*Appeal of Icenogle*, 34 Educ. Dep't Rep. 406 (1995)).

The fact that a pick-up point is located on a heavily traveled road or may require students to wait or travel on unlit narrow roadways with no sidewalks or walkways is insufficient to prove that the pick-up point is unsafe (*Appeal of Behan*, 34 Educ. Dep't Rep. 368 (1995); *Appeal of Krauciunas*, 35 Educ. Dep't Rep. 107 (1995); *Appeal of Jett*, 33 Educ. Dep't Rep. 446 (1994); *Appeal of Waklatsi*, 33 Educ. Dep't Rep. 552 (1994)).

It is the responsibility of the parent, not the school district, to see that his or her child reaches the pick-up point safely (*Appeal of Pauldine*, 35 Educ. Dep't Rep. 54 (1995)).

To afford the greatest possible protection to school children, the school board or superintendent may designate drive-off places on public highways for school buses to be driven off the highway to receive or discharge students. The state or municipality having jurisdiction over a highway so designated is authorized to provide construction and maintenance of drive-offs (§ 3635(5)).

22:17. What is the distance a student can be made to walk to a pick-up point?

The policy on walking distance established for a school district may be applied to side roads as well as to the distance from the student's home to the school itself. For example, if a school policy provides that student who lives more than 4/10ths of a mile will be transported to school, than students can be required to walk up to 4/10ths of a mile to reach the pick-up point (*Appeal of Marsh*, 36 Educ. Dep't Rep. 134 (1996)).

22:18. May a school district establish and maintain shelters for students who take school buses at various places along its bus routes?

There is nothing in the law that prevents school districts from doing this. A district may be ordered to provide additional transportation for children who live off a main route in cases where it is unwilling to provide these children with suitable shelter to wait for the bus, and where the district provides transportation for all other children at a point near their homes (*Matter of Spicer*, 73 St. Dep't Rep. 167 (1952)).

School Buses

22:19. What is the statutory definition of a school bus?

A *school bus* may be "any motor vehicle owned by a public or governmental agency or private school and operated for the transportation of students, teachers and other persons acting in a supervisory capacity, to or from school or school activities or privately owned and operated for compensation for the transportation of students, children of students, teachers and other persons acting in a supervisory capacity to or from school or school activities" (Veh. & Traf. Law § 142).

22:20. What are some of the legitimate and proper uses of district-owned school buses?

In addition to the transportation of students to and from school and/or school activities, district-owned buses and conveyances may be used legitimately for the following:

- Transportation for students and teachers to school-related events such as field trips and athletic events (*Cook v. Griffin*, 47 A.D.2d 23 (4th Dep't 1975); *Matter of O'Donnell*, 18 Educ. Dep't Rep. 259 (1978); see also § 2023(1)).
- Lease to another school district or Indian tribe for certain recreation projects or youth service projects (§ 1709(25)(c)).
- Lease to another school district, to a board of cooperative educational services (BOCES), to a county vocational education and extension board or to an American Indian tribe for educational purposes (§ 1709(25)(b)).
- Rent or lease to any senior citizens' center that is recognized and funded by the office for the aging (§ 1501-b(1)(a)).
- Rent or lease to any non-profit incorporated organization serving senior citizens (§1501-b(1)(b)).
- Rent or lease to any non-profit incorporated organization serving the physically or mentally disabled (§ 1501-b(1)(c)).
- Rent or lease to any not-for-profit organization that provides recreation youth services or runs neighborhood playgrounds or recreation centers (§§ 1501-b(1)(d); 1604(21)).
- Rent or lease to any municipal corporation, as defined in the General Construction Law (§ 1501-b(1)(e)).
- Transportation for certain infants and toddlers of students

enrolled in school district or BOCES programs. This is eligible for state aid (§ 3635(1)(f)).

- For districts wholly or partially located in rural areas, transportation to district residents enrolled in educational, job-training or other programs; children under age five traveling between home and day-care or preschool programs; and employees of school districts or other educational institutions (§ 1502(1)).

Whenever a bus is leased or rented, the consideration to be paid may not be less than the full amount of the costs and expenses incurred as a result thereof. In addition, the lessee must maintain insurance on each bus so leased, protecting the lessor district from all claims by reason of personal injury to persons and property damage (see **22:77**). The lessee also is required to carry fire insurance as well as compensation insurance on the driver of the leased bus. To protect the lessor district against further loss, the lessee also is required to carry collision insurance in the amount of the value of the bus. The cost of this insurance must be paid by the school district or other organization that leases the bus (§§ 1501-b(4); 1604(21); 1709(25)(f)).

Transportation for school purposes does not include the use of school buses for transportation of high school seniors or other groups of students to Washington, D.C. or to any other distant point for activities such as class trips, unless the trip is sponsored and supervised by the school (*Appeal of Bean*, 34 Educ. Dep't Rep. 437 (1995); *Appeal of Thompson*, 21 Educ. Dep't Rep. 287 (1981)).

22:21. Can a district use its school buses to transport its residents to parent-teacher meetings or on shopping trips, for example?

No. These are not authorized uses of school buses.

22:22. Who has ultimate authority for regulating safety and certification of school buses?

The commissioner of transportation in consultation with the commissioner of education is responsible for the adoption, promulgation, and the enforcement of rules, standards, and specifications regulating and controlling the efficiency and equipment of school buses used to transport students. Particular attention is made toward the safety and convenience of students and adaptability of such school buses to the requirements of the school district. No school bus shall be purchased by a school district or used to transport students unless and until it has been approved by the commissioner of transportation as complying with the rules, standards and specifications (§ 3623).

22:23. How often must school buses in New York State be inspected?

School buses in New York State must be inspected every six months. State Department of Transportation regulations provide that school buses cannot be operated unless they carry a certificate of inspection for the preceding six months, prominently displayed in the lower right-hand corner on the interior surface of the windshield (17 NYCRR § 721(3)).

22:24. Must a school bus be identified by a sign?

Yes. Buses having a seating capacity greater than 15 passengers must have the designation "School Bus" displayed conspicuously on two signs located on the exterior of the bus. The black letters must be at least eight inches high, and each stroke of each letter must be at least one inch wide. The background of the signs must be a yellow color known as "national school bus chrome" (Veh & Traf. Law § 375(20)(b)(1)).

These signs must be mounted securely on top of the bus. One must face forward and one must face backward, and each sign must be visible and readable from a distance of at least 200 feet. While the bus is being operated at night, the signs must be illuminated to be visible from a distance of at least 500 feet (Veh. & Traf. Law § 375(20)(b)(2)).

In addition to this, the flashing red signal lamps with which school buses must be equipped must be attached securely in the proper position (15 NYCRR § 46.2(g)). This law applies to vehicles with a seating capacity of seven or more passengers used exclusively to transport pupils, teachers, and other persons acting in a supervisory capacity to and from school or school activities (15 NYCRR § 46.2(a)).

22:25 Must a school bus identify the owner and/or operator of the vehicle?

All school buses purchased, leased or acquired on or after September 1, 1997 must have the area code and telephone number of the owner and/or operator printed in three-inch bold type on the left rear of the bus (Veh. & Traf. Law § 1223-a).

22:26. Must all school buses be painted the same color?

Yes. All school buses, regardless of ownership, having a seating capacity of more than seven passengers, must be painted the yellow color known as "national school bus chrome" (Veh. & Traf. Law § 375(21)).

22:27. Must school buses have safety equipment, such as special mirrors in front of the bus body?

Yes. Under section 375(20-e) of the Vehicle and Traffic Law, each school bus with a seating capacity of more than 12 and with the engine located ahead of the driver must be equipped with a convex mirror mounted in front of the bus. In this way the seated driver can observe the road directly in front of the bus. This is for the protection of students passing in front of the bus after they leave the bus.

School buses must also be equipped with safety glass and backup beepers to alert others when the bus is put in reverse, in addition to other safety equipment (Veh. & Traf. Law §§ 375(11); 375(21-g); 15 NYCRR Part 46).

With certain exceptions, school buses used by contractors that provide transportation to a school district must meet the same safety specifications and requirements as district-owned buses (§ 3623(1)(b)).

22:28. May a school district standardize its fleet with certain makes of school buses?

Yes. A school board may adopt a resolution, by at least a two-thirds vote, which states that for reasons of efficiency or economy, it will standardize the bus fleet. This resolution must include the reasons for its adoption (Gen. Mun. Law § 103(5)).

A need for standardization does not permit a school district to dispense with competitive bidding. It merely authorizes it to specify a particular type or brand. For further information, see "Competitive Bidding under General Municipal Law Section 103" (Opn. St. Comp., 1982, Research Paper, pp. 3017, 3034).

22:29. Must all vehicles owned by the school district and used to transport students meet the requirements that apply to regular school buses?

There are certain requirements for vehicles having seating capacities in excess of seven passengers and other requirements for those with seating capacities in excess of 12 and/or 15 passengers. In addition, special requirements exist for mirrors for vehicles with engines located in front of the driver (see **22:27**). However, the commissioner of transportation is authorized to grant exemptions to the requirements (see Veh. & Traf. Law § 375(20), (21)).

School Bus Safety

22:30. Who is responsible for the supervision and safety of students taking the school bus?

Courts have generally determined that school districts are not liable for the supervision and safety of students who are outside the district's physical custody or authority prior to boarding or after disembarking from a school bus. Custodial control and responsibility at those times rest with the parents (*Pratt v. Robinson*, 39 N.Y.2d 554 (1976)).

However, a court refused to dismiss a lawsuit brought against a school district by a parent who charged the district was responsible for a student's injuries where a district representative had promised to ensure that the student rode the school bus home rather than travel in another student's car. The court held that while a school district does not have a duty to compel students to ride the school bus home, by making the promise, the district may have undertaken a special duty to the student (*Wenger v. Goodell,* 220 A.D.2d 937 (3rd Dep't 1995)).

By contrast, another district was sued by the parent of a student who suffered severe injuries when struck by her school bus after she had disembarked (*Chainani v. Board of Education of the City of New York,* 87 N.Y.2d 370 (1995)). The school bus was driven by the employee of a bus company serving as an independent contractor. The court ruled that the district was not directly liable for the student's injuries because the student was not within the custody of the school district at the time of the accident but rather was in the custody of the independent contractor. The court also refused to hold the school district vicariously liable for the student's injuries because the activity of transporting students is not inherently dangerous.

22:31. Must students cross in front of the school bus when they are being picked up or discharged from it?

Yes. The driver of the school bus must instruct those students who must cross the highway or street to cross 10 feet in front of the bus, and the driver must keep the school bus halted with red signal lights flashing until they have reached the opposite side of the highway or street (Veh. & Traf. Law § 1174(b); 8 NYCRR § 156.3(4)).

22:32. May the school district employ a school crossing guard to direct traffic for school buses on a public highway?

No. However, section 2080-a of the General Municipal Law gives any city, town or village the authority to appoint school crossing guards for these purposes (see Inf. Opn. Att'y Gen. 84-30; see also § 806; *Matter of Glasner,* 7 Educ. Dep't Rep. 15 (1967)).

22:33. Does a school district have the right to regulate or restrict traffic on school property?

Yes. School districts may regulate, restrict or prohibit parking or standing, the direction and speed of traffic, and movement of motor traffic on any parking fields, driveways or public ways accessory to any school, playground or facility under their jurisdiction (Veh. & Traf. Law

§ 1670). Any violation of district traffic regulations will be considered a traffic infraction (Opn. St. Comp. 79-26).

In addition, section 1174 of the Vehicle and Traffic Law prohibits motorists from passing stopped school buses while they are boarding or discharging school children on school property.

22:34. What is the state law in relation to vehicles overtaking or meeting buses transporting children to or from school?

A vehicle overtaking or meeting a bus transporting children to and from school that is stopped to receive or discharge passengers on a public highway must come to a complete stop and remain stationary until the bus resumes motion or until signaled by the driver or a police officer to proceed, provided the bus carries flashing red signal lights and signs designating it as a school bus that are displayed as required by law (Veh. & Traf. Law § 1174).

22:35. Are school buses permitted to have stop-arm devices and two-way radios?

Yes. These devices are authorized as allowable transportation expenses but are not required (§ 3623-a(2)(c); 15 NYCRR §§46.6, 46.7).

22:36. Are seat belts for students required equipment on all school buses?

All school buses manufactured after July 1, 1987 must be designed to include seat belts and increased seat padding on the passenger seats. In addition, all motor vehicles weighing 10,000 pounds or less and used to transport students must have seat belts, regardless of the date of first use. The seat belts must be approved by the commissioner of transportation (15 NYCRR § 49.6; Veh. & Traf. Law § 383 (5)(a)). Drivers' seat belts are required on all school bus vehicles owned or leased by the district (Veh. & Traf. Law § 383(4-a)).

22:37. Are school districts required to compel students to wear seat belts while on the school bus?

No. However, after a public hearing, a school board may choose to adopt a resolution that provides for the use of seat belts on school buses (§ 3635-a).

Chapter 684 of the Laws of 1995 directs the State Education Department, in conjunction with various other state agencies, to develop and disseminate materials explaining the safety advantages of seat belt use on school buses.

According to section 3813(4) of the Education Law, when a lawsuit is brought against a school district, a school bus operator under contract with a district, or an operator of a school bus (including a driver, matron or teacher serving as a chaperon), no such person shall be held liable solely because the injured party was not wearing a seat belt.

22:38. Are school districts required to provide students with instruction on the use of seat belts?

Districts which transport students on school buses equipped with seat belts must insure that all students who are transported on any school bus owned, leased or contracted for by the district receive instruction on the use of seat belts. Instruction must be provided to both public and nonpublic school students at least three times a year (8 NYCRR § 156.3(i)).

22:39. Is there a law regarding standees on a school bus?

Currently, "20 percent of seated capacity" legally are permitted to stand (8 NYCRR § 156.2(b)). However, section 1229-b of the Vehicle and Traffic Law makes unlawful the operation of a school, camp or charter omnibus for 10 or more miles with any passenger standing.

22:40. May a school district use video cameras on school buses to ensure the safety of the driver and passengers?

Yes, video cameras may be used on school buses that transport students (8 NYCRR § 156.9(d)(1)). These cameras may be used to record the students' conduct to ensure their safety and to serve as evidence of their conduct for disciplinary purposes, if necessary.

22:41. Are emergency drills required on all school buses?

Yes. The commissioner's regulations (8 NYCRR § 156.3(h)) require emergency drills on school buses. These drills must include practice and instruction in the location, use and operation of the emergency door, fire extinguisher, first-aid equipment and windows as a means of escape in case of fire or accident (§ 3623)(1)(c)).

Drills also must include instruction in safe boarding and exiting procedures with specific emphasis on when and how to approach, board, disembark and move away from the bus after disembarking. They must include specific instructions for students to advance at least 10 feet in front of the bus before crossing the highway after disembarking. They must address specific hazards encountered by students during snow, ice, rain and other inclement weather, including, but not necessarily limited to, poor driver visibility, reduced vehicular control and reduced hearing. They must include instruction in the importance of orderly conduct by all school bus passengers, with emphasis on student discipline. This instruction and the conduct of the drills must be given by a member or members of the teaching or student transportation staff.

Students attending public and nonpublic schools who do not participate in these drills must also be provided with drills on school buses, or, as an alternative, must be provided with classroom instruction covering their content. A minimum of three drills must be held during the school year, the first to be conducted during the first week of the fall term, the second between November 1 and December 31, and the third between March 1 and April 30. No drills should be conducted when buses are en route.

School authorities must certify in their annual report to the State Education Department that their district has complied with this requirement.

22:42. Is there an established speed limit for school buses?

Yes. Although the Vehicle and Traffic Law specifies a maximum speed limit of 55 miles per hour, and 65 miles per hour on certain stretches of specified state highways located in rural areas, the Education Law specifies that the maximum speed at which school vehicles may be operated shall be 55 miles per hour (§ 3624).

Other restrictions on speed in populated areas and elsewhere as conditions warrant are imposed by cities, villages and the state Department of Transportation. School bus drivers should observe these regulations conscientiously at all times, and also should operate at speeds that are reasonable in terms of prevailing road, traffic and weather conditions. Speed should be reduced at curves, blind crossings, crests of hills, in fog or wherever the view is curtailed so the bus will be able to stop within the distance of clear vision.

22:43. Must a school bus keep its headlights illuminated when transporting students?

Yes. School buses must keep their lights on, day or night, when transporting students (Veh. & Traf. Law § 375(20)(i)).

22:44. Is a school bus permitted to turn right at a red traffic signal?

If the school bus is transporting students, the driver cannot turn right for any purpose if the bus is facing a steady red signal (Veh. & Traf. Law § 1111(5)).

22:45. Must school buses stop at all railroad crossings?

Yes. School buses must stop at all railroad crossings, whether or not they carry students, and proceed only when the driver can do so safely. While crossing the tracks, the driver must not shift gears. Drivers are not required to open school bus doors when crossing railroad tracks (Veh. & Traf. Law § 1171(a)).

Section 3636 of the Education Law provides a school district may not use an unguarded railroad crossing when transporting students to and from school or other places unless a public hearing has been held and a resolution adopted by the school board has determined using another route would be impractical. This resolution must be filed with the State Education Department and the state Department of Transportation. Additionally, the district must prepare and maintain a map indicating the bus route used and must make it available for inspection by any resident of the district at a place designated by the school board.

22:46. May a school district have a policy which limits the type of objects a student may bring onto a school bus?

Yes. State Department of Transportation regulations provide that the main aisle and the aisle to the door of a school bus may not be obstructed (15 NYCRR §721.7(a)). In one case, the commissioner of education upheld a district policy which prohibited students from carrying items on the bus which could not fit on their laps. The items listed in the policy which were not allowed on the bus included all musical instruments, other than flutes or clarinets, hockey sticks, lacrosse sticks, baseball bats, ski equipment, large equipment bags, large art displays, and any other item of similar size and shape (*Appeal of Moyer*, 37 Educ. Dep't Rep. 335 (1998)).

School Bus Drivers

22:47. How is a school bus driver defined under the commissioner's regulations?

A *school bus driver* is any person who drives a school bus owned, leased or contracted for by a public school district for the purpose of transporting students. However, a driver of a passenger or suburban type of vehicle is not considered a school bus driver if he or she is a school district employee who does not ordinarily transport students and is operating that vehicle to transport one or more students to a hospital or other medical facility, a physician's office, or home for medical treatment or because of illness. Likewise, a driver of a suburban intercity coach or transit bus who transports students on trips other than between home and school, such as field trips and athletic trips, is not considered to be a school bus driver. A parent who transports only his or her own children is also excluded from this definition (8 NYCRR §156.3(a)).

22:48. What are the qualifications for a school bus driver?

Although the superintendent of schools must approve the employment of each bus driver for each bus owned or operated within the district, the qualifications of school bus drivers are determined by regulations of the commissioner of education and the commissioner of motor vehicles (Educ. Law § 3624).

For an individual to be qualified as a school bus driver, he or she must:

- Be at least 21 years of age (8 NYCRR § 156.3(b)).
- Have a currently valid driver's license or permit that is valid for the operation of a bus in New York State (8 NYCRR § 156.3(d)).
- Pass a physical examination established by the commissioners of education and motor vehicles (8 NYCRR § 156.3(c)(1),(2)).
- Pass a physical performance test established by the commissioner of education (8 NYCRR § 156.3(c)(3)).
- Furnish to the superintendent at least three statements from three different persons not related to the applicant assessing his or her moral character and reliability (8 NYCRR § 156.3(e)).
- Not be disqualified to drive a school bus because of a conviction, violation or infraction listed in section 509-c or section 509-cc of the Vehicle and Traffic Law, or under any other provision of article 19-A of that law.
- Meet all other licensing and training requirements for driving a school bus (Veh. & Traf. Law §§ 501, 509–b, 509–c; 8 NYCRR § 156.3).

22:49. What are the licensure requirements for school bus drivers?

Licensure requirements for all school bus drivers currently are covered by article 19–A of the Vehicle and Traffic Law (§ 509–a to 509–o), part 6 of the rules and regulations of the commissioner of motor vehicles and part 156 of the regulations of the commissioner of education.

Federal and state laws require all school bus drivers to be issued a commercial driver's license (CDL) (Veh. & Traf. Law §§ 501-a(1), 509-b; 49 USC § 31308). This CDL is required of all commercial drivers, including school bus drivers.

The Education Law allows schools to receive transportation aid for certain approved costs associated with the new licensing regulations such as the training of drivers for the CDL and the expenses incurred in fingerprinting drivers for background checks (Educ. Law § 3602(7)(b); see also **22:55**).

22:50. What course of training is required for school bus drivers?

Each school bus driver initially employed by a school board or transportation contractor after July 1, 1973 must complete at least two hours of instruction on school bus safety practices. Each driver initially employed after January 1, 1976 who transports only students with disabilities must receive an additional hour of instruction concerning the special needs of such students (8 NYCRR § 156.3(d)(2)).

During his or her first year of employment, each driver must complete a course of instruction in school bus safety practices approved by the commissioner of education that includes two hours of instruction concerning the special needs of students with disabilities. All school bus drivers must complete a minimum of two hours of refresher instruction in school bus safety at least two times a year, at sessions conducted before the first day of school and before February 1 of each year. Refresher courses for drivers who transport students with disabilities exclusively also must include instruction relating to the special needs of such students (8 NYCRR § 156.3(d)(2)).

All training must be provided by or under the direct supervision of a school bus driver instructor approved by the commissioner of education, with the exception of pre-service training (8 NYCRR § 156.3(d)(3)). An approved school bus driver instructor's physical presence is not required during training conducted on the initial employment of a school bus driver by the board or transportation contractor, provided such training is conducted under the general supervision of such an instructor (8 NYCRR § 156.3(d)(3)(i).

Upon completion of the training requirements described above, each driver's compliance should be verified through the district's record-keeping system.

22:51. Must occasional drivers receive the training specified in 22:50?

No. Under the commissioner of education's regulations, an *occasional driver* is defined as a certified teacher employed by a school district or board of cooperative educational services (BOCES) who is not primarily employed as a school bus driver or substitute school bus driver on either a full-time or part-time basis. Occasional drivers used for other than regular routes are not required to fulfill the training described in **22:50** (8 NYCRR § 156.3(d)(2)).

22:52. Are school bus drivers required to meet basic physical requirements?

Yes. Each school bus driver must meet the requirements of section 6.11 of the regulations of the commissioner of motor vehicles, and the basic minimum physical requirements specified in the regulations of the commissioner of education, concerning, for example, vision and hearing. The superintendent must consider the physician's written report in determining the driver's fitness to operate or continue to operate any transportation vehicle used by students (Educ. Law § 3624).

22:53. Are school bus drivers required to undergo physical examinations?

Yes. Each regular or substitute driver of a school bus owned, leased or contracted for by a school district must be examined every year by a physician. When a driver is initially hired, he or she must be examined within four weeks prior to the beginning of service. The results of these physical examinations must be reported immediately to the superintendent on forms prescribed by the commissioner of education (8 NYCRR § 156.3(c)).

22:54. Are school bus drivers required to pass a physical performance test?

Yes. After September 1, 1997, all bus drivers must pass a physical performance test approved by the commissioner of education, at least once every two years. Drivers employed as of this date have until July 1, 2000 to take and pass the test.

The test is to be conducted by a certified school bus driver instructor. To pass the test, a bus driver must be able to perform the following functions:

- Repeatedly open and close a manually operated bus entrance door.
- Climb and descend bus steps.
- Operate hand controls simultaneously and quickly.
- Have quick reaction time from throttle to brake.
- Carry or drag individuals in a bus emergency evacuation.
- Repeatedly depress clutch and/or brake pedals.
- Exit quickly oneself and students from an emergency door.

A bus driver who fails any part of the test may not operate a school bus until he or she passes a re-examination test. The re-examination must be taken no sooner than three days from the prior test. The employer will be responsible for paying for the re-examination if the bus driver passes; the bus driver is responsible for the cost if he or she fails the re-examination (8 NYCRR § 156.3(3); see also "School Bus Driver Performance Test Guidelines," State Education Department, August, 1997).

22:55. Must school bus drivers be fingerprinted?

Yes. Section 509–d(2) of the Vehicle and Traffic Law and section 6.4(b) of the motor vehicle regulations require all school bus drivers to be fingerprinted so a school district may obtain any criminal record from state and federal authorities. In addition, driving and employment records must be obtained (see **22:56-58**).

Districts can obtain reimbursement for most costs associated with fingerprinting school bus drivers as a result of legislative changes accompanying the commercial driver's license (Educ. Law § 3602(7)); see **22:49**).

22:56. Is a school district required to check a person's employment record before employing him or her as a school bus driver?

Yes. The school district must conduct an investigation of the driver's employment record during the preceding three years, in a manner prescribed by the commissioner of motor vehicles (Veh. & Traf. Law § 509-d(1)(iii)).

22:57. Is a school district required to check a person's driving record before employing that person as a school bus driver?

Yes. A school district must obtain the driving record of each bus driver it employs from the appropriate agency in every state in which that driver resided or worked and/or held a driver's license or learner's permit during the preceding three years, in a manner prescribed by the commissioner of motor vehicles (Veh. & Traf. Law § 509-d(1)(ii)). A copy of the response by each state, showing the driving record or certifying that no driving record exists for that driver, must be kept on file by the school district for three years (§ 509-d(3)). The driving record must be updated annually, and all records must be retained for three years (§ 509-f).

22:58. Is a school bus driver required to report his or her convictions for violations of the Vehicle and Traffic Law to his or her employer?

Yes. A school bus driver who is convicted of a misdemeanor or felony under the Vehicle and Traffic Law, or who has his or her driver's license revoked, suspended or withdrawn, must notify his or her employer by the end of the business day following the date when the driver received notice of such action. Failure to provide this notice will subject the driver to a suspension of five working days or a suspension equivalent to the number of working days that the driver was not in compliance with this requirement, whichever is longer (Veh. & Traf. Law § 509-i(1)).

A school bus driver convicted of a traffic infraction in any jurisdiction must notify his or her employer within five working days of such a conviction. Failure to provide such notice within the required time period will subject the driver to a suspension of five working days (Veh. & Traf. Law § 509-i(1-a)).

22:59. Is a school bus driver required to report his or her involvement in an accident to his or her employer?

Yes. A driver who is involved in an accident as defined in section 509-a of the Vehicle and Traffic Law, in any jurisdiction, must notify his or her employer within five working days from the date of the accident. Failure to so notify within the required time period will subject the driver to a suspension of five working days (Veh. & Traf. Law § 509–i(1-b), see also **22:62**).

22:60. Does the school bus driver have responsibility to maintain order on the bus?

Yes. School bus drivers are held responsible for reasonable behavior of students in transit (8 NYCRR § 156.3(f)(2)). However, drivers have no authority to suspend students for disorderly conduct. They should report those students who violate established rules to the school principal who should take appropriate action (see **22:11**).

22:61. Are school bus drivers subject to alcohol and drug testing?

Yes. School bus drivers who operate a commercial motor vehicle and are required to have commercial drivers licenses (CDLs) are subject to alcohol and drug testing, according to federal regulations adopted to implement the Omnibus Transportation Employee Testing Act of 1991 (49 CFR Parts 382, 391). A school bus driver is subject to this requirement only when driving a vehicle which is designed to transport 16 or more passengers, including the driver (49 CFR §§ 382.103, 382.107).

Operating a school bus while under the influence of alcohol and drugs is a crime under state law, punishable by fines, imprisonment or both (Veh. & Traf. Law §§ 1193(1)(d)(1-a), (4-a); (2)(b)(4-a)).

22:62. When must bus drivers submit to alcohol and drug testing?

The regulations require school districts to have programs in place that will test school bus drivers for alcohol and drugs:

- Before they are employed as bus drivers, they must submit to drug testing (49 CFR § 382.301; see The Federal Register, vol. 60, no. 90, 24765 (May 10, 1995)).
- After a bus accident has occurred, if there was a fatality, or if the driver was cited for a moving violation in connection with the accident and there is an injury treated away from the scene of the accident or a disabled vehicle is towed away from the scene (49 CFR § 382.303(a)(1),(2); see **22:59**).

- If there is reasonable suspicion that the driver has used drugs or alcohol (49 CFR § 382.307).
- Randomly, a minimum percentage of a district's average number of bus drivers per year — 25 percent for alcohol and 50 percent for drugs. These percentages may vary, depending upon the Federal Highway Authority. Random tests must be unannounced and spread reasonably throughout the year (49 CFR § 382.305).
- A return-to-duty test for drivers who have previously tested positive and who have been evaluated by a substance abuse professional, before returning to work (49 CFR § 382.309).
- Unannounced follow-up tests on drivers referred by substance abuse professionals for alcohol or drug counseling and who have returned to work (49 CFR § 382.311).

Prior to implementing the testing programs, school districts must provide school bus drivers with information regarding the policy and regulation requirements, as well as information on alcohol and drug treatment programs and resources (49 CFR §§ 382.113; 382.601).

22:63. Are bus driver alcohol and drug testing results confidential?

The general rule is that alcohol and drug testing records are confidential and may not be revealed to anyone other than the employer without the driver's consent. However, under federal regulations, employers must make these records available to an authorized representative of the U.S. Department of Transportation, when requested, or any local or state official with regulatory authority over the employer or drivers. In addition, an employer may disclose the test results in proceedings related to benefits sought by the employee, such as worker's compensation or unemployment insurance compensation. Post-accident records may also be disclosed to the National Transportation Safety Board in the course of an accident investigation, or as required by state law (49 CFR § 382.405; News Alert, U.S. Department of Transportation, Federal Highway Administration, Region One, March 27, 1998).

22:64. May a school bus driver be precluded from driving a school bus based upon alcohol and/or drug consumption?

Yes. In accordance with federal and state law a school bus driver must not drive a school bus if he or she:

1. Possesses, consumes or is reasonably believed to possess or have consumed alcohol or a controlled substance, while on duty.

2. Uses or is under the influence of alcohol or a controlled substance within six hours or less before duty.

3. Has an alcohol concentration of 0.02 or higher, or tests positive for a controlled substance; or refuses to take a required alcohol or controlled substance test.

Any employee who is tested and found to have an alcohol concentration of at least 0.02, but less than 0.04, shall be removed from the position until his or her next regularly scheduled duty period, but not less than 24 hours following the test.

If the driver has an alcohol concentration of 0.04 or greater, or has engaged in prohibited alcohol or controlled substance use, he or she will be removed from driving duties, and referred to a substance abuse professional. No driver who has abused controlled substances or alcohol may return to duty unless he or she has successfully passed a required return to duty test (49 CFR § 382.307(e)(2); Veh. & Traf. Law § 509-l).

22:65. Are school districts required to pay for the rehabilitation of bus drivers who fail an alcohol or drug test?

No. Any treatment or rehabilitation program must be provided in accordance with the employer's policy or labor/management contracts. The regulations do not require the employer to provide rehabilitation, pay for treatment or reinstate the employee (49 CFR § 382.605(d)).

Purchase and Lease of School Buses and Transportation Services

22:66. How are contracts for the transportation of children awarded?

At the school board's discretion, contracts for the transportation of students that involve an annual expenditure in excess of $10,000, as specified in the bidding requirements of the General Municipal Law, may be awarded through the competitive bidding process or through an evaluation of proposals process (Educ. Law § 305(14)(a),(e); 8 NYCRR § 156.12). All contracts for the transportation of students must be approved by the commissioner of education (§ 305(14)(a)).

A school board is not required to undergo either process if it chooses to extend an existing contract for the transportation of students for up to five years or needs to amend a transportation contract in order to comply with federal or state regulations, or to enhance safety, so long as there is no increased cost associated with the amendment (§§ 305 (14)(a), (d); 8 NYCRR § 156.5).

22:67. What procedures must a school district follow if it elects to award a transportation contract by the competitive bidding process?

If a school board elects to award a transportation contract through competitive bidding, the transportation contract must be advertised in the same manner as purchase contracts under section 103 of the General Municipal Law (§ 305(14)(a)). All advertisements for bids must be published in a newspaper or newspapers, designated by the school board or trustees, with general circulation within the district. The advertisement must state when and where bids will be publicly opened and read, either by school authorities or their designee. At least five days must elapse between the first publication of the advertisement and the opening of bids (§ 305(14)(a)).

If a district is faced with an emergency affecting student transportation services and must take immediate action, the school board may negotiate interim transportation contracts for a period not to exceed one month. During this time, the board or a district trustee must advertise for bids and award a contract as required by the law. The approved costs of the interim contracts will be eligible for transportation aid (§ 305(14)(b)).

22:68. What is a request for proposals?

A *request for proposals* is an alternative to the competitive bidding process for the award of transportation contracts (§ 305(14)(e)). If a school board elects to award a transportation contract through the request for proposal process, it must take the following criteria into account:

- The previous experience of the contractor in transporting students.
- The name of each transportation company of which the contractor has been an owner or manager.
- A description of any safety programs implemented by the contractor.
- A record of motor vehicle accidents under control of the contractor.
- The driving history of the contractor's employees.
- Inspection and maintenance records and model year of each motor vehicle under control of the contractor.
- A financial analysis of the contractor.
- Documentation of compliance with motor vehicle insurance requirements.
- Total cost of the proposal (§ 305(14)(f); 8 NYCRR § 156.12).

A school district soliciting proposals must specify the criteria to be used in evaluating each proposal as well as the weightings that the board will assign to each criteria. No single criteria may be weighted in excess of 50 percent of the total weight of all of the criteria to be used (8 NYCRR § 156.12(c)).

Proposals for transportation contracts for the following school year must be requested no later than June 1, except for contracts for transporting students with disabilities, which must be requested by July 1 of the school year for which such contracts are to be awarded (8 NYCRR § 156.12(e)).

Interim contracts may be awarded for a period not to exceed one month in the case of an emergency or unforeseen occurrence or condition affecting transportation services (8 NYCRR § 156.12(f)).

22:69. Must transportation contracts be approved by the commissioner of education?

Yes. The standard transportation contract states that it will not become valid and binding upon either party until it has been approved by the commissioner of education (§ 3635(4)). Any such contract must be filed with the State Education Department within 120 days of the commencement of service under the contract. The contract must state the contractor agrees to come to a full stop before crossing any railroad track or state highway (§ 3625(1), (2)).

Transportation contracts may be made for a period not exceeding five years if the terms are approved by the district voters (§§ 1604(23), 1709(27)). These must be in writing, approved by the school superintendent, and signed by the superintendent and the school board president (§ 3625(1), (2)).

A contract extension may exceed the maximum amount specified, referenced by the consumer price index, to compensate for the criminal history and driver licensing testing fees attributable to special requirements for school bus drivers (Veh. & Traf. Law Arts. 19 and 19-A). These costs must be approved by the commissioner (§ 305(14)(c)) .

The state comptroller also is authorized to audit the financial records relating to contracts of school bus contractors that provide school transportation to districts (§ 3625(2)).

22:70. Must a school district competitively bid the purchase of a school bus?

Yes. Section 103 of the General Municipal Law requires competitive bidding on all purchase contracts involving all expenditures of more than $10,000 (see **19:45-50** for more information on the bidding process).

22:71. Must a school bus purchase be approved by the commissioner of education?

Yes. Any school bus purchase by a district must be approved by the commissioner of education (see 8 NYCRR § 156.4)

The bus purchase and financing must be approved by the school board. Financing may be by a bond, note or authorized as a specific item in the budget.

22:72. May school districts participate in cooperative purchasing of school buses?

Yes. School districts may purchase school buses and other items cooperatively (Gen. Mun. Law 5-g). This method requires the adoption of specifications that will be agreeable to all in the group. The voters of each district must grant the necessary appropriation or authorization to borrow money. The major benefit is the possibility of securing lower prices through quantity buying. Each district must award its own contract for purchase.

22:73. May a school district purchase a school bus through an installment purchase contract?

Yes. However, these contracts are subject to competitive bidding requirements, and installment payments may not be financed by the issuance of bonds or notes (Gen. Mun. Law § 109(b)). For further information, see "Competitive Bidding Under General Municipal Law Section 103" (Opn. St. Comp., 1982, Research Paper, pp. 3027-29).

22:74. May school districts lease school buses?

Yes. School buses may be leased under emergency conditions that include, but are not limited to, strikes, delay in delivery date, theft, vandalism, fire and accident (§ 1709(25)(e)). Such approval should be for no more than 90 days unless the emergency continues (8 NYCRR § 156.6). Additionally, the school board may replace a school bus because of damage or loss. It may be purchased by the board without voter approval, using any unencumbered funds, or by using budget notes (§ 1709(25)(a)); Loc. Fin. Law § 29.00).

In addition, the board may lease a motor vehicle to be used to transport students to and from school or BOCES for one school year, or for up to five years with voter approval. Once the initial lease expires, any additional lease for the same or equivalent vehicles requires voter approval (§§ 1604(31-a); 1709(25)(i); 2503(12-a)). No voter approval is required in the Big 5 school districts (§ 2554(19-a)).

22:75. Are motor vehicle fees required for district-owned conveyances?

No. School buses are exempt from these fees. School buses are also exempt from registration fees for license plates, as are district-owned snowplowing and grass-cutting tractors (Veh. & Traf. Law § 401(11)). They are also exempt from all state and federal taxes.

22:76. What transportation-related items may districts purchase through state contracts?

The state Division of Standards and Purchases gives school districts the opportunity to purchase, through state contracts, items such as school buses, gasoline, tires, spark plugs and motor oil, all at considerable savings. The purchase or series of purchases of a specific item should exceed $500; however, the amount need not be spent at any one time but may be spread over a period of time.

Inquiries about state contracts can be directed to the Office of General Services, Division of Purchasing, Empire State Plaza Albany, N.Y. 12242. Nonpublic schools may purchase state contract items through local school districts (Gen. Mun. Law § 109-a).

22:77. What insurance must be carried on a school bus?

Minimum and maximum levels for public liability and property damage insurance for school buses are contained in section 370 of the Vehicle and Traffic Law. The law establishes a minimum amount of indemnity for damages and injuries to persons and for property damage.

Each board must determine whether the statutory minimum sufficiently protects the district. If a board desires insurance in excess of the minimum, the amount of coverage must be specified in the district's advertisement for transportation contract bids. No-fault automobile insurance applies to school vehicles, although this law does not apply to losses incurred through property damage.

State Aid for Transportation

22:78. How is student transportation aid calculated?

Transportation aid is paid on general operations and on bus purchases. All school districts are entitled to transportation aid, between 6.5 percent and 90 percent of their approved transportation expense (§§ 3602(7); 3622-a; 3623-a).

If the voters approve transportation beyond the state-mandated mileage limitations, the transportation for the distance beyond one and one-half and two or three miles and over 15 miles is eligible for transportation aid (§§ 3621(2)(a); 3635(1)(a); 8 NYCRR § 156.2(a)).

The amount of state aid payable on the purchase of a school bus is limited to the state contract price for a similar bus, or, if no similar bus is available under a state contract, to the statewide median cost of similar buses. Aid on bus purchases may be reduced based on calculations made by the State Education Department (§ 3602(7)(c)).

Section 3602(7)(b) of the Education Law makes the following additional expenses eligible for transportation aid: health, life and other insurance premiums for transportation personnel for whom salaries are approved; premiums for collision and other insurance coverage; uniforms; equipment; and other expenses approved by the commissioner's regulations.

22:79. Do school districts receive state aid for out-of-district transportation of students to nonpublic schools?

Yes. State aid for transportation of students to nonpublic schools is based on the same criteria as that of aid to public schools (§ 3622-a(4); see 22:8).

22:80. Is state aid available for the transportation of students above grade six to another school district when the district does not furnish instruction for these grades?

Yes. Districts that do not maintain a secondary school must provide transportation, when necessary, for their students who have completed the work in the sixth grade and are receiving instruction in another district. These districts are eligible for transportation aid under the same rules that apply to other transportation (§ 3622-a(2)).

22:81. Is state aid available for the transportation of students with disabilities?

Yes. The Education Law provides that school districts transporting students with disabilities to and from school are eligible for state aid reimbursement of between 6.5 percent and 90 percent of the approved cost of such transportation provided.

However, it also provides that this transportation may not be in excess of 50 miles from the home of such a student to the appropriate special service or program, unless the commissioner of education certifies that no appropriate nonresidential special service or program is available within 50 miles. In this case, the commissioner may establish, by regulation, a maximum number of trips between a student's home and the private residential school that provides special services or programs (§ 4405(2); see also 8 NYCRR § 200.12).

Transportation to Nonpublic Schools

22:82. Are school districts required to provide transportation to nonpublic school students?

Yes. The Education Law requires that school districts must provide transportation to nonpublic school students within the same mileage limits established for resident students attending public schools (§ 3635). A school district is not required to transport students to a nonpublic school by private carrier rather than public transportation (*Appeal of Lavin*, 32 Educ. Dep't Rep. 249 (1992)).

To determine eligibility, the distance to be measured is from the student's home to the nonpublic school (see **22:4**). To the extent a school district provides transportation to public school students beyond what is required by law, it must also provide such additional transportation equally to students who attend nonpublic schools (§ 3635(1); *Appeal of Defeis*, 34 Educ. Dep't Rep. 408 (1995); *Appeal of Whitaker*, 33 Educ. Dep't Rep. 59 (1993); *Matter of Eberhardt*, 25 Educ. Dep't Rep. 263 (1986); *Matter of McIntyre*, 25 Educ. Dep't Rep. 156 (1985)).

If a district provides transportation to students who attend a particular nonpublic school and live within the district's mileage limitations, it must designate one or more public schools as a centralized pick-up point for the transportation of students who attend the nonpublic school but live outside the district's mileage limitations (§ 3635(1)(b)(i); *Appeal of Defeis*). The nonpublic school students that live beyond the mileage limitations must be transported from the centralized pick-up point to their respective nonpublic schools.

A school district may also provide transportation from a centralized pick-up point to a nonpublic school student whose school is located more than 15 miles from the student's residence if the district has provided transportation to that school in at least one of the three prior years, and the distance between the pick-up point and the nonpublic school is not more than 15 miles (§ 3635(1)(b)(ii); *Defeis*).

The school district is responsible for the supervision of students at a centralized pick-up point. However, once children are transported to the nonpublic school, responsibility for their supervision belongs to the nonpublic school even if the children arrive before the start of the school day (*Appeal of Hamilton*, 21 Educ. Dep't Rep. 30 (1981)).

The cost of providing transportation between centralized pick-up points and nonpublic schools is an ordinary contingent expense (§ 3635(1)(b)(ii)).

22:83. Under what circumstances may a school district deny transportation to an otherwise eligible nonpublic school student?

A parent must submit a request in writing for transportation to a nonpublic school no later than April 1, unless the family moves into the district after April 1, in which case the request must be made within 30 days of establishing residency (§ 3635(2)). A change in designation of a nonpublic school after the April 1 deadline constitutes a separate request

(*Appeal of Galvani,* 34 Educ. Dep't Rep. 370 (1995); *Appeal of McNair,* 33 Educ. Dep't Rep. 418 (1994)).

The filing of a late request may result in a denial of transportation, even where the district has previously accepted late requests (*Appeal of Beer,* 33 Educ. Dep't Rep. 620 (1994)).

No late request may be denied, however, if a reasonable explanation is provided for the delay. The school board has discretion to determine the reasonableness of the excuse, and its decision will not be set aside unless it constitutes an abuse of discretion *(Matter of Skinner,* 29 Educ. Dep't Rep. 200 (1990)). A board, for example, need not accept ignorance or forgetfulness of the April 1 deadline as a reasonable excuse (*Appeal of Haque,* 34 Educ. Dep't Rep. 496 (1995)). Similarly, a belated parental decision to enroll a child in a nonpublic school is not a reasonable excuse (*Appeal of Hause,* 34 Educ. Dep't Rep. 374 (1995); *Appeal of Young,* 34 Educ. Dep't Rep. 350 (1995); *Appeal of Somer,* 34 Educ. Dep't Rep. 16 (1994)).

On the other hand, the commissioner of education ruled a parent offered a reasonable excuse for failing to meet the April 1 deadline where the student had been admitted to a private boarding school but was subsequently denied enrollment after April 1 *(Appeal of Lamba,* 32 Educ. Dep't Rep. 473 (1993); *Application to Reopen the Appeal of Lamba,* 32 Educ. Dep't Rep. 611 (1993)).

Reliance on a nonpublic school to submit a list of students requiring transportation (see **22:88**) is not a reasonable excuse for filing a late request *(Matter of Hendricks,* 21 Educ. Dep't Rep. 302 (1981)).

Even in the absence of a reasonable explanation for the delay, a late request must be granted if the transportation request can be provided under existing transportation arrangements at no additional cost to the district (*Appeal of Mendoza,* 34 Educ. Dep't Rep. 402 (1995); *Appeal of Frasier,* 34 Educ. Dep't Rep. 404 (1995)).

22:84. Must public school districts provide transportation to nonpublic schools on days when public schools are not in session?

No. However, New York City must provide transportation to nonpublic schools for a maximum of five days, or a maximum of 10 days in any year in which the last day of Passover and Easter Sunday are separated by more than seven days, when public schools are not in session. Such five or 10 additional days are limited to the Wednesday, Thursday and Friday after Labor Day; Rosh Hashanah; Yom Kippur; the week in which public schools are closed for spring recess; and the week between Christmas Day and New Year's Day (§ 3635(2-a)).

22:85. Are school districts responsible for providing transportation to nonpublic school students between their home and a centralized pick-up point?

No. A district is not obligated to provide transportation to nonpublic school students to and from the centralized pick-up point. However, the Education Law allows a district to provide a nonpublic school student residing outside the mileage limitation required for transportation to the nonpublic school with transportation to the centralized pick-up point if the student lives on an established bus route for the transportation of students to the public school serving as the centralized pick-up point, and from there on to the nonpublic school (§ 3635(1)(b)(i)).

22:86. Must a school district transport students who attend release-time religious instruction from the public school to a church or parochial school?

No. School districts have no legal authority to provide this service (*Appeal of Fitch*, 2 Educ. Dep't Rep. 394 (1963); see also *Appeal of Santicola*, 37 Educ. Dep't Rep. 79 (1997)).

22:87. Are school districts required to alter their schedule to accommodate the transportation needs of nonpublic school students?

No. However, the commissioner of education has noted repeatedly that public and nonpublic schools have an obligation to cooperate in a reasonable manner in the scheduling of classes and transportation (*Appeal of Post*, 33 Educ. Dep't Rep. 151 (1993); *Matter of Jeffers*, 26 Educ. Dep't Rep. 408, 411 (1987); *Matter of Berger*, 22 Educ. Dep't Rep. 443 (1983)).

While public school authorities may not dictate the opening or closing hours for a nonpublic school (*Berger*), they are not required to alter their own schedules in order to provide transportation to nonpublic school students. Accordingly, the commissioner has ruled that a transportation scheme that delivers nonpublic school students to their school just five minutes (*Berger*) or even 20 minutes (*Matter of Stickley*, 27 Educ. Dep't Rep. 328 (1988)) before the start of the school day does not impose an unreasonable burden on the nonpublic school.

However, a transportation scheme that consistently delivers students late to nonpublic schools and on time to public schools is not reasonable (*Matter of Hacker*, 28 Educ. Dep't Rep. 141, 143 (1988); *Matter of Osgood*, 25 Educ. Dep't Rep. 274 (1986); *Matter of Tyo*, 20 Educ. Dep't Rep. 384 (1981)).

In addition, the adoption of an "unreasonable" schedule by a nonpublic school will not result in an obligation on the part of the public school district to provide special transportation services at additional expense in

order to meet that schedule. This was the case, for example, where a
nonpublic school dismissed its elementary and middle school students
at 3:20 p.m., but classes for high school students didn't end until 5:00 p.m.
(*Berger*).

22:88. May a nonpublic school submit a list of students who require transportation?

Yes. However, while the nonpublic school may submit a list of nonpublic
students requiring transportation, it is the responsibility of the parent or
guardian of a nonpublic school student to ensure a written request is filed
on time or transportation may be denied (see **22:83**).

This list should contain the name, address, age and grade of each child,
and a signed affidavit which states that the school has been authorized by
the parents or guardian of each child to act as his or her representative.
This affidavit also should indicate that a copy of this authorization duly
signed by the parents is on file in the school office *(Matter of Hendricks,*
21 Educ. Dep't Rep. 302 (1981)).

23. Religion in the Public Schools

23:1. What constitutional provisions govern the role of religion in the public schools?

The role of religion in the public schools is primarily governed by the Establishment and Free Exercise Clauses of the First Amendment of the United States Constitution.

The Establishment Clause states: "Congress shall make no law respecting an establishment of religion." It has been interpreted to require the separation of church and state and is applicable to the states and their subdivisions, including school districts. It requires that government "pursue a course of complete neutrality toward religion," and not promote religion or entangle itself in religious matters (see *Board of Educ. of the Kiryas Joel Village School Dist. v. Grumet*, 512 U.S. 687 (1994); *Lee v. Weisman*, 505 U.S. 577 (1992); *Wallace v. Jaffree*, 472 U.S. 38, 60 (1985); *Larson v. Valente*, 456 U.S. 228 (1982), *reh'g denied*, 457 U.S. 1111 (1982)).

However, not all governmental conduct that confers a benefit on or gives special recognition to religion is automatically prohibited. It depends on all the circumstances surrounding the particular church-state relationship (*Lynch v. Donnelly*, 465 U.S. 668, 678-79 (1984); see **23:2**).

The Free Exercise Clause addresses the freedom of individual belief and religious expression. It states: "Congress shall make no law prohibiting the free exercise" of religion. This clause is also applicable to the states and their political subdivisions, and prohibits government from restricting the right of an individual to believe in whatever he or she may choose. This right, however, may not be read "to require the Government to conduct its own internal affairs in ways that comport with the religious beliefs of particular citizens" *(Bowen v. Roy*, 476 U.S. 693, 699-700 (1986); *Lyng v. Northwest Indian Cemetery Protective Ass'n*, 485 U.S. 439 (1988)). Although "government may accommodate the free exercise of religion" it may not "supersede the fundamental limitations imposed by the Establishment Clause" (*Lee* at 587; see also *Kiryas Joel v. Grumet*).

In addition, article 11, section 3 of the New York State Constitution, also known as the Blaine Amendment, provides that neither the state nor any state subdivision, which includes school districts, may authorize the use of its property, credit or public funds, directly or indirectly, to assist any school under the control of any religious denomination or which teaches any denominational tenet or doctrine. The purpose of this article is to prevent state aid to religion, but the article has been interpreted as not prohibiting every state action that may provide some benefit to religious schools *(Board of Educ. v. Allen*, 392 U.S. 236 (1968)). For example, this article specifically exempts the transportation of students to and from nonpublic schools, and the district's examination or inspection of such schools.

23:2. Are there standards to determine whether a certain government action violates the Establishment Clause?

The most commonly used standard to determine whether governmental action violates the separation of church and state principles of the Establishment Clause is the *Lemon* test, a three-pronged test established by the United States Supreme Court and named after the lawsuit that gave rise to it, *Lemon v. Kurtzman* (403 U.S. 602 (1971), *reh'g denied,* 404 U.S. 876 (1971), *on remand,* 348 F.Supp. 300 (E.D. Pa. 1972), *aff'd,* 411 U.S. 192 (1973)). To be constitutional, an action: (1) must not have a religious purpose; (2) nor have a principal or primary effect of advancing or inhibiting religion; (3) and must not foster excessive government entanglement with religion.

However, the Supreme Court has decided more recent cases without reference to the test, and several justices have questioned the continued appropriateness of the test (see *Board of Educ. of the Kiryas Joel Village School District v. Grumet*, 512 U.S. 687 (1994); *Zobrest v. Catalina Foothills Sch. Dist.*, 509 U.S. 1 (1993); *Lambs Chapel v. Center Moriches Union Free School Dist.*, 508 U.S. 384 (1993), *remanded without op.*, 17 F.3d 1425 (2nd Cir. 1994); *Lee v. Weisman*, 505 U.S. 577 (1992)).

Thus far, the high court has not overruled the *Lemon* decision, but it seems to be moving toward an Establishment Clause analysis that focuses on global principles of neutrality not linked to a specific test. Under these neutrality principles, the Establishment Clause is violated when government acts in a non-neutral manner toward religion either by favoring religion over nonreligion, nonreligion over religion, or a particular denomination over another (see, e.g., *Kiryas Joel v. Grumet; Wallace v. Jaffree*, 472 U.S. 38, 60 (1985); *Larson v. Valente*, 456 U.S. 228 (1982), *reh'g denied,* 457 U.S. 1111 (1982)).

23:3. Are there standards to determine whether a certain government action violates the Free Exercise Clause?

Claims of violations of the Free Exercise Clause in an educational context traditionally have been measured by balancing the state's interest in providing public education against the right of the parent, student or employee to freely exercise or practice his or her religion. However, the right to exercise one's religion freely is not burdened simply by mandating one to be exposed to ideas with which that person disagrees *(Mozert v. Hawkins County Bd. of Education,* 827 F.2d 1058 (6th Cir. 1987), *cert. denied,* 484 U.S. 1066 (1988)).

Until recently, a federal law known as the Religious Freedom Restoration Act (RFRA) (42 USC § 2000bb) required government entities, including school districts, to demonstrate a compelling governmental interest to justify imposing a burden on an individual's free exercise rights. However, the United States Supreme Court declared this law unconstitutional, determining that it was improper for Congress to legislate the manner in which the high court was required to interpret the Free Exercise Clause *(City of Boerne v. Flores,* 117 S.Ct. 2157 (1997)).

Prayer and Moments of Silence

23:4. May a public school district organize or require class participation in daily prayer?

No. Policies promoting school-sponsored prayer in public schools consistently have been struck down as unconstitutional acts of government. The United States Supreme Court has ruled repeatedly that the separation of church and state principles embodied in the Establishment Clause of the First Amendment prohibit school-sponsored prayers and religious exercises, even when the prayer is nondenominational and participation is voluntary.

For example, a prayer endorsed by the New York State Board of Regents for use in public schools was ruled unconstitutional *(Engle v. Vitale,* 370 U.S. 421 (1962)), as well as a state statute requiring readings from the Bible *(School Dist. v. Schempp,* 374 U.S. 203 (1963)), even if students were not required to engage in such prayers.

23:5. May a public school district permit students to lead their peers in organized prayer during school hours?

No. Although there is no United States Supreme Court case on this question, allowing a student club to broadcast inspirational readings from the Bible and sectarian prayers over the school intercom system after the school's morning announcements, and allowing student-initiated prayers in individual classrooms during classroom hours, violates the separation of church and state requirements of the Establishment Clause in that the school district will be perceived as endorsing such religious messages *(Herdahl v. Pontotoc County Sch. Dist.,* 887 F.Supp. 902 (N.D.Miss. 1995); see also *Ingebretsen v. Jackson Public School Dist.,* 88 F.3d 274 (5th Cir. 1996), *cert. denied,* 117 S.Ct. 388 (1996)).

23:6. Are prayers before, during or after school-sponsored extracurricular activities constitutionally permissible?

Although there is no United States Supreme Court case on prayer and school-sponsored athletic events, or other court decisions binding in New York, various courts across the country have uniformly prohibited school-sponsored prayer at school games, including prayer in locker rooms and on the playing field, during practice and prior to and after sporting events.

For example, the posting of a prayer over the entrance to a school gymnasium and the practice of reciting or singing a prayer at pep rallies, games and graduation ceremonies was ruled unconstitutional (*Doe v. Aldine Independent School Dist.*, 563 F.Supp. 883 (S.D.Tex. 1982), as well as a 40-year-old practice of delivering invocations prior to high school football games (*Jager v. Douglas County School Dist.*, 862 F.2d 824 (11th Cir. 1989) *cert. denied*, 490 U.S. 1090 (1989)). In both cases, the courts rejected school district arguments that attendance at the events was voluntary, and that the prayers were solely to add solemnity to the events.

The Fifth Circuit Court of Appeals, which in the past has allowed student-led prayer at high school graduations (see **23:7**), has nonetheless followed other courts in this area by upholding an injunction prohibiting a basketball coach from saying prayers at practices and after games (*Doe v. Duncanville Independent Sch. Dist.*, 994 F.2d 160 (5th Cir. 1993)). The court distinguished prayer at graduation by noting that a school athletic event was less solemn and extraordinary, and students could become subject to team prayer at an early age. According to the court, participation in prayer at these events "entangles the school district in religion and signals an unconstitutional endorsement of religion."

The Fifth Circuit Court of Appeals also ruled unconstitutional a state statute that permitted public elementary and high school students to initiate nonsectarian, nonproselytizing prayer at most school-related activities, including sporting events (*Ingebretsen v. Jackson Public School Dist.*, 88 F.3d 274 (5th Cir. 1996), *cert. denied*, 117 S.Ct. 388 (1996)). The deciding factor against prayer at sporting events has been that they are school-sponsored and controlled activities, and well-established precedent forbids religious exercises at such events.

23:7. Are benedictions and invocations permissible at public school graduation ceremonies?

In a case involving prayer at a high school graduation, the United States Supreme Court ruled that it is unconstitutional for public schools to permit invocations and benedictions delivered by religious leaders at graduation ceremonies because of a potential coercive effect on the impressionable students who attend these ceremonies (*Lee v. Weisman*, 505 U.S. 577 (1992)). In so ruling, the high court rejected the argument that attendance at graduation ceremonies is voluntary. According to the court, "high school graduation is one of life's most significant occasions [and] a student is not free to absent herself from the graduation exercise in any real sense of the term voluntary."

Shortly after the *Weisman* decision, however, the Fifth Circuit Court of Appeals upheld as constitutional a school district policy permitting graduation prayer delivered by student volunteers chosen by students because "high school graduation is a significant once-in-a-lifetime event that could be appropriately marked with a prayer, the students involved were mature high school seniors, and the challenged prayer was nonsectarian and nonproselytizing" (*Jones v. Clear Creek Independent School Dist.*, 977 F.2d 963 (5th Cir. 1992), *cert denied,* 508 U.S. 967 (1993)).

Some courts have followed the *Jones* decision (*Ingebretsen v. Jackson Public School Dist.*, 88 F.3d 27, (5th Cir. 1996), *cert. denied,* 117 S.Ct. 388 (1996); *Adler s. Duval County Sch. Bd.,* 851 F.Supp. 446 (M.D. Fla. 1994), *vacated as moot,* 112 F.3d 1475 (11th Cir. 1997), *reh'g en banc denied,* 120 F.3d 276 (11th Cir. 1997).

Other courts have refused to follow *Jones* (*Harris v. Joint School Dist. No. 241*, 41 F.3d 447 (9th Cir. 1994), *judgment vacated as moot,* 515 U.S. 1154 (1995); *remanded,* 62 F.3d 1233 (9th Cir. 1995); *mot. denied,* 516 U.S. 803 (1995); *American Civil Liberties Union of New Jersey v. Black Horse Pike Regional Board of Educ.*, 84 F.3d 1471 (3rd Cir. en banc 1996); *Gearon v. Loudoun County Sch. Bd.*, 844 F.Supp. 1097 (E.D.Va. 1993)).

In addition, a federal circuit court of appeals ruled that a school district did not violate a prior injunction against prayer at graduation when members of the senior class recited the Lord's Prayer while assembling themselves for the processional, absent any evidence that the school district sponsored or supported the prayer (*Goluba v. School Dist. of Rippon*, 45 F.3d 1035 (7th Cir. 1995)).

Schools in New York State should continue to exercise caution in determining whether to include student-initiated invocations or benedictions in graduation programs, since neither the United States Supreme Court nor courts with jurisdiction over the state have addressed the specific issue of whether student-initiated prayer at graduation ceremonies is constitutionally permissible.

23:8. May student groups gather to openly pray or conduct Bible study meetings on school premises?

Yes, but only during noninstructional time, if the students are high school students, if the activity is not school-sponsored, and if the school district already allows other student-run, noncurriculum-related student groups to meet on school premises during "non-instructional time" which generally means before or after school.

The federal Equal Access Act (20 USC §§ 4071-4074) prohibits a public secondary school that receives federal assistance from denying "equal access" to student groups based on the "religious, political, philosophical, or other content" of the speech at meetings if the district has allowed other noncurriculum-related student groups to meet on school property during noninstructional time.

A student group is noncurriculum-related unless the subject matter of that group is actually taught or concerns the body of courses as a whole, or participation in such a group is a course requirement or provides the participants with academic credit.

According to the United States Supreme Court, the Equal Access Act does not violate the Establishment Clause, because, under the act, schools are not endorsing religious speech; they are merely permitting such speech on a nondiscriminatory basis (*Board of Educ. of Westside Community Schools v. Mergens,* 496 U.S. 226 (1990); see **16:44** for information on conditions imposed by the act for the use of public school facilities by student religious groups). In one case, the United States Court of Appeals for the Ninth Circuit ruled that a public high school's lunch break was "noninstructional time" within the meaning of the Equal Access Act, rejecting the district's position that only time set aside before and after school constituted "noninstructional time" (*Ceniceros v. Board of Trustees of San Diego Unified School District* (66 F.3d 1535 (9th Cir. 1995)).

A related issue involves the question of whether a religious group that uses school property under the Equal Access Act may limit participation in the group to members of that religion. In *Hsu v. Roslyn Union Free School Dist. No. 3,* 85 F.3d 839 (2nd Cir. 1996), *cert. denied,* 117 S.Ct. 608 (1996), the United States Court of Appeals for the Second Circuit, with jurisdiction over New York, ruled that a school district may not enforce a pre-existing nondiscrimination policy to prohibit a student Bible club from meeting on school property under the act because the group allowed only Christians to serve as officers of the club.

23:9. Are school-sponsored moments of silent meditation constitutional?

In 1985, the United States Supreme Court struck down a state statute requiring a one-minute period of silence for "meditation or voluntary prayer" during the school day *(Wallace v. Jaffree,* 472 U.S. 38 (1985)). In *Jaffree,* the legislative history of the statute reviewed by the court made it clear that the purpose was to permit prayer. Therefore, the statute was found to be unconstitutional.

Similarly, a New Jersey moment-of-silence statute that required public schools to permit students to observe one minute of silence "for quiet and private contemplation or introspection" was struck down also as a violation of the Establishment Clause *(Karcher v. May,* 780 F.2d 240 (3rd Cir. 1985), appeal dismissed for lack of jurisdiction, 484 U.S. 72 (1987)). The Supreme Court declined to rule on the merits of the case.

In contrast, however, the United States Court of Appeals for the Eleventh Circuit upheld a state law requiring a one-minute period of quiet reflection in public classrooms *(Bown v. Gwinnet County School District,* 112 F.3d 1464 (11th Cir. 1997)).

New York's Education Law allows for a moment of silence in the public schools (§ 3029-a). It specifically provides: "The silent meditation authorized . . . is not intended to be, and shall not be conducted as, a religious service or exercise, but may be considered an opportunity for silent meditation on a religious theme by those who are so disposed, or a moment of silent reflection on the anticipated activities of the day." Students may remain seated and may not be required to stand.

However, this statute has not been challenged in the courts. According to a 1964 Formal Opinion of Counsel from the State Education Department, the application of the statute would be impermissible if the statutory moment of silence were prefaced with the statement: "We will now have a moment of silence to acknowledge our Supreme Being" (Opn. Educ. Dep't, 3 Educ. Dep't Rep. 255 (1964)). Since the legislative history of that statute does not indicate that it was enacted to foster organized religious prayer, it may pass constitutional muster.

23:10. Is it constitutional to open a school board meeting with a prayer or a moment of silent meditation?

Although the United States Supreme Court has made no determination on the issue of opening school board meetings with a prayer or a moment of silent meditation, it has ruled on the opening of state legislative sessions with prayer.

Reviewing the Nebraska Legislature's 200-year-old practice of opening legislative sessions with a nondenominational prayer delivered by a chaplain paid by the state, the United States Supreme Court ruled the practice was not an unconstitutional "'establishment'" of religion, but was "a tolerable acknowledgment of beliefs widely held among the people of this country" (*Marsh v. Chambers*, 463 U.S. 783, 792 (1983)).

Prior to the *Marsh* decision, however, the Eighth Circuit Court of Appeals had permitted the use of prayer at county board meetings where no public funds were expended (*Bogen v. Doty*, 598 F.2d 1110 (8th Cir. 1979)). Applying the test (see **23:2**), the Eighth Circuit found no violation of the Establishment Clause because its primary effect was to establish order, not to promote religion. Although this decision may be persuasive, it is not binding on courts with jurisdiction in New York State.

In determining the constitutionality of prayers at school board meetings, courts may also consider whether the prayer involved is nonsectarian or nondenominational in nature, the degree of official involvement or sponsorship of the activity, and the absence or presence of compulsion of those participating in the activity (see *Marsa v. Wernik*, 430 A.2d 888 (N.J. 1981), *cert. denied*, 454 U.S. 958 (1981)). Courts may also consider whether school facilities are places which require the exercise of greater sensitivity regarding separation of church and state principles (see *County of Allegheny v. Amer. Civil Liberties Union, Greater Pittsburgh Chapter*, 492 U.S. 573 (1989), *on remand*, 887 F.2d 260 (3rd Cir. 1989)).

Religious Observances

23:11. May a school district close school for the observance of a religious holiday?

Although courts with jurisdiction over New York have not yet ruled on this matter, the United States Court of Appeals for the Seventh Circuit declared unconstitutional an Illinois statute which required all public schools to close on Good Friday because its legislative history reflected that the statute was intended to "accord special recognition to Christianity beyond anything ... necessary to accommodate the needs of [Illinois'] Christian majority (*Metzl v. Leininger*, 57 F.3d 618 (7th Cir. 1995)). However, the court explained its decision might have been different if the state had shown that the majority of students were Christians and would not attend school on Good Friday. Under such circumstances, the court noted it would make sense to close school to prevent the wasteful expenditure of resources.

23:12. May public schools acknowledge the observance of religious holidays through plays, pageants and other programs containing religious themes?

School districts may acknowledge religious holidays by conducting programs that have religious significance as long as these programs also contain some educational or cultural purpose (*Florey v. Sioux Falls School Dist. 49-5*, 619 F.2d 1311 (8th Cir. 1980), *cert. denied*, 449 U.S. 987 (1980)).

In *Matter of Rosenbaum*, 28 Educ. Dep't Rep. 138 (1988), the commissioner of education upheld a school district's policy permitting religious music and art where it was taught as part of a genuine secular program of education and where the policy excused students from participating in those parts of the curriculum which conflicted with their religious beliefs.

In addition, the commissioner upheld a school district's adoption of guidelines for the treatment of religious and cultural holidays in the instructional program (*Appeal of Pasquale*, 30 Educ. Dep't Rep. 361 (1991)). According to the commissioner, the adoption of such guidelines falls within the broad statutory authority of school boards to adopt bylaws and rules for the governance of the schools (§ 1709).

However, the commissioner has also ruled that a school board's resolution to change the name of its "Winter" music concert to the "Christmas" concert violated the Establishment Clause. The resolution began: "We, being a Christian community . . ." which the commissioner found indicated an unconstitutional religious purpose (*Appeal of Sebouhian*, 31 Educ. Dep't Rep. 397 (1992)).

23:13. May a student be absent or released from school to observe a religious holiday and for religious instruction?

Yes. School absences for the observance of religious holidays outside of the official state holidays and for attendance at religious instruction are permitted by state law and regulation upon written request from a parent or guardian (§ 3210(1)(b); 8 NYCRR § 109.2(a)). Students may be released to take such religious instruction in accordance with the commissioner's regulations (8 NYCRR § 109.2), as long as that instruction is not provided at the public school (*Zorach v. Clauson*, 343 U.S. 306 (1952)).

23:14. Must school districts accommodate a teacher's request for time off for religious observances?

Title VII of the Civil Rights Act of 1964 prohibits discrimination by an employer on the basis of an employee's religion. It requires that reasonable accommodations be made for an employee's desire to observe religious holidays, unless to do so would create an undue hardship.

Generally, courts have permitted teachers to take approximately five to 10 days off for religious reasons, even where substitutes must be hired (see *Wangsness v. Watertown School Dist.*, 541 F.Supp. 332 (D.S.D. 1982); *Niederhuber v. Camden County Vocational & Technical School Dist. Bd. of Education*, 495 F.Supp. 273 (D.N.J. 1980), *aff'd without op.*, 671 F.2d 496 (D.N.J. 1980)). Presumably, more than five or 10 teacher absences for religious observances would be considered an undue hardship for a school district and outside the scope of an employee's Title VII protection.

Public employers must permit an employee to use unpaid leave for religious observances if the days required are in excess of personal days already provided (*Ansonia Board of Educ. v. Philbrook*, 479 U.S. 60 (1986)). The Public Employment Relations Board (PERB) has ruled in two cases that a school district did not violate its duty to bargain in good faith by unilaterally rescinding a past practice of allowing employees to take extra paid leave for religious observances, finding that it was an unconstitutional practice and therefore not mandatorily negotiable (*Auburn Teachers Ass'n. v. Auburn Enlarged City SD*, 29 PERB ¶ 4671 (1997); *CSEA v. Eastchester U.F.S.D.*, 29 PERB ¶ 3041 (1996)). However, one court has ruled that paid leave for religious observance is a permissive subject of bargaining (*Binghamton City School District v. Andreatta*, 30 PERB 7504 (Broome County Sup. Ct. 1997)).

Like Title VII, the New York State Human Rights Law (Exec. Law § 296(10)) also makes it unlawful for any employer to discriminate against an employee because the employee observes a particular Sabbath day or days in accordance with his or her religious beliefs. Moreover, except in emergencies, a district cannot require a teacher to work on a Sabbath or holy day and must allow the teacher time to travel to his or her home or to places of religious observance (Exec. Law § 296(1)(b)).

In *New York City Transit Authority v. Div. of Human Rights*, 89 N.Y.2d 79 (1996), the New York State Court of Appeals held that an employer unlawfully discriminated against an employee by firing her when she refused to work at any time from sundown on Friday to sundown on Saturday because the tenets of her religion. The Court of Appeals ruled that the law requires employers to make a "good-faith" effort to accommodate Sabbath observing employees, even though an accommodation ultimately may not be available. The employer argued that it could not accommodate the employee, because the collective bargaining agreement required it to give senior employees preference in selecting days off. The court determined that the employer still had an obligation under the law to attempt to accommodate the employee's religious observance, despite this provision of the collective bargaining agreement, and that the employer had not made any effort to do so.

Religious Symbols

23:15. May school districts display religious symbols?

A school district's temporary display of religious symbols associated with religious holidays does not violate the Establishment Clause, according to one federal appeals court, if the display is not proselytizing in nature and merely acknowledges cultural and historical aspects of the holiday *(Florey v. Sioux Falls School Dist. 49-5*, 619 F.2d 1311 (8th Cir. 1980), *cert. denied*, 449 U.S. 987 (1980)).

By contrast, another federal appeals court ruled that a school district violated the Establishment Clause when it displayed for 30 years a portrait of Jesus Christ in the hallway of a public school *(Washegesic v. Bloomingdale Public Sch.*, 33 F.3d 679 (6th Cir. 1994), *cert. denied*, 514 U.S. 1095 (1995)). However, the court indicated that its decision would have been different if the school had placed representative symbols of many of the world's religions on a common wall.

Similarly, a federal district court in New York ordered a school district to remove a mural depicting a crucifixion that was painted by a former student and displayed on a wall in the school auditorium *(Joki v. Board of Educ. of Schuylerville Cent. School Dist.*, 745 F.Supp. 823 (N.D.N.Y. 1990)). The court held that since the mural was patently religious, it violated the Establishment Clause because impressionable students might assume school sponsorship of religion.

These decisions are consistent with a number of cases regarding religious displays on municipal property, including the United States Supreme Court decision in *Stone v. Graham*, 449 U.S. 39 (1980, *reh'g denied*, 449 U.S. 1104 (1981), *on remand*, 612 S.W.2d 133 (Ky. 1981)). In this case, a statute requiring the posting of the Ten Commandments inside public classrooms was found to violate the Establishment Clause.

The Supreme Court also found that a nativity scene inside a county courthouse by itself violated the separation of church and state. However, the display of a large Christmas tree and a Hanukkah menorah with the message "A Salute to Liberty" outside that same county courthouse did not *(County of Allegheny v. Amer. Civil Liberties Union, Greater Pittsburgh Chapter*, 492 U.S. 573 (1989)).

Similarly, a city's inclusion of a nativity scene in its Christmas display, along with a Santa Claus, a Christmas tree, a reindeer, a clown, a teddy bear and other holiday items, was found not to violate the Establishment Clause (*Lynch v. Donnelly*, 465 U.S. 668 (1984), *rehearing denied*, 466 U.S. 994 (1984)).

More recently, in *Elewski v. City of Syracuse*, 123 F.3d 51 (2nd Cir. 1997), *cert. denied*, 118 S.Ct. 1186 (1998), the United State Court of Appeals for the Second Circuit, which has jurisdiction over New York State, ruled that the display of a city-owned creche in a downtown public park at public expense did not violate the Establishment Clause. According to the court, ownership of the creche was not the critical factor. Instead, the test was whether a reasonable observer would perceive a message of endorsement from the display. In this case, the court determined that the government-owned display, when viewed together with a privately-sponsored menorah displayed nearby and other traditional religious and secular decorations in the area, did not endorse religion, but instead celebrated the "diversity of the holiday season . . ."

In yet another case, the United States Court of Appeals for the Seventh Circuit upheld a complete ban by a local government on all displays in the lobby of a government building, finding that the policy was a content-neutral law of general applicability which did not violate the first amendment (*Grossbaum v. Indianapolis-Marion County Building Authority*, 100 F.3d 1287 (7th Cir. 1996), *cert. denied*, 117 S.Ct. 1822 (1997)).

These cases provide guidance on the types of displays that will pass scrutiny under the Establishment Clause. Particularly in the *Allegheny* case, the Supreme Court noted several factors helpful in making such a determination. These factors include:

- The location of the display.
- Whether the display is part of a larger configuration that includes nonreligious items.
- The religious intensity of the display.
- Whether the display is shown in connection with a general secular holiday.
- The degree of public participation in the ownership and maintenance of the display.
- The existence of disclaimers of public sponsorship. Most notably, the court indicated that a greater level of sensitivity must be exercised with respect to the public schools.

23:16. Is the display of items associated with Halloween permissible?

In a case which the United States Supreme Court declined to hear, a Florida state court ruled that the depiction of witches, cauldrons and brooms, and related costumes during a school Halloween celebration did not violate the Establishment Clause *(Guyer v. School Board of Alachua County,* 634 So.2d 806 (Fla. App. 1 Dist. 1994), *cert. denied,* 513 U.S. 1044 (1994)). The Florida court rejected the argument that use of the symbols and costumes endorsed and promoted the "Wicca" religious faith (a variety of witchcraft and religion), after finding that the symbols were not "singularly" or "distinctively" religious. Although the decision is not binding in New York, it might be persuasive to courts with jurisdiction over the state.

23:17. Can the use of certain symbols such as school mascots be unconstitutional?

Litigation on the issue of school mascots and the religion clauses of the First Amendment of the United States Constitution has been scarce. However, the focus has been on whether the use of a particular symbol advances religion in violation of separation of church and state principles. For example, in *Kunselman v. Western Reserve Local Sch. Dist. Bd. of Educ.,* 70 F.3d 931 (6th Cir. 1995), parents unsuccessfully argued that use and display of a "blue devil" as the school's mascot violated the Establishment Clause by encouraging devil worship. In the court's opinion, "No reasonable person would think that the school authorities here are advocating Satanism . . . when they use the name and symbol" *(Kunselman* at 933).

Aside from the constitutionality issue, a determination as to the appropriateness of a school mascot rests with the local school board. Such a determination will be put aside only upon a showing that the board has abused its discretion *(Appeal of Tobin,* 25 Educ. Dep't Rep. 301 (1986), 30 Educ. Dep't Rep. 315 (1991)).

23:18. May school districts prevent a teacher from wearing religious garb while teaching?

In a decision from the turn of the century, the New York State Court of Appeals upheld a prohibition against the wearing of religious clothing by teachers *(O'Connor v. Hendrick,* 184 N.Y. 421 (1906)). The court found that the teacher's religious attire might unduly influence impressionable students, and that this sectarian influence was unconstitutional.

However, at least one modern court has struck down a school's prohibition against teachers' religious garb as violative of Title VII and the duty to make a reasonable accommodation for an employee's religious practices *(United States v. Board of Educ. for School Dist.,* 911 F.2d 882 (3rd Cir. 1990)). Consequently, in order to continue to ban religious garments, a school district may have to show that an accommodation of the teacher's wishes would cause undue hardship to the district.

In addition, one federal district court in New York upheld the right of a prison guard who was a Native American and practitioner of the traditional religion of the Mohawk Nation to wear long hair because it was an important spiritual tenet of his religion *(Rourke v. New York State Dep't. of Correctional Servs.*, 915 F.Supp. 525 (N.D.N.Y. 1995), *remanded,* 224 A.D.2d 815 (3rd Dep't 1996)). Therefore, it is questionable whether the *O'Connor* decision is still a valid legal precedent.

24. Nonpublic Schools and Home Instruction

Nonpublic Schools

24:1. Must a school district allow students of compulsory education age to withdraw from its public schools and attend a nonpublic school?

Yes. A school district must permit a child of compulsory education age to attend a nonpublic school. However, parents withdrawing children of compulsory education age from the public school must furnish proof that their child is receiving required instruction elsewhere. Failure to furnish such proof raises a presumption that the child is not receiving the required instruction, which is a violation of the Education Law, and which may result in a finding of educational neglect (§ 3212(2)(d); *Appeal of White*, 29 Educ. Dep't Rep. 511 (1990), citing *Matter of Christa H.*, 127 A.D.2d 997 (4th Dep't 1987) and *In re Andrew "T. T.,"* 122 A.D.2d 362 (3rd Dep't 1986); see also Fam. Ct. Act § 1012(f)(i)).

24:2. Do school districts owe any responsibility to resident children who attend nonpublic schools?

Yes. Public school boards must ensure that resident children attending other than a public school receive instruction from "competent teachers" that is "at least substantially equivalent," in terms of both "time and quality," to the instruction they would receive if they attended the public schools in the district where they reside (§§ 3204(2), 3210(2); *In re Adam D.*, 132 Misc.2d 797 (Fam. Ct. 1986)).

The responsibility for determining substantial equivalency rests with the local school board (Formal Op. of Counsel No. 78, 1 Educ. Dep't Rep. 778 (1952)). However, the board may delegate the responsibility for making any such initial determination to the superintendent of schools (see *Matter of Adam D.; In re Kilroy*, 121 Misc.2d 98 (Fam. Ct. 1983); *Appeal of Brown*, 34 Educ. Dep't Rep. 33 (1994); § 1711).

24:3. How can a school district determine if a student attending a nonpublic school is receiving a substantially equivalent education?

The superintendent of schools may visit the nonpublic schools of resident children to evaluate the educational programs they are receiving outside the public schools. The substantial equivalency of unregistered nonpublic schools must be determined through local review. However, if the nonpublic school is registered, the State Education Department (SED) recommends that the school board of the district in which a nonpublic school is located accept the registration of the school with SED as

591

evidence that the nonpublic school has an equivalent program of instruction (NY State Education Department: "Guidelines for Determining Equivalency of Instruction in Nonpublic Schools," March 1993; see **24:6**).

24:4. What steps should be taken if it is determined that a nonpublic school does not provide a substantially equivalent education to that provided in the public school?

The superintendent and the nonpublic school administrator should discuss any perceived deficiencies, determine whether these deficiencies can be corrected within a reasonable period of time, and create a schedule for the corrections to be made. If the nonpublic school is unable or unwilling to remedy its deficiencies, and the superintendent determines that the program does not provide a "substantially equivalent education," the superintendent should notify his or her board and the board of cooperative educational services (BOCES) district superintendent where appropriate (NY State Education Department: "Guidelines for Determining Equivalency of Instruction in Nonpublic Schools," March 1993, p. 4).

24:5. Are nonpublic schools subject to the same legal requirements that apply to public schools?

Generally, nonpublic schools are not bound by all of the requirements that apply to public schools. For example, the law does not require that nonpublic school teachers and administrators meet the state's requirements for certification. In addition, the rights of students in private schools generally are governed by the contractual arrangement between the school and the parents or by regulations or procedures set forth in a student handbook or school catalogue. Accordingly, nonpublic schools may impose tighter restrictions on students' speech and conduct than those possible within the public schools (see **12:77-94; 12:95-126**).

However, where nonpublic schools receive federal funds, they may become subject to various federal civil rights laws such as:

- Title IX of the Federal Education Amendments of 1972, which bars sexual discrimination in education programs.
- Title VI of the Civil Rights Act of 1964, which bans discrimination by race, color, religion or national origin in federally funded programs.
- Section 504 of the Rehabilitation Act of 1973, which prohibits discrimination against students with disabilities in such programs.
- The Family Educational Rights and Privacy Act, 20 U.S.C. § 1232g, which requires parental review of and consent to the release of student educational records.

In addition, certain state laws are applicable to nonpublic schools, such as section 807–a of the Education Law, which requires that nonpublic elementary or secondary schools enrolling 25 or more students file a fire-inspection report with the state. The Education Law and commissioner's regulations also require that any registered nonpublic nursery school or kindergarten attended by six or more pupils must meet certain safety standards to prevent fire, health or other safety hazards (§ 807-a(10)(b); 8 NYCRR § 125.3).

While a public school board is not responsible for enforcing these provisions, if a fire inspection reveals "an apparently serious deficiency," the board may take appropriate steps to inform the parents of students at the nonpublic school (NY State Education Department: "Guidelines for Determining Equivalency of Instruction in Nonpublic Schools," March 1993, p. 8).

24:6. Must nonpublic schools be registered with the State Education Department?

Nonpublic schools are not required to be registered with the State Education Department (see 8 NYCRR § 100.2(p)). However, the commissioner's regulations provide for the voluntary registration of nonpublic nursery schools and kindergartens (8 NYCRR Part 125). In addition, nonpublic high schools may be registered by the Board of Regents upon the recommendation of the commissioner of education. Only registered nonpublic high schools may issue diplomas and administer Regents examinations (8 NYCRR § 100.2(p)).

Inquiries concerning the requirements and procedures for the registration of nonpublic secondary schools or nursery schools and kindergartens should be addressed to the State Education Department's Office of Nonpublic School Services, Albany, N.Y. 12234.

24:7. Is there any State Education Department review of registered nonpublic high schools?

Yes. The commissioner's regulations provide that a registered nonpublic high school shall be placed under review by the commissioner whenever the school scores below the registration review criteria on one (or more) of the measures adopted by the Board of Regents, and the student achievement on such measures has not shown improvement over the preceding three school years, or when other sufficient cause exists to warrant registration review, as determined by the commissioner (8 NYCRR §100.2(p)(6)(i),(7)).

The school then develops an improvement plan with technical assistance from the commissioner if needed (8 NYCRR § 100.2(p)(6)(ii)). If the nonpublic high school under registration review does not show progress on the registration criteria, the commissioner notifies the nonpublic high school that it is at risk of having its registration revoked. Then, if after a further period of time the nonpublic high school still does not show progress, the commissioner will recommend to the Board of Regents that it revoke the school's registration (8 NYCRR §100.2(p)(6)(iii),(iv)).

24:8. Is there any State Education Department review of unregistered nonpublic schools?

Yes. The commissioner's regulations provide for State Education Department (SED) review of unregistered nonpublic schools, when any such school reports student scores below one or more of the review criteria on indicators of student achievement as provided in the commissioner's regulations; has not shown improvement on such indicators over the preceding three school years; and has not otherwise demonstrated satisfactory performance on other student achievement indicators determined by the commissioner in consultation with the appropriate nonpublic school officials (8 NYCRR § 100.2(z); see **14:74**).

Nonpublic schools under SED review are required to notify parents, develop a school improvement plan (with technical assistance from SED if requested), and submit the plan to SED. If, after a time period established by the commissioner in consultation with the appropriate nonpublic school officials, the school has not demonstrated progress, the commissioner will formally notify the nonpublic school officials that the school is at risk of being determined to be an "unsound educational environment." If thereafter the commissioner has determined there is still insufficient progress, he will determine that the school is an unsound educational environment. The commissioner and the nonpublic school officials must then develop a plan to ensure that the educational welfare of the students is protected (8 NYCRR § 100.2(z)).

24:9. Are there any steps a public school district should take when a new nonpublic school is established within its boundaries?

Yes. Public school officials should determine whether the new nonpublic school building is a safe place by reviewing, for example, building structure reports and fire inspection reports, whether the length of the school day and school calendar are substantially equivalent to that required for public schools, and whether the program of instruction covers essentially the same subject areas as are covered in the public schools (§§ 807–a, 3204(2), 3210(2)).

The superintendent of schools should ask to visit the new school prior to its opening, and ask the administrator of the nonpublic school for information such as the names and grade levels of students from the district, the school calendar and curriculum guides. If this information appears to be satisfactory and it is determined that the new nonpublic school will provide a substantially equivalent education, the superintendent should notify the public school board of this in writing, forward a copy of the notification to the nonpublic school and, where appropriate, notify the board of cooperative educational services (BOCES) district superintendent of the findings of the review. The superintendent should contact the State Education Department's (SED) Office of Nonpublic School Services to ensure that the new school will be placed on SED's mailing list and that its head will be invited to the annual fall conference for nonpublic school administrators (NY State Education Department: Guidelines for Determining Equivalency of Instruction in Nonpublic Schools, March 1993, pp. 4-5).

24:10. Are nonpublic schools entitled to any state aid?

Yes. Nonpublic schools are eligible for state financial aid for costs incurred by them in complying with state mandates relating to the administration of state testing and evaluation programs and participation in state programs for the reporting of basic educational data (Laws of 1974, Chs. 507 and 508).

Although the New York State Constitution provides that neither the state nor any state subdivision may provide funding or use its property or credit to assist a sectarian school (NYS Const. Art. 11, § 3), the authorized apportionment of state aid funds for nonpublic schools is limited to the services nonpublic schools are required to perform for the state in connection with the state's own responsibility to evaluate students through a system of uniform testing and reporting procedures to ensure students are being adequately educated (Laws of 1974, Chs. 507 and 508). The United States Supreme Court has upheld the constitutionality of these provisions under separation of church and state principles of the Establishment Clause of the First Amendment of the United States Constitution (§ 3601; *Committee for Public Education and Religious Liberty v. Regan*, 444 U.S. 646 (1980)).

Services for Nonpublic School Students

24:11. Are there any type of services that public school districts must provide to nonpublic school students?

Yes. As authorized by law, public school districts must provide nonpublic school students with, for instance, health and welfare services (§ 912, see **12:53**) and transportation (§ 3635, see **22:82-88**); and loan them textbooks

(§ 701; **24:14-15**), computer software (§ 752, see **24:16**) and library materials (**24:17**) (see also NY State Education Department: "Handbook on Services to Pupils Attending Nonpublic Schools," 1990).

In addition, under section 3602-c of the Education Law (also known as the dual-enrollment law), and upon parental request, school districts must provide students attending nonpublic schools located in the district with educational services in the areas of instruction for the gifted, career education, and special education and related services for students with disabilities (§ 3602-c(1)).

Parental requests for dual-enrollment services must be filed with the student's school district of residence by June 1 preceding the school year for which services are requested (§ 3602-c(2)). School districts may contract for such services with boards of cooperative educational services (BOCES) or the school district in which the nonpublic school is located (§ 3602-c(2),(3)). Transportation must be furnished between the nonpublic school and the site where the program is offered if the distance is more than one-fourth of a mile. The district may claim state aid for this transportation (§ 3602-c(4)).

Under federal law, school districts also may be required to provide educational services to students attending nonpublic schools, such as remedial instruction, counseling and other supplementary services where federal funds are appropriated and distributed in accordance with programs proposed by local school districts and approved by the State Education Department (Elementary and Secondary Education Act, 20 USC § 6321, see § 3602(10); 8 NYCRR subpart 149-1 *et seq.*).

24:12. Are school districts required to provide dual-enrollment services on site at the nonpublic schools?

No. The dual-enrollment law indicates that the services be provided in the regular classes of the public schools, with public school students in attendance (§ 3602-c (9); see **24:13**).

24:13. Is a school district required to provide on-site special education and related services to students with disabilities who attend private schools, including parochial schools?

The United States Supreme Court has ruled that the federal constitution does not prevent a school district from providing services to students on-site at the premises of their parochial school (*Agostini v. Felton*, 117 S.Ct. 1997 (1997)). Under the Individuals with Disabilities Education Act (IDEA), special education services may be provided to students with disabilities on the premises of private schools, including parochial schools, to the extent consistent with law (20 USC §1412(a)(10)(A)(i)).

However, a school district is not required under federal law to provide on-site special education services to children with disabilities voluntarily enrolled in private schools. It is still uncertain as to whether state law requires public school districts to provide such services on the premises of the private school (*Russman by Russman v. Mills*, 1998 WL 417452 (2nd Cir.).

In an earlier case, the New York State Court of Appeals ruled that a public school district was not required to provide special education services under the state's dual enrollment law on the premises of a private school (*Board of Educ. v. Wieder*, 72 N.Y.2d 174 (1988)).

24:14. Must public school districts purchase and loan textbooks to students attending nonpublic schools?

Yes. Section 701 of the Education Law requires all school boards to purchase and to loan "upon individual request" textbooks, workbooks, and manuals, for example, to all children residing in the district who attend kindergarten through 12th grade in any public school and in any nonpublic school that complies with the Education Law. Items such as encyclopedias, almanacs, atlases, certain audiovisual materials and review books are not considered "textbooks" (see 8 NYCRR § 21.2(a)).

Textbooks may be purchased only for resident students (see 8 NYCRR § 21.2(a)). Children who reside outside of the district in which the nonpublic school they attend is located must have their textbooks provided by their district of residence (§ 701(3)).

Under the statute, both the power and the duty to purchase and loan textbooks depend upon individual requests to the school board for such textbooks. To comply with the law, the nonpublic school may either forward individual student requests as a group to the school board or keep the requests on file and forward a summary of the requests to the school board (see 8 NYCRR § 21.2(b)). Section 701(6) of the Education Law provides that school districts receive an additional apportionment of state aid to comply with the statute. No school district is required to spend more on purchasing textbooks than the amount of state aid it receives for this purpose (§ 701(4)).

The commissioner of education has held that a school board must establish a procedure to ensure equitable distribution of all available textbooks, "both those on hand from prior years and those newly purchased." This "procedure must assure that in each subject area students are treated equally regardless of the school attended" (*Matter of Gross*, 25 Educ. Dep't Rep. 382, 384 (1986); see also *Appeal of Kelly*, 35 Educ. Dep't Rep. 235 (1996); *Matter of Caunitz*, 30 Educ. Dep't Rep. 396 (1991); § 701(4); 8 NYCRR § 21.2(c)).

Although the Education Law requires public schools to loan text-books upon individual request, it does not authorize school districts to reimburse individuals who have purchased textbooks on their own (*Appeal of Kelly*, 35 Educ. Dep't Rep. 235 (1996)).

For more information, see **14:53-59** and New York State Textbook Loan Program: Recommended Procedures for Textbook Purchases, Loans and Inventory Control, NY State Education Department, December 1994.

24:15. Is it constitutionally permissible for a public school district to purchase and loan textbooks to students attending parochial schools?

Yes. The United States Supreme Court has upheld the constitutionality of New York State's Education Law textbook provisions (*Board of Educ. v. Allen*, 392 U.S. 236 (1968); see also *Meek v. Pittenger*, 421 U.S. 349 (1975), *reh'g denied*, 422 U.S. 1049 (1975)). However, textbooks purchased and loaned to parochial school students must be nonsectarian and designated for use in any public elementary or secondary school of the state or approved by any school board (§ 701(3)).

24:16. May school districts purchase and loan computer software programs to nonpublic school students?

Yes. The law provides that school districts may purchase computer soft-ware programs and must loan these software programs upon individual request to nonpublic school students (§§ 751-752, 8 NYCRR § 21.3(c)). This software must be made available on an equitable basis to all eligible pupils, in both public and nonpublic schools (8 NYCRR § 21.3(d)).

Computer software does *not* include microcomputers, blank diskettes, cassettes or tapes, chips, computer correction devices, consoles, cords, disk drives or other similar items of hardware (8 NYCRR § 21.3(a)). Moreover, only computer software programs that do not contain material of a reli-gious nature may be purchased by a public school district (8 NYCRR § 21.3(b); see also *Wolman v. Walter*, 433 U.S. 229 (1977); *Meek v. Pittenger*, 421 U.S. 349 (1975), *reh'g denied*, 422 U.S. 1049 (1975); *Board of Educ. v. Allen*, 392 U.S. 236 (1968)).

No school district is required to purchase or otherwise acquire soft-ware programs that will cost more than the "software factor" (which is $4.80 for 1997-98 and 1998-99; $7.50 for 1999-2000; and $14.90 for 2001-2002) multiplied by the sum of the public school district enrollment and the enrollment of nonpublic school students within the school district (§§ 751(3),(4); 3603(n)(2),(3)).

24:17. May nonpublic school students borrow library materials?

Yes. School library materials owned or acquired by a public school district pursuant to section 711 of the Education Law must be made available on an equitable basis to all eligible pupils enrolled in grades kindergarten through 12 in both public and nonpublic schools located within the public school district (8 NYCRR § 21.4(d)).

Such library materials must be loaned free of charge upon the individual request of eligible nonpublic school students. Requests may be presented directly to the lending district, or with the consent of the district, to an appropriate official at the nonpublic school attended by the student (8 NYCRR § 21.4(c)).

School authorities must establish lending procedures consistent with the commissioner's regulations and must inform authorities at the nonpublic schools within the boundaries of the public school district of these procedures (8 NYCRR § 21.4(e)).

Home Instruction

24:18. Are parents permitted to educate their children at home?

Yes. The Education Law permits the education of children at home, provided that children of compulsory education age receive full-time instruction, and are taught by competent teachers and receive instruction that is substantially equivalent to that provided at the public schools of the student's district of residence (§§ 3204(2), 3210(2), 3212(2); 8 NYCRR 100.10; see *In re Franz*, 55 A.D.2d 424, 427 (2nd Dep't 1977); *People v. Turner*, 277 A.D. 317, 319 (4th Dep't 1950)). However, state law does not require any specific credentials for the person providing home instruction (NY State Education Department: Revised Questions and Answers on Home Instruction, February 1994, p. 2).

24:19. What specific provisions govern home instruction?

Sections 3204(2), 3210(12) and 3212 of the Education Law, and section 100.10 of the commissioner's regulations set forth the requirements that must be met by parents who wish to educate their children at home. Parents must, for instance, develop an individualized home instruction plan (IHIP) (8 NYCRR § 100.10(c)); *Appeal of Brown*, 34 Educ. Dep't Rep. 33 (1994); *Matter of White*, 29 Educ. Dep't Rep. 511 (1990)); submit quarterly reports (8 NYCRR § 100.10(g)); and file an annual assessment indicating the student's progress (8 NYCRR § 100.10(h)). The regulations also provide detailed requirements for courses to be taught, required attendance and student evaluation (8 NYCRR § 100.10(e-h)).

24:20. Must parents educating their children at home adhere to laws and regulations regarding home instruction?

Yes. The Education Law imposes upon parents a duty to ensure that their children receive appropriate instruction (§ 3212(2); *Appeal of Brown,* 34 Educ. Dep't Rep. 33 (1994); *Matter of White,* 29 Educ. Dep't Rep. 511 (1990); *Matter of Thomas H.,* 78 Misc.2d 412, 413 (1974)). Further, the state has a legitimate and compelling interest in ensuring that its children receive an education that will prepare them to be productive members of society *(Blackwelder v. Safnauer,* 689 F.Supp. 106 (N.D.N.Y. 1988), *appeal dismissed,* 866 F.2d 548 (2nd Cir. 1989)).

24:21. What are the responsibilities of parents who educate their children at home?

The parents or other persons in parental relation to students of compulsory education age wishing to educate their children at home must do the following:

- Notify the superintendent of schools in writing each year by July 1 of their intention to educate their child at home. If they move into the district or decide to educate their child at home after the start of the school year, they must provide notice within 14 days of commencing home instruction (8 NYCRR § 100.10(b)).
- Submit an individualized home instruction plan (IHIP) for each child of compulsory attendance age to be instructed at home within four weeks of receipt of the form provided by the district or by August 15, whichever is later (8 NYCRR § 100.10(c)(2)). The plan must contain, among other items, a list of the syllabi, curriculum materials, textbooks or plan of instruction to be used in each of the required subjects noted in the regulations, and the names of the person(s) to provide instruction (8 NYCRR § 100.10(d); see 8 NYCRR § 100.10(e) for a list of required courses). The school district will provide assistance in developing the IHIP, if the parent so requests (8 NYCRR § 100.10(c)(2)).
- Submit quarterly reports for each child to the school district on the dates specified in the IHIP. Each report must contain the number of hours of instruction; a description of the material covered in each subject; either a grade for the child in each subject or a written narrative evaluating the child's progress; and a written explanation if less than 80 percent of the course material set out in the IHIP was covered (8 NYCRR § 100.10(g)).
- File an annual assessment of the student at the same time as the fourth quarterly report. The assessment must be based on the results

of a commercially published norm-referenced achievement test, such as the Iowa or California Test, or an alternative form of evaluation. The test must be administered at a public or nonpublic school or at the child's home by a certified teacher, with the superintendent's consent (8 NYCRR § 100.10(h)). The commissioner of education has ruled that a student must take a commercially prepared achievement test despite his parents' objection that the test "conflicted with their personal philosophy" (*Appeal of Abbokire*, 33 Educ. Dep't Rep. 473 (1994)).

24:22. What are the school district's responsibilities over the individualized home instruction plan (IHIP) developed by parents educating their children at home?

- Within 10 business days of receiving notice from a child's parents of their intention to education their child at home, the school district must send to the parents a copy of the home instruction regulations, along with a form on which the parents must submit an individualized home instruction plan (IHIP) for any child educated at home (8 NYCRR § 100.10(c)(1)).
- Within 10 business days of receipt of the IHIP, or by August 31, whichever is later, the school district must either notify the parents that the IHIP is satisfactory or give the parents written notice of any deficiencies (8 NYCRR §100.10(c)(3)).
- The superintendent is responsible for ensuring the home student's IHIP complies with the commissioner's regulations, subject to review on an appeal to the board (8 NYCRR § 100.10(c)). If there are deficiencies, the parent must, within 15 days of receipt of such notice or by September 15, whichever is later, submit a revised IHIP which corrects the deficiencies (8 NYCRR § 100.10(c)(4)). The superintendent of schools then reviews the revised IHIP, and will issue a notice of noncompliance within 15 days of receipt of the revised IHIP if the indicated deficiencies have not been corrected (8 NYCRR § 100.10(c)(5)) .

24:23. What happens if a school district determines that the individualized home instruction plan (IHIP) of a student educated at home is deficient?

If the parents disagree with the school superintendent's determination of noncompliance (see **24:22**), they have a right to present evidence of compliance in their appeal to the school board (8 NYCRR §100.10(c)(5)). If the school board upholds the superintendent's determination, the parents may appeal to the commissioner of education within 30 days of receipt of notice of the school board's decision (8 NYCRR §100.10(c)(6)).

If parents lose their appeal or fail to contest the determination that their child's IHIP is deficient, they must "immediately provide for the instruction of their children at a public school or elsewhere in compliance with the Education Law." Further, the parents must provide to the superintendent written notice of the arrangements they have made, unless they have enrolled their child in the public school (8 NYCRR § 100.10(c)(7),(8)).

24:24. May students educated at home receive instruction at a location outside their parents' primary residence?

Yes. Instruction for students educated at home may be provided outside the parents' primary residence, provided the building where instruction takes place is in compliance with the local building code (8 NYCRR § 100.10(f)(5)).

24:25. May parents engage a tutor to provide home instruction?

Yes. Parents may engage the services of a tutor to provide instruction for all or part of the home instruction program. Moreover, parents providing home instruction to their children also can arrange to have their children receive group instruction in particular subjects. But where parents organize to have a "majority" of their children's education provided by a tutor in a group setting, they will be deemed to be operating a nonpublic school and will have to satisfy state law and regulations ensuring the substantial equivalency of instruction provided by nonpublic schools (NY State Education Department: "Revised Questions and Answers on Home Instruction," February 1994, p. 1).

24:26. Are there any attendance requirements for students educated at home?

Yes. Children in grades one through six must receive 900 hours of instruction and those in grades seven through 12 must receive 990 hours, with attendance substantially equivalent to 180 days per year. Absences are allowed on the same basis as prescribed by the school district for students attending the public schools. Parents must maintain records of attendance to be provided to the district upon request (8 NYCRR § 100.10(f)).

Instruction at home is usually given within the general time-frame of the normal school day, but greater flexibility in scheduling is possible. For example, parents may choose to provide instruction on weekends or in the evening. However, the total amount of instructional time per week should be generally comparable to that of the public school (NY State Education Department: "Revised Questions and Answers on Home Instruction," February 1994, p. 2).

24:27. Are there any courses that students instructed at home are required to take?

Yes. The commissioner's regulations set forth the courses that children educated at home must study (8 NYCRR § 100.10(e)). Among other things, bilingual education and/or English as a second language must be provided as needed (8 NYCRR § 100.10(e)(2)(i)). Although every student must have a physical education program, activities may differ provided that the outcomes are similar to those established for students in the public school.

24:28. Are students educated at home required to take state mandated standardized tests?

No. Home-instructed students are not required to take, for instance, Pupil Evaluation Program Tests (PEP) or Regents Competency Tests (RCTs), although the tests may be used to meet annual assessment requirements (8 NYCRR §100.10(h); see **14:65-66**).

In addition, if a request is made, school officials are encouraged to admit a student receiving home instruction to a Regents examination. If a Regents examination has a lab requirement, the student may be admitted to the examination if there is evidence that the student has met the lab requirement. The student's individualized home instruction plan (IHIP), quarterly reports and/or verification from the student's teacher can provide such evidence. However, Regents examinations may only be administered at the public school or registered nonpublic school because they are secure examinations. The test results can be helpful to the student and also to public school officials (NY State Education Department: "Revised Questions and Answers on Home Instruction," February 1994, p. 13).

24:29. What happens if a student educated at home does not perform adequately on the annual assessment?

If a student does not receive an adequate score on an annual assessment, the home instruction program will be placed on probation for a period of up to two years. The parent must submit a plan of remediation to be reviewed by the school district (8 NYCRR § 100.10(i)(1)). To be adequate, a student's annual assessment must reflect a composite score above the 33rd percentile on national norms, or indicate one academic year of growth as compared to a test administered during or subsequent to the prior school year (8 NYCRR § 100.10(h)(1)(v)).

If the objectives of the remediation plan are not met, the superintendent of schools will issue a notice of noncompliance, subject to school board review (8 NYCRR § 100.10(i)(2)), and ultimately require that the parent enroll the child in a public or other school which meets the requirements of the Education Law (8 NYCRR § 100.10(c)(7)).

During the period of probation, the superintendent or a designee may require one or more home visits, if he or she has reasonable grounds to believe that the program of home instruction does not comply with the regulations. The superintendent may include members of a home instruction peer review panel in the home visit team (8 NYCRR § 100.10(i)(3)). If the home instruction program is not on probation, school officials may request a home visit, but the parents are not required to consent to the request (NY State Education Department: "Revised Questions and Answers on Home Instruction," February 1994, p. 6).

24:30. May a student instructed at home be awarded a local or Regents diploma?

No. A high school diploma may only be awarded to a student enrolled in a registered secondary school who has completed all program requirements set by the Regents, the school or the district (8 NYCRR § 100.2(p); see also NY State Education Department: "Revised Questions and Answers on Home Instruction," February 1994, p. 5).

24:31. Are students who receive home instruction entitled to participate in interscholastic sports at the public school?

No. A home-schooled student does not have a property right in participation in sports, only a mere expectation, and the regulation restricting participation to public school students serves the legitimate purpose of "promoting school spirit, providing role models, and maintaining academic standards" (*Bradstreet v. Sobol*, 165 Misc. 2d 931 (Sup. Ct. 1995), *aff'd*, 225 A.D.2d 175 (3rd Dep't. 1996); see also *Appeal of Pelletier*, 27 Educ. Dep't Rep. 265 (1988); 8 NYCRR §§ 135.1(g), 135.4(c)(7)(ii)(b)(2)). Further, the court found that participation in athletics was quasi-curricular and one of the privileges of attending school. As such, it should not be available to students who opt out of the regular school program.

However, according to SED, children who are not educated in a public school may participate in the public school district's intramural activities, at the discretion of the board of education, which should adopt a written policy in this regard (NY State Education Department: "Revised Questions and Answers on Home Instruction," February 1994, p. 2, question 11).

24:32. Do students who receive home instruction have a right to borrow textbooks, computer software and library materials that are available to students enrolled in nonpublic schools?

No. The state law which requires districts to loan these items to nonpublic school students does not apply to students who receive home instruction, because such students are not enrolled in a nonpublic school. However, school districts may voluntarily loan such items to home-schooled students, subject to availability after the district has satisfied its legal obligations (NY State Education Department: "Revised Questions and Answers on Home Instruction," February 1994, p. 3; see also **24:14-17**).

24:33. Are students educated at home subject to the same immunization requirements as students attending school?

No. The provisions of Public Health Law section 2164 which require parents to submit proof of immunization prior to admission of their children to a school (see **12:58-59**) do not apply to students being educated at home. However, if the commissioner of health notifies school officials of the outbreak of a disease for which immunization is required, parents of children on home instruction who seek to participate in testing or other activities on the premises of a public or nonpublic school must produce proof of immunization or be denied access (NY State Education Department: Revised Questions and Answers on Home Instruction, February 1994, p. 3).

24:34. Is homebound instruction the same thing as home instruction?

No. Homebound instruction is provided on a temporary basis by the public school district when a student is unable to attend school, usually for reasons of illness, disability or discipline, whereas home instruction is typically provided by a parent on a more permanent basis.

24:35. Under what circumstances is homebound instruction provided?

If a prolonged absence due to physical, mental or emotional illness is anticipated, the administrator of the student's school should talk with the student's parents about arranging for homebound instruction. According to the State Education Department (SED), an absence of at least two weeks is considered a prolonged absence. Any such absence based upon an illness should be verified by the student's physician (see NY State Education Department: "Revised Handbook on Services to Pupils Attending Nonpublic Schools," 1990).

The district in which the student resides is responsible for providing an appropriately certified teacher to tutor the homebound student.

However, the district of residence may contract with another district to provide this service. According to SED, when a nonpublic school student requires homebound instruction, that student should enroll in the public school during the period of time that the nonpublic school student is receiving homebound instruction from the public school, so that the public school district may count the student in its attendance report for state aid purposes (see NY State Education Department: "Revised Handbook on Services to Pupils Attending Nonpublic School" 1990, addressing homebound instruction for nonpublic school students).

Commensurate with the commissioner's regulations on instruction for students in hospitals and other institutions, elementary school students on homebound instruction must receive at least five hours of instruction per week and secondary school students 10 hours per week. To the extent possible, homebound instruction should be staggered proportionately throughout the week (8 NYCRR § 175.21; see also NY State Education Department: "Revised Handbook on Services to Pupils Attending Nonpublic School," 1990).

It must be noted that, according to the U.S. Department of Education Office of Civil Rights, a school policy that provided for only four hours of instruction per week to homebound students and which failed to provide for make-up sessions when teachers were unable to provide the services during a particular week violated the Americans with Disabilities Act and section 504 of the Rehabilitation Act of 1973 (OCR Decision (*Boston Pub. Sch.*, 21 IDELR 170 (1994)).

25. Federal Laws and Public Schools

25:1. Is the federal government responsible for the provision of public education within the individual states?

No. Education is a state function under the Tenth Amendment of the United States Constitution, which reserves to the states those powers not delegated to the federal government. Furthermore, a number of United States Supreme Court decisions support the reserved powers of states in the field of public education. In *Brown v. Board of Educ.*, 347 U.S. 483 (1954), for example, the court stated that "education is perhaps the most important function of state and local governments." In 1972, the court recognized that "providing public schools ranks at the very apex of the function of a state" *(Wisconsin v. Yoder,* 406 U.S. 205 (1972)).

Additionally, in 1970, the General Education Provisions Act (20 USC §§ 1221–1235g) was amended to include a "prohibition against federal control of education" including any "direction, supervision, or control over the curriculum, program of instruction, administration, or personnel of any education institution, school, or school system, or over the selection of library resources, textbooks, or other printed or published instructional materials by any educational institution or school system" (20 USC § 1232a).

However, the federal role in public education has grown steadily as the availability of federal funds to state education departments and local school districts depends on local compliance with federal laws and regulations. For instance, if school districts accept federal funds, they must comply with, among others, the Hatch Amendment (20 USC § 1232h) which gives parents the right to inspect classroom materials used in connection with federally funded programs (see **14:57**); the Family Educational and Privacy Rights Act (also known as the Buckley Amendment) (20 USC § 1232g), which requires school districts to adopt policies to ensure student privacy rights (see **2:70, 2:80**); the Individuals with Disabilities Education Act (IDEA) (20 USC §§ 1400-1487), which requires schools to meet certain guidelines for serving children with disabilities (see chap. 13); and the Equal Access Act (20 USC § 4071), which declares that schools that permit student groups to use school facilities for noncurriculum-related purposes may not deny access to student religious or political groups based on anticipated content of the meeting (see **16:44**).

Additionally, the United States Constitution affects public education through its amendments, largely the First, Fifth and Fourteenth Amendments, protecting the rights of individuals. United States Supreme Court decisions interpreting these amendments have affected schools in areas such as school desegregation, separation of church and state, freedom of speech, corporal punishment and compulsory attendance.

Although the United States Constitution does not guarantee the right of public education, it precludes states, when determining for whom education must be provided, from categorically denying education to students on the basis of race, origin, alienage, indigence or illegitimacy (*San Antonio Independent Sch. Dist. v. Rodriguez*, 411 U.S. 1 (1973)). For instance, children who are illegal aliens may, in some circumstances, be entitled to a free public education (*Plyler v. Doe*, 457 U.S. 202 (1982)).

25:2. By what authority does the federal government legislate in the area of public education?

The authority of the federal government to legislate in the area of public education is derived from article 1, section 8, of the United States Constitution, which pertains to the power of Congress to provide for the general welfare and the Equal Protection Clause of the Fourteenth Amendment.

25:3. What federal agency has responsibility for coordinating federal support of education?

The United States Department of Education was created by the 96th Congress to assume responsibility for education (20 USC § 3411). The 1998 budget authority for this department is an estimated $29.4 billion in discretionary funds, most of which is distributed to the states' education departments and local schools.

25:4. Must school districts accept federal funds?

No. School districts and states are not obligated to accept federal funds, but if they do, they must accept the conditions under which federal funds are granted (see *Grove City College v. Bell*, 465 U.S. 555 (1984)). Congress may set these conditions (*Oklahoma v. United States Civil Service Comm.*, 330 U.S. 127 (1947)).

25:5. Are nonpublic schools in New York State eligible for federal programs and federal aid?

Yes. Nonpublic schools are eligible for certain federal programs and aid. Those schools that receive this aid are accountable for how the funds are spent, and they are prohibited from using these funds for religious worship or instruction (20 USC § 8897).

25:6. What is the total amount of federal aid for elementary, middle and secondary education in New York State?

In the federal fiscal year 1998 (October 1, 1997 – September 30, 1998), an estimated $1.24 billion in federal aid for elementary and secondary education was administered by the State Education Department.

25:7. What are the major programs through which federal education aid is allocated to elementary and secondary schools in New York State?

The following are the major federal education aid programs and the federal fiscal year 1998 (October 1, 1997 – September 30, 1998) allocations for New York State:

- **Title I of the Improving America's Schools Act (IASA)** (20 USC §§ 6301-6514), which was the vehicle for reforming the Elementary and Secondary Education Act (ESEA), ($711 million). This program serves educationally disadvantaged children in school attendance areas having a high concentration of children from low-income families (see **25:8**).
- **Individuals with Disabilities Education Act** (20 USC §§ 1400-1487) ($320.6 million). This legislation provides various programs to strengthen the educational services received by students with disabilities.
- **Goals 2000: Educate America Act** (20 USC §§ 5801-6084) ($35.2 million). This federal law provides grants to states and individual school districts to fund educational reform initiatives.
- **Title VI of the Improving America's Schools Act (IASA)** (20 USC §§ 7301-7373) ($21.6 million). This legislation contains various programs within several broad categories of basic skills, school improvement, innovation and meeting the needs of at-risk and high-cost students.

25:8. What federal programs are contained in Improving America's Schools Act?

The Improving America's Schools Act (IASA) of 1994 (20 USC §§ 6301-8962b), which enacted reforms to the Elementary and Secondary Education Act (ESEA), contains several programs, including:

- **Title I – Helping Disadvantaged Children Meet High Standards.** Provides states and local schools with funding for disadvantaged students. Funding is based upon the number of children living below the federal poverty line as counted in the U.S. census. Programs funded under this act must be used to serve these children.

- **Title II – Dwight D. Eisenhower Professional Development Program.** Provides grants for professional development for teachers with significant set-asides for mathematics and science teachers.
- **Title III – Technology For Education.** Provides grants to incorporate technology into the classroom to improve learning.
- **Title IV – Safe and Drug-Free Schools and Communities.** Provides grants to help school districts improve safety and reduce drug-related activity.
- **Title V – Promoting Equity.** Designed for districts with magnet school programs, enabling students and their families to choose among school buildings within a district which are established to focus student learning on such themes as the sciences, arts and humanities. These programs have been implemented to ensure desegregation and greater educational equity. Also includes women's educational equity to promote gender equity in education and assistance to address school dropout problems.
- **Title VI – Innovative Education Program Strategies.** Provides local grants to improve certain functions within schools, including professional development for teachers, administrators, and school board members. Other uses include technology acquisition and program coordination with other child-service agencies. This funding is the most flexible of all federal programs.
- **Title VII – Bilingual Education, Language Enhancement and Language Acquisition Programs.** Provides grants for programs designed to improve learning of English for non-English-speaking students.
- **Title VIII – Impact Aid.** Provides aid to districts that serve children of employees of the federal government, especially for students who are children of military employees that live on federal installations which are exempt from local taxes. Another section of this program provides payments in lieu of taxes (PILOTs) when the federal government acquires land previously on the tax roll.
- **Title IX – Indian, Native Hawaiian and Native Alaskan Education.** Provides funding for schools that serve Native American populations.
- **Title X – Programs of National Significance.** Funds educational research designed to help implement systemic reforms in order to reach higher academic standards.
- **Title XI – Coordinated Services.** Funds programs at the state and local levels which are designed to coordinate services for students who receive various forms of federal assistance.

- **Title XII – School Facilities Infrastructure Improvement.** Provides funding for schools in need of renovation. At press time, this program was not funded.
- **Title XIII – Support and Assistance Programs to Improve Education.** Provides grants for technical assistance needed to implement new reform efforts.
- **Title XIV – General Provisions.** Contains several miscellaneous programs, including the Gun-Free Schools Act, flexibility provisions and waiver requirements.

25:9. Does the Improving America's Schools Act (IASA) impose any requirements on school districts?

Yes. The Gun-Free Schools Act, which was adopted as part of the Improving America's Schools Act (20 USC § 8921), requires that in order to receive federal education funds under this section, a state must enact a law that requires at least a one-year suspension for any student who is found to have brought a firearm to school. The policy may enable the superintendent of schools to modify this requirement on a case-by-case basis.

In addition, under the Gun-Free Schools Act, a school district must have a policy in place to refer students who bring a firearm or weapon to school to the criminal justice or juvenile delinquency system (20 USC § 8922). The New York State Legislature has satisfied these requirements by enacting amendments to the Education Law (§ 3214(3)(d)) (see **12:119-125**).

25:10. What is the Goals 2000: Educate America Act?

The federal Goals 2000: Educate America Act provides a framework for state and local education reform initiatives designed to meet the National Education Goals, now established as part of federal law (20 USC § 5812). It gives states and school districts flexibility in the use of federal dollars, in exchange for improved educational performance. The National Education Goals are not mandates; rather, they are voluntary goals set by the federal government for school districts across the country.

The National Education Goals stipulate that:
- All children will start school ready to learn.
- At least 90 percent of students will finish high school.
- Students will leave grades four, eight and 12 with demonstrated competence in English, math, science, foreign languages, civics and government, economics, arts, history and geography.

- Teachers will have access to programs for the continued improvement of their skills.
- The United States will be first in the world in math and science achievement.
- Every adult will be literate and possess the skills to compete in a global economy.
- Every school will be free of drugs and violence.
- Every school will promote involvement of parents in their children's education.

The Goals 2000: Educate America Act also establishes a framework for the Improving America's Schools Act (IASA) The sections of IASA, including Title I (formally Chapter 1), and Title VI (formally Chapter 2), are geared towards meeting the National Education Goals.

25:11. Does the Goals 2000: Educate America Act require school districts to adopt reform programs?

No. The Goals 2000: Educate America Act is a voluntary competitive grant-based reform effort designed to help schools meet the National Education Goals. For example, Title III, State and Local Systematic Education Improvement (20 USC §§ 5881-5900), provides competitive grants to local school districts to implement reform. A district must establish a committee of members of the community to develop a reform plan designed to help district students meet the National Education Goals. In the case of school districts in New York, the shared-decision-making committees already in place under the Compact for Learning fill this role, and the grant monies can be used to implement districts' shared-decision-making plans (8 NYCRR § 100.11; see **3:26-27**).

Title IV, Parental Assistance (20 USC §§ 5911-5918), establishes a grant program for the creation of parental information resource centers, designed to improve parenting and child development in order to prepare all children for school. The centers must provide information and support to parents of young children and school-age children, and to those individuals who work with parents. The centers may be established by nonprofit organizations, either by themselves or with local school districts.

Title VII, Safe Schools (20 USC §§ 5961-5968) is a grant program which stipulates that school districts must develop a comprehensive plan to identify and assess school violence and discipline problems, and develop strategies for resolving these problems. These grants can be used to conduct school safety and violence prevention reviews; train personnel in violence prevention, conflict intervention, and peer mediation; create community education programs, parental involvement in the promotion of school safety; and coordinate school-based activities designed to promote school safety and reduce or prevent school violence and discipline problems through coordination with law enforcement, judicial, social service and other appropriate agencies.

25:12. Does the Goals 2000: Educate America Act impose any requirements on school districts?

Yes. The Pro-Children Act of 1994, which is part of Goals 2000 (20 USC § 6081), prohibits smoking in any enclosed school facility used to provide education services for children in kindergarten through 12th grade, in any school district that receives federal education aid.

25:13. Are there any federal laws which help prepare students for work?

Yes. The School-to-Work Opportunities Act (20 USC §§ 6101-6251) was created to help states and local schools better prepare non-college-bound students for work. The law provides money for state, local school district, and business partnerships to develop and implement a combination of vocational education and on-the-job training, to give students the skills needed to find work after high school. Additionally, most states, including New York, have received implementation grants for statewide coordination of school-to-work programs and for subgrants to local school/ business partnerships to implement grants at the local level. In New York, these programs are monitored by the state School-to-Work Opportunities Advisory Committee.

School districts may also receive Job-Training Partnership Act (JTPA) funds to operate JTPA programs (29 USC § 1517(c)).

25:14. Are public school districts eligible for federal public works funds for such projects as new school buildings, renovation or repair of existing schools?

Yes. When the Local Public Works Employment Law was authorized by Congress (42 USC §§ 6701-6735), school districts retained the right to equal treatment in the distribution of the funds. (42 USC § 6702(a)). Conditions are applied to the receipt of federal funds for construction projects. For instance, school districts must engage in projects pursuant to a contract awarded to the lowest competitive bidder (42 USC § 6705e).

In addition, school districts in receipt of federal funds for public works projects must pay all laborers and mechanics at least the prevailing wage in the locality as determined by the Secretary of Labor (42 USC § 6708) in accordance with the Davis Bacon Act (40 USC § 276a-276a-5).

Bibliography

Alexander, Kern, and M. David Alexander. *Law of Schools, Students and Teachers in a Nutshell.* St. Paul, Minn.: West Publishing Co., 1984.

___. *American Public School Law.* St. Paul, Minn.: West Publishing Co., 1985.

Asbestos: A Handbook for School Board Members and Administrators. Albany, N.Y.: New York State School Boards Association, 1989.

Best's Key Rating Guide. Odwick, N.J.: A.M. Best Co., 1987.

Black's Law Dictionary. 5th ed. St. Paul, Minn.: West Publishing Co., 1983.

BOCES Administrative Handbook. Vol. 1. Albany, N.Y.: New York State Education Department, January 1990.

BOCES: A Tradition of Educational Sharing. Albany, N.Y.: New York State School Boards Association, 1990.

Copyright Basics. Washington, D.C.: Library of Congress, 1989.

Disciplining School Employees. Albany, N.Y.: New York State School Boards Association, 1994.

Environmental Quality in Schools. Albany, N.Y.: New York State Education Department, 1994.

Fiscal Management: A Handbook for School Board Members. Albany, N.Y.: New York State School Boards Association, 1997.

Fischer, Louis, and Gail Paulus Sorenson. *School Law for Counselors, Psychologists and Teachers, 2nd edition.* New York: Longman, 1991.

"A Guide to the Reorganization of School Districts in New York State." Albany, N.Y.: New York State Education Department, 1993.

"Handbook One: Regulations of the Commissioner of Education." Albany, N.Y.: New York State Education Department, Office of Counsel, 1996.

"Handbook on Requirements for Elementary and Secondary Schools in Education Law, Rules of the Board of Regents, and Regulations of the Commissioner of Education." Albany, N.Y.: New York State Education Department, 1989.

Hudgins, H.C., Jr., and Richard S. Vacca. *Law and Education: Contemporary Issues and Court Decisions.* Charlottesville, Va.: Michie Co., 1985.

LaMorte, Michael W. *School Law: Cases and Concepts.* St. Paul, Minn.: West Publishing Co., 1987.

McKinney's Consolidated Laws of New York, Annotated. St. Paul, Minn.: West Publishing Co.

Menacker, Julius. *School Law: Theoretical and Case Perspectives.* Englewood Cliffs, N.J.: Prentice Hall, Inc., 1987.

Morris, A.A. *The Constitution and American Education.* St. Paul, Minn.: West Publishing Co., 1980.

Negotiations 1991: A Handbook on School District Negotiations. Albany, N.Y.: New York State School Boards Association, 1989.

"New York's Local Industrial Development Agencies: A Closer Look." Albany, N.Y.: New York State Legislative Commission on State-Local Relations, September 1989 (interim report).

"New York State Textbook Loan Program: Recommended Procedures for Textbook Purchases, Loans and Inventory Control." Albany, N.Y.: New York State Education Department, 1993.

Official Compilation of Codes, Rules and Regulations of the State of New York. Albany, N.Y.: Lenz & Riecker.

Official Decisions, Opinions and Related Matters: Public Employment Relations Board. Horsham, Pa.: LRP Publications.

Prosser & Keaton on the Law of Torts, 5th ed. St. Paul, Minn.: West, 1984.

"Questions and Answers on the BOCES Reform Act." Albany, N.Y.: New York State Education Department, October 1993.

"Radon Detection and Control in New York State Schools: An Interim Program Guideline." Albany, N.Y.: New York State Education Department, 1990.

Reutter, Edward. *The Law of Public Education.* Mineola, N.Y.: Foundation Press, 1985.

"Revised Handbook on Services to Pupils Attending Nonpublic Schools." Albany, N.Y.: New York State Education Department, 1990.

"Revised Questions and Answers on Home Instruction." Albany, N.Y.: New York State Education Department, February 1994.

Roberts III, Henry M., and William J. Evans, eds. *Robert's Rules of Order,* Newly Revised. Glenview, Ill.: Scott, Forsman, 1990.

"Safeguards, Accounting and Auditing of Extra Classroom Activity Funds." Albany, N.Y.: New York State Education Department, 1992.

A School Board Member's Guide to Shared Decision Making. Albany, N.Y.: New York State School Boards Association, 1993.

The Sunshine Laws: A Handbook for School Board Members. Albany, N.Y.: New York State School Boards Association, 1991.

Uniform System of Accounts for School Districts. Albany, N.Y.: Office of the State Comptroller.

Valente, W.D. *Law in the Schools.* Columbus, Ohio: Merrill Publishing Co., 1987.

"What Everyone Should know About Physical Education in New York State." Albany, N.Y.: New York State Education Department, 1989.

Index

Absences (*See also* Attendance)
  excessive absences, students
    as cause for denial of credit, 12:22, 13:44
    as cause for drop from enrollment, 12:25
    as cause for lowering of course grade, 12:116
  excessive absences, teachers
    job actions, 10:50
    salary adjustment, 8:130
  indigent children, lack of food or clothing as
    cause of absence, 12:69
  parental consent, 12:21
  for religious observance
    students, 12:17, 23:13
    teachers, 8:138, 23:14
  suspension days as, 12:23
Accident and health insurance
  district employees, 18:44
  school board members, 18:46
Accidents
  school bus drivers, 22:59
  school district's liability for, 18:7
Accounting
  major accounting funds, 19:13
  Uniform System of Accounts for School
    Districts, 19:12
ADA (*See* Americans with Disabilities Act (ADA))
ADEA (*See* Age Discrimination in Employment Act
  (ADEA))
Administrative employees
  probationary employees
    due process rights of, 7:13
Administrative tenure area, 7:7, 8:64
Administrators, school
  abolishment of position, 7:12
  "acting" positions, effect on probationary
    period, 7:9
  appointment of, 7:6, 7:17
  certification requirements, 7:2, 8:43
    waiver of, 7:3
  compensation when multiple districts share
    administrator's services, 7:5
  criminal charges
    service rendered outside tenure area
      pending outcome, effect on probationary
      period, 7:10
  discipline when multiple districts share
    administrator's services, 7:5
  dismissal of probationary administrators, 7:11
    abolishment of position as alternative to, 7:12
  employment contracts, 7:17
    probationary employees, 7:13
  multiple districts, shared administrator's
    services, 7:5
  Preferred Eligibility List (PEL), 7:12
  probationary employees
    "acting" positions, effect on probationary
      period, 7:9

criminal charges, service rendered outside
    tenure area pending outcome of, 7:10
  dismissal of, 7:11
  employment contracts, 7:13
  substitute positions, effect on probationary
    period, 7:8
  sharing administrator's services with multiple
    districts, 7:5
  substitute positions, effect on probationary
    period, 7:8
  tenure, 7:7, 8:64
    multiple districts, shared administrator's
      services, 7:5
Admissions
  BOCES programs, vocational education, 14:27
  first grade, 12:8
  homeless students, 12:43
  immunizations requirements, 12:58
    exceptions, 12:59
  kindergarten, 12:6, 12:7
  nonresident students, 12:29, 12:30
  private and parochial schools, 12:7
Adoptive parents
  leaves of absence, 8:136, 9:21
Adult education programs
  state aid, 21:12
Ad valorem levies, 20:21
Advertising
  bidding requirements, as part of, 19:47
    transportation, 22:67
  school buildings, construction of, 16:24
    printed brochure describing bond issue, 16:18
After-school programs
  emergency-management plans, 17:4
  fire drills, 17:4
Age
  compulsory attendance, 12:1, 12:3, 12:6, 12:13
  prekindergarten programs, 12:5
  retirement age, mandatory, 11:1
  school bus drivers, 22:48
  of student (*See* Age of students)
Age Discrimination in Employment Act (ADEA)
  teachers, 8:8, 8:125, 18:22
Agency shop fees
  allowability of, 10:26
  authorized uses, 10:28
  payroll deductions, 10:28
  refund procedures, 10:28
  strike, loss during, 10:51
Age of students
  for compulsory school attendance, 12:1, 12:3,
    12:4, 12:6, 12:13
  as criterion for admission, 12:6, 12:7, 12:8
  first grade, admission to, 12:8
  kindergarten, entrance to, 12:6, 12:7
  minimum age as criterion for admission, 12:6,
    12:7, 12:8

suspension of student over age 16, home
    instruction requirements, 12:108
AIDS
    ADA, rights granted under, 12:64
    classification of, 12:63, 12:64
    condoms and AIDS curriculum
        demonstrations on use, 14:34
        distribution of condoms as part of, 14:33
    confidentiality requirements, 12:65
    defined, 12:63
    as disability, 12:64, 13:2
    exposure control plans, 12:66, 17:24
    instruction in, state-mandated curriculum, 14:32
        condom distribution as part of, 14:33
        condom use demonstrations, 14:34
        religion as basis for excusal from, 14:28,
            14:32, 14:58
    nondiscrimination requirements, 12:64
    parental opposition to curriculum on, 14:28,
        14:32, 14:58
    prevention of, state-mandated instruction in,
        14:32
    protection from exposure to HIV, 12:66, 17:24
    religion as basis for excusal from AIDS-
        prevention instruction, 14:28, 14:32, 14:58
Air quality
    asbestos, exposure to (See Asbestos)
    indoors (See Indoor air quality)
Albany City School District
    annual district meeting, timing of, 4:3
Alcohol abuse
    prevention curriculum, 12:57, 14:36
        driver education classes, inclusion in, 14:48
    Safe and Drug-Free School and Communities
Act (SDFSCA), 12:57, 16:55, 16:56
    school bus drivers
        rehabilitation programs, 22:65
        removal or exclusion from driving, use as
            cause for, 22:64
Alcohol and drug testing
    collective bargaining, 10:37
    school bus drivers, 22:61
        confidentiality requirements, 22:63
        method of testing, 22:62
        program requirements, 22:62
        rehabilitation programs, 22:65
        removal or exclusion from driving, use as
            cause for, 22:64
    students
        with parental consent, 12:90
        random drug testing of athletes, 12:91
American Indians (See Native Americans)
Americans with Disabilities Act (ADA)
    AIDS, classification of, 12:64
    disabled children, 13:1
    disabled teachers, 8:6, 8:31, 18:22
        reasonable accommodation requirements, 8:7
    illegal drugs exclusion, 8:6
    reasonable accommodation requirements, 8:7
    school buildings, construction of, 16:27
Annexation, school district reorganization, 15:3
    collective bargaining agreements, 15:19

debt, assumption of, 15:18
employment contracts, 15:19, 15:22
employment rights
    central school district, annexation to, 15:21
    superintendents, 15:22
    union free school district, annexation to, 15:20
superintendent of schools, 15:22
teacher tenure
    central school district, annexation to, 15:21
    union free school district, annexation to, 15:20
voter approval, 15:3, 15:12
Annual district elections
    ballot propositions, 4:25
    election districts, division of district into, 4:72
    incorrect time or date, ramifications of holding
election at, 4:6
    poll watchers, appointment of, 4:76
    set aside of results, causes for, 4:59, 4:81
    time of, 4:3, 4:5
Annual district meeting
    absentee ballots
        allowability of, 4:86
        challenges to, 4:91
        deadline for submission of, 4:87
        list of persons requesting, public notice, 4:90
        multiple ballot applications, 4:89
        procedure for, 4:88
    Albany City School District, timing of meeting,
        4:3
    board's responsibilities
        budget contents, requirements, 4:13, 4:14,
            4:15, 4:16
        budget, presentation of, 4:13, 4:29
        proposed district budget, presentation of,
            4:13, 4:29
    bond issues, public notice requirements, 4:10,
        4:11
    budget actions, 4:1
        anonymous literature regarding budget, 4:27
        changes to proposed budget before actual
            vote, 4:22, 4:24
        completion of budget, deadline for, 4:18
        contents of budget, requirements, 4:14,
            4:15, 4:16
        deadline for completion of budget, 4:18
        defeat of proposed budget, 4:28
        limit on number of times board can submit
            budget, 4:29
        lobbying on behalf of budget, 4:26
        postponement of vote due to pending
            contract action, allowability of, 4:7
        presentation of budget to voters, 4:13, 4:29
        prior year's budget information, 4:17
        public notice requirements, 4:10, 4:11, 4:13
    budget contents, requirements
        administrative component of budget, 4:16
        capital component of budget, 4:15
        prior year's budget information, 4:17
        program component of budget, 4:14
    call to order, person responsible for, 4:9
    chairperson, powers of, 4:9, 4:58
    challenges to election results
        absentee ballots, 4:91

board actions taken pending appeal,
   effect on, 4:48
person's qualification to vote, challenges to,
   4:83, 4:84, 4:85
challenges to person's qualification to vote
   in districts without personal registration, 4:83
   in districts with personal registration, 4:84
   time and place requirements, 4:85
changes to proposed budget
   board initiated, 4:23
   voter initiated, 4:22, 4:24
clerk of district, 4:79
date of, 4:2, 4:5, 4:6
election districts, division of district into, 4:72
election inspectors, 4:75
election of school board members, 4:1
failure to have meeting, 4:4
improperly held meeting, 4:81
incorrect time or date, ramifications of holding
   meeting at, 4:6
lobbying on behalf of budget, 4:26
location of, 4:8
poll lists, 4:65, 4:78
postponement of vote due to pending contract
   action, allowability of, 4:7
prior year's budget information, 4:17
proposed district budget, presentation of
   limit of number of times board can submit
     budget, 4:29
proxy voting, 4:73
public hearing requirements, 4:19
public notice requirements, 4:10, 4:11, 4:19
   budget actions, 4:10, 4:11, 4:13, 4:21
   noncompliance with, consequences of, 4:12
purpose of, 4:1, 4:2
record keeping of proceedings, 4:79
set aside of results, causes for, 4:81
special meetings (See Special school district
   meeting)
time of, 4:3, 4:5, 4:6
voting at
   absentee ballots, 4:86, 4:87, 4:88, 4:89
   ballot voting, 4:69, 4:71
   booths, use of, 4:68
   challenges to person's qualification to vote,
     4:83, 4:84, 4:85
   closing of polls, people waiting in line at, 4:77
   counting of votes, 4:80
   electioneering, 4:74
   election inspectors, 4:75
   New York State Election Law, applicability
     of, 4:67
   proxy voting, 4:73
   qualified voters, 4:57
   residency requirements, 4:82
   set aside of results, causes for, 4:59, 4:81
   unqualified voters, penalties for, 4:59
   voting machines, 4:70, 4:71
Annuity plans, tax-sheltered, 11:19
   salary reduction as means of investing in, 8:129
Appeals
   arbitration, 10:58

to commissioner of education (See Commissioner
   of Education)
CSE determinations (See Committee on
   Special Education (CSE))
disciplinary penalties, civil service employees
   non-section 75 employees, 9:32
   tenured employees, 9:31
Appointment
   administrators, school, 7:2, 7:17
   BOCES staff members, 6:18
   district superintendent, 6:4
   principals, 7:6
   school board members, 1:22, 2:4
   superintendent of schools, 2:13, 7:2, 7:17
   teacher tenure, 8:68, 8:71
     notice requirements, 8:69
     part-time teachers, 8:73
     waiver of right to probationary appointment,
       8:72
Arbitration
   advisory, 10:57, 10:58
   agreement, 10:56
   American Arbitration Association (AAA), 10:59
   appeals, 10:58
   arbitrator selection process, 10:59
   binding arbitration, 10:39, 10:57, 10:58
   computerized database services, 10:10, 10:59
   coordinated bargaining, 10:39
   grievances, as resolution to (See Grievances)
   New York School Boards Association services
     available, 10:10, 10:59
   Public Employment Relations Board (PERB),
     10:59
Architects, preparation of plans and specifications,
   16:17
Arrest warrants, on school premises, 12:93
Asbestos
   air sampling, 17:56
   asbestos-abatement projects
     air sampling, 17:56
     containment area, 17:57
     contractors, 17:58, 17:59, 17:60
     defined, 17:44
     unanticipated projects, 17:54
     voter approval, 17:53
   asbestos-containing materials (ACMs), 17:41,
     17:44, 17:45, 17:47, 17:50
   asbestos designees, 17:49, 17:50
   asbestos handler defined, 17:61
   Asbestos Hazard Emergency Response Act
     (AHERA), 17:43, 17:44, 17:45
   building aid, 17:52
   clerk of the works, 17:62
   compliance with laws, person responsible for,
     17:49, 17:50
   containment area, 17:57
   contractors
     certification requirements, 17:59
     defined, 17:58
     employees of, 17:59
     licensing requirements, 17:59
     qualifications, 17:58

record keeping requirements, 17:60
defined, 17:41, 17:42
encapsulation defined, 17:47
enclosure defined, 17:47
friable asbestos defined, 17:42
funding
  building aid, 17:52
  grants, 17:52
  state aid, 17:52
grants, 17:52
Industrial Code Rule 56, 17:44
  air sampling, 17:56
  contractors defined, 17:58
  projects defined, 17:44
inspections, 17:51
liability, 17:48
licensing and certification, 17:59, 17:61
management plan, 17:44, 17:45
notification requirements, 17:55
operation and maintenance program, 17:47
projects defined, 17:44
record keeping
  contractors, 17:60
  management plan, copies of, 17:44
removal defined, 17:47
repair defined, 17:47
responses to presence of, 17:46
state aid, 17:52
Assessment of property
assessment roll (See Assessment roll)
assessors, 20:8
Board of Assessment Review, 20:6
certiorari proceedings, 20:14, 20:15
changing of assessment, procedures for,
  20:13, 20:14
complaints, filing of, 20:13
definitions, 20:7
information about, additional, 20:51
real property, defined, 20:7
review procedures, 20:13
State Board of Equalization and Assessment
  (See State Board of Real Property Services)
State Board of Real Property Services, 20:5,
  20:8, 20:30, 20:32, 20:51
state equalization rate, defined, 20:7
tax roll, defined, 20:7
tax warrant, defined, 20:7
timetable for, 20:11
Assessment of students (See Examinations; Testing
  of students)
Assessment roll
accuracy of, 20:10
collecting officer, return of roll by, 20:44
correction of, 20:12
preparation of, 20:9
return of roll and warrant by collecting officer,
  20:44
Assistant principals
certification requirements, 7:2
statutory requirement for, 7:27
Assistant superintendents
certification requirements, 7:2

sharing superintendent's services with multiple
  districts, 7:5
Associate superintendents
certification requirements, 7:2
sharing superintendent's services with multiple
  districts, 7:5
Athletics and competitive sports
admission fees, 16:48
broadcasting of, 16:48
coaches and coaching
  first aid and CPR skills, 8:42
  teacher certification, 8:42
  teachers, extra pay for, 8:17
detention precluding participation, 12:112
disabled students, 13:13
home instruction students, eligibility of, 24:31
injuries, school district liability for
  non-student participants, 18:16
  spectator injuries, 18:3, 18:17
  student participants, 18:15
insurance coverage for student participating
  in, 18:48
non-student participants, school district liability
  for injuries to, 18:16
prayers and benedictions at games or practices,
  23:6
school buses to events, 22:12, 22:20
sexual discrimination, prohibition against, 14:26
spectator injuries, school district liability for,
  18:3, 18:17
teachers, extra pay for coaching, 8:17
use of school buildings, 16:48
Attendance
absences (See Absences)
average daily attendance (ADA), 12:12
  state aid formulation, 21:15
compulsory attendance (See Compulsory
  attendance)
contagious diseases, students with, 12:62
disabled students, 13:44
dual-enrollment law, 12:15
employed students, 12:3
enforcement of, 12:12, 12:20
exemptions from compulsory attendance, 12:2
legal right to attend school, 12:6
  suspension, impact of, 12:103, 13:38, 13:40,
    13:41
married students, 12:3
parental opposition to school building
  conditions as reason for nonattendance, 12:16
part-time students, allowability of, 12:15
poor attendance as cause for drop from
  enrollment, 12:25
post-graduates under 21, right to attend school,
  12:9, 12:10
prekindergarten programs, 12:5
private and parochial schools, 12:4
record keeping requirements, 12:12
registers, 12:12
reports to parents, 14:70
state aid and, 21:9, 21:15, 21:18
transportation privileges, impact of suspension
  of, 12:110

truancy
   defined, 12:19
   enforcement, 12:20
   suspension of student for, permissibility of,
      12:97
   zones, 16:33
Attendance zones, 16:33
Attorneys (*See* Legal counsel)
At-will employees, 10:3
   manuals as contracts, 10:4
Audits
   Board of Cooperative Educational Services
      (BOCES) finances, 5:46
   district funds, 19:20
   federal audits, 19:20
   independent audits, 19:20
   internal audits, 19:20
   purchasing audits, 19:20
   school bus contractors, 22:69
   state audits, 19:20
Austerity budget, 19:37

Back pay, civil service employee reinstatement, 9:29
Balance, planned, 19:35
Bank accounts
   bond sales, deposit of proceeds of, 19:75
Banks or trust companies
   conflicts of interest, 3:17, 19:74
   designation as depository of district funds,
      3:16, 19:14
   district treasurer, permissibility as, 3:15
   official school depository, designation as,
      3:16, 19:14
Benefits
   collective bargaining, 10:36
   district superintendent, legal limits, 6:11
   Family and Medical Leave Act (*See* Family and
      Medical Leave Act (FMLA))
   limits on, district superintendent, 6:11
   retirement plan benefits (*See* Retirement plans)
   sick leave (*See* Sick leave)
   vacation pay
      district superintendent, legal limits, 6:12
      unused leave time, payment for, 8:141
Bidding requirements for school district purchases
   competitive bid requirements (*See* Competitive
      bidding requirements)
   noncompetitive bidding, procedures for,
      19:48, 19:49
   professional services, 19:48
Bilingual education
   Federal aid programs, 25:8
   limited English proficiency
      education policies, 14:30
      state aid, 21:12
      testing requirements, 14:30
      program requirements, 14:30
      state aid programs, 21:12
      teacher certification, 8:34
Binding arbitration, collective bargaining, 10:39,
   10:57, 10:58
Bingo and similar games, use of school premises
   for, 16:40

Board of Assessment Review, 20:6
Board of Cooperative Educational Services
   (BOCES), 1:24, 5:1
   annual meeting
      public notice requirements, 5:17, 5:18, 5:19
      purpose of, 5:16
      timing of, 5:17
   audits of, state and independent, 5:46
   budget of, 5:40
      adoption of, 5:39, 5:41
      approval requirements for, 5:41, 5:42, 5:45
      capital budget, 5:44, 5:45
      component districts' responsibilities for,
         5:38, 5:41
      contingency administrative budget, 5:42, 5:43
      deadline for adoption of, 5:39
      disclosure requirements, 5:18, 5:19, 5:20
      final adoption of, time limits on, 5:43
      program budget, 5:44, 5:45
      rejection of, result of, 5:42
      resident weighted daily attendance
         (RWADA), 5:38
      source of funds for, 5:38
      voting on, 5:41
   capital budget, 5:44
      approval requirements, 5:45
   chief executive officer, defined, 7:15
   as civil service employees, 9:2, 9:5
   contracting powers, 5:22
   disabled students
      registration requirements, 13:9
      shared services for, 5:30, 21:12, 21:23
   district superintendent (*See* District superin-
      tendent)
   election of members of board, 5:7
      component school districts' failure to vote,
         effect of, 5:14
      nomination process, 5:9, 5:10
      procedure for, 5:11
      quorum on election day, failure to obtain, 5:13
      tie vote in election, 5:12
      vacancies on board, procedures for filling, 5:15
   emergency-management plans (*See* Emergency-
      management plans)
   funds for, sources of
      component districts, cost sharing by, 5:38
      state aid, 5:34, 5:38, 21:3, 21:12, 21:15
   legal defense, indemnification for, 18:33,
      18:34, 18:35
   legal status, 5:1
   maintenance of buildings and grounds,
      prohibition against sharing of services for,
      5:37
   membership, district, 5:3
      termination of, 5:4
   members of board, 2:3, 2:4
      election of, 5:7, 5:9, 5:10, 5:11, 5:12, 5:13,
         5:14, 5:15
      eligibility requirements, 5:8
      limitations on membership, 5:7, 5:8
      multiple members from same component
         district, 5:7

nominations, 5:7, 5:9, 5:10
number of, 5:5
residency requirements, 5:8
restrictions on nominations, 5:7, 5:10
term of office, 5:6
vacancies on board, procedures for filling, 5:15
non-component district using services of, 5:36
number of BOCES, 5:2
oath of office, 2:8
performance of BOCES district, report card
for, 5:29, 14:73
powers and duties, 5:1, 5:20, 5:21, 5:22, 5:23
authority to suspend students, 12:99
private and parochial schools, 24:9
program budget, 5:44
approval requirements, 5:45
prohibited shared services, 5:37
property of
construction of, 5:23, 5:24
leasing of personal property, 5:28
leasing of unneeded facilities, 5:26
ownership rights, 5:23
purchasing of real property by BOCES, 5:23
renovations of BOCES buildings, 5:25
rental of real property, 5:27
report cards for academic and fiscal performance
of BOCES district, 5:29, 14:73
school-based planning and shared-decision-
making plans (See Shared decision making)
school buses leased to, 22:20
self-insurance fund, 18:43
services of, 5:1, 5:22
contracting requirements, 5:31
itinerant teachers or workers, maximum
time quotas for, 5:33
non-component district using, 5:36
procedure for securing, 5:31
prohibited shared services, 5:37
shared services, 5:21, 5:30, 5:33
state aid for purchase of, 5:34
transportation of students to BOCES classes,
5:35
teachers
revocation of certification, 8:48
shared services for, 5:30
shared time, 5:33
tenure, eligibility for, 8:55, 8:93
termination of membership by district, 5:4
transportation services for, 22:20
vocational education, shared services for,
5:22, 5:30
prerequisites for admission to, 14:27
quotas for classes, allowability of, 5:32
Board of Education Retirement System (BERS),
New York City, 11:4
Board of Regents
authority for public education, 1:2
authority over colleges and universities, 1:7
bond issuance, consent for, 19:70
compensation of, 1:9
composition of board, 1:8
construction projects, approval of, 16:20

examinations (See Regents examinations)
graduation standards adopted by, 14:15, 14:19
learning standards adopted by (See Learning
standards adopted by Board of Regents)
legal status of, 1:7
powers and duties of, 1:2, 1:5, 1:9
private and parochial schools, registration of,
24:6
selection of board members, 1:8
State Education Department (SED) (See State
Education Department (SED))
tenure rules (See Teacher tenure, Tenure)
BOCES (See Board of Cooperative Educational
Services (BOCES))
Bomb threats, 17:1, 17:5
Bonding
by district treasurer, 19:4
by tax collector, 19:4
Bonds
after school district reorganization, 15:18
attorney, hiring of, 19:78
auditor, bonding of, 3:21
authorization for issuance of, 19:68
Board of Regents
approval, 16:20
consent of, 19:70
bond anticipation notes (BANs), 19:65
bonds anticipation notes (BANs), 19:60,
19:61, 19:64
combining of projects, 19:73
construction of school buildings
Board of Regents' approval, 16:20
net bonded indebtedness, 16:20
printed brochure describing bond issue, 16:18
surety bonds, 18:49
destruction of canceled bonds, 2:75
investment of sale proceeds, 19:76
issuance of
authorization for, 19:68
comptroller's consent, 19:70
printed brochure describing bond issue, 16:18
public notice requirements, 4:10, 4:11
voter approval, 19:69, 19:77
limitations on amounts, 19:61
net bonded indebtedness, 16:20
printed brochure describing bond issue, 16:18
private sale of, 19:71
public sale of, 19:71
serial bonds, 19:60, 19:63
special bank accounts, 19:75
statutory installment bonds, 19:60, 19:63
tax collector, bonding of, 3:21
treasurer, bonding of, 3:21
voter approval for issuance of, 19:69, 19:77
Borrowing
bond anticipation notes (BANs), 19:65
bonds anticipation notes (BANs), 19:60, 19:61,
19:64
budget notes, 19:60, 19:64
capital notes, 19:60, 19:64
conflicts of interest, 19:74
50 percent rule, 19:62

information about, additional, 19:79
interest rates, 19:66, 19:67
limitations, 19:61
long-term borrowing instruments, 19:60, 19:63
revenue anticipation notes, 19:60
serial bonds, 19:60, 19:63
short-term borrowing instruments, 19:60
statutory installment bonds, 19:60, 19:63
tax anticipation notes, 19:60, 19:64
types of, 19:60
Breakfast programs, student (*See* School breakfast programs)
Broadcasting, of athletic events, 16:48
Buckley Amendment (*See* Family Educational Rights and Privacy Act (FERPA))
Budget notes, 19:60, 19:64
Budget, school
    annual budget, voter approval requirements, 19:31
    anonymous literature regarding budget, 4:27
    austerity budget, 4:28, 19:37
    board's responsibilities, 2:10
    BOCES' budgets (*See* Board of Cooperative Educational Services (BOCES))
    city school districts, 4:20
    commission of education, right to impose budget, 4:30
    contingent budget and expenses (*See* Contingent budget and expenses)
    defeat of proposed budget, 4:28
        limit of number of times board can submit budget after, 4:29
    excess spending, 19:15
    fund balance, 19:34
    legal expenses, 19:41
    limit of number of times board can submit budget, 4:29
    planned balance, 19:35
    residents' participation, 19:31, 19:33 (*See also* Contingent budget and expenses)
        changes to proposed budget, 4:22, 4:24
    statutory expenditures, 19:41
    transfers between budget categories, 19:36, 19:44
    transportation, 19:43, 22:8, 22:67
    unanticipated expenses, allowability of line for, 19:32
Buffalo
    school board membership, 2:3, 2:4
    state aid, 21:16
    teacher certification requirements, 8:27
Building aid
    asbestos-abatement projects, 17:52
    federal funds, 25:8, 25:14
    joint facilities, 16:29
    leasing of school buildings, 16:30
    reorganization incentive aid, 15:23
    state building aid, 16:29
Buildings, school (*See* School buildings)
Bureau of Facilities Planning, SED
    building permits, 16:23
    long-range plans on fiscal and program projections, 16:1

Bus transportation
    public carriers as student transportation, 22:1, 22:9, 22:82
    school buses (*See* School buses)

Camps
    school camps, establishment of, 2:17
    use of public school property for, 2:17
Capital Assets Preservation Program (CAPP), 16:1
Capital notes, 19:60, 19:64
Capital reserve fund, 19:24
CAPP (*See* Capital Assets Preservation Program (CAPP))
CAR, annual (*See* Comprehensive Assessment Report (CAR), annual)
Census
    board's responsibilities, 2:16
    disabled students, inclusion of, 13:9
Central high school districts, 1:21
    annual school board reorganization meetings, timing of, 3:2
    board membership, 2:3, 2:4
    naming of new district, 15:17
Centralization, school district reorganization (*See also* Annexation, school district reorganization)
    debt, assumption of, 15:18
    defined, 15:2
    employment contracts, 15:19
    employment rights, 15:21
    naming of new district, 15:17
    procedures for, 15:11
    teacher tenure, 15:21
    voter approval, 15:11
Central school districts, 1:20
    annexation, 15:3, 15:12
        employment rights, 15:21
        teacher tenure, 15:21
        voter approval, 15:12
    annual district meetings
        chairperson of, 4:9
        clerk of, 4:79
    annual school board reorganization meetings, timing of, 3:2
    board membership, 2:3, 2:4, 2:5
        vacancies, filling of, 2:29
    naming convention for, 1:26, 15:17
    personal voter registration systems, 4:60, 4:61
    school district reorganization, 15:2, 15:3, 15:11
Certification
    administrators, school, 7:2, 8:43
        waiver of certification, 7:3
    annulment of, 7:4
    asbestos-abatement projects, 17:59, 17:61
    collective bargaining unit, 10:18
    decertification procedure, 7:4
    guidance counselors, 8:43
    librarians, school, 8:43
    principals, 7:2
    private and parochial schools, 24:5
    psychologists, school, 8:43
    revocation of, 7:4
    School Administrator and Supervisor (SAS)

certification, 7:2
  school buses, 22:22
  School Business Administrator certification, 7:2
  School District Administrator (SDA) certifica-
    tion, 7:2
  superintendent of schools, 7:2, 8:43
    decertification procedure, 7:4
    waiver of certification, 7:3
  suspension of, 7:4
  teachers (*See* Teacher certification)
  teacher's aide, 8:41
  teaching assistants, requirements for, 8:40
  waivers of, 7:3
Certiorari proceedings, 20:14
  school district as party to, 20:15
Certiorari reserve fund, 19:24
Charities and charitable institutions
  collection of money on school premises, 16:61
  district funds, contributions from, 19:7
  exemption from school district taxation, 20:16
Cheating by student
  as cause for lowering of course grade, 12:116
  due process rights, 14:69
Checks
  board's approval, issuance before, 19:18
  signing of, 19:19
Chemical Hygiene Plan, 18.25
Chemicals, use in school labs, 18.26
Child abuse, reporting requirements, 12:74
Child care
  Latchkey Children Law, 16:39
  school buildings, use of, 16:39
  transportation, 22:6
Child Safety Act of 1992
  transportation safety zones under, 22:3
Citizenship requirements
  constitutionality of, 8:4
  district superintendent, 6:3
  school board members, 2:18
  teachers, 8:2, 8:4
City school districts
  annual school board reorganization meetings,
    timing of, 3:2
  Big 5 city school districts, 1:22
  board members
    appointment of, cities that practice, 1:22
    citizenship requirement, 2:18
    election of, cities that practice, 1:22
    number of, 1:22
    qualifications for membership, 2:18
    residency requirement, 2:18
    vacancies, filling of, 2:29
  budget process, 4:20
  consolidation with contiguous districts, 15:14
  defined, 1:22
  Education Law provisions that apply specifically
    to, 1:22
Civil rights, violation of
  compensatory damages, 18:21
  damages, district liability for, 18:18, 18:21
    school board members or district employees,
      18:19, 18:20

district employees, personal liability, 18:20
  legislative activities, when performing, 18:19
  policy or custom, determination of, 18:18
  school board members, personal liability, 18:20
    legislative activities, when performing, 18:19
  school district liability, 18:18, 18:21
    for district employees, 18:19, 18:20
    for school board members, 18:19, 18:20
Civil service, 9:1
  abolishment of position as means of discipline,
    notice and hearing requirements, 9:25
  administration of Civil Service Law, 9:2
  appointments
    permanent status, requirements for, 9:12
    procedures for, 9:8
    school board's role in, 9:3
  BOCES employees and, 9:2, 9:5
  classifications, 9:1, 9:5
    classified positions (*See* classified positions
      below)
    cross-sharing of duties appropriate to
      another position, 9:16
    school board's powers, 9:7
    unclassified positions, 9:1
  classified positions, 9:4
    administration of Civil Service Law, 9:2
    competitive class positions (*See* competitive
      class positions *below*)
    defined, 9:1
    enforcement of Civil Service Law, 9:2
    exempt class positions, defined, 9:6
    labor-class positions, defined, 9:6
    non-competitive class positions, defined, 9:6
    school board's role in appointments to, 9:3
  competitive class positions
    appointments, 9:8, 9:9, 9:10
    defined, 9:6
    examinations, 9:8
    probationary period, 9:12
    promotions, 9:8
    provisional appointments, 9:9
    residency requirements, 9:14
    temporary appointments, 9:10, 9:11
    tenure, 9:12
    transfers, 9:15
    veterans, 9:13
  county or city civil service commissions, 9:19
  covered employees, 9:4
  cross-sharing of duties assigned to another
    position, 9:16
  disabled veterans, 9:13
  discharge of employees
    non-section 75 employees, 9:32
    section 75 employees, 9:30
  disciplinary proceedings
    nontenured employees (*See* disciplinary
      proceedings for non-section 75 employees
      below)
    tenured employees (*See* disciplinary
      proceedings for section 75 employees
      below)
  disciplinary proceedings for non-section 75
    employees

discharge of employee as result, 9:32
due process rights, 9:23
name-clearing hearing, rights to, 9:33
procedures for, 9:32
disciplinary proceedings for section 75 employees
abolishment of position as means of
discipline, notice and hearing requirements,
9:25
appeal, right to, 9:31
back pay upon successful appeal, 9:29, 9:31
critical letter in file as disciplinary
reprimand, 9:34
discharge as result of, 9:30
due process rights, 9:23, 9:27
exempt employees, 9:23
hearing requirements for, 9:25
noncompetitive class employees, 9:23
notice requirements, 9:25, 9:26
penalties available, 9:30
procedure for, 9:24
statute of limitation on, 9:28
suspension without pay pending outcome
of hearing, 9:29
union representation, right to, 9:26
waiver of due process rights under collective
bargaining agreement, 9:27
whistle-blower protections, 9:35
dismissal
non-section 75 employees, 9:32
section 75 employees, 9:30
enforcement of Civil Service Law, 9:2
examinations, 9:8
exempt class positions, defined, 9:6
Fair Labor Standards Act, 9:18
information requests, 9:36
instructional employees, 9:5
labor-class positions, defined, 9:6
leaves of absence
Family and Medical Leave Act provisions, 9:21
military leave, 9:22
lunch breaks, 9:20
military leave, 9:22
minimum wage laws, 9:18
new positions, 9:7
non-competitive class positions, defined, 9:6
non-instructional positions, 9:4
oath of office, 9:17
overtime pay, 9:18
payroll
back pay, 9:29, 9:31
submissions, 9:19
wage structure, 9:19
principals, 9:5
probationary period, 9:12
promotions
procedures for, 9:8
provisional appointments
procedures for, 9:9
Public Employees' Fair Employments Act
(See Taylor Law)
reclassification of positions, 9:7
residency requirements, 9:14

school board's role in appointments to, 9:3
state Civil Service Commission, classification
of positions by, 9:6
superintendents, 9:5
Taylor Law (See Taylor Law)
teachers, 9:5
temporary appointments
eligibility lists, necessity of using, 9:11
procedure for, 9:10
tenured employees, 9:12, 10:4
disciplinary proceedings for (See disciplinary
proceedings for section 75 employees above)
unclassified positions, defined, 9:1
veterans, 9:13
wages
minimum wage laws, 9:18
payroll structure, 9:19
whistle-blower law, 9:35
Clergy, school board membership, 2:22
Closed or unused school buildings
gifts to public corporations, 16:13
procedures for closing, 16:34
rental of, 16:14
sale of, 16:12
Closing of schools
bomb threats, 17:1, 17:5
decision-making authority, 17:6
emergency closings, 17:1
epidemics as cause, 17:1
natural or human disasters, 17:1
religious holiday, in observance of, 23:11
state aid, effect on, 21:19
teacher salaries, payment of, 8:127
weather-related closings, 17:1
Clothing (See Dress code)
Coaches, athletic
extra pay for teachers serving as, 8:17
first aid and CPR skills, 8:42
teacher certification, 8:42
COBRA, continuation coverage under, 8:142
Code of ethics
posting requirements, 2:32
public employees, 2:31
school boards, 2:31, 2:32
school district officers, 2:31, 2:32
teachers, 8:19
Collective bargaining, 10:29
agency shop fees, 10:26, 10:28
agreement, 10:9
alcohol and drug testing, 10:37
annexation, school district reorganization, 15:19
approval, 10:6, 10:7
arbitration (See Arbitration)
bargaining unit
agency shop fees, 10:26, 10:28
authorized representative of employees,
procedure for becoming, 10:16
certification, 10:18
confidential employees, 10:23
covered employees, 10:15, 10:17, 10:21,
10:22, 10:23, 10:26
defined, 10:15
dues deductions, 10:27

"employee organization," defined, 10:16
employer recognition, 10:17, 10:18
exclusion of employees, 10:22
managerial employees, 10:23
newly hired employees, 10:20
rights of, 10:12, 10:13, 10:25
subcontracting as subject of, 10:38
substitute teachers, 10:19
benefits, 10:36
binding arbitration, 10:39, 10:57, 10:58
board's rights and responsibilities, 10:5
changes in employment contract, 10:7
loss of right to ratify, 10:7, 10:8
prior board action as cause loss of right to
ratify, 10:8
ratification rights, 10:5, 10:6, 10:7
renegotiation of employment contract, 10:7
confidential employees, 10:23, 10:24
conflicts of interest, 2:38
contract of employment compared, 10:3
coordinated bargaining, 10:39
costs associated with, payment of, 10:45
database services available, 10:10
deadline, 10:35
defined, 10:29
drug testing, 10:37
expiration of current agreement before
successor agreement negotiated, 10:46
Family and Medical Leave Act (FMLA)
implications on bargaining, 10:64
preemption of FMLA leave by agreement
leave, 10:62
good faith negotiation, 10:30
grievances, 10:36, 10:54
arbitration (See Arbitration)
database research services, 10:10
procedures for resolution, 10:55, 10:56
ground rules, 10:34
hours of employment, 10:36, 10:37
impact negotiations, 10:38, 10:40
past practice and, 10:41
impasse
costs associated with, payment of, 10:45
defined, 10:42
procedures, 10:43
Public Employment Relations Board (PERB),
role of, 10:44
improper practices under Taylor Law (See
Taylor Law)
information requests, 10:10
judicial review, 10:14
leaves of absence, 8:132, 9:21, 10:36, 10:37, 10:62
lunch period, right to free, 9:20
managerial employees, 10:23, 10:24
mandatory subjects of negotiation, 10:20, 10:37,
10:38
medical leave, preemption of FMLA leave, 10:62
negotiating team, 10:5, 10:31, 10:32, 10:33
negotiations procedures, 10:34
New York State School Boards Association
services available, 10:10
past practice and impact negotiations, 10:41

permissive subjects of negotiation, 10:37
procedures, 10:34
prohibited subjects of negotiation, 10:37
Public Employment Relations Board (PERB),
supervision by, 10:7, 10:14, 10:33
ratification of agreement, 10:6, 10:34
loss of board's right to, 10:7, 10:8
prior board action as cause of loss of board's
right to, 10:8
reinstatement of employees, 10:38
renegotiation of terms of agreement, 10:9
requirement for, 10:30
retiree health benefits, 11:2
right of association, 10:26
right to engage in, 10:12, 10:13
right to work, 10:26
salaries, 10:36, 10:37
principals, 7:28, 7:29
teachers, 8:121
school district reorganization, 15:19
settlements, 10:39
sexual harassment, employee discipline issues
concerning, 18:28
shared decision making plans, required
involvement, 3:35
sick leave, preemption of FMLA leave, 10:62
smoke-free schools, 17:40
strikes (See Strikes)
subcontracting as subject of, 10:38
subjects of negotiation, 10:36, 10:37
sunset clause, 10:46
superintendent's authority, modification of, 7:22
superintendent's responsibilities, 10:5, 10:32
Taylor Law provisions (See Taylor Law)
teachers
annuity plans, salary reduction as means of
investing in tax-sheltered, 8:129
dress code, 8:21
duty-free period, right to, 8:16
emergency closings, payment of salaries
during, 8:127
extracurricular supervision or participation,
extra pay for, 8:17
lunch period, right to free, 8:16
minimum salary requirements, 8:121, 8:123
part-time teachers, seniority credit, 8:73, 8:91
probationary teachers, 8:70, 8:73, 8:77
salary issues subject to negotiation, 8:124
waiver of right to paid suspension pending
disciplinary actions, 8:114
workday, maximum length, 8:14
work load, maximum, 8:15
tentative agreement, 10:7, 10:33
transfers, 10:37
unused leave time, payment for, 8:141
Colleges and universities
applications processed by school district, 14:75
Board of Regents, authority of, 1:7
Regents College Examinations Program, 1:7
scholarships for (See College scholarships)
College scholarships
grants available, state and federal, 14:76

loans programs available, state, 14:76
Commissioner of Education
  appeals, 1:16
    immunization record, 12:58
    judicial review of commissioner's decisions,
      1:17
    reopening of, 1:16
    statute of limitations on, 1:16
  attendance records, record keeping requirements
    prescribed for, 12:12
  budget, right to impose, 4:30
  building administration, assignment and
    employment of, 7:26
  decisions of, 1:16
    judicial review of, 1:17
    publishing of, 1:17
  instructional year, exceptions to minimum
    length requirements, 14:4
  judicial review of commissioner's decisions, 1:17
  powers and duties of, 1:14
  publishing of decisions of, 1:17
  record keeping requirements prescribed by, 12:12
  regulations of, defined, 1:15
  role of, 1:13
  school buildings
    fire-safety inspections, 17:12
    plans and specifications, approval of, 16:5,
      16:22, 16:23, 16:24, 17:7
    safety requirements, approval of, 17:7, 17:8
  school day, exceptions to minimum length
    requirements, 14:7
  school district reorganization, role in, 15:8,
    15:9, 15:16
  transportation contracts, 22:66, 22:69
Commissioner of Health
  immunization education programs, 12:61
  immunization surveys, 12:60
Committee on Preschool Special Education
    (CPSE), 13:7, 13:9, 13:45, 13:46, 13:47
  CSE distinguished, 13:48
  itinerant special education services recommen-
    dations, 13:46, 13:47
  membership, 13:48
  registration of disabled children, 13:8, 13:9
  surrogate parents, assignment of, 13:46
Committee on Special Education (CSE), 13:7
  appeal of district's determination, by parents
    appeal of hearing officer's determination, 13:32
    independent educational evaluation (IEE)
      at public expense, 13:35
    legal costs of parents, district liability for, 13:33
    out-of-district placement and tuition,
      district's responsibilities, 13:37
    pending outcome of, student's placement,
      13:34, 13:36
    private school placement at public expense
      as solution, 13:36
    selection of hearing officer, 13:31
    "stay-put" provisions, 13:34
  appeal of district's determination, school
    board's, 13:23
  attorney of school district, attendance at CSE
    meeting, 13:29

CPSE distinguished, 13:48
  function of, 13:18
  independent educational evaluation (IEE) at
    public expense, parental right to, 13:35
  meetings of
    attorney of school district, attendance by, 13:29
    parental attendance and participation
      requirements, 13:27
    tape-recording of, 13:28
  membership of, 13:19
    subcommittees, 13:21, 13:22
  number of committees allowed per district, 13:20
  parental attendance and participation
    requirements, 13:27
  parental consent requirements, 13:26
  registration of disabled children, 13:8, 13:9, 13:18
  review and revision of IEP, frequency
    requirements for, 13:25
  school board disagreement with CSE
    recommendation, procedure when, 13:23
  "stay-put" provisions, 13:34
  subcommittees of, 13:20, 13:22
    membership, 13:21, 13:22
  testing and evaluation of children, 13:18
    frequency requirements, 13:25
    independent educational evaluation (IEE)
      at public expense, 13:35
    parental consent requirement, 13:26
Common school districts, 1:18
  board membership, 2:3, 2:4, 2:6
    vacancies, filling of, 2:29
  consolidation, 15:4, 15:13
  trustee of, 2:6
Community school districts (New York City)
  board membership, 2:3, 2:4
  creation of, 15:6
  responsibilities of, 1:22
Community service
  as form of student discipline, 12:114
  as requirement for graduation, 12:94
Compensation (See also Salaries)
  administrative personnel
    multiple districts, shared administrator's
      services, 7:5
    salary schedule, requirement for, 7:28
  district superintendent (See District superin-
    tendent)
  principals
    reduction in, allowability of, 7:29
    salary schedule, requirement for, 7:28
  school board members, 2:34
  superintendent's services shared with multiple
    districts, 7:5
  tax collector, 20:45
Competitive bidding requirements, 19:45, 19:47,
  19:50
  advertising, 19:47
    transportation, 22:67
  determination if competitive bidding required,
    9:50
  emergency contract bidding, 19:48, 22:67
  exceptions to, 19:48

identical bidders, 19:47
insurance, 18:41
legal counsel, selection of, 18:32
noncompetitive bidding, procedures for, 19:48,
    19:49
personal property, leasing of, 19:46
professional services, 19:48
recycled paper, 19:55
request for proposals as alternative, 22:68
school bus purchases, 22:28, 22:70
secondhand supplies, 19:48
surplus supplies, 19:48
transportation contracts, 22:66, 22:67, 22:69
Competitive sports (*See* Athletics and competitive
    sports)
Comprehensive Assessment Report (CAR), annual
    incidental teaching assignments, 8:44
Comprehensive operating aid (*See* State aid)
Comptroller, State of New York
    bond issuance, consent for, 19:70
    debt statement, filing of, 19:72
    ERS, responsibility for operation of, 11:45
    school districts, annual financial report filing
        requirements, 19:21
Compulsory attendance, 12:1, 12:6, 12:13
    age requirements, 12:1, 12:3, 12:6, 12:13
    employed students, 12:3
    exemptions from, 12:2
    home instruction as legal alternative to, 12:1,
        12:4, 12:14, 24:19, 24:26
    married students, 12:3
    private and parochial schools, 12:4, 24:1
    truancy
        defined, 12:19
        enforcement, 12:20
        suspension of student for, permissibility of,
            12:97
Computer hardware
    federal aid, 25:8
    private and parochial schools, purchase or
        loans from district, 24:16
    state aid, 21:12
Computer software
    copyright guidelines, 14:63
    federal aid, 25:8
    home instruction students, borrowing rights
        of, 24:32
    private and parochial schools, purchase or
        loans from district, 24:16
    state aid, 21:12
Condoms and AIDS curriculum
    demonstrations on use, 14:34
    distribution of condoms as part of, 14:33
Confidential employees
    defined, 10:24
    designation of, 10:23
    managerial employees distinguished, 10:24
Confidentiality requirements
    AIDS, students with, 12:65
    alcohol and drug testing of school bus drivers,
        22:63

Conflicts of interest
    bank officers, 3:17, 19:74
        as board members, 2:35
    board members, 2:35, 2:36, 2:40, 3:23
        bank officers as, 2:35
        compatibility of office requirement, 2:41,
            2:42, 2:43, 2:44
        contracting with district, 2:35, 2:36, 2:39
        as current employee of district, 2:41
        determination of conflict, 2:39
        exceptions to provisions, 2:37
        judgeship at same time, 2:44
        political office holder at same time, 2:41,
            2:43, 2:44
        PTA members as, 1:28
        public officer at same time, 2:41, 2:42,
            2:43, 2:44
        relative of, 2:21, 2:35, 2:36
        teachers as, 1:28, 2:38
        violation of law, penalties for, 2:40
    collective bargaining agreements, 2:38
    contract, defined, 2:35
    district superintendent, 2:43, 3:23
        concurrent engagement in other business,
            permissibility of, 6:15
    district treasurer, 2:43, 3:17
    interest, defined, 2:35
    school district officers, 2:43, 3:13, 3:17, 3:23,
        19:74
    teachers, 2:38, 8:19
Consolidation, school district reorganization, 15:4
    city school district and contiguous districts, 15:14
    common school districts, 15:13
    employment contracts, 7:21, 15:19
    employment rights, 15:21
        superintendent of schools, pre-merger, 15:22
    superintendent of schools, pre-merger
        contract rights, 7:21, 15:22
    teacher tenure, 15:21
    union free school districts, 15:13
    voter approval, 15:13, 15:14
Construction or renovation of school buildings
    advertising for bids, 16:24
    Americans with Disabilities Act (ADA),
        compliance with, 16:27
    Board of Regents' approval, 16:20
    bonds for
        Board of Regents' approval, 16:20
        net bonded indebtedness, 16:20
        printed brochure describing bond issue, 16:18
        surety bonds, 18:49
    commissioner's approval of construction
        advertising for bids, 16:24
        plans and specifications, 16:5, 16:22, 17:7
        procedure for, 16:23
    environmental impact statement, 16:25
    federal funds, 25:8, 25:14
    joint facilities, building aid for, 16:29
    maximum expenditure, 16:19
    net bonded indebtedness, 16:20
    occupation before completion, 16:26

plans and specifications, 16:21
    architects, contracts with, 16:17
    commissioner's approval, 16:5, 16:22, 17:7
    safety requirements, 17:7
    printed brochure describing bond issue, 16:18
    state building aid, 16:29
    voter approval of funding for, 16:16
    wages for workers, 16:28
    zoning regulations, 16:15
Contagious diseases
    AIDS, classification of, 12:63, 12:64
    attendance of students with, 12:62
Contingent budget and expenses, 4:28, 19:37
    adoption of contingent budget, required times,
        19:38
    authority on interpretation of, 19:37
    determination of expenses for, 19:40
    legal obligations to be included in, 19:41
    limitations imposed by, 19:39
    required times for adoption of, 19:38
    salary increases for employees, 19:42
    transfers from non-contingent budget
        categories, 19:44
    transportation requirements, impact on, 19:43
    types of, 19:41
    unanticipated expenses, allowability of line for,
        19:32
Contracts
    competitive bidding requirements (See
        Competitive bidding requirements)
    employment contracts (See Employment contracts)
    retirement benefits (See Retirement plans)
    transportation
        installment contracts, 22:73
        request for proposals as option, 22:68
    transportation contracts
        bidding process, awarded through, 22:66,
            22:67, 22:69
        request for proposals process, awarded
            through, 22:68
Conventions, expenses for participation in, 19:9
Cooperative purchasing agreements, 19:51
Copying equipment, purchase of, 19:57
Copyrighted materials
    computer software, 14:63
    fair use, defined, 14:63
    school district liability, 14:63
Corporal punishment of students
    allowability of, 8:22, 12:117
    legal action resulting from, 8:25
    reporting requirements, 12:118
Correctional facilities
    inmates
        equivalency diploma (GED) earned by, 12:11,
            12:26
        right to educational services, 12:26
        state student aid, 12:26, 21:12
    purchases from, 19:53
    state aid, 12:26, 21:12
Cost-of-living allowances
    disabled teacher retirees, supplemental benefits
        for, 11:36

Counseling
    Guidance counselors (See Guidance counselors)
    student disciplinary proceeding, as penalty in,
        12:115
Course credit, attendance requirements, 12:22,
    13:44
Court systems
    federal system, structure of, 1:3
    New York State system, structure of, 1:4
CPSE (See Committee on Preschool Special
    Education (CPSE))
Credit cards, school, use by school board
    members, 19:10
Criminal charges
    administrative probationary periods and
        service rendered outside tenure area
        pending outcome of, 7:10
Criminal records
    teachers, conviction as cause for revocation
        of certification, 8:49
CSE (See Committee on Special Education (CSE))
Curricula
    academic freedom, guidelines, 8:20
    AIDS instruction
        condoms and, 14:33, 14:34
        parental opposition to, 14:28, 14:32, 14:58
        state-mandated, 14:32
        state syllabi, 14:32
    alcohol abuse by students, prevention of, 14:36
    child abduction prevention programs, 14:42
    child development, instruction in, 14:37
    dissections of animals, curricular alternatives
        for those objecting to, 14:44
    driver education classes, 14:48
        Saturday sessions, permissibility of, 14:4
    drug abuse by students, prevention of, 14:36
    environmental conservation, 14:40
    fire and arson prevention, 14:38
    firearms use and safety, 14:39
    fire drills, 14:38
    foreign language instruction, 14:20
    gifted and talented students, programs for, 14:31
    health care services training, 14:46
    health education (See Health education)
    Holocaust, curricular requirements, 14:41
    home instruction, 24:27
    homework, legal requirements, 14:25
    humane treatment of animals and birds,
        elementary school instruction in, 14:43
    human rights issues, curricular requirements,
        14:41
    instructional year, 14:1, 14:2, 14:3
    local district requirements exceeding state
        mandates, 14:22
    opt-out policies established by district, 14:32,
        14:44
    parental opposition to curriculum materials,
        14:57, 14:58, 14:59
    parenting skills training, 14:37
    prerequisites, allowability of, 14:27
    religious instruction in public schools, 14:35
        art and music, religious, 23:12

beliefs as cultural or historical topic, 14:28
music and art, religious, 23:12
plays and pageants, religious, 23:12
remediation requirements, 14:21
parental notification requirements, 14:74
SURR schools, 14:74
school day, length of
double or overlapping (split) session, 14:7
minimum length by law, 14:6, 14:7
school year, length of, 14:3, 14:4
science instruction, opt-out policy established
by district, 14:44
sexual discrimination in curriculum materials,
14:26
State Education Department approval
requirements, 14:23
state mandates, 14:14
AIDS instruction, 14:32
local district requirements exceeding, 14:22
state syllabi, 14:24
AIDS instruction, 14:32
health education, 14:36
student's right to choose courses, 14:27
substance abuse by students, prevention of, 14:36
textbooks (See Textbooks)
tobacco use by students, prevention of, 14:36

Damages, district liability for
civil rights, violation of, 18:18, 18:21
school board members or district employees,
18:19, 18:20
sexual harassment, 18:28
Damage to school property, rewards for
information on, 12:126
Data-processing equipment, purchase of, 19:57
Day care programs, school bus transportation, 22:20
Debt service, reserve fund for, 19:24
Debt statement, filing of, 19:72
De Facto segregation, 12:28
Demonstrations and protests, student, 12:78
Dental hygienist, school, tenure area, 8:60
Diploma, high school
adults over 21, equivalency diploma for, 12:11
alternative means to attain, 12:11
equivalency diploma (GED), 12:10, 12:11, 12:26
physical education requirements, 14:51
post-graduates under 21, right to attend school,
12:9, 12:10
prison inmates, equivalency diploma earned by,
12:11, 12:26
Regents diploma
home instruction students, 24:30
state requirements for, 14:74
local district requirements exceeding, 14:22
physical education requirements, 14:51
SURR schools, 14:74
Disability insurance, 18:38
Disabled children
classification of, 13:2, 13:4
definition of, 13:2
identification of, 13:7, 13:8
registration of, 13:8, 13:9

as students (See Disabled students)
Disabled persons
installment payment of real property taxes, 20:39
purchasing of products or services from, 19:54
reasonable accommodation requirements, 8:7
school bus transportation, 22:20, 22:81
services for, 13:6, 13:12
tax notification procedure, 20:37
as teachers, 8:6, 8:31
reasonable accommodation requirements, 8:7
veterans, civil service appointments, 9:13
Disabled students
absences, excessive, as cause for denial of
course credit, 13:44
adult students, services requirements for, 13:12
Americans with Disabilities Act of 1990 (ADA),
13:1
"assistive technology service," defined, 13:6
athletics, participation in, 13:13
attendance, 13:44
BOCES programs, shared services provided by,
5:30
census, inclusion in, 13:9
classification of, 13:2, 13:4
Committee on Special Education (CSE) (See
Committee on Special Education (CSE))
"continuum of alternative placements"
requirement, 13:5
discipline of, 13:38
dual-enrollment requirements, 24:11
Education of Handicapped Children Act
(EHA), 13:1
emotional disturbed children, 13:2
extracurricular activities, participation in, 13:13
"free appropriate public education," defined, 13:3
full inclusion, defined, 13:5
Gun-Free Schools Act and, 12:125
HIV or HIV-related conditions, 13:2
home instruction, 13:6, 24:34
identification of, 13:7, 13:8
individualized education program (IEP)
(See Individualized Education Program (IEP))
Individuals with Disabilities Education Act
(IDEA), 1:2, 13:1, 13:2, 25:1
review of student's IEP, 13:24, 13:25
interaction with nondisabled children,
mainstreaming requirements, 13:5
interim alternative placement
causes of, 13:39, 13:41
parental consent and, 13:41
procedures for, 13:41
requirements for, 13:40
learning disabled children, 13:2
"least restrictive environment"
defined, 13:5
responsibility of school district to provide, 13:7
mainstreaming of, 13:5
maximum statutory age for special education
services, 13:12
medical services required, 13:10
mental retardation, 13:2
orthopedically impaired children, 13:2

out-of-district placement and tuition, 12:30
district's responsibilities, 13:37
parents or guardians of
CSE meetings, attendance and participation
requirements, 13:27
private school, right to place child in, 13:36
procedural safeguards to insure rights of,
13:16, 13:17, 13:24
rights of, procedural safeguards to insure,
13:16, 13:17, 13:24
parochial schools, attendance at, 24:11
anti-discrimination requirements, 24:5
special education and services provided by
district, 13:15
physical education requirements, 14:49
placement of, 13:7
preschool children (See Preschool students)
private schools, attendance at, 24:11
anti-discrimination requirements, 24:5
dual-enrollment requirements, 24:11
special education and services provided by
district, 13:14, 13:36, 24:13, 24:15
recreation programs for, 13:6
registration of, 13:8, 13:9
related services, defined, 13:6
school buildings, special provisions in, 16:27
school bus transportation, 22:81
services and programs for
available programs, 13:6
district's responsibilities in providing, 13:6,
13:7
itinerant special education services, 13:47
medical services, 13:10
preschool children, 13:45, 13:46, 13:47
related services, defined, 13:6
year-round services, 13:4, 13:11
special education requirements for, 13:3, 13:7
parochial school, district responsibilities
when child attending, 13:15
preschool children, 13:45, 13:46
private school, district responsibilities when
child attending, 13:14, 13:15, 13:36, 24:13
state aid, 13:7, 21:12, 21:23, 22:81
statutory law governing, 13:1
suspension of
drug possession or selling as cause, 13:39, 13:41
due process rights, 13:42, 13:43
in excess of 10 days, 13:38, 13:39, 13:40, 13:41
Gun-Free Schools Act, 12:125
interim alternative placement requirements,
13:39, 13:40, 13:41
of less than 10 days, 13:38, 13:42
procedures for, 13:38, 13:39, 13:41
weapons possession as cause, 13:39, 13:41
testing and evaluation of, 13:7
CSE role in, 13:18
medical services needed, 13:10
Regents Competency Tests, phase-out of,
14:15, 14:65, 14:66
visually impaired children, 13:2
Vocational and Educational Services for

Individuals with Disabilities (VESID), 1:12
year-round services, 13:4, 13:11
Disabled teachers, 8:6
certification, nondiscrimination, 8:31
reasonable accommodation requirements, 8:7
retirement benefits, supplemental, 11:36, 11:38
Disadvantaged students
federal aid, 25:8
state aid, 21:21
Disasters, natural or human (See Emergencies;
Emergency-management plans)
Discipline
administrative personnel
multiple districts, shared administrator's
services, 7:5
board's responsibilities, 2:10, 22:11
civil service employees (See Civil service)
dress codes
religious exceptions, 23:18
students, 12:81, 12:82
teachers, 8:21
school buses, 22:11, 22:40, 22:60
students (See Student discipline)
suspension of students (See Suspension of
students)
teacher discipline (See Teacher discipline;
3020-a disciplinary hearings)
Disclosure requirements, public (See Public notice
and/or disclosure requirements)
Discrimination
age, 8:8, 8:125, 18:22
disability, 8:6, 8:31, 8:125
employment (See Employment discrimination)
federal protections against, 8:5, 8:6, 8:7, 8:8,
8:9, 14:26
marital status, 8:5, 8:125
national origin, 8:5, 8:125, 12:28
pregnancy, 8:5, 8:134, 8:135, 12:27, 18:22
private and parochial schools, 24:5
race, 8:5, 8:125, 12:28
religion, 8:5, 8:125, 8:138
school facilities, nondiscrimination requirements for use by outside groups, 16:42, 16:46
school facilities, use by outside groups,
nondiscrimination requirements, 23:8
sex (See Sexual discrimination)
Dismissal (See also Removal from office)
administrators, probationary school, 7:11
abolishment of position as alternative to
dismissal, 7:12
at-will employees, 10:4
civil service employees (See Civil service)
superintendent of schools, 2:15, 7:17
due process protections given to, 7:25
supervisors, probationary, 7:11
of teachers
abolishment of position as alternative, 8:96
name-clearing hearing, allowability of, 8:80
during probationary period, notice
requirements, 8:78, 8:79, 8:82
tenured teachers (See 3020-a disciplinary
hearings)

Dissolution, school district reorganization, 15:5, 15:15
  district superintendent, powers and duties of, 6:20
  employment rights, 15:20
  sale of district property, 15:18
  teacher tenure, 15:20
  voters' rights, 15:15
Distance limitations, transportation, 22:2
  child safety zones, 22:3
  length of commute, 22:5
  measurement of, 22:4
  walking distance for students, 22:17
District superintendent, 3:7 (See also Superintendent of schools)
  appointment of, 6:4
  benefits, legal limits on, 6:12
  BOCES relationship
    appointment and tenure recommendations for BOCES staff members, 6:18
    duties of BOCES to superintendent, 5:20, 6:11
    duties of superintendent to BOCES, 6:16, 6:18
  citizenship requirement for, 6:3
  compensation, 6:10
    legal limits on, 6:11, 6:12
    tie-ins to other collective bargaining agreements within district, 6:13
    withholding of salary by commissioner, permissibility of, 6:14
  employment contract, legal limits on duration of, 6:5
  engagement in other business, permissibility of concurrent, 6:15
  indemnification under Public Officers Law section 17, 6:22
  oath of office, 6:6
  powers and duties of, 6:1, 6:17, 6:20
    alteration of school districts, 6:20
    BOCES-related duties, 6:16, 6:18
    dissolution of school districts, 6:20
    formation of school districts, 6:20
    revocation of teacher's certificate, 6:19
    state aid claims, submission of, 21:4
    teacher probation and tenure decisions, 6:18
  prohibited actions defined by statute, 2:33
  Public Officers Law section 17, entitlement to protections of, 6:22
  qualifications for, 6:3
  removal of, 3:24, 6:7, 6:8
  residency requirements, 3:10, 6:3
  resignation of, 6:8
  responsibilities of, 6:1
    collective bargaining negotiations, 10:5, 10:32
    emergency-management plans, 6:21, 17:1
    teacher probation and tenure decisions, 6:18
  superintendent of schools distinguished, 6:1, 7:15
  supervisory district, defined, 6:2
  supervisory district of (See Supervisory district)
  vacancy in office
    causes of, 6:8
    filling of vacancy, 6:9

  withholding of salary by commissioner, permissibility of, 6:14
District treasurer
  bonding by, 19:4
  check issuance before board's approval, 19:18
  prohibited actions defined by statute, 2:33
Divorced or separated parents
  Missing children, 12:72
  multiple addresses listed for student, district transportation requirements, 22:7
  release of student from school, permission for, 12:72
  residency of student, determination of, 12:32, 12:33
  transportation of students and, 22:7
Doors, safety of electronically-operated doors, 17:9
Dress codes
  religious exceptions, 23:18
  students, 12:81, 12:82
  teachers, 8:21, 23:18
Driver education
  curricula, 14:48
  Saturday sessions, permissibility of, 14:4
Drivers, school buses (See School bus drivers)
Drug abuse
  ADA exclusion due to, 8:6
  drug-free school zones, 16:56
  prevention curriculum, 12:57, 14:36
    driver education classes, inclusion in, 14:48
  rehabilitation programs, school bus drivers, 22:65
  Safe and Drug-Free School and Communities Act (SDFSCA), 12:57, 16:55, 16:56
Drug-free School and Communities Act (DFSCA) (See Safe and Drug-Free School and Communities Act (SDFSCA))
Drug-free school zones, 16:56
  Federal aid, 25:8
Drug-related crime conviction, revocation of teacher's certification for, 8:49
Drug-related searches of students or lockers, 12:87
  with scent dogs, 12:89
Drug testing (See Alcohol and drug testing)
Dual enrollment law, 21:23, 24:11
  on-site requirements, 24:11, 24:12
Due process rights
  Employment contracts
    probationary employees, 7:13
    superintendent of schools, 7:25
  probationary employees, 7:13
  students
    cheating by student, 14:69
    disabled students, suspension of, 13:42, 13:43
    extracurricular activities, exclusion from, 12:111
    fraud by students, 14:69
    Gun-Free Schools Act, 12:123
    suspension of students (See Suspension of students)
  superintendent of schools, dismissal of, 7:25
Dues
  deductions from salaries, 10:27
  strikes, loss during, 10:51

Easements, schools granting to municipalities, 16:14
Educational malpractice, 18:8
Education of Handicapped Children Act (EHA)
    (See Individuals with Disabilities Education Act
    (IDEA))
Education, public (See Public education, generally)
Elections
    school board member (See School board members)
Elementary and Secondary Education Act (ESEA)
    (See Improving America's Schools Act (IASA))
Elementary, Middle, Secondary and Continuing
    Education (EMSC), Office of, 1:12
Elementary school students
    humane treatment of animals and birds,
        curricula requirements, 14:43
    learning standards adopted by Board of
        Regents, 14:17
    school breakfast programs, 12:136
Elementary school teachers, certification
    requirements, 8:28
Emergencies (See also Health and safety)
    closing of schools in emergencies, 17:1
        decision-making authority, 17:6
        teacher salaries, payment of, 8:127
    emergency-management plans (See Emergency-
        management plans)
    fire-related emergencies (See Fire and fire safety)
    home phone numbers of student and parents,
        12:68
    release of student from school, 12:71
    transportation
        contracts, 22:67, 22:74
        school bus leases, 22:74
Emergency drills, school buses, 22:41
Emergency management drills, 17:2
    after school programs, 17:4
Emergency-management plans, 17:1
    after school programs, 17:4
    bomb threats, 17:1, 17:5
    closing of schools, 17:1
    district superintendent, responsibilities of,
        6:21, 17:1
    emergency management drills, 17:2
    Fire drill requirements, 17:3
Employee Benefit Accrued Liability Reserve Fund,
    19:24
Employees
    at-will employees, 10:3
    civil service (See Civil service)
    former district employees
        letters of recommendations for, district
            liability, 18:10
        as school board members, 2:20
    manuals as contracts, 10:4
    noninstructional (See Noninstructional employees)
    reinstatement, 10:38
Employees' Retirement System (ERS), New York
    State, 11:4, 11:42
    administrator and trustee of, state comptroller
        as, 11:45
    benefits available, 11:42
    contributions

employee contributions, 11:47
        employer contributions, 11:47, 11:48
        underpayments by employer, 11:48
    early retirement incentives, effect on age
        requirements, 11:10
    eligible employees, 11:42
    funding, 11:46
    information requests, 11:50
    lump sum retirement payments, 11:35
    membership requirements, 11:43, 11:44
    noncontributory plans, 11:12
    public employment, returning to, 11:22
    state comptroller, responsibility for operation
        of, 11:45
    Tier systems (See specific tiers under Retirement
        plans)
    transfer of membership, 11:15, 11:16
    trustee and administrator of, state comptroller
        as, 11:45
    vesting, defined, 11:17
    workers' compensation leave, effect of, 11:49
Employees' safety (See Workplace safety)
Employment
    attendance requirements for students, 12:3
    certificates of, student, 12:3, 12:127, 12:128,
        12:129, 12:130
        minors, 14 and 15 years old, 12:128, 12:131
    contracts (See Employment contracts)
    death benefits, illegally employed minors,
        12:134
    discrimination in (See Employment discrimination)
    farm work permit, students, 12:128
    illegally employed minors, compensation and
        death benefits, 12:134
    minors, 14 and 15 years old
        certificates of employment, 12:128, 12:131
        illegal employment of, compensation and
            death benefits, 12:134
    of students, 12:127
        attendance requirements, 12:3
        certificates of employment, 12:3, 12:127,
            12:128, 12:129, 12:130, 12:131
        farm work permit, 12:128
        illegally employed minors, compensation and
            death benefits, 12:134
        maximum number of hours, 12:132, 12:133
        in school lunch and breakfast programs,
            12:142
Employment contracts, 10:1
    administrators, school, 7:17
        probationary employees, 7:13
    board's responsibilities, 10:5
    change in terms, 10:9
    collective bargaining unit compared, 10:3
    consolidation of school districts, 7:21, 15:19,
        15:21
        superintendent of schools, 7:21, 15:22
    discrimination in (See Employment discrimination)
    district superintendent's contract, legal limits
        on duration of, 6:5
    employee manuals as contracts, 10:4
    formation, 10:2

New York State School Boards Association
services available, 10:10
probationary employees, due process rights of,
7:13
provisions within, 10:1, 10:9, 10:10
requirement for, 10:4
school district reorganization, 15:19
subcontracting, collective bargaining, 10:38
superintendent of schools (See Superintendent
of schools)
Employment discrimination, 8:5, 8:6, 8:7, 8:8,
8:31, 8:125
definition of, 18:22
employer liability for, 18:24
Federal law governing, 18:22
legal recourse, 8:9
New York State laws governing, 18:23
Title VII (See Title VII, employment discrimination)
Employment record, school bus drivers, 22:56
Employment references
school bus drivers, 22:48
school district liability for recommendations
given for former employees, 18:10
Employment rights
post-school district reorganizations, 15:20, 15:21
English as a Second Language (ESL) (See Bilingual
education)
Enrollment
board's responsibilities, 2:10
dropping student from, 12:25
re-enrollment rights, notification requirements,
12:25
state aid
dual enrollment provision, 21:23, 24:11, 24:12
increased enrollment, 21:20
Environmental conservation
curricula requirements, 14:40
firearms curricula, approval requirements, 14:39
Environmental Impact Statement (EIS), building
projects, 16:25
Environmental Quality Review Act, site selection
for school buildings, 16:5
Equal Access Act, use of school premises, 16:44, 25:1
Equal Protection Clause, Fourteenth Amendment,
25:2
Equipment
disposal of school equipment, 16:12
lending of school equipment, 16:14
as prohibited gift, 16:49
sale of unused school property, 16:12
surplus equipment, sale of, 19:48
Equivalency diploma (GED), 12:11
Correctional facility inmates, 12:11, 12:26
right to attend high school after attaining, 12:10
ERS, New York State (See Employees' Retirement
System (ERS), New York State)
ESL (English as a Second Language) (See Bilingual
education)
Establishment Clause, U.S. Constitution, 23:1, 23:2
artwork of student with religious themes,
display of, 23:15

disabled students, special education of, 13:15
displays of religious symbols on school
property, 23:15
Halloween-related items, display of, 23:16
Lemon test, 23:2, 23:10
mascot of school as violation of, 23:17
meditation period, silent, 23:9
school board meeting, opening of, 23:10
moment of silence, 23:9
school board meeting, opening of, 23:10
observances, religious, in schools, 23:12
prayers and benedictions (See Prayers and
benedictions)
religious instruction in public schools (See
Religion)
Examinations (See also Testing of students)
home instruction students (See Home
instruction)
medical examinations (See Medical examinations)
physical examinations, school bus drivers,
22:48, 22:52
Pupil Evaluation Program (PEP) tests, phase-
out of, 14:66
Regents College Examinations Program, 1:7
Regents Competency Tests, phase-out of, 14:15,
14:65, 14:66
Regents examinations (See Regents examinations)
Excise taxes, exemption from, 19:59
Excursions, school-sponsored
permission slips for, 18:7
Expressive activities, student, 12:78, 12:81
censorship of, 12:80
Expulsion of students, 12:96
Extracurricular activities
academic standards as prerequisite to, 12:111
athletics (See Athletics and competitive sports)
disabled students, rights of, 13:13
eligibility for, academic standards as prerequisite to, 12:111
exclusion from, due process requirements, 12:111
funds for, 19:11
prayers and benedictions at, 23:6
security guards, 9:37
sexual discrimination, prohibition against, 14:26
teachers, extra pay for supervision or
participation in, 8:17
transportation, 22:12, 22:20
Extraordinary needs aid (ENA) (See State aid)

Fair Labor Standards Act (FSLA), 9:18
Family and Medical Leave Act (FMLA), 10:60, 10:61
adoptive parents, 8:136, 9:21
COBRA health coverage during leave, 8:142
collective bargaining
implications of FMLA on, 10:64
preemption of FMLA leave by agreement
leave, 10:62
family leave defined, 10:61
maternity leave, 8:135
medical leave defined, 10:61
noninstructional employees, 9:21
preemption of FMLA leave by medical or sick
leave, 10:62

right to return to old job after leave, 9:21, 10:63
teachers, 8:132, 8:133, 8:137
   COBRA health coverage during leave, 8:142
   maternity leaves, 8:135
Family Educational Rights and Privacy Act
   (FERPA), 2:70, 24:5, 25:1
Feasibility study, school district reorganization, 15:9
   state aid for, 15:10
Federal aid, 25:3
   amount of available aid, 25:6, 25:7
   bilingual education, 25:8
   computers and other technology for classrooms,
      25:8
   conditions for acceptance of, 25:4
   coordinated services, 25:8
   disadvantaged students, 25:8
   drug-free schools, 25:8
   educational equity, promotion of, 25:8
   Impact aid, 25:8
   magnet schools, 25:8
   major programs in New York State funded by,
      25:7
   Native Americans, 25:8
   nonacceptance of, 25:4
   obligation of states and districts to accept, 25:4
   payments in lieu of taxes (PILOTs), 25:8
   private and parochial schools, 24:11, 25:5
   professional development for teachers, 25:8
   school construction projects, 25:8, 25:14
   school lunch and breakfast programs, 12:137,
      12:141, 12:143
   surplus foods and price-supported commodities,
      12:143
   teachers, professional development for, 25:8
Federal authority
   public education, generally, 1:2
Federal court system, structure of, 1:3
Federal education aid (See Federal aid)
Federal income tax
   retirement plans
      benefits, 11:18
      contributions, 11:13
Fees and charges
   agency shop fees, 10:26, 10:28
   for laboratory equipment, 12:38
   for lockers, 12:38
   school buses, 22:12
   for textbooks, 12:38, 14:55
   for yearbooks, 12:38
FERPA (See Family Educational Rights and Privacy
   Act (FERPA))
Field trips, detention precluding participation in,
   12:112
Finances
   board members
      financial disclosure statement requirements,
         2:9, 4:40
   school boards, financial reporting requirements,
      19:21
   state aid (See State aid)
Fingerprinting, school bus drivers, 22:55
Fire and fire safety

arson, instruction in prevention of, 14:38
emergency-management plans (See Emergency-
   management plans)
failure to pass inspection, result of, 17:13
fire alarm system requirements, 17:15, 17:16
fire drills, 14:38, 17:3
   summer school, 14:38
inspection of school buildings, 17:11, 17:13
   public disclosure requirements, 17:14
   responsibility for, 17:12
instruction about, 14:38
prevention, instruction about, 14:38
private and parochial schools, 24:5
Firearms on campus (See also Gun-Free Schools Act)
curricula, 14:39
   Junior ROTC, as part of, 14:45
student possession
   confiscation of weapons, 12:85
   curriculum, as part of, 14:39
   parental notification requirements, 12:85
   police notification requirements, 12:85
   suspension requirements, 12:120, 12:123,
      12:124, 25:9
Firing (See Dismissal; Removal from office)
Fiscal dependence, 20:2
Fiscal independence, 20:2
Fiscal management
   audits, 19:20
   fiscal year, 19:1
   responsibility for, 19:2, 19:3
Fiscal year, 19:1
Flag, United States
   abstention from salute to, Free Exercise Clause
      rights, 16:51
   curricular instruction on respect and display of,
      14:52
   display of
      curricular instruction on, 14:52
      legal requirements for, 16:50
FMLA (See Family and Medical Leave Act (FMLA))
FOIL (See Freedom of Information Law (FOIL))
Food and food service
   breakfast programs, school (See School breakfast
      programs)
   cafeteria use by community groups, 12:145
   lunch programs, school (See School lunch
      programs)
   sales tax on school meals, 12:139
   sanitation rules and regulations, applicability
      of, 12:146
   sweetened foods on school grounds, sale of,
      16:58
Foreign language instruction
   curriculum requirements, state-mandated, 14:20
Fourteenth Amendment, protections
   Equal Protection Clause, 25:2
   student community service requirements and,
      12:94
Fraternities and sororities, student, 12:84
Freedom of Information Law (FOIL), 2:66, 2:67,
   2:69, 2:73
   exemptions, 2:69, 2:70

penalties for denial of access, 2:74
records access officer, role of, 2:73
records management officer, role of, 2:76
shared decision making process and, 3:37
student records, access to, 2:70
3020-a settlement agreements, access to, 2:71,
    8:118
Free Exercise Clause, First Amendment, 23:1, 23:3
abstention from salute to flag or pledge of
    allegiance, 16:51
Religious Freedom Restoration Act (RFRA),
    overturning of, 23:3
religious holidays or observances, 8:138
Free Exercise of Religion (See Free Exercise Clause,
First Amendment)
Free speech protections
students, 12:78, 12:79, 12:80
    clothing as free speech, 12:82
    distribution of literature on school grounds,
        12:83
teachers, 8:18
Fund balance, 19:34
Funding
asbestos-abatement projects
    building aid, 17:52
    grants, 17:52
    state aid, 17:52
    unanticipated projects, 17:54
Employees' Retirement System (ERS), New York
    State, 11:46
federal aid (See Federal aid)
local funding, 21:1
state aid (See State aid)
Teachers' Retirement System (TRS), New York
    State, 11:28

Gender, discrimination (See Sexual discrimination)
Gifted and talented students
programs requirements, 14:31
state aid, 21:12
dual-enrollment requirements, 24:11
Gifts
closed school buildings, 16:13
loans of school equipment to community
    members as, 16:49
site acquisition for school buildings, 16:8
Goals 2000: Educate America Act, 25:7, 25:10
National Education Goals, 25:10
parental assistance, 25:11
Pro-Children Act of 1994, 25:12
reforms activities sponsored by, 25:10, 25:11
requirements on school districts, 25:12
Graduation ceremonies, prayers and benedictions
at, 23:7
Graduation requirements
community service requirements, 12:94
for Regents examinations, 14:15, 14:19
Graffiti, on school buildings, 16:54
Grievances
arbitration as means of resolving, 10:56
advisory arbitration, 10:57, 10:58
appeals of arbitration, 10:58

binding arbitration, 10:57, 10:58
selection of arbitrators, 10:59
collective bargaining, 10:36, 10:54
arbitration (See Arbitration)
database research services, 10:10
procedures for resolution, 10:55
Guardians of students (See Parents or guardians
of students)
Guidance counselors
certification requirements, 8:43
student's right to choose courses, 14:27
tenure areas, 8:60
Gun-Free Schools Act, 12:119, 25:8, 25:9
alternative educational services requirements,
    12:124
BB gun as weapon under, 12:121
curricular instruction on safe firearms use and,
    14:39
disabled students and, 12:125
due process requirements, 12:123
school district's responsibilities under, 12:122
suspension requirements, 12:120, 12:123,
    12:124, 25:9
weapon defined under, 12:121
Guns (See Firearms on campus; Gun-Free Schools
Act)
Gym (See Physical education)

Hatch Act, rights of parents to inspect classroom
materials, 14:57, 25:1
Hazard-Communication Standard, 17:25
failure of compliance, 17:27
material safety data sheet (MSDS), 17:25, 17:26
Hazardous waste, 17:35
Head Start programs
disabled preschool age children, 13:45
Health and safety
AIDS (See AIDS)
child safety transportation zones, 22:3
exposure control plans, 12:66
Family and Medical Leave Act (See Family and
Medical Leave Act (FMLA))
health services (See Health services)
hypodermic syringes and needles, instructional
    use of, 14:64
private and parochial schools, 24:11, 24:12
sanitation rules and regulations, applicability
    to school meal programs, 12:146
school buildings (See School buildings)
school buses, safety regulations (See School buses)
security guards (See Security guards)
Health benefits
COBRA, continuation coverage under, 8:142
retirement benefits, 11:2
Health care services training, curricula requirements, 14:46
Health certificates, 12:54
immunization certificate, 12:58
medical examination provided by district, 12:55
Health education
AIDS instruction as part of, 14:32
opt-out policies established by district, 14:32

religion as basis for excusal from, 14:28, 14:32, 14:58
child development, instruction in, 14:37
parenting skills training as part of curriculum, 14:37
religion as basis for excusal from, 14:28, 14:32, 14:58
state syllabi, 14:36
substance abuse by students, prevention of, 14:36
Health insurance (*See* Accident and health insurance)
Health services programs, 12:50
  commissioner's regulations, 12:52
  disabled children, 13:10
  health certificates, 12:54, 12:55
  parental notification requirements, 12:55
  private school students, 12:53
  scoliosis screening, 12:52, 12:56
  screening for health problems, 12:52, 12:55, 12:56
  for students, 12:50, 12:52, 12:54, 12:55
    condom distribution, 14:33
    drug testing, 12:90, 12:91
    immunization, 12:58
    private school students, 12:53
    screening for health problems, 12:52, 12:55, 12:56
    treatment requirements, 12:55
  treatment requirements, 12:55
Hearings
  CSE determinations, parental appeals of, 13:33
  disciplinary proceedings
  civil service employees (*See* Civil service)
Hepatitis infections, protection from, 17:24
Highway equipment, leasing of, 16:31
HIV (*See* AIDS)
Holidays
  public holidays, New York state, 14:5
  religious holidays (*See* Religious holidays)
  transportation for private school students on public school holidays, 22:84
Holocaust, curricular requirements, 14:41
Homebound instruction
  arrangements for, 24:35
  district responsibilities for, 24:35
  home instruction distinguished, 24:34
Home economics, parenting skills training as part of curriculum, 14:37
Home instruction
  adequacy of, 12:4, 12:14, 24:19, 24:21, 24:23, 24:29
  allowability of, 24:18
  athletics and competitive sports at public school, eligibility to participate in, 24:31
  attendance requirements, 12:1, 12:4, 12:14, 12:15, 24:19, 24:26
  computer software borrowing privileges, eligibility for, 24:32
  course requirements, 24:28
  curriculum requirements, 24:27
  disabled children, 13:6, 24:34

duty of parents, 24:18, 24:20, 24:21
Education Law, compliance with, 24:1, 24:20, 24:21
equivalency standards, 24:18
  enforcement of, 24:3, 24:4
homebound instruction distinguished, 24:34
immunization requirements, 24:33
individualized home instruction plan (IHIP), 24:2, 24:21, 24:28
  school district responsibilities, 24:22, 24:23
library borrowing privileges, eligibility for, 24:32
at location outside of parent's primary residence, 24:24
part-time attendance at public school, allowability of, 12:15
PEP tests, option to take, 24:28
physical education requirements, 24:27
poor performance by student, district's options, 24:29
pregnant students, 12:27
proof of instruction, 24:21
Regents diploma, eligibility of student for, 24:30
Regents examinations, option to take, 24:28
responsibilities of parents, 24:21
school board's responsibilities, 12:4, 12:14, 24:2, 24:22, 24:23, 24:29
supervision of, 24:2
during suspension of student, 12:107, 12:108, 12:124
testing and evaluation of
  eligible assessments, 24:21
  poor performance by student, district's options, 24:29
  state examinations offered, 24:21, 24:28
textbook borrowing privileges, eligibility for, 24:32
tutor as source of, 24:25
Homeless children
  admissions procedure, 12:43
  continuation of attendance when residence changes
    within district, 12:45
    out-of-district housing, temporary, 12:46
  defined, 12:39
  residency determination, 12:40, 12:42, 12:43
    change of, 12:41
    out-of-state, previously, 12:42
  transportation services, 12:47
    mileage limitations, 12:48
    state aid, 12:49
  tuition payments, 12:44
Home schools (*See* Home instruction)
Homestead property-classification system, 20:32, 20:33, 20:34
Homework, legal requirements, 14:25
Hours of employment, collective bargaining, 10:36
Human rights issues, curricular requirements, 14:41
Hypodermic syringes and needles, instructional use of, 14:64

IDEA (*See* Individuals with Disabilities Education Act (IDEA))
IEP for disabled students (*See* Individualized Education Program (IEP))
Immunization
  as admissions requirement, 12:58
    exceptions, 12:59
  educational programs on, 12:61
  home instruction student, 24:33
  surveys on, state, 12:60
Impact aid, Federal aid program, 25:8
Impasse
  collective bargaining, 10:42, 10:43
    costs associated with impasse, payment of, 10:45
    Public Employment Relations Board (PERB), role of, 10:44
    Public Employment Relations Board (PERB), role of, 10:44
Improving America's Schools Act (IASA), 25:7
  Gun-Free Schools Act, 25:9
  programs included in, 25:8, 25:9
Incarcerated students (*See* Correctional facilities)
Incidental teaching
  teacher certification, 8:44
  teacher's duties, 8:44
Income
  federal income tax (*See* Federal income tax)
  New York state income tax (*See* New York State Income Tax)
  school lunch and breakfast programs, free or reduced-price participation, 12:138
  state aid, property value per pupil, 21:14, 21:17
Independent study students
  Regents examinations, admission to, 14:67
Indigent students, 12:69
  tuition payments, 12:44
Individualized Education Program (IEP), 13:3, 13:4
  classification of student's disability, 13:4
    parental notification rights, 13:24, 13:26
    parental notice rights, 13:24, 13:26
    parental participation requirement, 13:27
  physical education program, development of, 14:49
  review and revision of
    district's refusal to change child's IEP, parental notification rights, 13:24
    frequency requirements for, 13:25
    parental consent requirements, 13:26
    parental notification rights, 13:24, 13:26
  special education requirements, 13:4
  suspension of student, impact of, 13:38
  year-round services as part of, 13:4, 13:11
Individualized home instruction plan (IHIP), 24:2, 24:21, 24:28
  deficiencies in, school district responsibilities, 24:23
  school district responsibilities, 24:22, 24:23
Individuals with Disabilities Education Act (IDEA), 25:1
  disabled children, 1:2, 13:1
    defined, 13:2

review of student's IEP, 13:24, 13:25
  funding for, 25:7
  private and parochial schools, on-site special education services for, 13:15
Indoor air quality
  defined, 17:37
  radon, exposure to, 17:31
  regulations, 17:38
  smoke-free schools requirement, 17:39, 17:40, 25:12
Industrial development agencies
  board members, 20:47
  defined, 20:46
  payments in lieu of taxes
    notification requirements, 20:50
  payments in lieu of taxes (PILOTs)
    Federal Impact aid program, as part of, 25:8
    PILOT revenues, distribution of, 20:48, 20:49
  taxable status, 20:48
  uniform tax exemption policy, 20:48
Injunctions
  strikes, 10:51, 10:52
Inspections
  private and parochial schools
    registered high schools, 24:7
    unregistered schools, 24:8
  school buildings
    asbestos, exposure to, 17:51
    fire-safety inspections, 17:11, 17:12, 17:13, 17:14
    health and safety inspections, 12:52
    by school board members, 16:2, 16:3
    structural inspections, 17:10
  school buses, 22:23
Installment bonds, 19:60
Installment contracts, 19:57
Instructional supplies, fees or charges for, 12:38
Instructional year, 14:1, 14:2, 14:3
Insurance
  accident and health insurance
    district employees, 18:44
    school board members, 18:46
  amount of coverage required, 18:40
  bidding requirements, 18:41
  disability insurance, 18:38
  group insurance programs, 18:44
    withholding from employee salaries to fund, 18:45
  insurance company, information on reliability of, 18:42
  legal counsel costs, indemnification requirements (*See* Legal counsel)
  life insurance, 18:44
  school buildings, 18:36
  school buses, 22:20, 22:77
  school libraries, 18:36
  security guards, 9:37
  self-insurance fund, 18:43
  student insurance, 18:47, 18:48
  surety bonds for school construction jobs, 18:49
  types of, 18:37
  unemployment insurance, 18:39

withholding from employee salaries to fund
group plans, 18:45
workers' compensation insurance, 18:38
Insurance companies
information on reliability of, 18:42
Insurance Reserve Fund, 19:24
Interest rates
bonds and notes, sale of, 19:66, 19:67
Interscholastic athletics (*See* Athletics and
competitive sports)
Interstate Agreement on Qualification of
Educational Personnel, 8:45
Investments
annual review of policies concerning, 2:81
bond sale proceeds, 19:76
general fund, 19:28
policies concerning, annual review requirements, 2:81
policy for, 19:30
of reserve funds, 19:27, 19:29
short-term investments, 19:28
temporary investments, IRC rebate requirements, 19:67

Jarema credit, 8:75, 8:92
Job-training programs
Job-Training Partnership Act (JTPA), funding
for, 25:13
school buses, 22:20
School-to-Work Opportunities Act, 14:47, 25:13
Joint facilities, building aid for construction of,
16:29
Junior ROTC, 14:45
Juul agreements, probationary teachers, 8:77

Kindergarten
admissions to, 12:6, 12:7, 14:8
age for entrance to, 12:6, 12:7, 14:8
AIDS instruction, state-mandated, 14:32
omission of, 12:7, 14:8
part-time teachers, seniority credit, 8:73, 8:91
private or parochial schools, 12:7, 22:20
program requirements, 14:8
transportation, 22:1
Knives (*See* Weapons)

Laboratory equipment
fees for, 12:38
safety equipment requirements, 12:67
Latchkey Children Law, 16:39
Lead, exposure to, 17:32
water supply, lead in, 17:33, 17:34
Learning standards adopted by Board of Regents,
14:15
elementary school grades, 14:17
foreign language requirements, 14:20
grades one through six, 14:17
grades seven and eight, 14:18
grades nine through twelve, 14:19
graduation standards for, 14:19
kindergarten, 14:16
prekindergarten, 14:16

Regents exams, revisions to meet new
standards, 14:66
remediation requirements, 14:21
schedule of phase-in of new Regents exams
based on, 14:66
Lease-purchase agreements
for instructional equipment, 19:56
for school buildings, 16:11
Leases and rentals
BOCES board powers, 5:22
highway equipment, 16:31
lease-purchase agreements
for instructional equipment, 19:56
for school buildings, 16:11
personal property, 19:46
school buildings, 16:10, 16:14, 16:30
school buildings, unused, 16:14
school buses, 22:74
"Least Restrictive Environment," disabled
children, 13:7
"Least restrictive environment," disabled children,
13:5
Leaves of absence
adoptive parents, 8:136, 9:21
collective bargaining, 8:132, 9:21, 10:36, 10:37,
10:62
exchange teachers, 8:140
Family and Medical Leave Act (*See* Family and
Medical Leave Act (FMLA))
military leave, 9:22
noninstructional employees, 9:21
policies on, school board powers and duties,
8:132
religious holidays or observances, 8:138
Legal counsel
bidding process in selection of, 18:32
bond attorney, hiring of, 19:78
fees, 19:41
parental appeal of district's CSE determination, 13:33
indemnification for costs of counsel
pre-indemnification procedures required,
18:34
school board members, 18:33, 18:34, 18:35
school district superintendent, 6:22
statutory requirements, 18:33, 18:35
teachers or other district employees, 8:25,
18:33, 18:34, 18:35
retention of counsel by school district, 18:31
school board members, indemnification for
costs of counsel, 18:33, 18:34, 18:35
school district attorneys, 18:31
appointment of, 3:1
attendance at CSE meetings, 13:29
status as district employee or officer, 3:9
school district superintendent, indemnification
for costs of counsel, 6:22
teachers or other district employees,
indemnification for costs of counsel, 8:25,
18:33, 18:34, 18:35
Legal expenses, 19:41

Legal status
    New York State education system, generally, 1:1
    school board members, 2:1
    school boards, 2:1
Liability
    defined, 18:1
    immunity from
        school board member's immunity, 18:2
    personal liability (*See* Personal liability)
    rules of, 18:1
    school district liability (*See* Liability, school
        district)
Liability, school district
    asbestos, exposure to, 17:48
    athletic or competitive events, injuries incurred
        in school sponsored (*See* Athletics and
        competitive sports)
    athletic or competitive events, school-
        sponsored, 18:3
    civil rights, violation of (*See* Civil rights,
        violation of)
    educational malpractice, 18:8
    employment practices, 18:9, 18:22
    errands, students sent on, 18:14
    independent contractors hired by district, 18:12
    insurance (*See* Insurance)
    legal action, procedure for, 18:4, 18:5
    letters of recommendations for former
        employees, 18:10
    negligence (*See* Negligence)
    notice of claim
        filing requirements, 18:6
        statute of limitations, 18:5
    off school grounds injuries, 18:14
    outside organization's use of school facility,
        injuries incurred during, 18:3
    permission slips as protection, 18:7
    school bus accidents, 18:12, 18:13
    school-sponsored trips, 18:7
    sexual harassment claims (*See* Sexual harassment)
    statute of limitations, 18:5
    student assaults on teachers, 18:11
    transportation accidents, 18:12, 18:13
Libraries, school
    board's responsibilities, 14:60, 14:62
    contents of, minimum holdings requirements,
        14:60
    home instruction students, borrowing privileges
        for, 24:32
    insurance for, 18:36
    library media specialist
        certification requirements, 8:43
        district's responsibility to employ, 14:61
        tenure areas, 8:60
    private and parochial schools, borrowing
        privileges for, 24:17
    removal of books from, constitutional issues,
        14:62
    state aid, 21:12
Library media specialist
    certification requirements, 8:43
    district's responsibility to employ, 14:61
    tenure areas, 8:60

Licensing
    certification (*See* Certification)
    school bus drivers, 22:49, 22:57
Life insurance, 18:44
Lockers
    fees or charges for, 12:38
    search of students', 12:86, 12:88
Loitering, on school grounds, 16:53
Lottery, state aid from, 21:2
Low-performing schools, SURR designation, 14:74
Lunch period, right to free
    noninstructional employees, 9:20
    teachers, 8:16
Lunch programs, student (*See* School lunch
    programs)

Magnet schools, federal aid for, 25:8
Mainstreaming of disabled children, 13:5
Managerial employees
    confidential employees distinguished, 10:24
    defined, 10:24
    designation of, 10:23
    principals as, allowability of, 7:30
Married students
    attendance requirements, 12:3
    nondiscrimination, right to equal educational
        opportunities, 12:27
    pregnancy, nondiscrimination, 12:27
Married teachers, nondiscrimination protections,
    8:5
Mascot, school, 23:17
Master Plan, school district reorganization, 15:7
Maternity leave
    Family and Medical Leave Act, 8:135
    noninstructional employees, 9:21
    teachers, 8:135
Medical examinations
    disabled children, 12:55, 13:10
    health certificates, for students who have not
        furnished, 12:55
    parental notification requirements, 12:55
    physician to perform, district hiring require-
        ments, 12:51
    religion as basis for excusal from school-based,
        12:55, 14:28
    school-based exams
        drug testing of students, 12:90, 12:91
        hearing tests, 12:56
        parental notification requirements, 12:55,
            12:56
        physician, school district, 12:51
        religion as basis for excusal from, 12:55,
            12:56, 14:28
        scoliosis screening, 12:52, 12:56
        sickle-cell anemia testing, 12:55
        for students who have not furnished health
            certificates, 12:55
        vision tests, 12:56
    school bus drivers, 22:48, 22:53
    teachers
        current employees, 8:12
        pre-employment exams, 8:11, 12:52

psychiatric examinations, procedures and rights, 8:12

Medical leave
Family and Medical Leave Act, 8:132, 8:135, 10:61

Medical services (*See* Health services programs)

Meditation period, silent, constitutionality, 23:9, 23:10

"Megan's Law" (*See* Sex Offender Registration Act ("Megan's Law"))

Military
instruction in public schools, 14:45
Junior ROTC, 14:45
leaves of absence for service in, 9:22
recruiting on school property, 16:41
veterans (*See* Veterans)

Minimum wage laws
civil service employees, 9:18
Fair Labor Standards Act, applicability of, 9:18

Missing children
abduction prevention programs, 12:71, 14:42
release of student from school, 12:71
divorced or separated parents, 12:72
school district's responsibility, 12:70, 12:71

National Education Goals, as part of Goals 2000, 25:10

Native Americans
dress code, 23:18
Federal aid, 25:8
property owned by, exemption from taxation, 20:16
school bus use for nonschool activities, 22:20

Negligence
accidents to students, school district's liability for, 8:25, 18:7
athletic or competitive events, school-sponsored (*See* Athletics and competitive sports)
defined, 18:7
employment practices, 18:9, 18:22
errands, students sent on, 18:14
independent contractors hired by district, 18:12
off school grounds injuries, 18:14
school-sponsored trips, 18:7
statutory protection for employees, 8:25, 18:33, 18:35
transportation to and from school by bus, 18:12, 18:13

New learning standards (*See* Learning standards adopted by Board of Regents)

Newspapers
annual district meeting, public notice requirements, 4:10, 4:11
transportation contract bids, advertising, 22:67

New York City
central board of education, role and responsibilities of, 1:22
community school districts
board membership, 2:3, 2:4
creation of, 15:6
responsibilities of, 1:22
school budget, 4:20
state aid, 21:16

New York State court system, structure of, 1:4

New York State Department of Transportation
school bus safety regulations (*See* School buses)

New York State Higher Education Service Corporation
Guaranteed Student Loan Program of, 14:76

New York State income tax
on retirement plans
benefits, 11:18
contributions, 11:13

New York State School Boards Association
AIDS instruction advisory council membership, legal challenge to, 14:32
arbitration services available, 10:10, 10:59
conventions, expenses for participation in, 19:9
dues, payment of, 19:8
policy development assistance to local boards, 2:84

New York State School Tax Relief Program (STAR) (*See* School Tax Relief Program (STAR))

New York State teacher certification examination, 8:29

Nondiscrimination protections (*See* Discrimination)

Noninstructional employees (*See also* Civil service)
board's responsibilities, 2:10
child abuse, reporting requirements, 12:74
Family and Medical Leave Act (*See* Family and Medical Leave Act (FMLA))
leaves of absence (*See* Leaves of absence)
mandatory reporter status for child abuse reporting, 12:74
prohibited actions defined by statute, 2:33
retirement plans for (*See* Employees' Retirement System (ERS), New York State)
sexual abuse of child, reporting requirements, 12:74
Social Security, 11:52

Nonpublic schools (*See* Private and parochial schools; private and parochial schools)

Nonresident students
disabled students, 12:30
refusal of by school district, 12:30
tuition charges for, 12:9, 12:35, 12:36

Nonteaching employees (*See* Noninstructional employees)

Northeast regional credential, teacher certification, 8:45

Notes, financial
after school district reorganization, 15:18
authorization for issuance of, 19:68
bond anticipation notes (BANs), 19:65
bonds anticipation notes (BANs), 19:60, 19:61, 19:64
budget notes, 19:60, 19:64
capital notes, 19:60, 19:64
destruction of canceled notes, 2:75
limitations on amounts, 19:61
revenue anticipation notes, 19:60
special bank accounts, 19:75
tax anticipation notes, 19:60, 19:64
voter approval for issuance of, 19:69, 19:77

Notice
  to employers
    accidents, school bus drivers, 22:59
    school bus driver traffic violations, 22:58
  parents or guardians of students (*See* Parents
    or guardians of students)
  public notice and/or disclosure requirements
    (*See* Public notice and/or disclosure
    requirements)
  special school district meeting, 2:48, 2:52
Nurse, school
  employment requirements, 12:51

Oath of allegiance, teacher's, 8:2
Oath of office
  board members, 2:8, 3:20, 4:46
  BOCES member, 2:8
  civil service employees, 9:17
  district superintendent, 6:6
Occupational education
  dual-enrollment requirements, 24:11
  state syllabi for, 14:24
  teacher certification requirements, 8:34
Occupational Safety and Health Act (OSHA),
  17:20 (*See also* State Occupational Safety and
  Health Act (SOSHA))
  chemical hygiene plan, 17:30
  hazard communication standard, 17:25
  hepatitis infections, 17:24
  HIV, exposure to, 17:24
  material safety data sheet (MSDS), 17:26
  shop classes, 17:23
Office of General Services, purchasing through,
  19:52
On-the-job training programs, funding for, 25:13
Open Meetings Law, 2:46, 2:54, 2:57, 2:65, 4:19
  shared decision making process and, 3:36
Operating aid, reorganization incentive aid, 15:23
Option agreements, school site acquisition, 16:9
OSHA (*See* Occupational Safety and Health Act
  (OSHA))
Overtime pay
  civil service employees, 9:18

Paper products, recycled paper, 19:55
Parenting skills, instruction in as part of student
  curricula, 14:37
Parents or guardians of students
  consent
    absences of student, 12:21
    condom distribution to students, 14:33
    drug-testing of students, 12:90
    Junior ROTC, 14:45
    police interrogations, in school buildings,
      12:93
    release of student from school, 12:18, 12:71
  disabled students
    Individualized Education Program (IEP),
      participation requirements, 13:27
    private school, right of parents to place child
      in, 13:36
    procedural safeguards to insure rights of,
      13:16, 13:17

    rights of parents, procedural safeguards to
      insure, 13:16, 13:17
    SCE meetings, attendance and participation
      requirements, 13:27
  discipline proceedings against students
    school buses, misbehavior on, 22:11
    suspensions of less than five days, 12:103
    suspensions of less than ten days, 13:38
  divorced or separated parents
    release of student from school, permission
      for, 12:72
    residency of student, determination of,
      12:32, 12:33
    transportation of students and, 22:7
  duty to educate their children, 24:20
  home instruction by (*See* Home instruction)
  Individualized Education Program (IEP),
    participation requirements, 13:27
  legal residence, 12:31, 12:33, 12:35
  notification requirements
    absences of child, 12:20
    dropping of student from enrollment, 12:25
    exemption from school's participation in
      breakfast programs, 12:137
    extracurricular activities available to disabled
      students, 13:13
    incidental teaching assignments, 8:44
    involuntary transfer of child, 12:24
    medical examinations, school-based, 12:55,
      12:56
    procedural rights available to parents of
      disabled students, 13:17
    remediation requirements, 14:74
    school buses, discipline resulting from
      misbehavior on, 22:11
    SED review of private or parochial school,
      24:8
    suspensions of less than five days, 12:103
    termination of school's participation in
      breakfast programs, 12:137
  opposition by
    AIDS-prevention instruction, 14:28, 14:32,
      14:58
    as cause for removal of textbook, 14:59
    to conditions of school, 12:16
    to curriculum materials, 14:57, 14:58, 14:59
  Parent-Teacher Associations (*See* Parent-Teacher
    Associations (PTA))
  release of student from school, permission for,
    12:18, 12:71
    divorced or separated parents, 12:72
  requests by
    for absence by child for religious reasons, 12:17
    for release of child during school hours for
      religious instruction, 12:18
    transportation, 22:8
  rights
    to conference to discuss involuntary transfer
      of child, 12:24
    to inspect classroom materials, 14:57
  SCE meetings for disabled students
    attendance and participation requirements
      for parents, 13:27

tape-recording of, 13:28
student weapons possession on campus,
    notification requirements, 12:85
transportation
    provided by, compensation, 22:13
    requests, 22:8
Parent-Teacher Associations (PTA), 1:27
    conflict-of-interest concerns for members, 1:28
    information requests, 1:29
    membership, 1:28
    relationship to public schools, 1:27
    school board membership, concurrent, 1:28
    school bus transportation to meetings, 22:21
Parochial schools (See Private and parochial schools)
Part-time students, allowability of, 12:15
Payments in lieu of taxes (PILOTs)
    Federal Impact aid program, as part of, 25:8
    PILOT revenues, distribution of, 20:48, 20:49
Payroll
    civil service employees, 9:19
    strike penalty, 10:52
PEL (See Preferred Eligibility List (PEL))
Pell Grants, federal, 14:76
Penalties
    strikes, 10:51, 10:52
PEP (Pupil Evaluation Program) tests, phase-out
    of, 14:66
PERB (See Public Employment Relations Board
    (PERB))
Personal liability, school board members, 2:1
Personal Privacy Protection Law
    records access officer, role of, 2:76
Personal property
    leasing of, 19:46
    purchasing requirements, 19:46
PESH bureau (See Public Employees' Safety and
Health (PESH) Bureau)
Pesticides, use of, 17:28, 17:29
    integrated pest management, 17:29
Petroleum, underground storage tanks, 17:36
Petty cash funds, establishment of, 19:22
Photographs, sale on school premises, 16:60
Physical education
    alternatives to participation requirements, 14:50
    disabled students, 14:49
    high school diploma, as prerequisite for, 14:51
    home instruction students, 24:27
    participation requirements, 14:49, 14:51
        alternatives to, 14:50
Physical examinations (See Medical examinations)
Physician, school district, 12:51
PILOTs (See Payments in lieu of taxes (PILOTs))
Planned balance, 19:35
Pledge of Allegiance
    abstention from, Free Exercise Clause rights,
        16:51
    instruction and participation requirements, 16:51
Police
    Miranda rights of students, 12:92
    in school buildings, 12:93
    Miranda rights of students, 12:92
    weapons possession on campus, notification
        requirements, 12:85

Polling place
    annual district meetings, 4:8
    general elections, use of school buildings in,
        16:38
    special school district meetings, 4:54
Poll lists, annual district meetings, 4:65, 4:78
Post-graduates under 21, right to attend school,
    12:9, 12:10
Prayers and benedictions
    at athletic games or practices, 23:6
    bible study meetings on school premises, 16:44,
        23:8
    in classroom, 16:44, 23:4, 23:5, 23:8
    at extracurricular activities, 23:6
    at graduation ceremonies, 23:7
    intercom system, student-led prayer broadcasts
        over, 23:5
    moment of silence, 23:9
    school board meeting, opening of, 23:10
    school board meeting, opening of, 23:10
    student-led prayer, 16:44, 23:5, 23:7, 23:8
    voluntary prayer, 16:44, 23:4, 23:5, 23:8
Preferred Eligibility List (PEL)
    administrators, school, 7:12
    teachers, 8:94, 8:98, 8:100, 8:103
Pregnancy
    nondiscrimination
        students, right to equal educational
            opportunities, 12:27
        teachers, 8:5, 8:134, 18:22
    students
        home instruction, 12:27
        right to equal educational opportunities, 12:27
    teachers
        Family and Medical Leave Act, 8:135
        mandatory sick leave, allowability of, 8:134
        maternity leave policies, 8:135
        nondiscrimination, 8:5, 8:134, 18:22
        Title VII protections, 8:5, 18:22
Prekindergarten programs (See also Preschool
    students)
    admissions to, 12:5
    advisory board, prekindergarten policy
        appointment of board members, 14:10
        deadline for formation of, 14:11
        formation of, 14:10, 14:11
        role of, 14:12, 14:13
    age requirements, 12:5
    attendance policies for, 12:5
    learning standards adopted by Board of
        Regents, 14:16
    New York State Experimental Pre-Kindergarten
    Program, 14:9
        phase-in schedule for, 14:9
        program requirements, 14:9
        school board responsibility for, 14:10, 14:12,
            14:13
Preschool students (See also Prekindergarten
    programs)
    Committee on Preschool Special Education
        (CPSE) (See Committee on Preschool Special
        Education (CPSE))
    disabled children

Committee on Preschool Special Education
(CPSE) (*See* Committee on Preschool
Special Education (CPSE))
Head Start programs, 13:45
itinerant special education services, 13:46,
13:47
placement of, 13:45
school district's responsibilities to, 13:45,
13:46
services and programs available to, 13:46
testing and evaluation of, 13:7, 13:8, 13:18,
13:45
private schools, transportation to, 22:82
school buses, 22:20, 22:82
school lunch program, eligibility for, 12:144
state aid, 21:12
President, school board
voting rights, 2:61
Principals
appointment of, 7:6
assistant principals
statutory requirement for, 7:27
certification requirements, 7:2
as civil service employees, 9:5
compensation
reduction in, allowability of, 7:29
salary schedule, requirement for, 7:28
managerial employee designation, 7:30
one-per-school requirements, 7:26
powers and duties, 14:27
authority to suspend students, 12:99
statutory requirement for, 7:1
statutory requirements for, 7:26
tenure, 7:6, 7:7
salary, allowability of reduction in, 7:29
Prisons (*See* Correctional facilities)
Privacy rights
alcohol and drug test results, school bus
drivers, 22:63
Family Educational Rights and Privacy Act
(FERPA), 2:70, 25:1
Personal Privacy Protection Law, 2:76
Private and parochial schools
academic performance tests, 24:10
antidiscrimination laws, compliance with, 24:5
Board of Cooperative Educational Services
(BOCES), 24:9
Board of Regents, registration with, 24:6
board's responsibilities, 24:2, 24:9
breakfast programs, school, 12:136
certification of new schools, 24:5, 24:9
certification of teachers, 8:36, 24:5
compulsory attendance, 12:4
computer software programs, loans from public
schools, 24:16
constitutional restraints and, 24:12
disabled students, 24:11
anti-discrimination requirements, 24:5
on-site services, 24:13
special education and services provided by
district, 13:14, 13:15, 13:36, 24:13
"stay-put" provisions, 13:34

dual enrollment law, 21:23, 24:11, 24:12
Education Law, compliance with, 24:1
equivalency standards, 24:1, 24:2, 24:5
enforcement of, 24:3, 24:4
Family Educational Rights and Privacy Act
(FERPA), 24:5
federal aid, 24:11, 25:5
federal laws, compliance with, 24:5, 24:12
fire and fire safety, 14:38, 24:5
health and welfare services, provided by public
school district, 12:53, 24:12
homebound instruction, district responsibilities
for, 24:35
inspections, 24:7, 24:8
kindergarten requirements, 12:7, 24:6
mandated services law, 24:11
new schools, 24:9
preschools and nursery schools, 24:6
transportation to, 22:82
public school district, services provided by, 24:11
computer software programs, purchase of
loan of, 24:16
dual-enrollment requirements, 24:11
dual enrollment services, 24:11, 24:12
library materials, borrowing of, 24:17
special education services, 13:14, 13:36,
24:13, 24:15
textbooks, purchase and loan of, 24:14, 24:15
religious instruction, release time for, 12:18,
22:86, 23:13
safety standards, compliance with, 24:5, 24:7,
24:8
scholastic achievement tests, 24:10
standards, 24:3
state aid, 21:5, 21:12, 24:10
closings, displacement aid regarding, 21:22
disabled students, 21:23
mandated services law, 24:11
operating aid, 21:5
school buses, out-of-district transportation
of students, 22:79
testing and data collection services, 21:12
State Education Department (SED), 24:10
registration with, 24:6
supervisory role, 1:11
state laws and, 24:11, 24:12
substandard performance assessment, remedy
for, 24:7, 24:8
superintendent of schools, role of, 24:3, 24:9
supervision of, 24:2, 24:5
teacher certification requirements, 8:2, 8:36,
24:5
textbooks, loan or purchase by public school
district, 24:14, 24:15
limits on frequency of, 14:56
transportation
accommodation of private school's schedule,
public district's, 22:87
central pickup points, 22:82, 22:85
denial of transportation, causes for, 22:83
holidays of public school, status regarding,
22:84

late requests, 22:83
public district's accommodation of private
    school's schedule, 22:87
religious instructional classes, 22:86
requests, 22:1
requests for, 22:83
requirements, 22:1, 22:82, 24:11
submission of lists of eligible students, 22:88
supervision requirements, 22:82
Probationary employees
administrative employees (*See* Administrative
    employees)
due process rights of, 7:13
Probationary teachers
appointment of, 8:68, 8:69, 8:71, 8:73
    waiver of right to probationary appointment,
        8:72
defined, 8:67
denial of tenure, 8:81
    notice requirements, 8:82
dismissal after, notice requirements, 8:82
dismissal during, notice requirements, 8:78,
    8:79, 8:82
early tenure, granting of, 8:76
employment contracts, 8:70
extension of, 8:77
granting of tenure, procedures, 8:85, 8:86
Jarema credit, 8:75, 8:92
Juul agreements, 8:77
length of, 8:74
notice of appointment, 8:69
notice requirements
    for denial of tenure, 8:82
    for dismissal, 8:79
notice requirements for dismissal, 8:82
part-time teachers, 8:73
substitute teachers, 8:74
tenure by estoppel, 8:77, 8:87
transfers from one district to another, 8:56
waiver of probationary period, 8:72
waiver of right to probationary appointment, 8:72
Probation, employee
strikes as cause for, 10:53
Probation, student, 12:96
Pro-Children Act of 1994, smoke-free schools,
    17:39, 25:12
Professional services, exemption from competitive
    bidding requirements, 19:48
Program Evaluation Test (PET), phase-out of, 14:66
Progress reports, students', 14:70
Property Loss and Liability Reserve Fund, 19:24
Property rights, post-school district reorganization,
    15:18
Protests and demonstrations, student, 12:78
Psychologists, school
certification requirements, 8:43
tenure areas, 8:60
PTA (*See* Parent-Teacher Associations (PTA))
Public carriers, as student transportation, 22:1,
    22:9, 22:82
Public education, generally
aliens, illegal, right to public education, 25:1

authority for, 1:1, 25:1, 25:2
federal authority, 25:1, 25:2
federal funding (*See* Federal aid)
legal framework for, 1:1, 1:2
responsibility for, 1:2
    federal support agency, 25:3
right to, basis for, 25:1
Public employees
code of ethics, 2:31
prohibited actions defined by statute, 2:33
retirees as
    retirement allowance, impact on, 11:20,
        11:21, 11:22
    school district employees, 11:22
    teachers, 11:20, 11:21
retirement age, mandatory, 11:1
retirement plans (*See* Retirement plans)
Taylor Law (*See* Taylor Law)
Public Employees' Fair Employments Act
    (*See* Taylor Law)
Public Employees' Safety and Health (PESH)
    Bureau, 17:19
financial assistance for compliance, 17:22
hepatitis infections, 17:24
HIV, exposure to, 17:24
requirements, 17:19
violation of rules, 17:21
Public Employment Relations Board (PERB)
designation of managerial employee, 7:30
paid leave for religious observance, rulings on,
    8:138
strike, role during, 8:23, 10:14, 10:33, 10:52
Public holidays, New York state, 14:5
Public notice and/or disclosure requirements
annual district meeting, 4:10, 4:11, 4:19
    budget actions, 4:10, 4:11, 4:13, 4:21
    noncompliance with notice requirements,
        consequences of, 4:12
BOCES annual meetings, 5:17, 5:18, 5:19
BOCES budget, 5:18, 5:19, 5:20
bond issues, 4:10, 4:11
budget actions by board, 4:10, 4:11, 4:13, 4:21
fire-safety inspections of school buildings, 17:14
noncompliance with notice requirements,
    consequences of, 4:12
school board meetings, 2:52
school board member elections, 4:11
Sex Offender Registration Act ("Megan's Law"),
    12:75, 12:76
special school district meetings, 2:48, 2:52,
    4:10, 4:53, 4:54
Sunshine Laws (*See* Sunshine Laws)
Pupil Evaluation Program (PEP) tests
home instruction students, 24:28
phase-out of, 14:66
Purchasing
audits, 19:20
bidding requirements (*See* Competitive bidding
    requirements)
cooperative purchasing agreements, 19:51
copying equipment, 19:57
correctional institutions, purchases from, 19:53

data-processing equipment, 19:57
disabled persons, products or services of, 19:54
federal excise taxes, 19:59
installment contracts, 19:57
lease-purchase agreements
   for instructional equipment, 19:56
   for school buildings, 16:11
Office of General Services, purchases through, 19:52
paper products, 19:55
personal property, 19:46
state sales taxes, 19:58
surplus equipment, 19:48
taxation
   federal excise taxes, 19:59
   state sale taxes, 19:58

Race, discrimination, 8:5, 8:125, 12:28
Radio and television, promotional activities on school premises, 16:59
Radon, exposure to, 17:31
Real property
   leasing of (See Leases and rentals)
   renting of (See Leases and rentals)
   taxation (See Taxation)
Recess, detention precluding participation in, 12:112
Records
   asbestos management plan
      contractors, 17:60
      copies of, 17:44
   definition of, 2:68
   denial of access
      appeals, 2:73
      penalties for, 2:74
   destruction of, 2:75
   improvement of records management, public funding for, 2:77
   Local Government Records Management Improvement Fund, 2:77
   management of records, public funding for improvement of, 2:77
   microfilm preservation of, 2:75
   minutes of meetings, 2:54, 2:64
      public access to, 2:65
   personnel records
      school board members, access rights, 2:72
   preservation of, 2:75
   public inspection of, 2:66, 2:68
      denial of access, 2:67, 2:69, 2:74
      exemptions, 2:68, 2:69
      procedure for, 2:73
   records access officer
      appointment of, 3:1
      role of, 2:73
   records management officer
      appointment of, 3:1
      role of, 2:76
   responsibility for, 2:76
   school district clerk, role of, 2:76
   student records (See Students)
   tape recording of meetings, allowability of, 2:55

Recreation (See also Athletics and competitive sports)
   disabled children, programs for, 13:6
   use of school bus for nonschool recreational purposes, 22:20
Recycled paper
   bidding requirements, 19:55
Regents, Board of (See Board of Regents)
Regents College Examinations Program (See Regents examinations)
Regents Competency Tests, phase-out of, 14:15, 14:65, 14:66
Regents diploma, 14:19
   graduation standards for, 14:15, 14:19
   home instruction students, 24:30
Regents examinations, 1:7, 14:65
   admissions requirements, 14:67, 14:68
   alternative testing, 14:66
   cheating by students, due process rights, 14:69
   equivalency diploma (GED) attained through, 12:11
   fraud by students, due process rights, 14:69
   graduation standards for, 14:15
   home instruction students wishing to take, 14:68, 24:28
   local qualifying exams, allowability of, 14:68
   modification of exams to meet new learning standards, 14:66
   new learning standards, modification of exams to meet, 14:66
   schedule of phase-in of exams based on new learning standards, 14:66
   types of exams available, 14:15, 14:66
Regional transportation systems, for multiple school districts, 22:10
Registration
   private and parochial schools, with State Education Department (SED), 24:6
   school buses, 22:75
   security guards, 9:37
Rehabilitation programs, drug and alcohol school bus drivers, 22:65
Reimbursement
   fingerprinting, school bus drivers, 22:55
Relatives, conflicts of interest
   school board members, 2:21, 2:35, 2:36, 8:10
   teachers, 8:10
Release time, for religious instruction, 23:13
   transportation requirements, 22:86
Religion
   absences for religious observance
      students, 12:17, 23:13
      teachers, 8:138, 23:14
   AIDS-prevention instruction, excusal from, 14:28, 14:32, 14:58
   artwork of student with religious themes, display of, 23:15
   basis for abstention from pledge and flag salute, 16:51
   basis for excusing child from classes, 12:17, 12:18, 14:28, 14:32, 14:58, 23:13
   displays of religious symbols on school property, 23:15

distribution of religious literature on school grounds, student rights, 12:83
dress code, 23:18
Establishment Clause, U.S. Constitution (*See* Establishment Clause, U.S. Constitution)
Free Exercise Clause, First Amendment (*See* Free Exercise Clause, First Amendment)
Halloween-related items, display of, 23:16
health education, excusal from, 14:28, 14:32, 14:58
holidays (*See* Religious holidays)
immunization requirements, excusal from, 12:59
instruction (*See* Religious instruction)
mascot of school and, 23:17
medical examination, excusal from school-based, 12:55, 14:28
   drug testing, 12:90
nondiscrimination protections, teachers, 8:5, 8:125, 8:138, 23:14
religious garb, 23:18
observances, religious (*See* Religious holidays)
opt-out policy established by district, 14:32, 14:44
parochial schools (*See* Private and parochial schools)
prayers and benedictions (*See* Prayers and benedictions)
property used for worship, exemption from taxation, 20:16
religious literature, distribution on school grounds, student rights, 12:83
separation of church and state (*See* Establishment Clause, U.S. Constitution)
symbols, religious, display in schools, 23:15
teachers, nondiscrimination protections, 8:5, 8:125, 8:138
Title VII nondiscrimination protections, 23:14, 23:18
worship, use of school premises for, 16:43, 16:44, 23:8
Religious Freedom Restoration Act (RFRA), overturning of, 23:3
Religious holidays
   closing of school in óbservance of, 23:11
   Halloween-related items, display of, 23:16
   leaves of absence, teachers, 8:138
   observances in public schools, 23:11, 23:12
   religious symbols in schools, display of, 23:15, 23:16
   student absences for, 12:17, 23:13
   teacher absences for, 8:138, 23:14
Religious instruction
   art and music, religious, 23:12
   beliefs as cultural or historical topic, 14:35
   music and art, religious, 23:12
   in public schools, 14:35
   release time for, 12:18, 22:86, 23:13
   use of school premises for, 16:45, 23:8
Religious worship, use of school premises for, 16:43, 16:44, 23:8
Remediation requirements, 14:21
   SURR schools, 14:74
Removal from office (*See also* Dismissal)

district superintendent, 6:7, 6:8
school board members, 2:25, 2:27
superintendent of schools, 2:15
   multiple districts, superintendent's services shared with, 7:5
Rentals (*See* Leases and rentals)
Reorganization, school district (*See* School district reorganization)
Repair Reserve Fund, 19:24
Report cards
   BOCES report cards, 5:29, 14:73
   school report cards (*See* School report cards)
   student report cards, 14:70
Reserve funds
   defined, 19:23
   establishment of, 19:23
   excess funds, transfer of, 19:26
   investment of, 19:27, 19:29
   kinds of, 19:24
   voter approval, 19:25
Reserve Officer Training Corps (ROTC), high school (*See* Junior ROTC)
Residency requirements, 12:29
   annual district meetings, voting at, 4:82
   BOCES board members, 5:8
   citizenship (*See* Citizenship requirements)
   civil service employees, 9:14
   determination of child's entitlement to attend school in particular district, 12:34
   district superintendent, 6:3
   entitlement to attend school in particular district, determination of child's, 12:34
   homeless children, 12:40, 12:41, 12:42, 12:43
      continuation of attendance when residence changes, 12:45, 12:46
      out-of-state, previously, 12:42
   parents, legal residence, defined, 12:31, 12:33
      divorced or separated parents, 12:32, 12:33
   physical presence alone as insufficient, 12:31
   school board members, 2:18
   special school district meetings, voting at, 4:49
   students, legal residence, defined, 12:31
      divorced or separated parents, 12:32, 12:33
   tuition charges for nonresidents, 12:9, 12:35
Resignation of teacher
   denial of tenure, rights when teacher chooses resignation rather than, 8:84
   tenured teachers
      3020-a decision, prior to, 8:106
      unused leave time, payment for, 8:141
Respondeat superior, defined, 18:1
Retirement
   mandatory retirement age, 11:1
   plans covering (*See* Retirement plans)
   sick leave, cash payment for unused leave at retirement, 7:14
Retirement plans, 11:4
   Age 55 Plan, 11:12
   Age 60 Plan, 11:12
   annuity plans, tax-sheltered, 8:129, 11:19
   benefits
      disability allowances, 11:38

health benefits, 11:2
retirement allowances for funding of plan
    participation, 11:3
supplemental benefits, 11:36, 11:38
Career Plan, 11:12
changes in benefits, allowability of, 11:11
contributions (*See also* specific plans)
    borrowing against, 11:39
    income taxation of, 11:13
    retirement allowances as, 11:3
disabled teachers, supplemental allowances for,
    11:36, 11:38
Employees' Retirement System (ERS), New York
    State
    generally (*See* Employees' Retirement System
        (ERS), New York State)
    tier structures (*See specific Tiers below*)
health benefits, 11:2
Improved Career Plan, 11:12
Improved 1/60th Plan, 11:12
income taxation
    of benefits, 11:18
    of contributions, 11:13
lump sum retirement payments, 11:35
noncontributory plans, 11:12
1/60th Plan, 11:12
service credits, 11:14, 11:16
Social Security, integration with (*See* Social
    Security)
taxation of contributions, 11:13
for teachers
    New York City system (*See* Teachers'
        Retirement System, New York City)
    New York State system (*See* Teachers'
        Retirement System (TRS), New York State)
    tier structures (*See specific Tiers below*)
Tier I members, 11:5
    changes in benefits, 11:11
    contribution requirements, 11:29
    early retirement incentives, effect of, 11:10
    lump sum retirement payments, 11:35
    noncontributory plans available to, 11:12
    service credits, 11:14
    service requirements, 11:6
Tier II members, 11:5
    changes in benefits, 11:11
    contribution requirements, 11:29
    early retirement incentives, effect of, 11:10
    lump sum retirement payments, 11:35
    noncontributory plans available to, 11:12
    service, contribution and benefit require-
        ments, 11:7
    service credits, 11:14
Tier III members, 11:5
    benefits available, 11:8
    borrowing from accumulated deposits, 11:39
    changes in benefits, 11:11
    contribution requirements, 11:29
    early retirement incentives, effect of, 11:10
    lump sum retirement payments, 11:35
    service credits, 11:14
    service requirements, 11:8

taxability of contributions, 11:13
workers' compensation leave, effect of, 11:49
Tier IV members, 11:5
    benefits available, 11:9
    borrowing from accumulated deposits, 11:39
    changes in benefits, 11:11
    contribution requirements, 11:29
    early retirement incentives, effect of, 11:10
    lump sum retirement payments, 11:35
    service credits, 11:14
    service requirements, 11:9
    taxability of contributions, 11:13
    workers' compensation leave, effect of, 11:49
    transfer of membership, 11:15, 11:16
vesting, defined, 11:17
Revenue anticipation notes, 19:60
Revocation
    of superintendent's certification, 7:4
    of teacher's certification, 6:19, 7:4
Right-of-way, schools granting to municipalities,
    16:14
Rochester
    school board membership, 2:3, 2:4
    state aid, 21:16
ROTC, high school (*See* Junior ROTC)
Routes, school bus
    distance limitations, 22:2
        child safety zones, 22:3
        hazardous routes as exception to, 22:3
        length of commute, 22:5
        measurement of, 22:4
        walking distance for students, 22:17
    drive-off places for buses, 22:16
    hazardous routes, 22:3, 22:14
    hazards on, 22:14
    length of commute, 22:5
    pick-up places for buses, 22:16
    on private land or roads, 22:15
    shelters for riders, 22:18
    unsafe or impassable roads, 22:14
    walking distance, policy, 22:17

Safe and Drug-Free School and Communities Act
    (SDFSCA), 12:57, 16:55, 16:56
Safe Schools program, violence prevention, 25:11
Safety
    building safety (*See* School buildings)
    employees' safety (*See* Workplace safety)
    Federal aid to increase, 25:8
    fire safety (*See* Fire and fire safety)
    health and (*See* Health and safety)
    school buses (*See* School buses)
    workplace safety (*See* Workplace safety)
Safety equipment, vocational and laboratory
    classes, 12:67
Salaries (*See also* Compensation)
    collective bargaining, 10:36, 10:37
    as contingent expense, 19:42
Sale
    of school buildings, 16:12
    of sweetened foods on school grounds, 16:58

Sales taxes
    allocation of county tax for school district
        purposes, 20:4
    breakfast and lunch programs, school-based,
        12:139
    exemption from, 19:58
    food services, school-based, 12:139
    as revenue source for school districts, 20:3, 20:4
Scholarship funds
    for college (See College scholarships)
    and school districts
        administration of fund by district, 19:5
        donations by district, prohibition against, 19:6
School administrators (See Administrators, school)
School-based management (See Shared decision
    making)
School-based planning (See Shared decision
    making)
School board
    advisory committees, 3:6
    appointment of superintendent, 2:13, 7:17
    arbitration services, 10:10, 10:59
    bank as official school depository, designation
        of, 3:16, 3:17, 19:14
    bonds, authorization for issuance of, 19:68
    budget appropriations, spending funds in
        excess of, 19:15
    camp, establishment of school, 2:17
    census responsibilities of, 2:16, 13:9
    charitable contributions, 19:7
    city school boards (See City school districts)
    civil service employees
        new employees, 9:7
        reclassification, 9:7
    code of ethics, 2:31
    composition of, 2:2
    conduct on school premises, responsibility for,
        12:95, 16:52
    conflicts of interest (See Conflicts of interest)
    county government, relationship with, 1:25
    curriculum requirements for district,
        authorization of, 14:14
    disabled children
        disagreement with CSE recommendations,
            procedure when, 13:23
        responsibilities to, 13:7
    disciplinary actions by
        student transportation privileges, suspension
            of, 12:110, 22:11, 22:60
    extracurricular activity funds, responsibility for,
        19:11
    feasibility study, school district reorganization,
        15:9
    fiscal responsibilities, 19.1, 19.3
    home instruction, responsibilities, 12:4, 12:14,
        24:2, 24:22, 24:23, 24:29
    individual member's right to act of behalf of
        board, 2:12
    instructional year, role in determining length
        of, 14:3
    investment of funds
        general fund, 19:28

    policy for, 19:30
    legal status, 2:1
    libraries, removal of books from, constitutional
        issues, 14:62
    local governments, relationship with, 1:25
    managerial employee designation by,
        allowability of, 7:30
    marking periods, role in determining, 14:3
    New York State School Boards Association
        (See New York State School Boards
        Association)
    notes, authorization for issuance of, 19:68
    payment of bills and invoices
        advance payments, 19:17
        vouchers, 19:16
    personnel records of district employees, access
        rights, 2:72
    petty cash funds, establishment of, 19:22
    policies of, 2:78
        annual review requirements, 2:81
        documentation requirements, 2:82
        function of, 2:79
        legal status, 2:79
        New York State School Boards Association's
            assistance in development of, 2:84
        regulations distinguished, 2:83
        School Policy Encyclopedia, 2:84
        statutory requirements, 2:80
    powers and duties of, 2:10
        authority to suspend students, 12:99
        collective bargaining (See Collective
            bargaining)
        curriculum requirements for district,
            authorization of, 14:14
        devolution of, 2:11
        employment contracts, 10:5
        extracurricular activities, setting academic
            standards for participation in, 12:111
        free textbooks, duty to provide, 14:55
        leaves of absence, policies on, 8:132
        school year, role in determining length of,
            14:3
        transportation, 22:5, 22:11, 22:66, 22:67
    prekindergarten programs, responsibility for,
        14:10, 14:12, 14:13
    private and parochial schools, responsibilities,
        24:2
    proposed district budget, presentation of, 4:13
    quorum defined for meetings of, 2:50
    regulations, policies distinguished, 2:83
    rescission of previous action taken, 2:62
    scholarship funds
        donations to, 19:6
        responsibility for, 19:5
    school-based planning and shared-decision-
        making plans (See Shared decision making)
    School Policy Encyclopedia, 2:84
    school year, role in determining length of, 14:3
    standing committees, 3:6
    statutory authority of, 1:2
    superintendent of schools and
        appointment of, 2:13, 7:17

changes in superintendent duties by school
 board, 7:23
employment contract terms, 7:18
extension of employment contract by
 outgoing board, 2:14, 7:20
removal of, 2:15
rights with regard to board, 7:16
termination of employment contract by
 board, 7:24
textbooks
 free textbooks, duty to provide, 14:55
 selection of, 14:54
travel expenses, reimbursement of teachers'
 work-related, 8:131
trust funds, responsibility for, 19:5
vacancies (*See under* School board members)
vouchers for payment of bills and invoices,
 19:16
waiver of superintendent's certification
 requirements, request for, 7:3
School board meetings
absences of member, 2:28
abstention from voting, 2:63
agenda requirements, 2:53
annual district meeting, 2:45
audience participation in, 2:60
call of meeting, 2:48
committee meetings, public access requirements,
 2:57
executive sessions, 2:58, 2:59
location requirements, 2:46
minutes of, 2:48, 2:62, 2:64
 public access to, 2:65
moment of silence at opening of, 23:10
number required by law, 2:47
organizational meeting, 2:45
planning meetings, public access requirements,
 2:56
prayer or benediction at opening of, 23:10
public access to, 2:46, 2:52, 2:54, 2:56, 2:57, 2:59
 audience participation, 2:60
 tape recording of meetings, allowability of, 2:55
public notice requirements, 2:52
quorum defined for, 2:50
reorganizational meeting, 2:45, 3:1
 annual district meeting distinguished, 3:1
 officers elected and appointed at, 3:1, 3:3, 3:8
 timing of, 3:2
requirements for holding of, 2:49
rescission of previous action taken, 2:62
special district meeting (*See* Special school
 district meeting)
tape recording of meetings, allowability of, 2:55
telephone, allowability of voting by, 2:51
types of, 2:45
video conference, allowability of voting by, 2:51
voting at, 2:50
 abstention from voting, 2:63
 president or presiding officer, 2:61
 public access to, 2:54
 rescission of previous action taken, 2:62
 by telephone, allowability of, 2:51

by video conference, allowability of, 2:51
work sessions, public access to, 2:56
School board members, 3:7
absences from meetings as cause for vacancy, 2:28
abstention from voting, effect of, 2:63
acceptance of office, 4:45
accident and health insurance, participation in,
 18:46
appointment of, 2:4
 city school districts, 1:22, 2:4
BOCES employees as, 5:8
BOCES member as, 5:5
Buffalo school board, 2:3
building inspections, 16:2, 16:3
call of meeting by, 2:48
campaign expenditure statement requirements,
 2:9
censure of, 2:26
central high school districts, 2:3, 2:4
central school districts, 2:3, 2:4
challenges to election results, 4:47
 board actions taken pending appeal, effect
  on, 4:48
change in number of, 2:5
citizenship requirements, 2:18
civil rights cases, personal liability, 18:20
 legislative activities, when performing, 18:19
clergy person as, 2:22
common school districts, 2:3, 2:4, 2:6
community school districts (NYC), 2:3, 2:4
compensation for, 2:34
conflicts of interest (*See* Conflicts of interest)
credit cards, use of school, 19:10
election of, 2:4, 4:1, 4:41
 acceptance of office, 4:45
 city school districts, 1:22
 death of candidate, 4:38
 disputes involving, resolution of, 4:47, 4:48
 financial disclosure statement requirements,
  4:40
 ineligible candidates, 4:38
 nomination, method of, 4:31
 not enough candidates, 4:37
 order of names on ballot, 4:42
 rejection of nominating petition by board, 4:35
 resubmission of candidacy, 4:39
 results, official notice of, 4:43
 set aside of results, causes for, 4:59, 4:81
 tie vote, 4:44
 withdrawal of candidate, 4:38, 4:39
 write-in candidates, 4:36, 4:37
fees or gratuities, 2:34
felony conviction, removal from office for, 2:27
financial disclosure statement requirements,
 2:9, 4:40
former district employee as, 2:20
hospitalization and medical service plans,
 participation in, 18:46
IDA governing boards, allowability of service
 on, 20:47
individual member's right to act of behalf of
 board, 2:12

legal defense costs, indemnification for, 18:33, 18:34, 18:35
legal status, 2:1, 2:12
liability
  civil rights violations, 18:19, 18:20
  immunity available, 18:2
lobbying on behalf of budget, 4:26
local versus state officer status, 2:7
misconduct as cause for removal from office, 2:25, 2:27
New York City school board, 2:3, 2:4
nomination of, 4:31
  rejection of petition by board, 4:35
number of, 2:3, 2:5
oath of office, 2:8, 3:20, 4:46
personal liability of, 2:1
personnel records of district employees, access rights, 2:72
president, 2:2
  election of, 3:3
  fiscal management, responsibility for, 19:2
  vacancy in office of, 3:5
  voting rights, 2:61
prohibited actions defined by statute, 2:33
PTA membership, concurrent, 1:28
qualifications for membership, 2:18, 2:19, 3:10
  clergy person as member, 2:22
  former district employee as member, 2:20
reimbursement of expenses, 2:34
relative as district employee, 2:21, 2:36, 8:10
removal from office, 2:25, 2:27, 3:24
  hearing requirements, 2:25
reprimand of, 2:26
residency requirements, 2:18, 3:10
resignation of, 2:23
  withdrawal of, 2:24
Rochester school board, 2:3
as school district clerk, 3:11
as school district treasurer, 3:18
shared decision making committees, ineligibility for service on, 3:32
spouse as district employee, 2:21, 2:36
state versus local official status, 2:7
superintendent of schools, membership rights of, 7:16
Syracuse school board, 2:3
term of office, 2:4, 4:46
transaction of district business by individual, 2:12
trustee distinguished from, 2:6
union free school districts, 2:3, 2:4
vacancies, 2:27
  absences, declared for, 2:28
  obligation of district to fill, 2:30
  president's office, 3:5
  procedure for filling of, 2:29, 3:5
vice president
  election of, 3:3
  powers of, 3:4, 3:5
Yonkers school board, 2:3
School breakfast programs, 12:136
  exemption from participation, notice requirements, 12:137

food-service management company, operation by, 12:140
reimbursement eligibility, federal and state, 12:141
free or reduced-price participation, 12:138
private schools, 12:136
sales tax on school meals, 12:139
sanitation rules and regulations, applicability of, 12:146
severe need public elementary schools, 12:136
state aid, 21:12
student employment in, 12:142
surplus foods and price-supported commodities, eligibility for federal, 12:143
termination of participation, notice requirements, 12:137
School buildings
  advertising for bids, 16:24
    printed brochure describing bond issue, 16:18
  Americans with Disabilities Act (ADA), compliance with, 16:27
  architects, contracts with, 16:17
  asbestos (See Asbestos)
  athletic events, admission fees for, 16:48
  bingo and similar games, use for, 16:40
  board's responsibilities, 2:10
  bomb threats, 17:1, 17:5
  building aid, 16:30
  building permit, 16:24
  Bureau of Facilities Planning, 16.1
  Capital Assets Preservation Program (CAPP), 16:1
  charities, collection of money for, 16:61
  child-care services, use for, 16:39
  closed buildings (See Closed or unused school buildings)
  closing of schools in emergencies (See Closing of schools)
  condition of building as basis for parent's refusal to send child to school, 12:16
  construction or renovation (See Construction or renovation of school buildings)
  electronically-operated doors, 17:9
  emergency-management plans (See Emergency-management plans)
  environmental impact statement, 16:25
  Equal Access Act, federal, 16:44
  equipment lending, 16:14
    as prohibited gift, 16:49
  federal funds, 25:8, 25:14
  fire alarm system requirements, 17:15, 17:16
  fire drills, 14:38, 17:3
  fire-safety inspections (See Fire and fire safety)
  flag displays, 16:50
  gift of closed buildings to public corporations, 16:13
  graffiti, 16:54
  hazardous waste, 17:35
  health and safety inspections, 12:52
  health and safety regulations
    asbestos (See Asbestos)
    authority for, 17:7

bomb threats, 17:1, 17:5
closing of schools, 17:1
electronically-operated doors, 17:9
emergency-management plans (See
    Emergency-management plans)
fire alarm system, 17:15, 17:16
fire drills, 14:38, 17:3
fire-safety inspections (See Fire and fire safety)
hazardous waste, 17:35
indoor air quality, 17:37, 17:38
integrated pest management, 17:29
lead, exposure to, 17:32, 17:33, 17:34
pesticides, use of, 17:28
plans and specifications, approval of, 17:7
radon, exposure to, 17:31
smoke-free schools requirement, 17:39,
    17:40, 25:12
structural inspections, 17:10
subjects covered by, 17:8
underground storage tanks, 17:36
indoor air quality (See Indoor air quality)
inspections (See Inspections)
insurance for, 18:36
integrated pest management, 17:29
joint facilities, building aid for, 16:29
lead, exposure to, 17:32
    water supply, lead in, 17:33, 17:34
lease-purchase agreements, 16:11
leasing of, 16:10, 16:14
    building aid, 16:30
loitering, 16:53
long-range plans on fiscal and program
    projections, 16:1
maintenance of buildings and grounds,
    prohibition against sharing of services for, 5:37
maximum expenditure on construction, 16:19
military recruiting in, 16:41
net bonded indebtedness, 16:20
occupation before completion, 16:26
outside groups, use of building by
    fees for, 16:46, 16:47
    non-discrimination protections, 16:42, 16:46,
        23:8
    religious organizations, 16:42
    student-run Bible meetings, 16:44
parental refusal to send child to school based
    on condition of, 12:16
permissible uses, 16:35
pesticides, use of, 17:28, 17:29
plans and specification for construction or
    renovation (See Construction or renovation
    of school buildings)
police presence and activity in
    Miranda rights of students, 12:92
polling place in general elections, use as, 16:38
printed brochure describing bond issue, 16:18
private meetings, use for, 16:37
radio and television promotional activities, 16:59
radon, exposure to, 17:31
religious instruction, use for, 16:45, 23:8
religious organization, use by, 16:42
religious worship, use for, 16:43, 16:44, 23:8

renovation of (See Construction or renovation
    of school buildings)
rental of unused buildings, 16:14
right-of-way, granting of, 16:14
sale of unused buildings, 16:12
site acquisition
    gifts, 16:8
    methods of, 16:6
    option agreements, 16:9
    selection of site, 16:6
    voter approval, 16:4, 16:7, 16:8
smoke-free schools requirement, 17:39, 17:40,
    25:12
state aid, 21:12
state building aid, 16:29
structural inspections (See Inspections)
student photographs, sale of, 16:60
sweetened foods, sale of, 16:58
traffic regulation, 16:57
trespassing, 16:53
underground storage tanks, 17:36
unlawful entry, 16:53
unsafe areas, 16:32
use of
    athletic events, admission fees for, 16:48
    authority in granting, 16:36
    bingo and similar games, 16:40
    cafeteria use by community groups, 12:145
    charging fees for, 16:46, 16:47
    charities, collection of money for, 16:61
    child-care services, 16:39
    Equal Access Act, federal, 16:44
    leasing, 16:14
    nondiscrimination requirements, 16:42,
        16:44, 23:8
    by outside groups, 16:42, 16:46, 16:47, 23:8
    permissible uses, 16:35
    polling place in general elections, 16:38
    private meetings, 16:37
    radio and television promotional activities,
        16:59
    religious instruction, 16:45, 23:8
    by religious organization, 16:42
    for religious worship, 16:43
    right-of-way, granting of, 16:14
    school board's responsibility, 16:52
    student photographs, sale of, 16:60
    sweetened foods, sale of, 16:58
vandalism of, rewards for information on,
    12:126
zoning regulations, 16:15
School bus drivers
    accidents, 22:59
    age requirement, 22:48
    alcohol and drug testing (See Alcohol and drug
        testing)
    approval, 22:48
    background checks, 22:48, 22:56, 22:57
    character references, 22:48
    commissioner of education, qualifications set
        by, 22:48
    crosswalk instructions, responsibility for, 22:31

defined, 22:47
driving record, 22:57
employment record, 22:56
fingerprinting, 22:55
licenses, 22:57
licensure requirements, 22:49
mandatory reporter status for child abuse
    reporting, 12:74
occasional drivers, 22:51
physical examination, 22:48, 22:53
physical performance tests, 22:54
physical requirements, 22:52, 22:54
qualifications, 22:48, 22:57
    age, 22:48
    character references, 22:48
    commissioner of education, determination
        by, 22:48
    driving record, 22:57
    physical examination, 22:48, 22:53
    physical performance tests, 22:54
    physical requirements, 22:52, 22:54
    superintendent of schools, approval by, 22:48
rehabilitation programs for, 22:65
removal or exclusion from driving, alcohol or
    drug use as cause for, 22:64
responsibilities
    crosswalk instructions, 22:31
    supervision, 22:30, 22:60
safety instruction courses, 22:50
sexual abuse of child, reporting requirements,
    12:74
substitute drivers, 22:51, 22:53
superintendent of schools, approval by, 22:48
supervision of students, 22:30, 22:60
suspension of driver's license, reporting
    requirements, 22:58
traffic violations, reporting requirements, 22:58
training, 22:50, 22:51
School buses (See also Transportation)
accidents, school district's responsibility for,
    18:12, 18:13
approval, 22:70
athletic events, 22:12, 22:20
board's responsibilities, 22:11, 22:70
BOCES, leases to, 22:20
carry-on items, limits on size of, 22:46
certification, 22:22
competitive bidding
    purchases of buses, 22:28, 22:70
    transportation contracts (See Transportation)
cooperative purchasing, 22:72
costs and expenses, 22:12, 22:78
day care programs, 22:20
defined, 22:19
disabled, organizations for, 22:20
discipline, 22:11, 22:40, 22:60
distance limitations, 22:2
    child safety zones, 22:3
    length of commute, 22:5
    measurement of, 22:4
    standee regulation, 22:39
    walking distance for students, 22:17

divorced or separated parents, student has
    multiple addresses due to, 22:7
drive-off places, 22:16
drivers (See School bus drivers)
emergencies, leases during, 22:74
emergency drills, 14:38
exemptions for, 22:75
extracurricular activities, 22:20
fees, 22:75
fees for student use, 22:12
financing, 22:70
fire drills, 14:38
identification requirements for owner/
    operators, 22:25
inspection requirements, 22:23
insurance requirements, 22:20, 22:77
job-training programs, 22:20
leases of, 22:74
leasing of bus to another school district or
    organization, 22:20
length of commute, 22:5
license plate fee exemption, 22:75
motor vehicle fee exemption, 22:75
multiple addresses listed for student due to
    divorced or separated parents, 22:7
municipal corporations, 22:20
operating expenses, 22:78
owner/operator identification requirements,
    22:25
parent-teacher meetings, 22:21
pick-up places, 22:16
preschool programs, 22:20, 22:82
private and parochial schools (See Private and
    parochial schools)
purchases
    approval by commissioner of education, 22:71
    competitive bidding, 22:28, 22:70
    cooperative purchasing, 22:72
    installment contracts, 22:73
    standardization of fleet, 22:28
    state aid for, 22:78
    through state contracts, 22:76
railroad crossings, 22:45
recreational uses, 22:20
regional (multi-district) systems, 22:10
registration fee exemption, 22:75
routes (See Routes, school bus)
safety equipment requirements, 22:27
safety regulations
    alcohol and drug testing of drivers (See
        Alcohol and drug testing)
    carry-on items, limits on size of, 22:46
    certification that buses meet, 22:22
    color of school bus, 22:26
    crossing, 22:31
    emergency drills, 22:41
    equipment specifically for safety, 22:27
    headlight illumination, 22:43
    inspection requirements, 22:23
    instruction courses, 22:50
    New York State Department of Transportation,
        role of, 22:22

responsibility for student safety, 22:30
right turn on red, 22:44
safety equipment, 22:27
school district liability for student safety, 22:30
seat belts, presence and usage of, 22:36,
    22:37, 22:38
seating capacity and vehicle configuration,
    22:29
signal lights, 22:31, 22:34
signs, 22:24
speed limit, 22:42
standees, 22:39
station wagons, use of, 22:29
stop-arm devices, 22:35
traffic regulations on school property, 22:33
training for drivers, 22:50, 22:51
turning right on red, 22:44
two-way radios, 22:35
vehicles overtaking or meeting buses, 22:34
video cameras, use of, 22:40
school crossing guards, 22:32
seat belt requirements
    instruction on use of belts, 22:38
    presence of belts, 22:36
    wearing of belts by students, 22:37
senior citizens, 22:20
shelters, 22:18
shopping trips, 22:21
signs, 22:24
sporting events, 22:12, 22:20
standardization of fleet, 22:28
standees, 22:39
state aid for, 22:20, 22:78
    disabled students, 22:81
    out-of-district transportation of students to
        non-public schools, 22:79
    post-elementary education in another
        district, 22:80
supervision of students, 22:30
uses of, 22:20
vandalism of, rewards for information on, 12:126
video cameras, use of, 22:40
walking distance, policy, 22:17
School crossing guards, 22:32
School day, length of
    double or overlapping (split) session, 14:7
    minimum length by law, 14:6, 14:7
School district reorganization
    abolishment of administrative position, 7:12
    abolishment of teaching position, 8:95
        as alternative to firing, 8:96
        improperly excessed, rights and damages
            allowed, 8:101, 8:102
        reappointment rights, 8:98
        seniority rights, 8:97
    annexation (See Annexation, school district
        reorganization)
    assumption of debt, 15:18
    bonds, assumption of, 15:18
    centralization (See Centralization, school
        district reorganization)
    commissioner of education, role of, 15:8, 15:9,
        15:16

consolidation (See Consolidation, school district
    reorganization)
debt, assumption of, 15:18
defined, 15:1
dissolution of (See Dissolution, school district
    reorganization)
division into smaller districts, 15:6
efficiency study, 15:9
    state aid for, 15:10
employment contracts, 15:19, 15:22
employment rights, 15:20, 15:21, 15:22
feasibility study, 15:9
    state aid for, 15:10
information requests, 15:24
Master Plan, 15:7
methods of, 15:1
notes, assumption of, 15:18
property rights, 15:18, 15:22
proposal defeated, resubmission limits, 15:16
resubmission of proposal for, limits on, 15:16
smaller districts, division into, 15:6
state aid, 21:12
State Plan, 15:7
teacher tenure, 15:20, 15:21
School districts
    accident and health insurance
        district employees, 18:44
        school board members, 18:46
    accounting funds, 19:13
    auditor
        appointment of, 3:8, 3:19
        bonding of, 3:21
        conflicts of interest, 3:19
    Big 5 city school districts, 21:16
    Board of Cooperative Educational Services
        (BOCES) (See Board of Cooperative
        Educational Services (BOCES))
    BOCES (See Board of Cooperative Educational
        Services (BOCES))
    borrowing (See Borrowing)
    boundaries of, 6:20
    camp, establishment of school, 2:17
    Capital Reserve Fund, 19:24
    central high school district, defined, 1:21
    central school district, defined, 1:20
    Certiorari Reserve Fund, 19:24
    checks, signing of, 19:19
    chief executive officer, defined, 7:15
    city school districts (See City school districts)
    civil rights cases, immunity in, 18:18
    civil service employees of (See Civil service)
    clerk of, 3:7
        annual district meeting proceedings, 4:79
        appointment of, 3:8
        board member as, 3:11
        compensation, 3:22
        oath of office, 3:20
        record keeping, role in, 2:76
        removal from office, 3:25
        residency requirement, 3:10
        school board election responsibilities, 4:42,
            4:43

stand-in for, appointment of, 3:12
code number, relevance to state aid, 21:14
college applications processed by, 14:75
Committee on Special Education (CSE), role of
   (See Committee on Special Education (CSE))
common school district, defined, 1:18
copyrighted materials, liability for classroom
   use of, 14:63
county government, relationship with, 1:25
curricula (See Curricula)
debt service, reserve fund for, 19:24
disabled children, responsibilities to, 13:6, 13:7
   Committee on Special Education (CSE), role
      of (See Committee on Special Education
      (CSE))
   medical services required, 13:10
   preschool children, 13:45, 13:46
   registration and record keeping requirements,
      13:9, 13:45
dissolution of (See Dissolution, school district
   reorganization)
educational malpractice, 18:8
election districts, division into, 4:72
emergency-management plans (See Emergency-
   management plans)
Employee Benefit Accrued Liability Reserve
   Fund, 19:24
Federal aid (See Federal aid)
fiscally dependent districts, 20:2
fiscally independent districts, 20:2
formation of, district superintendent's powers
   and duties concerning, 6:20
former employee as board member, 2:20
Improving America's Schools Act (IASA) (See
   Improving America's Schools Act (IASA))
insurance requirements (See Insurance)
Insurance Reserve Fund, 19:24
investment of funds
   general fund, 19:28
   policy for, 19:30
   reserve funds, 19:27, 19:29
   short-term investments, 19:28
   types allowed, 19:29
Job-Training Partnership Act (JTPA), funding
   for, 25:13
legal counsel for (See Legal counsel)
legal status of, 1:2
liability (See Liability, school district)
life insurance, 18:44
local governments, relationship with, 1:25
long-range plans on fiscal and program
   projections, 16:1
naming conventions for, 1:26
negligence, actions for (See Negligence)
nonresident students (See Nonresident students)
officers of (See also specific officers)
   conflicts of interest, 2:43, 3:17, 3:23
   defined, 3:7
planned balance, 19:35
Property Loss and Liability Reserve Fund, 19:24
purchasing (See Purchasing)
records of (See Records)

Religious Freedom Restoration Act (RFRA),
   impact of overturned, 23:3
reorganization of (See School district
   reorganization)
Repair Reserve Fund, 19:24
reserve funds
   establishment of, 19:23
   excess funds, transfer of, 19:26
   investment of, 19:27, 19:29
   kinds of, 19:24
   voter approval, 19:25
retirement plan contributions, 11:30
school-based management (See Shared decision
   making)
school buses (See School buses)
school year, role in determining length of, 14:3
shared decision making (See Shared decision
   making)
Social Security, allowability of withdrawal from
   coverage, 11:53
special act school district, defined, 1:23
special meetings (See Special school district
   meeting)
state aid (See State aid)
strikes, responsibilities during, 10:52
superintendent of (See Superintendent of schools)
Tax Certiorari Reserve Fund, 19:24
tax collector, 3:7
   appointment of, 3:8
   bonding of, 3:21
   compensation, 3:22
   conflicts of interest, 3:13
   dismissal of, 3:24
   residency requirements, 3:10
Tax Reduction, Reserve Fund for, 19:24
traffic regulations and restrictions imposed
   by, 22:33
transportation (See Transportation)
treasurer, 3:7
   appointment of, 3:8
   bank as, permissibility of, 3:15
   board member as, 3:18
   bonding of, 3:18, 3:21
   compensation, 3:22
   conflicts of interest, 2:43, 3:13, 3:17
   deputy treasurer, 3:14
   dismissal of, 3:24
   oath of office, 3:20
   residency requirements, 3:10
21st Century Schools, 14:29
Uncollected Taxes, Reserve Fund for, 19:24
unemployment insurance, 18:39
Unemployment Insurance Payment Reserve
   Fund, 19:24
Uniform System of Accounts for School
   Districts, 19:12
union free school district, defined, 1:19
Workers' Compensation Reserve Fund, 19:24
School grounds
   camps, use for, 2:17
   distribution of literature, student rights, 12:83
School labs
   chemical hygiene plan, 18.25

chemicals, use of, 18:26
School lunch programs, 12:135
    food-service management company, operation
        by, 12:140
    reimbursement eligibility, federal and state,
        12:141
    free or reduced-price participation, 12:138
    milk, provision of, 12:135
    preschool students, 12:144
    sales tax on school meals, 12:139
    sanitation rules and regulations, applicability
        of, 12:146
    state aid, 21:12
    student employment in, 12:142
    surplus foods and price-supported commodities,
        eligibility for federal, 12:143
School principals (See Principals)
School report cards
    BOCES report cards, 5:29, 14:73
    content requirements, 14:72
    distribution requirements, 14:72
    state test results as part of, 14:71
School Tax Relief Program (STAR)
    additional information sources, 20:29
    application procedure, 20:25
    basic STAR program, 20:24
    components of, 20:22
    eligibility requirements, 20:22, 20:23, 20:24
    enhanced STAR program, 20:23
    school district's responsibilities, 20:26
    senior citizens, 20:22, 20:23
    state aid and, 20:28
    tax rate and, 20:27
    tax shortfalls, state reimbursement for, 20:28
School-to-Work Opportunities Act, 14:47, 25:13
School trustees, 3:7
    oath of office, 3:20
    residency requirements, 3:10
School Under Registration Review (SURR), 14:74
School year
    length of, 14:3
        minimum length by law, 14:4
    public holidays, New York state, 14:5
School yearbook, sale on school premises, 16:60
Searches
    student book bags or other belongings, 12:86
        with scent dogs, 12:89
    student lockers, 12:86, 12:88
        with scent dogs, 12:89
    of students, 12:87, 12:93
        with scent dogs, 12:89
Search warrants, 12:86, 12:87, 12:88, 12:93
Second-language instruction (See Foreign language
    instruction)
Section 1983 actions (See Civil rights, violation of)
Section 3020-a, discipline of tenured teachers (See
    3020-a disciplinary hearings)
Security Guard Act of 1992, 9:37, 9:38
Security guards
    insurance, 9:37
    registration, 9:37
    responsibilities, 9:37

Security Guard Act of 1992, 9:37, 9:38
SED (See State Education Department (SED))
Segregation, prohibitions against, 12:28
Senior citizens
    installment payment of real property taxes, 20:39
    real property taxation of, 20:18, 20:39
        School Tax Relief Program (STAR), 20:22,
            20:23
    school bus use by, 22:20
    School Tax Relief Program (STAR), 20:22, 20:23
    tax notification procedure, 20:37
Seniority credit, teacher tenure
    calculation of, 8:90
    Jarema credit, 8:75, 8:92
    nondistrict experience, 8:128
    part-time service, 8:73, 8:91
    substitute teachers, 8:74, 8:92
Seniority rights, 8:65, 8:66
    abolishment of administrative position, 7:12
    abolishment of teaching position, 7:12, 8:95, 8:97
    after takeover by BOCES or other district, 8:93
    alteration of, 8:89
    BOCES teachers, 8:93
    defined, 8:88
    school district reorganization, abolishment of
        teaching position after, 8:97
    tenure areas, effect of, 8:94
    tenure rights distinguished, 8:65
    waiver of, 8:89
Separation of church and state (See Establishment
    Clause, U.S. Constitution)
Serial bonds, 19:60
Sex Offender Registration Act ("Megan's Law")
    disclosure of information received under, 12:76
    public notice requirements, 12:75
    requirements, 12:75
Sexual abuse, of student
    legal action resulting from, 8:25
    reporting requirements, 12:74
    revocation of teacher's certification, grounds
        for, 8:49
Sexual discrimination
    academic programs, 14:26, 24:5
    curriculum materials, 14:26
    extracurricular activities, 14:26
    sexual harassment as form of, 18:25
    against teachers, 8:5, 8:125
    Title IX, rights and protections, 14:26
        private and parochial schools, 24:5
Sexual harassment
    burden of proof, 18:27
    defenses against, 18:28
    defined, 18:25, 18:26
    economic loss, burden of proof, 18:27
    employee discipline issues, 18:28
    hostile environment defined, 18:26
    liability for, district, 18:24
        economic loss, burden of proof, 18:27
        monetary damages, 18:28
        psychological harm, burden of proof, 18:27
        student as harasser (peer-on-peer), 18:30
        student as victim, 18:29, 18:30

men as victims of, 18:25
prevention programs, 18:28
psychological harm, burden of proof, 18:27
quid pro quo sexual harassment defined, 18:26
sexual discrimination, as form of, 18:25
student harassed, district liability for
  by student (peer-on-peer), 18:30
  by teacher, 18:29
teacher harassment of student, district liability
  for, 18:29
Title VII, employment discrimination filing
  under, 18:22, 18:25
Title IX, rights and protections, 14:26
  harassment of student, district liability,
    18:29, 18:30
  private and parochial schools, 24:5
types of, 18:25, 18:26
Shared decision making, 3:26
appeals, 3:34
areas addressed by, 3:28
board members, ineligibility for service on
  district-wide committees, 3:32
consultation defined, 3:27
employee tenure decisions as inappropriate for,
  3:29
exemptions to, 3:29
Freedom of Information Law, applicability of,
  3:37
limitations on, 3:29
meaningful participation defined, 3:27
membership, who's eligible for, 3:32, 3:33
Open Meetings Law, applicability of, 3:36
Persons eligible for membership, 3:32, 3:33
review of
  frequency requirements, 3:30
  persons involved in, 3:31
Teachers' participation in, 8:24
union involvement in, 3:35
Sick leave
accrued leave, cash payment for unused leave
  at retirement, 7:14
cash payment for unused leave at retirement,
  7:14
district superintendent, legal limits on benefits,
  6:12
Family and Medical Leave Act (*See* Family and
  Medical Leave Act (FMLA))
superintendent of schools, cash payment for
  unused leave at retirement, 7:14
teachers
  legal requirements, 8:133
  preemption of FMLA leave, collective
    bargaining agreement, 10:62
  pregnant teachers, mandatory leave, 8:134
  unused leave time, payment for, 8:141
Smoking regulations, 17:39, 25:12
Social security
information requests, 11:56
limits on post-retirement earnings, 11:54
noninstructional employees, coverage for, 11:52
post-retirement earnings, limits on, 11:54
school district, allowability of withdrawal from

coverage, 11:53
teachers
  eligible teachers, 11:51
  information requests, 11:56
  limits on post-retirement earnings, 11:54
  part-time teachers, 11:25
  post-age 65 employment, 11:55
  post-retirement earnings, limits on, 11:54
withdrawal from coverage by school district,
  allowability of, 11:53
Social worker, school, tenure areas, 8:60
Sororities and fraternities, student, 12:84
SOSHA (*See* State Occupational Safety and Health
  Act (SOSHA))
Sovereign immunity, abolishment in New York
  state, 18:1
Special act school district, defined, 1:23
Special district meeting (*See* Special school district
  meeting)
Special education, 13:3, 13:7
Committee on Preschool Special Education
  (CPSE) (*See* Committee on Preschool Special
  Education (CPSE))
Committee on Special Education (CSE) (*See*
  Committee on Special Education (CSE))
dual-enrollment requirements, 24:11
Individualized Education Program (IEP) (*See*
  Individualized Education Program (IEP))
itinerant special education services, 13:47
on-site services for private and parochial school
  students, 24:13
out-of-district placement and tuition, district's
  responsibilities, 13:37
parochial school, district responsibilities when
  attending, 13:15
  on-site services, 24:13
preschool children, 13:45, 13:46, 13:47
private schools, district responsibilities for
  students at, 13:14, 13:15, 13:36
  dual-enrollment requirements, 24:11
  on-site services, 24:13
teacher certification, 8:34
Special school district meeting, 2:48
absentee ballots
  allowability of, 4:86
  challenges to, 4:91
  deadline for submission of, 4:87
  list of persons requesting, public notice, 4:90
  multiple ballot applications, 4:89
  procedure for, 4:88
call of, 2:48, 4:51
call to order, 4:55
chairperson, voting rights of, 4:58
challenges to election results
  absentee ballots, 4:91
  board actions taken pending appeal, effect
    on, 4:48
  person's qualification to vote, challenges to,
    4:83, 4:84, 4:85
challenges to person's qualification to vote
  in districts without personal registration, 4:84
  in districts with personal registration, 4:83

time and place requirements, 4:85
clerk of district, record keeping of proceedings, 4:55
election districts, division of district into, 4:72
election inspectors, 4:75
location of, 4:54
minutes of, 2:48
proxy voting, 4:73
public access to, 2:48
public notice requirements, 2:48, 2:52, 4:10, 4:53, 4:54
time of, 2:45
time of day or week
    public notice requirements, 4:54
    requirements for, 4:50
voters' petition for, board refusal of, 4:52
voting at
    absentee ballots, 4:86, 4:87, 4:88, 4:89, 4:90, 4:91
    ballot voting, 4:69, 4:71
    booths, use of, 4:68
    challenges to person's qualification to vote, 4:83, 4:84, 4:85
    closing of polls, people waiting in line at, 4:77
    counting of votes, 4:80
    electioneering, 4:74
    election inspectors, 4:75
    New York State Election Law, applicability of, 4:67
    proxy voting, 4:73
    qualified voters, 4:56, 4:57, 4:59
    residency requirements, 4:82
    unqualified voters, penalties for, 4:59
    voting machines, 4:70, 4:71
Sporting events (See Athletics and competitive sports)
STAR Program (See School Tax Relief Program (STAR))
State aid, 21:1, 21:6
    asbestos-abatement projects, 17:52
    attendance and, 21:9, 21:15, 21:18
    average daily attendance, 21:15
    average daily attendance (ADA), 12:12, 21:9
    basis of distribution, 21:15
    Big 5 city school districts, 21:12, 21:16
    bilingual programs, 21:12
    BOCES, sources of funds for, 5:34, 5:38, 21:12, 21:15, 21:23
        payment schedule, 21:3
    breakfast programs, 21:12
    Buffalo, 21:16
    building aid, 21:12
    categorical aid, 21:6, 21:12, 21:16
    claims, processing of, 21:4
    comprehensive operating aid, 21:6
        allocation formula, 21:7, 21:8
        at-risk set-asides, 21:21
        calculation of, 21:8
        extraordinary needs aid (ENA), 21:7, 21:21
        pupil count, 21:9
        total aidable pupil units (TAPU), 21:8, 21:9
        transition adjustment and, 21:10

computation of
    daily sessions, minimum length of, 14:6, 14:7
    instructional year, minimum length of, 14:4
computer systems and software aid, 21:12
curriculum approval requirements, 14:23
disabled students, 13:7, 13:45, 21:12, 21:23, 22:81
disadvantaged students, 21:21
dual enrollment provision, 21:23, 24:11, 24:12
educationally related support services aid, 21:12
education technology incentive aid, 21:12
employment preparation education (EPE) aid, 21:12
equalization formulas
    tax equalization unrestricted aid, 21:11
    wealth-equalizing formulas, 21:15, 21:17
extraordinary needs aid (ENA), 21:6, 21:7, 21:21
feasibility study, school district reorganization, 15:10
food programs, 21:12
gifted and talented aid, 21:12
growth aid, 21:6
incarcerated youths, 21:12
increased enrollment, 21:20
information requests, 21:24
kindergarten (full-day) incentive aid, 21:12
library materials aid, 21:12
limitations, 21:7
limited English proficiency (LEP) aid, 21:12
lottery aid, 21:2
lunch programs, 21:12
maintenance and repair aid, 21:12
maintenance of effort allocation, 21:16
New York City, 21:16
payment schedule, 21:3
per pupil allocation, 21:15
prekindergarten aid, 21:12
private and parochial schools, 24:10
    closings, displacement aid regarding, 21:22
    disabled students, 21:23
    operating aid, 21:5
    testing and data collection services, 21:5, 21:12
reorganization incentive aid, 21:12
repair and maintenance aid, 21:12
Rochester, 21:16
school closings, effect of, 21:19
school construction projects, 16:29
school district code number, 21:14
school lunch and breakfast programs, 12:141
sources of funding, 21:2
speech therapy aid, 21:12
strikes and, 21:18
superintendent of schools, claims submission by, 21:4
Syracuse, 21:16
tax effort aid, 21:6, 21:11
tax equalization aid, 21:6, 21:11
Teachers' Retirement System (TRS), 21:3
textbook aid, 21:12
total aidable pupil units (TAPU), 21:9
transition adjustment and comprehensive operating aid, 21:10
transportation, 22:78

disabled students, 22:81
homeless students, 12:49
out-of-district transportation of students to
   nonpublic schools, 22:79
post-elementary education in another
   district, 22:80
transportation aid, 21:12
types of aid available, 21:6
types of state aid available, 21:12
unrestricted aid, 21:6
wealth-equalizing formulas, 21:15, 21:17
Yonkers, 21:16
State Board of Equalization and Assessment (See
   State Board of Real Property Services)
State Board of Real Property Services, 20:5, 20:8,
   20:30, 20:32, 20:51
State Education Department (SED), 1:2, 1:7, 1:10
adequacy of local curricula, 14:14, 14:23, 14:24
Board of Regents, relationship with, 1:10, 1:11
building permits, receipt of, 16:23
Bureau of Facilities Planning (See Bureau of
   Facilities Planning, SED)
chief executive officer of (See Commissioner of
   Education)
curricula, authority over local, 14:23
disabled children served in district, record
   keeping requirements, 13:9, 13:45
Elementary, Middle, Secondary and Continuing
   Education (EMSC), Office of, 1:12
employment rights, statement on post-school
   district reorganization, 15:21
environmental conservation education,
   curricula syllabi, 14:40
firearms curricula, approval of, 14:39
function of, legal, 1:11
health-education curriculum developed by, 14:36
homeless students, tuition payments for, 12:44
legal status of, 1:10
missing children, responsibilities to, 12:70
Office of Teaching, 8:47, 8:52, 8:53
organization of, 1:12
parenting skills curriculum development, 14:37
private and parochial schools, 24:10
   improvement plans, 24:7, 24:8
   registration of, 24:6
   review of, 24:7, 24:8
   supervisory role, 24:6, 24:7, 24:8
review of private and parochial schools, 24:7,
   24:8
   parental notification requirements, 24:8
School Under Registration Review (SURR)
   designation, 14:74
school year, role in determining length of, 14:3
supervisory responsibilities of, 1:11, 24:6
teacher certification, 8:27, 8:32, 8:34
   enforcement of law and regulations
      governing, 8:47
tuition payments for homeless students, 12:44
Vocational and Educational Services for
Individuals with Disabilities (VESID), Office of, 1:12
State Occupational Safety and Health Act
   (SOSHA), 17:18, 17:20

State Office of General Services
purchasing through, 19:52
   school buses and other transportation needs,
      22:76
State Plan, school district reorganization, 15:7
State University of New York (SUNY)
overview of, 1:6
retirement benefits, 11:24
University of the State of New York distinguished, 1:5
Statutory authority for public schools in New York
State, 1:2
Statutory expenditures, 19:41
Statutory installment bonds, 19:60, 19:63
Strikes (See also Taylor Law)
activities constituting, 10:50
definition, 8:23
employees' organization, 10:51
injunctions, 10:51, 10:52
instigating, 10:46
job actions, 10:50
no-strike provisions of Taylor Law, 10:13, 10:37,
   10:51
payroll penalty, 10:52
penalties, 10:51, 10:52
penalties for, 8:23
probation due to, 10:53
Public Employment Relations Board (PERB),
   role of, 8:23, 10:14, 10:33, 10:52
sanctions, 10:51
school district responsibilities, 10:52
state aid, effect on, 21:18
teachers, 8:23
Student clubs, extracurricular activity funds, 19:11
Student discipline, 12:95
absences, excessive
   as cause for denial of credit, 12:22, 13:44
   as cause for drop from enrollment, 12:25
   as cause for lowering of course grade, 12:116
annual review of policies concerning, 2:81
code of discipline, 12:95
   dress code as part of, 12:82
   penalties for violation of, 12:96
   violation of, penalties, 12:96
community service, allowability of, 12:114
corporal punishment, 8:22, 12:117
   legal action resulting from, 8:25
   reporting requirements, 12:118
counseling as penalty, allowability of, 12:115
detention, 12:96, 12:112
disabled students (See Disabled students)
extracurricular activities, exclusion from, 12:111
involuntary transfers, 12:24, 12:113
legal action resulting from, 8:25
lowering of course grade, 12:116
policies concerning, annual review requirements,
   2:81
probation, 12:96
reprimand, 12:96
Safe Schools program, 25:11
school buses, misbehavior on, 22:11, 22:60
   suspension of student transportation
      privileges, 12:110, 22:11, 22:60

suspension of (*See* Suspension of students)
by teachers, 8:22
    legal action resulting from, 8:25
    transfer to another school, allowability of, 12:113
types of discipline permissible, 12:96
warnings, verbal or written, 12:96
Student insurance, 18:47, 18:48
Students
    age of (*See* Age of students)
    aliens, illegal, right to public education, 25:1
    armbands or buttons, right to wear expressive, 12:78, 12:81
    arrest warrants for, 12:93
    assaults on teachers, school district liability for, 18:11
    attendance (*See* Attendance)
    bilingual education (*See* Bilingual education)
    breakfast program for (*See* School breakfast programs)
    cheating by
        as cause for lowering of course grade, 12:116
        due process rights, 14:69
    choice of courses, right to, 14:27
    clothing, 12:81, 12:82
    college applications processed by district, 14:75
    community service requirements, 12:94
    compulsory attendance (*See* Compulsory attendance)
    conduct of
        disciplinary code, 12:95
        report cards, 14:70
    consent
        Parental consent (*See* Parents or guardians of students)
        records, release of, 2:70
        release of student from school, 12:72
    constitutional protections, 12:77, 12:78
    contagious diseases, attendance with, 12:62
    corporal punishment of, 8:22, 12:117
        legal action resulting from, 8:25
        reporting requirements, 12:118
    demonstrations and peaceful protests, right to, 12:78
    disabled (*See* Disabled students)
    discipline of (*See* Student discipline)
    dress codes, 12:81, 12:82
    drug testing of
        with parental consent, 12:90
        random testing of athletes, 12:91
    dual-enrollment law, 12:15
    due process rights, 14:69
        involuntary transfers, 12:24
        suspension proceedings (*See* Suspension of students)
    employment of (*See* Employment)
    enrollment increases, state aid for, 21:20
    expressive activities
        censorship of, 12:80
        constitutional protections, 12:78, 12:81
    expulsion of, 12:96
    Fifth Amendment rights, 12:77
    firearms possession on campus (*See* Firearms on campus)

First Amendment rights, 12:77
Fourth Amendment rights, 12:77, 12:86, 12:87, 12:88, 12:93
fraternities and sororities, 12:84
free speech protections, 12:78
    clothing as free speech, 12:82
    distribution of literature on school grounds, 12:83
    nonpolitical or nonreligious in nature, 12:79
    student publications, 12:80
gifted and talented (*See* Gifted and talented students)
grades received, report cards, 14:70
gun possession on campus (*See* Firearms; Gun-Free Schools Act)
health services for (*See* Health services)
homeless students, 12:39
    admissions procedure, 12:43
    continuation of attendance when residence changes, 12:45, 12:46
    residency requirements, 12:40, 12:41, 12:42, 12:43
    transportation services, 12:47, 12:48, 12:49
    tuition payments, 12:44
incarcerated youths, state aid, 21:12
indigent students, 12:69
interim progress reports, 14:70
involuntary transfers, 12:24, 12:113
legal residence, determination of, 12:31, 12:35
legal rights
    choice of courses, right to, 14:27
    constitutional protections, 12:77, 12:78
    due process rights, 12:24, 12:103, 12:104, 12:105, 12:123, 13:42, 13:43, 14:69
    Fifth Amendment rights, 12:77
    First Amendment rights, 12:77
    Fourth Amendment rights, 12:77, 12:86, 12:87, 12:88, 12:93
lunch program for (*See* School lunch programs)
married students, attendance requirements for, 12:3
Miranda rights of students, 12:92
nonresident students
    disabled students, 12:30
    refusal of by school district, 12:30
    tuition charges for, 12:9, 12:35, 12:36
notification rights
    dropping of student from enrollment, 12:25
    re-enrollment rights, 12:25
part-time attendance, allowability of, 12:15
police interrogations, in school buildings, 12:93
    Miranda rights of students, 12:92
post-graduates under 21
    right to attend school, 12:9, 12:10
    tuition charges, 12:9, 12:35, 12:36
progress reports, 14:70
protests and demonstrations, 12:78
publications, 12:78
    censorship of, 12:80
    right to distribute on school grounds, 12:83
records of
    access rights, 2:67, 2:70

alteration of, penalties, 2:70
challenges to, 2:70
FERPA rights, 2:70
home phone numbers, 12:68
privacy rights, 2:70
release of student from school, 12:18, 12:71
divorced or separated parents, 12:72
report cards, 14:70
right to attend school, 12:6
equivalency diploma (GED) graduates, 12:10
post-graduates under 21, 12:9
suspension, impact of, 12:101, 13:38, 13:40
scholarships for college (*See* College scholarships)
search of lockers, 12:86, 12:88
with scent dogs, 12:89
search of student, 12:87, 12:93
with scent dogs, 12:89
sexual abuse of (*See* Sexual abuse, of student)
sexual harassment, district liability
by student (peer-on-peer), 18:30
by teacher, 18:29
sororities and fraternities, 12:84
state aid programs (*See* State aid)
suspension of (*See* Suspension of students)
textbooks (*See* Textbooks)
theatrical productions, 12:78
censorship of, 12:80
tobacco use by, prevention curriculum, 14:36
transfers, involuntary, 12:24, 12:113
transportation of (*See* School buses; Transportation)
tuition charges for nonresident students, 12:9, 12:35, 12:36
weapons possession on campus (*See* Gun-Free Schools Act; Weapons on campus)
Student teachers, 8:32, 8:38
as substitute teachers, 8:39
Subcontracting, collective bargaining, 10:38
Substance abuse
prevention curriculum, 14:36
testing for (*See* Alcohol and drug testing)
Substitutes
school bus drivers, 22:51, 22:53
teachers (*See* Substitute teachers)
Substitute teachers
certification requirements, 8:39
collective bargaining units, 10:19
Jarema credit, "regular substitute" defined for, 8:75
minimum salary requirements, 8:123
retirement options, 11:25
student teachers as, 8:39
teacher tenure
Jarema credit, 8:75
probationary period, length of, 8:74
seniority credit, 8:74, 8:75, 8:92
Summer school, fire drills during, 14:38
Sunshine Laws
Freedom of Information Law (FOIL) (*See* Freedom of Information Law (FOIL))
Open Meetings Law, 2:46, 2:54, 2:58, 2:65

public inspection of school district records (*See* Records)
student records (*See* Students)
SUNY (*See* State University of New York (SUNY))
Superintendent of schools, 3:7 (*See also* District superintendent)
appointment of, 2:13, 3:8, 7:2, 7:17
certification requirements, 7:2, 8:43
decertification procedure, 7:4
waiver of, 7:3
as civil service employees, 9:5
claims for state aid, role in, 21:4
collective bargaining, responsibilities regarding, 10:5, 10:32
compensation when multiple districts share administrator's services, 7:5
consolidation of school districts, employment contract, 7:21, 15:22
decertification of, 7:4
defined, 7:15
discipline when multiple districts share administrator's services, 7:5
dismissal of, 2:15, 3:24, 7:17
due process protections, 7:25
termination of employment contract, 7:24, 7:25
district superintendent distinguished, 6:1, 7:15
employment contracts, 7:17
changes in duties by school board, 7:23
consolidation of school districts, pre-merger contracts, 7:21, 15:22
extension of contract by outgoing board, 2:14, 7:20
necessity of contract, 7:18
school district reorganization, 15:22
school district reorganization, rights after, 7:21
termination of, 7:24, 7:25
term limits for, 7:17, 7:19
terms of contract, 7:18
extension of employment contract by outgoing board, 2:14, 7:20
legal status, 2:13
powers and duties of, 21:4
authority to suspend students, 12:99
changes in duties by school board, 7:23
school closing authority, 17:6
shared personnel agreements, approval of, 7:5
statutory powers and duties, 7:22
private and parochial schools, 24:9
private and parochial schools, review by, 24:3
recommendation of individual school district superintendent, 7:17
removal of, 2:15
residency requirements, 3:10
responsibilities of, 7:15, 7:22
teacher discipline, 7:22
school board, relationship with (*See* School board)
school bus drivers, approval, 22:48
school district reorganization, employment contract, 7:21, 15:22

sharing superintendent's services with multiple
districts, 7:5
statutory requirement for, 7:1
tenure
multiple districts, superintendent's services
shared with, 7:5
termination of employment contract, 7:24
due process rights, 7:25
term limits for, 7:17, 7:19
textbooks, selection of, 7:22, 14:54
Supervisors, dismissal of probationary supervisors, 7:11
Supervisory district, 6:2
Surety bonds for school construction projects, 18:49
SURR schools (See School Under Registration
Review (SURR))
Suspension of students, 12:96
absences, counting suspension days as, 12:23
authority to suspend, 12:99
disabled students (See Disabled students)
for drug possession or selling on campus,
13:39, 13:41
due process rights, 12:101
disabled students, 13:42, 13:43
five days or less, suspension for, 12:103
five days or more, suspension for, 12:104,
12:105
under Gun-Free Schools Act, 12:123
hearing requirements, 12:104, 12:105
particular class only, suspension from, 12:102
duration of, limitations on, 12:100
for firearms possession on campus, 13:39,
13:41, 25:9
under Gun-Free Schools Act, 12:120
hearings, 12:104, 12:105, 12:107
home instruction during, 12:107, 12:108, 12:124
in-school suspension, 12:109
instruction after, 12:107, 12:108
student over age 16, 12:108
limitations on duration of, 12:100
particular class only, suspension from, 12:102
procedures for, 12:101
disabled students (See Disabled students)
in-school suspension, 12:109
particular class only, suspension from, 12:102
revocation of suspension, 12:106
suspensions in excess of five days, 12:104,
12:105
suspensions of less than five days, 12:103
reasons for, 12:97, 12:98
revocation of, 12:106
right to attend school, impact on, 12:101, 13:38,
13:40, 13:41
supervision during, 12:107
for truancy, permissibility, 12:97
for weapons possession on campus, 12:120,
12:123, 12:124, 13:39, 13:41, 25:9
Suspension, school bus drivers, 22:58
Sweetened foods, sale on school grounds, 16:58
Syracuse
school board membership, 2:3, 2:4
state aid, 21:16

TAP (See Tuition Assistance Program (TAP), state)
Tax anticipation notes, 19:60, 19:64
Taxation (See also Assessment of property)
ad valorem levies, 20:21
assessed value defined, 20:31
certiorari proceedings, 20:14, 20:15
Certiorari Reserve Fund, 19:24
collection of taxes
assessment roll (See Assessment roll)
authorization of, 20:35
installment payments, 20:38, 20:39
non-realty taxes, 20:3
partial payments, 20:40
tax roll, return by collecting officer, 20:44
unpaid taxes, 20:42
wrong collector, taxes paid to, 20:41
commercial property versus residential
property rates, 20:32
constitutional limits on, 20:1
disabled persons, 20:39
excise taxes, exemption from, 19:59
exemptions
ad valorem levies, 20:21
charitable or religious property, 20:16
federal property, 20:16
municipal property, 20:16
New York State property, 20:16
partially exempt property, 20:17
School Tax Relief Program (STAR)
(See School Tax Relief Program (STAR))
senior citizens, 20:18, 20:22, 20:23
tax foreclosure sales, property acquired at,
20:20
veterans, property owned by, 20:19
wholly exempt property, 20:16
federal income tax (See Federal income tax)
fiscally independent districts, 20:2
homestead property-classification system, 20:32,
20:33, 20:34
Industrial Development Agencies
payments in lieu of taxes, 20:48, 20:49, 20:50
taxable status, 20:48
uniform tax exemption policy, 20:48
information about, additional, 20:51
installment payments, 20:38, 20:39
market value defined, 20:31
non-realty taxes as source of school district
revenue, 20:3
notification procedure, 20:36, 20:37
partial payments, 20:40
rates, determination of
assessed value, 20:31
commercial property versus residential
property rates, 20:32
homestead property-classification system,
20:32, 20:33, 20:34
market value, 20:31
methods, 20:30
under School Tax Relief Program (STAR),
20:27
tax equalization, 20:31
reduction in, reserve fund for, 19:24

sales taxes (*See* Sales taxes)
senior citizens, 20:18, 20:39
    School Tax Relief Program (STAR), 20:22,
    20:23
state tax (*See* New York State income tax)
tax equalization, 20:31
tax foreclosure sales, property acquired at, 20:20
Uncollected Taxes, Reserve Fund for, 19:24
unpaid taxes, 20:42
veterans, property owned by, 20:19
wrong collector, taxes paid to, 20:41
Tax Certiorari Reserve Fund, 19:24
Tax collectors, 3:7
    bonding by, 19:4
    bonding of, 3:21
    compensation of, 20:45
    conflicts of interest, 3:13
    notification procedure, 20:36, 20:37
    wrong collector, taxes paid to, 20:41
Taxes (*See* Taxation)
Tax warrant
    notification, 20:36, 20:37
    renewal of, 20:35
    signing of, 20:35
    tax list, affixation to, 20:35
Taylor Law, 8:23, 10:11
    administration of, 10:14
    appeals, 10:14
    authorized representative of employees,
        procedure for becoming, 10:16
    collective bargaining unit
        agency shop fees, 10:26, 10:28
        authorized representative of employees,
            procedure for becoming, 10:16
        certification, 10:18
        covered employees, 10:15, 10:17, 10:21,
            10:22, 10:23, 10:26
        defined, 10:15
        dues deductions, 10:27
        "employee organization," defined, 10:16
        employer recognition, 10:17, 10:18
        exclusion of employees, 10:22
        leaves of absence, 8:132
        mandatory subjects of negotiation, 10:20
        negotiation and execution of contracts, party
            responsible for, 10:5
        newly hired employees, 10:20
        religious holiday or observance, personal
            leave for, 8:138
        rights of, 10:12, 10:25
        salary issues in negotiation, 8:124
        substitute teachers, 10:19
    confidential designation of employees, 10:23
    "employee organization," defined, 10:16
    employee representation, 10:12
    enforcement, 10:14
    improper practices, 10:7, 10:30, 10:34, 10:35,
        10:46
        defined, 10:47
        by employee organization, examples, 10:46,
            10:49
        by employer, examples, 10:46, 10:48

judicial review, 10:14
managerial designation of employee, 10:23
Public Employment Relations Board (PERB),
    powers and duties of, 10:14, 10:33, 10:52
right of association, 10:26
right to negotiate, 10:12, 10:13
salary issues in negotiation, 8:124
strikes, 10:13, 10:46, 10:50, 10:51, 10:52
Triborough Amendment, 10:9, 10:46, 10:51
Teacher certification, 8:2, 8:26, 8:53
    aliens, 8:4
    application fee, 8:30
    area of certification, 8:34
        bilingual education, 8:34
        English as a second language, 8:34
        evening schools, 8:34
        middle school teachers, 8:35
        reading teacher, 8:34
        special education, 8:34
    bilingual education, 8:34
    Buffalo school district, special requirements,
        8:27
    certificate, defined, 8:26
    certificate of qualification, 8:32
        substitute teachers, 8:39
    classifications of, 8:34
    coaches, interscholastic sports, 8:42
    college preparation required, 8:28
    competency examination requirement, 8:29
    continuing certificate, teaching assistants, 8:40
    disabled teachers, 8:31
    enforcement of law and regulations governing,
        8:47
    exchange teachers, 8:46
    fee for certificate, 8:30
    hearings, procedure for, 8:51, 8:52
    incidental teaching, 8:44
    internship certificate, 8:32
    Interstate Agreement on Qualification of
        Educational Personnel, 8:45
    middle school teachers, 8:35
    New York State Teacher Certification
        Examination, 8:29
    Northeast Regional Credential, 8:45
    nurse-teacher, school, 12:51
    occupational education teachers, 8:34
    permanent certificate, 8:28, 8:29, 8:32
    private and parochial schools, 8:2, 8:36, 24:5
    provisional certificate, 8:28, 8:29, 8:32
        renewal of, 8:33
    reading teacher, 8:34
    reciprocity between states, 8:45
    as requirement for employment, 8:27
    revocation of, 6:19, 7:4, 8:48
        BOCES action, 8:48
        conviction of crime as grounds, 8:49, 8:51
        failure to complete contract of employment
            as grounds, 8:50
        grounds for, 8:50
        hearings, procedure for, 8:51, 8:52
        lack of good moral character as basis, 8:52
    special education, 8:34
    substitute teachers, 8:39

suspension of, 8:48
  hearings, procedure for, 8:52
  lack of good moral character as basis, 8:52
teaching assistants, requirements for, 8:40
temporary license, 8:3, 8:37
  teaching assistants, 8:40
types of, 8:32, 8:34
uncertified teachers, employment of, 8:3, 8:37,
  8:103
Teacher discipline
  absences, excessive
    job actions, 10:50
    salary adjustment, 8:130
  academic freedom, guidelines, 8:20
  superintendent's responsibilities, 7:22
  suspension
    pending resolution of 3020-a case, 8:114
    superintendent's responsibilities, 7:22
  tenured teachers (See 3020-a disciplinary
    hearings)
Teacher Education Certification and Practice
  Board (TECAP) (See Teacher Professional
  Standards and Practices Board)
Teacher Professional Standards and Practices
  Board, 8:51
Teachers
  abolishment of teaching position, 7:12, 8:95
    as alternative to firing, 8:96
    improperly excessed, rights and damages
      allowed, 8:101, 8:102
    preferred eligibility list (PEL), 7:12, 8:98,
      8:100
    reappointment rights, 8:98
    seniority rights, 7:12, 8:95, 8:97
  academic freedom, guidelines, 8:20
  adult education programs, state aid, 21:12
  advance compensation, 8:122
  after age 65, continued employment, 11:55
  age discrimination, 8:8, 8:125, 18:22
  age requirements, 8:2, 8:8
  aliens as, 8:4
  certification requirements (See Teacher
    certification)
  child abuse, reporting requirements, 12:74
  citizenship requirements, 8:2, 8:4
    constitutionality of, 8:4
  as civil service employees, 9:5
  claims against, 8:25
  code of ethics, 8:19
  collective bargaining (See Collective bargaining)
  compensation
    advance compensation, 8:122
    annuity plans, salary reduction as means of
      investing in tax-sheltered, 8:129
    collective bargaining issues, 8:124
    failure to provide services, salary adjustment,
      8:130
    minimum salary requirements, 8:121, 8:123
    nondistrict experience, impact on salary
      schedule, 8:128
    payment schedule requirements, 8:122
    school closed due to emergency, 8:127

summer months, extra salary for work
  during, 8:121
waiver or release, signing as condition of
  payment, 8:126
conflicts of interest, 8:19
  school board membership as, 1:28, 2:38
copyrighted materials, proper use of, 14:63
corporal punishment of students, 8:22
  legal action resulting from, 8:25
criminal records, revocation of teacher's
  certification for, 8:49
definition of, 8:1, 11:24
disabled individuals as, 8:6, 8:31, 18:22
  certification, 8:31
  retirement benefits, 11:36
disciplining of students (See Student discipline)
disciplining of teachers
  Generally (See Teacher discipline)
  tenured teachers (See 3020-a disciplinary
    hearings)
dismissal
  name-clearing hearing, allowability of, 8:80
  during probationary period, notice
    requirements, 8:78, 8:79, 8:82
  tenured teachers (See 3020-a disciplinary
    hearings)
district superintendent's responsibilities, 6:18,
  6:19
dress code, 8:21
duties of, 8:13
  code of ethics, 8:19
  extracurricular supervision or participation,
    extra pay for, 8:17
  legal action resulting from discharge of, 8:25
  workday, maximum length, 8:14
  workload, maximum, 8:15
duty-free period, right to, 8:16
excessed teachers, 8:97
  improperly excessed, rights and damages
    allowed, 8:101, 8:102
  reappointment rights, 8:98
  reassignment of, 8:103
  recalling of, procedure, 8:99
exchange teachers, 8:4, 8:140
  certification requirements, 8:46
  leave of absence to become, 8:140
extracurricular supervision or participation,
  extra pay for, 8:17
Family and Medical Leave Act (See Family and
  Medical Leave Act (FMLA))
free speech protections, 8:18
gifts to, 8:19
health benefits
  COBRA, continuation coverage under, 8:142
  retirement benefits, 11:2
kindergarten teachers
  part-time teachers, seniority credit, 8:73, 8:91
  seniority credit for part-time teachers, 8:73,
    8:91
leaves of absence (See Family and Medical Leave
  Act (FMLA); Leaves of absence)
legal actions against, 8:25

legal defense costs, indemnification for, 18:33,
    18:34, 18:35
legal definition, 8:1
lunch period, right to free, 8:16
mandatory reporter status for child abuse
    reporting, 12:74
marital status, nondiscrimination protections,
    8:5, 8:125
maximum length of workday, 8:14
medical examinations
    current employees, 8:12
    pre-employment exams, 8:11, 12:52
    psychiatric examinations, procedures and
        rights, 8:12
name-clearing hearing for terminated teachers,
    8:80
noncitizens as, exceptions to citizenship rule,
    8:4
nondiscrimination protections, 8:5, 8:6, 8:7,
    8:8, 8:31
    legal recourse, 8:9
nurse-teacher, school, 12:51
    tenure area, 8:60
oath of allegiance, 8:2
part-time teachers
    credit toward tenure, 8:73
    retirement options, 11:25
    Social Security benefits, 11:25
post-age 65 employment, 11:55
preferred eligibility list (PEL), 8:94, 8:98, 8:100,
    8:103
pregnancy, nondiscrimination protections, 8:5,
    8:134, 18:22
probationary period (See Probationary teachers)
professional development, Federal aid for, 25:8
prohibited actions defined by statute, 2:33
psychiatric examinations, procedures and
    rights, 8:12
relative of as school board member, 2:21, 2:36
relative serving as school board member,
    allowability of, 8:10
resignation of
    denial of tenure, rights when teacher chooses
        resignation rather than, 8:84
    3020-a decision, prior to, 8:106
    unused leave time, payment for, 8:141
retirees returning to employment, impact on
    retirement allowance
    private employment, 11:23
    public employment, 11:20, 11:21
retirement plans for (See Teachers' Retirement
    System, New York City; Teachers' Retirement
    System (TRS), New York State)
safety (See Workplace safety)
school-based planning, participation in, 8:24
school board membership, conflicts of interest,
    1:28, 2:38
school nurse-teacher, tenure area, 8:60
seniority credits (See Seniority credit, teacher
    tenure)
seniority rights (See Seniority rights)
sexual abuse of child, reporting requirements,
    12:74

sexual discrimination, 8:5
sexual harassment by, 18:26
    district liability for, 18:29
    student, harassment of, 18:29
shared BOCES service, 5:30, 5:33
shared decision making, participation in, 8:24
sick leave (See Sick leave)
Social Security (See Social Security)
strikes, subject to Taylor Law, 8:23
student assaults on teachers, school district
    liability for, 18:11
student progress reports, 14:70
student teachers, 8:32, 8:38
    as substitute teachers, 8:39
substitute teachers (See Substitute teachers)
summer months, extra salary for work during,
    8:121
suspension of (See Teacher discipline)
Taylor Law (See Taylor Law)
teaching load, maximum, 8:15
tenure (See Teacher tenure)
tenure areas (See Teacher tenure areas)
transfers, superintendent's responsibilities, 7:22
travel expenses, reimbursement of work-related,
    8:131
uncertified teachers, employment of, 8:3, 8:37
unqualified teachers, employment of, 8:3
unused leave time, payment for, 8:141
vote in election, right to time off to, 8:139
workday, maximum length, 8:14
work load, maximum, 8:15
Teacher's aide
    certification requirements, 8:41
    duties of, 8:41
Teachers' Retirement System, New York City, 11:4
Teachers' Retirement System (TRS), New York
    State, 11:4
    administration of, 11:26, 11:27
    annuity plans, tax-sheltered, 8:129, 11:19
    benefits
        supplemental pensions, 11:36, 11:38
    board members on TRS board, 11:27
    bonus termination pay, 11:40
    borrowing against contributions, 11:39
    changes in benefits, 11:11
    contributions
        ceasing to teach, impact of, 11:34
        member contributions, 11:29
        payment procedures, 11:32, 11:33
        retirees returning to public employment,
            status regarding, 11:21
        school district contributions, 11:30, 11:31
        unclaimed contributions, 11:34
        underpayment, procedures when, 11:33
    covered employees, 11:24, 11:25
    death benefits, 11:37
    disability allowances, 11:36, 11:38
    funding of, 11:28
    information requests, 11:41
    lump sum retirement payments, 11:35
    noncontributory plans, 11:12
    part-time teachers, 11:25

private employment, retirees returning to, 11:23
public employment, retirees returning to, 11:20, 11:21
public employment, returning to, 11:22
service credits, 11:14
state aid, 21:3
substitute teachers, 11:25
supplemental pensions, 11:36, 11:38
Tier systems (*See specific Tiers under* Retirement plans)
transfer of membership, 11:15, 11:16
vesting, defined, 11:17
Teacher tenure
    authority to grant tenure, 8:86
    BOCES teachers, 8:55, 8:56, 8:74, 8:93
    defined, 8:54, 8:57
    denial of tenure, 8:81
        final consideration, 8:83
        notice requirements, 8:82
        resignation rather than denial, rights when teacher chooses, 8:84
    disciplining tenured teachers (*See* 3020-a disciplinary hearings)
    district superintendent's responsibilities, 6:18
    early tenure, granting of, 8:76
    eligible teachers, 8:55
    granting of tenure, procedures, 8:85, 8:86
        early tenure, 8:76
        tenure by estoppel, 8:77, 8:87
    preferred eligibility list (PEL), 8:94, 8:98, 8:100, 8:103
    probationary period (*See* Probationary teachers)
    resignation
        denial of tenure, rights when teacher chooses resignation over, 8:84
        3020-a decision, prior to, 8:106
        unused leave time, payment for, 8:141
    school district reorganization, 15:20, 15:21
    seniority credits (*See* Seniority credit, teacher tenure)
    seniority rights (*See* Seniority rights)
    seniority rights distinguished, 8:65
    substitute teachers
        probationary period, length of, 8:74
        seniority credit, 8:74, 8:92
    tenure areas (*See* Teacher tenure areas)
    tenure by estoppel, 8:77, 8:87
    tenure rights, 8:65
    3020-a disciplinary hearings (*See* 3020-a disciplinary hearings)
    transferability from one district to next, 8:56
    vacant position, defined, 8:71
    waiver of, 8:72
Teacher tenure areas, 8:59
    administrative tenure area, 7:7, 8:64
    changes in, notice requirements, 8:69
    defined, 8:58
    50 percent rule, 8:64
    grade-level areas, 8:59, 8:66
    horizontal tenure practices, 8:61
    multiple area service, concurrent, 8:59, 8:64, 8:85

multiple tenure area service, concurrent, 8:63
preferred eligibility list (PEL), 8:94, 8:98, 8:100, 8:103
recognized areas of tenure under part 30 of Regents' Rules, 8:59, 8:60
seniority credits, accrual of, 8:90
seniority rights, effect on, 8:94
special subject tenure areas under Part 30 of Regents' Rules, 8:60
transfers to different area, 8:97
transfers to different tenure areas, 8:62
Teaching assistants
    certification requirements, 8:40
    duties of, 8:40
TECAP (*See* Teacher Education Certification and Practice Board (TECAP); now Teacher Professional Standards and Practices Board)
Telephone numbers
    student and parents, 12:68
Television
    promotional activities on school premises, 16:59
Tenure
    administrative personnel, 7:7, 8:64
        multiple districts, shared administrator's services, 7:5
    civil service employees (*See* Civil service)
    principals, 7:6, 7:7
        salary, allowability of reduction in, 7:29
    rescission of previous school board action, 2:62
    teacher tenure (*See* Teacher tenure; Teacher tenure areas)
Tenure areas, teacher (*See* Teacher tenure areas)
Termination (*See* Dismissal; Removal from office)
Testing of students (*See also* Examinations)
    disabled children, identification and placement of, 13:7, 13:8
    frequency requirements, 13:25
    home instruction students (*See* Home instruction)
    Regents College Examinations Program, 1:7
    Regents examinations (*See* Regents examinations)
Textbooks
    board's responsibilities, 14:54, 14:55
    changes in designated books
        frequency of change, limits on, 14:56
    contents of, complaints concerning
        religious objections, 14:58
        as subversive material, 14:54
        as vulgar and sexually explicit, 14:59, 14:62
    defined, 14:53
    designation of, 14:56
    fees or charges for, permissibility of, 12:38, 14:55
    frequency of change in, limits on, 14:56
    home instruction students, district responsibilities for, 24:32
    parental inspection rights, 14:57
    parental opposition to curricular material, 14:57, 14:58, 14:59
    parochial school students, district responsibilities for, 24:14, 24:15
        limits on frequency of new purchases, 14:56
    private school students, district responsibilities for, 24:15

limits on frequency of new purchases, 14:56
purchase of, 14:55
removal of, 14:59
selection of, 14:54, 14:56
state aid, 21:12
state's right to review, 14:54
superintendent's responsibilities, 7:22, 14:54
Thirteenth Amendment rights and student
    community service requirements, 12:94
3020-a disciplinary hearings, 8:104
    acquittal of charges, 8:117
    alternatives to 3020-a process, 8:120
    appeals, 8:119
    disclosure of settlement agreements under
    Freedom of Information Law, 2:71, 8:118
    disclosure to teacher of district's case against
        teacher, requirements for, 8:112
    dismissal of teacher, 8:104
        "just cause" requirement, 8:105
        as penalty for guilty verdict on 3020-a
            charge, 8:115
        procedure, 8:106
        right to hearing, 8:105
        unemployment benefits, eligibility for, 8:116
    filing of charges
        disclosure to teacher of district's case against
            teacher, requirements for, 8:112
        notice requirements, 8:108
        procedure, 8:108
        suspension pending resolution of charges,
            8:114
    Freedom of Information Law access to results
        of, 2:71, 8:118
    guilty verdict, penalties for, 8:115
    hearing officer
        responsibilities of, 8:111, 8:113
        selection of, 8:109
    "just cause" requirement, 8:105
    nondismissal-level discipline
        "just cause" requirement, 8:105
        procedure, 8:106
        right to hearing, 8:105, 8:107
    notice requirements for filing of charges, 8:108
    penalties for guilty verdict on 3020-a charge,
        8:115
    pre-hearing conference, 8:111
    procedures, 8:113
    resignation of teacher prior to resolution of,
        8:106
    right to hearing, 8:105, 8:107, 8:108
    suspension pending resolution of case, 8:114
    unemployment benefits, eligibility for, 8:116
    waiver of right to paid suspension, collective
        bargaining agreement, 8:114
    three-member 3020-a panel, 8:110
        acquittal of charges, 8:117
        appeals, 8:119
        guilty verdict, penalties for, 8:115
        penalties for guilty verdict on 3020-a charge,
            8:115
        single hearing officer, instead of, 8:110
    transcripts of, 8:113

waiver of right to hearing, 8:107
waiver of right to paid suspension, collective
    bargaining agreement, 8:114
Title VII, employment discrimination
    burden of proof, 18:22
    damage awards, 18:22
    pregnancy discrimination, 8:5, 18:22
    religious discrimination, 23:14, 23:18
    sexual harassment, 18:22, 18:25
Title IX, rights and protections, 14:26
    private and parochial schools, 24:5
    sexual harassment of student, district liability
        by student (peer-on-peer), 18:30
        by teacher, 18:29
Tobacco use by students, prevention curriculum,
    14:36
Traffic regulation
    directing of traffic, 22:33
    on school property, 16:57
    school speed zones, 22:33
    security guards, 9:37
    speed limit for buses, 22:42
Traffic violations, school bus driver, 22:58
Training, school bus drivers, 22:50, 22:51
Transfers
    civil service employees, 9:15
    collective bargaining, 10:37, 10:38
    students
        disciplinary measure, allowability as, 12:113
        due process rights, 12:24
        involuntary transfers, 12:24, 12:113
    teachers
        superintendent's responsibilities, 7:22
Transportation (See also School buses)
    accidents, school district's responsibility for,
        18:12, 18:13
    audits, 22:69
    board's responsibilities, 22:5, 22:11
    BOCES classes, 5:22, 5:35
    as budgetary item, 19:43, 22:8, 22:70
    child-care locations, to and from, 22:6
    Child Safety Act of 1992, 22:3
    child safety zone, 22:3
    city school districts, 22:1
    Commissioner of Education, approvals by
        contract bids, 22:66, 22:69
    as contingency budgetary item, 19:43
    contracts
        competitive bidding process, 22:66, 22:67,
            2:69
        emergency contract bidding, 22:67
    cooperative purchasing agreements, 22:72
    cost of, 22:1
    disabled individuals, 22:20, 22:81
    distance limitations, 22:2
        child safety zones, 22:3
        hazardous routes as exception to, 22:3
        length of commute, 22:5
        measurement of, 22:4
        walking distance for students, 22:17
    divorced or separated parents, student has
        multiple addresses due to, 22:7

emergency contract bidding, 22:67
extracurricular activities, 22:12, 22:20
homeless students, 12:47
    mileage limitations, 12:48
    state aid, 12:49
kindergarten, 22:1
multiple addresses listed for student due to
    divorced or separated parents, 22:7
New York State Department of Transportation,
    22:22
organizations outside school, 22:12, 22:20
parent or guardian providing, 22:13
private and parochial schools (See Private and
    parochial schools)
public carriers, use of, 22:1, 22:9, 22:82
regional (multi-district) systems, 22:10
requests by parents or guardians of students,
    22:1, 22:8
requirements for, 22:1
routes (See Routes, school bus)
safety regulations for buses (See School buses)
seatbelt requirements
    instruction on use of belts, 22:38
    presence of belts, 22:36
    wearing of belts by students, 22:37
state aid, 21:12, 22:78
    disabled students, 22:81
    homeless students, 12:49
    out-of-district transportation of students to
        nonpublic schools, 22:79
    post-elementary education in another
        district, 22:80
suspension of student transportation privileges,
    12:110, 22:11, 22:60
    attendance, impact on, 12:110
vocational education classes, non-district, 12:37
walking distance for students, 22:17
Travel expenses, reimbursement of teachers' work-
    related, 8:131
Treasurer
    bonding by, 19:4
    check issuance before board's approval, 19:18
Trespassing, school property, 16:53
TRS (See Teachers' Retirement System (TRS), New
    York State)
Truancy
    defined, 12:19
    enforcement, 12:20
    legal status of, 12:20
    suspension of student for, permissibility of, 12:97
Trust companies (See Banks or trust companies)
Trustee
    scholarship funds, 19:5
    school board member distinguished from, 2:6
Trust funds, administration of, 19:5
Tuition
    computation of, 12:36
    homeless students, 12:44
    nonresident students, 12:9, 12:35, 12:36
        vocational education, 12:37
    post-graduates under 21, 12:9, 12:35, 12:36

"tuitioning out", 12:37
    vocational education, 12:37
Tuition Assistance Program (TAP), state, 14:76
Tutor
    homebound instruction, as source of, 24:35
    home instruction, as source of, 24:25
21st Century Schools, 14:29

Underground storage tanks, 17:36
Unemployment insurance, 18:39
    teachers dismissed as result of 3020-a
        proceeding, eligibility for, 8:116
Unemployment Insurance Payment Reserve Fund,
    19:24
Uniform system of accounts for school districts,
    19:12
Union free school districts, 1:19
    annexation to, 15:12
        employment rights, 15:20
        teacher tenure, 15:20
        voter approval, 15:3
    annual district meetings
        chairperson of, 4:9
        clerk of, 4:79
    annual school board reorganization meetings,
        timing of, 3:2
    board membership, 2:3, 2:4, 2:5
        vacancies, filling of, 2:29
    consolidation, 15:4, 15:13
    personal voter registration systems, 4:60, 4:61
    transfers between budget categories without
        voter approval, 19:36
Unions
    collective bargaining (See Collective bargaining)
    shared decision making plans, required
        involvement, 3:35
University of the State of New York
    overview of, 1:5
    president of, 1:13
    private schools, admission of, 24:6
    SED supervision of, 1:11
    SUNY system distinguished, 1:5, 1:6
Unlawful entry, school property, 16:53
Unsafe areas in school buildings, 16:32

Vacancy in office
    BOCES vacancies, procedures for filling, 5:15
    district superintendent
        causes of vacancy, 6:8
        filling of vacancy, 6:9
    school board members (See School board
        members)
Vacation pay
    district superintendent, legal limits on benefits,
        6:12
    unused leave time, payment for, 8:141
Vandalism of school district property, rewards for
    information on, 12:126
VESID (See Vocational and Educational Services for
    Individuals with Disabilities (VESID), Office of)
Vesting, retirement plans, 11:17

Veterans
  civil service appointments, 9:13
  disabled veterans, civil service appointments, 9:13
  taxation of property owned by, 20:19
Video cameras, school buses, 22:40
Violence prevention
  Safe and Drug-Free Schools and Communities
    Act, 16:55
  Safe Schools program, 25:11
Vocational and Educational Services for
  Individuals with Disabilities (VESID), Office of,
  1:12
Vocational education
  BOCES programs and shared services for, 5:22,
    5:30
  prerequisites for admission to, 14:27
  quotas for classes, allowability of, 5:32
  dual-enrollment requirements, 24:11
  enrollment of resident in out-of-district courses,
    12:37
  health care services training, 14:46
  out-of-district tuition, district's responsibilities,
    12:37
  safety glasses, 12:67
  School-to Work Opportunities Act, 14:47, 25:13
  as tenure area, 8:60
  tuition payments for out-of-district enrollments,
    12:37
Voter approval
  annexation of school district, 15:3, 15:12
  asbestos-abatement projects, 17:53
  bond issuance, 19:69, 19:77
  consolidation of districts
    city school district and contiguous districts,
      15:14
    common school districts, 15:4, 15:13
    union free school districts, 15:4, 15:13
  construction or renovation of school building,
    funding for, 16:16
  dissolution of school district, 15:15
  school building site acquisition, 16:4, 16:7
    gifts, 16:8
    option agreements, 16:9
Voter registration, 4:60, 4:61
  information included in register, 4:63
  location of, 4:62
  personal voter registration systems, 4:60, 4:61
    alternatives to, 4:60
    discontinuation of, 4:66
    location of, 4:62
    time of, 4:62
  preparation of register, 4:64
  public inspection of poll and registration lists,
    4:65, 4:78
  time of, 4:62
Voting
  school board elections (See School board
    members)
  at school board meetings (See School board
    meetings)
  at special district meetings (See Special school
    district meeting)

teachers, time off to vote, 8:139
voting machines, use in district elections, 4:70,
  4:71
Vouchers, 19:16

Wages (See also Compensation; Salaries)
  school construction projects, 16:28
Water safety, exposure to lead, 17:33, 17:34
Weapons on campus (See also Firearms; Gun-Free
  Schools Act)
  BB gun as weapon, 12:121
  police notification requirements, 12:85
  student possession
    confiscation of, 12:85
    parental notification requirements, 12:85
    police notification requirements, 12:85
    suspension requirements, 12:120, 12:123,
      12:124, 25:9
Whistle-blower Law, 9:35
Workday, teachers, maximum length, 8:14
Workers' compensation insurance, 18:38
Workers' compensation leave
  Employees' Retirement System (ERS) retirement
    service, effect on, 11:49
Workers' Compensation Reserve Fund, 19:24
Workplace safety, 17:17
  chemical hygiene plan, 17:30
  hazard communication standard, 17:25
    failure of compliance, 17:27
    material safety data sheet (MSDS), 17:26
  HIV, exposure to, 17:24
  material safety data sheet (MSDS), 17:25, 17:26
  Occupational Safety and Health Act (OSHA),
    17:20
    chemical hygiene plan, 17:30
    hazard communication standard, 17:25
    hepatitis infections, 17:24
    HIV, exposure to, 17:24
    material safety data sheet (MSDS), 17:26
    shop classes, 17:23
  PESH Bureau, 17:18, 17:19
    financial assistance for compliance, 17:22
    hepatitis infections, 17:24
    HIV, exposure to, 17:24
    requirements, 17:19
    violation of rules, 17:21
  responsibility for, 17:17, 17:18
  science lab chemicals, use of, 17:30
    chemical hygiene plan, 17:30
  shop classes, compliance with OSHA standards,
    17:23
  State Occupational Safety and Health Act
    (SOSHA), 17:18, 17:20

Yearbooks, fees or charges for, 12:38
Yonkers
  school board membership, 2:3, 2:4
  state aid, 21:16

Zoning regulations
  attendance zones, 16:33
  school building projects, 16:15